John Locke

A Paraphrase and Notes on the Epistles of Saint Paul to the Galatians, I and II Corinthians, Romans and Ephesians

John Locke

A Paraphrase and Notes on the Epistles of Saint Paul to the Galatians, I and II Corinthians, Romans and Ephesians

ISBN/EAN: 9783337729585

Printed in Europe, USA, Canada, Australia, Japan

Cover: Foto ©Lupo / pixelio.de

More available books at **www.hansebooks.com**

A PARAPHRASE AND NOTES

ON THE

EPISTLES of St. *PAUL*

TO THE

| Galatians,
 I & II } Corinthians, | Romans, *and*
 Ephesians. |

To which is prefixed,

An ESSAY

FOR THE

Understanding of St. Paul's Epistles, by consulting St. Paul Himself.

By *JOHN LOCKE*, Esq;

THE SIXTH EDITION.

LONDON:
Printed for A. Millar, H. Woodfall, J. Whiston and B. White, J. Rivington, L. Davis and C. Reymers, R. Baldwin; Hawes, Clarke, and Collins; W. Johnston, W. Owen, J. Richardson, S. Crowder, T. Longman, B. Law, C. Rivington, E. Dilly, R. Withy, C. and R. Ware, S. Baker, T. Payne, A. Shuckburgh, and J. Hinxman.
MDCCLXIII.

AN ESSAY

For the UNDERSTANDING

St. *PAUL*'s Epistles, &c.

TO go about to explain any of St. *Paul*'s Epistles, after so great a Train of Expositors and Commentators, might seem an Attempt of Vanity, censurable for its Needlessness, did not the daily and approved Examples of pious and learned Men justify it. This may be some Excuse for me to the Publick, if ever these following Papers should chance to come abroad: But to myself, for whose Use this Work was undertaken, I need make no Apology. Though I had been conversant in these Epistles, as well as in other Parts of Sacred Scripture, yet I found that I understood them not; I mean, the doctrinal and discursive Parts of them: Though the practical Directions, which are usually dropped in the latter Part of each Epistle, appeared to me very plain, intelligible, and instructive.

I did not, when I reflected on it, very much wonder that this Part of Sacred Scripture had Difficulties in it; many Causes of Obscurity did readily occur to me. The Nature of Epistolary Writings, in general, disposes the Writer to pass by the mentioning of many Things, as well known to him to whom his Letter is addressed, which are necessary to be laid open to a Stranger, to make him comprehend what is said: And it not seldom falls out, that a well penned Letter, which is very easy and intelligible to the Receiver, is very obscure to a Stranger, who hardly knows what to make of it. The Matters that St. *Paul* writ about, were certainly Things well known to those he writ to, and which they had some peculiar

Concern in; which made them easily apprehend his Meaning, and see the Tendency and Force of his Discourse. But we having now at this Distance no Information of the Occasion of his Writing, little or no Knowledge of the Temper and Circumstances those he writ to were in, but what is to be gathered out of the Epistles themselves, it is not strange that many Things in them lie concealed to us, which, no doubt, they who were concerned in the Letter, understood at first sight. Add to this, that in many Places, 'tis manifest, he answers Letters sent, and Questions proposed to him; which, if we had, would much better clear those Passages that relate to them, than all the learned Notes of Criticks and Commentators, who in Aftertimes fill us with their Conjectures; for very often, as to the Matter in hand, they are nothing else.

The Language wherein these Epistles are writ, are another, and that no small Occasion of their Obscurity to us now. The Words are *Greek*, a Language dead many Ages since; a Language of a very witty, volatile People, Seekers after Novelty, and abounding with Variety of Notions and Sects, to which they applied the Terms of their common Tongue with great Liberty and Variety: And yet this makes but one small Part of the Difficulty in the Language of these Epistles; there is a Peculiarity in it, that much more obscures and perplexes the Meaning of these Writings, than what can be occasioned by the Looseness and Variety of the *Greek* Tongue. The Terms are *Greek*, but the Idiom or Turn of the Phrases may be truly said to be *Hebrew*, or *Syriack*: The Custom and Familiarity of which Tongues do sometimes so far influence the Expressions in these Epistles, that one may observe the Force of the *Hebrew* Conjugations, particularly that of *Hiphil*, given to *Greek* Verbs, in a Way unknown to the *Grecians* themselves. Nor is this all; the Subject treated of in these Epistles is so wholly new, and the Doctrines contained in them so perfectly remote from the Notions that Mankind were acquainted with, that most of the important Terms in it have quite another Signification from what they have in other Discourses: So that putting all together, we may truly say, that the New Testament is a Book written in a Language peculiar to itself.

To these Causes of Obscurity, common to St. *Paul* with most of the other Penmen of the several Books of the New Testament, we may add those that are peculiarly his, and owing to his Stile and Temper. He was, as 'tis visible, a Man of quick Thought, warm Temper, mighty well versed in the Writings of the Old Testament,

and

and full of the Doctrine of the New: All this put together, suggested Matter to him in abundance, on those Subjects which came in his way; so that one may consider him, when he was writing, as beset with a Crowd of Thoughts, all striving for Utterance. In this Posture of Mind it was almost impossible for him to keep that slow Pace, and observe minutely that Order and Method of ranging all he said, from which results an easy and obvious Perspicuity. To this Plenty and Vehemence of his, may be imputed those many large Parentheses, which a careful Reader may observe in his Epistles. Upon this Account also it is, that he often breaks off in the middle of an Argument, to let in some new Thought suggested by his own Words; which having pursued and explained, as far as conduced to his present Purpose, he re-assumes again the Thread of his Discourse, and goes on with it, without taking any Notice that he returns again to what he had been before saying; though sometimes it be so far off, that it may well have slipt out of his Mind, and requires a very attentive Reader to observe, and so bring the disjointed Members together, as to make up the Connection, and see how the scattered Parts of the Discourse hang together in a coherent, well-agreeing Sense, that makes it all of a Piece.

Besides the Disturbance in perusing St. *Paul*'s Epistles, from the Plenty and Vivacity of his Thoughts, which may obscure his Method, and often hide his Sense from an unwary, or over-hasty Reader; the frequent changing of the Personage he speaks in, renders the Sense very uncertain, and is apt to mislead one that has not some Clue to guide him: Sometimes by the Pronoun *I*, he means himself, sometimes any Christian; sometimes a *Jew*, and sometimes any Man, &c. If speaking of himself, in the first Person Singular, has so various Meanings, his Use of the first Person Plural is with a far greater Latitude; sometimes designing himself alone, sometimes those with himself whom he makes Partners to the Epistle; sometimes with himself comprehending the other Apostles, or Preachers of the Gospel, or Christians: Nay, sometimes he in that way speaks of the Converted *Jews*, other times of the Converted *Gentiles*, and sometimes of others, in a more or less extended Sense; every one of which varies the Meaning of the Place, and makes it to be differently understood. I have forborn to trouble the Reader with Examples of them here: If his own Observation hath not already furnished him with them, the following Paraphrase and Notes, I suppose, will satisfy him in the Point.

In

In the Current also of his Discourse, he sometimes drops in the Objections of others, and his Answers to them, without any Change in the Scheme of his Language, that might give Notice of any other speaking besides himself. This requires great Attention to observe, and yet, if it be neglected or over-looked, will make the Reader very much mistake, and misunderstand his Meaning, and render the Sense very perplexed.

These are intrinsick Difficulties arising from the Text itself, whereof there might be a great many other named; as the Uncertainty, sometimes, who are the Persons he speaks to, or the Opinions or Practices which he has in his Eye; sometimes in alluding to them, sometimes in his Exhortations and Reproofs. But those above mentioned being the chief, it may suffice to have opened our Eyes a little upon them; which, well examined, may contribute towards our Discovery of the rest.

To these we may subjoin two external Causes, that have made no small Increase of the Native and Original Difficulties that keep us from an easy and assured Discovery of St. *Paul*'s Sense, in many Parts of his Epistles; and those are,

First, The dividing of them into Chapters and Verses, as we have done; whereby they are so chopped and minced, and as they are now printed, stand so broken and divided, that not only the common People take the Verses usually for distinct Aphorisms, but even Men of more advanced Knowledge, in reading them, lose very much of the Strength and Force of the Coherence, and the Light that depends on it. Our Minds are so weak and narrow, that they have need of all the Helps and Assistances that can be procured, to lay before them undisturbedly, the Thread and Coherence of any Discourse; by which alone they are truly improved, and led into the genuine Sense of the Author. When the Eye is constantly disturbed with loose Sentences, that by their Standing and Separation, appear as so many distinct Fragments, the Mind will have much ado to take in, and carry on in its Memory, an uniform Discourse of dependent Reasonings; especially having from the Cradle been used to wrong Impressions concerning them, and constantly accustomed to hear them quoted as distinct Sentences, without any Limitation or Explication of their precise Meaning from the Place they stand in, and the Relation they bear to what goes before, or follows. These Divisions also have given Occasion to the Reading these Epistles by Parcels and in Scraps, which has farther confirmed the Evil arising

from

from such Partitions. And, I doubt not, but every one will confess it to be a very unlikely Way to come to the Understanding of any other Letters, to read them Piece-meal, a Bit to-day, and another Scrap to-morrow, and so on by-broken Intervals; especially if the Pause and Cessation should be made, as the Chapters the Apostle's Epistles are divided into, to end sometimes in the Middle of a Discourse, and sometimes in the Middle of a Sentence. It cannot therefore but be wondred at, that that should be permitted to be done to Holy Writ, which would visibly disturb the Sense, and hinder the Understanding of any other Book whatsoever. If *Tully*'s Epistles were so printed, and so used, I ask, whether they would not be much harder to be understood, less easy and less pleasant to be read, by much, than now they are.

How plain soever this Abuse is, and what Prejudice soever it does to the Understanding of the Sacred Scripture; yet if a Bible was printed as it should be, and as the several Parts of it were writ, in continued Discourses where the Argument is continued, I doubt not but the several Parties would complain of it, as an Innovation, and a dangerous Change in the publishing those holy Books. And indeed, those who are for maintaining their Opinions, and the Systems of Parties by Sound of Words, with a Neglect of the true Sense of Scripture, would have reason to make and foment the Outcry: They would most of them be immediately disarmed of their great Magazine of Artillery wherewith they defend themselves, and fall upon others. If the Holy Scripture were but laid before the Eyes of Christians in its due Connection and Consistency, it would not then be so easy to snatch out a few Words, as if they were separate from the rest, to serve a Purpose, to which they do not at all belong, and with which they have nothing to do. But as the Matter now stands, he that has a Mind to it, may at a cheap Rate be a notable Champion for the Truth; that is, for the Doctrines of the Sect, that Chance or Interest has cast him into. He need but be furnished with Verses of Sacred Scripture, containing Words and Expressions that are but flexible (as all general, obscure and doubtful ones are) and his System that has appropriated them to the Orthodoxy of his Church, makes them immediately strong and irrefragable Arguments for his Opinion. This is the Benefit of loose Sentences, and Scripture crumbled into Verses, which quickly turn into independent Aphorisms. But if the Quotation in the Verse produced, were considered as a Part of a continued, coherent Discourse, and so its

Sense

Sense were limited by the Tenor of the Context, most of those forward and warm Disputants would be quite stripped of those, which they doubt not now to call Spiritual Weapons; and they would have often nothing to say that would not shew their Weakness, and manifestly fly in their Faces. I crave leave to set down a Saying of the Learned and Judicious Mr. *Selden*. "In interpreting the Scripture,
"says he, many do as if a Man should see one have ten Pounds,
"which he reckoned by 1, 2, 3, 4, 5, 6, 7, 8, 9, 10. meaning four
"was but four Unites, and five five Unites, &c. and that he had in
"all but ten Pounds: The other that sees him, takes not the Figures
"together, as he doth, but picks here and there; and thereupon
"reports, that he had five Pounds in one Bag, and six Pounds in
"another Bag, and nine Pounds in another Bag, &c. when as, in
"truth, he has but ten Pounds in all. So we pick out a Text, here
"and there, to make it serve our Turn; whereas if we take it all to-
"gether, and consider what went before, and what followed after,
"we should find it meant no such Thing." I have heard sober Christians very much admire why ordinary, illiterate People, who were Professors, that shewed a Concern for Religion, seemed much more conversant in St. *Paul*'s Epistles, than in the plainer, and, as it seemed to them, much more intelligible Parts of the New Testament: They confessed, that though they read St. *Paul*'s Epistles with their best Attention, yet they generally found them too hard to be mastered; and they laboured in vain so far to reach the Apostle's Meaning all along in the Train of what he said, as to read them with that Satisfaction that arises from a Feeling that we understand and fully comprehend the Force and Reasoning of an Author; and therefore they could not imagine what those saw in them, whose Eyes they thought not much better than their own. But the Case was plain: These sober, inquisitive Readers, had a mind to see nothing in St. *Paul*'s Epistles but just what he meant; whereas those others of a quicker and gayer Sight, could see in them what they pleased. Nothing is more acceptable to Fancy than pliant Terms and Expressions, that are not obstinate; in such it can find its Account with Delight, and with them be illuminated Orthodox, infallible at pleasure, and in its own way. But where the Sense of the Author goes visibly in its own Train, and the Words, receiving a determined Sense from their Companions and Adjacents, will not consent to give Countenance and Colour to what is agreed to be right, and must be supported at any rate, there Men of established

Ortho-

Orthodoxy do not so well find their Satisfaction. And perhaps if it were well examined, it would be no very extravagant Paradox to say, that there are fewer that bring their Opinions to the Sacred Scripture to be tried by that infallible Rule, than bring the Sacred Scripture to their Opinions, to bend it to them, to make it, as they can, a Cover and Guard of them. And to this Purpose, its being divided into Verses, and brought as much as may be into loose and general Aphorisms, makes it most useful and serviceable. And in this lies the other great Cause of Obscurity and Perplexedness, which has been cast upon St. *Paul*'s Epistles from without.

St. *Paul*'s Epistles, as they stand translated in our *English* Bibles, are now, by long and constant Use, become a Part of the *English* Language, and common Phraseology, especially in Matters of Religion: This every one uses familiarly, and thinks he understands; but it must be observed, that if he has a distinct Meaning when he uses those Words and Phrases, and knows himself what he intends by them, it is always according to the Sense of his own System, and the Articles or Interpretations of the Society he is engaged in. So that all this Knowledge and Understanding, which he has in the Use of these Passages of Sacred Scripture, reaches no farther than this, that he knows (and that is very well) what he himself says, but thereby knows nothing at all what St. *Paul* said in them. The Apostle writ not by that Man's System, and so his Meaning cannot be known by it. This being the ordinary Way of understanding the Epistles, and every Sect being perfectly Orthodox in its own Judgment, what a great and invincible Darkness must this cast upon St. *Paul*'s Meaning to all those of that Way, in all those Places where his Thoughts and Sense run counter to what any Party has espoused for Orthodox; as it must unavoidably to all, but one of the different Systems, in all those Passages that any way relate to the Points in Controversy between them.

This is a Mischief, which, however frequent and almost natural, reaches so far, that it would justly make all those who depend upon them, wholly diffident of Commentators; and let them see, how little Help was to be expected from them in relying on them for the true Sense of the Sacred Scripture, did they not take care to help to cozen themselves, by choosing to use and pin their Faith on such Expositors as explain the Sacred Scripture in favour of those Opinions that they before-hand have voted Orthodox, and bring to the Sacred

Scripture, not for Trial, but Confirmation. No body can think that any Text of St. *Paul*'s Epistles has two contrary Meanings; and yet so it must have to two different Men, who taking two Commentators of different Sects, for their respective Guides into the Sense of any one of the Epistles, shall build upon their respective Expositions. We need go no farther for a Proof of it, than the Notes of the two celebrated Commentators on the New Testament, Dr. *Hammond* and *Beza*, both Men of Parts and Learning, and both thought by their Followers Men mighty in the Sacred Scriptures. So that here we see the Hopes of great Benefit and Light from Expositors and Commentators, is in a great part abated; and those who have most need of their Help, can receive but little from them, and can have very little Assurance of reaching the Apostle's Sense by what they find in them, whilst Matters remain in the same State they are in at present. For those who find they need Help, and would borrow Light from Expositors, either consult only those who have the good Luck to be thought sound and Orthodox, avoiding those of different Sentiments from themselves in the great and approved Points of their Systems, as dangerous, and not fit to be meddled with; or else, with Indifferency, look into the Notes of all Commentators promiscuously. The first of these take Pains only to confirm themselves in the Opinions and Tenets they have already; which, whether it be the way to get the true Meaning of what St. *Paul* delivered, is easy to determine. The others, with much more Fairness to themselves, though with reaping little more Advantage (unless they have something else to guide them into the Apostle's Meaning than the Comments themselves) seek Help on all Hands, and refuse not to be taught by any one, who offers to enlighten them in any of the dark Passages. But here, though they avoid the Mischief which the others fall into, of being confined in their Sense, and seeing nothing but that in St. *Paul*'s Writings, be it right or wrong; yet they run into as great on the other side, and instead of being confirmed in the Meaning, that they thought they saw in the Text, are distracted with an hundred, suggested by those they advised with; and so, instead of that one Sense of the Scripture which they carried with them to their Commentators, return from them with none at all.

This, indeed, seems to make the Case desperate; for if the Comments and Expositions of pious and learned Men cannot be depended on, whither shall we go for Help? To which I answer, I would not be mistaken, as if I thought the Labours of the Learned in this Case wholly lost, and fruitless. There is great Use and Benefit to be made of them, when we have once got a Rule to know which of their Expositions, in the great Variety there is of them, explains the Words and Phrases according to the Apostle's Meaning. 'Till then, 'tis evident, from what is above said, they serve for the most part to no other Use, but either to make us find our own Sense, and not his, in St. *Paul*'s Words; or else to find in them no settled Sense at all.

Here it will be ask'd, How shall we come by this Rule you mention? Where is that Touchstone to be had, that will shew us whether the Meaning we ourselves put, or take as put by others upon St. *Paul*'s Words in his Epistles, be truly his Meaning or no? I will not say the Way, which I propose, and have in the following Paraphrase followed, will make us infallible in our Interpretations of the Apostle's Text: But this I will own, that till I took this Way, St. *Paul*'s Epistles to me, in the ordinary Way of reading and studying them, were very obscure Parts of Scripture, that left me almost every where at a Loss; and I was at a great Uncertainty in which of the contrary Senses, that were to be found in his Commentators, he was to be taken. Whether what I have done, has made it any clearer and more visible now, I must leave others to judge. This I beg Leave to say for myself, that if some very sober, judicious Christians, no Strangers to the Sacred Scriptures, nay, learned Divines of the Church of *England*, had not professed, that by the Perusal of these following Papers, they understood the Epistles much better than they did before, and had not, with repeated Instances, pressed me to publish them, I should not have consented they should have gone beyond my own private Use, for which they were at first designed, and where they made me not repent my Pains.

If any one be so far pleased with my Endeavours, as to think it worth while to be informed what was the Clue I guided myself by through all the dark Passages of these Epistles, I shall minutely tell him the Steps by which I was brought into this Way, that he may judge whether I proceeded rationally, upon right Grounds or no, if so be any thing in so mean an Example as mine, may be worth his Notice.

After I had found, by long Experience, that the Reading of the Text and Comments in the ordinary Way, proved not so successful as I wished to the End proposed, I began to suspect, that in reading a Chapter as was usual, and thereupon sometimes consulting Expositors upon some hard Places of it, which at that Time most affected me, as relating to Points then under Consideration in my own Mind, or in Debate amongst others, was not a right Method to get into the true Sense of these Epistles. I saw plainly, after I began once to reflect on it, that if any one now should write me a Letter, as long as St. *Paul*'s to the *Romans*, concerning such a Matter as that is, in a Stile as foreign, and Expressions as dubious as his seem to be; if I should divide it into fifteen or sixteen Chapters, and read of them one to-day, and another to-morrow, *&c.* it was ten to one I should never come to a full and clear Comprehension of it. The Way to understand the Mind of him that writ it, every one would agree, was to read the whole Letter through, from one End to the other, all at once, to see what was the main Subject and Tendency of it; or if it had several Views and Purposes in it, not dependent one of another, nor in a Subordination to one chief Aim and End, to discover what those different Matters were, and where the Author concluded one, and began another; and if there were any Necessity of dividing the Epistle into Parts, to make the Boundaries of them.

In Prosecution of this Thought, I concluded it necessary, for the Understanding of any one of St. *Paul*'s Epistles, to read it all through at one Sitting, and to observe, as well as I could, the Drift and Design of his writing it. If the first Reading gave me some Light, the second gave me more; and so I persisted on reading constantly the whole Epistle over at once, till I came to have a good general View of the Apostle's main Purpose in writing the Epistle, the chief Branches of his Discourse wherein he prosecuted it, the Arguments he used, and Disposition of the whole.

This, I confess, is not to be obtained by one or two hasty Readings; it must be repeated again and again, with a close Attention to the Tenour of the Discourse, and a perfect Neglect of the Divisions into Chapters and Verses. On the contrary, the safest Way is to suppose, that the Epistle has but one Business, and one Aim, till by a frequent Perusal of it, you are forced to see there are distinct, independent Matters in it, which will forwardly enough shew themselves.

It requires so much more Pains, Judgment and Aplication, to find the Coherence of obscure and abstruse Writings, and makes them so much the more unfit to serve Prejudice and Pre-occupation when found, that it is not to be wondred that St. *Paul*'s Epistles have with many passed rather for disjointed, loose pious Discourses, full of Warmth and Zeal, and Overflows of Light, rather than for calm, strong, coherent Reasonings, that carried a Thread of Argument and Consistency all through them.

But this Muttering of lazy, or ill disposed Readers, hindred me not from persisting in the Course I had began: I continued to read the same Epistle over and over, and over again, till I came to discover, as appeared to me, what was the Drift and Aim of it, and by what Steps and Arguments St. *Paul* prosecuted his Purpose. I remembred that St. *Paul* was miraculously called to the Ministry of the Gospel, and declared to be a chosen Vessel; that he had the whole Doctrine of the Gospel from God by immediate Revelation, and was appointed to be the Apostle of the *Gentiles*, for the propagating of it in the Heathen World. This was enough to persuade me, that he was not a Man of loose and shattered Parts, uncapable to argue, and unfit to convince those he had to deal with: God knows how to choose fit Instruments for the Business he employs them in. A large Stock of *Jewish* Learning he had taken in at the Feet of *Gamaliel*; and for his Information in Christian Knowledge, and the Mysteries and Depths of the Dispensation of Grace by Jesus Christ, God himself had condescended to be his Instructor and Teacher. The Light of the Gospel he had received from the Fountain and Father of Light himself, who, I concluded, had not furnished him in this extraordinary Manner, if all this plentiful Stock of Learning and Illumination had been in danger to have been lost, or proved useless, in a jumbled and confused Head; nor have laid up such a Store of admirable and useful Knowledge in a Man, who, for want of Method and Order, Clearness of Conception, of Pertinency in Discourse, could not draw it out into Use with the greatest Advantages of Force and Coherence. That he knew how to prosecute his Purpose with Strength of Argument and close Reasoning, without incoherent Sallies, or the intermixing of Things foreign to his Business, was evident to me from several Speeches of his recorded in the *Acts*: And it was hard to think that a Man that could talk with so much Consistency and Clearness of Conviction, should not be able to write without Confusion, inextricable Obscurity,

rity, and perpetual Rambling. The Force, Order and Perspicuity of those Discourses, could not be denied to be very visible: How then came it that the like was thought much wanting in his Epistles? And of this there appeared to me this plain Reason: The Particularities of the History in which these Speeches are inserted, shew St. *Paul*'s End in speaking; which being seen, casts a Light on the whole, and shews the Pertinency of all that he says. But his Epistles not being so circumstantiated; there being no concurring History that plainly declares the Disposition St. *Paul* was in; what the Actions, Expectations, or Demands of those to whom he writ, required him to speak to, we are no where told. All this, and a great deal more, necessary to guide us into the true Meaning of the Epistles, is to be had only from the Epistles themselves, and to be gathered from thence with stubborn Attention, and more than common Application.

This being the only safe Guide (under the Spirit of God, that dictated these Sacred Writings) that can be relied on, I hope I may be excused, if I venture to say, that the utmost ought to be done to observe and trace out St. *Paul*'s Reasonings; to follow the Thread of his Discourse in each of his Epistles; to shew how it goes on still directed with the same View, and pertinently drawing the several Incidents towards the same Point. To understand him right, his Inferences should be strictly observed; and it should be carefully examined from what they are drawn, and what they tend to. He is certainly a coherent, argumentative, pertinent Writer; and Care, I think, should be taken in expounding of him, to shew that he is so. But though I say he has weighty Aims in his Epistles, which he steadily keeps in his Eye, and drives at in all that he says; yet I do not say that he puts his Discourses into an artificial Method; or leads his Reader into a Distinction of his Arguments, or gives them notice of new Matter by rhetorical, or studied Transitions. He has no Ornaments borrowed from the *Greek* Eloquence; no Notions of their Philosophy mixed with his Doctrine, to set it off. *The inticing Words of Man's Wisdom*, whereby he means all the studied Rules of the *Grecian* Schools, which made them such Masters in the Art of Speaking, he, as he says himself, 1 *Cor.* II. 4. wholly neglected: The Reason whereof he gives in the next Verse, and in other Places. But the Politeness of Language, Delicacy of Stile, Fineness of Expression, laboured Periods, artificial Transitions, and a very methodical Ranging of the Parts, with such other Imbellishments as make a

Discourse

Discourse enter the Mind smoothly, and strike the Fancy at first Hearing, have little or no Place in his Stile; yet Coherence of Discourse, and direct Tendency of all the Parts of it, to the Argument in hand, are most eminently to be found in him. This I take to be his Character, and doubt not but he will be found to be so upon diligent Examination. And in this, if it be so, we have a Clue, if we will take the Pains to find it, that will conduct us with Surety thro' those seemingly dark Places, and imagined Intricacies, in which Christians have wandered so far one from another, as to find quite contrary Senses.

Whether a superficial Reading, accompanied with the common Opinion of his invincible Obscurity, has kept off some from seeking in him the Coherence of a Discourse, tending with close, strong Reasoning to a Point; or a seemingly more honourable Opinion of one that had been wrapped up into the Third Heaven, as if from a Man so warmed and illuminated as he had been nothing could be expected but Flashes of Light, and Raptures of Zeal, hindred others to look for a Train of Reasoning, proceeding on regular and cogent Argumentation, from a Man raised above the ordinary Pitch of Humanity to an higher and brighter way of Illumination; or else, whether others were loth to beat their Heads above the Tenour and Coherence in St. *Paul*'s Discourses, which if found out, possibly might set him at a manifest and irreconcileable Difference with their Systems; 'tis certain, that whatever hath been the Cause, this Way of getting the true Sense of St. *Paul*'s Epistles, seems not to have been much made use of, or at least so thoroughly pursued as I am apt to think it deserves.

For, granting that he was full stored with Knowledge of the Things he treated of, for he had Light from Heaven, it was God himself furnished him, and he could not want; allowing also that he had Ability to make use of the Knowledge had been given him for the End for which it was given him, *viz.* the Information, Conviction, and Conversion of others; and, accordingly, that he knew how to direct his Discourse to the Point in hand, we cannot widely mistake the Parts of his Discourse employed about it, when we have any where found out the Point he drives at: Wherever we have got a View of his Design, and the Aim he proposed to himself in Writing, we may be sure that such or such an Interpretation does not give us his genuine Sense, it being nothing at all to his present Purpose. Nay, among various Meanings given a Text, it fails not to direct us to the best, and very often to assure us of the true: For it is no Presumption, when one sees a Man arguing for this or that Proposition, if he be a sober Man, Master of Reason or common Sense, and takes any Care of what he says, to pronounce, with Confidence in several Cases, that he could not talk thus or thus.

I do not yet so magnify this Method of studying St. *Paul's* Epistles, as well as other Parts of Sacred Scripture, as to think it will perfectly clear every hard Place, and leave no Doubt unresolved. I know Expressions now out of Use, Opinions of those Times, not heard of in our Days, Allusions to Customs lost to us, and various Circumstances and Particularities of the Parties, which we cannot come at, &c. must needs continue several Passages in the dark now to us at this Distance, which shone with full Light to those they were directed to. But for all that, the studying of St. *Paul's* Epistles in the Way I have proposed, will, I humbly conceive, carry us a great length in the right understanding of them, and make us rejoice in the Light we receive from those most useful Parts of Divine Revelation, by furnishing us with visible Grounds that we are not mistaken, whilst the Consistency of the Discourse, and the Pertinency of it to the Design he is upon, vouches it worthy of our great Apostle. At least, I hope, it may be my Excuse, for having endeavoured to make St. *Paul* an Interpreter to me of his own Epistles.

To this may be added another Help, which St. *Paul* himself affords us, towards the attaining the true Meaning contained in his Epistles. He that reads him with the Attention I propose, will easily observe, that as he was full of the Doctrine of the Gospel, so it lay all clear, and in order, open to his View. When he gave his Thoughts Utterance upon any Point, the Matter flowed like a Torrent: But, 'tis plain, 'twas a Matter he was perfectly Master of; he fully possessed the entire Revelation he had received from God; had thoroughly digested it; all the Parts were formed together in his Mind into one well contracted, harmonious Body: So that he was no way at Uncertainty, nor ever in the least at a loss concerning any Branch of it. One may see his Thoughts were all of a Piece in all his Epistles; his Notions were at all Times uniform, and constantly the same, though his Expressions very various: In them he seems to take great Liberty. This, at least, is certain, that no one seems less tied up to a Form of Words. If then having, by the Method before proposed, got into the Sense of the several Epistles, we will but compare what he says, in the Places where he treats of the same Subject,

Subject, we can hardly be mistaken in his Sense, nor doubt what it was, that he believed and taught concerning those Points of the Christian Religion. I know it is not unusual to find a Multitude of Texts heaped up for the maintaining of an espoused Proposition, but in a Sense often so remote from the true Meaning, that one can hardly avoid thinking that those who so used them, either sought not, or valued not the Sense; and were satisfied with the Sound, where they could but get that to favour them. But a verbal Concordance leads not always to Texts of the same Meaning; trusting too much thereto will furnish us but with slight Proofs in many Cases; and any one may observe how apt that is to jumble together Passages of Scripture not relating to the same Matter, and thereby to disturb and unsettle the true Meaning of Holy Scripture. I have therefore said, that we should compare together Places of Scripture treating of the same Point. Thus, indeed, one Part of the Sacred Text could not fail to give light unto another. And since the Providence of God hath so ordered it, that St. *Paul* has writ a great Number of Epistles, which, though upon different Occasions, and to several Purposes, yet are all confined within the Business of his Apostleship, and so contain nothing but Points of Christian Instruction, amongst which he seldom fails to drop in, and often to enlarge on the great and distinguishing Doctrines of our holy Religion; which, if quitting our own Infallibility in that Analogy of Faith which we have made to ourselves, or have implicitly adopted from some other, we would carefully lay together, and diligently compare and study, I am apt to think would give us St. *Paul*'s System in a clear and indisputable Sense, which every one must acknowledge to be a better Standard to interpret his Meaning by, in any obscure and doubtful Parts of his Epistles, if any such should still remain, than the System, Confession, or Articles of any Church or Society of Christians yet known; which, however pretended to be founded on Scripture, are visibly the Contrivance of Men, (fallible both in their Opinions and Interpretations) and, as is visible in most of them, made with partial Views, and adapted to what the Occasions of that Time, and the present Circumstances they were then in, were thought to require for the Support or Justification of themselves. Their Philosophy also has its Part in misleading Men from the true Sense of the Sacred Scripture. He that shall attentively read the Christian Writers after the Age of the Apostles, will easily find how much the Philosophy they were tinctured with, influenced them in

their

their Understanding of the Books of the Old and New Testament. In the Ages wherein *Platonism* prevailed, the Converts to Christianity of that School, on all Occasions, interpreted Holy Writ according to the Notions they had imbibed from that Philosophy. *Aristotle*'s Doctrine had the same Effect in its Turn; and when it degenerated into the Peripateticism of the Schools, that too brought its Notions and Distinctions into Divinity, and affixed them to the Terms of the Sacred Scripture. And we may still see how, at this Day, every one's Philosophy regulates every one's Interpretation of the Word of God. Those who are possessed with the Doctrine of Aerial and Ætherial Vehicles, have thence borrowed an Interpretation of the four first Verses of 2 *Cor.* V. without having any ground to think that St. *Paul* had the least Notion of any such Vehicles. 'Tis plain, that the teaching of Men Philosophy, was no Part of the Design of Divine Revelation; but that the Expressions of Scripture are commonly suited, in those Matters, to the vulgar Apprehensions and Conceptions of the Place and People where they were delivered. And as to the Doctrine therein, directly taught by the Apostles, that tends wholly to the setting up the Kingdom of Jesus Christ in this World, and the Salvation of Mens Souls; and in this, 'tis plain, their Expressions were conformed to the Ideas and Notions which they had received from Revelation, or were consequent from it. We shall therefore in vain go about to interpret their Words by the Notions of our Philosophy, and the Doctrines of Men delivered in our Schools. This is to explain the Apostle's Meaning by what they never thought of whilst they were writing; which is not the way to find their Sense in what they delivered, but our own, and to take up from their Writings not what they left there for us, but what we bring along with us in ourselves. He that would understand St. *Paul* right, must understand his Terms in the Sense he uses them; and not as they are appropriated, by each Man's particular Philosophy, to Conceptions that never entered the Mind of the Apostle. For Example; he that shall bring the Philosophy now taught and received, to the explaining of *Spirit, Soul,* and *Body,* mentioned 1 *Thess.* V. 23. will, I fear, hardly reach St. *Paul*'s Sense, or represent to himself the Notions St. *Paul* then had in his Mind. That is what we should aim at in reading him, or any other Author; and till we, from his Words, paint his very Ideas and Thoughts in our Minds, we do not understand him.

In the Division I have made, I have endeavoured, the best I could, to govern myself by the Diversity of Matter. But, in a Writer like St. *Paul*, it is not so easy always to find precisely where one Subject ends, and another begins. He is full of the Matter he treats, and writes with Warmth; which usually neglects Method, and those Partitions and Pauses, which Men educated in the Schools of Rhetoricians usually observe. Those Arts of Writing St. *Paul*, as well out of Design as Temper, wholly laid by: The Subject he had in hand, and the Grounds upon which it stood firm, and by which he inforced it, was what alone he minded; and, without solemnly winding up one Argument, and intimating any way that he began another, let his Thoughts, which were fully possessed of the Matter, run in one continued Train, wherein the Parts of his Discourse were wove one into another. So that it is seldom that the Scheme of his Discourse makes any Gap; and therefore, without breaking in upon the Connection of his Language, 'tis hardly possible to separate his Discourse, and give a distinct View of his several Arguments in distinct Sections.

I am far from pretending Infallibility in the Sense I have any where given in my Paraphrase or Notes; that would be to erect myself into an Apostle, a Presumption of the highest Nature in any one that cannot confirm what he says by Miracles. I have, for my own Information, sought the true Meaning, as far as my poor Abilities would reach: And I have unbiassedly embraced what, upon a fair Enquiry, appeared so to me. This I thought my Duty and Interest, in a Matter of so great Concernment to me. If I must believe for myself, it is unavoidable that I must understand for myself: For if I blindly, and with an implicit Faith, take the Pope's Interpretation of the Sacred Scripture, without examining whether it be Christ's Meaning, 'tis the Pope I believe in, and not in Christ; 'tis his Authority I rest upon; 'tis what he says I embrace; for what 'tis Christ says, I neither know, nor concern myself. 'Tis the same thing when I set up any other Man in Christ's Place, and make him the authentic Interpreter of Sacred Scripture to myself. He may possibly understand the Sacred Scripture as right as any Man, but I shall do well to examine myself, whether that which I do not know, nay which (in the way I take) I can never know, can justify me in making myself his Disciple, instead of Jesus Christ's, who of Right is alone, and ought to be, my only Lord and Master; and it will be no less Sacrilege in me to substitute to myself any other in his room, to be a Prophet to me, than to be my King or Priest.

 The same Reasons that put me upon doing what I have in these Papers done, will exempt me from all Suspicion of imposing my Interpretation on others. The Reasons that led me into the Meaning which prevailed on my Mind, are set down with it: As far as they carry Light and Conviction to any other Man's Understanding, so far I hope my Labour may be of some Use to him; beyond the Evidence it carries with it, I advise him not to follow mine, nor any Man's Interpretation. We are all Men, liable to Errors, and infected with them; but have this sure Way to preserve ourselves, every one from Danger by them, if, laying aside Sloth, Carelesness, Prejudice, Party, and a Reverence of Men, we betake ourselves in earnest to the Study of the Way to Salvation, in those holy Writings wherein God has revealed it from Heaven, and proposed it to the World; seeking our Religion where we are sure it is in Truth to be found, comparing spiritual Things with spiritual Things.

A PARAPHRASE and NOTES

ON THE
EPISTLE of St. *PAUL*
TO THE
GALATIANS.

Writ from Ephesus the Year of our Lord 57. Of Nero 3.

SYNOPSIS.

THE Subject and Design of this Epistle of St. *Paul* is much the same with that of his Epistle to the *Romans*, but treated in somewhat a different manner. The Business of it is to dehort and hinder the *Galatians* from bringing themselves under the Bondage of the Mosaical Law.

St. *Paul* himself had planted the Churches of *Galatia*, and therefore referring (as he does, *Ch.* I. 8, 9.) to what he had before taught them, does not in this Epistle lay down at large to them the Doctrine of the Gospel, as he does in that to the *Romans*; who having been converted to the Christian Faith by others, he did not know how far they were instructed in all those Particulars, which, on the Occasion whereon he writ to them, it might be necessary for them to understand: And therefore, writing to the *Romans*, he sets before them a large and comprehensive View of the chief Heads of the Christian Religion.

He also deals more roundly with his Disciples the *Galatians*, than, we may observe, he does with the *Romans*, to whom he, being a Stranger, writes not in so familiar a Stile, nor in his Reproofs and Exhortations uses so much the Tone of a Master, as he does to the *Galatians.*

St. *Paul* had converted the *Galatians* to the Faith, and erected several Churches among them in the Year of our Lord 51; between which.

Chap. I. which, and the Year 57, wherein this Epistle was writ, the Disorders following were got into those Churches.

First, Some Zealots for the *Jewish* Constitution, had very near persuaded them out of their Christian Liberty, and made them willing to submit to Circumcision, and all the Ritual Observances of the *Jewish* Church, as necessary under the Gospel: *Ch.* I. 7. III. 3. IV. 9, 10, 21. V. 1, 2, 6, 9, 10.

Secondly, Their Dissentions and Disputes in this matter had raised great Animosities amongst them, to the Disturbance of their Peace, and the setting them at Strife one with another: *Ch.* V. 6, 13---15.

The reforming them in these two Points seems to be the main Business of this Epistle, wherein he endeavours to establish them in a Resolution to stand firm in the Freedom of the Gospel, which exempts them from the Bondage of the Mosaical Law; and labours to reduce them to a sincere Love and Affection one to another; which he concludes with an Exhortation to Liberality, and general Beneficence, especially to their Teachers; *Ch.* VI. 6, 10. These being the Matters he had in his Mind to write to them about, he seems here as if he had done: But upon mentioning, *v.* 11. what a long Letter he had writ to them with his own Hand, the former Argument concerning Circumcision, which filled and warmed his Mind, broke out again into what we find, *v.* 12---17. of the VIth Chapter.

SECT. I.

CHAP. I. 1———5.

INTRODUCTION.

CONTENTS.

THE general View of this Epistle plainly shews St. *Paul's* chief Design in it to be, to keep the *Galatians* from hearkening to those Judaizing Seducers, who had almost persuaded them to be circumcised. These Perverters of the Gospel of Christ, as St. *Paul* himself calls them, *v.* 7. had, as may be gathered from *v.* 8, and 10. and from *Ch.* V. 11. and other Passages of this Epistle, made the *Galatians* believe, that St. *Paul* himself was for Circumcision. Till St. *Paul* himself had set them right in this Matter, and convinced them of the Falshood

hood of this Aspersion, it was in vain for him, by other Arguments, to attempt the re-establishing the *Galatians* in the Christian Liberty, and in that Truth which he had preached to them. The removing therefore of this Calumny was his first Endeavour; and to that Purpose, this Introduction, different from what we find in any other of his Epistles, is marvellously well adapted. He declares here at the Entrance, very expresly and emphatically, that he was not sent by Men on their Errands; nay, that Christ in sending him did not so much as convey his Apostolick Power to him by the Ministry, or Intervention of any Man; but that his Commission and Instructions were all entirely from God, and Christ himself, by immediate Revelation. This of itself was an Argument sufficient to induce them to believe, 1. That what he taught them when he first preached the Gospel to them, was the Truth, and they ought to stick firm to that. 2. That he changed not his Doctrine, whatever might be reported of him. He was Christ's chosen Officer, and had no Dependance on Men's Opinions, nor Regard to their Authority, or Favour, in what he preached; and therefore it was not likely he should preach one thing at one time, and another thing at another.

Thus this Preface is very proper in this Place to introduce what he is going to say concerning himself, and adds Force to his Discourse, and the Account he gives of himself in the next Section.

TEXT.

1 PAUL an Apostle (not of men, neither by man, but by Jesus Christ, and God the Father who raised him from the dead)

PARAPHRASE.

1. PAUL (an Apostle not of Men ^a, to serve their Ends, or carry on their Designs, nor receiving his Call, or Commission, by the Intervention of any Man ^b to whom he might be thought to owe any Respect, or Deference upon that account; but immediately from Jesus Christ, and from God the Father, who raised him up from

NOTES.

1 ^a 'Οὐκ ἀπ' ἀνθρώπων, *not of Men*, i. e. not sent by Men at their Pleasure, or by their Authority; not instructed by Men what to say or do, as we see *Timothy* and *Titus* were, when sent by St. *Paul*: And *Judas* and *Silas*, sent by the Church of *Jerusalem*.

^b 'Οὐδὲ δι᾽ ἀνθρώπου, *nor by Man*, i. e. His Choice and Separation to his Ministry and Apostleship, was so wholly an Act of God and Christ, that there was no Intervention of any thing done by any Man in the Case, as there was in the Election of *Matthias*. All this we may see explained at large, *v.* 10——12. and *v.* 16, 17. and *Cb.* II. 6——9.

GALATIANS.

PARAPHRASE.

2. the Dead;) and all the Brethren, that are with
3. me, unto the Churches ᶜ of *Galatia:* Favour be
to you and Peace ᵈ from God the Father, and
4. from our Lord Jesus Christ, who gave himself for
our Sins, that he might take us out of this present evil World ᵉ, according to the Will and good
5. Pleasure of God, and our Father, to whom be
Glory for ever and ever. *Amen.*

TEXT.

2 And all the brethren which are with me, unto the Churches of Galatia:

3 Grace be to you, and peace from God the Father, and from our Lord Jesus Christ;

4 Who gave himself for our sins, that he might deliver us from this present evil world, according to the will of God and our Father:

5 To whom be glory for ever and ever. Amen.

NOTES.

2 ᶜ *Churches of* Galatia. This was an evident Seal of his Apostleship to the Gentiles; since in no bigger a Country than *Galatia*, a small Province of the Lesser *Asia*, he had, in no long Stay among them, planted several distinct Churches.

3 ᵈ *Peace.* The wishing of *Peace* in the Scripture-Language, is the wishing of all manner of Good.

4 ᵉ *Ὅπως ἐξέληται ἡμᾶς ἐκ τοῦ ἐνεστῶτος αἰῶνος πονηροῦ*, *That he might take us out of this present evil World,* or *Age,* so the *Greek* Words signify: Whereby it cannot be thought, that St. *Paul* meant, that Christians were to be immediately removed into the other World. Therefore *ἐνεστὼς αἰὼν* must signify something else than *present World,* in the ordinary Import of those Words in *English.* Ἀιὼν οὗτος, 1 *Cor.* II. 6, 8. and in other Places, plainly signifies the *Jewish* Nation, under the Mosaical Constitution; and it suits very well with the Apostle's Design in this Epistle, that it should do so here. God has in this World but one Kingdom and one People. The Nation of the *Jews* were the Kingdom and People of God, whilst the Law stood. And this Kingdom of God, under the Mosaical Constitution, was called *ἀιὼν οὗτος, this Age,* or as it is commonly translated, *this World,* to which *ἀιὼν ἐνεστὼς, the present World,* or *Age,* here answers. But the Kingdom of God, which was to be under the Messiah, wherein the Oeconomy and Constitution of the *Jewish* Church, and the Nation itself, that in opposition to Christ adhered to it, was to be laid aside, is in the New Testament called *ἀιὼν μέλλων, the World,* or *Age to come*; so that Christ's *taking them out of the present World,* may, without any Violence to the Words, be understood to signify his setting them free from the Mosaical Constitution. This is suitable to the Design of this Epistle, and what St. *Paul* has declared in many other Places. See *Col.* II. 14——17, and 20. which agrees to this Place, and *Rom.* VII. 4, 6. The Law is said to be *contrary to us,* Col. II. 14. and to work Wrath, *Rom.* IV. 15. and St. *Paul* speaks very diminishingly of the Ritual Parts of it in many Places: But yet, if all this may not be thought sufficient to justify the applying of the Epithet *πονηρά, Evil,* to it, that Scruple will be removed, if we take *ἐνεστὼς ἀιὼν, this present World,* here, for the *Jewish* Constitution and Nation together, in which Sense it may very well be called *Evil,* though the Apostle, out of his wonted Tenderness to his Nation, forbears to name them openly, and uses a doubtful Expression, which might comprehend the Heathen World also, though he chiefly pointed at the *Jews.*

SECT.

GALATIANS.
SECT. II.
CHAP. I. 6.———II. 21.
CONTENTS.

WE have above obferved, that St. *Paul*'s firft Endeavour in this Epiftle, was to fatisfy the *Galatians*, that the Report fpread of him, that he preach'd Circumcifion, was falfe. Till this Obftruction, that lay in his way, was removed, it was to no purpofe for him to go about to diffuade them from Circumcifion, though that be what he principally aims at in this Epiftle. To fhew them, that he promoted not Circumcifion, he calls their hearkening to thofe who perfuaded them to be circumcifed, their being *removed* from him; and thofe that fo perfuaded them, *Perverters of the Gofpel of Chrift*, v. 6, 7. He farther affures them, that the Gofpel which he preached every where was that, and that only, which he had received by immediate Revelation from Chrift, and no Contrivance of Man, nor did he vary it to pleafe Men: That would not confift with his being a Servant of Chrift, v. 10. And he expreffes fuch a firm Adherence to what he had received from Chrift, and had preached to them, that he pronounces an *Anathema* upon himfelf, v. 8, 9. or any other Man or Angel, that fhould preach any thing elfe to them. To make out this to have been all along his Conduct, he gives an Account of himfelf for many Years backwards, even from the Time before his Converfion: Wherein he fhews, that from a zealous perfecuting Jew, he was made a Chriftian, and an Apoftle, by immediate Revelation; and that having no Communication with the Apoftles, or with the Churches of *Judea*, or any Man for fome Years, he had nothing to preach, but what he had receiv'd by immediate Revelation. Nay, when fourteen Years after he went up to *Jerufalem*, it was by Revelation, and when he there communicated the Gofpel, which he preach'd among the *Gentiles*, *Peter*, *James*, and *John* approved of it, without adding any thing, but admitted him as their Fellow-Apoftle. So that in all this he was guided by nothing but Divine Revelation, which he inflexibly ftuck to, fo far, that he openly oppofed St. *Peter*, for his Judaizing at *Antioch*. All which Account of himfelf tends clearly to fhew, that St. *Paul* made not the leaft Step towards complying with the *Jews* in favour of the Law, nor did,

B

Chap. I. did, out of Regard to Man, deviate from the Doctrine he had received by Revelation from God.

All the Parts of this Section, and the Narrative contain'd in it, manifestly *concenter* in this, as will more fully appear, as we go through them, and take a closer View of them; which will shew us, that the whole is so skilfully managed, and the Parts so gently slid into, that it is a strong, but not seemingly laboured Justification of himself, from the Imputation of Preaching up Circumcision.

PARAPHRASE.

6. I Cannot but wonder that you are so soon ᶠ removed from me ᵍ, (who called you unto the Covenant of Grace which is in Christ) unto another Sort of Gospel; which is not owing to any thing else ʰ, but only this, that you are troubled by a certain Sort of Men, who would overturn the Gospel of Christ, by making Circumcision, and the keeping of the Law necessary ⁱ under the

TEXT.

6 I Marvel that ye are so soon removed from him that called you into the grace of Christ, unto another gospel:

7 Which is not another; but there be some that trouble you, and would pervert the gospel of Christ.

NOTES.

6 ᶠ *So soon.* The first Place we find *Galatia* mentioned is *Acts* XVI. 6. And therefore St. *Paul* may be supposed to have planted these Churches there, in his Journey mentioned, *Acts* XVI. which was *Anno Domini* 51. He visited them again, after he had been at *Jerusalem*, Acts XVIII. 21———23. *Anno Domini* 54. From thence he returned to *Ephesus*, and staid there about two Years, during which Time this Epistle was writ: So that counting from his last Visit, this Letter was writ to them within two or three Years from the Time he was last with them, and had left them confirmed in the Doctrine he had taught them; and therefore he might with reason wonder at their forsaking him so soon, and that Gospel he had converted them to.

ᵍ *From him that called you.* These Words plainly point out himself. But then one might wonder how St. *Paul* came to use them; since it would have sounded better to have said, *Removed from the Gospel I preach'd to you, to another Gospel*, than *removed from me that preach'd to you, to another Gospel*. But if it be remembered that St. *Paul*'s Design here is to vindicate himself from the Aspersion cast on him, that he preached Circumcision, nothing could be more suitable to that Purpose, than this Way of expressing himself.

7 ʰ Ὃ οὐκ ἔστιν ἄλλο, I take to signify, *which is not any thing else.* The Words themselves, the Context, and the Business the Apostle is upon here, do all concur to give these Words the Sense I have taken them in. For, 1. If ⁰ had referred to ἐυαγγέλιον, it would have been more natural to have kept the Word ἕτερον, and not have changed it into ἄλλο. 2. It can scarce be supposed by any one who reads what St. *Paul* says, in the following Words of this Verse, and the two adjoining; and also *Chap.* III. 4. and *Ver.* 2——4, and 7. that St. *Paul* should tell them, that what he would keep them from *is not another Gospel.* 3. It is suitable to St. *Paul*'s Design here to tell them, that to their being *removed to another Gospel*, no body else had contributed, but it was wholly owing to those Judaizing Seducers.

ⁱ See *Acts* XV. 1, 5, 23, 24.

Gospel.

GALATIANS.

Chap. I.

TEXT.

8 But though we or an angel from heaven preach any other gospel unto you, than that which we have preached unto you, let him be accursed.

9 As we said before, so say I now again, if any man preach any other gospel unto you than that ye have received, let him be accursed.

10 For do I now persuade Men, or God? or do I seek to please men? for if I yet pleased men, I should not be the servant of Christ.

11 But I certify you, brethren, that the gospel which was preached of

PARAPHRASE.

Gospel. But if even I myself, or an Angel from Heaven, should preach any thing to you for Gospel, different from the Gospel I have preach'd unto you, let him be accursed. I say it again to you, if any one, under pretence of the Gospel, preach any other thing to you than what you have received from me, let him be accursed[k]. For can it be doubted of me, after having done and suffer'd so much for the Gospel of Christ, whether I do now[l] at this time of day make any Court to Men, or seek the Favour[m] of God? If I had hitherto made it my Business to please Men, I should not have been the Servant of Christ, nor taken up the Profession of the Gospel. But I certify you, Brethren, that the Gospel which has been

8.

9.

10.

11.

NOTES.

9[k] *Accursed.* Tho' we may look upon the Repetition of the *Anathema* here to be for the adding of Force to what he says, yet we may observe, that by joining himself with an Angel in the foregoing Verse, he does as good as tell them, that he is not guilty of what deserves it, by skilfully insinuating to the *Galatians*, that they might as well suspect an Angel might preach to them a Gospel different from his, *i. e.* a false Gospel, as that he himself should; and then in this Verse lays the *Anathema* wholly and solely upon the Judaizing Seducers.

10[l] *Ἄρτι Νῶν,* and *Ἔτι yet,* cannot be understood without a Reference to something in St. *Paul*'s past Life; what that was, which he had particularly then in his Mind, we may see by the Account he gives of himself in what immediately follows, (*viz.*) That before his Conversion he was employ'd by Men in their Designs, and made it his Business to please them, as may be seen, *Acts* IX. 1, 2. But when God called him, he received his Commission and Instructions from him alone, and set immediately about it without consulting any Man whatsoever, preaching that, and that only, which he had received from Christ. So that it would be senseless Folly in him, and no less than the forsaking his Master Jesus Christ, if he should *now,* as was reported of him, mix any thing of Men's with the pure Doctrine of the Gospel, which he had received immediately by Revelation from Jesus Christ, to please the *Jews*, after he had so long preach'd only that; and had, to avoid all Appearance or Pretence to the contrary, so carefully shunn'd all Communication with the Churches of *Judea*; and had not till a good while after, and that very sparingly, conversed with any, and those but a few, of the Apostles themselves, some of whom he openly reproved for their Judaizing. Thus the Narrative subjoined to this Verse explains the *νῶν* and *yet* in it, and tends to the same Purpose.

[m] Πείθω translated *persuade*, is sometimes used for making application to any one to obtain his good Will or Friendship; and hence *Acts* XII. 20. πείσαντες Βλάστον is translated, *having made Blastus their Friend*: The Sense here is the same which in 1 *Thess.* II. 4. he expresses in these Words, οὐχ ὡς ἀνθρώποις ἀρέσκοντες, ἀλλὰ τῷ Θεῷ, *not as pleasing Men, but God.*

| Chap. I. | PARAPHRASE. | TEXT. |

| | every where ⁿ preached by me, is not such as is pliant to human Interest, or can be accomodated to the pleasing of Men. (For I neither received it from Man, nor was I taught it by any one as his Scholar) but it is the pure and unmixed immediate Revelation of Jesus Christ to me. To satisfy you of this, my Behaviour, whilst I was of the Jewish Religion, is so well known, that I need not tell you, how excessive violent I was in persecuting the Church of God, and destroyed it all I could; and that being carried on by an extraordinary Zeal for the Traditions of my Forefathers, I out-stripp'd many Students of my own Age and Nation, in *Judaism*. But when it pleased God (who separated ᵒ me from my Mother's Womb, and by his especial Favour called ᵖ me to be a Christian, and a Preacher of the Gospel) to reveal his Son to me, that I might preach him among the *Gentiles*, I thereupon applied not myself to any Man ᑫ for Advice what to do ʳ: Neither went I up to *Jerusalem*, to those who were Apostles before me, to see whether they approved my Doctrine, or to have farther Instructions from | me, is not after man. For I neither received it of man, neither was I taught it, but by the Revelation of Jesus Christ. For ye have heard of my conversation in time past, in the Jews religion, how that beyond measure I persecuted the church of God, and wasted it; And profited in the Jews religion, above many my equals in mine own nation, being more exceedingly zealous of the traditions of my fathers. But when it pleased God, who separated me from my mother's womb, and called me by his grace, To reveal his Son in me, that I might preach him among the Heathen; immediately I conferred not with flesh and blood: Neither went I up to Jerusalem, to them which were Apostles before me, but I went into Arabia, and returned again unto Damascus. |

Verse numbers: 12, 13, 14, 15, 16, 17.

NOTES.

11 ⁿ Τὸ εὐαγγέλιον ὑπ' ἐμοῦ, *which has been preached by me*: This being spoken indefinitely, must be understood in general *every where*, and so is the Import of the foregoing Verse.

15 ᵒ *Separated*. This may be understood by *Jer.* I. 5.
ᵖ *Called*. The History of this Call, see *Acts* IX. 1, &c.

16 ᑫ *Flesh and Blood* is used for Man, see *Eph.* VI. 12.

ʳ *For Advice:* This, and what he says in the following Verse, is evidence to the *Galatians* the full Assurance he had of the Truth and Perfection of the Gospel, which he had received from Christ by immediate Revelation; and how little he was disposed to have any Regard to the pleasing of Men in preaching it; that he did not so much as communicate or advise with any of the Apostles about it, to see whether they approved of it.

them:

GALATIANS.

TEXT.

18 Then after three years I went up to Jerusalem to see Peter, and abode with him fifteen days.
19 But other of the apostles saw I none, save James the Lord's brother.
20 Now the things which I write unto you, behold, before God, I lie not.
21 Afterwards I came into the regions of Syria and Cilicia:
22 And was unknown by face unto the Churches of Judea, which were in Christ.
23 But they had heard only, That he which persecuted us in times past, now preached the faith which once he destroyed.
24 And they glorified God in me.

PARAPHRASE.

them: But I went immediately ᵗ unto *Arabia*, and from thence returned again to *Damascus*. Then after three Years ᵗ I went up to *Jerusalem*, 18. to see *Peter*, and abode with him fifteen Days. But other of the Apostles saw I none, but *James* 19. the Brother of our Lord. These things that I write 20. to you, I call God to witness, are all true; there is no Falshood in them. Afterwards I came into 21. the Regions of *Syria*, and *Cilicia*. But with the 22. Churches of Christ ᵘ in *Judea*, I had had no Communication, they had not so much as seen my Face ʷ; only they had heard that I, who 23. formerly persecuted the Churches of Christ, did now preach the Gospel, which I once endeavoured to suppress and extirpate. And they glorified 24. God upon my Account.

NOTES.

17 ᵗ Εὐθέως, *immediately*, tho' placed just before οὐ and προσανεθέμην, *I conferred not*, yet it is plain by the Sense and Design of St. *Paul* here, that it principally relates to, *I went into Arabia*; his Departure into *Arabia*, presently upon his Conversion, before he had consulted with any body, being made use of, to shew that the Gospel he had received by immediate Revelation from Jesus Christ, was compleat, and sufficiently instructed and enabled him to be a Preacher and an Apostle to the *Gentiles*, without borrowing any thing from any Man, in order thereunto, no not from any of the Apostles, no one of whom he saw till three Years after.

18 ᵗ *Three Years*, i. e. from his Conversion.

22 ᵘ *In Christ*, i. e. Believing in Christ, see *Rom.* XVI. 7.

ʷ This which he so particularly takes notice of, does nothing to the proving that he was a true Apostle, but serves very well to shew, that in what he preached, he had no Communication with those of his own Nation, nor took any Care to please the *Jews*.

GALATIANS.

CHAP. II.

PARAPHRASE.	TEXT.
1. THen fourteen Years after I went up again to *Jerusalem*, with *Barnabas*, and took *Titus* 2. also with me. And I went up by Revelation, and there laid before them the Gospel which I ˣ preached to the *Gentiles*, but privately to those who were of Note and Reputation amongst them, left the Pains that I have already taken ʸ. or should take in the Gospel, should be in 'vain ᶻ. 3. But tho' I communicated the Gospel which I preach'd to the *Gentiles*, to the eminent Men of	THen fourteen years 1 after I went up again to Jerusalem, with Barnabas, and took Titus with me also. And I went up by re- 2 velation, and communicated unto them that gospel which I preach among the *Gentiles*, but privately to them which were of reputation, lest by any means I should run, or had run in vain. But neither Titus, who 3

NOTES.

ˣ *I communicated.* The Conference he had in private with the chief of the Church of *Jerusalem*, concerning the Gospel which he preached among the *Gentiles*, seems not to have been barely concerning the Doctrine of their being free from the Law of *Moses*: That had been openly and hotly disputed at *Antioch*, and was known to be the Business they came about to *Jerusalem*; but it is probable it was to explain to them the whole Doctrine he had received by Revelation, by the Fulness and Perfection whereof, (for it is said, *ver.* 6. that in that Conference they added nothing to it) and by the Miracles he had done in Confirmation of it (see *ver* 8.) they might see and own what he preached to be the Truth, and him to be one of themselves both by Commission and Doctrine, as indeed they did. Ἀυτοῖς, *them*, signifies those at *Jerusalem*: κατ' ἰδίαν δὲ τοῖς δοκοῦσι, are exegetical, and shew the particular Manner and Persons, and import *nempe privatim eminentioribus.* 'Twas enough to his Purpose to be owned by those of greatest Authority, and so we see he was by *James*, *Peter* and *John*, *ver.* 9. and therefore it was safest and best to give an Account of the Gospel he preach'd in private to them, and not publickly to the whole Church.

ʸ *Running*, St. *Paul* uses for *taking Pains* in the Gospel, see *Col.* II. 16. A Metaphor, I suppose, taken from the Olympick Games, to express his utmost Endeavours to prevail in propagating the Gospel.

ᶻ *In vain.* He seems here to give two Reasons why at last, after 14 Years, he communicated to the chief of the Apostles at *Jerusalem*, the Gospel that he preach'd to the *Gentiles*, when, as he shews to the *Galatians*, he had formerly declined all Communication with the convert *Jews*. 1. He seems to intimate, That he did it by Revelation. 2. He gives another Reason, *viz.* That if he had not communicated, as he did, with the leading Men there, and satisfied them of his Doctrine and Mission, his Opposers might unsettle the Churches he had, or should plant, by urging that the Apostles knew not what it was that he preached, nor had ever owned it for the Gospel, or him for an Apostle. Of the Readiness of the Judaizing Seducers to take any such Advantage against him, he had lately an Example in the Church of *Corinth*.

the

GALATIANS.

TEXT.

was with me, being a Greek, was compelled to be circumcised:

4 And that because of false brethren unawares brought in, who came in privily to spy out our liberty, which we have in Christ Jesus, that they might bring us into bondage:

5 To whom we gave place by subjection, no not

PARAPHRASE.

the Church at *Jerusalem*, yet neither ᵃ *Titus*, who was with me, being a *Greek*, was forced to be Circumcised. Nor ᵇ did I yield any thing one Moment, by way of Subjection ᶜ to the Law, to those false Brethren, who by an unwary Admittance were slily crept in to spy out our Liberty from the Law, which we have under the Gospel; that they might bring us into Bondage ᵈ to the Law. But I stood my ground against it, that the

4.

5.

NOTES.

3 ᵃ οὐκ ἠναγκάσθη is rightly translated, *was not compelled*, a plain Evidence to the *Galatians* that the Circumcising of the convert *Gentiles* was no Part of the Gospel which he laid before these Men of Note, as what he preach'd to the *Gentiles*. For if it had, *Titus* must have been circumcised; for no Part of his Gospel was blamed or altered by them, *ver.* 6. Of what other Use his mentioning this of *Titus* here can be, but to shew to the *Galatians* that what he preach'd contain'd nothing of circumcising the convert *Gentiles*, it is hard to find. If it were to shew that the other Apostles, and Church at *Jerusalem*, dispensed with Circumcision, and other ritual Observances of the Mosaical Law, that was needless; for that was sufficiently declared by their Decree, *Acts* XV. which was made and communicated to the Churches before this Epistle was writ, as may be seen, *Acts* XVI. 4. much less was this of *Titus* of any Force to prove that St. *Paul* was a true Apostle, if that were what he was here labouring to justify. But considering his Aim here to be the clearing himself from a Report that he preach'd up Circumcision, there could be nothing more to his Purpose than this Instance of *Titus*, whom, uncircumcised as he was, he took with him to *Jerusalem*; uncircumcised he kept with him there, and uncircumcised he took back with him when he returned. This was a strong and pertinent Instance to persuade the *Galatians*, that the Report of his preaching Circumcision was a mere Aspersion.

4 ᵇ οὐδέ, *Neither*, in the 3d Verse, according to Propriety of Speech, ought to have a *Nor* to answer it, which is the οὐδέ, *nor*, here; which so taken answers the Propriety of the *Greek*, and very much clears the Sense; οὐδέ Τίτος ἠναγκάσθη, οὐδὲ πρὸς ὥραν εἴξαμεν. *Neither was Titus compelled, nor did we yield to them a Moment.*

ᶜ Τῇ ὑποταγῇ, *by Subjection*. The Point those false Brethren contended for, was, That the Law of *Moses* was to be kept, see *Acts* XV. 5. St. *Paul*, who on other Occasions was so complaisant, that to the *Jews* he became as a *Jew*, to those under the Law as under the Law, (see 1 *Cor.* IX. 19 — 22.) yet when Subjection to the Law was claim'd as due in any Case, would not yield the least Matter; this I take to be his Meaning of οἷς οὐδὲ πρὸς ὥραν εἴξαμεν τῇ ὑποταγῇ, for whe e Compliance was desired of him upon the Account of Expedience, and not of Subjection to the Law, we do not find him stiff and inflexible, as may be seen, *Acts* XXI. 18———26. which was after the Writing of this Epistle.

ᵈ *Bondage*. What this Bondage was, see *Acts* XV. 1, 5, 10.

Truth

Chap. II.

GALATIANS.

PARAPHRASE.

6. Truth [e] of the Gospel might remain [f] among you. But as for those [g] who were really Men [h] of Eminency and Value, what they were heretofore it matters not at all to me: God accepts not the Person of any Man, but communi-

TEXT.

for an hour; that the truth of the gospel might continue with you.
But of these, who 6 seemed to be somewhat, (whatsoever they were, it maketh no matter to

NOTES.

5 [e] *The Truth of the Gospel.* By it he means here the Doctrine of Freedom from the Law; and so he calls it again, *ver.* 14. and *chap.* III. 1. and IV. 19.

[f] *Might remain among you.* Here he tells the Reason himself why he yielded not to those Judaizing false Brethren: It was, that the true Doctrine which he had preach'd to the *Gentiles*, of their Freedom from the Law, might stand firm. A convincing Argument to the *Galatians*, that he preach'd not Circumcision.

4, 5. *And that,—to whom.* There appears a manifest Difficulty in these two Verses, which has been observed by most Interpreters, and is by several ascribed to a Redundancy, which some place in δὲ, in the Beginning of *ver.* 4. and others to οἷς, in the Beginning of *ver.* 5. The Relation between δὲ *ver.* 3. and δὲ *ver.* 5. methinks, puts an easy End to the Doubt, by the shewing St. *Paul's* Sense to be, that he *neither* circumcised *Titus*, *nor* yielded in the least to the false Brethren: He having told the *Galatians*, that upon his laying before the Men of most Authority in the Church at *Jerusalem*, the Doctrine which he preach'd, *Titus* was not circumcised; he, as a farther Proof of his not preaching Circumcision, tells them how he carried it towards the false Brethren, whose Design it was to bring the convert *Gentiles* into *Subjection* to the Law. *And*, or *Moreover* (for so δὲ often signifies) says he, *in regard to the false Brethren*, &c. Which Way of Entrance on the Matter would not admit of δὲ after it to answer δὲ, *ver.* 3. which was already writ; but without οἷς the Negation must be expressed by οἷς, as any one will perceive, who attentively reads the *Greek* Original. And thus οἷς may be allowed for an *Hebrew* Pleonasm, and the Reason of it to be the preventing the former δὲ to stand alone to the Disturbance of the Sense.

6 [g] He that considers the Beginning of this Verse, ἀπὸ δὲ τῶν δοκούντων, with regard to the Διὰ δὲ τὸ Ψευδαδέλφοις, in the Beginning of the 4th Verse, will easily be induced by the *Greek* Idiom to conclude, that the Author, by these Beginnings, intimates a plain Distinction of the Matter separately treated of, in what follows each of them, (viz.) what passed between the false Brethren and him, contained *ver.* 6 —— 10. And therefore some (and I think with Reason) introduce this Verse with these Words, *Thus we behaved ourselves towards the false Brethren: But,* &c.

[h] τῶν δοκούντων εἶναί τι, our Translation renders, *who seemed to be somewhat*, which however it may answer the Words, yet to an *English* Ear it carries a diminishing and ironical Sense, contrary to the Meaning of the Apostle, who speaks here of those for whom he had a real Esteem, and were truly of the first Rank; for it is plain by what follows, that he means *Peter, James* and *John*. Besides, οἱ δοκοῦντες being taken in a good Sense, *ver.* 2. and translated *those of Reputation*, the same Expression should have been kept to in rendering *ver.* 6. and 3. where the same Term occurs again three times, and may be presumed in the same Sense that it was at first used in *ver.* 2.

GALATIANS.

TEXT.

me: God accepteth no man's person) for they who seemed *to be somewhat*, in conference added nothing to me.

7 But contrariwise, when they saw that the Gospel of the uncircumcision was committed unto me, as the Gospel of the circumcision was unto Peter;

PARAPHRASE.

cates the Gospel to whom he pleases[i], as he has done to me by Revelation, without their Help; for in their Conference with me they added nothing to me, they taught me nothing new, nor that Christ had not taught me before, nor had they any thing to object against what I preached to the *Gentiles*. But on the contrary, [k] *James*, *Peter* and *John*, who were of Reputation, and justly esteemed to be Pillars, perceiving that the Gospel which was to be preached to the *Gentiles*, was committed to me, as that which was to be preached to the *Jews*, was com-

7.

NOTES.

[i] Every body sees that there is something to be supplied to make up the Sense; most Commentators that I have seen, add these Words, *I learned nothing*. But then that enervates the Reason that follows: *For in Conference they added nothing to me*; giving the same thing as a Reason for itself, and making St. *Paul* talk thus, *I learnt nothing of them, for they taught me nothing*. But it is very good Reasoning, and suited to his Purpose, that it was nothing at all to him, how much those great Men were formerly in Christ's Favour; this hindered not but that God, who was no Respecter of Persons, might reveal the Gospel to him also, as 'twas evident he had done, and that in its full Perfection. For those great Men, the most eminent of the Apostles, had nothing to add to it, or except against it. This was proper to persuade the *Galatians*, that he no where in his Preaching receded from that Doctrine of Freedom from the Law, which he had preached to them, and was satisfied it was the Truth, even before he had conferred with these Apostles. The bare Supplying of *ἐ*, in the Beginning of the Verse, takes away the Necessity of any such Addition. Examples of the like Elleipses we have, *Mat.* XXVII. 9. where we read ἀ-ὶ υἱῶν for οἱ ἀπὸ υἱῶν; and *John* XVI. 17. ἐκ τῶν μαθητῶν, for οἱ ἐκ τῶν μαθητῶ; and so here taking ἀπὸ τῶν δοκούντων, to be for οἱ ἀπὸ τῶν δοκούντων, all the Difficulty is removed; and St. *Paul* having in the foregoing Verse ended the Narrative of his Deportment towards the false Brethren, he here begins an Account of what passed between him and the chief of the Apostles.

7 *Peter*, *James* and *John*, who 'tis manifest by *ver.* 9. are the Persons here spoken of, seem of all the Apostles to have been most in Esteem and Favour with their Master during his Conversation with them on Earth. See *Mark* V. 37. and IX. 2. and XIV. 33. "But yet that," says St. *Paul*, "is of no Moment now to me. The Gospel which I preach, and which God, who is "no Respecter of Persons, has been pleased to commit to me, by immediate Revelation, is not "the less true, nor is there any Reason for me to recede from it in the little; for these Men of "the first Rank could find nothing to add, alter, or gainsay in it." This is suitable to St. *Paul's* Design here, to let the *Galatians* see that as he, in his Carriage, had never favoured Circumcision, so neither had he any Reason, by preaching Circumcision, to forsake the Doctrine of Liberty from the Law, which he had preached to them as a Part of that Gospel which he had received by Revelation.

GALATIANS.

Chap. II.

PARAPHRASE.

8. mitted to *Peter*; (For he that had wrought powerfully¹ in *Peter* to his executing the Office of an Apostle to the *Jews*, had also wrought powerfully in me in my Application and Apostleship, to the *Gentiles*;) And knowing ᵐ the Favour that was bestowed on me, gave me and *Barnabas* the Right Hand ⁿ of Fellowship, that we should preach the Gospel to the *Gentiles*, and they to the Children of *Israel*. All that they proposed was, that we should remember to make Collections among the *Gentiles*, for the poor Christians of *Judea*; which was a Thing that of myself I was forward to do. But when *Peter* came to *Antioch*, I openly opposed him ᵒ to his Face. For indeed he

TEXT.

8 (For he that wrought effectually in Peter to the apostleship of the circumcision, the same was mighty in me towards the Gentiles)

9 And when James, Cephas and John, who seemed to be pillars, perceived the grace that was given unto me, they gave to me and Barnabas the right hands of fellowship; that we should go unto the heathen, and they unto the circumcision.

10 Only they would that we should remember the poor; the same which I also was forward to do.

11 But when Peter was

NOTES.

8 ¹ Ἐνεργήσας, *working in*, may be understood here to signify, both the Operation of the Spirit upon the Mind of St. *Peter* and St. *Paul*, in sending them, the one to the *Jews*, the other to the *Gentiles*; and also the Holy Ghost bestowed on them, whereby they were enabled to do Miracles for the Confirmation of their Doctrine. In neither of which St. *Paul*, as he shews, was inferior, and so had as authentic a Seal of his Mission and Doctrine.

9 ᵐ Καὶ, *and*, copulates γνόντες, *knowing*, in this Verse, with ἰδόντες, *seeing*, ver. 7. and makes both of them to agree with the Nominative Case to the Verb ἔδωκαν, *gave*, which is no other but *James, Cephas* and *John*: and so justifies my transferring those Names to *ver.* 7. for the more easy Construction and Understanding of the Text, though St. *Paul* defers the Naming of them, till he is, as it were against his Will, forced to it before the End of his Discourse.

ⁿ The giving the Right Hand was a Symbol amongst the *Jews*, as well as other Nations, of Accord, and admitting Men into Fellowship.

11 ᵒ *I opposed him.* From this Opposition to St. *Peter*, which they suppose to be before the Council at *Jerusalem*, some would have it, that this Epistle to the *Galatians* was writ before that Council; as if what was done before the Council could not be mentioned in a Letter writ after the Council. They also contend, that this Journey mentioned here by St. *Paul*, was not that wherein he and *Barnabas* went up to that Council to *Jerusalem*, but that mentioned *Acts* XI. 30. but this with as little ground as the former. The strongest Reason they bring is, that, if this Journey had been to the Council, and this Letter, after that Council, St *Paul* would not certainly have omitted to have mentioned to the *Galatians* that Decree. To which I answer, 1ˢᵗ, The Mention of it was superfluous, for they had it already, see *Acts* XVI. 4. 2ᵈˡʸ, The Mentioning of it was impertinent to the Design of St. *Paul*'s Narrative here. For it is plain that his Aim in what he relates here of himself, and his past Actions, is to shew, that having received the Gospel from Christ by immediate Revelation, he had all along preached that, and nothing but that, every where; so that he could not be supposed to have preached Circumcision, or by his Carriage to have shewn any Subjection to the Law; all the whole Narrative following being to make good what he says, *Chap.* I. 11. That the Gospel which he preached was not accommodated to the Humouring of Men; nor did he seek to

please

GALATIANS.

Chap. II.

TEXT.	PARAPHRASE.
come to Antioch, I withstood him to the face, because he was to be blamed.	he was to be blamed. For he conversed there familiarly with the *Gentiles*, and eat with them till some *Jews* came thither from *James*; then he
12 For before that certain came from James, he did eat with the Gentiles, but when they were come, he withdrew, and separated himself, fearing them which were of the circumcision.	withdrew and separated from the *Gentiles*, for fear of those who were of the Circumcision: And the rest of the *Jews* joined also with him in this Hypocrisy, insomuch that *Barnabas* himself was carried away with the Stream, and dissembled as
13 And the other Jews dissembled likewise with him; insomuch that Barnabas also was carried away with their dissimulation.	they did. But when I saw they conformed not their Conduct to the Truth ᵖ of the Gospel, I said unto *Peter* before them all, If thou, being a *Jew*, takest the Liberty sometimes to live after
14 But when I saw that they walked not uprightly, according to the truth of the gospel, I said unto Peter before them all, If thou, being a Jew, livest after the manner of Gentiles, and not as do the Jews, why compellest thou the Gentiles to live as do the Jews?	the Manner of the *Gentiles*, not keeping to those Rules which the *Jews* observe, why dost thou constrain the *Gentiles* to conform themselves to the Rites, and Manner of Living of the *Jews*? We who are by ᑫ Nature *Jews*, born under the Instruction and Guidance of the Law, God's peculiar People, and not of the unclean and profligate Race of the *Gentiles*, abandoned to Sin and
15 We who are Jews by nature, and not sinners of the Gentiles,	Death; knowing that a Man cannot be justified by the Deeds of the Law, but solely by Faith
16 Knowing that a man is not justified by the works of the law, but by the faith of Jesus Christ, even we have believed	in Jesus Christ; even we have put ourselves upon believing on him, and embraced the Profession of the Gospel for the Attainment of Justification

	12.
	13.
	14.
	15.
	16.

NOTES.

please the *Jews* (who are the Men here meant) in what he taught. Taking this to be his Aim, we shall find the whole Account he gives of himself, from that 11th *ver.* of *Chap.* I. to the End of this IId. to be very clear and easy, and very proper to invalidate the Report of his preaching Circumcision.

14 ᵖ Ἀληθεια τῇ εὐαγγελίῳ, *The truth of the Gospel*, is put here for that Freedom from the Law of *Moses* which was a Part of the true Doctrine of the Gospel: For it was in nothing else but their undue and timorous observing some of the Mosaical Rites, that St. *Paul* here blames St. *Peter*, and the other Judaizing Converts at *Antioch*. In this sense he uses the Word *Truth*, all along through this Epistle, as *Chap.* II. 5, 14. and III. 1. and V. 7. insisting on it, that this Doctrine of Freedom from the Law was the true Gospel.

15 ᑫ Φύσει Ἰουδαῖοι, *Jews by Nature*. What the *Jews* thought of themselves in contradistinction to the *Gentiles*, see *Rom.* II. 17, 23.

C 2   by

GALATIANS.

PARAPHRASE.

by Faith in Christ, and not by the Works of the
17. Law: But if we seek to be justified in Christ,
even we ourselves also are found unjustified Sinners ʳ, (for such are all those who are under the
Law, which admits of no Remission nor Justification) is Christ therefore the Minister of Sin?
Is the Dispensation by him a Dispensation of Sin,
and not of Righteousness? Did he come into
the World, that those who believe in him should
still remain Sinners, *i. e.* under the Guilt of
their Sins, without the Benefit of Justification?
18. By no means. And yet certain it is, if I ˢ who
quitted the Law, to put myself under the Gospel, put myself again under the Law, I make
myself a Transgressor, I re-assume again the
Guilt of all my Transgressions; which by the
Terms of that Covenant of Works, I cannot be
19. justified from. For by the ᵗ Tenor of the Law
itself I by Faith in Christ am discharged ᵘ

TEXT.

in Jesus Christ; that we might be justified by the faith of Christ, and not by the works of the law: for by the works of the law shall no flesh be justified.

But if while we seek 17 to be justified by Christ, we ourselves also are found sinners, is therefore Christ the minister of sin? God forbid.

For if I build again 18 the things which I destroyed, I make myself a transgressor.

For I through the law 19 am dead to the law, that

NOTES.

17 ʳ *Sinners.* Those who are under the Law, having once transgressed, remain always Sinners unalterably so in the Eye of the Law; which excludes all from Justification. The Apostle, in this Place, argues thus; "We *Jews*, who are by Birth God's holy People, and "not as the profligate *Gentiles*, abandoned to all Manner of Pollution and Uncleanness, not "being nevertheless able to attain Righteousness by the Deeds of the Law, have believed in "Christ, that we might be justified by Faith in him. But if even we, who have betaken "ourselves to Christ for Justification, are ourselves found to be unjustified Sinners, liable "still to Wrath, as also under the Law, to which we subject ourselves; what Deliverance have we from Sin by Christ? None at all: We are as much concluded under Sin "and Guilt, as if we did not believe in him. So that by joining him and the Law together "for Justification, we shut ourselves out from Justification, which cannot be had under "the Law; and make Christ the Minister of Sin, and not of Justification; which God forbid."

18 ˢ Whether this be a Part of what St. *Paul* said to St. *Peter*, or whether it be addressed to the *Galatians*, St. *Paul*, by speaking in his own Name, plainly declares, that if he sets up the Law again, he must necessarily be an Offender; whereby he strongly insinuates to the *Galatians*, that he was no Promoter of Circumcision, especially when what he says, *Chap.* V. 2—4. is added to it

19 ᵗ *By the Tenor of the Law itself.* See *Rom.* III. 21. *Gal.* III. 24, 25. & IV. 21. &c.

ᵘ Being *discharged from the Law*, St. *Paul* expresses by *Dead to the Law*; compare *Rom.* VI. 14. with VII. 4.

from

GALATIANS.

TEXT.

I might live unto God.
20 I am crucified with Christ: nevertheless I live; yet not I, but Christ liveth in me: and the life which I now live in the flesh, I live by the faith of the Son of God, who loved me, and gave himself for me.
21 I do not frustrate the grace of God: for if righteousness come by the law, then Christ is dead in vain.

PARAPHRASE.

from the Law that I might be appropriated [w] to God, and live acceptably to him in his Kingdom, which he has now set up under his Son. I, 20. a Member of Christ's Body, am crucified [x] with him: But tho' I am thereby dead to the Law, I nevertheless live; yet not I, but Christ liveth in me; *i. e.* the Life which I now live in the Flesh, is upon no other Principle, nor under any other Law, but that of Faith in the Son of God [y], who loved me, and gave himself for me. And 21. in so doing I avoid frustrating the Grace of God; I accept of the Grace [z] and Forgiveness of God, as it is offered through Faith in Christ in the Gospel: But if I subject myself to the Law, as still in force under the Gospel, I do in effect frustrate Grace. For if Righteousness be to be had by the Law, then Christ died to no Purpose, there was no need of it [a].

Chap. II.

NOTES.

[w] *Live to God.* What St. *Paul* says here, seems to imply, that living under the Law, was to live not acceptably to God; a strange Doctrine certainly to the *Jews*, and yet it was true now under the Gospel: For God having put his Kingdom in this World wholly under his Son, when he raised him from the Dead, all who after that would be his People in his Kingdom, were to live by no other Law but the Gospel, which was now the Law of his Kingdom. And hence we see God cast off the *Jews*, because sticking to their old Constitution, they would not have this Man reign over them: so that what St. *Paul* says here, is in effect this; "By believing in "Christ, I am discharged from the Mosaical Law, that I may wholly conform myself to the "Rule of the Gospel, which is now the Law, which must be owned and observed by all those "who, as God's People, will live acceptably to him." This, I think, is visibly his Meaning, though the accustoming himself to Antitheses may possibly be the Reason why, after having said, *I am dead to the Law*, he expresses his putting himself under the Gospel, by *living to God*.

20 [x] *Crucified with Christ:* See this explained, *Rom.* VII. 4. and VI. 2 — 14.

[y] *i. e.* The whole Management of myself is conformable to the Doctrine of the Gospel of Justification in Christ alone, and not by the Deeds of the Law. This and the former Verse seems to be spoken in opposition to St. *Peter*'s owning a Subjection to the Law of *Moses*, by his Walking, mentioned *ver.* 14.

21 [z] *Grace of God*, see *Chap.* I. 6, 7. to which this seems here opposed.

[a] *In vain:* Read this explained in St. *Paul*'s own Works, *Chap.* V. 3 — 6.

SECT.

GALATIANS.

SECT. III.

CHAP. III. 1——5.

CONTENTS.

BY the Account St. *Paul* has given of himself in the foregoing Section, the *Galatians* being furnished with Evidence sufficient to clear him in their Minds from the Report of his preaching Circumcision, he comes now, the Way being thus opened, directly to oppose their being circumcised, and subjecting themselves to the Law. The first Argument he uses is, that they received the Holy Ghost, and the Gifts of Miracles, by the Gospel, and not by the Law.

PARAPHRASE.

1. O Ye foolish *Galatians*, who hath cast a Mist before your Eyes, that you should not keep to the Truth [b] of the Gospel; you to whom the Sufferings and Death of Christ [c] upon the Cross, had been by me so lively represented, as if it had
2. been actually done in your Sight? This one Thing I desire to know of you, Did you receive the miraculous Gifts of the Spirit, by the Works of the
3. Law, or by the Gospel preached to you? Have you so little Understanding, that having begun in the Reception of the Spiritual Doctrine of the Gospel, you hope to be advanced to higher Degrees

TEXT.

1. O Foolish Galatians, who hath bewitched you, that you should not obey the truth, before whose eyes Jesus Christ hath been evidently set forth, crucified among you?
2. This only would I learn of you, Received ye the Spirit by the works of the law, or by the hearing of faith?
3. Are ye so foolish? Ha-

NOTES.

1 [b] *Obey the Truth*, i. e. stand fast in the Liberty of the Gospel: *Truth* being used in this Epistle, as we have already noted, *Chap.* II. 14. for the Doctrine of being free from the Law; which St. *Paul* had delivered to them: The Reason whereof he gives *Chap.* V. 3 5.

[c] St. *Paul* mentions nothing to them here but *Christ crucified*, as knowing, that when formerly he had preached Christ crucified to them, he had shewn them, that by Christ's Death on the Cross, Believers were set free from the Law, and the Covenant of Works was removed, to make way for that of Grace. This we may find him inculcating to his other Gentile Converts. See *Eph.* II. 15, 16. *Col.* II. 14. 20. And accordingly he tells the *Galatians*, Chap. V. 2, 4. that if by Circumcision they put themselves under the Law, they were fallen from Grace, and Christ should profit them nothing at all : Things which they are supposed to understand at his writing to them.

GALATIANS.

| TEXT. | PARAPHRASE. | Chap. III. |

ving begun in the Spirit are ye now made perfect by the flesh?

4 Have ye suffered so many things in vain? if it be yet in vain.

5 He therefore that ministereth to you the Spirit, and worketh miracles among you, doth he it by the works of the law, or by the hearing of faith?

of Perfection, and to be compleated, by the Law^d? Have you suffered so many Things in vain; if at least you will render it in vain, by falling off from the Profession of the pure and uncorrupted Doctrine of the Gospel, and apostatizing to Judaism? The Gifts of the Holy Ghost that have been conferred upon you, have they not been conferred on you as Christians, professing Faith in Jesus Christ, and not as Observers of the Law? And hath not he^e, who hath conveyed these Gifts to you, and done Miracles amongst you, done it as a Preacher and Professor of the Gospel; the *Jews*, who stick to the Law of *Moses*, being not able by Virtue of that to do any such Thing?

4.

5.

NOTES.

3 ^d It is a Way of speaking, very familiar to St. *Paul*, in opposing the Law to the Gospel, to call the Law *Flesh*, and the Gospel *Spirit*: The Reason whereof is very plain to any one conversant in his Epistles.

5 ^e *He.* The Person meant here by ὁ ἐπιχορηγῶν, *he that ministereth*, and *Chap.* I. 6. by ὁ καλέσας, *he that called*, is plainly St. *Paul* himself, though out of Modesty he declines naming himself.

SECT. IV.

CHAP. III. 6———17.

CONTENTS.

HIS next Argument against Circumcision and Subjection to the Law, is, that the Children of *Abraham*, entitled to the Inheritance and Blessing promised to *Abraham* and his Seed, are so by Faith, and not by being under the Law, which brings a Curse upon those who are under it.

But

GALATIANS.

Chap. III.

PARAPHRASE.

6, 7. But to proceed. As *Abraham* believed in God, and it was accounted to him for Righteousness; so know ye, that those who are of Faith, *i. e.* who rely upon God and his Promises of Grace, and not upon their own Performances, they are the Children of *Abraham* who shall inherit. And this is
8. plain in the Scripture; for it being in the Purpose of God to justify the *Gentiles* by Faith, he gave *Abraham* a Fore-knowledge of the Gospel in these Words: ^f *In thee all the Nations of the Earth
9. shall be blessed*. So that they who are of ^g Faith are
10. blessed with *Abraham*, who believed. But as many as are of the Works of the Law, are under the ^h Curse: For it is written, ⁱ *Cursed is every one who remaineth not in all things which are written in
11. the Book of the Law, to do them*. But that no Man is justified by the Law in the sight of God, is evi-
12. dent, *for the Just shall live by Faith* ^k. But the Law says not so, the Law gives not Life to those who believe^l; but the Rule of the Law is, *He that doth
13. them, shall live in them* ^m. Christ hath redeemed us from the Curse of the Law, being made a Curse for us: For it is written, ⁿ *Cursed is every one that
14. hangeth on a Tree*. That the Blessing ^o promised

TEXT.

6. Even as Abraham believed God, and it was accounted to him for righteousness.
7. Know ye therefore, that they which are of faith, the same are the children of Abraham.
8. And the scripture foreseeing that God would justify the Heathen thro' faith, preached before the gospel unto Abraham, saying, In thee shall all nations be blessed.
9. So then they which be of faith, are blessed with faithful Abraham.
10. For as many as are of the works of the law, are under the curse: for it is written, Cursed is every one that continueth not in all things which are written in the book of the law to do them.
11. But that no man is justified by the law in the sight of God, it is evident: for, The just shall live by faith.
12. And the law is not of faith: but, The man that doth them, shall live in them.

NOTES.

8 ^f *Gen.* XII. 3.

9, 10. *Of Faith*, and *of the Works of the Law*: Spoken as of two Races of Men, the one as the genuine Posterity of *Abraham*, Heirs of the Promise, the other not.

^h *Blessed, and under the Curse*. Here again there is another *Division* (viz.) into the *Blessed*, and those *under the Curse*; whereby is meant such as are in a State of Life, or Acceptance with God, or such as are exposed to his Wrath, and to Death. See *Deut.* XXX. 19.

10 ⁱ Written *Deut.* XXVII. 26.
11 ^k *Hab.* II. 4.
12 ^l See *Act.* XIII. 39.
^m *Lev.* VIII. 15.
13 *Deut.* XXI. 23.
14 ^o *Blessing*. That Blessing, *ver.* 8, 9, 14. Justification, *ver.* 11. Righteousness, *ver.* 21. Life, *ver.* 11, 12, 21. Inheritance, *ver.* 18. being the Children of God, *ver.* 26. are in effect all the same on the one Side; and *the Curse, ver.* 13. the direct contrary on the other side, is so plain in St. *Paul*'s Discourse here, that no body who reads it with the least Attention will be in any Doubt about it.

GALATIANS.

TEXT.

13 Christ hath redeemed us from the curse of the law, being made a curse for us: for it is written, Cursed is every one that hangeth on a tree:

14 That the blessing of Abraham might come on the Gentiles through Jesus Christ; that we might receive the promise of the Spirit through faith.

15 Brethren, I speak after the manner of men; tho' it be but a man's covenant, yet if it be confirmed, no man disannulleth or addeth thereto.

16 Now to Abraham and his seed were the promises made. He saith not, And to seeds, as of many; but as of one, And to thy seed, which is Christ.

17 And this I say, that the covenant that was confirmed before of God in Christ, the law which

PARAPHRASE.

to *Abraham* might come on the *Gentiles* through *Jesus Christ*; that we who are Christians might, believing, receive the Spirit that was promised ᵖ. Brethren, this is a known and allowed Rule in human Affairs, that a Promise or Compact, tho' it be barely a Man's Covenant, yet if it be once ratified, so it must stand; no body can render it void, or make any Alteration in it. Now to *Abraham* and his Seed were the Promises made. God doth not say, *and to Seeds* ᵠ, as if he spoke of more Seeds than one, that were entitled to the Promise upon different Accounts, but only of one Sort of Men, who upon one sole Account were that Seed of *Abraham* which was alone meant and concerned in the Promise: So that *unto thy Seed* ʳ, designed Christ, and his mystical Body ˢ, *i. e.* those that become Members of him by Faith. This therefore I say, that the Law, which was not till 430 Years after, cannot disannul the Covenant that was long before made and ratified to Christ by God, so as

15.

16.

17.

NOTES.

ᵖ *Promised.* St. *Paul*'s Argument to convince the *Galatians*, that they ought not to be circumcised, or submit to the Law, from having received the Spirit from him, upon their having received the Gospel which he preached to them. *ver.* 2, and 5. stands thus: The Blessing promised to *Abraham*, and to his Seed, was wholly upon the Account of Faith, *ver.* 7. There were not different Seeds, who should inherit the Promise, the one by the Works of the Law, and the other by Faith; for there was but one Seed, which was Christ, *ver.* 16. and those who should claim in and under him by Faith. Among those there was no Distinction of *Jew* and *Gentile*. They, and they only, who believed, were all one and the same true Seed of *Abraham*, and Heirs according to the Promise, *ver.* 28, 29. And therefore the Promise made to the People of God, of giving them the Spirit under the Gospel, was performed only to those who believed in Christ: A clear Evidence that it was not by putting themselves under the Law, but by Faith in Jesus Christ, that they were the People of God, and Heirs of the Promise.

16 ᵠ *And to Seeds.* By Seeds St. *Paul* here visibly means the οἱ ἐκ πίστεως, *those of Faith*, and the οἱ ἐκ ἔργων νόμου, *those of the Works of the Law*, spoken of above, *ver.* 9, 10. as two distinct Seeds, or Descendants claiming from *Abraham*.

ʳ *And to thy Seed*, see Gen. XII. 7. Repeated again in the following Chapters.

ˢ *Mystical Body*, see *ver.* 27.

GALATIANS.

PARAPHRASE.

to set aside the Promise. For if the Right to the Inheritance be from the Works of the Law, it is plain that it is not founded in the Promise to *Abraham*, as certainly it is: For the Inheritance was a Donation and free Gift of God, settled on *Abraham* and his Seed by Promise.

TEXT.

was four hundred and thirty years after, cannot disannul, that it should make the promise of none effect.

SECT. V.

CHAP. III. 18——25.

CONTENTS.

IN Answer to this Objection, *To what then serveth the Law?* he shews that the Law was not contrary to the Promise: But since all Men were guilty of Transgression, *ver.* 22. the Law was added to shew the *Israelites* the Fruit and inevitable Consequence of their Sin, and thereby the Necessity of betaking themselves to Christ; but as soon as Men have received Christ, they have attained the End of the Law, and so are no longer under it. This is a farther Argument against Circumcision.

PARAPHRASE.

18. If the Blessing and Inheritance be settled on *Abraham* and Believers, as a free Gift by Promise, and was not to be obtained by the Deeds of the
19. Law, to what Purpose then was the Law? It was added because the *Israelites*, the Posterity of *Abraham*, were Transgressors[r], as well as other Men, to shew them their Sins, and the Punishment and Death they incurred by them, till Christ should

TEXT.

18 For if the inheritance be of the law, it is no more of promise: but God gave it to Abraham by promise.
19 Wherefore then serveth the law? It was added because of transgres-

NOTES.

19 [r] That this is the Meaning of, *because of Transgression*, the following Part of this Section shews, wherein St. *Paul* argues to this Purpose: The *Jews* were Sinners as well as other Men, *ver.* 22. The Law denouncing Death to all Sinners, could save none, *ver.* 21. but was thereby useful to bring Men to Christ, that they might be justified by Faith, *ver.* 24. See *Chap.* II. 15, 16.

come,

GALATIANS.

TEXT.

-sions, till the seed should come to whom the promise was made; and it was ordained by angels in the hand of a mediator.

20 Now a mediator is not a mediator of one, but God is one.

21 Is the law then against the promise of God? God forbid: for if there had been a law given which could have given life, verily righteousness

PARAPHRASE.

come, who was that Seed into whom both *Jews* and *Gentiles*, ingrafted by believing, become the People of God, and Children of *Abraham*; that Seed to which the Promise was made. And the Law was ordained by Angels in the Hand of a Mediator [u], whereby it is manifest, that the Law could not disannul the Promise; because a Mediator is a Mediator between two Parties concerned, but God is but one [w] of those concerned in the Promise. If then the promised Inheritance come not to the Seed of *Abraham* by the Law, is the Law opposite, by the Curse it denounces against Transgressors, to the Promise that God made of the Blessing to *Abraham?* No by no means. For if there had been a Law given which could have put

20.

21.

NOTES.

[u] *Mediator*, see *Deut.* V. 5. *Lev.* XXVI. 46. where it is said, the Law was made between God and the Children of *Israel by the Hand of Moses.*

20 [w] *But God is one.* To understand this Verse, we must carry in our Minds what St. *Paul* is here doing, and that from *ver.* 17. is manifest, that he is proving that the Law could not disannul the Promise; and he does it upon this known Rule, that a Covenant of Promise, once ratified, cannot be altered or disannulled by any other, but by the Parties concerned. Now, says he, God is but one of the Parties concerned in the Promise; the *Gentiles* and *Israelites* together made up the other, *ver.* 14. But *Moses* at the giving of the Law was a Mediator only between the *Israelites* and God, and therefore could not transact any thing to the disannulling the Promise which was between God and the *Israelites* and *Gentiles* together, because God was but one of the Parties to that Covenant; the other, which was the *Gentiles* as well as *Israelites*, *Moses* appeared or transacted not for. And so what was done at Mount *Sinai*, by the Mediation of *Moses*, could not affect a Covenant made between Parties, whereof one only was there. How necessary it was for St. *Paul* to add this, we shall see, if we consider, that without it, his Argument of 430 Years Distance would have been deficient and hardly conclusive. For if both the Parties concerned in the Promise had transacted by *Moses* the Mediator (as they might, if none but the Nation of the *Israelites* had been concerned in the Promise made by God to *Abraham*) they might by mutual Consent have altered or set aside the former Promise, as well four Hundred Years as four Days after. That which hindered it was, that at *Moses's* Mediation at Mount *Sinai*, God, who was but one of the Parties to the Promise, was present; but the other Party, *Abraham's* Seed, consisting of *Israelites* and *Gentiles* together, was not there; *Moses* transacted for the Nation of the *Israelites* alone: The other Nations were not concerned in the Covenant made at Mount *Sinai*, as they were in the Promise made to *Abraham* and his Seed, which therefore could not be disannulled without their Consent; for that both the Promise to *Abraham* and his Seed, and the Covenant with *Israel* at Mount *Sinai*, was National, is in itself evident.

GALATIANS.

PARAPHRASE.

us in a State of Life ˣ, certainly Righteousness should have been by Law ʸ. But we find the quite contrary by the Scripture, which makes no Distinction betwixt *Jew* and *Gentile* in this Respect, but has shut up together all Mankind ᶻ, *Jews* and *Gentiles*, under ᵃ Sin and Guilt, that the Blessing which was promised to that which is *Abraham*'s true and intended Seed by Faith ᵇ in Christ, might be given to those who believe. But before Christ, and the Doctrine of Justification by Faith ᶜ in him, came, we Jews were shut up as a Company of Prisoners, together, under the Custody and inflexible Rigor of the Law, unto the Coming of the Messiah, when the Doctrine of Justification by Faith ᵈ in him should be revealed. So that the Law by its Severity served as a School-master, to bring us to Christ, that we might be justified by Faith. But Christ being come, and with him the Doctrine of Justification by Faith, we are set free from this School-master; there is no longer any need of him.

TEXT.

should have been by the law.

But the scripture hath 22 concluded all under sin, that the promise by Faith of Jesus Christ might be given to them that believe.

But before faith came, 23 we were kept under the law, shut up unto the faith which should afterwards be revealed.

Wherefore the law 24 was our school-master to bring us unto Christ, that we might be justified by faith.

But after that faith is 25 come, we are no longer under a school-master.

NOTES.

21 ˣ Ζωοποιῆσαι, *Put into a State of Life*. The *Greek* word signifies to *make alive*. St. *Paul* considers all Men here as in a mortal State; and to be put out of that mortal State into a State of Life, he calls being *made alive*. This he says the Law could not do, because it could not confer Righteousness.

ʸ 'Εκ νόμου, *by Law*, i. e. by Works or Obedience to that Law, which tended towards Righteousness as well as the Promise, but was not able to reach or confer it; see *Rom.* VII. 3. *i. e.* Frail Men were not able to attain Righteousness by any exact Conformity of their Actions to the Law of Righteousness.

22 ᶻ Τὰ πάντα, *all*, is used here for *all Men*: The Apostle, *Rom.* III. 9, and 19. expresses the same Thing by πάντας, *all Men*; and πᾶς, ὁ Κόσμος, *all the World*. But speaking in the Text here of the *Jews* in particular, he says, *We*; meaning those of his own Nation, as is evident from ver. 24, 25.

ᵃ *Under Sin*, i. e. rank them all together, as one guilty Race of Sinners. See this proved *Rom.* III. 9. I. 18, &c. To the same Purpose of putting both *Jews* and *Gentiles* into one State, St. *Paul* uses συνέκλεισε πάντας, *hath shut them up all together*, Rom. XI. 32.

ᵇ The Thing *promised* in this Chapter, sometimes called *Blessing*, ver. 9, 14. sometimes *Inheritance*, ver. 18. sometimes *Justification*, ver. 11, 24. sometimes *Righteousness*, ver. 21. and sometimes *Life*, ver. 11, 21.

ᶜ 23 *By Faith*, see ver. 14.

ᵈ *Justification by Faith*, see ver. 24.

SECT.

GALATIANS.

SECT. VI.

CHAP. III. 26——29.

CONTENTS.

AS a further Argument to diſſuade them from Circumciſion, he tells the *Galatians*, that by Faith in Chriſt, all, whether *Jews* or *Gentiles*, are made the Children of God, and ſo they ſtood in no need of Circumciſion.

TEXT.

26 For ye are all the children of God by faith in Chriſt Jeſus.
27 For as many of you as have been baptized into Chriſt, have put on Chriſt.
28 There is neither Jew nor Greek, there is neither bond nor free, there is neither male nor female; for ye are all one in Chriſt Jeſus.
29 And if ye be Chriſt's, then are ye Abraham's ſeed, and heirs according to the promiſe.

PARAPHRASE.

26. For ye are ᵉ all the Children of God by Faith in Chriſt Jeſus.
27. For as many of you as have been baptized into Chriſt, have put on Chriſt ᶠ.
28. There is no Diſtinction of *Jew* or *Gentile*; of Bond or Free; of Male or Female. For ye are all one Body, making up one Perſon in Chriſt Jeſus: And if ye are all one in Chriſt Jeſus ᵍ, ye
29. are the true ones, Seed of *Abraham*, and Heirs according to the Promiſe.

NOTES.

26 ᵉ *All*, i. e. both *Jews* and *Gentiles*.

27 ᶠ *Put on Chriſt*. This, which, at firſt Sight, may ſeem a very bold Metaphor, if we conſider what St. *Paul* has ſaid, *v*. 16, and 26. is admirably adapted to expreſs his Thoughts in few Words, and has a great Grace in it. He ſays, ver. 16, that *the Seed* to which the Promiſe was made, *was but one, and that one was Chriſt*. And ver. 26. he declares, that *by Faith in Chriſt they all become the Sons of God*. To lead them into an eaſy Conception how this is done, he here tells them, that by taking on them the Profeſſion of the Goſpel, *they have*, as it were, *put on Chriſt*; ſo that to God, now looking on them, there appears nothing but Chriſt. They are, as it were, covered all over with him, as a Man is with the Clothes he hath put on. And hence he ſays, in the next Verſe, that *they are all one in Chriſt Jeſus*, as if there were but that one Perſon.

29 ᵍ The *Clermont* Copy reads εἰ δὲ ὑμεῖς εἷς ἐν Χριϛῷ Ἰησῦ, *And if ye are one in Chriſt Jeſus*, more ſuitable, as it ſeems, to the Apoſtle's Argument. For ver. 28. he ſays, *They are all one in Chriſt Jeſus*; from whence the Inference in the following Words of the *Clermont* Copy is natural; *And if ye be one in Chriſt Jeſus, then are ye Abraham's Seed, and Heirs according to Promiſe*.

SECT.

SECT. VII.

CHAP. IV. 1——11.

CONTENTS.

IN the first Part of this Section, he farther shews, that the Law was not against the Promise, in that the Child is not disinherited by being under Tutors. But the chief Design of this Section is to shew, that though both *Jews* and *Gentiles* were intended to be the Children of God, and Heirs of the Promise by Faith in Christ, yet they both of them were left in Bondage, the *Jews* to the Law, *v.* 3. and the *Gentiles* to false Gods, *v.* 8. till Christ, in due Time, came to redeem them both; and therefore it was Folly in the *Galatians*, being redeemed from one Bondage, to go backwards, and put themselves again in a State of Bondage, though under a new Master.

PARAPHRASE.

1. NOW I say that the Heir, as long as he is a Child, differeth nothing from a Bondman [h], tho' he be Lord of all; but is under Tutors
2. and Guardians, until the Time prefixed by his Father. So we [i] *Jews*, whilst we were Children,
3. were in Bondage under the Law [k]. But when the
4. Time appointed for the Coming of the Messias was accomplished, God sent forth his Son, made of a

TEXT.

1. NOW I say, that the heir as long as he is a child, differeth nothing from a servant, tho' he be lord of all;
2. But is under tutors and governors, until the time appointed of the Father.
3. Even so we, when we were children, were in bondage under the elements of the world:
4. But when the fulness

NOTES.

1 [h] *Bondman*, so δοῦλος signifies; and unless it be so translated, *v.* 1, 7, 8. *Bondage*, *v.* 3, 7. will scarce be understood by an *English* Reader; but St. *Paul*'s Sense will be lost to one, who, by *Servant*, understands not one in a State of *Bondage*.

3 [i] *We*. 'Tis plain St. *Paul* speaks here in the Name of the *Jews*, or Jewish Church, which, though God's peculiar People, yet was to pass its Nonage (so St. *Paul* calls it) under the Restraint and Tutorage of the Law, and not to receive the Possession of the promised Inheritance till Christ came.

[k] *The Law* he calls here στοιχεῖα τοῦ κόσμου, *Elements*, or *Rudiments of the World*; because the Observances and Discipline of the Law, which had Restraint and Bondage enough in it, led them not beyond the Things of this World, into the Possession or State of their spiritual and heavenly Inheritance.

Woman,

GALATIANS.

Chap. IV.

TEXT.	PARAPHRASE.

of the Time was come, God sent forth his Son made of a woman, made under the law,

5 To redeem them that were under the law, that we might receive the adoption of sons.

6 And because ye are sons, God hath sent forth the Spirit of his Son into your hearts, crying, Abba, Father.

7 Wherefore thou art no more a servant, but a son; and if a son, then an heir of God through Christ.

8 Howbeit, then when ye knew not God, ye did service unto them, which by nature are no gods.

9 But now after that ye have known God, or ra-

Woman, and subjected to the Law; That he 5. might redeem those who were under the Law, and set them free from it, that we who believe might be put out of the State of Bondmen into that of Sons. Into which State of Sons, it is evident 6. that you *Galatians*, who were heretofore *Gentiles*, are put; for as much as God hath sent forth his Spirit ᶦ into your Hearts, which enables you to cry *Abba*, Father; so that thou art no longer a 7. Bondman but a Son: And if a Son, then an Heir ᵐ of God, or of the Promise of God through Christ. But then, *i. e.* before ye were made the 8. Sons of God by Faith in Christ, now under the Gospel, ye, not knowing God, were in Bondage to those who were in truth no Gods. But now 9. that ye know God, yea rather, that ye are known ⁿ and taken into favour by him, how

NOTES.

6 ᶦ The same Argument of proving their Sonship from their having the *Spirit*, St. *Paul* uses to the *Romans*, Rom. VIII. 16. And he that will read 2 *Cor.* IV. 17.—V. 6. and *Eph.* I. 11—14. will find, that the Spirit is looked on as the Seal and Assurance of the Inheritance of Life to those *who have received the Adoption of Sons*, as St. *Paul* speaks here, *v.* 5. The Force of the Argument seems to lie in this, that as he that has the Spirit of a Man in him, has an Evidence that he is the son of Man, so he that hath the Spirit of God, has thereby an Assurance that he is the Son of God. Conformable hereunto, the Opinion of the *Jews* was, that the Spirit of God was given to none but themselves, they alone being the People, or Children of God; for God calls the People of *Israel* his Son, *Exod.* IV. 22, 23. And hence we see, that when, to the Astonishment of the *Jews*, the Spirit was given to the *Gentiles*, the *Jews* no longer doubted that the Inheritance of eternal Life was also conferred on the *Gentiles*. Compare *Acts* X. 44—48. with *Acts* XI. 15—18.

7 ᵐ St. *Paul*, from the *Galatians* having received the Spirit, (as appears, *Ch.* III. 2.) argues, that they are the Sons of God without the Law, and consequently Heirs of the Promise without the Law: For, says he, *v.* 1—6. the *Jews* themselves were fain to be redeemed from the Bondage of the Law by Jesus Christ, that as Sons they might attain to the Inheritance. But you *Galatians*, says he, have, by the Spirit that is given you by the Ministry of the Gospel, an Evidence that God is your Father; and, being Sons, are free from the Bondage of the Law, and Heirs without it. The same Sort of Reasoning St. *Paul* uses to the *Romans*, Ch. VIII. 14—17.

9 ⁿ *Known.* It has been before observed how apt St. *Paul* is to repeat his Words, though something varied in their Signification. We have here another Instance of it; having said, Ye have known God, he subjoins, or *rather are known of him*, in the *Hebrew* Latitude of the Word *known*, in which Language it sometimes signifies *knowing* with Choice and Approbation. See *Amos* III. 2. 1 *Cor.* VIII. 3.

can

GALATIANS.

PARAPHRASE.

can it be that you, who have been put out of a State of Bondage, into the Freedom of Sons, should go backwards, and be willing to put yourselves under the ° weak and beggarly Elements ᵖ of the
10. World, into a State of Bondage again? Ye observe Days, and Months, and Times, and Years, in Compliance with the *Mosaical* Institution. I
11. begin to be afraid of you, and to be in doubt, whether all the Pains I have taken about you, to set you at Liberty in the Freedom of the Gospel, will not prove lost Labour.

TEXT.

ther are *known of God*, how turn *ye again to the* weak and *beggarly elements*, whereunto ye desire again to be in bondage?

Ye observe days, and 10 months, and times, and years.

I am afraid of you, lest 11 I have bestowed upon you labour in vain.

NOTES.

° The Law is here called *weak*, because it was not able to deliver a Man from Bondage and Death, into the glorious Liberty of the Sons of God, *Rom* VIII. 1—3. And it is called *beggarly*, because it kept Men in the poor Estate of Pupils, from the full Possession and Enjoyment of the Inheritance, *v.* 1—3.

ᵖ The Apostle makes it Matter of Astonishment, how they, who had been in Bondage to false Gods, having been once set free, could endure the Thoughts of parting with their Liberty, and of returning into any Sort of Bondage again, even under the mean and beggarly Rudiments of the *Mosaical* Institution, which was not able to make them Sons, and instal them in the Inheritance. For St. *Paul*, *v.* 7. expressly opposes Bondage to Sonship; so that all who are not in the State of Sons, are in the State of Bondage. Πάλιν, *again*, cannot here refer to ςοιχεῖα, *Elements*, which the *Galatians* had never been under hitherto; but to *Bondage*, which he tells them, *v.* 8. they had been in to false Gods.

SECT. VIII.

CHAP. IV. 12——20.

CONTENTS.

HE presses them with the Remembrance of the great Kindness they had for him when he was amongst them; and assures them, that they have no Reason to be alienated from him, though that be it which the Judaizing Seducers aim at.

I beseech

GALATIANS.

TEXT.

12 Brethren, I beseech you be as I am; for I am as ye are: ye have not injured me at all.
13 Ye know how, through infirmity of the flesh, I preached the Gospel unto you at the first.
14 And my temptation, which was in my flesh, ye despised not, nor rejected: but received me as an angel of God, even as Christ Jesus.
15 Where is then the blessedness you spake of? for I bear you record, that if it had been possible, ye would have plucked out your own eyes, and have given them to me.
16 Am I therefore become your enemy, because I tell you the truth?
17 They zealously affect you, but not well; yea, they would exclude us, that you might affect them.
18 But it is good to be zealously affected always in a good thing, and not only when I am present with you.

PARAPHRASE.

I beseech you, Brethren, let you and I be as if we were all one. Think yourselves to be very me; as I in my own Mind put no Difference at all between you and myself, you have done me no Manner of Injury: On the contrary, ye know, that through Infirmity of the Flesh, I heretofore preached the Gospel to you, and yet ye despised me not for the Trial I underwent in the Flesh q, you treated me not with Contempt and Scorn; but you received me as an Angel of God, yea, as Jesus Christ himself. What Benedictions r did you then pour out upon me? For I bear you Witness, had it been practicable, you would have pulled out your very Eyes, and given them me. But is it so that I am become your Enemy s in continuing to tell you the Truth? They who would make you of that Mind, shew a Warmth of Affection to you: But it is not well; for their Business is to exclude me, that they may get into your Affection. It is good to be well and warmly affected towards a good Man t at all times, and not barely when I am present with you.

My

12.
13.
14.

15.

16.
17.

18.

NOTES.

14 q What this *Weakness* and *Trial in the Flesh* was, since it has not pleased the Apostle to mention it, is impossible for us to know: But may be remarked here as an Instance, once for all, of that unavoidable Obscurity of some Passages in epistolary Writings, without any Fault in the Author. For some Things, necessary to the understanding of what is writ, are usually, of course, and justly omitted, because already known to him the Letter is writ to; and it would be sometimes ungraceful, oftentimes superfluous, particularly to mention them.

15 r The Context makes this Sense of the Words so necessary and visible, that it is to be wondered how any one could over-look it.

16 s *Your Enemy*. See *Ch. I. 6.*

18 t That by καλῷ, he here means a Person, and himself, the Scope of the Context evinces. In the preceding *Verses* he speaks only of himself, and the Change of their Affection to him since he left them. There is no other Thing mentioned, as peculiarly deserving their Affection, to which the Rule given in this *Verse* could refer. He had said, *v.* 17. ζηλοῦσιν ὑμᾶς, *they affect you*; and ἵνα αὐτοὺς ζηλῶτε, *that you might affect them*; this is only of Persons, and therefore ζηλοῦσθαι ἐν καλῷ, which immediately follows, may best be understood of a Person, else the following Part of the *Verse*, though joined by the Copulative ϗ, *ana*, will make but a dis-jointed

Sense

GALATIANS.

PARAPHRASE.

19. My little Children, for whom I have again the Pains of a Woman in Child-birth till Christ be formed in you ⁿ, *i. e.* till the true Doctrine of Christianity be settled in your Minds. But I
20. would willingly be this very Moment with you, and change ʷ my Discourse as I should find Occasion; for I am at a Stand about you, and know not what to think of you.

TEXT.

19 My little children, of whom I travel in birth again until Christ be formed in you:

20 I desire to be present with you now, and to change my voice, for I stand in doubt of you.

NOTES.

Sense with the preceding. But there can be nothing plainer, nor more coherent than this, which seems to be St. *Paul's* Sense here. *You were very affectionate to me when I was with you. You are since estranged from me; it is the Artifice of the Seducers that hath cooled you to me. But if I am the good Man you took me to be, you will do well to continue the Warmth of your Affection to me, when I am absent; and not to be well affected towards me, only when I am present among you.* Though this be his Meaning, yet the Way he has taken to express it, is much more elegant, modest and graceful. Let any one read the Original, and see whether it be not so.

19 If this *Verse* be taken for an entire Sentence by itself, it will be a Parenthesis, and that not the most necessary or congruous that is to be found in St. *Paul's* Epistles; or α, *but*, must be left out, as we see it is in our Translation. But if τεκνία μȣ, *my little Children*, be joined on by Apposition to ὑμᾶς, *you*, the last Word of the foregoing *Verse*, and so the two *Verses* 18 and 19, be read as one Sentence, the 20th *ver.* with αι. *but*, in it, follows very naturally. But as we now read in our *English* Bible. αι, *but*, is forced to be left out, and the 20th *ver.* stands alone by itself, without any Connection with what goes before, or follows.

20 Ἀλλάξαι ϕωνὴν, to *change the Voice*, seems to signify the speaking higher or lower; changing the Tone of the Voice suitably to the Matter one delivers, *v. g.* whether it be Advice, or Commendation, or Reproof, &c. for each of these have their distinct Voices. St. *Paul* wishes himself with them, that he might accommodate himself to their present Condition and Circumstances, which he confesses himself to be ignorant of, and in doubt about.

SECT. IX.

CHAP. IV. 21.——V. 1.

CONTENTS.

HE exhorts them to stand fast in the Liberty with which Christ hath made them free, shewing those who are so zealous for the Law, that if they mind what they read in the Law, they will there

GALATIANS.

Chap. IV.

there find, that the Children of the Promise, or of the *New Jerusalem*, were to be free; but the Children after the Flesh, of the earthly *Jerusalem*, were to be in Bondage, and to be cast out, and not to have the Inheritance.

TEXT.

21 Tell me, ye that desire to be under the law, do ye not hear the law?
22 For it is written, that Abraham had two sons; the one by a bond-maid, the other by a free-woman.
23 But he who was of the bond-woman, was born after the flesh; but he of the free-woman was by promise.
24 Which things are an allegory; for these are the two covenants; the one from the mount Sinai, which gendereth to bondage, which is Agar.
25 For this Agar is mount Sinai in Arabia, and answereth to Jerusalem which now is, and is in bondage with her children.
26 But Jerusalem, which is above, is free, which is the mother of us all.
27 For it is written, Rejoice, thou barren that bearest not; break forth and cry thou that travailest not; for the desolate hath many more children than she which hath an husband.
28 Now we, brethren, as Isaac was, are the children of promise.

PARAPHRASE.

Tell me, you that would so fain be under the Law, do you not acquaint yourselves with what is in the Law, either by reading it[x], or having it read in your Assemblies? For it is there written[y], *Abraham* had two Sons; one by a Bond-Maid, the other by a Free-Woman: But he that was of the Bond-Woman, was born according to the Flesh, in the ordinary Course of Nature; but he that was of the Free-Woman, *Abraham* had by Virtue of the Promise, after he and his Wife were past the Hopes of another Child. These Things have an allegorical Meaning; for the two Women are the two Covenants; the one of them delivered from Mount *Sinai*, and is represented by *Agar*, who produces her Issue into Bondage. (For *Agar* is Mount *Sinai* in *Arabia*, and answers to *Jerusalem* that now is, and is in Bondage with her Children.) But the heavenly *Jerusalem*, which is above, and answers to *Sarah*, the Mother of the promised Seed, is free, the Mother of us all, both *Jews* and *Gentiles*, who believe. For it was of her that it is written[z], *Rejoice, thou barren that bearest not; break out into loud Acclamations of Joy, thou that hast not the Travails of Child-birth; for more are the Children of the Desolate than of her that hath an Husband.* And it is we, my Brethren, who, as *Isaac* was,

21.
22.
23.
24.
25.
26.
27.
28.

NOTES.

21 [x] The Vulgar has, after some *Greek* Manuscripts, *Read*.
22 [y] *Written there*, (viz.) *Gen.* XVI. 15. and XXI. 1. The Term *Law*, in the foregoing Verse, comprehends the five Books of *Moses*.
27 [z] *Written*, (viz.) *Isai.* LIV. 1.

E 2

are

GALATIANS.

PARAPHRASE.

29. are the Children of Promise. But as then *Ishmael*, who was born in the ordinary Course of Nature, persecuted *Isaac*, who was born by an extraordinary Power from Heaven, working miraculously; so is it now.
30. But what saith the Scripture [b]? *Cast out the Bond-Woman and her Son; for the Son of the Bond-Woman shall not share the Inheritance with the Son of the Free-Woman.*
31. So then, Brethren, we, who believe in Christ, are not the Children of the Bond-Woman, but
Ver. 1. of the Free [c]. Stand fast therefore in the Liberty wherewith Christ hath made you free, and do not put on again a Yoke of Bondage, by putting yourselves under the Law.

TEXT.

29 But as then he that was born after the flesh, persecuted him that was born after the Spirit, even so it is now.
30 Nevertheless, what saith the scripture? Cast out the bond-woman and her son; for the son of the bond-woman, shall not be heir with the son of the free-woman.
31 So then, brethren, we are not children of the bond-woman, but of the free.
1 Stand fast therefore in the liberty wherewith Christ hath made us free, and be not intangled again with the yoke of bondage.

NOTES.

29 Ὁ κατὰ σάρκα γεννηθεὶς, *Born after the Flesh*; and τὸν κατὰ πνεῦμα, *Born after the Spirit*. These Expressions have, in their Original Brevity, with regard to the whole View wherein St. *Paul* uses them, an admirable Beauty and Force, which cannot be retained in a Paraphrase.
30 [b] *Scripture*, (viz.) Gen. XX. 10.
31 [c] The Apostle, by this allegorical History, shews the *Galatians*, that they who are Sons of *Agar*, i. e. under the Law given at Mount *Sinai*, are in Bondage, and intended to be cast out, the Inheritance being designed for those only, who are the free-born Sons of God under the spiritual Covenant of the Gospel. And thereupon he exhorts them, in the following Words, to preserve themselves in that State of Freedom.

SECT. X.

CHAP. V. 2——13.

CONTENTS.

IT is evident, from *Ver.* 11. that, the better to prevail with the *Galatians* to be circumcised, it had been reported, that St. *Paul* himself preached up Circumcision. St. *Paul*, without taking express Notice

Notice of this Calumny, *Ch.* I. 6. and II. 21. gives an Account of his paſt Life in a large Train of Particulars, which all concur to make ſuch a Character of him, as renders it very incredible, that he ſhould ever declare for the Circumciſion of the *Gentile* Converts, or for their Submiſſion to the Law. Having thus prepared the Minds of the *Galatians*, to give him a fair Hearing, as a fair Man, ζηλῦσθαι ἐν καλῷ he goes on to argue againſt their ſubjecting themſelves to the Law. And having eſtabliſhed their Freedom from the Law by many ſtrong Arguments, he comes here at laſt openly to take Notice of the Report which had been raiſed of him, that he preached Circumciſion, and directly confutes it.

1. By poſitively denouncing to them himſelf, very ſolemnly, that they who ſuffered themſelves to be circumciſed, put themſelves into a perfect legal State, out of the Covenant of Grace, and could receive no Benefit by Jeſus Chriſt, *ver.* 2—4.

2. By aſſuring them, that he, and thoſe that followed him, expected Juſtification only by Faith, *v.* 5, 6.

3. By telling them, that he had put them in the right Way, and that this new Perſuaſion came not from him that converted them to Chriſtianity, *v.* 7, 8.

3. By inſinuating to them, that they ſhould agree to paſs Judgment on him that troubled them with this Doctrine, 9, 10.

5. By his being perſecuted, for oppoſing the Circumciſion of the Chriſtians. For this was the great Offence which ſtuck with the *Jews*, even after their Converſion, *v.* 11.

6. By wiſhing thoſe cut off that trouble them with this Doctrine, *v.* 12.

This will, I doubt not, by whoever weighs it, be found a very ſkilful Management of the argumentative Part of this Epiſtle, which ends here: For though he begins with ſapping the Foundation, on which the Judaizing Seducers ſeemed to have laid their main Streſs, (*viz.*) the Report of his preaching Circumciſion, yet he reſerves the direct and open Confutation of it to the End, and ſo leaves it with them, that it may have the more forcible and laſting Impreſſion on their Minds.

GALATIANS.

PARAPHRASE.

2. TAKE Notice that I *Paul*[d], who am falsly reported to preach up Circumcision in other Places, say unto you, that if you are circumcised, Christ shall be of no Advantage to you.

3. For I repeat here again what I have always preached, and solemnly testify to every one who yields to be circumcised, in Compliance with those who say, that now under the Gospel he cannot be saved without it[e], that he is under an Obligation to the whole Law, and bound to observe and

4. perform every Tittle of it. Christ is of no Use to you, who seek Justification by the Law: Whosoever do so, be ye what you will, ye are fallen

5. from the Covenant of Grace. But I[f], and those who with me are true Christians, we who follow the Truth of the Gospel[g], and the Doctrine of the Spirit of God, have no other Hope of Justi-

6. fication but by Faith in Christ. For in the State of the Gospel under Jesus the Messiah, 'tis neither Circumcision nor Uncircumcision, that is of any Moment; all that is available, is Faith

7. alone, working by Love[h]. When you first entered into the Profession of the Gospel, you were in a good Way, and went on well: Who has

TEXT.

2 Behold, I Paul say unto you, that if ye be circumcised, Christ shall profit you nothing.

3 For I testify again to every man that is circumcised, that he is a debtor to do the whole law.

4 Christ is become of no effect unto you, whosoever of you are justified by the law; ye are fallen from grace.

5 For we, through the Spirit, wait for the hope of righteousness by faith.

6 For in Jesus Christ, neither circumcision availeth any thing, nor uncircumcision, but faith which worketh by love.

7 Ye did run well, who did hinder you, that

NOTES.

2 [d] Ἰδὲ, ἐγὼ Παῦλος, *Behold, I Paul*, I the same *Paul*, who am reported to preach Circumcision, μαρτύρομαι δὲ πάλιν παντὶ ἀνθρώπῳ, v. 3. *witness again*, continue my Testimony, *to every Man*, to you and all Men. This, so emphatical Way of Speaking, may very well be understood to have Regard to what he takes Notice, v. 11. to be cast upon him, (viz.) his preaching Circumcision, and is a very significant Vindication of himself.

3 [e] *Cannot be saved.* This was the Ground upon which the *Jews* and *Judaizing* Christians urged Circumcision. See *Acts* XV. 1.

5 [f] *We.* 'Tis evident from the Context, that St. *Paul* here means himself: But *We* is a more graceful Way of Speaking than *I*, though he be vindicating himself alone from the Imputation of setting up Circumcision.

[g] *Spirit.* The Law and the Gospel opposed under the Titles of *Flesh* and *Spirit*, we may see, *Ch.* III. 3. of this Epistle. The same Opposition it stands in here to *the Law*, in the foregoing *Verse*, points out the same Signification.

6 [h] *Which worketh by Love.* This is added, to express the Animosities which were amongst them, probably raised by this Question about Circumcision. See v. 15——19.

put

GALATIANS. Chap. V.

TEXT.

ye should not obey the truth?
8 This persuasion cometh not of him that calleth you.
9 A little leaven leaveneth the whole lump.
10 I have confidence in you through the Lord, that you will be none otherwise minded: but he that troubleth you, shall bear his judgment, whosoever he be.
11 And I, brethren, if I yet preach circumcision, why do I yet suffer persecution? then is the

PARAPHRASE.

put a Stop to you, and hindered you, that you keep no longer to the Truth of the Christian Doctrine? This Persuasion, that it is necessary for you to be circumcised, cometh not from him ⁱ, by whose Preaching you were called to the Profession of the Gospel. Remember that a little Leaven leaveneth the whole Lump; the Influence of one Man ᵏ entertained among you, may mislead you all. I have Confidence in you, that, by the Help of the Lord, you will be all of this same Mind ˡ with me; and consequently he that troubles you shall fall under the Censure he deserves for it ᵐ, whoever he be. But as for me, Brethren, if I at last am become a Preacher of Circumcision, why am I yet persecuted ⁿ? If it be so that the *Gentile* Converts are to be circumcised, and so subjected to the Law, the great

8.
9.
10.
11.

NOTES.

8 ⁱ This Expression, of *him that called* or *calleth you*, he used before, *Ch.* I. 6. and in both Places means himself; and here declares, that this πεισμονη (whether taken for *Persuasion* or for *Subjection*, as it may be in St. *Paul*'s Stile, considering πειθεσθαι, in the End of the foregoing *Verse*) came not from him; for he called them to Liberty from the Law, and not Subjection to it. See *v.* 13. *You were going on well in the Liberty of the Gospel, who stopped you?* I, you may be sure, had no Hand in it; I, you know, called you to Liberty, and not to Subjection to the Law; and therefore you can by no means suppose that I should preach up Circumcision. Thus St. *Paul* argues here.

9 ᵏ By this and the next *Verse*, it looks as if all this Disorder arose from one Man.

10 ˡ *Will not be otherwise minded,* will beware of this Leaven, so as not to be put into a Ferment, nor shaken in your Liberty, which you ought to stand fast in; and to secure it, I doubt not (such Confidence I have in you) will, with one Accord, cast out him that troubles you. For, as for me, you may be sure I am not for Circumcision, in that the *Jews* continue to persecute me. This is evidently his Meaning, though not spoken out, but managed warily, with a very skilful and moving Insinuation: For, as he says himself, *Ch.* IV. 20. he knew not, at that Distance, what Temper they were in.

ᵐ Κριμα, *Judgment,* seems here to mean Expulsion by a Church-censure: See *v.* 12. We shall be the more inclined to this, if we consider, that the Apostle uses the same Argument of *a little Leaven leaveneth the whole Lump,* 1 Cor. V. 6. where he would persuade the *Corinthians* to purge out the Fornicator.

11 ⁿ *Persecution.* The Persecution St. *Paul* was still under, was a convincing Argument, that he was not for Circumcision and Subjection to the Law; for it was from the *Jews,* upon that Account, that at this Time rose all the Persecution which the Christians suffered, as may be seen through all the History of the *Acts.* Nor are there wanting clear Footsteps of it in several Places of this Epistle, besides this here, as *Ch.* III. 4. and VI. 12.

Offence

GALATIANS.

Chap. V.

PARAPHRASE.

12. Offence of the Gospel *, in relying solely on a crucified Saviour for Salvation, is removed. But I am of another Mind, and with that they may be cut off who trouble you about this Matter,
13. and they shall be cut off. For, Brethren, ye have been called by me unto Liberty.

TEXT.

offence of the cross ceased.
12 I would they were even cut off which trouble you.
13 For, brethren, ye have been called unto liberty.

NOTES.

* Offence of the Cross. See *Co.* VI. 12——14.

SECT. XI.

CHAP. V. 13——26.

CONTENTS.

FROM the Mention of Liberty, which he tells them they are called to under the Gospel, he takes a Rise to caution them in the Use of it, and so exhorts them to a spiritual, or true Christian Life, shewing the Difference and Contrariety between that and a carnal Life, or a Life after the Flesh.

PARAPHRASE.

13. Though the Gospel to which ye are called, be a State of Liberty from the Bondage of the Law, yet pray take great Care you do not mistake that Liberty, nor think it affords you an Opportunity, in the Abuse of it, to satisfy the Lust of the Flesh, but
14. serve ᵖ one another in Love. For the whole Law

TEXT.

13 Only use not liberty for an occasion to the flesh, but by love serve one another.
14 For all the law is fulfilled in one word, even

NOTES.

13 ᵖ Δουλεύετε, *Serve*, has a greater Force in the *Greek*, than our *English* Word *Serve* does, in the common Acceptation of it, express; for it signifies the opposite to ἐλευθερία, *Freedom*. And so the Apostle elegantly informs them, that though by the Gospel they are called to a State of *Liberty* from the Law, yet they were still as much bound and subjected to their Brethren in all the Offices and Duties of Love and good Will, as if, in that respect, they were their Vassals and Bondmen.

concerning

GALATIANS.

TEXT.

in this; Thou shalt love thy neighbour as thyself.
15 But if ye bite and devour one another, take heed that ye be not consumed one of another.
16 This I say then, Walk in the Spirit, and ye shall not fulfil the lust of the flesh.
17 For the flesh lusteth against the Spirit, and the Spirit against the flesh; and these are contrary the one to the other: so that ye cannot do the things that ye would.
18 But if ye be led by the

PARAPHRASE.

concerning our Duty to others, is fulfilled in observing this one Precept ᵠ, *Thou shalt love thy Neighbour as thyself.* But if you bite and tear one another, take heed that you be not destroyed and consumed by one another. This I say to you, conduct yourselves by the Light that is in your Minds ʳ, and do not give yourselves up to the Lusts of the Flesh, to obey them in what they put you upon. For the Inclinations and Desires of the Flesh are contrary to those of the Spirit; and the Dictates and Inclinations of the Spirit are contrary to those of the Flesh: So that under these contrary Impulses you do not do the Things that you purpose to yourselves ˢ. But if you give yourselves up to the Con-

15.

16.

17.

18.

NOTES.

14 ᵠ *Lev.* XIX. 18.

16 ʳ That which he here and in the next Verse calls *Spirit*, he calls, *Rom.* VII. 22. *the inward Man*, ver. 23. *the Law of the Mind*; ver. 25. *the Mind*.

17 ˢ *Do not:* So it is in the *Greek*; and ours is the only Translation that I know which renders it *cannot*.

16, 17. There can be nothing plainer, than that the State St. *Paul* describes here in these two Verses, he points out more at large, *Rom.* VII. 17, &c. speaking there in the Person of a *Jew*. This is evident, that St. *Paul* supposes two Principles in every Man, which draw him different Ways; the one he calls *Flesh*, the other *Spirit*. These, though there be other Appellations given them, are the most common and usual Names given them in the New Testament. By *Flesh* is meant all those vicious and irregular Appetites, Inclinations and Habitudes, whereby a Man is turned from his Obedience to that eternal Law of Right, the Observance whereof God always requires, and is pleased with: This is very properly called *Flesh*, this bodily State being the Source of which all our Deviations from the strait Rule of Rectitude, do for the most part take their Rise, or else do ultimately terminate in. On the other side, *Spirit* is the Part of a Man which is endowed with Light from God, to know and see what is righteous, just and good; and which, being consulted and hearkened to, is always ready to direct and prompt us to that which is good. The *Flesh* then, in the Gospel-Language, is that Principle which inclines and carries Men to Ill; the *Spirit*, that Principle which dictates what is right, and inclines to Good. But because, by prevailing Custom and contrary Habits, this Principle was very much weakened, and almost extinct in the *Gentiles*, see *Eph.* IV. 17 ———— 21. he exhorts them to be *renewed in the Spirit of their Minds*, ver. 23. and to *put off the Old Man*, i. e. fleshly corrupt Habits, and to put on the *New Man*, which he tells them, ver. 24. *is created in Righteousness and true Holiness.* This is also called *renewing of the Mind*, *Rom.* XII. 2. *renewing of the inward Man*, 2 Cor. IV. 16. which is done by the Assistance of the Spirit of God, *Eph.* III. 16.

F

duct

GALATIANS. Chap. V.

PARAPHRASE.

19. duct of the Gospel ᵗ by Faith in Christ, ye are not under the Law ᵘ. Now the Works of the Flesh as is manifest are these, Adultery, Fornication,
20. Uncleanness, Lasciviousness, Idolatry, Witchcraft ʷ, Enmities, Quarrels, Emulations, Animo-
21. sities, Strife, Seditions, Sects, Envyings, Murders, Drunkenness, Revellings ˣ, and such like; concerning which I forewarn you now, as heretofore I have done, that they who do such Things shall
22. not inherit the Kingdom of God. But on the other Side, the Fruit of the Spirit is Love, Joy, Peace, Long-suffering, Sweetness of Disposition,
23. Beneficence, Faithfulness, Meekness, Temperance:
24. Against these and the like there is no Law. Now they who belong ʸ to Christ, and are his Mem-

TEXT.

Spirit, ye are not under the Law.

Now the works of the 19 flesh are manifest, which are these, adultery, fornication, uncleanness, lasciviousness,

Idolatry, witchcraft, ha- 20 tred, variance, emulations, wrath, strife, seditions, heresies,

Envyings, murders, 21 drunkenness, revellings, and such like, of the which I tell you before, as I have also told you in time past, that they which do such things shall not inherit the kingdom of God.

But the fruit of the 22 Spirit is love, joy, peace, long-suffering, gentleness, goodness, faith,

NOTES.

18 ᵗ The Reason of this Assertion we may find, *Rom.* VIII. 14. *viz.* because, *they who are led by the Spirit of God, are the Sons of God*; and so Heirs, and free without the Law, as he argues here, *Chap.* III. and IV.

ᵘ This is plainly the Sense of the Apostle, who teaches all along in the former Part of this Epistle, and also that to the *Romans*, that those that put themselves under the Gospel, are not under the Law. The Question then that remains, is only about the Phrase, *led by the Spirit*: And as to that, it is easy to observe how natural it is for St. *Paul*, having in the foregoing Verses more than once mentioned the *Spirit*, to continue the same Word, though somewhat varied in the Sense. In St. *Paul*'s Phraseology, as the Irregularities of Appetite, and the Dictates of right Reason, are opposed under the Titles of *Flesh* and *Spirit*, as we have seen; so the Covenant of Works, and the Covenant of Grace, Law and Gospel, are opposed under the Titles of *Flesh* and *Spirit*. 2 *Cor.* III. 6, 8. he calls the Gospel *Spirit*; and *Rom.* VII. 5. *In the Flesh*, signifies in the legal State. But we need go no farther than *Chap.* III. 3. of this very Epistle, to see the Law and the Gospel opposed by St. *Paul* under the Titles of *Flesh* and *Spirit*. The Reason of thus using the Word *Spirit* is very apparent in the Doctrine of the New Testament, which teaches, that those who received Christ by Faith, with him receive his *Spirit*, and its Assistance against the Flesh, see *Rom.* VIII. 9 —— 11. Accordingly, for the attaining of Salvation, St. *Paul* joins together Belief of the Truth and Sanctification of the Spirit, 2 *Thess.* II. 13. And so *Spirit* here may be taken for the *Spirit of the Mind*, but renewed and strengthened by the *Spirit* of God; see *Eph.* III. 16. and IV. 23.

20 ʷ Φαρμακεία signifies *Witchcraft*, or *Poisoning*.

21 ˣ Κῶμοι, *Revellings*, were, amongst the *Greeks*, disorderly spending of the Night in Feasting, with a licentious indulging to Wine, good Chear, Musick, Dancing, &c.

24 ʸ Οἱ τοῦ Χριστοῦ, *those who are of Christ*, are the same with *those who are led by the Spirit*, ver. 18. and are opposed to *those who live after the Flesh*, *Rom.* VIII. 13. where it is said, conformably to what we find here, *they, through the Spirit, mortify the Deeds of the Body.*

bers,

GALATIANS.

TEXT.

23 Meekness, temperance: against such there is no law.
24 And they that are Christ's have crucified the flesh, with the affections and lusts.
25 If we live in the Spirit, let us also walk in the Spirit.
26 Let us not be desirous of vain-glory, provoking one onother, envying one another.

PARAPHRASE.

bers, have ᶻ crucified the Flesh, with the Affections and Lusts thereof. If our Life then (our Flesh having been crucified) be as we profess by the Spirit, whereby we are alive from that State of Sin we were dead in before, let us regulate our Lives and Actions by the Light and Dictates of the Spirit. Let us not be led by an Itch of Vain-glory to provoke one another, or to envy one another ᵃ.

25.

26.

NOTES.

ᶻ *Crucified the Flesh.* That Principle in us, from whence spring vicious Inclinations and Actions, is, as we have observed above, called sometimes the *Flesh*, sometimes the *Old Man*. The subduing and mortifying of this evil Principle, so that the Force and Power wherewith it used to rule in us is extinguished, the Apostle, by a very engaging Accommodation to the Death of our Saviour, calls, *crucifying the Old Man*, Rom. VI. 6. *crucifying the Flesh* here; *putting off the Body of the Sins of the Flesh*, Col. II. 11. *putting off the Old Man*, Eph. IV. 2. Col. III. 8, 9. It is also called, *Mortifying the Members which are on the Earth*, Col. III. 5. *Mortifying the Deeds of the Body*, Rom. VIII. 13.

26 ᵃ Whether the *Vain-glory* and *Envying* here were about their spiritual Gifts, a Fault which the *Corinthians* were guilty of, as we may see at large, 1 Cor. XII. 13, 14. or upon any other Occasion, and so contained in *ver.* 15. of this Chapter, I shall not curiously examine: Either Way the Sense of the Words will be much the same; and accordingly this Verse must end the 5th, or begin the 6th Chapter.

SECT. XII.

CHAP. VI. 1——5.

CONTENTS.

HE here exhorts the Stronger to Gentleness and Meekness towards the Weak.

TEXT.

1 BRethren, if a man be overtaken in a fault, ye which are spi-

PARAPHRASE.

BRethren, if a Man, by Frailty or Surprize, fall into a Fault, do you who are eminent in the Church for Knowledge, Practice, and Gifts ᵇ,

1.

NOTES.

1 ᵇ Πνευματικοὶ, *Spiritual*, in 1 *Cor.* III. 1. and XII. 1. taken together, has this Sense.

GALATIANS.

PARAPHRASE.

raise him up again, and set him right, with Gentleness and Meekness, considering that you yourselves are not out of the reach of Temptations.
2. Bear with one another's Infirmities, and help to support each other under your Burdens ⁶, and so
3. fulfil the Law of Christ ᵈ. For if any one be conceited of himself, as if he were something, a Man of Weight, fit to prescribe to others, when in-
4. deed he is not, he deceiveth himself. But let him take care that what he himself doth be right, and such as will bear the Test, and then he will have Matter of glorying ᵉ in himself, and not in ano-
5. ther. For every one shall be accountable only for his own Actions.

TEXT.

ritual, restore such an one in the spirit of meekness; considering thyself, lest thou also be tempted.
2 Bear ye one another's burdens, and so fulfil the law of Christ.
3 For if a man think himself to be something, when he is nothing, he deceiveth himself.
4 But let every man prove his own work, and then shall he have rejoicing in himself alone, and not in another.
5 For every man shall bear his own burden.

NOTES.

2 ᶜ See a parallel Exhortation, 1 *Thess.* V. 14. which will give light to this; as also *Rom.* XV. 1.

ᵈ See *John* XIII. 34, 35. and XIV. 2. There were some among them very zealous for the Observation of the Law of *Moses*; St. *Paul* here puts them in mind of a Law, which they were under, and were obliged to observe, *viz. the Law of Christ*. And he shews them how to do it, *(viz.)* by helping to bear one another's Burdens, and not increasing their Burdens by the Observances of the Levitical Law. Though the Gospel contain the Law of the Kingdom of Christ, yet I do not remember that St. *Paul* any where calls it *the Law of Christ*, but in this Place, where he mentions it in opposition to those who thought a Law so necessary, that they would retain that of *Moses* under the Gospel.

4 ᵉ Καύχημα, I think, should have been translated here *Glorying*, as Καυχήσωται is, *ver.* 13. the Apostle in both Places meaning the same Thing, *(viz.)* Glorying in another, in having brought him to Circumcision, and other ritual Observances of the Mosaical Law. For thus St. *Paul* seems to me to discourse in this Section: "Brethren, there be some among you that would "bring others under the ritual Observances of the Mosaical Law, a Yoke which was too heavy "for us and our Fathers to bear. They would do much better to ease the Burdens of the "Weak ; this is suitable to the Law of Christ, which they are under, and is the Law which "they ought strictly to obey. If they think, because of their spiritual Gifts, that they have "Power to prescribe in such Matters, I tell them, that they have not, but do deceive them- "selves. Let them rather take care of their own particular Actions, that they be right, and "such as they ought to be. This will give them Matter of glorying in themselves, and not "vainly in others, as they do when they prevail with them to be circumcised : For every Man "shall be answerable for his own Actions." Let the Reader judge whether this does not seem to be St. *Paul's* View here, and suit with his Way of Writing ?

Ἔχειν καύχημα, is a Phrase whereby St. *Paul* signifies *to have Matter of Glorying* ; and to that Sense it is rendered, *Rom.* IV. 2.

SECT.

GALATIANS.

SECT. XIII.

CHAP. VI. 6——10.

CONTENTS.

ST. *Paul* having laid some Restraint upon the Authority and Forwardness of the Teachers, and leading Men amongst them, who were, as it seems, more ready to impose on the *Galatians*, what they should not, than to help them forward in the Practice of Gospel-Obedience; he here takes care of them in respect of their Maintenance, and exhorts the *Galatians* to Liberality towards them; and in general, towards all Men, especially Christians.

TEXT.

6 Let him that is taught in the word, communicate unto him that teacheth, in all good things.
7 Be not deceived; God is not mocked: for whatsoever a man soweth, that shall he also reap.
8 For he that soweth to his flesh, shall of the flesh reap corruption: but he that soweth to the Spirit, shall of the Spirit reap life everlasting.
9 And let us not be weary in well-doing: for in due season we shall reap, if we faint not.
10 As we have therefore opportunity, let us do good unto all men, especially unto them who are of the houshold of faith.

PARAPHRASE.

6. Let him that is taught the Doctrine of the Gospel, freely communicate the good Things of this World to him that teaches him: Be not deceived, God will not be mocked: For as a Man soweth ᶠ, so also shall he reap.
7.
8. He that lays out the Stock of good Things he has, only for the Satisfaction of his own bodily Necessities, Conveniencies or Pleasures, shall at the Harvest find the Fruit and Product of such Husbandry to be Corruption and Perishing ᵍ. But he that lays out his worldly Substance according to the Rules dictated by the Spirit of God in the Gospel, shall of the Spirit reap Life everlasting.
9. In doing thus what is good and right, let us not wax weary; for in due Season, when the Time of Harvest comes, we shall reap, if we continue on to do good, and flag not.
10. Therefore, as we have Opportunities, let us do good unto all Men, especially to those who profess Faith in Jesus Christ, *i. e.* the Christian Religion.

NOTES.

7 ᶠ *Soweth*; a Metaphor used by St. *Paul* for Mens laying out their worldly Goods. See 2 *Cor.* IX. 6, &c.
8 *Rom.* VIII. 13. and II. 12.

GALATIANS.

SECT. XIV.

CHAP. VI. 11.——18.

CONTENTS.

ONE may see what lay upon St. *Paul*'s Mind, in writing to the *Galatians*, by what he inculcates to them here, even after he had finished his Letter. The like we have in the last Chapter to the *Romans*. He here winds up all with Admonitions to the *Galatians*, of a different End and Aim they had to get the *Galatians* circumcised, from what he had in preaching the Gospel.

PARAPHRASE.

11. You see how long a Letter I have writ to you
12. with my own Hand [h]. They who are willing to carry so fairly in the ritual Part of the Law, and to make Ostentation of their Compliance therein, constrain you to be circumcised, only to avoid Persecution, for owning their Dependance for Salvation solely on a crucified Messiah [i], and not on the
13. Observances of the Law. For even they themselves who are circumcised do not keep the Law; but they will have you to be circumcised, that this Mark in your Flesh may afford them Matter of glorying, and of recommending themselves to the
14. good Opinion of the *Jews* [k]. But as for me, whatever may be said of me [l], God forbid that I should glory in any thing, but in having Jesus Christ, who

TEXT.

11. Ye see how large a letter I have written unto you with mine own hand.
12. As many as desire to make a fair shew in the flesh, they constrain you to be circumcised; only lest they should suffer persecution for the cross of Christ.
13. For neither they themselves who are circumcised keep the law; but desire to have you circumcised that they may glory in your flesh.
14. But God forbid that I

NOTES.

11 [h] St. *Paul* mentions the *Writing with his own Hand*, as an Argument of his great Concern for them in the Case: For it was not usual for him to write his Epistles with his own Hand, but to dictate them to others, who writ them from his Mouth. See *Rom.* XVI. 22. 1 *Cor.* XVI. 21.

12 [i] *In the Flesh*, i. e. in the ritual Observances of the Law, which, *Heb.* IX. 10. are called, δικαιώματα σαρκός.

13 [k] See *Chap.* V. 11

14 [l] See *Chap.* V. 11.

GALATIANS.   43
                              Chap. V.

TEXT.   PARAPHRASE.

should glory save in the   was crucified, for my sole Lord and Master, whom
cross of our Lord Jesus   I am to obey and depend on; which I so entire-
Christ, by whom the   ly do, without regard to any thing else, that I
world is crucified unto   am wholly dead to the World, and the World
me, and I unto the   dead to me, and it has no more Influence on me
world.   than if it were not. For as to the obtaining a 15.
15 For in Christ Jesus   Share in the Kingdom of Jesus Christ, and the
neither circumcision a-   Privileges and Advantages of it, neither Circum-
vaileth any thing, nor   cision nor Uncircumcision, such outward Diffe-
uncircumcision, but a   rences in the Flesh, avail any thing, but the New
new creature.   Creation, wherein, by a thorough Change, a Man
16 And as many as walk   is disposed to Righteousness and true Holiness in
according to this rule,   good Works^m. And on all those who walk by 16.
peace be on them, and   this Rule, *viz.* that it is the New Creation alone,
mercy, and upon the Is-   and not Circumcision, that availeth under the
rael of God.   Gospel, Peace and Mercy shall be on them, they
17 From henceforth let   being that *Israel* which are truly the People of
no man trouble me; for   God^n. From henceforth let no Man give me 17.
I bear in my body the   Trouble by Questions, or Doubt, whether I preach
marks of the Lord Jesus.   Circumcision or no. It is true, I am circumcised:
18 Brethren, the grace of But yet the Marks I now bear in my Body, are
our Lord Jesus Christ be   the Marks of Jesus Christ, that I am his: The
with your spirit, Amen.   Marks of the Stripes which I have received from
¶ Unto the Galatians,   the *Jews*, and which I still bear in my Body for
written from Rome.   preaching Jesus Christ, are an Evidence that I
                            am not for Circumcision. Brethren, *the Favour* 18.
                            of our Lord Jesus Christ be with your Spirit,
                            Amen.

                 NOTES.

15 ^m See *Eph.* II. 10. and IV. 24.
16 ^n St. *Paul* having in the foregoing Verse asserted, that it is the New Creation alone that
puts Men into the Kingdom of Christ, and into the Possession of the Privileges thereof, this Verse
may be understood also as assertory, rather than as a Prayer, unless there were a Verb that expressed it; especially considering that he writes this Epistle to encourage them to refuse Circumcision. To which End, the assuring them, that those who do so shall have Peace and Mercy from
God, is of more Force than to tell them, that he prays that they may have Peace and Mercy. And
for the same Reason I understand the *Israel of God* to be the same with *those who walk by this Rule*,
though joined with them by the Copulative Καὶ, *And*; no very unusual Way of Speaking.

                                                                            A

A PARAPHRASE *and* NOTES

ON THE

First EPISTLE of St. *PAUL*

TO THE

CORINTHIANS.

An. Ch.
57. *Nero-*
nis 3.

SYNOPSIS.

Saint *Paul*'s first coming to *Corinth* was *Anno Christi* 52. where he first applied himself to the Synagogue, *Acts* XVIII. 4. But finding them obstinate in their Opposition to the Gospel, he turned to the *Gentiles*, *ver*. 6. out of whom this Church at *Corinth* seems chiefly to be gathered, as appears, *Acts* XVIII. and 1 *Cor.* XII. 2.

His Stay here was about two Years, as appears from *Acts* XVIII. 11, 18. compared: In which Time it may be concluded he made many Converts, for he was not idle there, nor did he use to stay long in a Place where he was not encouraged by the Success of his Ministry. Besides what his so long Abode in this one City, and his indefatigable Labour every where, might induce one to presume of the Number of Converts he made in that City, the Scripture itself, *Acts* XVIII. 10. gives sufficient Evidence of a numerous Church gathered there.

Corinth itself was a rich Merchant-Town, the Inhabitants *Greeks*, a People of quick Parts, and inquisitive, 1 *Cor.* I. 22. but naturally vain and conceited of themselves.

These Things considered, may help us in some Measure the better to understand St. *Paul*'s Epistles to this Church, which seems to be in greater Disorder than any other of the Churches which he writ to.

This

I CORINTHIANS.

This Epistle was writ to the *Corinthians Anno Christi* 57, between two and three Years after St. *Paul* had left them. In this Interval there was got in amongst them a new Instructor, a *Jew* by Nation, who had raised a Faction against St. *Paul*. With this Party, whereof he was the Leader, this false Apostle had gained great Authority; so that they admired, and gloried in him, with an apparent Disesteem and Diminishing of St. *Paul*.

Why I suppose the Opposition to be made to St. *Paul* in this Church by one Party under one Leader, I shall give the Reasons that make it probable to me, as they come in my Way, going through these two Epistles; which I shall leave to the Reader to judge, without positively determining on either Side: And therefore shall, as it happens, speak of these Opposers of St. *Paul* sometimes in the singular, and sometimes in the plural Number.

This at least is evident, that the main Design of St. *Paul* in this Epistle, is to support his own Authority, Dignity, and Credit, with that Part of the Church which stuck to him; to vindicate himself from the Aspersions and Calumnies of the opposite Party; to lessen the Credit of the chief and leading Men in it, by intimating their Miscarriages, and shewing their no Cause of glorying, or being gloried in; that so withdrawing their Party from the Admiration and Esteem of those their Leaders, he might break the Faction; and putting an end to the Division might re-unite them with the uncorrupted Part of the Church, that they might all unanimously submit to the Authority of his Divine Mission, and with one Accord receive and keep the Doctrine and Directions he had delivered to them.

This is the whole Subject from *Ch.* I. 10. to the End of *Ch.* VI. In the remaining Part of this Epistle he answers some Questions they had proposed to him; and resolves some Doubts, not without a Mixture, on all Occasions, of Reflections on his Opposers, and of other Things that might tend to the breaking of their Faction.

I CORINTHIANS.

SECTION. I.

CHAP. I. Ver. 1—9.

INTRODUCTION.	TEXT.
1. PAUL an Apostle of *Jesus Christ*, called to be so by the Will of God[a], and *Sosthenes* 2. [b] our Brother in the Christian Faith; to the Church of God which is at *Corinth*; to them that are separated from the rest of the World by Faith in *Christ Jesus*[c], called to be Saints, with all that are every where called by the Name of 3. *Jesus Christ*[d], their Lord[e], and ours; Favour and Peace be unto you from God our Father, 4. and from the Lord *Jesus Christ*. I thank God always on your Behalf, for the Favour of God which is bestowed on you through *Jesus Christ*; 5. so that by him you are inriched with all Knowledge and Utterance, and all extraordinary	PAUL, called to be an 1 apostle of Jesus Christ, through the will of God, and Sosthenes our brother, Unto the church of God 2 which is at Corinth, to them that are sanctified in Christ Jesus, called to be saints, with all that in every place call upon the name of Jesus Christ our Lord, both theirs and ours. Grace be unto you, and 3 peace from God our Father, and from the Lord Jesus Christ. I thank God always 4 on your behalf, for the grace of God, which is given you by Jesus Christ; That in every thing ye 5 are enriched by him in all utterance, and in all knowledge:

NOTES.

[a] St. *Paul* in most of his Epistles mentions his being *called to be an Apostle by the Will of God*, which Way of Speaking being peculiar to him, we may suppose him therein to intimate his extraordinary and miraculous Call, *Acts* IX. and his receiving the Gospel by immediate Revelation, *Gal.* I. 11, 12. for he doubted not of the Will and Providence of God governing all Things.

[b] *Acts* XVIII. 17.

[c] Ἡγιασμένοις ἐν Χριστῷ Ἰησοῦ, *Sanctified in Christ Jesus*, does not signify here, whose Lives are pure and holy, for there were many amongst those he writ to, who were quite otherwise; but *sanctified* signifies separate from the common State of Mankind, to be the People of God, and to serve him. The heathen World had revolted from the true God, to the Service of Idols and false Gods, *Rom.* I. 18—25. The *Jews* being separated from this corrupted Mass, to be the peculiar People of God, were called *holy*, Exod. XIX. 5, 6. Numb. XV. 40. They being cast off, the Professors of Christianity were separated to be the People of God, and so became *holy*, 1 *Pet.* II. 9. 10.

[d] Ἐπικαλουμένοις ὄνομα Χριστοῦ, *that are called Christians*; these *Greek* Words being a Periphrasis for Christians, as is plain from the Design of this Verse. But he that is not satisfied with that, may see more Proofs of it in Dr. *Hammond* upon the Place.

[e] What the Apostle means by *Lord*, when he attributes it to Christ, see *Chap.* VIII. 6.

Gifts;

I CORINTHIANS.

TEXT.	INTRODUCTION.	Chap. I.
6 Even as the testimony of Christ was confirmed in you.	Gifts; as at first by those miraculous Gifts the Gospel of *Christ* was confirmed among you: So that in no spiritual Gift are you short or deficient [f], waiting for the coming of our Lord *Jesus Christ*; who also shall confirm you unto the End, that in the Day of the Lord *Jesus Christ* there may be no Charge against you. For God, who has called you unto the Fellowship of his Son *Jesus Christ* our Lord, may be relied on for what is to be done on his Side.	6. 7. 8. 9.
7 So that ye come behind in no gift; waiting for the coming of our Lord Jesus Christ:		
8 Who shall also confirm you unto the end, that ye may be blameless in the day of our Lord Jesus Christ.		
9 God is faithful, by whom ye were called unto the fellowship of his Son Jesus Christ our Lord.		

NOTES.

7 [f] Vid. 2 *Cor.* XII. 12, 13.

SECT. II.
CHAP. I. 10——VI. 20.
CONTENTS.

THERE were great Disorders in the Church of *Corinth*, caused chiefly by a Faction raised there against St. *Paul*: The Partisan of the Faction mightily cried up and gloried in their Leaders, who did all they could to disparage St. *Paul*, and lessen him in the Esteem of the *Corinthians*. St. *Paul* makes it his Business in this Section, to take off the *Corinthians* from siding with, and glorying in this pretended Apostle, whose Followers and Scholars they professed themselves to be; and to reduce them into one Body, as the Scholars of Christ united in a Belief of the Gospel, which he had preached to them, and in an Obedience to it, without any such Distinction of Masters or Leaders, from whom they denominated themselves. He also here and there intermixes a Justification of himself against the Aspersions which were cast upon him by his Opposers. How much St. *Paul* was set against their Leaders, may be seen, 2 *Cor.* XI. 13—15.

Chap. I. The Arguments used by St. *Paul* to break the opposite Faction, and put an end to all Divisions amongst them, being various, we shall take notice of them under their several Heads, as they come in the Order of his Discourse.

SECT. II. *N.* 1.

CHAP. I. 10——16.

CONTENTS.

Saint *Paul*'s first Argument is, That in Christianity, they all had but one Maker, *viz. Christ*; and therefore were not to fall into Parties denominated from distinct Teachers, as they did in their Schools of Philosophy.

PARAPHRASE.

10. Now I beseech you, Brethren, by the Name [g] of our Lord *Jesus Christ*, that ye hold the same Doctrine, and that there be no Divisions amongst you; but that ye be framed together into one intire Body, with one Mind, and one Affection. For I understand, my Brethren [h], by some of the House of *Chloe*, that there are Quarrels and Dissentions amongst you:

11.

TEXT.

10 Now I beseech you, brethren, by the name of our Lord Jesus Christ, that ye all speak the same thing, and that there be no divisions among you; but that ye be perfectly joined together in the same mind, and in the same judgment.

11 For it hath been declared unto me of you, my brethren, by them which are of the house of Chloe, that there are contentions among you.

NOTES.

10 [g] Of whom the whole Family in Heaven and Earth, is, and ought to be named. If any one has thought St *Paul* a loose Writer, it is only because he was a looser Reader. He that takes notice of St. *Paul*'s Design, shall find that there is not a Word, scarce, or Expression that he makes use of, but with relation and tendency to his present main Purpose; as here, intending to abolish the Names of Leaders they distinguished themselves by, he beseeches them by the Name of Christ, a Form that I do not remember he elsewhere use.

11 [h] *Brethren*, a Name of Union and Friendship used here twice together by St. *Paul*, in the entrance of his Persuasion to them, to put an end to their Divisions.

I CORINTHIANS.

TEXT.

12 Now this I say, that every one of you faith, I am of Paul, and I of Apollos, and I of Cephas, and I of Chrift.
13 Is Chrift divided? was Paul crucified for you? or were ye baptized in the name of Paul?
14 I thank God that I baptized none of you but Crifpus and Gaius:
15 Left any fhould fay that I had baptized in mine own name.
16 And I baptized also the houfhold of Stephanas: befides, I know not whether I baptized any other.

PARAPHRASE.

So that ye are all fallen into Parties, ranking yourfelves under different Leaders, or Mafters; one faying, I am of *Paul*, another, I of *Apollos*, I of *Cephas*, I of *Chrift*. Is *Chrift*, who is our only Head and Mafter, divided? Was *Paul* crucified for you? Or were you baptized into ⸠ the Name of *Paul*? I thank God that I baptized none of you, but *Crifpus* and *Gaius*; left any one fhould fay I had baptized into my own Name. I baptized alfo the Houfhold of *Stephanas*: Farther, I know not whether I baptized any other.

12.
13.
14.
15.
16.

NOTES.

13 ⸠ 'Εις properly fignifies *into*: So the *French* tranflate it here. The Phrafe βαπτιςθῆναι εἰς, *to be baptized into any one's Name, or into any one*, is folemnly, by that Ceremony, to enter himfelf a Difciple of him into whofe Name he was baptized, with Profeffion to receive his Doctrine and Rules, and fubmit to his Authority: A very good Argument here why they fhould be called by no one's Name but *Chrift*'s..

SECT. II. N. 2.

CHAP. I. 17——31.

CONTENTS.

THE next Argument of St. *Paul*, to ftop their Followers from glorying in thefe falfe Apoftles, is, that neither any Advantage of Extraction, nor Skill in the Learning of the *Jews*, nor in the Philofophy and Eloquence of the *Greeks*, was that for which God chofe Men to be Preachers of the Gofpel. Thofe whom he made choice of for overturning the Mighty and the Learned, were mean, plain, illiterate Men.

For

I CORINTHIANS.

Chap. I.

PARAPHRASE.

17. For *Christ* sent me not to baptize, but to preach the Gospel; not with learned and eloquent Harangues, lest thereby the Virtue and Efficacy of *Christ*'s Sufferings and Death should be overlooked and neglected, if the Stress of our Persuasion should be laid on the Learning and
18. Quaintness of our Preaching. For the plain insisting on the Death of a crucified Saviour, is, by those who perish, received as a foolish, contemptible Thing; though to us, who are saved, it be the Power of God, conformable to what
19. is prophesied by *Isaiah*: I will destroy the Wisdom of the Wise, and I will bring to nothing
20. the Understanding of the Prudent. Where is the Philosopher skilled in the Wisdom of the *Greeks*? Where the Scribe ᵏ studied in the Learning of the *Jews*? Where the Professor of Human Arts and Sciences? Hath not God rendered all the Learning and Wisdom of this World foolish and useless, for the Discovery
21. of the Truths of the Gospel? For since the World, by their natural Parts and Improvements in what with them passed for Wisdom, acknowledged not the one only true God, though he had manifested himself to them in the wise Contrivance and admirable Frame of the visible Works of the Creation, it pleased God by the plain, and (as the World esteems it) foolish Doctrine of the Gospel, to save those who

TEXT.

For Christ sent me not 17 to baptize, but to preach the gospel; not with wisdom of words, lest the cross of Christ should be made of none effect.

For the preaching of 18 the cross is to them that perish, foolishness: but unto us which are saved, it is the power of God.

For it is written, I will 19 destroy the wisdom of the wise, and will bring to nothing the understanding of the prudent.

Where is the wise? 20 where is the scribe? where is the disputer of this world? hath not God made foolish the wisdom of this world?

For after that, in the 21 wisdom . of God, the world by wisdom knew not God, it pleased God by the foolishness of preaching to save them that believe.

NOTES.

20 ᵏ *Scribe* was the Title of a learned Man amongst the *Jews*; one versed in their Law and Rites, which was the Study of their Doctors and Rabbies. It is likely the false Apostle, so much concerned in these two Epistles to the *Corinthians*, who was a *Jew*, pretended to something of this Kind, and magnified himself thereupon; otherwise it is not probable that Saint *Paul* should name to the *Corinthians* a Sort of Men not much known or valued amongst the *Greeks*. This therefore may be supposed to be said to take off their glorying in their false Apostle.

receive

TEXT.

22 For the Jews require a sign, and the Greeks seek after wisdom:
23 But we preach Christ crucified, unto the Jews a stumbling-block, and unto the Greeks foolishness;
24 But unto them which are called, both Jews and Greeks, Christ, the power of God, and the wisdom of God.
25 Because the foolishness of God is wiser than men; and the weakness of God is stronger than men.
26 For ye see your calling, brethren, how that not many wise men after the flesh, not many mighty, not many noble are called.
27 But God hath chosen the foolish things of the world, to confound the wise; and God hath chosen the weak things of the world, to confound the things which are mighty;

PARAPHRASE.

receive and believe it. Since [1] both the *Jews* demand extraordinary Signs and Miracles, and the *Greeks* seek Wisdom; but I have nothing else to preach to them but Christ crucified, a Doctrine offensive to the Hopes and Expectations of the *Jews*, and foolish to the acute Men of Learning, the *Greeks*; but yet it is to these, both *Jews* and *Greeks* (when they are converted) *Christ*, the Power of God, and *Christ*, the Wisdom of God: Because that which seems Foolishness in those who came from God, surpasses the Wisdom of Man; and that which seems Weakness in those sent by God, surpasses the Power of Men. For, reflect upon yourselves, Brethren, and you may observe, that there are not many of the wise and learned Men, not many Men of Power or of Birth among you, that are called. But God hath chosen the foolish Men in the Account of the World to confound the Wise; and God hath chosen the weak Men of the World to confound

NOTES.

22 [1] Ἐπειδὴ καὶ, *since both*. The Words used here by St. *Paul*, are not certainly idle and insignificant, and therefore I see not how they can be omitted in the Translation.
Ἐπειδὴ is a Word of Reasoning, and, if minded, will lead us into one of St. *Paul*'s Reasonings here, which the Neglect of this Word makes the Reader overlook. St. *Paul*, in *v.* 21. argues thus in general: "Since the World, by their natural Parts and Improvements, did not attain
"to a right and saving Knowledge of God, God by the Preaching of the Gospel, which seems
"Foolishness to them, was pleased to communicate that Knowledge to those who believed."
In the three following Verses he repeats the same Reasoning, a little more expresly applied to the People he had here in his View, *viz. Jews* and *Greeks*; and his Sense seems to be this.
"Since the *Jews*, to make any Doctrine go down with them, require extraordinary Signs of
"the *Power* of God to accompany it, and nothing will please the nice Palates of the learned
"*Greeks* but *Wisdom*, and though our preaching of a crucified *Messiah* be a Scandal to the *Jews*,
"and Foolishness to the *Greeks*, yet we have what they both seek; for both *Jew* and *Gentile*,
"when they are called, find the *Messiah*, whom we preach, to be the *Power* of God, and
"*Wisdom* of God."

the

I CORINTHIANS.

Chap. I.

PARAPHRASE.

28. the Mighty: The mean Men of the World, and contemptible, has God chosen; and those that are of no account, are nothing ᵐ, to displace those
29. that are: That so there might be no Room or Pretence for any one to glory in his Presence.
30. Natural Human Abilities, Parts or Wisdom, could never have reached this Way to Happiness: 'Tis to his Wisdom alone that ye owe the Contrivance of it: To his revealing of it that ye owe the Knowledge of it; and 'tis from him alone that you are in *Christ Jesus*, whom God has made to us *Christians* Wisdom, and Righteousness, and Sanctification, and Redemption, which is all the Dignity and Pre-eminence, all that is of any Value amongst us *Christians*: That as it is written,
31. He that glorieth, should glory only in the Lord.

TEXT.

23 And base things of the world, and things which are despised, hath God chosen; yea, and things which are not, to bring to nought things that are:
29 That no flesh should glory in his presence.
30 But of him are ye in Christ Jesus, who of God is made unto us wisdom, and righteousness, and sanctification, and redemption:
31 That, according as it is written, He that glorieth, let him glory in the Lord.

NOTES.

25, 27, 28. He that will read the Context, cannot doubt but that St. *Paul*, by what he expresses in these Verses in the Neuter Gender, means Persons; the whole Argument of the Place being about Persons, and their glorying, and not about Things.

28 ᵐ Τὰ μὴ ὄντα, *Things that are not*, I think may well be understood of the *Gentiles*, who were not the People of God, and were counted as nothing by the *Jews*; and we are pointed to this Meaning by the Words καταισχύνῃ & καταργήσῃ. By *the foolish and weak Things*, i. e. by simple, illiterate and mean Men, God would *make ashamed* the learned Philosophers and great Men of the Nation: But by the μὴ ὄντα, the Things that are not, he would abolish the Things that are, as in effect he did abolish the *Jewish* Church by the Christian, taking in the *Gentiles* to be his People, in the Place of the rejected *Jews*, who till then were his People. This St. *Paul* mentions here not by chance, but pursuant to his main Design, to stay their glorying in their false Apostle, who was a *Jew*; by shewing that whatever that Head of the Faction might claim under that Pretence, as it is plain he did stand upon it (see 2 Cor. XI. 21, 22.) he had not any the least Title to any Esteem or Respect upon that Account, since the *Jewish* Nation was laid aside, and God had chosen the *Gentiles* to take their Place, and to be his Church and People instead of them. *Vid*. Note on *Chap*. II. *v*. 6. there one may see, who are the καταργούμενοι, *the Abolished*, whom God says here, καταργήσῃ, he will abolish.

I CORINTHIANS.

SECT. II. N. 3.

CHAP. II. 1——5.

CONTENTS.

Farther, to keep them from glorying in their Leaders, he tells them, that as the Preachers of the Gospel of God's choosing were mean and illiterate Men, so the Gospel was not to be propagated, nor Men to be established in the Faith by human Learning and Eloquence, but by the Evidence it had from the Revelation contained in the Old Testament, and from the Power of God accompanying and confirming it with Miracles.

TEXT.

3 AND I, brethren, when I came to you, came not with excellency of speech, or of wisdom, declaring unto you the testimony of God.

2 For I determined not to

PARAPHRASE.

AND I, Brethren, when I came and preached the Gospel to you, I did not endeavour to set it off with any Ornaments of Rhetoric, or the Mixture of human Learning or Philosophy, but plainly declared it to you as a Doctrine coming from God, revealed and attested ⁿ by him. For I resolved to own

1.

2.

NOTES.

1 ⁿ Τὸ μαρτύριον τȣ̃ Θεȣ̃, *The Testimony of God*, i. e. what God hath revealed and testifies in the Old Testament. The Apostle here declares to the *Corinthians*, that when he brought the Gospel to them, he made no use of any human Science, Improvement, or Skill; no Insinuations of Eloquence, no philosophical Speculations, or Ornaments of human Learning appeared in any thing he said to persuade them: All his Arguments were, as he tells them, *ver.* 4. from the Revelation of the Spirit of God in the Predictions of the Old Testament, and the Miracles which he, *Paul*, did among them, that their Faith might be built wholly upon the Spirit of God, and not upon the Abilities and Wisdom of Man. Tho' μαρτύριον τȣ̃ Θεȣ̃, *the Testimony of God*, agrees very well with so much of St. *Paul*'s Meaning, as relates to his founding his Preaching on the Testimony of God, yet those Copies which read μυστήριον, *Mystery*, for μαρτύριον, *Testimony*, seem more perfectly to correspond with St. *Paul*'s Sense in the whole Latitude of it. For tho' he owns the Doctrine of the Gospel dictated by the Spirit of God, to be contained in the Scriptures of the Old Testament, and builds upon Revelation; yet he every where teaches, that it remained a Secret there, not understood till they were led into the hidden Evangelical Meaning of those Passages by the Coming of *Jesus Christ*, and by the Assistance of the Spirit in the Times of the *Messiah*, and then published to the World by the Preachers of the Gospel: And therefore he calls it, especially that Part of it which relates to the *Gentiles*, almost every where, μυστήριον, *Mystery*. See particularly *Rom.* XVI. 25, 26.

H

or

PARAPHRASE.

or shew no other Knowledge among you, but the Knowledge ° or Doctrine of *Jesus Christ*, and of him crucified.

3. All my Carriage among you had nothing in it but the Appearance of Weakness, and Humility, and Fear of offending you ᵖ.

4. Neither did I in my Discourse, or Preaching, make use of any human Art of Persuasion to inveigle you. But the Doctrine of the Gospel which I proposed, I confirmed, and inforced by what the Spirit ᑫ had revealed and demonstrated of it in the Old Testament, and by the Power of God accompanying it with miraculous Operations;

5. that your Faith might have its Foundation not in the Wisdom and Endowments of Men, but in the Power of God ʳ.

TEXT.

know any thing among you, save Jesus Christ, and him crucified.

3. And I was with you in weakness, and in fear, and in much trembling.

4. And my speech, and my preaching was not with enticing words of man's wisdom, but in demonstration of the Spirit, and of power:

5. That your Faith should not stand in the wisdom of men, but in the power of God.

NOTES.

2 ° St. *Paul*, who was himself a learned Man, especially in the *Jewish* Knowledge, having in the foregoing Chapter told them, that neither the *Jewish* Learning, nor *Grecian* Sciences, give a Man any Advantage, as a Minister of the Gospel; he here reminds them, that he made no shew or Use of either when he planted the Gospel amongst them: Intimating thereby, that those were not Things for which their Teachers were to be valued or followed.

3 ᵖ St. *Paul*, by thus setting forth his own modest and humble Behaviour amongst them, reflects on the contrary Carriage of their false Apostle, which he describes in the Words at length, 2 *Cor.* XI. 20.

4 ᑫ There were two Sorts of Arguments wherewith the Apostle confirmed the Gospel: The one was the Revelations made concerning our Saviour by Types and Figures, and Prophecies of him under the Law: The other, Miracles and miraculous Gifts accompanying the first Preachers of the Gospel, in the publishing and propagating of it. The latter of these St. *Paul* here calls *Power*; the former in this Chapter he terms *Spirit*: So *ver.* 12, 14. *Things of the Spirit of God*, and *spiritual Things*, are Things which are revealed by the Spirit of God, and not discoverable by our natural Faculties.

5 ʳ Their Faith being built wholly on Divine Revelation and Miracles, whereby all human Abilities were shut out, there could be no Reason for any of them to boast themselves of their Teachers, or value themselves upon their being the Followers of this or that Preacher; which St. *Paul* hereby obviates.

I CORINTHIANS.

SECT. II. N. 4.

CHAP. II. 6——16.

CONTENTS.

THE next Argument the Apostle uses, to shew them that they had no Reason to glory in their Teachers, is, that the Knowledge of the Gospel was not attainable by our natural Parts, however they were improved by Arts and Philosophy, but was wholly owing to Revelation.

TEXT.

6. Howbeit we speak wisdom among them that are perfect: yet not the wisdom of this world; nor of

PARAPHRASE.

6. Howbeit that which we preach is Wisdom, and known to be so among those who are thoroughly instructed in the *Christian* Religion, and take it upon its sound and true Principles [a]: But not the Wisdom of this World [b], nor of

NOTES.

6 [a] *Perfect* here is the same with Spiritual, *ver.* 15. one that is so perfectly well apprized of the Divine Nature and Original of the *Christian* Religion, that he sees and acknowledges it to be all a pure Revelation from God, and not in the least the Product of human Discovery, Parts, or Learning; and so deriving it wholly from what God hath taught by his Spirit in the sacred Scriptures, allows not the least Part of it to be ascribed to the Skill or Abilities of Men, as Authors of it, but received as a Doctrine coming from God alone. And thus *perfect* is opposed to *carnal*, Chap. III. 1, 3. *i. e.* such *Babes* in Christianity, such weak and mistaken Christians, that they thought the Gospel was to be managed as human Arts and Sciences amongst Men of the World, and those were better instructed, and were more in the right, who followed this Master or Teacher rather than another; and so glorying in being the Scholars, one of *Paul*, and another of *Apollos*, fell into Divisions and Parties about it, and vaunted one over another: Whereas, in the School of *Christ*, all was to be built on the Authority of God alone, and the Revelation of his Spirit in the sacred Scriptures.

[b] *Wisdom of this World*, i. e. the Knowledge, Arts and Sciences attainable by Man's natural Parts and Faculties; such as Man's Wit could find out, cultivate and improve: *Or of the Princes of this World*, i. e. such Doctrines, Arts and Sciences, as the Princes of the World approve, encourage, and endeavour to propagate.

the

1 CORINTHIANS.

PARAPHRASE.

the Princes ᵘ or Great Men of this World ʷ, who will in a short Time be brought
7. to nought ˣ. But we speak the Wisdom of

TEXT.

the princes of this world, that come to nought.
But we speak the wis- 7

NOTES.

ᵘ Tho' by ἀρχόντων τοῦ αἰῶνος τούτου, may here be understood the *Princes* or *Great Men of this World*, in the ordinary Sense of these Words; yet he that well considers *ver.* 28. of the foregoing Chapter, and *ver.* 8. of this Chapter, may find reason to think that the Apostle here principally designs the Rulers and Great Men of the *Jewish* Nation. If it be objected, that there is little ground to think that St. *Paul*, by the Wisdom he disowns, should mean that of his own Nation, which the *Greeks* of *Corinth* (whom he was writing to) had little Acquaintance with, and had very little Esteem for; I reply, that to understand this right, and the Pertinency of it, we must remember, that the great Design of St. *Paul*, in writing to the *Corinthians*, was to take them off from the Respect and Esteem that many of them had for a false Apostle that was got in among them, and had there raised a Faction against St. *Paul*. This pretended Apostle, it is plain from 2 *Cor.* XI. 22. was a *Jew*; and, as it seems, 2 *Cor.* V. 16, 17. valued himself upon that Account, and possibly boasted himself to be a Man of Note, either by Birth, or Alliance, or Place, or Learning, among that People, who counted themselves the holy and illuminated People of God, and therefore to have a right to sway among these new Heathen Converts. To obviate this Claim of his to any Authority, St. *Paul* here tells the *Corinthians*, that the Wisdom and Learning of the *Jewish* Nation led them not into the Knowledge of the Wisdom of God, *i. e.* the Gospel revealed in the Old Testament, evident in this, that it was their Rulers and Rabbies, who stiffly adhering to the Notions and Prejudices of their Nation, had crucified *Jesus* the Lord of Glory, and were now themselves, with their State and Religion, upon the point to be swept away and abolished. It is to the same Purpose that, 2 *Cor.* V. 16——19. he tells the *Corinthians*, that he *knows no Man after the Flesh*, *i. e.* that he acknowledges no Dignity of Birth, or Descent, or outward national Privileges. The old Things of the *Jewish* Constitution are past and gone; whoever is in *Christ*, and entered into his Kingdom, is in a new Creation, wherein all Things are new, all Things are from God; no Right, no Claim or Preference derived to any one from any former Institution, but every one's Dignity consists solely in this, that God hath reconciled him to himself, not imputing his former Trespasses to him.

ʷ Αἰῶν οὗτος, which we translate *this World*, seems to me to signify commonly, if not constantly, in the New Testament, that State which, during the Mosaical Constitution, Men, either *Jews*, or *Gentiles*, were in, as contra-distinguished to the Evangelical State or Constitution, which is commonly called Αἰῶν μέλλων ἐρχόμενος, *The World to come*.

ˣ Τῶν καταργουμένων, *Who are brought to nought, i. e.* who are vanishing. If *the Wisdom of this World, and of the Princes of this World*, be to be understood of the Wisdom and Learning of the World in general, as contra-distinguished to the Doctrine of the Gospel, then the Words are added, to shew what Folly it is for them to glory as they do in their Teachers, when all that worldly Wisdom and Learning, and the Great Men, the Supporters of it, would quickly be gone; whereas all true and lasting Glory came only from *Jesus Christ*, the Lord of Glory. But if these Words are to be understood of the *Jews*, as seems most consonant both to the main Design of the Epistle, and to St. *Paul*'s Expressions here; then his telling them that the *Princes of the Jewish Nation are brought to nought*, is to take them off from glorying in their Judaizing false Apostle, since the Authority of the Rulers of that Nation, in Matters of Religion, was now at an end, and they with all their Pretences, and their very Constitution itself, were upon the point of being abolished and swept away, for having rejected and crucified the Lord of Glory.

God,

I CORINTHIANS.

Chap. II.

TEXT.
dom of God in a mystery, even the hidden wisdom which God ordained be-

PARAPHRASE.
God [z], contained in the mysterious and the obscure Prophecies of the Old Testament [a], which has been therein concealed and hid; though it be what God predetermined in his own Purpose before the *Jewish* Constitution [b], to the

NOTES.

7 [z] *Wisdom of God*, is used here for the Doctrine of the Gospel coming immediately from God by the Revelation of his Spirit, and in this Chapter is set in opposition to all Knowledge, Discoveries and Improvements whatsoever, attainable by human Industry, Parts, and Study; all which he calls *the Wisdom of the World*, and *Man's Wisdom*; thus distinguishing the Knowledge of the Gospel which was derived wholly from Revelation, and could be had no other Way, from all other Knowledge whatsoever.

[a] What the Spirit of God had revealed of the Gospel, during the Times of the Law, was so little understood by the *Jews*, in whose sacred Writings it was contained, that it might well be called the *Wisdom of God in a Mystery*, i. e. declared in obscure Prophecies, and mysterious Expressions and Types. Tho' this be undoubtedly so, as appears by what the *Jews* both thought and did when *Jesus the Messiah*, exactly answering what was foretold of him, came amongst them; yet by *the Wisdom of God in Mystery wherein it was hid, though purposed by God before the settling of the* Jewish Oeconomy, St. *Paul* seems more particularly to mean what the *Gentiles*, and consequently the *Corinthians*, were more peculiarly concerned in, (*viz.*) God's Purpose of calling the *Gentiles* to be his People under the *Messiah*, which, tho' revealed in the Old Testament, yet was not in the least understood till the Times of the Gospel, and the Preaching of St. *Paul* the Apostle of the *Gentiles*, which therefore he so frequently calls a *Mystery*. The reading and comparing *Rom.* XVI. 25, 26. *Eph.* III. 3 — 9. *Chap.* VI. 19, 20. *Col.* I. 26, 27. & II. 1 — 8. & IV. 3, 4. will give light to this. To which give me leave to observe upon the Use of the Word *Wisdom* here, that St. *Paul* speaking of God's calling the *Gentiles*, cannot in mentioning it forbear Expressions of his Admiration of the great and incomprehensible Wisdom of God therein. See *Eph.* III. 8, 10. *Rom.* XI. 33.

[b] Πρὸ τῶ αἰώνων signifies properly, *before the Ages*; and I think it may be doubted whether these Words, *before the World*, do exactly render the Sense of the Place. That αἰὼν or αἰῶνες, should not be translated *the World*, is in many Places they are. I shall give one convincing Instance among many that might be brought, *viz. Eph.* III. 9. compared with *Col.* I. 26. The Words in *Colossians* are, τὸ μυστήριον τὸ ἀποκεκρυμμένον ἀπὸ τῶν αἰώνων; thus rendered in the *English* Translation, *which hath been hidden from Ages*; but in *Eph.* III. 9. a parallel Place, the same Words, τῆς μυστηρίου τοῦ ἀποκεκρυμμένου ἀπὸ τῶν αἰώνων, are translated, *the Mystery which from the Beginning of the World hath been hid*: Whereas it is plain, from *Col.* I. 26. ἀπὸ τῶν αἰώνων does not signify the Epoch or Commencement of the Concealment, but those from whom it was concealed. 'Tis plain, the Apostle in the Verse immediately preceding, and that following this which we have before us, speaks of the *Jews*; and therefore πρὸ τῶν αἰώνων here, may be well understood to mean, *before the Ages of the Jews*; and so Ἀπ' αἰώνων, *from the Ages of the Jews*, in the other two mentioned Texts. Why αἰῶνες in these, and other Places, as *Luke* I. 70. and *Acts* III. 21. and elsewhere, should be appropriated to the Ages of the *Jews*, may be owing to their counting by Ages or Jubilees: *Vid.* Dr. *Burthogge* in his Judicious Treatise, *Christianity a revealed Mystery*, c. 2. p. 17.

Glory

1 CORINTHIANS.

Chap. II.

PARAPHRASE.

8. Glory of us ᵉ, who understand, receive, and preach it. Which none of the Rulers amongst the Jews understood: For if they had, they would not have crucified the Lord Christ, who has in his Hands the disposing of all true Glory.

9. But they knew it not; as it is written, Eye hath not seen, nor Ear heard, nor have the Things that God hath prepared for them that love him, entered into the Heart or Thoughts of Man.

10. But these Things which are not discoverable by Man's natural Faculties and Powers, God hath revealed to us by his Spirit, which searcheth out all Things, even the deep Counsels of God, which are beyond the reach of our Abilities to discover.

11. For as no Man knoweth what is in the Mind of another Man, but only the Spirit of the Man himself that is in him; so much less doth any Man know or can discover the Thoughts and Counsels of God, but only the Spirit of God.

12. But we ᵈ have received not the Spirit of the

TEXT.

fore the world unto our glory.

8 Which none of the princes of this world knew: for had they known it, they would not have crucified the Lord of glory.

9 But as it is written, Eye hath not seen, nor ear heard, neither have entered into the heart of man, the things which God hath prepared for them that love him.

10 But God hath revealed them unto us by his Spirit: for the Spirit searcheth all things; yea, the deep things of God.

11 For what man knoweth the things of a man, save the spirit of a man, which is in him? even so the things of God knoweth no man, but the Spirit of God.

12 Now we have received not the spirit of the

NOTES.

ᵉ St. *Paul* opposes here the true *Glory* of a *Christian* to the *Glorying* which was amongst the *Corinthians*, in the Eloquence, Learning, or any other Quality of their factious Leaders; for St. *Paul*, in all his Expressions, has an Eye on his main Purpose: As if he should have said; "Why do you make Divisions, by glorying, as you do, in your distinct Teachers? The Glory "that God has ordained us *Christian* Teachers and Professors to, is to be Expounders, Preachers, "and Believers of those revealed Truths and Purposes of God, which, though contained in the "sacred Scriptures of the Old Testament, were not understood in former Ages. This is all "the Glory that belongs to us the Disciples of *Christ*, who is the Lord of *all* Power and "Glory, and herein has given us what far excels all that either *Jews* or *Gentiles* had any Ex- "pectation of from what they gloried in; *vid.* ver. 9." Thus St. *Paul* takes away all Matter of Glorying from the false Apostle, and his factious Followers among the *Corinthians*. The Excellency of the Gospel-Ministration see also, 2 *Cor.* III. 6 ――― 11.

12 ᵈ *We*, the true Apostles, or rather *I*; for tho' he speaks in the Plural Number to avoid Ostentation, as it might be interpreted, yet he is here justifying himself, and shewing the *Corinthians*, that none of them had Reason to forsake and slight him, to follow and cry up their false Apostle. And that he speaks of himself, is plain from the next Verse, where he saith, *We speak not in the Words which Man's Wisdom teacheth*; the same which he says of himself, Ch. I. 17. *I was sent to preach, not with Wisdom of Words*. And *Ch.* II. 1. *I came to you, not with Excellency of Speech, or of Wisdom*.

World,

I CORINTHIANS.

Chap. II.

TEXT.

world, but the Spirit which is of God; that we might know the things that are freely given to us of God.

13 Which things also we speak, not in the words which man's wisdom teacheth, but which the Holy Ghost teacheth; comparing spiritual things with spiritual.

14 But the natural man receiveth not the things of the Spirit of God; for they are foolishness unto him: neither can he know them, because they are spiritually discerned.

15 But he that is spiritual, judgeth all things; yet

PARAPHRASE.

World *e*, but the Spirit which is of God, that we might know what Things are in the Purpose of God, out of his free Bounty to bestow upon us: Which Things we not only know, but declare also; not in the Language and Learning taught by Human Eloquence and Philosophy, but in the Language and Expressions which the Holy Ghost teacheth in the Revelations contained in the Holy Scriptures, comparing one Part of Revelation *f* with another. But a Man *g* who hath no other Help but his own natural Faculties, how much soever improved by Human Arts and Sciences, cannot receive the Truths of the Gospel, which are made known by another Principle only, *viz.* the Spirit of God revealing them, and therefore seem foolish and absurd to such a Man; nor can he by the bare Use of his natural Faculties, and the Principles of Human Reason, ever come to the Knowledge of them, because it is by the Studying of Divine Revelation alone that we can attain the Knowledge of them. But he that lays his Foundation in Divine Revelation *g*, can judge what is, and what

13.

14.

15.

NOTES.

e As he puts Princes of the World, *ver.* 6, and 8. for the Rulers of the *Jews*, so here he puts *Spirit of the World* for the Notions of the *Jews*, that worldly Spirit wherewith they interpreted the Old Testament, and the Prophecies of the *Messiah* and his Kingdom; which Spirit, in Contra-distinction to the Spirit of God, which the *Roman* Converts had received, he calls *the Spirit of Bondage,* Rom. VIII. 15.

13 *f* 'Tis plain the *spiritual Things* he here speaks of, are the unsearchable Counsels of God, revealed by the Spirit of God; which therefore he calls *spiritual Things.*

14, 15. *g* Ψυχικὸς, *the animal Man,* and πνευματικὸς, *the spiritual Man,* are opposed by St. *Paul* in *ver.* 14, 15. the one signifying a Man that has no higher Principles to build on than those of natural Reason; the other, a Man that founds his Faith and Religion on Divine Revelation. This is what appears to be meant by *natural,* or rather *animal* Man, and *Spiritual,* as they stand opposed in these two Verses.

is

Chap. III.

PARAPHRASE.

is not the Doctrine of the Gospel and of Salvation; he can judge who is, and who is not a good Minister and Preacher of the Word of God: But others, who are bare Animal Men, that go not beyond the Discoveries made by the natural Faculties of human Understanding, without the Help and Study of Revelation, cannot judge of such an one, whether he preacheth right and well, or not.

16. For who, by the bare Use of his natural Parts, can come to know the Mind of the Lord in the Design of the Gospel, so as to be able to instruct him [h] [the spiritual Man] in it? But I, who renouncing all human Learning and Knowledge in the Case, take all that I preach from Divine Revelation alone, I am sure that therein I have the Mind of Christ; and therefore there is no reason why any of you should prefer other Teachers to me, glory in them who oppose and vilify me, and count it an Honour to go for their Scholars, and be of their Party.

TEXT.

he himself is judged of no man.

For who hath known 16 the mind of the Lord, that he may instruct him? but we have the mind of Christ.

NOTES.

16 [h] Αὐτὸν, *him*, refers here to *spiritual Man* in the former Verse, and not to *Lord* in this: For St. *Paul* is shewing here, not that a *natural Man* and a mere Philosopher cannot instruct Christ, this nobody pretending to be a Christian could own; but that a Man by his bare natural Parts, not knowing the Mind of the Lord, could not instruct, could not judge, could not correct a Preacher of the Gospel who built upon Revelation, as he did, and therefore 'twas sure he had the Mind of Christ.

SECT. II. N. 5.
CHAP. III. 1.——IV. 20.

CONTENTS.

THE next Matter of Boasting which the Faction made use of to give the Pre-eminence and Preference to their Leader above St. *Paul*, seems to have been this, that their new Teacher had led them farther, and given them a deeper Insight into the Mysteries of the Gospel than St. *Paul* had done. To take away their

Glorying

glorying on this Account, St. *Paul* tells them, that they were carnal, Chap.III. and not capable of those more advanced Truths, or any thing beyond the first Principles of Christianity which he had taught them; and though another had come and watered what he had planted, yet neither Planter, nor Waterer, could assume to himself any Glory from thence, because it was God alone that gave the Increase. But whatever new Doctrines they might pretend to receive from their magnified new Apostle, yet no Man could lay any other Foundation in a Christian Church, but what he, St. *Paul*, had laid, *viz.* that *Jesus* is the *Christ*; and therefore there was no Reason to glory in their Teachers, because, upon this Foundation, they possibly might build false or unsound Doctrines, for which they should receive no Thanks from God, though continuing in the Faith, they might be saved. Some of the particular Hay and Stubble which this Leader brought into the Church at *Corinth*, he seems particularly to point at, *Chap.* III. 16, 17. *viz.* their defiling the Church by retaining, and, as it may be supposed, patronizing the Fornicator, who should have been turned out, *Ch.* V. 7—13. He further adds, that these extolled Heads of their Party were at best but Men; and none of the Church ought to glory in Men: For even *Paul,* and *Apollos,* and *Peter,* and all the other Preachers of the Gospel, were for the Use and Benefit, and Glory of the Church, as the Church was for the Glory of Christ.

Moreover, he shews them, that they ought not to be puffed up upon the Account of these their new Teachers, to the undervaluing of him, though it should be true, that they had learned more from them, than from himself; for these Reasons:

1. Because all the Preachers of the Gospel are but Stewards of the Mysteries of God; and whether they have been faithful in their Stewardship cannot be now known; and therefore they ought not to be some of them magnified and extolled, and others depressed and blamed by their Hearers here, till *Christ* their Lord came, and then he, knowing how they have behaved themselves in their Ministry, will give them their due Praises. Besides, these Stewards have nothing but what they have received, and therefore no Glory belongs to them for it.

2. Because, if these Leaders were (as was pretended) Apostles, Glory, and Honour, and outward Affluence here, was not their Portion, the Apostles being destined to Want, Contempt, and Persecution.

I   3. They

Chap. III. 3. They ought not to be honoured, followed, and gloried in as Apostles, because they had not the Power of Miracles; which he intended shortly to come and shew they had not.

PARAPHRASE.

1. AND I, Brethren, found you so given up to Pride and Vain-Glory, in Affectation of Learning and Philosophical Knowledge ^{i}, that I could not speak to you as Spiritual ^{k}, *i. e.* as to Men not wholly depending on Philosophy, and the Discoveries of natural Reason, as to Men who had resigned themselves up in Matters of Religion to Revelation, and the Knowledge which comes only from the Spirit of God; but as to Carnal ^{l}, even as to Babes who yet retained a great many childish and wrong Notions about it: This hindered me that I could not go so far as I desired in the Mysteries of the *Christian* Religion, but was fain to content myself with instructing you in the first Prin-

TEXT.

AND I, brethren, 1 could not speak unto you as unto spiritual, but as unto carnal, even as unto babes in Christ.

NOTES.

^{i} Vid. *Chap.* I. 22. & III. 18.

^{k} Here πνευματικος, *Spiritual*, is opposed to σαρκικὸ·, *Carnal*, as *Chap.* II. 14. it is to Ψυχικὸ·, *Natural*, or rather *Animal*; so that here we have three Sorts of Men: 1. *Carnal*, i. e. such as are swayed by fleshly Passions and Interests; 2. *Animal*, i. e. such as seek Wisdom, or a Way to Happiness only by the Strength and Guidance of their own natural Parts, without any supernatural Light coming from the Spirit of God, *i. e.* by Reason without Revelation, by Philosophy without Scripture; 3. *Spiritual*, i. e. such as seek their Direction to Happiness, not in the Dictates of natural Reason and Philosophy, but in the Revelations of the Spirit of God in the Holy Scriptures.

^{l} Here σαρκικὸς, *carnal*, is opposed to πνευματικὸς, *Spiritual*, in the same Sense that ψυχικὸς, *natural* or *animal*, is opposed to πνευματικὸς, *Spiritual*, Chap. II. 14. as appears by the Explination which St. *Paul* himself gives here to σαρκικὸς, *carnal*: For he makes the *Carnal* to be all one with *Babes in Christ*, ver. 1. *i. e.* such as had not their Understandings yet fully opened to the true Grounds of the Christian Religion, but retained a great many childish Thoughts about it, as appeared by their Divisions, one for the Doctrine of his Master *Paul*, another for that of his Master *Apollos*; which, if they had been *spiritual*, i. e. had looked upon the Doctrine of the Gospel to have come solely from the Spirit of God, and to be had only from Revelation, they could not have done; for then all human Mixtures of any thing, derived either from *Paul* or *Apollos*, or any other Man, had been wholly excluded. But they in these Divisions professed to hold their Religion, one from one Man, and another from another; and were thereupon divided into Parties. This he tells them was to be *carnal*, and περιπατεῖν κατὰ ἄνθρωπον, to be led by Principles purely human, *i. e.* to found their Religion upon Mens natural Parts and Discoveries; whereas the Gospel was wholly built upon Divine Revelation, and nothing else, and from thence alone those who were πνευματικοι took it.

ciples

I CORINTHIANS.

TEXT.	PARAPHRASE.

2. I have fed you with milk, and not with meat: for hitherto ye were not able to bear it, neither yet now are ye able.

ciples ᵐ and more obvious and easy Doctrines of it. I could not apply myself to you, as to spiritual Men ⁿ, that could compare spiritual Things with spiritual, one Part of Scripture with another, and thereby understand the Truths revealed by the Spirit of God, discerning true from false Doctrines, good and useful from evil ᵒ and vain Opinions. A further Discovery of the Truths and Mysteries of Christianity, depending wholly on Revelation, you were not able to bear then, nor are you yet able to bear;

3. For ye are yet carnal: for whereas there is among you envying, and strife, and divisions, are ye not carnal, and walk as men?
4. For while one saith, I am of Paul, and another,

because you are carnal, full of Envyings, and Strife, and Factions upon the account of your Knowledge, and the Orthodoxy of your particular Parties ᵖ. For whilst you say, one, I am of *Paul*; and another, I am of *Apollos* ᵍ; are ye not carnal, and manage yourselves in the Conduct both of your Minds and Actions, according to barely human Principles, and do

NOTES.

ᵐ That this is the Meaning of the Apostle's Metaphor of *Milk* and *Babes*, may be seen *Heb.* V. 12——14.

2 ⁿ Vid. *Chap.* II. 13.

ᵒ Vid. *Heb.* V. 14.

3 ᵖ Κατ' ἄνθρωπον. Speaking according to Man, signifies speaking according to the Principles of natural Reason, in Contra-distinction to Revelation, *vid.* 1 Cor. IX. 8. Gal. I. 11. and so *walking according to Man* must be here understood.

4 ᵍ From this 4th Verse, compared with *Chap.* V. 6. it may be no improbable Conjecture that the Division in this Church was only into two opposite Parties; whereof the one adhered to St. *Paul*, the other stood up for their Head, a false Apostle, who opposed St. *Paul*: For the *Apollos* whom St. *Paul* mentions here, was one (as he tells us, ver. 6.) who came in and watered what he had planted, *i. e.* when St. *Paul* had planted a Church at *Corinth*, this *Apollos* got into it, and pretended to instruct them farther, and boasted in his Performances amongst them, which St. *Paul* takes notice of again, 2 *Cor.* X. 15, 16. Now the *Apollos* that he here speaks of, he himself tells us, *Chap.* IV. 6. was another Man under that borrowed Name. 'Tis true, St. *Paul*, in his Epistles to the *Corinthians*, generally speaks of these his Opposers in the Plural Number; but it is to be remembered, that he speaks so of himself too, which as it was the less invidious Way in regard to himself, so it was the softer Way towards his Opposer, though he seems to intimate plainly, that it was one Leader that was set up against him.

I CORINTHIANS.

PARAPHRASE.

not as spiritual Men acknowledge all that Information, and all those Gifts wherewith the Ministers of Jesus Christ are furnished for the Propagation of the Gospel, to come wholly from
5. the Spirit of God? What then are any of the Preachers of the Gospel, that you should glory in them, and divide into Parties under their Names? Who, for Example, is *Paul*, or who *Apollos*? What are they else but bare Ministers, by whose Ministry, according to those several Abilities and Gifts which God has bestowed upon each of them, ye have received the Gospel? They are only Servants, employed to bring unto you a Religion derived entirely from Divine Revelation, wherein human Abilities, or Wisdom, had nothing to do. The Preachers of it are only Instruments by whom this Doctrine is conveyed to you; which, whether you look on it in its Original, is not a Thing of human Invention or Discovery; or whether you look upon the Gifts of the Teachers who instruct you in it, all is intirely from God alone, and affords you not the least Ground to
6. attribute any thing to your Teachers. For Example, I planted it amongst you, and *Apollos* watered it, but nothing can from thence be ascribed to either of us; there is no Reason for your calling yourselves, some of *Paul*, and others
7. of *Apollos:* For neither the Planter nor the Waterer have any Power to make it take Root and grow in your Hearts; they are as nothing in that respect, the Growth and Success is ow-
8. ing to God alone. The Planter and the Waterer on this account are all one, neither of them to be magnified or preferred before the other; they are but Instruments concurring to the same End, and therefore ought not to be distin-

TEXT.

I am of Apollos, are ye not carnal?

5 Who then is Paul, and who is Apollos, but ministers by whom ye believed, even as the Lord gave to every man?

6 I have planted, Apollos watered; but God gave the increase.

7 So then, neither is he that planteth any thing, neither he that watereth; but God that giveth the increase.

8 Now he that planteth, and he that watereth, are one: and every man shall receive his own reward,

I CORINTHIANS.

TEXT.

according to his own labour.

9 For we are labourers together with God: ye are God's husbandry, ye are God's building.

10 According to the grace of God which is given unto me, as a wise master-builder I have laid the foundation, and another buildeth thereon. But let every man take heed how he buildeth thereupon.

11 For other foundation can no man lay, than that is laid, which is Jesus Christ.

12 Now if any man build upon this foundation, gold, silver, precious stones, wood, hay, stubble:

PARAPHRASE.

distinguished, and set in opposition one to another, or cried up as more deserving one than another. We, the Preachers of the Gospel, are but Labourers employed by God about that which is his Work, and from him shall receive Reward hereafter, every one according to his own Labour; and not from Men here, who are liable to make a wrong Estimate of the Labours of their Teachers, preferring those who do not labour together with God, who do not carry on the Design or Work of God in the Gospel, or perhaps do not carry it on equally with others who are undervalued by them. Ye who are the Church of God, are God's Building; in which I, according to the Skill and Knowledge which God of his free Bounty has been pleased to give me, and therefore ought not to be to me, or any other, Matter of glorying, as a skilful Architect, have laid a sure Foundation, which is Jesus the Messiah, the sole and only Foundation of Christianity, besides which no Man can lay any other. But tho' no Man, who pretends to be a Preacher of the Gospel, can build upon any other Foundation, yet you ought not to cry up your new Instructor¹, (who has come and built upon the Foundation that I laid) for the Doctrines he builds thereon, as if there were no other Minister of the Gospel but he: For it is possible a Man may build upon that true Foundation, Wood, Hay, and Stubble, Things that will not bear the Test, when the Trial by Fire at the

9.

10.

11.

12.

NOTES.

11 ¹ *Chap.* IV. 15. In this he reflects on the false Apostle, 2 *Cor.* X. 15, 16.

last

I CORINTHIANS.

PARAPHRASE.

13. last Day ˢ shall come. At that Day every Man's Work shall be tried, and discovered of what
14. sort it is: If what he hath taught be found and good, and will stand the Trial, as Silver and Gold, and precious Stones, abide in the Fire, he shall be rewarded for his Labour in the
15. Gospel: But if he hath introduced false or unsound Doctrines into Christianity, he shall be like a Man, whose Building being of Wood, Hay and Stubble, is consumed by the Fire; all his Pains in Building is lost, and his Works consumed and gone, though he himself should
16. escape and be saved. I told you, that ye are God's Building ᵗ; yea, more than that, ye are the Temple of God, in which his Spirit dwell-
17. eth. If any Man by corrupt Doctrine or Discipline defileth ᵘ the Temple of God, he shall not be saved with Loss, as by Fire, but him will God destroy; for the Temple of God is
18. holy, which Temple ye are. Let no Man deceive himself by his Success in carrying his Point ʷ: If any one seemeth to himself or

TEXT.

13. Every man's work shall be made manifest: for the day shall declare it, because it shall be revealed by fire; and the fire shall try every man's work, of what sort it is.

14. If any man's work abide which he hath built thereupon, he shall receive a reward.

15. If any man's work shall be burnt, he shall suffer loss: but he himself shall be saved; yet so, as by fire.

16. Know ye not that ye are the temple of God, and that the Spirit of God dwelleth in you?

17. If any man defile the temple of God, him shall God destroy: for the temple of God is holy, which temple ye are.

18. Let no man deceive himself: if any man among you seemeth to be

NOTES.

13 ˢ When the Day of Trial and Recompense shall be, see *Chap.* IV. 5. where he speaks of the same Thing.

16 ᵗ Vid. *Ver.* 9.

17 ᵘ It is not incongruous to think, that by *any Man* here, St. *Paul* designs one particular Man, *viz.* the false Apostle, who, 'tis probable, by the Strength of his Party supporting and retaining the Fornicator mentioned *Chap.* V. in the Church, had defiled it; which may be the Reason why St. *Paul* so often mentions Fornication in this Epistle, and that in some Places with particular Emphasis, as Chap. V. 9. & VI. 13—20. Most of the Disorders in this Church we may look on as owing to this false Apostle, which is the Reason why St. *Paul* sets himself so much against him in both these Epistles, and makes almost the whole Business of them to draw the *Corinthians* off from this Leader; judging, as 'tis like, that this Church could not be reformed as long as that Person was in Credit, and had a Party among them.

18 ʷ What it was wherein the Craftiness of the Person mentioned had appeared, it was not necessary for St. *Paul*, writing to the *Corinthians*, who knew the Matter of Fact, to particularize to us, therefore it is left to guess; and possibly we shall not be much out, if we take it to be the keeping the Fornicator from Censure, so much insisted on by St. *Paul*, Chap. V.

others

I CORINTHIANS.

Chap. III.

TEXT.

wife in this world, let him become a fool, that he may be wife.

19 For the wifdom of this world is foolifhnefs with God: for it is written, He taketh the wife in their own craftinefs.
20 And again, The Lord knoweth the thoughts of the wife, that they are vain.
21 Therefore let no man glory in men: for all things are yours.
22 Whether Paul, or Apollos, or Cephas, or the world, or life, or death, or things prefent, or things to come; all are yours:
23 And ye are Chrift's; and Chrift is God's.

1 Let a man fo account of us, as of the minifters

PARAPHRASE.

others wife [x], in worldly Wifdom, fo as to pride himfelf in his Parts and Dexterity, in compaffing his Ends, let him renounce all his natural and acquired Parts, all his Knowledge and Ability, that he may become truly wife in embracing and owning no other Knowledge but the Simplicity of the Gofpel. For all other Wifdom, all the Wifdom of the World, is Foolifhnefs with God: For it is written, He taketh the Wife in their own Craftinefs. And again, The Lord knoweth the Thoughts of the Wife, that they are vain. Therefore let none of you glory in any of your Teachers, for they are but Men. For all your Teachers, whether *Paul*, or *Apollos*, or *Peter*, even the Apoftles themfelves, nay, all the World, and even the World to come, all Things are yours, for your Sake and Ufe; as you are Chrift's Subjects, of his Kingdom, for his Glory, and Chrift and his Kingdom for the Glory of God. Therefore if all your Teachers, and fo many other greater Things are for you, and for your Sakes, you can have no reafon to make it a Glory to you, that you belong to this or that particular Teacher amongft you; your true Glory is, that you are Chrift's, and Chrift and all his are God's, and not that you are this or that Man's Scholar or Follower.

19.
20.
21.
22.
23.

As for me, I pretend not to fet up a School amongft you, and, as a Mafter, to have my Scholars denominated from me; no, let no Man have higher Thoughts of me than as a

Chap. IV.
1.

NOTES.

[x] That by σοφὸς here, the Apoftle means a cunning Man in Bufinefs, is plain from his Quotation in the next Verfe, where the Wife fpoken of are the Crafty.

Minifter

I CORINTHIANS.

PARAPHRASE.

Minister of Christ, employed as his Steward to dispense the Truths and Doctrines of the Gospel, which are the Mysteries which God wrapped up in Types and obscure Predictions, where they have lain hid, till by us, his Apostles, he now reveals them. Now that which is principally required and regarded in a Steward, is that he be faithful in dispensing what is committed to his Charge. But as for me, I value it not, if I am censured by some of you, or by any Man, as not being a faithful Steward: Nay, as to this, I pass no Judgment on myself. For though I can truly say that I know nothing by myself, yet am I not hereby justified to you: But the Lord, whose Steward I am, at the last Day will pronounce Sentence on my Behaviour in my Stewardship, and then you will know what to think of me. Then judge not either me or others before the Time, until the Lord come, who will bring to light the dark and secret Counsels of Men's Hearts, in preaching the Gospel; and then shall every one have that Praise, that Estimate set upon him by God himself, which he truly deserves. But Praise ought not to be given them before the Time by their Hearers, who are ignorant, fallible Men. On this Occasion, I have named *Apollos* and myself [y], as the magnified and opposed Heads of distinct Factions amongst you, not that we are so, but out of respect to you, that I might offend no body by naming them; and that you may learn by us, of whom I have written [z], that we are but Planters,

TEXT.

of Christ, and stewards of the mysteries of God.

2 Moreover, it is required in stewards, that a man be found faithful.

3 But with me it is a very small thing that I should be judged of you, or of man's judgment: yea, I judge not mine own self.

4 For I know nothing by myself, yet am I not hereby justified: but he that judgeth me is the Lord.

5 Therefore judge nothing before the time, until the Lord come, who both will bring to light the hidden things of darkness, and will make manifest the counsels of the hearts: and then shall every man have praise of God.

6 And these things, brethren, I have in a figure transferred to myself, and to Apollos, for your sakes: that ye might learn in us, not to think of men

NOTES.

6 [y] Vid. *Chap.* III. 4.
[z] Vid. *Chap.* III. 6——9. *Chap.* IV. 1.

Waterers,

I CORINTHIANS.

TEXT.

above that which is written, that no one of you be puffed up for one against another.

7 For who maketh thee to differ from another? and what hast thou that thou didst not receive? now if thou didst receive it, why dost thou glory, as if thou hadst not received it?

8 Now ye are full, now ye are rich, ye have reigned as kings without us: and I would to God ye did reign, that we also might reign with you.

9 For I think that God hath set forth us the apostles last, as it were appointed to death: For we are made a spectacle unto the world, and to angels, and to men.

10 We are fools for Christ's sake, but ye are wise in Christ: we are weak, but ye are strong: ye are honourable, but we are despised.

11 Even unto this present hour we both hunger, and thirst, and are naked, and are buffeted, and have no certain dwelling-place;

PARAPHRASE.

Waterers, and Stewards, not to think of the Ministers of the Gospel above what I have written to you of them, that you be not puffed up, each Party, in the vain Glory of their one extolled Leader, to the Crying-down and Contempt of any other who is well esteemed of by others. For what maketh one to differ from another? or what Gifts of the Spirit, what Knowledge of the Gospel, has any Leader amongst you, which he received not, as intrusted to him of God, and not acquired by his own Abilities? And if he received it as a Steward, why does he glory in that which is not his own? However, you are mightily satisfied with your present State; you are now full, you now are rich, and abound in every thing you desire; you have not need of me, but have reigned like Princes without me: And I wish truly you did reign, that I might come and share in the Protection and Prosperity you enjoy now you are in your Kingdom. For I being made an Apostle last of all, it seems to me as if I were brought last [a] upon the Stage, to be, in my Sufferings and Death, a Spectacle to the World, and to Angels, and to Men. I am a Fool for Christ's Sake, but you manage your Christian Concerns with Wisdom. I am weak, and in a suffering Condition [b]; you are strong and flourishing. You are honourable; but I am despised. Even to this present Hour I both hunger and thirst, and want Clothes, and am buffeted, wander-

7.

8.

9.

10.

11.

NOTES.

9 [a] The Apostle seems here to allude to the Custom of bringing those last upon the Theatre, who were to be destroyed by wild Beasts.

10 [b] So he uses the Word *Weakness* often, in his Epistles to the *Corinthians*, applied to himself. *Vid.* 2 Cor. XII. 10.

I CORINTHIANS.

PARAPHRASE.

12. ing without House or Home, and maintain myself with the Labour of my Hands. Being reviled, I bless; being persecuted, I suffer pa-
13. tiently; being defamed, I intreat: I am made as the Filth of the World, and the Off-scouring
14. of all things unto this Day. I write not these Things to shame you; but as a Father, to warn ye, my Children, that ye be not the devoted, zealous Partizans and Followers of such whose Carriage is not like this; under whom, however, you may flatter yourselves, in truth, you do not reign; but, on the contrary, are domi-
15. neered over, and fleeced by them [c]. I warn you, I say, as your Father: For how many Teachers soever you may have, you can have but one Father; it was I that begot you in Christ, *i. e.* I converted you to Christianity:
16. Wherefore, I beseech you, be ye Followers of
17. me [d]. To this Purpose I have sent my beloved Son *Timothy* to you, who may be relied upon: He shall put you in mind, and inform you, how I behave myself every where in the Mi-
18. nistry of the Gospel [e]. Some indeed are puffed up, and make their Boasts, as if I would not

TEXT.

12. And labour, working with our own hands: being reviled, we bless: being persecuted, we suffer it:
13. Being defamed, we intreat: we are made as the filth of the world, and are the off-scouring of all things unto this day.
14. I write not these things to shame you, but as my beloved sons I warn you.
15. For though you have ten thousand instructors in Christ, yet have we not many fathers: for in Christ Jesus I have begotten you through the gospel.
16. Wherefore, I beseech you, be ye followers of me.
17. For this cause have I sent unto you Timotheus, who is my beloved son, and faithful in the Lord, who shall bring you into remembrance of my ways which be in Christ, as I teach every where in every church.
18. Now some are puffed up, as though I would not come to you.

NOTES.

14 [c] *Vid.* 2 *Cor.* XI. 20. St. *Paul* here, from *ver.* 3, to 17. by giving an Account of his own Carriage, gently rebukes them for following Men of a different Character, and exhorts them to be Followers of himself.

16 [d] This he presses again, *Chap.* XI. 1. and 'tis not likely he would have proposed himself over and over again to them, to be followed by them, had the Question and Contest amongst them been only whose Name they should have borne, his or their new Teacher's. His proposing himself therefore thus to be followed, must be understood in direct Opposition to the false Apostle, who misled them, and was not to be suffered to have any Credit or Followers amongst them.

17 [e] This he does to shew that what he taught them, and pressed them to, was not in a Pique against his Opposer, but to convince them, that all he did at *Corinth* was the very same, and no other than what he did every where, as a faithful Steward and Minister of the Gospel.

come

I CORINTHIANS.

TEXT.

19 But I will come to you shortly, if the Lord will, and will know, not the speech of them which are puffed up, but the power.
20 For the kingdom of God is not in word, but in power.

PARAPHRASE.

come to you. But I intend, God willing, to 19. come shortly, and then will make Trial, not of the Rhetorick or Talking of these Boasters, but of what miraculous Power of the Holy Ghost is in them. For the Doctrine and Prevalency of 20. the Gospel, the Propagation and Support of Christ's Kingdom, by the Conversion and Establishment of Believers, does not consist in Talking, nor in the Fluency of a glib Tongue and a fine Discourse, but in the miraculous Operations of the Holy Ghost.

SECT. II. *N.* 6.
CHAP. IV. 21——VI. 20.

CONTENTS.

ANother Means which St. *Paul* makes use of to bring off the *Corinthians* from their false Apostle, and to stop their Veneration of him, and their glorying in him, is by representing to them the Fault and Disorder which was committed in that Church, by not judging and expelling the Fornicator; which Neglect, as may be guessed, was owing to that Faction:

1. Because it is natural for a Faction to support and protect an Offender that is of their Side.

2. From the great Fear St. *Paul* was in, whether they would obey him in censuring the Offender, as appears by the second Epistle; which he could not fear, but from the opposite Faction: they who had preserved their Respect to him, being sure to follow his Orders.

3. From what he says, *Chap.* IV. 16. after he had told them, *ver.* 6. of that Chapter, that they should not be puffed up for any other against him, for so the whole Scope of his Discourse here imports; he beseeches them to be his Followers, *i. e.* leaving their other

Guides to follow him in punishing the Offender. For that we may conclude, from his immediately insisting on it so earnestly, he had in his View, when he beseeches them to be Followers of him; and consequently, that they might join with him, and take him for their Leader, *Chap.* V. 3, 4. he makes himself by his Spirit, as his Proxy, the President of their Assembly, to be convened for the punishing that Criminal.

4. It may further be suspected, from what St. *Paul* says, *Ch.* VI. 1. that the opposite Party, to stop the Church-Censure, pretended that this was a Matter to be judged by the Civil Magistrate: Nay, possibly from what is said, *ver.* 6. of that Chapter, it may be gathered, that they had got it brought before the Heathen Judge; or at least, from *ver.* 12. that they pleaded, that what he had done was lawful, and might be justified before the Magistrate: For the Judging spoken of, *Ch.* VI. must be understood to relate to the same Matter it does *Ch.* V. it being a Continuation of the same Discourse and Argument; as is easy to be observed by any one who will read it without regarding the Divisions into Chapters and Verses, whereby ordinary People (not to say others) are often disturbed in reading the Holy Scripture, and hindered from observing the true Sense and Coherence of it. The whole VIth Chapter is spent in prosecuting the Business of the Fornicator, began in the Vth. That this is so, is evident from the latter End, as well as Beginning of the VIth Chapter. And therefore what St. *Paul* says of *lawful*, Chapter VI. 12. may, without any Violence, be supposed to be said in answer to some, who might have alledged in favour of the Fornicator, that what he had done was *lawful*, and might be justified by the Laws of the Country, which he was under; why else should St. *Paul* subjoin so many Arguments (wherewith he concludes this VIth Chapter, and this Subject) to prove the Fornication in Question to be, by the Law of the Gospel, a great Sin, and consequently fit for a Christian Church to censure in one of its Members, however it might pass for *lawful* in the Esteem, and by the Laws, of *Gentiles*?

There is one Objection, which, at first sight, seems to be a strong Argument against this Supposition, that the Fornication here spoken of, was held lawful by the *Gentiles* of *Corinth*, and that possibly this very Case had been brought before the Magistrate there and not condemned. The Objection seems to lie in these Words; *Chap.* V. 1. *There is Fornication heard of amongst you, and such Fornication as is not heard of amongst the* Gentiles, *that one should have his Father's*

Father's Wife. But yet I conceive the Words, duly considered, have nothing in them contrary to my Supposition.

To clear this, I take liberty to say, it cannot be thought that this Man had his Father's Wife, whilst by the Laws of the Place she actually was his Father's Wife; for then it had been μοιχεία and Adultery, and so the Apostle would have called it, which was a Crime in *Greece*; nor could it be tolerated in any Civil Society, that one Man should have the Use of a Woman, whilst she was another Man's Wife, *i. e.* another Man's Right and Possession.

The Case therefore here seems to be this: The Woman had parted from her Husband; which it is plain, from *Ch.* VII. 10, 11, 13. at *Corinth* Women could do: For if by the Law of that Country a Woman could not divorce herself from her Husband, the Apostle had there in vain bid her not leave her Husband.

But however known and allowed a Practice it might be amongst the *Corinthians*, for a Woman to part from her Husband, yet this was the first Time it was ever known that her Husband's own Son should marry her. This is that which the Apostle takes notice of in these Words, *Such a Fornication as is not named amongst the* Gentiles. Such a Fornication this was, so little known in Practice amongst them, that it was not so much as heard named, or spoken of by any of them: But whether they held it unlawful that a Woman, so separated, should marry her Husband's Son, when she was looked upon to be at liberty from her former Husband, and free to marry whom she pleased, that the Apostle says not. This indeed he declares, that by the Law of Christ a Woman's leaving her Husband, and marrying another, is unlawful, *Ch.* VII. 11. and this Woman's marrying her Husband's Son, he declares, *Ch.* V. 1. (the Place before us) to be Fornication; a peculiar Sort of Fornication, whatever the *Corinthians*, or their Law, might determine in the Case: And therefore a Christian Church might and ought to have censured it within themselves, it being an Offence against the Rule of the Gospel; which is the Law of their Society: And they might and should have expelled this Fornicator out of their Society, for not submitting to the Laws of it; notwithstanding that the Civil Laws of the Country, and the Judgment of the Heathen Magistrate, might acquit him. Suitably hereunto, it is very remarkable, that the Arguments that St. *Paul* uses, in the Close of this Discourse, *Ch.* VI. 13—20. to prove Fornication unlawful, are all drawn solely from the Christian Institution, *ver.* 9. That our Bodies are made for the Lord, *ver.* 13. That our Bodies are

are Members of Christ, *ver.* 15. That our Bodies are the Temples of the Holy Ghost, *ver.* 19. That we are not our own, but bought with a Price, *ver.* 20. All which Arguments concern Christians only; and there is not in all this Discourse against Fornication, one Word to declare it to be unlawful by the Law of Nature to Mankind in general: That was altogether needless, and besides the Apostle's Purpose here, where he was teaching and exhorting Christians what they were to do as Christians, within their own Society, by the Law of Christ, which was to be their Rule, and was sufficient to oblige them; whatever other Laws the rest of Mankind observed, or were under, those he professes, *Chap.* V. 12, 13. not to meddle with, nor to judge: For having no Authority amongst them, he leaves them to the Judgment of God, under whose Government they are.

These Considerations afford Ground to conjecture, that the Faction which opposed St. *Paul*, had hindered the Church of *Corinth* from censuring the Fornicator; and that St. *Paul*, shewing them their Miscarriage herein, aims thereby to lessen the Credit of their Leader, by whose Influence they were drawn into it: For as soon as they had unanimously shewn their Obedience to St. *Paul* in this Matter, we see his Severity ceases, and he is all Softness and Gentleness to the Offender, 2 *Cor.* II. 5——8. and he tells them, in express Words, *ver.* 9. that his End, in writing to them of it, was to try their Obedience. To which let me add, that this Supposition, though it had not all the Evidence for it which it has, yet being suited to St. *Paul*'s principal Design in this Epistle, and helping us the better to understand these two Chapters, may deserve to be mentioned.

I CORINTHIANS.

TEXT.

21 What will ye? shall I come unto you with a rod, or in love, and in the spirit of meekness?
1 It is reported commonly that there is fornication among you, and such fornication as is not so much as named amongst the Gentiles, that one should have his father's wife.
2 And ye are puffed up, and have not rather mourned, that he that hath done this deed, might be taken away from among you.
3 For I verily, as absent in body, but present in spirit, have judged already, as though I were present concerning him that hath so done this deed;
4 In the name of our Lord Jesus Christ, when ye are gathered together, and my spirit, with the power of our Lord Jesus Christ,
5 To deliver such an one

PARAPHRASE.

I Purposed to come unto you: But what would you have me do? Shall I come to you with a Rod, to chastise you? or with Kindness, and a peaceable Disposition of Mind ᶠ? In short, it is commonly reported, that there is Fornication ᵍ among you, and such Fornication as is not known ʰ ordinarily among the Heathen, that one should have his Father's Wife; and yet ye remain puffed up, though it would better have become you to have been dejected for this scandalous Fact amongst you, and, in a mournful Sense of it, to have removed the Offender out of the Church. For I truly, though absent in Body, yet, as present in Spirit, have thus already judged, as if I were personally with you, him that committed this Fact. When in the Name of the Lord Jesus ye are assembled, and my Spirit, *i. e.* my Vote, as if I were present, making one by the Power of our Lord Jesus Christ, deliver the Offender up to Satan, that being put thus into

Chap. V.

21.

1.

2.

3.

4.

5.

NOTES.

21 ᶠ He that shall carefully read 2 *Cor.* I. 20 —— II. 11. will easily perceive that this last Verse here of this IVth Chapter is an Introduction to the severe Act or Discipline which St. *Paul* was going to exercise amongst them, tho' absent, as if he had been present; and therefore this Verse ought not to have been separated from the following Chapter, as if it belonged not to that Discourse.

1 ᵍ Vid. *Chap.* IV. 8, 10. The Writers of the New Testament seem to use the *Greek* Word πορνεια, which we translate Fornication, in the same Sense that the *Hebrews* used זנה, which we also translate Fornication; tho' it be certain both these Words, in sacred Scripture, have a larger Sense than the Word *Fornication* has in our Language: For זנה, amongst the *Hebrews*, signified, *Turpitudinem*, or *Rem turpem*, Uncleanness, or any flagitious scandalous Crime; but more especially the Uncleanness of unlawful Copulation and Idolatry, and not precisely Fornication in our Sense of the Word, *i. e.* the unlawful Mixture of an unmarried Couple.

ʰ *Not known*. That the marrying of a Son-in-law and a Mother-in-law, was not prohibited by the Laws of the *Roman* Empire, may be seen in *Tully*; but yet it was looked on as so scandalous and infamous, that it never had any Countenance from Practice. His Words in his Oration *pro Cluentio*, § 4. are so agreeable to the present Case, that it may not be amiss to set them down: *Nubit genero socrus, nullis auspiciis, nullis auctoribus. O scelus incredibile, & præter hanc unam in omni vita inauditum!*

the

I CORINTHIANS.

Chap. IV.

PARAPHRASE.

the Hands and Power of the Devil, his Body may be afflicted and brought down, that his Soul may be saved when our Lord Jesus comes
6. to judge the World. Your glorying ⁱ, as you do in a Leader, who drew you into this scandalous Indulgence ᵏ in this Case, is a Fault in you; ye that are knowing, know you not that a little Leaven leaveneth the whole ˡ Lump?
7. Therefore laying by that Deference and Veneration ye had for those Leaders you gloried in, turn out from among you that Fornicator, that the Church may receive no Taint from him; that you may be a pure new Lump, or Society, free from such a dangerous Mixture, which may corrupt you. For Christ, our Passover,
8. is slain for us; therefore let us, in commemoration of his Death, and our Deliverance
9. by him, be a holy People to him ᵐ. I wrote to you before, that you should not keep com-
10. pany with Fornicators. You are not to understand by it, as if I meant, that you are to avoid all unconverted Heathens, that are Fornicators, or Covetous, or Rapacious, or Idolaters; for then you must go out of the
11. World. But that which I now write unto you, is, that you should not keep company, no, nor eat with a Christian by Profession, who is lascivious, covetous, idolatrous, a Rai-

TEXT.

6 unto Satan for the destruction of the flesh, that the spirit may be saved in the day of the Lord Jesus.
Your glorying is not good: know ye not that a little leaven leaveneth the whole lump?
7 Purge out therefore the old leaven, that ye may be a new lump, as ye are unleavened: for even Christ our passover is sacrificed for us.
8 Therefore let us keep the feast, not with old leaven, neither with the leaven of malice and wickedness; but with the unleavened bread of sincerity and truth.
9 I wrote unto you in an epistle, not to company with fornicators.
10 Yet not altogether with the fornicators of this world, or with the covetous or extortioners, or with idolaters; for then must ye needs go out of the world.
11 But now I have written unto you, not to keep company, if any man that is called a brother be a fornicator, or covetous, or an idolater, or a railer, or a drunkard, or an extortioner; with such an one, no not to eat.

NOTES.

6 ⁱ Glorying is all along in the Beginning of this Epistle spoken of the Preference they gave to their new Leader, in opposition to St. *Paul*.
ᵏ If their Leader had not been guilty of this Miscarriage, it had been out of St. *Paul*'s Way, here to have reproved them for their glorying in him. But St. *Paul* is a close Writer, and uses not to mention Things, where they are impertinent to his Subject.
ˡ What reason he had to say this, *vid*: 2 Cor. XII. 21.——*Grex totus in agris*
Unius scabie cadit, & porrigine porci.
7 & 8. ᵐ In these two Verses he alludes to the *Jews* cleansing their Houses at the Feast of the Passover from all Leaven, the Symbol of Corruption and Wickedness.

ler,

I CORINTHIANS.

TEXT.

12 For what have I to do to judge them also that are without? do not ye judge them that are within?
13 But them that are without God judgeth. Therefore put away from among yourselves that wicked person.
1 Dare any of you, having a matter against another, go to law before the unjust, and not before the saints?
2 Do ye not know that the saints shall judge the world? and if the world shall be judged by you, are ye unworthy to judge the smallest matters?
3 Know ye not that we shall judge angels? how much more things that pertain to this life?
4 If then ye have judgments of things pertaining to this life, let them to judge who are least esteemed in the church.
5 I speak to your shame. Is it so, that there is not a wise man amongst you? no not one that shall be able to judge between his brethren?

PARAPHRASE.

12. ler, Drunkard, or rapacious. For what have I to do to judge those who are out of the Church? Have ye not a Power to judge those who are Members of your Church?
13. But as for those who are out of the Church, leave them to God; to judge them belongs to him: Therefore do ye what is your Part; remove that wicked one, the Fornicator, out of the Church.
1. Dare any of you, having a Controversy with another, bring it before an Heathen Judge to be tried, and not let it be decided by Christians[n]?
2. Know ye not that Christians shall judge the World; and if the World shall be judged by you, are ye unworthy to judge ordinary small Matters?
3. Know ye not that we Christians have Power over evil Spirits? How much more over the little Things relating to this animal Life?
4. If then ye have at any time Controversies amongst you concerning Things pertaining to this Life, let the Parties contending choose Arbitrators[o] in the Church, *i. e.* out of Church-Members.
5. Is there not among you, I speak it to your Shame, who stand so much upon your Wisdom, one[p] wise Man, whom ye can think able enough to refer

NOTES.

1 [n] Ἅγιοι, Saints, is put for Christians; ἄδικοι, Unjust, for Heathens.

4 [o] Ἐξουθενημένους, Judices non Authenticos. Among the Jews there was *concessus triumviralis authenticus,* who had Authority, and could hear and determine Causes *ex Officio.* There was another *concessus triumviralis,* which were chosen by the Parties; these, though they were not *authentick,* yet could judge and determine the Causes referred to them; these were those whom St. Paul calls here ἐξουθενημένους, Judices non Authenticos, i. e. Referees chosen by the Parties: See *de Dieu.* That St. Paul does not mean by ἐξουθενημένους, those *who are least esteemed,* as our *English* Translation reads it, is plain from the next Verse.

5 [p] Σοφὸς, *wise Man.* If St. Paul uses this Word in the Sense of the Synagogue, it signifies one ordained, or a Rabbi, and so capacitated to be a Judge; for such were called *wise Men:* If in the Sense of the *Greek* Schools, then it signifies a Man of Learning, Study and Parts; if it be taken in the latter Sense, it may seem to be with some Reflection on their pretending to Wisdom.

I CORINTHIANS.

PARAPHRASE.

6. your Controversies to? But one Christian goeth to Law with another, and that before the Unbelievers, in the Heathen Courts of Justice:
7. Nay, verily, it is a Failure and Defect in you, that you so far contest Matters of Right one with another, as to bring them to Trial or Judgment: Why do ye not rather suffer Loss and
8. Wrong? But it is plain, by the Man's having his Father's Wife, that ye are guilty of doing Wrong ^q one to another, and stick not to do Injustice, even to your Christian Brethren.
9. Know ye not that the Transgressors of the Law of Christ shall not inherit the Kingdom of God? Deceive not yourselves; neither Fornicators, nor Idolaters, nor Adulterers, nor Effeminate, nor Abusers of themselves with Man-
10. kind, nor Thieves, nor Covetous, nor Drunkards, nor Revilers, nor Extortioners, shall in-
11. herit the Kingdom of God. And such were some of you; but your past Sins are washed away and forgiven you, upon your receiving of the Gospel by Baptism: But ye are sanctified ^r, *i. e.* ye are Members of Christ's Church, which consists of Saints, and have made some

TEXT.

6. But brother goeth to law with brother, and that before the unbelievers.
7. Now therefore there is utterly a fault among you, because ye go to law one with another: why do ye not rather take wrong? why do ye not rather suffer yourselves to be defrauded?
8. Nay, you do wrong and defraud, and that your brethren.
9. Know ye not that the unrighteous shall not inherit the kingdom of God? be not deceived: neither fornicators, nor idolaters, nor adulterers, nor effeminate, nor abusers of themselves with mankind,
10. Nor thieves, nor covetous, nor drunkards, nor revilers, nor extortioners, shall inherit the kingdom of God.
11. And such were some of you: but ye are washed, but ye are sanctified, but ye are justified in the name of the Lord Jesus,

NOTES.

8 ^q That the Wrong here spoken of, was the Fornicator's taking and keeping his Father's Wife, the Words of St. *Paul*, 2 Cor. VII. 12. instancing this very Wrong, are a sufficient Evidence. And it is not wholly improbable there had been some Hearing of this Matter before a Heathen Judge, or at least talked of; which, if supposed, will give a great Light to this whole Passage, and several others in these Chapters. For thus visibly runs St. *Paul*'s Argument, *Chap.* V. 12, 13. *Chap.* VI. 1, 2, 3. *&c.* coherent and easy to be understood, if it stood together, as it should, and were not chopped in pieces, by a Division into two Chapters. Ye have a Power to judge those who are of your Church, therefore put away from among you that Fornicator: You do ill to let it come before a Heathen Magistrate. Are you, who are to judge the World and Angels, not worthy to judge such a Matter as this?

11 ^r Ἡγιασμένοι, *sanctified, i. e.* have Remission of your Sins; so *sanctified* signifies, *Heb.* X. 10, & 18. compared. He that would perfectly comprehend, and be satisfied in the Meaning of this Place, let him read *Heb.* IX. 10. particularly IX. 13——23.

Advances

I CORINTHIANS.

TEXT.

and by the Spirit of our God.

12 All things are lawful unto me, but all things are not expedient: all things are lawful for me, but I will not be brought under the power of any.

PARAPHRASE.

Advances in the Reformation of your Lives ⁵, by the Doctrine of Christ, confirmed to you by the extraordinary Operations of the Holy Ghost. But ᵗ supposing Fornication were in itself as lawful as eating promiscuously all Sorts of Meat that are made for the Belly, on purpose to be eaten; yet I would not so far indulge either Custom, or my Appetite, as to bring my Body thereby into any disadvantageous State of Subjection: As in Eating and Drinking, though Meat be made purposely for the Belly, and the Belly for Meat; yet because it may not be expedient ᵘ for me, I will not, in so evidently a lawful Thing as that, go to the utmost Bounds of

12.

NOTES.

ˢ Ἐξυπνώσατε, ye are become just, i. e. are reformed in your Lives. See it so used, Rev. XXII. 11.

12 ᵗ St. *Paul* having, upon occasion of Injustice amongst them, particularly in the Matter of the Fornicator, warned them against that and other Sins that exclude Men from Salvation, he here re-assumes his former Argument about Fornication; and by his Reasoning here, it looks as if some among them had pleaded that Fornication was lawful. To which he answers, that granting it to be so, yet the Lawfulness of all wholesome Food reached not the Case of Fornication; and shews, by several Instances (as particularly the degrading the Body, and making what in a Christian is the Member of Christ, the Member of an Harlot) that Fornication, upon several Accounts, might be so unsuitable to the State of a Christian Man, that a Christian Society might have Reason to animadvert upon a Fornicator, though Fornication might pass for an indifferent Action in another Man.

ᵘ *Expedient*, and *brought under Power*, in this Verse seems to refer to the two Parts of the following Verse; the first of them to Eating, in the first Part of the 13th Verse, and the latter of them to Fornication, in the latter Part of the 13th Verse. To make this the more intelligible, it may be fit to remark, that St. *Paul* here seems to obviate such a Sort of Reasoning as this, in behalf of the Fornicator. "All Sorts of Meats are lawful to Christians who are set
" free from the Law of *Moses*, and why are they not so in regard of Women who are at their
" own Disposals? To which St. *Paul* replies: Though my Belly was made only for eating, and
" all Sorts of Meat were made to be eaten, and so are lawful for me; yet I will abstain from
" what is lawful, if it be not convenient for me, though my Belly will be certain to receive no
" Prejudice by it, which will affect it in the other World, since God will there put an end
" to the Belly, and all Use of Food. But as to the Body of a Christian, the Case is quite other-
" wise; that was not made for the Enjoyment of Women, but for a much nobler End, to be
" a Member of Christ's Body, and so shall last for ever, and not be destroyed as the Belly shall
" be. Therefore supposing Fornication to be lawful in itself, I will not so debase and subject
" my Body, and do it that Prejudice, as to take that which is a Member of Christ, and make
" it the Member of an Harlot; this ought to be had in detestation by all Christians." The Context

I CORINTHIANS.

Chap. VI.

PARAPHRASE.

13. of my Liberty, though there be no Danger that I should thereby bring any lasting Damage upon my Belly, since God will speedily put an end both to Belly and Food. But the Case of the Body, in reference to Women, is far different from that of the Belly, in reference to Meats. For the Body is not made to be joined to a Woman [w], much less to be joined to an Harlot in Fornication; as the Belly is made for Meat, and then to be put an end to when that Use ceases. But the Body is for a much nobler Purpose, and shall subsist when the Belly and Food shall be destroyed. The Body is for our Lord Christ, to be a Member of him; as our Lord Christ has taken a Body [x], that he might partake of our Nature, and be our Head.

14. So that as God has already raised him up, and given him all Power, so he will raise us up likewise, who are his Members, to [y] the partaking in the Nature of his glorious Body, and

TEXT.

Meats for the belly, and 13 the belly for meats: but God shall destroy both it and them. Now the body is not for fornication, but for the Lord; and the Lord for the body.

And God hath both 14 raised up the Lord, and will also raise up us by his own power.

NOTES.

Context is so plain in the Case, Interpreters allow St. *Paul* to discourse here upon a Supposition of the Lawfulness of Fornication. Nor will it appear at all strange that he does so, if we consider the Argument he is upon. He is here convincing the *Corinthians*, that though Fornication were to them an indifferent Thing, and were not condemned in their Country more than eating any Sort of Meat, yet there might be Reasons why a Christian Society might punish it in their own Members by Church-Censures, and Expulsion of the Guilty. Conformably hereunto we see, in what follows here, that all the Arguments used by St. *Paul* against Fornication, are brought from the Incongruity it hath with the State of a Christian as a Christian; but nothing is said against it as a Fault in a Man as a Man, no Plea used that it is a Sin in all Men by the Law of Nature. A Christian Society, without entering into that Enquiry, or going so far as that, had reason to condemn and censure it, as not comporting with the Dignity and Principles of that Religion which was the Foundation of their Society.

13 *Woman.* I have put in this to make the Apostle's Sense understood the easier; for he arguing here as he does, upon the Supposition that Fornication is in itself lawful, Fornication in these Words must mean the supposed lawful Enjoyment of a Woman, otherwise it will not answer the foregoing Instance of the Belly and Eating.

[x] *And the Lord for the Body,* see Heb. II. 5 — 18.

14 [y] Διὰ τῆς δυνάμεως αὐτοῦ, *To his Power.* The Context and Design of St. *Paul* here, strongly incline one to take διὰ here to signify as it does, 2 *Pet.* I. 3. *to,* and not *by.* St. *Paul* is

I CORINTHIANS.

Chap. VI.

TEXT.

15 Know ye not, that your bodies are the members of Christ? shall I then take the members of Christ, and make them the members of an harlot? God forbid.

16 What, know ye not that he which is joined to an harlot, is one body? for two (saith he) shall be one flesh.

17 But he that is joined unto the Lord, is one spirit.

18 Flee fornication. Every sin that a man doth, is without the body: but he that committeth fornication, sinneth against his own body.

PARAPHRASE.

and the Power he is vested with in it. Know ye not, you who are so knowing, that our Bodies are the Members of Christ? will you then take the Members of Christ, and make them the Members of an Harlot? What? know ye not that he who is joined to an Harlot, is one Body with her? for two, saith God, shall be united into one Flesh. But he who is joined to the Lord, is one with him, by that one Spirit that unites the Members to the Head; which is a nearer and stricter Union, whereby what in Dignity is done to the one, equally affects the other. Flee Fornication: All other Sins that a Man commits, debase only the Soul, but are, in that respect, as if they were done out of the Body; the Body is not debased, suffers no Loss of its Dignity by them; but he who committeth Fornication, sinneth against the End for which his Body was made, degrading his Body from the Dignity and Honour it was designed to, making that the Member of an Harlot, which

15.

16.

17.

18.

NOTES.

is here making out to the *Corinthian* Converts, that they have a Power to judge. He tells them that they shall judge the World, ver. 2. And that they shall judge Angels, much more then Things of this Life, ver. 3. And for their not judging he blames them, and tells them it is a lessening to them, not to exercise this Power, ver. 7. And for it he gives a Reason in this Verse, viz. That Christ is raised up into the Power of God, and so shall they be. Unless it be taken in this Sense, this Verse seems to stand alone here: For what Connection has the Mention of the Resurrection, in the ordinary Sense of this Verse, with what the Apostle is saying here, but raising us up with Bodies to be Members of his glorious Body, and to partake in his Power in judging the World? This adds a great Honour and Dignity to our Bodies, and is a Reason why we should not debase them into the Members of an Harlot. These Words also give a Reason of his saying, *he would not be brought under the Power of any Thing*, ver. 12. (viz) "Shall I, "whose Body is a Member of Christ, and shall be raised to the Power he has now in Heaven, "suffer my Body to be a Member, and under the Power of an Harlot? That I will never do, "let Fornication in itself be never so lawful." If this be not the Meaning of St. *Paul* here, I desire to know to what purpose it is that he so expresly declares that the Belly and Meat shall be destroyed, and does so manifestly put an Opposition between the Body and the Belly, ver. 13.

was

Ch. VII.

I CORINTHIANS.

PARAPHRASE.

19. was made to be a Member of Christ. What, know ye not * that your Body is the Temple of the Holy Ghost that is in you; which Body you have from God, and so it is not your own
20. to bestow on Harlots? Besides, ye are bought with a Price, viz. the precious Blood of Christ, and therefore are not at your own Disposal; but are bound to glorify God with both Body and Soul: For both Body and Soul are from him, and are God's.

TEXT.

19 What, know ye not that your body is the temple of the Holy Ghost which is in you, which ye have of God, and ye are not your own?

20 For ye are bought with a price: therefore glorify God in your body, and in your spirit, which are God's.

NOTES.

19 * This Question, *Know ye not?* is repeated six Times in this one Chapter; which may seem to carry with it a just Reproach to the *Corinthians*, who had got a new and better Instructor than himself, in whom they so much gloried, and may not unfitly be thought to set on his Irony, Chap. IV. 10. where he tells them they are *wise*.

SECT. III.

CHAP. VII. 1——40.

CONTENTS.

THE chief Business of the foregoing Chapters we have seen to be the lessening the false Apostle's Credit, and the extinguishing that Faction. What follows, is in answer to some Questions they had proposed to St. *Paul*. This Section contains conjugal Matters, wherein he dissuades from Marriage those who have the Gift of Continence. But Marriage being appointed as a Remedy against Fornication, those who cannot forbear, should marry, and render to each other due Benevolence. Next he teaches that Converts ought not to forsake their unconverted Mates, insomuch as Christianity changes nothing in Mens civil Estate, but leaves them under the same Obligations they were tied by before. And last of all, he gives Directions about marrying, or not marrying their Daughters.

I CORINTHIANS.

Ch. VII.

TEXT.	PARAPHRASE.
1 NOW concerning the things whereof ye wrote unto me: it is good for a man not to touch a woman.	1. Concerning those Things that ye have written to me about, I answer, it is most convenient not to have to do with a Woman.
2 Nevertheless, to avoid fornication, let every man have his own wife, and let every woman have her own husband.	2. But because every one cannot forbear, therefore they that cannot contain, should, both Men and Women, each have their own peculiar Husband and Wife, to avoid Fornication.
3 Let the husband render unto the wife due benevolence: and likewise also the wife unto the husband.	3. And those that are married, for the same Reason, are to regulate themselves by the Disposition and Exigency of their respective Mates; and therefore let the Husband render to the Wife that Benevolence^a which is her due, and so likewise the Wife to the Husband, *vice versa*.
4 The wife hath not power of her own body, but the husband: and likewise also the husband hath not power of his own body, but the wife.	4. For the Wife has not Power or Dominion over her own Body, to refuse the Husband when he desires; but this Power and Right to her Body is in the Husband: And, on the other Side, the Husband has not the Power and Dominion over his own Body, to refuse his Wife when she shews an Inclination; but this Power and Right to his Body, when she has Occasion, is in the Wife^b.
5 Defraud you not one the other, except it be with consent for a time, that ye may give yourselves to fasting and prayer; and come together again, that Satan tempt you not for your incontinency.	5. Do not, in this Matter, be wanting one to another, unless it be by mutual Consent for a short Time, that you may wholly attend to Acts of Devotion, when ye fast upon some solemn Occasion; and when this Time of solemn Devotion is over, return to your former Freedom and Conjugal Society, lest the Devil, taking advantage of your Inability to con-

NOTES.

3 ^a Ευνοια, *Benevolence*, signifies here that Complaisance and Compliance which every married Couple ought to have for each other, when either of them shews an Inclination to Conjugal Enjoyments.

4. The Woman (who in all other Rights is inferior) has here the same Power given her over the Man's Body, that the Man has over hers: The Reason whereof is plain; because if she had not her Man, when she had need of him, as well as the Man his Woman, when he had need of her, Marriage would be no Remedy against Fornication.

tain,

I CORINTHIANS.

| | PARAPHRASE. | TEXT. |

6. tain, should tempt you to a Violation of the Marriage-Bed. As to marrying in general, I wish that you were all unmarried, as I am; but this
7. I say unto you by way of Advice, not of Command. Every one has from God his own proper Gift, some one way, and some another,
8. whereby he must govern himself. To the Unmarried and Widows, I say it, as my Opinion, that it is best for them to remain unmarried, as
9. I am. But if they have not the Gift of Continency, let them marry; for the Inconveniences of Marriage are to be preferred to Flames of Lust.
10. But to the Married, I say not by way of Counsel from myself, but of Command from the Lord, that a Woman should not leave her Husband:
11. But if she has separated herself from him, let her return and be reconciled to him again, or at least let her remain unmarried: And let
12. not the Husband put away his Wife. But as to others, 'tis my Advice, not a Commandment from the Lord, That if a Christian Man hath an Heathen Wife that is content to live with him, let him not break company with her ᶜ, and dissolve the Marriage:
13. And if a Christian Woman hath an Heathen Husband that is content to live with her, let her not break company with him ᶜ,
14. and dissolve the Marriage. You need have no Scruple concerning this Matter, for the Heathen Husband or Wife, in respect of Conjugal Duty, can be no more refused, than if they

6. But I speak this by permission, and not of commandment.
7. For I would that all men were even as I myself: but every man hath his proper gift of God, one after this manner, and another after that.
8. I say therefore to the unmarried and widows, it is good for them if they abide even as I.
9. But if they cannot contain, let them marry: for it is better to marry than to burn.
10. And unto the married I command, yet not I, but the Lord, Let not the wife depart from her husband:
11. But and if she depart, let her remain unmarried, or be reconciled to her husband: and let not the husband put away his wife.
12. But to the rest speak I, not the Lord, If any brother hath a wife that believeth not, and she be pleased to dwell with him, let him not put her away.
13. And the woman which hath an husband that believeth not, and he be pleased to dwell with her, let her not leave him.
14. For the unbelieving husband is sanctified by the wife, and the unbeliev-

NOTES.

12 & 13. ᶜ Ἀφίετω, the *Greek* Word in the Original, signifying *put away*, being directed here in these two Verses both to the Man and the Woman, seems to intimate the same Power and the same Act of Dismissing in both; and therefore ought in both Places to be translated alike.

were

I CORINTHIANS.

Ch. VII.

TEXT.

ing Wife is sanctified by the Husband: else were your Children unclean; but now are they holy.

15 But if the unbelieving depart, let him depart. A brother or a sister is not under bondage in such cases: but God hath called us to peace.

16 For what knowest thou, O wife, whether thou shalt save thy husband? or how knowest thou, O man, whether thou shalt save thy wife?

17 But as God hath distributed to every man, as the Lord hath called every one, so let him walk: and so ordain I in all churches.

PARAPHRASE.

were Christian: For in this Case the unbelieving Husband is sanctified ᵈ, or made a Christian, as to his Issue, in his Wife, and the Wife sanctified in her Husband. If it were not so, the Children of such Parents would be unclean ᵈ, *i. e.* in the State of Heathens; but now are they holy ᵈ, *i. e.* born Members of the Christian Church. But if the unbelieving Party will separate, let them separate. A Christian Man or Woman is not inslaved in such a Case; only it is to be remembered, that it is incumbent on us, whom God in the Gospel has called to be Christians, to live peaceably with all Men, as much as in us lieth; and therefore the Christian Husband or Wife is not to make a Breach in the Family, by leaving the unbelieving Party, who is content to stay. For what knowest thou, O Woman, but thou mayest be the Means of converting, and so saving thy unbelieving Husband, if thou continuest peaceably as a loving Wife with him? Or what knowest thou, O Man, but after the same Manner thou mayest save thy Wife? On this Occasion let me give you this general Rule; whatever Condition God has allotted to any of you, let him continue and go on contentedly in the same ᵉ State wherein he was called, not look-

15.

16.

17.

NOTES.

14 ᵈ Ἡγίασαι, *sanctified*, ἅγια, *holy*, and ἀκάθαρτα, *unclean*, are used here by the Apostle in the *Jewish* Sense. The *Jews* called all that were *Jews*, holy; and all others they called *unclean*. Thus *proles genita extra sanctitatem*, was a Child begot by Parents whilst they were yet Heathens; *genita intra sanctitatem*, was a Child begot by Parents after they were Proselytes. This Way of Speaking St. *Paul* transfers from the *Jewish* into the Christian Church, calling all that are of the Christian Church *Saints*, or *holy*; by which Reason all that were out of it were *unclean*. See *Note*, Chap. i. 2.

17 ᵉ ὡς signifies here not the Manner of his Calling, but the State and Condition of Life he was in when called; and therefore ὅτως must signify the same too, as the next Verse shews.

M

I CORINTHIANS.

Ch. VII.

PARAPHRASE.

ing on himself as set free from it by his Conversion to Christianity. And this is no more
18. than what I order in all the Churches. For example, was any one converted to Christianity, being circumcised? let him not become uncircumcised: Was any one called, being un-
19. circumcised? let him not be circumcised. Circumcision or Uncircumcision are nothing in the Sight of God; but that which he has a Regard
20. to, is an Obedience to his Commands. Christianity gives not any one any new Privilege to change the State, or put off [f] the Obligations of Civil Life, which he was in before.
21. Wert thou called, being a Slave? think thyself not the less a Christian for being a Slave; but yet prefer Freedom to Slavery, if thou canst
22. obtain it. For he that is converted to Christianity, being a Bond-man, is Christ's Freedman [g]: And he that is converted, being a Free-man, is Christ's Bond-man, under his Com-

TEXT.

Is any man called being 18 circumcised? let him not become uncircumcised: is any called in uncircumcision? let him not become circumcised.

Circumcision is nothing, 19 and uncircumcision is nothing; but the keeping of the commandments of God.

Let every man abide in 20 the same calling wherein he was called.

Art thou called being a 21 servant? care not for it; but if thou mayest be made free, use it rather.

For he that is called in 22 the Lord, being a servant, is the Lord's freeman: likewise also he that is called being free, is Christ's servant.

NOTES.

20 [f] Μενέτω, Let him abide. 'Tis plain from what immediately follows, that this is not an absolute Command; but only signifies, that a Man should not think himself discharged by the Privilege of his Christian State, and the Franchises of the Kingdom of Christ, which he was entered into, from any Ties or Obligations he was in as a Member of the Civil Society. And therefore, for the settling a true Notion thereof in the Mind of the Reader, it has been thought convenient to give that which is the Apostle's Sense to *ver.* 17, 20, & 24. of this Chapter, in Words somewhat different from the Apostle's. The thinking themselves freed by Christianity from the Ties of Civil Society and Government, was a Fault, it seems, that those Christians were very apt to run into. For St. *Paul*, for the preventing their Thoughts of any Change of any thing of their Civil State upon their embracing Christianity, thinks it necessary to warn them against it three Times in the Compass of seven Verses, and that in the Form of a direct Command not to change their Condition or State of Life: Whereby he intends that they should not change upon a Presumption that Christianity gave them a new or peculiar Liberty so to do. For, notwithstanding the Apostle's positively bidding them remain in the same Condition in which they were at their Conversion; yet it is certain it was lawful for them, as well as the others, to change, where it was lawful for them to change without being Christians.

22 [g] Ἀπελεύθερος, in *Latin Libertus*, signifies not simply a *Free-man*; but one who having been a Slave, has had his Freedom given him by his Master.

I CORINTHIANS.   Ch. VII.

TEXT.

23 Ye are bought with a price; be not ye the servants of men.
24 Brethren, let every man wherein he is called, therein abide with God.

25 Now concerning virgins, I have no commandment of the Lord: yet I give my judgment as one that hath obtained mercy, of the Lord, to be faithful.
26 I suppose therefore, that this is good for the present distress: I say, that it is good for a man so to be.
27 Art thou bound unto a wife? seek not to be loosed: Art thou loosed from a wife? seek not a wife.
28 But, and if thou marry, thou hast not sinned; and if a virgin marry, she hath not sinned: nevertheless,

PARAPHRASE.

mand and Dominion. Ye are bought with a Price [h], and so belong to Christ; be not, if you can avoid it, Slaves to any body. In whatsoever State a Man is called, in the same he is to remain, notwithstanding any Privileges of the Gospel, which gives him no Dispensation or Exemption from any Obligation he was in before to the Laws of his Country. Now concerning Virgins [i], I have no express Command from Christ to give you; but I tell you my Opinion, as one whom the Lord has been graciously pleased to make credible [k], and so you may trust and rely on in this Matter. I tell you therefore, that I judge a single Life to be convenient, because of the present Streights of the Church; and that it is best for a Man to be unmarried. Art thou in the Bonds of Wedlock? seek not to be loosed: Art thou loosed from a Wife? seek not a Wife. But if thou marriest, thou sinnest not; or if a Virgin marry, she sins not: But those that are married, shall have worldly Troubles: But I spare you, by not representing to you, how little Enjoy-

NOTES.

23 [h] Slaves were bought and sold in the Market, as Cattle are; and so by the Price paid, there was a Propriety acquired in them. This therefore here, is a Reason for what he advised, *ver.* 21. that they should not be Slaves to Men, because Christ had paid a Price for them, and they belonged to him. The Slavery he speaks of, is Civil Slavery; which he makes use of here to convince the *Corinthians*, that the Civil Ties of Marriage were not to be dissolved by a Man's becoming a Christian, since Slavery itself was not: And in general, in the next Verse he tells them, that nothing in any Man's Civil Estate or Rights, is altered by his becoming a Christian.

25 [i] By *Virgins*, 'tis plain St. *Paul* here means those of both Sexes, who are in a celibate State. 'Tis probable he had formerly dissuaded them from Marriage in the present State of the Church. This, it seems, they were uneasy under, *ver.* 28, & 35. and therefore sent some Questions to St. *Paul* about it; and particularly, What then should Men do with their Daughters? Upon which Occasion, *ver.* 27——37. he gives Directions to the Unmarried about their marrying or not marrying; and, in the close, *ver.* 38. answers to the Parents about marrying their Daughters; and then, *ver.* 39, & 40. he speaks of Widows.

[k] In this Sense he uses πιστὸς ἄνθρωπος, & πιστὸς λόγος, 2 Tim. II. 2.

Ch. VII.

PARAPHRASE.   *TEXT.*

ment Christians are like to have from a married Life in the present State of Things; and so I leave
29. you the liberty of marrying. But give me leave to tell you, that the Time for enjoying Husbands and Wives, is but short [l]: But be that as it will, this is certain, that those who have Wives, should be as if they had them not, and not set their
30. Hearts upon them: And they that weep, as if they wept not; and they that rejoice, as if they rejoiced not; and they that buy, as if they possessed not: All these Things should be done with
31. Resignation, and a Christian Indifferency. And those who use this World, should use it without an Over-relish of it [m], without giving themselves up to the Enjoyment of it; for the Scene of Things is always changing in this World,
32. and nothing can be relied on in it [n]. All the Reason why I dissuade you from Marriage, is, that I would have you free from anxious Cares: He that is unmarried, has Time and Liberty to mind Things of Religion, how he may please
33. the Lord: But he that is married, is taken up with the Cares of the World, how he may
34. please his Wife. The like Difference there is between a married Woman and a Maid: She that is unmarried, has Opportunity to mind the Things of Religion, that she may be holy in Mind and Body; but the married Woman is taken up with the Cares of the World, how to

such shall have trouble in the flesh; but I spare you.

23 But this I say, brethren, the time is short: It remaineth, that both they that have wives, be as though they had none;

30 And they that weep, as though they wept not; and they that rejoice, as though they rejoiced not; and they that buy, as though they possessed not;

31 And they that use this world, as not abusing it: for the fashion of this world passeth away.

32 But I would have you without carefulness. He that is unmarried, careth for the things that belong to the Lord, how he may please the Lord.

33 But he that is married, careth for the things that are of the world, how he may please his wife.

34 There is difference also between a wife and a virgin: the unmarried woman careth for the things of the Lord, that she may be holy, both in body and in spirit: but she that is married, careth for the things of the world, how she may please her husband.

NOTES.

28 [l] Said possibly out of a prophetical Foresight of the approaching Persecution under *Nero*.
31 [m] Καταχρωμενοι does not here signify *abusing*, in our *English* Sense of the Word, but *intently using*.
[l] All from the Beginning of *ver.* 28. to the End of this *ver.* 31. I think may be looked on as a Parenthesis.

please

I CORINTHIANS.

Ch. VII.

TEXT.	PARAPHRASE.

35 And this I speak for your own profit, not that I may cast a snare upon you, but for that which is comely, and that you may attend upon the Lord without distraction.

36 But if any man think that he behaveth himself uncomely towards his virgin, if she pass the flower of her age, and need so require, let him do what he will, he sinneth not: let them marry.

37 Nevertheless, he that standeth stedfast in his heart, having no necessity, but hath power over his own will, and hath so decreed in his heart, that

35. please her Husband. This I say to you for your particular Advantage, not to lay any Constraint upon you°, but to put you in a Way wherein you may most suitably, and as best becomes Christianity, apply yourselves to the Study and Duties of the Gospel, without Distraction. 36. But if any one thinks that he carries not himself as becomes him to his Virgin, if he lets her pass the Flower of her Age unmarried, and need so requires, let him do as he thinks fit; he sins not, if he marry her. 37. But whoever is settled in a firm Resolution of Mind, and finds himself under no Necessity of marrying, and is Master of his own Will, or is at his own Disposal, and has so determined in his Thoughts, that he will keep his Virginity ᵖ, he chooses

NOTES.

35 ° Βρόχ⊙·, which we translate a *Snare*, signifies a *Cord*; which possibly the Apostle might, according to the Language of the *Hebrew* School, use here for Binding; and then his Discourse runs thus: Though I have declared it my Opinion, that it is best for a Virgin to remain unmarried, yet I bind it not; *i. e.* I do not declare it to be unlawful to marry.

37 ᵖ Παρθένον seems used here for the Virgin-State, and not the Person of a Virgin; whether there be Examples of the like Use of it, I know not, and therefore I propose it as my Conjecture, upon these Grounds. 1. Because the Resolution of Mind here spoken of, must be in the Person to be married, and not in the Father that has the Power over the Person concerned; for how will the Firmness of Mind of the Father hinder Fornication in the Child, who has not that Firmness? 2. The Necessity of Marriage can only be judged of by the Persons themselves. A Father cannot feel the Child's Flames which make the Need of Marriage: The Persons themselves only know whether they burn, or have the Gift of Continence. 3. Ἐξουσίαν ἔχει περὶ τοῦ ἰδίου θελήματος, *hath the Power over his own Will*, must either signify, *can govern his own Desires*, *is Master of his own Will*: But this cannot be meant here, because it is sufficiently expressed before by ἕδραῖος τῇ καρδίᾳ, *stedfast in Heart*; and afterwards too by κέκρικεν ἐν τῇ καρδίᾳ, *decreed in Heart*: Or must signify, *has the Disposal of himself*, *i. e.* is free from the Father's Power of disposing their Children in Marriage; for I think the Words should be translated, *hath a Power concerning his own Will*, *i. e.* concerning what he willeth: For if by it St. *Paul* meant a Power over his own Will, one might think he would have expressed that Thought, as he does *Chap.* IX. 12. and *Rom.* IX. 21. without περὶ; or by the Preposition ἐπὶ, as it is, *Luke* IX. 1. 4. Because, if *keep his Virgin*, had here signified keep his Children from marrying, the Expression had been more natural to have used the Word τέκνα, which signifies both Sexes, than παρθένον, which belongs only to the Female. If therefore παρθένον be taken abstractly for Virginity, the precedent Verse must be understood thus: *But if any one think it a Shame to pass the Flower of his Age unmarried, and he finds it necessary to marry,*

	PARAPHRASE.	TEXT.
38.	chooses the better ᵠ Side. So then, he that marrieth, doth well; but he that marrieth ʳ not, doth better. It is unlawful for a Woman to leave her Husband as long as he lives; but when he is dead, she is at liberty to marry, or not marry, as she pleases, and to whom she pleases; which Virgins cannot do, being under the Disposal of their Parents; only she must take care to marry as a Christian, fearing God. But, in my Opinion, she is happier if she remain a Widow; and permit me to say, that whatever any among you may think or say of me, I have the Spirit of God, so that I may be relied on in this my Advice, that I do not mislead you.	he will keep his virgin, doth well. So then, he that giveth 38 her in marriage, doth well: but he that giveth her not in marriage, doth better. The wife is bound by 39 the law, as long as her husband liveth: but if her husband be dead, she is at liberty to be married to whom she will; only in the Lord. But she is happier if she 40 so abide, after my judgment: and I think also that I have the Spirit of God.

NOTES.

let him do as he pleases, he sins not; let such marry. I confess it is hard to bring these two Verses to the same Sense, and both of them to the Design of the Apostle here, without taking the Words in one or both of them very figuratively. St. *Paul* here seems to obviate an Objection that might be made against his Dissuasion from Marriage, *viz.* that it might be an Indecency one should be guilty of, if one should live unmarried past one's Prime, and afterwards be forced to marry. To which he answers, that no body should abstain upon the account of being a Christian; but those who are of steady Resolutions, are at their own Disposal, and have fully determined it in their own Minds.

Καλῶς here, as in *ver.* 1, 8, and 26. signifies not simply good, but preferable.

38 ᵠ Παρθένος being taken in the Sense before-mentioned, it is necessary in this Verse to follow the Copies which read γαμίζων, *marrying*, for ἐκγαμίζων, *giving in Marriage*.

I CORINTHIANS.

SECT. IV.

CHAP. VIII. 1——13.

CONTENTS.

THIS Section is concerning the eating Things offered to Idols; wherein one may guess, by St. *Paul*'s Answer, that they had writ to him, that they knew their Christian Liberty herein, that they knew that an Idol was nothing, and therefore that they did well to shew their Knowledge of the Nullity of the Heathen Gods, and their Disregard of them, by eating promiscuously, and without Scruple, Things offered to them. Upon which the Design of the Apostle here seems to be, to take down their Opinion of their Knowledge, by shewing them, that notwithstanding all the Knowledge they presumed on, and were puffed up with, yet the eating of those Sacrifices did not recommend them to God; *vid. ver.* 8. and that they might sin, in their Want of Charity, by offending their weak Brother. This seems plainly, from *ver.* 1—3. and 11, 12. to be the Design of the Apostle's Answer here, and not to resolve the Case of eating Things offered to Idols in its full Latitude; for then he would have prosecuted it more at large here, and not have deferred the doing of it to *Chap.* X. where, under another Head, he treats of it more particularly.

TEXT.

NOW, as touching things offered unto idols, we know that we all have knowledge. Knowledge puffeth up, but charity edifieth.

PARAPHRASE.

1. AS for Things offered up unto Idols, it must not be questioned but that every one of you, who stand so much upon your Knowledge, know that the imaginary Gods, to whom the *Gentiles* sacrifice, are not in reality Gods, but meer Fictions: But with this pray remember, that such a Knowledge, or Opinion of their Knowledge, swell Men with Pride and Vanity; but Charity it is that improves and advances

	PARAPHRASE.	TEXT.
2.	advances Men in Christianity ˢ. But if any one be conceited of his own Knowledge, as if Christianity were a Science for Speculation and Dispute, he knows nothing yet of Christianity as he ought to know it.	And if any man think that he knoweth any thing, he knoweth nothing yet as he ought to know. 2
3.	But if any one love God, and consequently his Neighbour for God's sake, such an one is made to know ᵗ, or has got true Knowledge from God himself.	But if any man love God, the same is known of him. 3
4.	To the Question then, of eating Things offered to Idols: I know, as well as you, that an Idol, *i. e.* that the fictitious Gods, whose Images are in the Heathen Temples, are no real Beings in the World; and there is, in truth, no other but one God.	As concerning therefore the eating of those things that are offered in sacrifice unto idols, we know that an idol is nothing in the world, and that there is none other God but one. 4
5.	For tho' there be many imaginary nominal Gods, both in Heaven and Earth ᵘ, as are indeed all their many Gods, and many Lords, which are merely titular;	For though there be that are called gods, whether in heaven or in earth, (as there be gods many, and lords many.) 5
6.	yet to us Christians, there is but one God, the Father and Author of all Things, to whom alone we address all our Worship and Service; and but one Lord, *viz.* Jesus Christ, by whom all Things come from God to us, and by whom	But to us there is but one God, the Father, of whom are all things, and we in him; and one Lord Jesus Christ, by whom are all things, and we by him. 6

NOTES.

1 ˢ To continue the Thread of the Apostle's Discourse, the 7th Verse must be read as joined on to the 1st, and all between looked on as a Parenthesis.

3 ᵗ Ἔγνωϛαι, *is made to know*, or *is taught*. The Apostle, though writing in *Greek*, yet often uses the *Greek* Verbs according to the *Hebrew* Conjugation. So *Chap.* XIII. 12. ἐπιγνώσομαι, which, according to the *Greek* Propriety, signifies *I shall be known*, is used for *I shall be made to know*; and so *Gal.* IV. 9. γνωσθέντες, is put to signify *being taught*.

5 ᵘ *In Heaven and Earth.* The Heathens had supreme Sovereign Gods, whom they supposed eternal, remaining always in the Heavens; these were called Θεοὶ, *Gods*. They had besides another Order of inferior Gods, *Gods upon Earth*; who, by the Will and Direction of the heavenly Gods, governed terrestrial Things, and were the Mediators between the Supreme heavenly Gods and Men, without whom there could be no Communication between them. These were called in Scripture *Baalim*, i. e. *Lords*; and by the *Greeks*, Δαίμονες. To this the Apostle alludes here, saying, Though there be, in the Opinion of the Heathens, *Gods many*, i. e. many celestial Sovereign Gods in Heaven, and *Lords many*, i. e. many *Baalims*, or Lord's Agents, and Presidents over earthly Things; yet to us Christians there is but one Sovereign God, the Father, of whom are all Things, and to whom, as Supreme, we are to direct all our Services; and but one Lord-Agent, Jesus Christ, by whom are all Things that come from the Father to us, and through whom alone we find Access unto him, *Mede Disc.* on 2 *Pet.* II. 1.

I CORINTHIANS.

TEXT.

7 Howbeit there is not in every man that knowledge: for some with conscience of the idol unto this hour, eat it as a thing offered unto an idol; and their conscience being weak, is defiled.

8 But meat commendeth us not to God: for neither if we eat, are we the better; neither if we eat not, are we the worse.

9 But take heed, lest by any means this liberty of yours become a stumbling-block to them that are weak.

10 For if any man see thee which hast knowledge, sit at meat in the idol's temple, shall not the conscience of him which is weak, be emboldened to eat those things which are offered to idols:

PARAPHRASE.

we have Access to the Father. For, notwithstanding all the great Pretences to Knowledge that are amongst you, every one doth not know that the Gods of the Heathens are but Imaginations of the Fancy, mere nothing. Some, to this Day, conscious to themselves that they think those Idols to be real Deities, eat Things sacrificed to them, as sacrificed to real Deities, whereby doing that, which they in their Consciences, not yet sufficiently enlightened, think to be unlawful, they are guilty of Sin. Food, of what kind soever, makes not God regard us[w]: For neither if in Knowledge and full Persuasion, that an Idol is nothing, we eat Things offered to Idols, do we thereby add any thing to Christianity; or, if not being so well informed, we are scrupulous and forbear, are we the worse Christians, or are lessened by it[x]. But this you knowing Men ought to take especial Care of, that the Power or Freedom you have to eat, be not made such an Use of, as to become a Stumbling-block to weaker Christians, who are not convinced of that Liberty. For if such an one should see thee, who hath this Knowledge of thy Liberty, to sit feasting in an Idol-Temple, shall not his weak Conscience, not thoroughly instructed in the Matter of Idols, be drawn in by thy Example to eat what is offered to Idols, tho' he in his

7.

8.

9.

10.

NOTES.

8 [w] Ου παρίστησι, sets us not before God, *i. e.* to be taken notice of by him.
[x] It cannot be supposed that St. *Paul*, in answer to a Letter of the *Corinthians*, should tell them, that if they eat Things offered to Idols, they were not the better; or if they eat not, were not the worse, unless they had expressed some Opinion of Good in Eating.

PARAPHRASE.

11. Conscience doubt of its Lawfulness? and thus thy weak Brother, for whom Christ died, is destroyed by thy Knowledge, wherewith thou justi-
12. fiest thy Eating. But when you sin thus against your Brethren, and wound their weak Consci-
13. ences, you sin against Christ. Wherefore if Meat make my Brother offend, I will never more eat Flesh, to avoid making my Brother offend.

TEXT.

11. And through thy knowledge shall the weak brother perish, for whom Christ died?
12. But when ye sin so against the brethren, and wound their weak conscience, ye sin against Christ.
13. Wherefore if meat make my brother to offend, I will eat no flesh while the world standeth, lest I make my brother to offend.

SECT. V.

CHAP. IX. 1——27.

CONTENTS.

ST. *Paul* had preached the Gospel at *Corinth* about two Years, in all which Time he had taken nothing of them, 2 *Cor.* XI. 7—9. This by some of the opposite Faction, and particularly, as we may suppose, by their Leader, was made use of to call in question his Apostleship, 2 *Cor.* XI. 5, 6. For why, if he were an Apostle, should he not use the Power of an Apostle, to demand Maintenance where he preached? In this Section St. *Paul* vindicates his Apostleship; and in answer to these Enquiries, gives the Reason why, though he had a Right to Maintenance, yet he preached *gratis* to the *Corinthians*. My Answer, says he, to these Inquisitors, is, That tho', as being an Apostle, I know that I have a Right to Maintenance, as well as *Peter*, or any other of the Apostles, who all have a Right, as is evident from Reason and from Scripture; yet I neither have, nor shall make use of my Privilege amongst you, for fear that, if it cost you any thing, that should hinder the Effect of my Preaching: I would neglect nothing that might promote the Gospel. For I do not content myself with doing barely what is my Duty; for by my extraordinary Call and Commission, it is now incumbent on me to preach

the

I CORINTHIANS.

the Gospel; but I endeavour to excel in my Ministry, and not to execute my Commission overtly, and just enough to serve the Turn: For if those, who in the *Agonistick* Games aiming at Victory, to obtain only a corruptible Crown, deny themselves in eating and drinking, and other Pleasures, how much more does the eternal Crown of Glory deserve, that we should do our utmost to obtain it? to be as careful in not indulging our Bodies, in denying our Pleasures, in doing every thing we could in order to get it, as if there were but one that should have it? Wonder not therefore if I, having this in view, neglect my Body, and those outward Conveniencies that I, as an Apostle, sent to preach the Gospel, might claim, and make use of: Wonder not that I prefer the propagating of the Gospel, and making of Converts, to all Care and Regard of myself. This seems the Design of the Apostle, and will give light to the following Discourse; which we shall now take in the Order St. *Paul* writ it.

TEXT.

AM I not an apostle? am I not free? have I not seen Jesus Christ our Lord? are not you my work in the Lord?

If I be not an apostle unto others, yet doubtless I am to you: for the seal of mine apostleship are ye in the Lord.

Mine answer to them that do examine me, is this,

Have we not power to eat and to drink?

Have we not power to lead about a sister, a wife,

PARAPHRASE.

AM I not an Apostle? And am I not at liberty^a, as much as any other of the Apostles, to make use of the Privilege due to that Office? Have I not had the Favour to see Jesus Christ, our Lord, after an extraordinary Manner? And are not you yourselves, whom I have converted, an Evidence of the Success of my Employment in the Gospel? If others should question my being an Apostle, you at least cannot doubt of it; your Conversion to Christianity is, as it were, a Seal set to it, to make good the Truth of my Apostleship. This then is my Answer to those who set up an Inquisition upon me: Have not I a Right to Meat and Drink where I preach? Have not I and *Barnabas* a Power to take along with us, in our Travelling, to propagate the Gospel, a

1.

2.

3.

4.

5.

NOTES.

1 ^a It was a Law amongst the *Jews*, not to receive Alms from the *Gentiles*.

I CORINTHIANS.

PARAPHRASE.

Christian Woman[b], to provide our Conveniencies, and be serviceable to us, as well as *Peter*, and the Brethren of the Lord, and the rest of the
6. Apostles? Or is it I only and *Barnabas*, who are excluded from the Privilege of being maintain-
7. ed without Working? Who goes to the War any where, and serves as a Soldier at his own Charges? Who planteth a Vineyard, and eateth not of the Fruit thereof? Who feedeth a Flock, and eateth not of the Milk? This is allowed to be Reason, that those who are so employed, should be maintained by their Employments; and so like-
8. wise a Preacher of the Gospel. But I say not this barely upon the Principles of human Reason, Revelation teaches the same Thing in the
9. Law of *Moses*; where it is said, Thou shalt not muzzle the Mouth of the Ox, that treadeth out the Corn. Doth God take care to pro-
10. vide so particularly for Oxen by a Law? No, certainly; it is said particularly for our Sakes, and not for Oxen, that he who sows, may sow in hope of enjoying the Fruits of his Labour at Harvest, and may then thresh out and eat the
11. Corn he hoped for. If we have sowed to you spiritual Things, in preaching the Gospel to you, is it unreasonable that we should expect a little Meat and Drink from you, a little Share
12. of your carnal Things? If any partake of this

TEXT.

as well as other apostles, and as the brethren of the Lord, and Cephas?
6. Or I only and Barnabas, have not we power to forbear working?
7. Who goeth a warfare any time at his own charges? who planteth a vineyard, and eateth not of the fruit thereof? or who feedeth a flock, and eateth not of the milk of the flock?
8. Say I these things as a man? or saith not the law the same also?
9. For it is written in the law of Moses, Thou shalt not muzzle the mouth of the ox that treadeth out the corn. Doth God take care for oxen?
10. Or saith he it altogether for our sakes? For our sakes, no doubt, this is written: that he that ploweth, should plow in hope; and that he that thresheth in hope, should be partaker of his hope.
11. If we have sown unto you spiritual things, is it a great thing if we shall reap your carnal things?
12. If others be partakers of this power over you, are not we rather? Nevertheless, we have not used this power; but suffer all things, lest we

NOTES.

5 [b] There were not in those Parts, as among us, Inns, where Travellers might have their Conveniencies; and Strangers could not be accommodated with Necessaries unless they had some body with them, to take that care, and provide for them. They who would make it their business to preach, and neglect this, must needs suffer great Hardships.

Power

I CORINTHIANS.

Chap. IX.

TEXT.	PARAPHRASE.

should hinder the gospel of Christ.

13. Do ye not know, that they which minister about holy things, live of the things of the temple? and they which wait at the altar, are partakers with the altar?

14. Even so hath the Lord ordained, that they which preach the gospel, should live of the gospel.

15. But I have used none of these things. Neither have I written these things, that it should be so done unto me: for it were better for me to die, than that any man should make my glorying void.

16. For though I preach the gospel, I have nothing to glory of: for necessity is laid upon me; yea, wo is unto me, if I preach not the gospel.

17. For if I do this thing willingly, I have a reward: but if against my will, a dispensation of the gospel is committed unto me.

18. What is my reward then? verily that when I preach the gospel, I may make the gospel of Christ without charge, that I abuse not my power in the gospel.

Power over you [c], why not we much rather? But I made no use of it, but bear with any thing, that I may avoid all Hindrance to the Progress of the Gospel. Do ye not know, that they who in the Temple serve about holy Things, live upon those holy Things? And they who wait at the Altar, are Partakers with the Altar? So has the Lord ordained, that they who preach the Gospel, should live of the Gospel. But though, as an Apostle and Preacher of the Gospel, I have, as you see, a Right to Maintenance, yet I have not taken it, neither have I written this to demand it; for I had rather perish for Want, than be deprived of what I glory in, viz. preaching the Gospel freely. For if I preach the Gospel, I do barely my Duty; but have nothing to glory in, for I am under an Obligation and Command to preach [d]: And wo be to me, if I preach not the Gospel; which if I do willingly, I shall have a Reward; if unwillingly, the Dispensation is nevertheless intrusted to me, and ye ought to hear me as an Apostle. How therefore do I make it turn to account to myself? Even thus: If I preach the Gospel of Christ of Free-cost, so that I exact not the Maintenance I have a Right to by the Gospel.

13.
14.
15.
16.
17.
18.

NOTES.

12 [c] For τῆς ἐνεξίας, I should incline to read τῆς ὑσίας, if there be, as *Vossius* says, any MSS to authorize it: And then the Words will run thus, *If any partake of your Substance.* This better suits the foregoing Words, and needs not the Addition of the Word *this*, to be inserted in the Translation; which, with Difficulty enough, makes it refer to a Power which he was not here speaking of, but stands eight Verses off. Besides, in these Words St. *Paul* seems to glance at what they suffered from the false Apostle, who did not only pretend to Power of Maintenance, but did actually devour them: *Vid.* 2 Cor. XI. 20.

16 [d] *Vid.* Acts XXII. 15——21.

For

PARAPHRASE.	TEXT.
19. For being under no Obligation to any Man, I yet subject myself to every one, to the end that I may make the more Converts to Christ.	For though I be free from all men, yet have I made myself servant unto all, that I might gain the more.
20. To the *Jews*, and those under the Law of *Moses*, I became as a *Jew*, and one under that Law, that I might gain the *Jews*, and those under	And unto the Jews, I became as a Jew, that I might gain the Jews; to them that are under the law, as under the law, that I might gain them that are under the law;
21. the Law: To those without the Law of *Moses*, I applied myself as one not under that Law, (not indeed as if I were under no Law to God, but as obeying and following the Law of Christ) that I might gain those who were	To them that are without law, as without law, (being not without law to God, but under the law to Christ) that I might gain them that are without law.
22. without the Law. To the Weak I became as weak, that I might gain the Weak. I became all Things to all Men, that I might leave no lawful Thing untried, whereby I might save	To the weak became I as weak, that I might gain the weak: I am made all things to all men, that I might by all means save some.
23. People of all sorts. And this I do for the Gospel's sake, that I myself may share in the Be-	And this I do for the gospel's sake, that I might be partaker thereof with you.
24. nefits of the Gospel. Know ye not, that they who run a Race, run not lazily, but with their utmost Force? they all endeavour to be first, because there is but one that gets the Prize: It is not enough for you to run, but so to run that ye may obtain; which they cannot do, who running only because they are bid, do not	Know ye not, that they which run in a race, run all, but one receiveth the prize? so run, that ye may obtain.
25. run with all their Might. They who propose to themselves the getting the Garland in your Games, readily submit themselves to severe Rules of Exercise and Abstinence; and yet theirs is but a fading transitory Crown; that which we propose to ourselves is everlasting, and therefore deserves that we should endure	And every man that striveth for the mastery, is temperate in all things: now, they do it to obtain a corruptible crown, but we an incorruptible.
26. greater Hardships for it. I therefore so run, as not to leave it to Uncertainty: I do what I do, not as one who fences for Exercise or Ostenta-	I therefore so run, not as uncertainly: so fight I, not as one that beateth the air:
27. tion; but I really and in earnest keep under my Body, and entirely inslave it to the Service of the Gospel, without allowing any thing to the	But I keep under my body, and bring it into subjection: lest that by

I CORINTHIANS.

TEXT.	PARAPHRASE.
any means when I have preached to others, I myself should be a cast-away.	the Exigencies of this animal Life, which may be the least Hindrance to the Propagation of the Gospel, lest that I, who preach to bring others into the Kingdom of Heaven, should be disapproved of, and rejected myself.

SECT. VI. N. I.
CHAP. X. 1——22.

CONTENTS.

IT seems, by what he here says, as if the *Corinthians* had told St. *Paul*, that the Temptations and Constraints they were under, of going to their Heathen Neighbours Feasts upon their Sacrifices, were so many and so great, that there was no avoiding it: And therefore they thought they might go to them without any Offence to God, or Danger to themselves; since they were the People of God, purged from Sin by Baptism, and fenced against it, by partaking of the Body and Blood of Christ in the Lord's Supper. To which St. *Paul* answers, that notwithstanding their Baptism, and partaking of that spiritual Meat and Drink, yet they, as well as the *Jews* of old did, might sin, and draw on themselves Destruction from the Hand of God; that eating of Things that were known and owned to be offered to Idols, was partaking in the idolatrous Worship; and therefore they were to prefer even the Danger of Persecution before such a Compliance, for God would find a Way for them to escape.

I Would

I CORINTHIANS.

Chap. X.

PARAPHRASE.

1. I Would not have you ignorant, Brethren, that all our Fathers, the whole Congregation of the Children of *Israel*, at their coming out of *Egypt*, were, all to a Man, under the Cloud, and
2. all passed through the Sea: And were all, by this Baptism ᵉ in the Cloud, and passing through the Water, initiated into the Mosaical Institution and Government, by these two Miracles, of the
3. Cloud and the Sea: And they all eat the same Meat, which had a typical and spiritual Signi-
4. fication. And they all drank the same spiritual typical Drink, which came out of the Rock, and followed them; which Rock typified Christ: All which were typical Representations of Christ, as well as the Bread and Wine, which we eat and drink in the Lord's Supper, are typical Re-
5. presentations of him. But yet tho' every one of the Children of *Israel*, that came out of *Egypt*, were thus solemnly separated from the rest of the profane idolatrous World, and were made God's peculiar People, sanctified and holy, every one of them to himself, and Members of his Church: Nay, tho' they did all ᶠ partake of the same Meat, and the same Drink, which

TEXT.

1 Moreover, brethren, I would not that ye should be ignorant, how that all our fathers were under the cloud, and all passed through the sea;

2 And were all baptized unto Moses in the cloud, and in the sea;

3 And did eat all the same spiritual meat;

4 And did drink all the same spiritual drink: (for they drank of that spiritual Rock that followed them; and that Rock was Christ.)

5 But with many of them God was not well pleased; for they were overthrown in the wilderness.

NOTES.

2 ᵉ The Apostle calls it Baptism, which is the initiating Ceremony into both the *Jewish* and *Christian* Church: And the Cloud and Sea both being nothing but Water, are well suited to that typical Representation; and that the Children of *Israel* were washed with Rain from the Cloud, may be collected from *Psal.* LXVIII. 9.

5 ᶠ It may be observed here, that St. *Paul* speaking of the *Israelites*, uses the Word πάντες, *all*, five times in the four foregoing Verses; besides that, he carefully says, τὸ αὐτὸ βρῶμα, the same Meat, and τὸ αὐτὸ πόμα, the same Drink; which we cannot suppose to be done by chance, but emphatically, to signify to the *Corinthians*, who probably presumed too much upon their Baptism, and eating the Lord's Supper, as if that were enough to keep them right in the Sight of God; that tho' the *Israelites*, all to a Man, eat the very same spiritual Food, and all to a Man drank the very same spiritual Drink, yet they were not all to a Man preserved, but many of them, for all that, sinned and fell under the avenging Hand of God in the Wilderness.

did

I CORINTHIANS.

Chap. X.

TEXT.

6 Now these things were our examples, to the intent we should not lust after evil things, as they also lusted.
7 Neither be ye idolaters, as were some of them; as it is written, The people sat down to eat and drink, and rose up to play.
8 Neither let us commit fornication, as some of them committed: and fell in one day three and twenty thousand.
9 Neither let us tempt Christ, as some of them also tempted, and were destroyed of serpents.
10 Neither murmur ye, as some of them also murmured, and were destroyed of the destroyer.
11 Now all these things happened unto them for ensamples: and they are written for our admonition, upon whom the ends of the world are come.

PARAPHRASE.

did typically represent Christ, yet they were not thereby privileged from Sin, but great Numbers of them provoked God, and were destroyed in the Wilderness, for their Disobedience. Now these Things were set as Patterns to us, that we, warned by these Examples, should not set our Minds a-longing, as they did, after Meats [g] that would be safer let alone. Neither be ye Idolaters, as were some of them; as it is written, The People sat down to eat and to drink, and rose up to play [h]. Neither let us commit Fornication, as some of them committed, and fell in one Day Three and twenty Thousand. Neither let us provoke Christ, as some of them provoked, and were destroyed of Serpents. Neither murmur ye, as some of them murmured, and were destroyed of the Destroyer [i]. Now all these Things [k] happened to the *Jews* for Examples, and are written for our [l] Admonition, upon whom

6.

7.

8.

9.

10.

11.

NOTES.

6 [g] Κακῶν, *evil Things*. The Fault of the *Israelites*, which this Place refers to, seems to be their longing for Flesh, *Num.* XI. which cost many of them their Lives: And that which he warns the *Corinthians* of here, is their great Propension to the Pagan Sacrifice-Feasts.

7 [h] *Play*, i. e. Dance: Feasting and Dancing usually accompanied the Heathen Sacrifices.

10 [i] Ὀλοθρευτῇ, *Destroyer*, was an Angel that had the Power to destroy, mentioned *Exod.* XII. 23. *Heb.* XI. 28.

11 [k] It is to be observed, that all these Instances, mentioned by the Apostle, of Destruction, which came upon the *Israelites*, who were in Covenant with God, and Partakers in those typical Sacraments above-mentioned, were occasioned by their luxurious Appetites about Meat and Drink, by Fornication, and by Idolatry; Sins which the *Corinthians* were inclined to, and which he here warns them against.

[l] So I think τὰ τέλη τῶν αἰώνων should be rendered, and not, contrary to Grammar, *the End of the World*; because it is certain that τέλη and συντέλεια τῦ αἰῶνος, or τῶν αἰώνων, cannot signify every where, as we render it, *the End of the World*, which denotes but one certain Period of Time, for the World can have but one End; whereas these Words signify, in different Places, different Periods of Time, as will be manifest to any one who will compare these Texts where they occur, *viz. Mat.* XIII. 39, 40. & XXIV. 3. & XXVIII. 20. 1 *Cor.* X. 11. *Heb.* IX. 26. It may be worth while therefore to consider whether αἰών hath not ordinarily a more natural Signification in the New Testament, by standing for a considerable Length of Time, passing under some one remarkable Dispensation.

I CORINTHIANS.

PARAPHRASE.

12. the End of the Ages are come. Wherefore, taught by these Examples, let him that thinks himself safe, by being in the Church, and partaking of the Christian Sacraments, take heed lest he fall into Sin, and so Destruction from
13. God overtake him. Hitherto the Temptations you have met with, have been but light and ordinary: If you should come to be pressed harder, God, who is faithful, and never forsakes those who forsake not him, will not suffer you to be tempted above your Strength; but will either enable you to bear the Perse-
14. cution, or open you a Way out of it. Therefore, my Beloved, take care to keep off from Idolatry; and be not drawn to any Approaches near it, by any Temptation or Persecution whatsoever. You are satisfied that you want not
15. Knowledge. ᵐ And therefore, as to knowing Men, I appeal to you; and make you Judges of what I am going to say in the Case.
16. They who drink of the Cup of Blessing ⁿ, which we bless in the Lord's Supper, do they not thereby partake of the Benefits purchased by Christ's Blood shed for them upon the Cross, which they here symbolically drink? And they who eat of the Bread broken ᵒ there, do they not partake in the Sacrifice of the Body of Christ, and profess to be Members of
17. him? For by eating of that Bread, we, though many in Number, are all united, and make but one Body; as many Grains of Corn are united

TEXT.

12. Wherefore let him that thinketh he standeth, take heed lest he fall.

13. There hath no temptation taken you, but such as is common to man: but God is faithful, who will not suffer you to be tempted above that ye are able; but will with the temptation also make a way to escape, that ye may be able to bear it.

14. Wherefore, my dearly beloved, flee from idolatry.

15. I speak as to wise men: judge ye what I say.

16. The cup of blessing which we bless, is it not the communion of the blood of Christ? The bread which we break, is it not the communion of the body of Christ?

17. For we being many, are one bread, and one body: for we are all partakers of that one bread.

NOTES.

15 ᵐ Vid. *Chap.* VIII. 1.

16 ⁿ *Cup of Blessing*, was a Name given by the *Jews* to a Cup of Wine, which they solemnly drank in the Passover, with Thanksgiving.

ᵒ This was also taken from the Custom of the *Jews* in the Passover, to break a Cake of Unleavened Bread.

into

I CORINTHIANS. 103

Chap. X.

| TEXT. | PARAPHRASE. |

18 Behold Israel after the flesh: are not they which eat of the sacrifices, partakers of the altar?

19 What say I then? that the idol is any thing, or that which is offered in sacrifice to idols, is any thing?

20 But I say, that the things which the Gentiles sacrifice, they sacrifice to devils, and not to God: and I would not that ye should have fellowship with devils.

21 Ye cannot drink the cup of the Lord, and the cup of devils: ye cannot be partakers of the Lord's table, and of the table of devils.

18. into one Loaf. See how it is among the *Jews*, who are outwardly, according to the Flesh, by Circumcision the People of God: Among them, they who eat of the Sacrifice, are Partakers of God's Table, the Altar, have Fellowship with him, and share in the Benefit of the Sacrifice, as if it were offered for them.

19. Do not mistake me, as if I hereby said, that the Idols of the *Gentiles* are Gods in reality; or that the Things offered to them change their Nature, and are any thing really different from what they were before, so as to affect us in our Use of them?:

20. No, but this I say, that the Things which the *Gentiles* sacrifice, they sacrifice to Devils, and not to God; and I would not that you should have Fellowship, and be in League with Devils, as they who by eating of the Things offered to them, enter into Covenant, Alliance and Friendship, with them.

21. You cannot eat and drink with God, as Friends at his Table in the Eucharist, and entertain Familiarity and Friendship with Devils, by eating with them, and partaking of the Sacrifices offered to them ^q: You cannot be Christians, and Idolaters too; nor if you should endeavour to join these inconsistent Rites, will it avail you any thing. For your partaking in the Sacraments of the Christian Church, will no more exempt you from the Anger of God, and Punishment

NOTES.

19 ^p This is evident from what he says, *ver.* 25, 27. that Things offered to Idols may be eaten as well as any other Meat, so it be without partaking in the Sacrifice, and without Scandal.

21 ^q 'Tis plain, by what the Apostle says, that the Thing he speaks against here, is their assisting at the Heathen Sacrifices, or at least at the Feasts in their Temples, upon the Sacrifice, which was a foederal Rite.

O 2 due

I CORINTHIANS.

PARAPHRASE.

due to your Idolatry, than the Eating of the spiritual Food, and Drinking of the spiritual Rock, kept the baptized *Israelites*, who offended God by their Idolatry, or other Sins, from
22. being destroyed in the Wilderness. Dare you then, being espoused to Christ, provoke the Lord to Jealousy by Idolatry, which is spiritual Whoredom? Are you stronger than he, and able to resist him, when he lets loose his Fury against you?

TEXT.

22 Do ye provoke the Lord to jealousy? are we stronger than he?

SECT. VI. N. 2.
CHAP. X. 23.——XI. 1.

CONTENTS.

WE have here another of his Arguments against Things offered to Idols; wherein he shews the Danger might be in it, from the Scandal it might give, supposing it a Thing lawful in itself. He had formerly treated of this Subject, *Chap.* VIII. so far as to let them see, that there was no Good nor Virtue in eating Things offered to Idols, notwithstanding they knew that Idols were nothing, and they might think that their free eating without Scruple, shewed that they knew their Freedom in the Gospel, that they knew that Idols were in reality nothing, and therefore they slighted and disregarded them and their Worship, as nothing; but that there might be Evil in Eating, by the Offence it might give to weak Christians, who had not that Knowledge: He here takes up the Argument of Scandal again, and extends it to *Jews* and *Gentiles, vid.* ver. 32. and shews, that it is not enough to justify them in any Action, that the Things they do is in itself lawful, unless we seek in it the Glory of God, and the Good of others.

Farther,

I CORINTHIANS.

TEXT.

23 All things are lawful for me, but all things are not expedient: all things are lawful for me, but all things edify not.
24 Let no man seek his own: but every man another's wealth.
25 Whatsoever is sold in the shambles, that eat, asking no question for conscience sake.
26 For the earth is the Lord's, and the fulness thereof.
27 If any of them that believe not, bid you to a feast, and ye be disposed to go; whatsoever is set before you, eat, asking no question for conscience sake.
28 But if any man say unto you, This is offered in sacrifice unto idols, eat not, for his sake that shewed it, and for conscience sake. For the earth is the Lord's, and the fulness thereof.
29 Conscience, I say, not thine own, but of the others: for why is my liberty judged of another man's conscience?
30 For, if I by grace be a partaker, why am I evil spoken of for that for which I give thanks?
31 Whether therefore ye eat or drink, or whatsoever ye do, do all to the glory of God.

PARAPHRASE.

Farther, supposing it lawful to eat Things offered to Idols; yet all Things that are lawful, are not expedient: Things that in themselves are lawful for me, may not tend to the Edification of others, and so may be fit to be forborn. No one must seek barely his own private, particular Interest alone; but let every one seek the Good of others also. Eat whatever is sold in the Shambles, without any Enquiry or Scruple, whether it had been offered to any Idol or no: For the Earth, and all therein, are the good Creatures of the true God, given by him to Men for their Use. If an Heathen invite you to an Entertainment, and you go, eat whatever is set before you, without making any Question or Scruple about it, whether it had been offered in Sacrifice or no: But if any one say to you, This was offered in Sacrifice to an Idol, eat it not, for his sake that mentioned it, and for Conscience-sake ʳ. Conscience, I say, not thine own (for thou knowest thy Liberty, and that an Idol is nothing) but the Conscience of the other: For why should I use my Liberty, so that another Man should in Conscience think I offended? And if I, with Thanksgiving, partake of what is lawful for me to eat, why do I order the Matter so, that I am ill spoken of for that which I bless God for? Whether therefore ye eat or drink, or whatever you do, let your Care and Aim be the Glory of God. Give no

23.

24.

25.

26.

27.

28.

29.

30.

31.

NOTES.

28 ʳ The Repetition of these Words, *The Earth is the Lord's, and the Fulness thereof*, does so manifestly disturb the Sense, that the *Syriac*, *Arabic*, Vulgar and *French* Translations, have omitted them, and are justified in it by the *Alexandrian*, and some other *Greek* Copies.

Offence

PARAPHRASE.

32. Offence to the *Jews*, by giving them occasion to think that Christians are permitted to worship Heathen Idols; nor to the *Gentiles*, by giving them occasion to think that you allow their Idolatry, by partaking of their Sacrifices; nor to weak Members of the Church of God, by drawing them, by your Example, to eat of Things offered to Idols, of the Lawfulness whereof they

33. are not fully satisfied: As I myself do, who abridge myself of many Conveniences of Life, to comply with the different Judgments of Men, and gain the good Opinion of others, that I may be instrumental to the Salvation of as many as is possible.

1. Imitate herein my Example, as I do that of our Lord Christ, who neglected himself for the Salvation of others[f].

TEXT.

32. Give none offence, neither to the Jews, nor to the Gentiles, nor to the church of God:

33. Even as I please all men in all things, not seeking mine own profit, but the profit of many, that they may be saved.

1. Be ye followers of me, even as I also am of Christ.

NOTES.

1 [f] Vid. *Rom.* XV. 3. This Verse seems to belong to the precedent, wherein he had proposed himself as an Example; and therefore this Verse should not be cut off from the former Chapter. In what St. *Paul* says in this and the preceding Verse, taken together, we may suppose he makes some Reflection on the false Apostle, whom many of the *Corinthians* followed as their Leader. At least it is for St. *Paul*'s Justification, that he proposes himself to be followed no farther than as he sought the Good of others, and not his own, and had Christ for his Pattern, *vid.* Chap. IV. 16.

I CORINTHIANS.

SECT. VII.

CHAP. XI. 2——16.

CONTENTS.

ST. *Paul* commends them for obferving the Orders he had left with them, and ufes Arguments to juftify the Rule he had given them, that Women fhould not pray or prophefy in their Affemblies uncovered; which it feems there was fome Contention about, and they had writ to him to be refolved in it.

TEXT.

2 NOW I praife you, brethren, that you remember me in all things, and keep the ordinances, as I delivered them to you.
3 But I would have you know, that the head of

PARAPHRASE.

2. I Commend you, Brethren, for remembering all my Orders, and for retaining thofe Rules I delivered to you, when I was with you.
3. But for your better underftanding what concerns Women ᵗ in your Affemblies, you are to

NOTES.

3 ᵗ This about Women feeming as difficult a Paffage as moft in St. *Paul*'s Epiftles, I crave leave to premife fome few Confiderations, which I hope may conduce to the clearing of it.

(1.) It is to be obferved, that it was the Cuftom for Women who appeared in public, to be vailed, *ver.* 13——16. Therefore it could be no Queftion at all, whether they ought to be vailed when they affifted at the Prayers and Praifes in the publick Affemblies; or if that were the Thing intended by the Apoftle, it had been much eafier, fhorter and plainer, for him to have faid, that Women fhould be covered in the Affemblies.

(2.) It is plain that this covering the Head in Women, is reftrained to fome particular Actions which they performed in the Affembly, expreffed by the Words, *Praying and Prophefying*, ver. 4, and 5. which, whatever they fignify, muft have the fame Meaning, when applied to the Women, in the 5th Verfe, that they have when applied to the Men, in the 4th Verfe.

It will poffibly be objected, If Women were to be vailed in the Affemblies, let thofe Actions be what they will, the Women joining in them were ftill to be vailed.

Anfw. This would be plainly fo, if their Interpretation were to be followed, who are of opinion, that by *Praying* and *Prophefying* here, was meant to be prefent in the Affembly, and joining with the Congregation in the Prayers that were made, or Hymns that were fung; or in hearing the Reading and Expofition of the Holy Scriptures there. But againft this, that the hearing of Preaching or Prophefying was never called *Preaching* or *Prophefying*, is fo unanfwerable an Objection, that I think there can be no Reply to it.

The Cafe, in fhort, feems to be this: The Men prayed and prophefied in the Affemblies, and did it with their Heads uncovered: The Women alfo fometimes prayed and prophefied too in the Affemblies; which when they did, though, during their performing that Action, they were

PARAPHRASE.	TEXT.
to take notice, that Christ is the Head to which every Man is subjected; and the Man is the Head	every man is Christ; and the head of the woman, is

NOTES.

were excused from being vailed, and might be bare-headed, or at least open-faced, as well as the Men. This was that which the Apostle restrains in them, and directs, that tho' they prayed or prophesied, they were still to remain vailed.

(3.) The next Thing to be considered, is, what is here to be understood by *Praying* and *Prophesying*. And that seems to me to be the performing of some particular publick Action in the Assembly by some one Person, which was for that Time peculiar to that Person, and whilst it lasted the rest of the Assembly silently assisted. For it cannot be supposed, that when the Apostle says, a Man praying or prophesying, that he means an Action performed in common by the whole Congregation; or if he did, what Pretence could that give the Woman to be unvailed more during the Performance of such an Action, than at any other Time? A Woman must be vailed in the Assembly; what Pretence then or Claim could it give her to be unvailed, that she joined with the rest of the Assembly, in the Prayer that some one Person made? Such a Praying as this could give no more Ground for her being unvailed, than her being in the Assembly could be thought a Reason for her being unvailed. The same may be said of Prophesying, when understood to signify a Woman's joining with the Congregation in singing the Praises of God. But if the Woman prayed as the Mouth of the Assembly, &c. then it was like she might think she might have the Privilege to be unvailed.

Praying and *Prophesying*, as has been shewn, signifying here the doing some peculiar Action in the Assembly, whilst the rest of the Congregation only assisted; let us, in the next Place, examine what that Action was. As to *Prophesying*, the Apostle in express Words tells us, *Ch.* XIV. 3, & 12. that it was speaking in the Assembly. The same is evident as to *Praying*; that the Apostle means by it praying publickly with an audible Voice in the Congregation, *vid. Ch.* XIV. 14——19.

(4.) It is to be observed that whether any one prayed or prophesied, they did it alone, the rest remaining silent, *Ch.* XIV. 27——33. So that even in these extraordinary Praises, which any one sung to God by the immediate Motion and Impulse of the Holy Ghost, which was one of the Actions called Prophesying, they sung alone. And indeed how could it be otherwise? For who could join with the Person so prophesying, in Things dictated to him alone by the Holy Ghost, which the others could not know, till the Person prophesying uttered them?

(5.) Prophesying, as St. *Paul* tells, *Chap.* XIV. 3. was speaking unto others to Edification, Exhortation and Comfort: But every Speaking to others to any of these Ends, was not Prophesying, but only then when such Speaking was a spiritual Gift, performed by the immediate and extraordinary Motion of the Holy Ghost, *vid. Ch.* XIV. 1, 12, 24, 30. For example, singing Praises to God was called Prophesying; but we see when *Saul* prophesied, the Spirit of God fell upon him, and he was turned into another Man, 1 *Sam.* X. 6. Nor do I think any Place in the New Testament can be produced, wherein Prophesying signifies bare reading of the Scripture, or any other Action performed without a supernatural Impulse and Assistance of the Spirit of God. This we are sure, that the Prophesying which St. *Paul* here speaks of, is one of the extraordinary Gifts given by the Spirit of God, *vid. Ch.* XII. 10. Now that the Spirit of God, and the Gift of Prophecy should be poured out upon Women as well as Men, in the Time of the Gospel, is plain from *Acts* II 17. and then where could be a fitter Place for them to utter their Prophecies in, than the Assemblies?

Mr. Mede Disc. 16. It is not unlikely, what one of the most learned and sagacious of our Interpreters of Scripture suggests upon this Place, viz. That Christian Women might, out of a Vanity incident to that Sex, propose to themselves, and affect an Imitation of the Priests and Prophetesses of the *Gentiles*, who had

I CORINTHIANS.

TEXT.
the man; and the head of Chriſt, is God.

PARAPHRASE.
Head to which every Woman is ſubjected; and that the Head or Superior to Chriſt him-

NOTES.

had their Faces uncovered when they uttered their Oracles, or officiated in their Sacrifices: But I cannot but wonder that that very acute Writer ſhould not ſee that the bare being in the Aſſembly could not give a Chriſtian Woman any Pretence to that Freedom. None of the *Bacchai* or *Pythiai* quitted their ordinary modeſt Guiſe, but when ſhe was, as the Poets expreſs it, *rapta* or *plena Deo*, poſſeſſed and hurried by the Spirit ſhe ſerved. And ſo, poſſibly, a Chriſtian Woman, when ſhe found the Spirit of God poured out upon her, as *Joel* expreſſes it, exciting her to pray or ſing Praiſes to God, or diſcover any Truth immediately revealed to her, might think it convenient, for her better uttering of it, to be uncovered, or, at leaſt, to be no more reſtrained in her Liberty of ſhewing herſelf, than the Female Prieſts of the Heathens were when they delivered their Oracles: But yet even in theſe Actions the Apoſtle forbids the Women to unvail themſelves.

St. *Paul*'s forbidding Women to ſpeak in the Aſſemblies, will, probably, ſeem a ſtrong Argument againſt this; but when well conſidered, will perhaps prove none. There be two Places wherein the Apoſtle forbids Women to ſpeak in the Church, 1 *Cor.* XIV. 34, 35. & 1 *Tim.* II. 11, 12. He that ſhall attentively read and compare theſe together, may obſerve that the Silence injoined the Woman is for a Mark of their Subjection to the Male Sex: And therefore what in the one is expreſſed by *keeping Silence, and not ſpeaking, but being under Obedience*, in the other is called, *being in Silence with all Subjection, not teaching nor uſurping Authority over the Man*. The Women in the Churches were not to aſſume the Perſonage of Doctors, or ſpeak there as Teachers; this carried with it the Appearance of Superiority, and was forbidden. Nay, they were not ſo much as to aſk Queſtions there, or to enter into any Sort of Conference. This ſhews a Kind of Equality, and was alſo forbidden: But yet, tho' they were not to ſpeak in the Church in their own Names, or as if they were raiſed by the Franchiſes of Chriſtianity, to ſuch an Equality with the Men, that where Knowledge or Preſumption of their own Abilities emboldened them to it, they might take upon them to be Teachers and Inſtructors of the Congregation, or might at leaſt enter into Queſtionings and Debates there; this would have had too great an Air of ſtanding upon even Ground with the Men, and would not have well comported with the Subordination of the Sex: But yet this Subordination which God, for Order's ſake, had inſtituted in the World, hindered not, but that by the ſupernatural Gifts of the Spirit, he might make uſe of the weaker Sex, to any extraordinary Function, whenever he thought fit, as well as he did of the Men. But yet, when they thus either prayed or propheſied by the Motion and Impulſe of the Holy Ghoſt, Care was taken that whilſt they were obeying God, who was pleaſed by his Spirit to ſet them a ſpeaking, the Subjection of their Sex ſhould not be forgotten, but owned and preſerved by their being covered. The Chriſtian Religion was not to give Offence, by any Appearance or Suſpicion that it took away the Subordination of the Sexes, and ſet the Women at liberty from their natural Subjection to the Man. And therefore we ſee, that in both theſe Caſes, the Aim was to maintain and ſecure the confeſſed Superiority and Dominion of the Men, and not permit it to be invaded ſo much as in appearance. Hence the Arguments in the one Caſe for Covering, and in the other for Silence, are all drawn from the natural Superiority of the Man, and the Subjection of the Woman. In the one, the Woman, without an extraordinary Call, was to keep ſilent, as a Mark of her Subjection; in the other, where ſhe was to ſpeak by an extraordinary Call and Commiſſion from God, ſhe was yet to continue the Profeſſion of her Subjection in keeping herſelf covered. Here, by the way, it is to be obſerved, that there was extraordinary Praying to God by the Impulſe of the Spirit, as well as Speaking unto Men for their Edification, Exhortation and Comfort: *Vid.* Chap. XIV. 15. *Rom.* VIII. 26. *Jude* 20. Theſe Things being premiſed, let us follow the Thread of St *Paul*'s Diſcourſe.

P   ſelf,

I CORINTHIANS.

Chap. XI.

PARAPHRASE.

4. self, is God. Every Man that prayeth or prophesieth, *i. e.* by the Gift of the Spirit of God, speaketh in the Church for the edifying, exhorting, and comforting of the Congregation, having his Head covered, dishonoureth Christ his Head, by appearing in a Garb not becoming the Authority and Dominion which God, thro' Christ, has given him over all the Things of this World; the covering of the Head being a Mark of Sub-
5. jection. But, on the contrary, a Woman praying or prophesying in the Church with her Head uncovered, dishonoureth the Man, who is her Head, by appearing in a Garb that disowns her Subjection to him: For to appear bare-headed in publick, is all one as to have her Hair cut off; which is the Garb and Dress of the other
6. Sex, and not of a Woman. If therefore it be unsuitable to the Female Sex, to have their Hair shorn or shaved off, let her, for the same Reason,
7. be covered. A Man indeed ought not to be vailed, because he is the Image and Representative of God in his Dominion over the rest of the World, which is one Part of the Glory of
8. God: But the Woman, who was made out of the Man, made for him, and in Subjection to
9. him, is Matter of Glory to the Man. But the Man not being made out of the Woman, nor for her, but the Woman made out of, and for the
10. Man, she ought, for this Reason, to have a Vail on her Head, in token of her Subjection, be-
11. cause of the Angels ⁿ. Nevertheless, the Sexes have not a Being one without the other; nei-

TEXT.

4 Every man praying or prophesying, having his head covered, dishonoureth his head.

5 But every woman that prayeth, or prophesieth with her head uncovered, dishonoureth her head: for that is even all one as if she were shaven.

6 For if the woman be not covered, let her also be shorn: but if it be a shame for a woman to be shorn or shaven, let her be covered.

7 For a man indeed ought not to cover his head, forasmuch as he is the image and glory of God: but the woman is the glory of the man.

8 For the man is not of the woman, but the woman of the man.

9 Neither was the man created for the woman, but the woman for the man.

10 For this cause ought the woman to have power on her head, because of the angels.

11 Nevertheless, neither is the man without the wo-

NOTES.

10 "What the Meaning of these Words is, I confess I do not understand.

ther

I CORINTHIANS.

Chap. XI.

TEXT.

man, neither the woman without the man, in the Lord.

12 For as the woman is of the man, even so is the man also by the woman: but all things of God.

13 Judge in yourselves: is it comely that a woman pray unto God uncovered?

14 Doth not even nature itself teach you, that if a man have long hair, it is a shame unto him?

15 But if a woman have long hair, it is a glory to her: for her hair is given her for a covering.

16 But if any man seem to be contentious, we have no such custom, neither the churches of God.

PARAPHRASE.

ther the Man without the Woman, or the Woman without the Man; the Lord so ordering it. For as the first Woman was made out of the Man, so the Race of Men ever since is continued and propagated by the Female Sex: But they and all other Things had their Being and Original from God. Be you yourselves Judges, whether it be decent for a Woman to make a Prayer to God in the Church uncovered. Does not even Nature, that has made, and would have the Distinction of Sexes preserved, teach you, that if a Man wear his Hair long, and dressed up after the manner of Women, it is misbecoming and dishonourable to him? But to a Woman, if she be curious about her Hair, in having it long, and dressing herself with it, it is a Grace and Commendation, since her Hair is given her for a Covering. But if any shew himself to be a Lover of Contention [w], we the Apostles have no such Custom, nor any of the Churches of God.

12.

13.

14.

15.

16.

NOTES.

16 [w] Why may not this *any one* be understood of the false Apostle here glanced at?

P 2 SECT.

SECT. VIII.

CHAP. XI. 17——34.

CONTENTS.

ONE may observe, from several Passages in this Epistle, that several *Judaical* Customs were crept into the *Corinthian* Church. This Church being of St. *Paul*'s own planting, who spent two Years at *Corinth* in forming it; it is evident these Abuses had their Rise from some other Teacher, who came to them after his leaving them, which was about five Years before his writing this Epistle. These Disorders therefore may with reason be ascribed to the Head of the Faction that opposed St. *Paul*, who, as has been remarked, was a *Jew*, and probably *judaized*. And that, 'tis like, was the Foundation of the great Opposition between him and St. *Paul*, and the Reason why St. *Paul* labours so earnestly to destroy his Credit amongst the *Corinthians*; this Sort of Men being very busy, very troublesome, and very dangerous to the Gospel, as may be seen in other of St. *Paul*'s Epistles, particularly that to the *Galatians*.

The celebrating the Passover amongst the *Jews*, was plainly the eating of a Meal distinguished from other ordinary Meals by several peculiar Ceremonies. Two of these Ceremonies were, eating of Bread solemnly broken, and drinking a Cup of Wine, called the Cup of Blessing. These two our Saviour transferred into the Christian Church, to be used in their Assemblies for a Commemoration of his Death and Sufferings. In celebrating this Institution of our Saviour, the *Judaizing Corinthians* followed the *Jewish* Custom of eating their Passover: They eat the Lord's Supper as a Part of their Meal, bringing their Provisions into the Assembly; where they eat, divided into distinct Companies, some feasting to Excess, whilst others, ill provided, were in want. This eating thus in the public Assembly, and mixing the Lord's Supper with their ordinary Meal, as a Part of it, with other Disorders and Indecencies accompanying it, is the Matter of this Section. These Innovations, he tells them here, he as much blames, as in the Beginning of this Chapter he commends them, for keeping to his Directions in some other Things.

Tho'

I CORINTHIANS.

Chap. XI.

TEXT.

17 NOW in this that I declare unto you, I praise you not, that ye come together not for the better, but for the worse.
18 For first of all, when ye come together in the church, I hear that there be divisions among you; and I partly believe it.
19 For there must be also heresies among you, that they which are approved, may be made manifest among you.
20 When ye come together therefore into one place, this is not to eat the Lord's supper.
21 For in eating every one taketh before other, his own supper: and one is hungry, and another is drunken.
22 What, have ye not houses to eat and to drink in?

PARAPHRASE.

THO' what I said to you, concerning Women's Behaviour in the Church, was not without Commendation of you; yet this that I am now going to speak to you of, is without praising you, because you so order your Meetings in your Assemblies, that they are not to your Advantage, but Harm. For first I hear, that when you come together in the Church, you fall into Parties; and I partly believe it: Because there must be Divisions and Factions amongst you, that those who stand firm upon Trial, may be made manifest amongst you. You come together, it's true, in one Place, and there you eat; but yet this makes it not to be the Eating of the Lord's Supper. For in eating you eat not together, but every one takes his own Supper, one before another[x]. Have ye not Houses to eat and drink in at home, for satisfying your Hunger and Thirst? Or have ye

17.

18.

19.

20.

21.

22.

NOTES.

21 [x] To understand this, we must observe,

(1.) That they had sometimes Meetings on purpose only for eating the Lord's Supper, *ver.* 33.

(2.) That to those Meetings they brought their own Supper, *ver.* 21.

(3.) That tho' every one's Supper were brought into the common Assembly, yet it was not to eat in common, but every one fell to his own Supper apart, as soon as he and his Supper were there ready for one another, without staying for the rest of the Company, or communicating with them in eating, *ver.* 21, 33.

In this St. *Paul* blames three Things especially;

1*st*. That they eat their common Food in the Assembly, which was to be eaten at home in their Houses, *ver.* 22, 34.

2*dly*. That tho' they eat in the common Meeting-place, yet they eat separately every one his own Supper apart. So that the Plenty and Excess of some, shamed the Want and Penury of others, *ver.* 22. Hereby also the Divisions amongst them were kept up, *ver.* 18. they being as so many separated and divided Societies; not as one united Body of Christians commemorating their common Head, as they should have been in celebrating the Lord's Supper, *Chap* X. 16, 17.

3*dly*. That they mixed the Lord's Supper with their own, eating it as a Part of their ordinary Meal; where they made not that Discrimination between it and their common Food, as they should have done, *ver.* 29.

4

a Con-

I CORINTHIANS.

Chap. XI.

PARAPHRASE.

23. a Contempt for the Church of God, and take a Pleasure to put those out of Countenance, who have not wherewithal to feast there as you do? What is it I said to you, that I praise you ʸ for retaining what I delivered to you? In this Occasion indeed I praise you not for it. For what I received concerning this Institution from the Lord himself, that I delivered unto you when I was with you; and it was this,

24. *viz.* That the Lord Jesus, in the Night wherein he was betrayed, took Bread: And having given Thanks brake it, and said, Take, eat, this is my Body, which is broken for you; this

25. do in remembrance of me. So likewise he took the Cup also when he had supped, saying, This Cup is the New Testament in my Blood: This do ye, as often as ye do it, in re-

26. membrance of me. So that the eating of this Bread, and the drinking of this Cup of the Lord's Supper, is not to satisfy Hunger and Thirst, but to shew forth the Lord's Death

27. till he comes. Insomuch, that he who eats this Bread, and drinks this Cup of the Lord, in an unworthy manner ᶻ, not suitable to that End, shall be guilty of a Misuse of the

TEXT.

Or despise ye the church of God, and shame them that have not? what shall I say to you? shall I praise you in this? I praise you not.

23 For I have received of the Lord, that which also I delivered unto you, that the Lord Jesus, the same night in which he was betrayed, took bread:

24 And when he had given thanks, he brake it, and said, Take, eat; this is my body, which is broken for you: this do in remembrance of me.

25 After the same manner also he took the cup, when he had supped, saying, This cup is the new testament in my blood: this do ye, as oft as ye drink it, in remembrance of me.

26 For as often as ye eat this bread, and drink this cup, ye do shew the Lord's death till he come.

27 Wherefore, whosoever shall eat this bread, and drink this cup of the Lord unworthily, shall be guilty of the body and blood of the Lord.

NOTES.

22 ʸ He here plainly refers to what he had said to them, *ver.* 2. where he praised them for remembring him in all Things, and for retaining τὰς παραδόσεις καθὼς παρέδωκα, what he had delivered to them. This Commendation he here retracts; for in this Matter of eating the Lord's Supper, they did not retain ὃ παρέδωκα, *ver.* 23. what he had *delivered* to them, which therefore in the immediately following Words he repeats to them again.

27 ᶻ Ἀναξίως, *unworthily.* Our Saviour, in the Institution of the Lord's Supper, tells the Apostles, that the Bread and the Cup were sacramentally his Body and Blood, and that they were to be eaten and drank in remembrance of him; which, as St. *Paul* interprets it, *ver.* 26. was to shew forth his Death till he came. Whoever therefore eat and drank them, so as not solemnly to shew forth his Death, followed not Christ's Institution, but used them *unworthily,* i. e. not to the End to which they were instituted. This makes St. *Paul* tell them, *ver.* 20. that their coming together to eat it as they did, *viz.* the Sacramental Bread and Wine promiscuously with their other Food, as a Part of their Meal, and that tho' in the same Place, yet not all together at one Time and in one Company, was not the Eating of the Lord's Supper.

Body

I CORINTHIANS.

Chap. XI.

TEXT.	PARAPHRASE.
28 But let a man examine himself, and so let him eat of that bread, and drink of that cup.	Body and Blood of the Lord ᵃ. By this Institution therefore of Christ, let a man examine himself ᵇ; and according to that ᶜ, let 28.

NOTES.

ᵃ Ἔνοχος ἔσται, shall be liable to the Punishment due to one who makes a wrong Use of the Sacramental Body and Blood of Christ in the Lord's Supper. What that Punishment was, *vid. ver.* 30.

ᵇ 28 "St. *Paul*, as we have observed, tells the *Corinthians*, ver. 20. that to eat it after the manner they did, was not to eat the Lord's Supper. He tells them also, *ver.* 29. that to eat it without a due, direct and immediate Regard had to the Lord's Body (for so he calls the Sacramental Bread and Wine, as our Saviour did in the Institution) by separating the Bread and Wine from the common Use of Eating and Drinking for Hunger and Thirst, was to eat unworthily. To remedy their Disorders herein, he sets before them Christ's own Institution of this ᶜacrament; that in it they might see the Manner and End of its Institution, and by that every one might examine his own Comportment herein, whether it were conformable to that Institution, and suited to that End. In the Account he gives of Christ's Institution, we may observe that he particularly remarks to them, that this Eating and Drinking was no Part of common Eating and Drinking for Hunger and Thirst; but was instituted in a very solemn Manner, after they had supped, and for another End, *viz.* to represent Christ's Body and Blood, and to be eaten and drank in remembrance of him: Or, as St. *Paul* expounds it, to shew forth his Death. Another Thing which they might observe in the Institution, was, that this was done by all who were present, united together in one Company at the same Time. All which put together, shews us what the Examination here proposed, is. For the Design of the Apostle here being to reform what he found fault with, in their celebrating the Lord's Supper, 'tis by that alone we must understand the Directions he gives them about it, if we will suppose he talked pertinently to this captious and touchy People, whom he was very desirous to reduce from the Irregularities they were run into in this Matter, as well as several others. And if the Account of Christ's Institution be not for their examining their Carriage by it, and adjusting it to it, to what Purpose is it here? The Examination therefore proposed, was no other but an Examination of their Manner of eating the Lord's Supper by Christ's Institution, to see how their Behaviour herein comported with the Institution, and the End for which it was instituted. Which farther appears to be so, by the Punishment annexed to their Miscarriages herein; which was, Infirmities, Sickness, and temporal Death, with which God chastened them, that they might not be condemned with the unbelieving World, *ver.* 30, 32. For if the Unworthiness here spoke of were either Unbelief, or any of those Sins which are usually made the Matter of Examination, 'tis to be presumed the Apostle would not wholly have passed them over in Silence: This, at least, is certain, that the Punishment of these Sins is infinitely greater than that which God here inflicts on unworthy Receivers, whereby they who are guilty of them received the Sacrament or no.

ᶜ Καὶ οὕτως. These Words, as to the Letter, are rightly translated *and so*. But that Translation, I imagine, leaves generally a wrong Sense of the Place in the Mind of an *English* Reader: For in ordinary Speaking, these Words, *Let a Man examine, and so let him eat*, are understood to import the same with these, *Let a Man examine, and then let him eat*; as if they signified no more, but that Examination should precede, and Eating follow; which I take to be quite different from the Meaning of the Apostle here, whose Sense the whole Design of the Context shews to be this: *I here set before you the Institution of Christ, by that let a Man examine his Carriage*, καὶ οὕτως, *and according to that let him eat*; let him conform the Manner of his eating to that.

him

Chap. XI.

PARAPHRASE.

29. him eat of this Bread, and drink of this Cup. For he who eats and drinks after an unworthy manner, without a due Respect had to the Lord's Body, in a discriminating ^{d} and purely sacramental Use of the Bread and Wine that represents it, draws Punishment ^{e} on himself
30. by so doing. And hence it is many among you are weak and sick, and a good Number
31. are gone to their Graves. But if we would discriminate ^{f} ourselves, *i. e.* by our discriminating Use of the Lord's Supper, we should
32. not be judged, *i. e.* ^{g} punished by God. But being punished by the Lord, we are corrected ^{h}, that we may not be condemned hereafter with the unbelieving World. Wherefore

TEXT.

For he that eateth and 29 drinketh unworthily, eateth and drinketh damnation to himself, not discerning the Lord's body.

For this cause many are 30 weak and sickly among you, and many sleep.

For if we would judge 31 ourselves, we should not be judged.

But when we are judg- 32 ed, we are chastened of the Lord, that we should not be condemned with the world.

NOTES.

29 ^{d} Μὴ διακρίνων, *not discriminating*, not putting a Difference between the Sacramental Bread and Wine (which St. *Paul*, with our Saviour, calls Christ's Body) and other Bread and Wine, in the solemn and separate Use of them. The *Corinthians*, as has been remarked, eat the Lord's Supper in, and with their own ordinary Supper, whereby it came not to be sufficiently distinguished (as became a religious and Christian Observance so solemnly instituted) from common Eating for bodily Refreshment, nor from the *Jewish* Paschal Supper, and the Bread broken, and the Cup of Blessing used in that; nor did it, in this Way of eating it, in separate Companies, as it were in private Families, shew forth the Lord's Death, as it was designed to do by the Concurrence and Communion of the whole Assembly of Christians, jointly united in the partaking of Bread and Wine in a Way peculiar to them with reference solely to Jesus Christ. This was that, as appears by this Place, which St. *Paul*, as we have already explained, calls *eating unworthily*.

^{e} *Damnation*, by which our Translation renders κρίμα, is vulgarly taken for eternal Damnation in the other World; whereas κρίμα here signifies Punishment of another Nature, as appears by *ver.* 30, 32.

31 ^{f} Διακρίνειν does no where, that I know, signify *to judge*, as it is here translated, but always signifies to *distinguish* or *discriminate*; and in this Place has the same Signification, and means the same Thing, that it does *ver.* 29. He is little versed in St. *Paul's* Writings, who has not observed how apt he is to repeat the same Word he had used before to the same Purpose, though in a different, and sometimes in a pretty hard Construction; as here he applies διακρίνειν, to the Persons discriminating, as in the 29th Verse, to the Thing to be discriminated, though in both Places it be put to denote the same Action.

^{g} Ἐκρινόμεθα here signifies the same that κρίμα does, *ver* 19.

32 ^{h} Παιδευόμεθα properly signifies to be corrected, as Scholars are by their Master, for their good.

my

I CORINTHIANS.

TEXT.	PARAPHRASE.	Ch. XII.

33 Wherefore, my brethren, when ye come together, to eat, tarry one for another.

33. my Brethren, when you have a Meeting for celebrating the Lord's Supper, stay for one another, that you may eat it all together, as Partakers all in common of the Lord's Table, without Division or Distinction. But if any one be hungry, let him eat at home to satisfy his Hunger, that so the Disorder in these Meetings may not draw on you the Punishment above-mentioned. What else remains to be rectified in this Matter, I will set in order when I come.

34 And if any man hunger, let him eat at home; that ye come not together unto condemnation. And the rest will I set in order when I come.

SECT. IX.

CHAP. XII. 1.——XIV. 40.

CONTENTS.

THE *Corinthians* seem to have enquired of St. *Paul*, What Order of Precedency and Preference Men were to have in their Assemblies, in regard of their spiritual Gifts? Nay, if we may guess by his Answer, the Question they seem more particularly to have proposed, was, Whether those who had the Gift of Tongues, ought not to take place, and speak first, and be first heard in their Meetings? Concerning this there seems to have been some Strife, Maligning and Disorder amongst them, as may be collected from *Ch.* XII. 21—25. and XIII. 45. and XIV. 40.

To this St. *Paul* answers, in these three Chapters, as followeth:

1. That they had all been Heathen Idolaters, and so being Deniers of Christ, were in that State none of them *Spiritual:* But that now being Christians, and owning Jesus to be the Lord, (which could not be done without the Spirit of God) they were all πνευματικοί, *Spiritual;* and so there was no reason for one to undervalue another, as if he were not Spiritual as well as himself, *Ch.* XII. 1——3.

2. That

Ch. XII. 2. That tho' there be Diversity of Gifts, yet they are all by the same Spirit, from the same Lord, and the same God, working them all in every one, according to his good Pleasure. So that in this Respect also there is no Difference or Precedency; no Occasion for any one's being puffed up, or affecting Priority, upon account of his Gifts, *Chap.* XII. 4—11.

3. That the Diversity of Gifts is for the Use and Benefit of the Church, which is Christ's Body; wherein the Members (as in the natural Body) of meaner Functions, are as much Parts, and as necessary in their Use to the Good of the Whole, and therefore to be honoured as much as any other. The Union they have as Members in the same Body, makes them all equally share in one another's Good and Evil; gives them a mutual Esteem and Concern one for another, and leaves no room for Contests or Divisions amongst them about their Gifts, or the Honour and Place due to them upon that Account, *Chap.* XII. 12——31.

4. That tho' Gifts have their Excellency and Use, and those who have them may be zealous in the Use of them; yet the true and sure Way for a Man to get an Excellency and Preference above others, is the enlarging himself in Charity, and excelling in that; without which a Christian, with all his spiritual Gifts, is nothing.

5. In the Comparison of Spiritual Gifts, he gives those the Precedency which edify most, and, in particular, prefers Prophesying to Tongues, *Chap.* XIV. 1——40.

SECT. IX. N. 1.

CHAP. XII. 1——3.

CONTENTS.

TEXT.	PARAPHRASE.
1 NOW concerning spiritual gifts, brethren, I would not have you ignorant. 2 Ye know that ye were Gentiles, carried away unto these dumb idols, even as ye were led. 3 Wherefore I give you to understand, that no man speaking by the Spirit of God, calleth Jesus accursed: and that no man can say that Jesus is the Lord, but by the Holy Ghost.	1. AS to spiritual Men, or Men assisted and acted by the Spirit ^{i}, I shall inform you, for I would not have you be ignorant. 2. You yourselves know that you were Heathens, engaged in the Worship of Stocks and Stones, dumb, senseless Idols, by those who were then your Leaders. 3. Whereupon let me tell you, that no one who opposes Jesus Christ, or his Religion, has the Spirit of God ^{k}. And whoever is brought to own Jesus to be the Messiah, the Lord ^{l}, does it by the Holy Ghost. And therefore upon account of having the Spirit, you can none of you lay any claim to Superiority; or have any pretence to slight any of your Brethren, as not having the Spirit of God as well as you. For all that own our Lord Jesus Christ, and believe in him, do it by the Spirit of God, *i. e.* can do it upon no other Ground, but Revelation coming from the Spirit of God.

NOTES.

^{i} 1 Πνευματικῶν, *Spiritual*. We are warranted by a like Use of the Word in several Places of St. *Paul*'s Epistles, as *Ch.* II. 15. and XIV. 37. of this Epistle, and *Gal.* VI. 1. to take it here in the Masculine Gender, standing for Persons, and not Gifts. And the Context obliges us to understand it so: For if we will have it stand for Gifts, and not Persons, the Sense and Coherence of these three first Verses will be very hard to be made out. Besides, there is Evidence enough, in several Parts of it, that the Subject of St. *Paul*'s Discourse here is πνευματικοί, Persons endowed with spiritual Gifts, contending for Precedency in consideration of their Gifts. See *ver.* 13, &c. of this Chapter: And to what Purpose else, says he, *Chap.* XIV. 5. *Greater is he that prophesieth, than he that speaketh with Tongues?*

^{k} 3 This is spoken against the *Jews*, who pretended to the Holy Ghost, and yet spoke against *Jesus* Christ; and denied that the Holy Ghost was ever given to the *Gentiles*, vid. *Acts* X. 45. Whether their Judaizing false Apostle were at all glanced at in this, may be considered.

^{l} *Lord.* What is meant by Lord, see *Note*, Chap. VIII. 5.

SECT.

I CORINTHIANS.
SECT. IX. N. 2.
CHAP. XII. 4——11.

CONTENTS.

ANother Consideration which St. *Paul* offers against any Contention for Superiority, or Pretence to Precedency, upon account of any spiritual Gift, is, that those distinct Gifts are all of one and the same Spirit, by the same Lord, wrought in every one by God alone, and all for the Profit of the Church.

PARAPHRASE.   TEXT.

4. BE not mistaken by the Diversity of Gifts; for though there be Diversity of Gifts amongst Christians, yet there is no Diversity of Spirits, they all come from one and the same
5. Spirit. Though there be Diversities of Offices in the Church, yet all the Officers ᵐ have but
6. one Lord. And though there be various Influxes whereby Christians are enabled to do extraordinary Things ⁿ, yet it is the same God that works ᵒ all these extraordinary Gifts in every
7. one that has them. But the Way or Gift wherein every one, who has the Spirit, is to shew it is given him not for his private Advantage or Honour ᵖ, but for the Good and

4. NOW there are diversities of gifts, but the same Spirit.

5. And there are differences of administrations, but the same Lord.

6. And there are diversities of operations, but it is the same God, which worketh all in all.

7. But the manifestation of the Spirit is given to every man to profit withal.

NOTES.

5 ᵐ These different Offices are reckoned up, *ver.* 28, &c.

6 ⁿ What these ἐνεργήματα were, see *ver.* 8 —— 11.

ᵒ They were very properly called ἐνεργήματα *In Workings*, because they were above all human Power: Men of themselves could do nothing of them at all, but it was God, as the Apostle tells us here, who in these extraordinary Gifts of the Holy Ghost, did all that was done: It was the Effect of his immediate Operation, as St. *Paul* assures us in that parallel Place, *Phil.* II. 13. In which Chapter, *ver.* 3, and 14. we find that the *Philippians* stood a little in need of the same Advice which St. *Paul* so at large presses here upon the *Corinthians*.

7 ᵖ Vid. *Rom.* XII. 3 —— 8.

I CORINTHIANS.

Ch. XII.

TEXT.	PARAPHRASE.	
8 For to one is given by the Spirit the word of wisdom; to another the word of knowledge by the same Spirit;	Advantages of the Church. For instance, to one is given by the Spirit, the Word of Wisdom ^q, or the Revelation of the Gospel of Jesus Christ, in the full Latitude of it, such as was given to the Apostles; to another by the same Spirit, the Knowledge ^r of the true Sense and true Meaning of the Holy Scriptures of the Old Testament, for the Explaining and Confirmation of the Gospel:	8.
9 To another faith by the same Spirit; to another the gifts of healing by the same Spirit;	To another by the same Spirit, is given an undoubting Persuasion ^s and stedfast Confidence of performing what he is going about; to another the Gift of curing Diseases, by the same Spirit:	9.
10 To another the working of miracles; to another prophecy; to another discerning of spirits; to another divers kinds of tongues; to another the interpretation of tongues.	To another the Working of Miracles; to another Prophecy ^t; to another the Discerning by what Spirit Man did any extraordinary Operation; to another Diversity of Languages; to another the Interpretation of Languages.	10.
11 But all these worketh that one and the self-same Spirit, dividing to every man severally as he will.	All which Gifts are wrought in Believers by one and the same Spirit, distributing to every one in particular as he thinks fit.	11.

NOTES.

8 ^q Σοφία: The Doctrine of the Gospel is more than once, in the Beginning of this Epistle, called the *Wisdom of God*.

^r Γνῶσις is used by St. *Paul* for such a *Knowledge* of the Law and the Prophets.

9 ^s In this Sense πίστις, *Faith*, is sometimes taken in the New Testament; particularly *Chap.* XIII. 2. It is difficult, I confess, to define the precise Meaning of each Word which the Apostle uses in the 8th, 9th, and 10th Verses here. But if the Order which St. *Paul* observes, in enumerating by 1st, 2d, 3d, the three first Officers set down, *ver.* 28. viz. *First*, *Apostle*; *Secondly*, *Prophets*; *Thirdly*, *Teachers*; have any Relation, or may give any Light to these three Gifts which are set down in the first Place here, *viz. Wisdom, Knowledge,* and *Faith,* we may then properly understand by σοφία, *Wisdom*, the whole Doctrine of the Gospel, as communicated to the Apostles: By γνῶσις, *Knowledge*, the Gifts of Understanding the mystical Sense of the Law and the Prophets; and by πίστις, *Faith*, the Assurance and Confidence in delivering and confirming the Doctrine of the Gospel, which became διδασκαλία, *Doctors* or *Teachers*. This at least, I think, may be presumed, that since σοφία and γνῶσις have λόγος joined to them, and it is said *the Word of Wisdom,* and *the Word of Knowledge,* Wisdom and Knowledge here signify such Gifts of the Mind as are to be employed in Preaching.

10 ^t Prophecy comprehends these three Things; Prediction, Singing by the Dictate of the Spirit, and understanding and explaining the mysterious hidden Sense of Scripture by an immediate Illumination and Motion of the Spirit, as we have already shewn: And that the Prophesying here spoken of, was by immediate Revelation, *vid.* Chap. XIV. 29 —— 31.

SECT.

I CORINTHIANS.

SECT. IX. N. 3.

CHAP. XII. 12——31.

CONTENTS.

FROM the necessarily different Functions in the Body, and the strict Union, nevertheless, of the Members adapted to those different Functions, in a mutual Sympathy and Concern one for another, St. *Paul* here farther shews, that there ought not to be any Strife or Division amongst them about Precedency and Preference, upon account of their distinct Gifts.

PARAPHRASE.

12. FOR as the Body being but one, hath many Members, and all the Members of the Body, tho' many, yet make but one Body; so is Christ, in respect of his mystical Body the
13. Church. For by one Spirit we are all baptized into one Church, and are thereby made one Body, without any Pre-eminence to the *Jew* [u] above the *Gentile*; to the Free above the Bond-man: And the Blood of Christ, which we all partake of in the Lord's Supper, makes us all have one Life, one Spirit; as the same Blood, diffused through the whole Body, communicates the same Life and Spirit to all the
14. Members. For the Body is not one sole Member, but consists of many Members, all vitally united in one common Sympathy and Use-

TEXT.

FOR as the body is 12 one, and hath many members, and all the members of that one body, being many, are one body; so also is Christ.

For by one Spirit are 13 we all baptized into one body, whether we be Jews or Gentiles, whether we be bond or free; and have been all made to drink into one Spirit.

For the body is not one 14 member, but many.

NOTES.

13 [u] The naming of the *Jews* here with *Gentiles*, and setting both on the same Level when converted to Christianity, may probably be done here by St. *Paul* with reference to the false Apostle, who was a *Jew*, and seems to have claimed some Pre-eminence as due to him upon that Account: Whereas, among the Members of Christ, which all make but one Body, there is no Superiority or other Distinction, but as, by the several Gifts bestowed on them by God, they contribute more or less to the Edification of the Church.

I CORINTHIANS. Ch. XII.

TEXT.	PARAPHRASE.

15 If the foot shall say, Because I am not the hand, I am not of the body; is it therefore not of the body?

16 And if the ear shall say, Because I am not the eye, I am not of the body; is it therefore not of the body?

17 If the whole body were an eye, where were the hearing? If the whole were hearing, where were the smelling?

18 But now hath God set the members, every one of them in the body, as it hath pleased him.

19 And if they were all one member, where were the body?

20 But now are they many members, yet but one body.

21 And the eye cannot say unto the hand, I have no need of thee: nor again, the head to the feet, I have no need of you.

22 Nay, much more those members of the body which seem to be more feeble are necessary.

23 And those members of the body, which we think to be less honourable, upon these we bestow more abundant honour, and our uncomely parts have more abundant comeliness.

24 For our comely parts have no need: but God hath tempered the body together, having given more abundant honour to that part which lacked:

25 That there should be no schism in the body: but that the members should

15. fulness. If any one have not that Function or Dignity in the Church which he desires, he
16. must not therefore declare that he is not of the Church; he does not thereby cease to be a
17. Member of the Church. There is as much need of several and distinct Gifts and Functions in the Church, as there is of different Senses and Members in the Body; and the meanest and least honourable would be missed if it were wanting, and the whole Body would
18. suffer by it. Accordingly, God hath fitted several Persons, as it were so many distinct Members, to several Offices and Functions in the Church, by proper and peculiar Gifts and Abilities, which he has bestowed on them according to his good Pleasure. But if all were but
19. one Member, what would become of the Body? There would be no such Thing as a human Body; no more could the Church be edified, and framed into a growing, lasting Society, if the Gifts of the Spirit were all reduced to
20. one. But now, by the various Gifts of the Spirit bestowed on its several Members, it is as a well organized Body, wherein the most eminent Member cannot despise the meanest.
21. The Eye cannot say to the Hand, I have no need of thee; nor the Head to the Feet, I have
22. no need of you. It is so far from being so, that the Parts of the Body that seem in themselves weak, are nevertheless of absolute Necessity.
23. And those Parts which are thought least honourable, we take care always to cover with the more Respect; and our least graceful Parts have thereby a more studied and adventitious Comeliness. For our comely Parts have no
24. need of any borrowed Helps or Ornaments.
25. But God hath contrived the Symmetry of the

PARAPHRASE.

26. the Body, that he hath added Honour to those Parts that might seem naturally to want it; that there might be no Disunion, no Schism in the Body, but that the Members should have the same Care and Concern one for another, and all equally partake and share in the Harm or Honour that is done to any one of them in particular.
27. Now in like manner you are, by your particular Gifts, each of you in his peculiar Station and Aptitude, Members of the Body of Christ,
28. which is the Church; wherein God hath set first some Apostles, secondly Prophets, thirdly Teachers, next Workers of Miracles, then those who have the Gifts of Healing, Helpers [w], Governors [x], and such as are able to speak Diversity of Tongues.
29. Are all Apostles? are all Prophets? are all Teachers? are all Workers of
30. Miracles? Have all the Gift of Healing? do all speak Diversity of Tongues? are all Inter-
31. preters of Tongues? But ye contest one with another, whose particular Gift is best, and most preferable [y]; but I will shew you a more excellent Way, viz. Mutual Good-will, Affection, and Charity.

TEXT.

have the same care one for another.

26. And whether one member suffer, all the members suffer with it; or one member be honoured, all the members rejoice with it.
27. Now ye are the body of Christ, and members in particular.
28. And God hath set some in the church, first apostles, secondarily prophets, thirdly teachers, after that miracles, then gifts of healings, helps, governments, diversities of tongues.
29. Are all apostles? are all prophets? are all teachers? are all workers of miracles?
30. Have all the gifts of healing? do all speak with tongues? do all interpret?
31. But covet earnestly the best gifts: And yet shew I unto you a more excellent way.

SECT.

NOTES.

28 [w] Ἀντιλήψεις, Helps, Dr. Lightfoot takes to be those who accompanied the Apostles, were sent up and down by them in the Service of the Gospel, and baptized those that were converted by them.

[x] Κυβερνήσεις, to be the same with discerning of Spirits, ver. 10.

31 [y] That this is the Apostle's Meaning here, is plain, in that there was an Emulation amongst them, and a Strife for Precedency, on account of the several Gifts they had, (as we have already observed from several Passages in this Section) which made them in their Assemblies desire to be heard first. This was the Fault the Apostle was here correcting: and 'tis not likely he should exhort them all promiscuously to seek the principal and most eminent Gifts at the End of a Discourse, wherein he had been demonstrating to them, by the Example of the human Body, that there ought to be Diversities of Gifts and Functions in the Church, but that there ought to be no Schism, Emulation, or Contest among them, upon the Account of the Exercise of those Gifts. That they were all useful in their Places, and no Member was at all

to

I CORINTHIANS.

SECT. IX. N. 4.

CHAP. XIII. 1——13.

CONTENTS.

ST. *Paul* having told the *Corinthians*, in the last Words of the precedent Chapter, that he would shew them a more excellent Way than the emulous producing of their Gifts in the Assembly; he in this Chapter tells them, that this more excellent Way is Charity, which he at large explains, and shews the Excellency of.

TEXT.	PARAPHRASE.	
1 Though I speak with the tongues of men and of angels, and have not charity, I am become as sounding brass, or a tinkling cymbal.	IF I speak all the Languages of Men and Angels [z], and yet have not Charity to make use of them entirely for the Good and Benefit of others, I am no better than a sounding Brass, or noisy Cymbal [a], which fills the Ears of others, without any Advantage to itself by the Sound it makes. And if I have the Gift of Prophecy, and see in the Law and the Pro-	1.
2 And though I have the gift of prophecy, and understand all mysteries, and		2.

NOTES.

to be the less honoured or valued for the Gift he had, though it were not one of the first Rank. And in this Sense the Word ζηλοῦτε, is taken in the next Chapter, *ver.* 4. where St. *Paul* pursuing the same Argument, exhorts them to mutual Charity, Good-will and Affection, which he assures them is preferable to any Gifts whatsoever.] Besides, to what purpose should he exhort them to *covet earnestly the best Gifts*, when the obtaining of this or that Gift did not at all lie in their Desires or Endeavours? the Apostle having just before told them, *ver.* 11. that *the Spirit divides those Gifts to every Man severally, as he will*; and those he writ to, had their Allotment already. He might as reasonably, according to his own Doctrine, in this very Chapter, bid the Foot covet to be the Hand, or the Ear to be the Eye. Let it be remembered therefore, to rectify this, that St. *Paul* says, *ver.* 17. of this Chapter, *If the whole Body were the Eye, where were the Hearing?* &c. St. *Paul* does not use to cross his own Design, nor contradict his own Reasoning.

1 [z] *Tongues of Angels* are mentioned here according to the Conception of the *Jews*.
[a] A Cymbal consisted of two large hollowed Plates of Brass, with broad Brims, which were struck one against another, to fill up the Symphony in great Concerts of Musick; they made a great deep Sound, but had scarce any Variety of musical Notes.

I CORINTHIANS.

PARAPHRASE.

3. phets all the Mysteries [b] contained in them, and comprehend all the Knowledge they teach; and if I have Faith to the highest Degree, and Power of Miracles, so as to be able to remove Mountains [c], and have not Charity, I am nothing; I am of no Value: And if I bestow all I have in Relief of the Poor, and give myself to be burnt, and have not Charity, it profits me nothing.
4. Charity is long-suffering, is gentle and benign, without Emulation, Insolence, or being puffed up; is not ambitious, nor at all
5. self-interested; is not sharp upon others Failings,
6. or inclined to ill Interpretations: Charity rejoices with others when they do well; and when any thing is amiss, is troubled, and covers their Failings:
7. Charity believes well, hopes well of every one, and patiently bears with every thing [d]:
8. Charity will never cease, as a Thing out of use; but the Gifts of Prophecy, and Tongues, and the Knowledge whereby Men look into, and explain the Meaning of the Scriptures, the Time will be when they will
9. be laid aside, as no longer of any Use: For the Knowledge we have now in this State, and the Explication we give of Scripture, is short, par-

TEXT.

all knowledge; and tho' I have all faith, so that I could remove mountains, and have no charity, I am nothing.

3. And though I bestow all my goods to feed the poor, and though I give my body to be burned, and have not charity, it profiteth me nothing.

4. Charity suffereth long, and is kind; charity envieth not; charity vaunteth not itself, is not puffed up:

5. Doth not behave itself unseemly, seeketh not her own, is not easily provoked, thinketh no evil,

6. Rejoiceth not in iniquity, but rejoiceth in the truth:

7. Beareth all things, believeth all things, hopeth all things, endureth all things.

8. Charity never faileth: but whether there be prophecies, they shall fail; whether there be tongues, they shall cease; whether there be knowledge, it shall vanish away.

9. For we know in part, and we prophesy in part.

NOTES.

2 [b] Any Predictions relating to our Saviour, or his Doctrine, or the Times of the Gospel, contained in the Old Testament, in Types, or figurative and obscure Expressions, not understood before his coming, and being revealed to the World, St. *Paul* calls *Mystery*, as may be seen all through his Writings. So that *Mystery* and *Knowledge* are Terms here used by St. *Paul* to signify Truths concerning Christ to come, contained in the Old Testament; and *Prophecy*, the understanding of the Types and Prophecies containing those Truths, so as to be able to explain them to others.

[c] *To remove Mountains*, is to do what is next to impossible.

7 [d] May we not suppose, that in this Description of Charity, St. *Paul* intimates, and tacitly reproves their contrary Carriage, in their Emulation and Contests about the Dignity and Preference of their spiritual Gifts.

tial

I CORINTHIANS.

Ch. XIII.

TEXT.

10 But when that which is perfect is come, then that which is in part shall be done away.

11 When I was a child, I spake as a child, I understood as a child, I thought as a child: but when I became a man, I put away childish things.

12 For now we see thro' a glass darkly; but then face to face: now I know in part; but then shall I know even as also I am known.

13 And now abideth faith, hope, charity, these three; but the greatest of these is charity.

PARAPHRASE.

10. tial and defective. But when hereafter we shall be got into the State of Accomplishment and Perfection, wherein we are to remain in the other World, there will no longer be any need of these imperfecter Ways of Information, whereby we arrive at but a partial Knowledge here.

11. Thus when I was in the imperfect State of Childhood, I talked, I understood, I reasoned after the imperfect manner of a Child; but when I came to the State and Perfection of Manhood, I laid aside those childish Ways.

12. Now we see but by Reflection, the dim, and as it were enigmatical, Representation of Things; but then we shall see Things directly, and as they are in themselves, as a Man sees another when they are Face to Face. Now I have but a superficial, partial Knowledge of Things, but then I shall have an intuitive comprehensive Knowledge of them; as I myself am known, and lie open to the View of superior Seraphic Beings, not by the obscure and imperfect Way of Deductions and Reasoning.

13. But then even in that State, Faith, Hope, and Charity will remain: But the greatest of the three is Charity.

R 2

SECT.

I CORINTHIANS.

SECT. IX. N. 5.

CHAP. XIV. 1——40.

CONTENTS.

ST. *Paul* in this Chapter concludes his Answer to the *Corinthians*, concerning spiritual Men and their Gifts; and having told them that those were most preferable that tended most to Edification, and particularly shewn that Prophecy was to be preferred to Tongues, he gives them Directions for the decent, orderly, and profitable Exercise of their Gifts in their Assemblies.

PARAPHRASE.	*TEXT.*
1. LET your Endeavours, let your Pursuit therefore be after Charity; not that you should neglect the Use of your spiritual Gifts^e, especially the Gift of Prophecy: For he that	1. Follow after charity, and desire spiritual gifts; but rather that ye may prophesy.

NOTES.

1 ^e Ζηλῦτε τὰ πνευματικά. That ζηλῦν does not signify to *covet* or *desire*, nor can be understood to be so used by St. *Paul* in this Section, I have already shewn, *Chap.* XII. 31. That it has here the Sense that I have given it, is plain from the same Direction concerning spiritual Gifts, repeated *ver*. 39. in these Words, ζηλῦτε τὸ προφητεύειν, ἢ τὸ λαλεῖν γλώσσαις μὴ κωλύετε; the Meaning in both Places being evidently this: That they should not neglect the Use of their spiritual Gifts; especially they should, in the first Place, cultivate and exercise the Gift of Prophesying, but yet should not wholly lay aside the Speaking with Variety of Tongues in their Assemblies. It will, perhaps, be wondered why St. *Paul* should employ the Word ζηλῦν in so unusual a Sense; but that will easily be accounted for, if what I have remarked, *Chap.* XIV. 15. concerning St. *Paul*'s Custom of repeating Words, be remembered. But besides what is familiar in St. *Paul*'s Way of Writing, we may find a particular Reason for his repeating the Word ζηλῦν here, though in a somewhat unusual Signification. He having, by Way of Reproof, told them, that they did ζηλῦν τὰ χαρίσματα τὰ χρίσσονα, had an Emulation, or made a Stir about whose Gifts were best, and were therefore to take place in their Assemblies, to prevent their thinking that ζηλῦν might have too harsh a Meaning, (for he is, in all this Epistle, very tender of offending them, and therefore sweetens all his Reproofs as much as possible) he here takes it up again, and uses it more than once, in a Way that approves and advises that they should ζηλῦν πνευματικά; whereby he means no more, than that they should not neglect their spiritual Gifts: He would have them use them in their Assemblies, but yet in such Method and Order as he directs.

speaks

I CORINTHIANS.

Ch. XIV.

TEXT.	PARAPHRASE.
2 For he that speaketh in an unknown tongue, speaketh not unto men, but unto God: for no man understandeth him: howbeit in the spirit he speaketh mysteries.	speaks in an unknown Tongue ᶠ, speaks to God alone, but not to Men, for nobody understands him; the Things he utters by the Spirit in an unknown Tongue, are Mysteries, Things not understood by those who hear them.
3 But he that prophesieth, speaketh unto men to edification, and exhortation and comfort.	But he that prophesieth ᵍ, speaks to Men; who are exhorted and comforted thereby, and helped forwards in Religion and Piety. He that
4 He that speaketh in an unknown tongue, edifieth himself: but he that prophesieth, edifieth the church.	speaks in an unknown Tongue ʰ, edifies himself alone; but he that prophesieth, edifieth the Church. I wish that ye had all the Gift of
5 I would that ye all spake with tongues, but rather that ye prophesied: for greater is he that prophesieth, than he that speaketh	Tongues, but rather that ye all prophesied; for greater is he that prophesieth, than he that speaks with Tongues, unless he interprets what

NOTES.

2 ᶠ He who attentively reads this Section, about spiritual Men and their Gifts, may find reason to imagine that it was those who had the Gift of Tongues, who caused the Disorder in the Church at *Corinth*, by their Forwardness to speak, and striving to be heard first; and so taking up too much of the Time in their Assemblies, in speaking in unknown Tongues. For the remedying this Disorder, and better regulating this Matter, amongst other Things, they had recourse to St. *Paul*. He will not easily avoid thinking so, who considers,

1ˢᵗ, That the first Gift which St. *Paul* compares with Charity, *Chap.* XIII. and extremely undervalues, in comparison of that Divine Virtue, is the Gift of Tongues: As if that were the Gift they most affected to shew, and most valued themselves upon; as indeed it was in it self most fitted for Ostentation in their Assemblies, of any other, if any one were inclined that way: And that the *Corinthians*, in their present state, were not exempt from Emulation, Vanity and Ostentation, is very evident.

2dly, That, *Chap.* XIV. when St. *Paul* compares their spiritual Gifts one with another, the first, nay, and only one, that he debases and depreciates in comparison of others, is the Gift of Tongues, which he discourses of for above twenty Verses together, in a Way fit to abate a too high Esteem, and a too excessive Use of it in their Assemblies; which we cannot suppose he would have done, had they not been guilty of some such Miscarriages in the Case, whereof the 24th Verse is not without an Intimation.

3dly, When he comes to give Directions about the Exercise of their Gifts in their Meetings, this of Tongues is the only one that he restrains and limits, *ver.* 27, 28.

3 ᵍ What is meant by Prophesying, see *Chap.* XII. 10.

4 ʰ By γλώσσῃ, *unknown Tongue*, Dr. *Lightfoot* in this Chapter understands the *Hebrew* Tongue; which, as he observes, was used in the Synagogue in reading the sacred Scripture, in Praying, and in Preaching. If that be the Meaning of *Tongue* here, it suits well the Apostle's Design, which was to take them off from their *Jewish* false Apostle, who probably might have encouraged and promoted this Speaking of *Hebrew* in their Assemblies.

he

I. CORINTHIANS.
Ch. XIV.

PARAPHRASE.

6. he delivers in an unknown Tongue, that the Church may be edified by it. For Example, should I apply myself to you in a Tongue you knew not, what Good should I do you, unless I interpreted to you what I said, that you might understand the Revelation, or Knowledge, or Prophecy, or Doctrine [i] contained in it?
7. Even inanimate Instruments of Sound, as Pipe, or Harp, are not made use of to make an insignificant Noise; but distinct Notes, expressing Mirth, or Mourning, or the like, are played upon them; whereby the Tune and Composure is understood.
8. And if the Trumpet sound not some Point of War that is understood, the Soldier is not thereby instructed
9. what to do. So likewise ye, unless with the Tongue which you use, you utter Words of a clear and known Signification to your Hearers, you talk to the Wind, for your Auditors under-
10. stand nothing that you say. There is a great Number of significant Languages in the World, I know not how many, every Nation has its
11. own; if then I understand not another's Language, and the Force of his Words, I am to him, when he speaks, a Barbarian, and what-

TEXT.

with tongues, except he interpret, that the church may receive edifying.

6 Now, brethren, if I come unto you speaking with tongues, what shall I profit you, except I shall speak to you either by revelation, or by knowledge, or by prophesying, or by doctrine?

7 And even things without life giving sound, whether pipe or harp, except they give a distinction in the sounds, how shall it be known what is piped or harped?

8 For if the trumpet give an uncertain sound, who shall prepare himself to the battle?

9 So likewise you, except ye utter by the tongue words easy to be understood, how shall it be known what is spoken? for ye shall speak into the air.

10 There are, it may be, so many kinds of voices in the world, and none of them is without signification.

11 Therefore if I know not the meaning of the voice,

NOTES.

6 [i] 'Tis not to be doubted but these four distinct Terms used here by the Apostle, had each its distinct Signification in his Mind and Intention; whether what may be collected from these Epistles, may sufficiently warrant us to understand them in the following Significations, I leave to the Judgment of others. 1st, Ἀποκάλυψις, *Revelation*, something revealed by God immediately to the Person, vid. ver. 30. 2dly, Γνῶσις, *Knowledge*; the understanding the mystical and evangelical Sense of Passages in the Old Testament, relating to our Saviour and the Gospel. 3dly, Προφητεία, *Prophecy*, an inspired Hymn, vid. ver. 26. 4thly, Διδαχή, *Doctrine*; any Truth of the Gospel concerning Faith or Manners. But whether this, or any other precise Meaning of these Words can be certainly made out now, it is perhaps of no great Necessity to be over-curious; it being enough, for the understanding the Sense and Argument of the Apostle here, to know that these Terms stand for some intelligible Discourse tending to the Edification of the Church, though of what Kind each of them was in particular, we certainly know not.

ever

I CORINTHIANS.

TEXT.

I shall be unto him that speaketh, a barbarian; and he that speaketh, shall be a barbarian unto me.

12 Even so ye, forasmuch as ye are zealous of spiritual gifts, seek that ye may excel to the edifying of the church.

13 Wherefore let him that speaketh in an unknown tongue, pray that he may interpret.

14 For if I pray in an unknown tongue, my spirit prayeth, but my understanding is unfruitful.

15 What is it then? I will pray with the Spirit, and I will pray with the understanding also: I will

PARAPHRASE.

ever he says, is all gibberish to me: And so is it with you; ye are Barbarians to one another, as far as ye speak to one another in unknown Tongues. But since there is Emulation amongst 12. you concerning spiritual Gifts, seek to abound in the Exercise of those which tend most to the Edification of the Church. Wherefore let him 13. that speaks an unknown Tongue, pray that he may interpret what he says. For if I pray in 14. the Congregation in an unknown Tongue, my Spirit, it is true, accompanies my Words which I understand, and so my Spirit prays ^{k}; but my Meaning is unprofitable to others, who understand not my Words. What then is to 15. be done in the Case? Why, I will, when moved to it by the Spirit, pray in an unknown Tongue, but so that my Meaning ^{l} may be understood by others; *i. e.* I will not do it, but when there is some body by to interpret ^{m}:

NOTES.

14 ^{k} This is evident from *ver.* 4. where it is said, *He that speaketh with a Tongue, edifies himself.*

15 ^{l} I will not pretend to justify this Interpretation of τῷ νοΐ, by the exact Rules of the *Greek* Idiom; but the Sense of the Place will, I think, bear me out in it. And, as there is occasion often to remark, he must be little versed in the Writings of St. *Paul,* who does not observe, that when he has used a Term, he is apt to repeat it again in the same Discourse in a Way peculiar to himself, and somewhat varied from its ordinary Signification; so having here, in the foregoing Verse, used νοῦς for the Sentiment of his own Mind, which was unprofitable to others when he prayed in a Tongue unknown to them, and opposed it to πνεῦμα, which he used there for his own Sense, accompanying his own Words, intelligible to himself, when by the Impulse of the Spirit he prayed in a foreign Tongue, he here, in this Verse, continues to use Praying, τῷ πνεύματι, and τῷ νοΐ, in the same Opposition; the one for praying in a strange Tongue, which alone his own Mind understood and accompanied; the other for praying so, as that the Meaning of his Mind, in those Words he uttered, was made known to others, so that they were also benefited. This Use of πνεῦμα is farther confirmed in the next Verse, and what he means by νοΐ here, he expresses by διὰ νοὸς, *ver.* 19. and there explains the Meaning of it.

^{m} For so he orders in the Use of an unknown Tongue, *ver.* 27.

And

I CORINTHIANS.

PARAPHRASE.

And so I will do also in Singing ⁿ; I will sing by the Spirit in an unknown Tongue, but I will take care that the Meaning of what I sing shall be understood by the Assistants. And thus ye shall all do in all like Cases. For if thou, by the Impulse of the Spirit, givest Thanks to God in an unknown Tongue, which all understand not; how shall the Hearer, who in this Respect is unlearned, and being ignorant in that Tongue, knows not what thou sayest, how shall he say Amen? How shall he join in the Thanks which he understands not? Thou indeed givest Thanks well, but the other is not at all edified by it. I thank God, I speak with Tongues more than you all; but I had rather speak in the Church five Words that are understood, that I might instruct others also, than in an unknown Tongue ten thousand, that others understand not. My Brethren, be not in Understanding Children, who are apt to be taken with the Novelty or Strangeness of Things: In Temper and Disposition be as Children, void of Malice °; but in Matters of Understanding be ye perfect Men, and use your Understanding ^p. But not so zealous for the Use of unknown Tongues in the Church, they are not so proper there: It is written in the

TEXT.

sing with the spirit, and I will sing with the understanding also.

16 Else when thou shalt bless with the spirit, how shall he that occupieth the room of the unlearned, say Amen at thy giving of thanks, seeing he understandeth not what thou sayest?

17 For thou verily givest thanks well, but the other is not edified.

18 I thank my God, I speak with Tongues more than you all:

19 Yet in the church I had rather speak five words with my understanding, that by my voice I might teach others also, than ten thousand words in an unknown tongue.

20 Brethren, be not children in understanding: howbeit in malice be ye children, but in understanding be men.

21 In the law it is written, With men of other tongues, and other lips,

NOTES.

ⁿ Here it may be observed, that as in their public Prayer one prayed, and the others held their Peace, so it was in their Singing; at least, in that Singing which was of extempore Hymns, by the Impulse of the Spirit.

20 ° By ἀκακία, Malice, I think is here to be understood all Sorts of ill Temper of Mind, contrary to the Gentleness and Innocence of Childhood; and in particular their Emulation and Strife about the Exercise of their Gifts in their Assemblies.

^p Vid. *Rom*. XVI. 19. *Eph*. IV. 13—15.

Law,

I CORINTHIANS. Ch. XIV.

TEXT.

will I speak unto this people: and yet for all that will they not hear me, saith the Lord.

22 Wherefore tongues are for a sign, not to them that believe, but to them that believe not: but prophesying serveth not for them that believe not, but for them which believe.

23 If therefore the whole church be come together into one place, and all speak with tongues, and there come in those that are unlearned, or unbelievers, will they not say that ye are mad?

24 But if all prophesy, and there come in one that believeth not, or one unlearned, he is convinced of all, he is judged of all:

25 And thus are the secrets of his heart made manifest; and so falling down on his face he will worship God, and report that God is in you of a truth.

26 How is it then, brethren? when ye come together, every one of you hath a psalm, hath doc-

PARAPHRASE.

Law q, With Men of other Tongues, and other Lips, will I speak unto this People; and yet for all that will they not hear me, saith the Lord. So that you see the speaking of strange Tongues miraculously, is not for those who are already converted, but for a Sign to those who are Unbelievers: But Prophecy is for Believers, and not for Unbelievers; and therefore fitter for your Assemblies. If therefore, when the Church is all come together, you should all speak in unknown Tongues, and Men unlearned, or Unbelievers, should come in, would they not say that you are mad? But if ye all prophesy, and an Unbeliever or ignorant Man come in, the Discourses he hears from you reaching his Conscience, and the secret Thoughts of his Heart, he is convinced, and wrought upon; and so falling down, worships God, and declares that God is certainly amongst you. What then is to be done, Brethren? When ye come together, every one is ready r, one with a Psalm, another with a Doctrine, another with a strange Tongue, another with a Revelation, another with Interpretation. Let

22.

23.

24.

25.

26.

NOTES.

21 q The Books of Sacred Scripture, delivered to the *Jews* by Divine Revelation, under the Law, before the Time of the Gospel, which we now call the Old Testament, are in the Writings of the New Testament called sometimes *the Law, the Prophets,* and *the Psalms,* as *Luke* XXIV. 44. sometimes *the Law and the Prophets,* as *Acts* XXIV. 14. And sometimes they are all comprehended under this one Name, *the Law,* as here; for the Passage cited is in *Isaiah*.

26 r 'Tis plain, by this whole Discourse of the Apostle's, that there were Contentions and Emulations amongst them for Precedency of their Gifts; and therefore I think ἕκαστος ἔχει may be rendered, *every one is ready,* as impatient to be first heard. If there were no such Disorder amongst them, there would have been no need for the Regulations given in the End of this Verse, and the seven Verses following; especially *ver.* 31, 32. where he tells them, they all may prophesy one by one, and that the Motions of the Spirit were not so ungovernable, as not to leave a Man Master of himself. He must not think himself under a Necessity of speaking, as soon as he found any Impulse of the Spirit upon his Mind.

S all

I CORINTHIANS.

PARAPHRASE.

27. all Things be done to Edification, even though ˢ any one speak in an unknown Tongue, which is a Gift that seems least intended for Edification ᵗ; let but two or three at most, at any one Meeting, speak in an unknown Tongue, and that separately one after another; and let there
28. be but one Interpreter ᵘ. But if there be no body present that can interpret, let not any one use his Gift of Tongues in the Congregation, but let him silently within himself speak to himself, and to God. Of those who have the Gift
29. of Prophecy, let but two or three speak at the same Meeting, and let the others examine
30. and discuss it. But if, during their Debate, the Meaning of it be revealed to one that sits by, let him that was discoursing of it before
31. give off. For ye may all prophesy one after another, that all may in their Turns be Hearers, and receive Exhortation and Instruction.
32. For the Gifts of the Holy Ghost are not like the Possession of the Heathen Priests, who are not Makers of the Spirit that possesses them: But Christians, however filled

TEXT.

trine, hath a tongue, hath a revelation, hath an interpretation. Let all things be done to edifying.

27 If any man speak in an unknown tongue, let it be by two, or at the most by three, and that by course; and let one interpret.

28 But if there be no interpreter, let him keep silence in the church; and let him speak to himself, and to God.

29 Let the prophets speak two or three, and let the other judge.

30 If any thing be revealed to another that sitteth by, let the first hold his peace.

31 For ye may all prophesy one by one, that all may learn, and all may be comforted.

32 And the spirits of the prophets are subject to the prophets.

NOTES.

27 ˢ St. *Paul* has said in this Chapter as much as conveniently could be said to restrain their speaking in unknown Tongues in their Assemblies; which seems to be that wherein the Vanity and Ostentation of the *Corinthians* was most forward to shew itself. It is not, says he, a Gift intended for the Edification of Believers; however, since you will be exercising it in your Meetings, let it always be so ordered, that it may be for Edification. εἴτε I have rendered *altho'*: So I think it is sometimes used, but no where, as I remember, simply for *if*, as in our Translation; nor will the Sense here bear *and either*, which is the common Signification of εἴτε. And therefore I take the Apostle's Sense to be this: You must do nothing but to Edification, though you speak in an unknown Tongue; even an unknown Tongue must be made use of, in your Assemblies, only to Edification.

ᵗ Vid. *Ver.* 2. and 4.

ᵘ The Rule of the Synagogue was, In the Law let one read, and one interpret: In the Prophets let one read, and two interpret: In *Esther* ten may read, and ten interpret. 'Tis not improbable that some such Disorder had been introduced into the Church of *Corinth* by their Judaizing false Apostle, which St. *Paul* would here put an end to.

with

I CORINTHIANS.

TEXT.	PARAPHRASE.

33 For God is not the author of confusion, but of peace, as in all churches of the saints.

34 Let your women keep silence in the churches: for it is not permitted unto them to speak; but they are commanded to be under obedience, as also faith the law.

35 And if they will learn any thing, let them ask their husbands at home: for it is a shame for women to speak in the church.

36 What? came the word of God out from you? or came it unto you only?

37 If any Man think himself to be a prophet, or spiritual, let him acknow-

with the Holy Ghost, are Masters of their own Actions; can speak or hold their Peace as they see occasion, and are not hurried away by any Compulsion. It is therefore no reason 33. for you to speak more than one at once, or to interrupt one another, because you find yourselves inspired and moved by the Spirit of God; for God is not the Author of Confusion and Disorder, but of Quietness and Peace: And this is what is observed in all the Churches of God. As to your Women, let them keep 34. Silence in your Assemblies; for it is not permitted them to discourse there, or pretend to teach; that does no way suit their State of Subjection appointed them in the Law. But 35. if they have a mind to have any thing explained to them that passes in the Church, let them for their Information ask their Husbands at home; for it is a Shame for Women to discourse and debate with Men publickly in the Congregation ʷ. What, do you pretend to 36. give Laws to the Church of God, or to a Right to do what you please amongst yourselves, as if the Gospel began at *Corinth*, and issuing from you, was communicated to the rest of the World, or as if it were communicated to you alone of all the World? If any 37. Man amongst you think that he hath the Gift of Prophecy, and would pass for a Man know-

NOTES.

34, 35. ʷ Why I apply this Prohibition of speaking only to Reasoning and purely voluntary Discourse, but suppose a Liberty left Women to speak, where they had an immediate Impulse and Revelation from the Spirit of God, *vid.* Chap. XI. 3. In the Synagogue it was usual for any Man, that had a mind, to demand of the Teacher a farther Explication of what he had said; but this was not permitted to the Women.

PARAPHRASE.

ing in the revealed Will of God [x], let him acknowledge that thefe Rules which I have here given, are the Commandments of the Lord. But if any Man [y] be ignorant that they are fo, I have no more to fay to him; I leave him to his Ignorance. To conclude, Brethren, let Prophecy have the Preference in the Exercife of it [z]; but forbid ye not the fpeaking unknown Tongues. But whether a Man prophefies, or fpeaks with Tongues, whatever fpiritual Gift he exercifes in your Affemblies, let it be done without any Indecorum or Diforder.

38.
39.
40.

TEXT.

ledge that the things that I write unto you, are the commandments of the Lord.

38 But if any man be ignorant, let him be ignorant.

39 Wherefore, brethren, covet to prophefy, and forbid not to fpeak with tongues.

40 Let all things be done decently, and in order.

NOTES.

37 [x] Πνευματικὸς, *a fpiritual Man*, in the Senfe of St. *Paul*, is one who founds his Knowledge in what is revealed by the Spirit of God, and not in the bare Difcoveries of his natural Reafon and Parts; *vid.* Chap. II. 15.

38 [y] By the *any Man* mentioned in this, and the foregoing Verfe, St. *Paul* feems to intimate the falfe Apoftle, who pretended to give Laws amongft them; and, as we have obferved, may well be fuppofed to be the Author of thefe Diforders, whom therefore St. *Paul* reflects on, and preffes in thefe three Verfes.

39 [z] Ζηλοῦν, in this whole Difcourfe of St. *Paul*, taken to refer to the Exercife, and not to the obtaining the Gifts to which it is joined, will direct us right in underftanding St. *Paul*, and make his Meaning very eafy and intelligible.

SECT. X.

CHAP. XV. 1——58.

CONTENTS.

After St. *Paul* (who had taught them another Doctrine) had left *Corinth*, fome among them denied the Refurrection of the Dead. This he confutes by Chrift's Refurrection, which the Number of Witneffes yet remaining, that had feen him, put paft Queftion; befides the conftant inculcating of it by all the Apoftles

every

every where. From the Resurrection of Christ thus established, he Ch. XV. infers the Resurrection of the Dead; shews the Order they shall rise in, and what Sort of Bodies they shall have.

TEXT.

1 Moreover, brethren, I declare unto you the Gospel which I preached unto you, which also you have received, and wherein ye stand;
2 By which also ye are saved, if ye keep in memory what I preached unto you, unless ye have believed in vain.
3 For I delivered unto you first of all, that which I also received, how that Christ died for our sins, according to the scriptures:
4 And that he was buried, and that he rose again the third day, according to the scriptures:
5 And that he was seen of Cephas, then of the twelve.
6 After that, he was seen of above five hundred brethren at once: of whom the greater part remain unto this present, but some are fallen asleep:
7 After that he was seen of James; then of all the apostles.
8 And last of all, he was seen of me also, as of one born out of due time.
9 For I am the least of the apostles, that am not meet to be called an apostle, because I persecuted the church of God.
10 But by the grace of God,

PARAPHRASE.

1. IN what I am now going to say to you, Brethren, I make known to you no other Gospel than what I formerly preached to you, and you received, and have hitherto professed,
2. and by which alone you are to be saved. This you will find to be so, if you retain in your Memories what it was that I preached to you; which you certainly do, unless you have taken up the Christian Name and Profession to no
3. purpose. For I delivered to you, and particularly insisted on this, which I had received, *viz.* that Christ died for our Sins, according to the Scriptures; and that he was buried, and that
4. he was raised again the third Day, according to the Scriptures; and that he was seen by
5. *Peter*, afterwards by the twelve Apostles; and
6. after that, by above five hundred Christians at once, of whom the greatest Part remain alive to this Day, but some of them are deceased: Afterwards he was seen by *James*; and after
7. that by all the Apostles. Last of all, he was
8. seen by me also, as by one born before my Time [a]. For I am the least of the Apostles, not worthy
9. the Name of an Apostle, because I persecuted the Church of God. But by the free Bounty
10. of God, I am what it hath pleased him to make me: And this Favour which he hath bestowed

NOTES.

8 [a] An abortive Birth that comes before its Time, which is the Name St. *Paul* gives himself here, is usually sudden and at unawares; and is also weak and feeble, scarce deserving to be called or counted a Man. The former Part agrees to St. *Paul's* being made a Christian and an Apostle, though it be in regard of the latter that in the following Verse St. *Paul* calls himself abortive.

on

PARAPHRASE.

11. on me, hath not been altogether fruitless, for I have laboured in preaching of the Gospel more than all the other Apostles [b]; which yet I do not ascribe to any thing of myself, but to the Favour of God which accompanied me. But whether I, or the other Apostles preached, this was that which we preached, and this was the Faith ye were baptized into, *viz.* that Christ died,
12. and rose again the third Day. If therefore this be so, if this be that which has been preached to you, *viz.* that Christ has been raised from the Dead, how comes it that some [c] amongst you say, as they do, that there is no Resurrection
13. of the Dead? And if there be no Resurrection of the Dead, then even Christ himself is not
14. risen: And if Christ be not risen, our Preaching
15. is idle Talk, and your believing it is to no purpose. And we who pretend to be Witnesses for God and his Truth, shall be found Liars, bearing Witness against God and his Truth, affirming that he raised Christ, whom in truth he did not raise, if it be so that the Dead are
16. not raised. For if the Dead shall not be raised,
17. neither is Christ raised: And if Christ be not risen, your Faith is to no purpose; your Sins are

TEXT.

I am what I am: and his grace which was bestowed upon me, was not in vain: but I laboured more abundantly than they all; yet not I, but the grace of God which was with me.

11. Therefore whether it were I or they, so we preach, and so ye believed.
12. Now if Christ be preached that he rose from the dead, how say some among you, that there is no resurrection of the dead?
13. But if there be no resurrection of the dead, then is Christ not risen.
14. And if Christ be not risen, then is our preaching vain, and your faith is also vain.
15. Yea, and we are found false witnesses of God; because we have testified of God, that he raised up Christ: whom he raised not up, if so be that the dead rise not.
16. For if the dead rise not, then is not Christ raised:
17. And if Christ be not raised, your faith is vain, ye are yet in your sins.

NOTES.

10 [b] St. *Paul* drops in this Commendation of himself to keep up his Credit in the Church of *Corinth*, where there was a Faction labouring to discredit him.

12 [c] This may well be understood of the Head of the contrary Faction, and some of his Scholars. *1st*, Because St. *Paul* introduces this Confutation by asserting his Mission, which these his Opposers would bring in question. *2dly*, Because he is so careful to let the *Corinthians* see he maintains not the Doctrine of the Resurrection, in opposition to these their new Leaders; it being the Doctrine he had preached to them at their first Conversion, before any such false Apostle appeared among them, and misled them about the Resurrection. Their false Apostle was a *Jew*, and in all appearance judaized; may he not also be suspected of Sadducism? For 'tis plain, he, with all his Might, opposed St. *Paul*; which must be from some main Difference in Opinion at the bottom, for there are no Footsteps of any personal Provocation.

not

I CORINTHIANS.

Ch. XV.

| TEXT. | PARAPHRASE. |

13 Then they also which are fallen asleep in Christ, are perished.

18. not forgiven, but you are still liable to the Punishment due to them. And they also who died in the Belief of the Gospel, are perished and lost.

19 If in this life only we have hope in Christ, we are of all men most miserable.

19. If the Advantages we expect from Christ are confined to this Life, and we have no Hope of any Benefit from him in another Life hereafter, we Christians are the most miserable of all Men.

20 But now is Christ risen from the dead, and become the first-fruits of them that slept.

20. But in truth Christ is actually risen from the Dead, and is become the First-Fruits[d] of those who were dead.

21 For since by man came death, by man came also the resurrection of the dead.

21. For since by Man came Death, by Man came also the Resurrection of the Dead, or Restoration to Life.

22 For as in Adam all die, even so in Christ shall all be made alive.

22. For as the Death that all Men suffer is owing to *Adam*, so the Life that all shall be restored to again is procured them by Christ.

23 But every man in his own order: Christ the first-fruits, afterward they that are Christ's, at his coming.

23. But they shall return to Life again; not all at once, but in their proper Order: Christ, the First-Fruits, is already risen; next after him shall rise those who are his People, his Church; and this shall be at his second Coming.

24 Then cometh the end, when he shall have delivered up the kingdom to God, even the Father; when he shall have put down all rule, and all authority and power.

24. After that shall be the Day of Judgment, which shall bring to a Conclusion, and finish the whole Dispensation to the Race and Posterity of *Adam* in this World; when Christ shall have delivered up the Kingdom to God and the Father, which he shall not do till he hath destroyed all Empire, Power and Authority, that shall be in the World besides.

25 For he must reign till he hath put all enemies under his feet.

25. For he must reign till he has totally subdued and brought all his Enemies into Subjection to his Kingdom.

26 The last enemy that shall be destroyed, is death.

26. The last Enemy that shall be destroyed, is Death.

27 For he hath put all things under his feet. But

27. For God hath subjected all Things to Christ; but when it is said all Things

NOTES.

20 [d] The First-Fruits was a small Part, which was first taken and offered to God, and sanctified the whole Mass which was to follow.

are

I CORINTHIANS.

PARAPHRASE.

28. are subjected, it is plain that he is to be excepted, who did subject all things to him. But when all Things shall be actually reduced under Subjection to him, then even the Son himself, *i. e.* Christ and his whole Kingdom, he and all his Subjects and Members, shall be subjected to him that gave him this Kingdom and universal Dominion, that God may immediately govern
29. and influence all. Else ^e what shall they do who
30. are baptized for the Dead ^f? and why do we
31. venture our Lives continually? As to myself, I am exposed, vilified, treated so that I die daily: And for this I call to witness your glorying against me, in which I really glory, as coming on me for our Lord Jesus Christ's Sake.
32. And particularly, to what purpose did I suffer myself to be exposed to wild Beasts at *Ephesus*, if the Dead rise not? If there be no Resurrection, 'tis wiser a great deal to preserve ourselves as long as we can in a free Enjoyment of all the Pleasures of this Life; for when Death comes, as it shortly will, there is an End of us for ever.
33. Take heed that ye be not misled by such Discourses; for evil Communication is apt to cor-
34. rupt even good Minds. Awake from such Dreams, as 'tis fit you should, and give not

TEXT.

when he saith all things are put under him, it is manifest that he is excepted which did put all things under him.

28 And when all things shall be subdued unto him, then shall the Son also himself be subject unto him that put all things under him, that God may be all in all.

29 Else what shall they do which are baptized for the dead, if the dead rise not at all? why are they then baptized for the dead?

30 And why stand we in jeopardy every hour?

31 I protest by your rejoicing, which I have in Christ Jesus our Lord, I die daily.

32 If after the manner of men I have fought with beasts at Ephesus, what advantageth it me, if the dead rise not? let us eat and drink, for to morrow we die.

33 Be not deceived: Evil communications corrupt good manners.

34 Awake to righteousness, and sin not; for some have

NOTES.

29 ^e *Else* here relates to *ver.* 20. where it is said, *Christ is risen*. St. *Paul* having in that Verse mentioned Christ being the First-Fruits from the Dead, takes occasion from thence, now that he is upon the Resurrection, to inform the *Corinthians* of several Particularities relating to the Resurrection, which might enlighten them about it, and could not be known but by Revelation. Having made this Excursion in the eight preceding Verses, he here, in the 29th, re-assumes the Thread of his Discourse, and goes on with his Arguments for believing the Resurrection.

^f What this Baptizing for the Dead was, I confess I know not; but it seems, by the following Verses, to be something wherein they exposed themselves to the Danger of Death.

your

I CORINTHIANS. Ch. XV.

TEXT.	PARAPHRASE.

not the knowledge of God: I speak this to your shame.

35 But some man will say, How are the dead raised up? and with what body do they come?

36 Thou fool, that which thou sowest is not quickened except it die.

37 And that which thou sowest, thou sowest not that body that shall be, but bare grain; it may chance of wheat, or of some other grain.

38 But God giveth it a body as it hath pleased him, and to every seed his own body.

39 All flesh is not the same flesh: but there is one kind of flesh of men, ano-

yourselves up sinfully to the Enjoyments of this Life? for there are some ᵍ atheistical People among you: This I say to make you ashamed. But possibly it will be asked, How comes it to 35. pass that dead Men are raised? and with what Kind of Bodies do they come ʰ? Shall they have at the Resurrection such Bodies as they have now? Thou Fool, does not daily Experience 36. teach thee, that the Seed which thou sowest corrupts and dies, before it springs up and lives again? That which thou sowest is the bare 37. Grain of Wheat or Barley, or the like; but the Body which it has when it rises up, is different from the Seed that is sown. For it is not the 38. Seed that rises up again, but a quite different Body, such as God has thought fit to give it, viz. a Plant of a particular Shape and Size, which God has appointed to each Sort of Seed. And so likewise it is in Animals, there are diffe- 39. rent Kinds of Flesh ⁱ; for the Flesh of Men is of

NOTES.

34 ᵍ May not this probably be said to make them ashamed of their Leader, whom they were so forward to glory in? For 'tis not unlikely, that their questioning and denying the Resurrection, came from their new Apostle, who raised such Opposition against St. Paul.

35 ʰ If we will allow St. Paul to know what he says, it is plain from what he answers, that he understands these Words to contain two Questions. 1ˢᵗ, How comes it to pass that dead Men are raised to Life again? would it not be better they should live on? Why do they die to live again? 2dly, With what Bodies shall they return to Life? To both these he distinctly answers, viz. That those who are raised to an heavenly State, shall have other Bodies: And next, that it is fit that Men should die, Death being no improper Way to the attaining other Bodies. This he shews there is so plain and common an Instance of, in the sowing of all Seeds, that he thinks it a foolish Thing to make a Difficulty of it; and then proceeds to declare, that as they shall have others, so they shall have better Bodies than they had before, viz. spiritual and incorruptible.

39 ⁱ The Scope of the Place makes it evident, that by Flesh, St. Paul here means Bodies, viz. That God has given to the several Sorts of Animals, Bodies, in Shape, Texture and Organization, very different one from another, as he has thought good; and so he can give to Men, at the Resurrection, Bodies of very different Constitutions and Qualities from those they had before.

T one

PARAPHRASE.

one Kind; the Flesh of Cattle is of another Kind; that of Fish is different from them both; and the Flesh of Birds is of a peculiar Sort,
40. different from them all. To look yet farther into the Difference of Bodies, there be both heavenly and earthly Bodies; but the Beauty and Excellency of the heavenly Bodies is of one Kind, and that of earthly Bodies of ano-
41. ther. The Sun, Moon and Stars, have each of them their particular Beauty and Brightness; and one Star differs from another in Glory.
42. And so shall the Resurrection of the Dead ^{k} be; That

TEXT.

ther flesh of beasts, another of fishes, and another of birds.

There are also celestial 40 bodies, and bodies terrestrial: but the glory of the celestial is one, and the glory of the terrestrial is another.

There is one glory of 41 the sun, and another glory of the moon, and another glory of the stars; for one star differeth from another star in glory.

So also is the resurrec- 42 tion of the dead. It is sown in corruption, it is raised in incorruption:

NOTES.

42 ^{k} *The Resurrection of the Dead* here spoken of, is not the Resurrection of all Mankind in common, but only the Resurrection of the Just. This will be evident to any one, who observes that St. *Paul* having, *ver.* 22. declared that all Men shall be made alive again, tells the *Corinthians*, ver. 23. that it shall not be all at once, but at several Distances of Time. First of all Christ rose, afterwards, next in Order to him, the Saints should all be raised; which Resurrection of the Just is that which he treats, and gives an Account of to the End of this Discourse and Chapter, and so never comes to the Resurrection of the Wicked, which was to be the third and last in Order: So that from the 23d Verse to the End of this Chapter, all that he says of the Resurrection, is a Description only of the Resurrection of the Just, though he calls it here by the general Name of the Resurrection of the Dead. That this is so, there is so much Evidence, that there is scarce a Verse, from the 41st to the End, that does not evince it.

1*st*, What in this Resurrection is raised, St. *Paul* assures us, *ver.* 43. is raised in Glory; but the Wicked are not raised in Glory.

2*dly*, He says *we* (speaking in the Name of all that shall be then raised) shall bear the Image of the heavenly *Adam*, ver. 49. which cannot belong to the Wicked. *We* shall all be changed, that by putting on Incorruptibility, and Immortality, Death may be swallowed up of Victory, which God giveth us through our Lord Jesus Christ, *ver.* 51, 52, 53, 54, 57. which cannot likewise belong to the Damned. And therefore *we* and *us* must be understood to be spoken in the Name of the Dead that are Christ's, who are to be raised by themselves before the rest of Mankind.

3*dly*, He says, *ver.* 52. that when the Dead are raised, they who are alive shall be changed in the Twinkling of an Eye. Now that these Dead are only the Dead in Christ, which shall rise first, and shall be caught up in the Clouds to meet the Lord in the Air, is plain from 1 *Thess.* IV. 16, 17.

4*thly*, He teaches, *ver.* 54. that by this Corruptible's putting on Incorruption, is brought to pass the saying, that Death is swallowed up of Victory. But, I think, no body will say that the Wicked have Victory over Death; yet that, according to the Apostle here, belongs to all those whose corruptible Bodies have put on Incorruption, which therefore must be only those that rise the second in Order. From whence it is clear, that their Resurrection alone is that which is here mentioned and described.

5*thly*,

I CORINTHIANS

Ch. XV.

TEXT.	PARAPHRASE.
43 It is sown in dishonour, it is raised in glory: it is sown in weakness, it is raised in power:	That which is sown in this World¹, and comes to die, is a poor, weak, contemptible, corruptible Thing; when it is raised again, it shall be powerful, glorious, and incorruptible. The

NOTES.

5thly, A farther Proof whereof is *ver.* 56, 57. in that their Sins being taken away, the Sting whereby Death kills is taken away. And hence St. *Paul* says, God has given *us* the Victory; which is the same *us* or *we* who should bear the Image of the heavenly *Adam*, ver. 49. and the same *we*, who should all be changed, *ver.* 51, 52. All which Places can therefore belong to none but those who are Christ's, who shall be raised by themselves, the second in Order, before the rest of the Dead.

'Tis very remarkable what St. *Paul* says in this 51st Verse, We *shall not all sleep, but we shall all be changed in the Twinkling of an Eye*. The Reason he gives for it, *ver.* 53. is, because this corruptible Thing must put on Incorruption, and this mortal Thing must put on Immortality. How? Why, by putting off Flesh and Blood by an instantaneous Change, because, as he tells us, *ver.* 50. Flesh and Blood cannot inherit the Kingdom of God; and therefore, to fit Believers for that Kingdom, those who are alive at Christ's coming, shall be changed in the Twinkling of an Eye, and those that are in their Graves, shall be changed likewise at the Instant of their being raised; and so all the whole Collection of Saints, all the Members of Christ's Body, shall be put into a State of Incorruptibility, *ver.* 52. in a new Sort of Bodies: Taking the Resurrection here spoken of, to be the Resurrection of all the Dead promiscuously, St. *Paul*'s Reasoning in this Place can hardly be understood: But, upon a Supposition that he here describes the Resurrection of the Just only, that Resurrection which, as he says, *ver.* 23. is to be the next after Christ's, and separate from the rest, there is nothing can be more plain, natural and easy, than St. *Paul*'s Reasoning; and it stands thus: Men alive are Flesh and Blood, the Dead in the Graves are but the Remains of corrupted Flesh and Blood, but Flesh and Blood cannot inherit the Kingdom of God, neither Corruption inherit Incorruption, *i. e.* Immortality; therefore to make all those who are Christ's capable to enter into his eternal Kingdom of Life, as well those of them who are alive, as those of them who are raised from the Dead, shall in the Twinkling of an Eye be all changed, and their Corruptible shall put on Incorruption, and their Mortal shall put on Immortality: And thus God gives them the Victory over Death, through their Lord Jesus Christ. This is, in short, St. *Paul*'s Arguing here, and the Account he gives of the Resurrection of the Blessed. But how the Wicked, who are afterwards to be restored to Life, were to be raised, and what was to become of them, he here says nothing, as not being to his present Purpose, which was to assure the *Corinthians*, by the Resurrection of Christ, of a happy Resurrection to Believers, and thereby to encourage them to continue stedfast in the Faith which had such a Reward. That this was his Design, may be seen by the Beginning of his Discourse, *ver.* 12——21. and by the Conclusion, *ver.* 58. in these Words: *Wherefore, my beloved Brethren, be ye stedfast, unmoveable, always abounding in the Work of the Lord; forasmuch as ye know that your Labour is not in vain in the Lord.* Which Words shew that what he had been speaking of in the immediately preceding Verses, *viz.* their being changed, and the putting on of Incorruption and Immortality, and their having thereby the Victory through Jesus Christ, was what belonged solely to the Saints, as a Reward to those who remained stedfast, and abounded in the Work of the Lord.

The like Use, of the like, though shorter Discourse of the Resurrection, wherein he describes only that of the Blessed, he makes to the *Thessalonians*, 1 Thess. IV. 13——18. which he concludes thus: *Wherefore comfort one another with these Words*.

I CORINTHIANS.

PARAPHRASE.

44. The Body we have here [1], surpasses not the animal Nature; at the Resurrection it shall be spiritual. There are both animal [m] and spi-
45. ritual [n] Bodies. And so it is written, The first Man *Adam* was made a living Soul, *i. e.* made of an animal Constitution, endowed with an animal Life; the second *Adam* was made of a spiritual Constitution, with a Power to
46. give Life to others. Howbeit, the spiritual was not first, but the animal; and afterwards the
47. spiritual. The first Man was of the Earth, made up of Dust or earthly Particles; the se-
48. cond Man is the Lord from Heaven. Those who have no higher an Extraction than barely from the earthy Man, they, like him, have barely an animal Life and Constitution. But

TEXT.

44 It is sown a natural body, it is raised a spiritual body. There is a natural body, and there is a spiritual body.
45 And so it is written, The first man Adam was made a living soul, the last Adam was made a quickening spirit.
46 Howbeit, that was not first which is spiritual, but that which is natural; and afterward that which is spiritual.
47 The first man is of the earth, earthy; the second man is the Lord from heaven.
48 As is the earthy, such are they also that are earthy: and as is the

NOTES.

Nor is it in this Place alone that St. *Paul* calls the Resurrection of the Just by the general Name of the Resurrection of the Dead. He does the same, *Phil.* III. 11. where he speaks of his Sufferings, and of his Endeavours, if by any means he might attain unto the Resurrection of the Dead; whereby he cannot mean the Resurrection of the Dead in general, which, since he has declared in this very Chapter, *ver.* 22. all Men, both good and bad, shall as certainly partake of, as that they shall die, there needs no Endeavours to attain to it. Our Saviour likewise speaks of the Resurrection of the Just in the same general Terms of the Resurrection, *Matt.* XXII. 30. *and the Resurrection from the Dead*, Luke XX. 35. by which is meant only the Resurrection of the Just, as is plain from the Context.

43 [l] The Time that Man is in this World affixed to this Earth, is his being sown, and not when being dead he is put in the Grave, as is evident from St. *Paul's* own Words: For dead Things are not sown; Seeds are sown being alive, and die not till after they are sown. Besides, he that will attentively consider what follows, will find reason from St. *Paul's* arguing to understand him so.

44 [m] Σῶμα ψυχικόν, which, in our Bibles, is translated *natural Body*, should, I think, more suitably to the Propriety of the *Greek*, and more conformably to the Apostle's Meaning, be translated *animal Body*: For that which St. *Paul* is doing here, is to shew, that as we have animal Bodies now (which we derived from *Adam*) endowed with an animal Life, which, unless supported with a constant Supply of Food and Air, will fail and perish, and at last, do what we can, will dissolve and come to an End, so at the Resurrection we shall have from Christ, the second *Adam*, *spiritual Bodies*, which shall have an essential and natural inseparable Life in them, which shall continue and subsist perpetually of itself, without the Help of Meat and Drink, or Air, or any such foreign Support, without Decay, or any Tendency to a Dissolution; of which our Saviour speaking, Luke XX. 35. says, *They who shall be accounted worthy to obtain that World, and the Resurrection from the Dead, cannot die any more, for they are equal to the Angels*, i. e. of an angelical Nature and Constitution.

[n] *Vid.* Phil. III. 21.

those

I CORINTHIANS.

Ch. XV.

TEXT.	PARAPHRASE.

heavenly, such are they also that are heavenly.

49 And as we have borne the image of the earthy, we shall also bear the image of the heavenly.

those who are regenerate, and born of the heavenly Seed, are as he that is heavenly, spiritual, and immortal. And as in the animal, corruptible, mortal State we were born in, we have been like him that was earthy; so also shall we, who at the Resurrection partake of a Spiritual Life from Christ, be made like him, the Lord from Heaven, heavenly, *i. e.* live as the Spirits in Heaven do, without the Need of Food or Nourishment to support it, and without Infirmities, Decay and Death, enjoying a fixed, stable, unfleeting Life. This I say to you, Brethren, to satisfy those that ask with what Bodies the Dead shall come, that we shall not at the Resurrection have such Bodies as we have now: For Flesh and Blood cannot enter into the Kingdom which the Saints shall inherit in Heaven: nor are such fleeting, corruptible Things as our present Bodies are, fitted to that State of immutable Incorruptibility. To which let me add, what has not been hitherto discovered, *viz.* that we shall not all die, but we shall all be changed in a Moment, in the Twinkling of an Eye, at the Sounding of the last Trumpet; for the Trumpet shall sound, and the Dead shall rise; and as many of us Believers as are then alive, shall be changed. For this corruptible ° Frame and Constitution of ours must put on Incorruption, and from mortal

49.

50 Now this I say, brethren, that flesh and blood cannot inherit the kingdom of God; neither doth corruption inherit incorruption.

50.

51 Behold, I shew you a mystery; we shall not all sleep, but we shall all be changed,

52 In a moment, in the twinkling of an eye, at the last trump (for the trumpet shall sound) and the dead shall be raised incorruptible, and we shall be changed.

51.

52.

53 For this coruptible must put on incorruption, and

53.

NOTES.

53 ° Τὸ φθαρτὸν, *corruptible*, and τὸ θνητὸν, *mortal*, have not here σῶμα, *Body*, for their Substantive, as some imagine, but are put in the Neuter Gender absolute, and stand to represent νεκροὶ, *dead*, as appears by the immediately preceding Verse; and also ver. 42. οὕτω κ̀ ἡ ἀνάστασις τῶν νεκρῶν· σπείρεται ἐν φθορᾷ. *So is the Resurrection of the Dead; it is sown in Corruption, i. e.* mortal, corruptible Men, are sown, being corruptible and weak. Nor can it be thought strange or strained, that I interpret φθαρτὸν and θνητὸν as Adjectives of the Neuter Gender, to signify Persons, when, in this very Discourse, the Apostle uses two Adjectives in the Neuter

PARAPHRASE.

54. mortal become immortal. And when we are got into that State of Incorruptibility and Immortality, then shall be fulfilled what was foretold in these Words, Death is swallowed up of Victory ᵖ; *i. e.* Death is perfectly subdued and exterminated by a compleat Victory over it, so
55. that there shall be no Death any more. Where, O Death, is now that Power whereby thou deprivest Men of Life? What is become of the Dominion of the Grave, whereby they were
56. detained Prisoners there ᑫ? That which gives Death the Power over Men is Sin; and 'tis the
57. Law by which Sin has this Power. But Thanks be to God, who gives us Deliverance and Victory over Death, the Punishment of Sin by the Law, through our Lord Jesus Christ, who has delivered us from the Rigor of the Law.

TEXT.

this mortal must put on immortality.

54 So when this corruptible shall have put on incorruption, and this mortal shall have put on immortality, then shall be brought to pass the saying that is written, Death is swallowed up in victory.

55 O Death, where is thy sting? O grave, where is thy victory?

56 The sting of death is sin; and the strength of sin is the law.

57 But thanks be to God, which giveth us the victory, through our Lord Jesus.

NOTES.

Neuter Gender, to signify the Persons of *Adam* and *Christ*, in such a way, as it is impossible to understand them otherwise. The Words no farther off than *ver.* 46. are these: Ἀλλὰ ἡ πρῶτον τὸ πνευματικὸν ἀλλὰ τὸ ψυχικὸν, ἔπειτα τὸ πνευματικὸν. The like Way of speaking we have *Mat.* I. 20. and *Luke* I. 35. in both which the Person of our Saviour is expressed by Adjectives of the Neuter Gender. To any of all which Places I do not think any one will add the Substantive σῶμα, *Body*, to make out the Sense. That then which is meant here being this, that this *mortal Man* shall put on Immortality, and this *corruptible Man* Incorruptibility, any one will easily find another Nominative Case to σπείρεται, *is sown*, and not σῶμα, *Body*, when he considers the Sense of the Place; wherein the Apostle's Purpose is to speak of νεκροὶ, *mortal Men*, being dead, and raised again to Life, and made immortal. Those with whom Grammatical Construction, and the Nominative Case weighs so much, may be pleased to read this Passage in *Virgil*;

> Linquebant dulces animas, aut ægra trahebant
> Corpora,   Æneid. l. 3. ver. 140.

where, by finding the Nominative Case to the two Verbs in it, he may come to discover that Personality, as, contra-distinguished to both Body and Soul, may be the Nominative Case to Verbs.

54 Νῖκος, *Victory*, often signifies End and Destruction. See *Vossius de LXX interpret. cap.* 24.

55 ᑫ This has something the Air of a Song of Triumph, which St. *Paul* breaks out into upon a View of the Saints Victory over Death, in a State wherein Death is never to have place any more.

I CORINTHIANS.

Ch. XVI.

TEXT.

58 Therefore, my beloved brethren, be ye ſtedfaſt, unmoveable, always abounding in the work of the Lord, foraſmuch as ye know that your labour is not in vain in the Lord.

PARAPHRASE.

58. Wherefore, my beloved Brethren, continue ſtedfaſt and unmoveable in the Chriſtian Faith, always abounding in your Obedience to the Precepts of Chriſt, and in thoſe Duties which are required of us by our Lord and Saviour; knowing that your Labour will not be loſt, whatſoever you ſhall do or ſuffer for him, will be abundantly rewarded by eternal Life.

SECT. XI.

CHAP. XVI. 1.——4.

CONTENTS.

HE gives Directions concerning their Contribution to the poor Chriſtians at *Jeruſalem*.

TEXT.

1 NOW concerning the collection for the ſaints, as I have given order to the churches of Galatia, even ſo do ye.

2 Upon the firſt day of the week, let every one of you lay by him in ſtore, as God hath proſpered him, that there be no gatherings when I come.

PARAPHRASE.

1. AS to the Collection for the Converts to Chriſtianity, who are at *Jeruſalem*, I would have you do as I have directed the Churches of *Galatia*. 2. Let every one of you, according as he thrives in his Calling, lay aſide ſome Part of his Gain by itſelf; which the firſt Day of the Week let him put into the common Treaſury ʳ of the Church, that there may be no need of any Gathering when I come.

NOTES.

2 ʳ Θησαυρίζων ſeems uſed here in the Senſe I have given it. For 'tis certain, that the Apoſtle directs that they ſhould every Lord's Day bring to the Congregation what their Charity had laid aſide the foregoing Week, as their Gain came in, that there it might be put into ſome publick Box appointed for that purpoſe, or Officers Hands. For if they only laid it aſide at home, there would neverthelefs be need of a Collection when he came.

And

I CORINTHIANS.

PARAPHRASE.

3. And when I come, those whom you shall approve of¹, will I send with Letters to *Jerusa-*
4. *lem*, to carry thither your Benevolence: Which, if it deserves that I also should go, they shall go along with me.

TEXT.

3 And when I come, whomsoever you shall approve by your letters, them will I send to bring your liberality unto Jerusalem.

4 And if it be meet that I go also, they shall go with me.

NOTES.

3 ¹ Δοκιμάσητε, δι᾽ ἐπιστολῶν τούτους πέμψω, this Pointing that makes δι᾽ ἐπιστολῶν belong to πέμψω, and not δοκιμάσητε, the Apostle's Sense justifies: He telling them here, that finding their Collection ready when he came, he would write by those they should think fit to send it by, or go himself with them, if their Present were worthy of it. There needed no Approbation of their Messengers to him by their Letters, when he was present: And if the *Corinthians*, by their Letters, approved of them to the Saints at *Jerusalem*, how could St. *Paul* say he would send them?

SECT. XII.
CHAP. XVI. 5——12.

CONTENTS.

HE gives them an Account of his own, *Timothy*'s, and *Apollos*'s Intention of coming to them.

PARAPHRASE.

5. I Will come unto you, when I have been in *Macedonia*, for I intend to take that in my
6. Way: And perhaps I shall make some Stay, nay winter with you, that you may bring me go-
7. ing on my Way, whithersoever I go. For I do not intend just to call in upon you, as I pass by; but I hope to spend some Time with
8. you, if the Lord permit. But I shall stay at
9. *Ephesus* till *Pentecost*, i. e. *Whitsuntide*. For now I have a very fair and promising Opportunity given me of propagating the Gospel, tho' there

TEXT.

5 NOW I will come unto you, when I shall pass through Macedonia: (for I do pass through Macedonia)

6 And it may be that I will abide, yea, and winter with you, that ye may bring me on my journey whithersoever I go.

7 For I will not see you now by the way, but I trust to tarry a while with you, if the Lord permit.

8 But I will tarry at Ephesus until Pentecost.

9 For a great door and effectual is opened unto me,

I CORINTHIANS.
Ch. XVI.

TEXT.

and there are many adversaries.
10 Now if Timotheus come, see that he may be with you without fear: for he worketh the work of the Lord, as I also do.
11 Let no man therefore despise him: but conduct him forth in peace, that he may come unto me: for I look for him with the brethren.
12 As touching our brother Apollos, I greatly desired him to come unto you with the brethren: but his will was not at all to come at this time; but he will come when he shall have convenient time.

PARAPHRASE.

there be many Opposers. If *Timothy* come to you, pray take care that he be easy, and without Fear amongst you; for he promotes the Work of the Lord in preaching the Gospel, even as I do. Let no body therefore despise him, but treat him kindly, and bring him going, that he may come unto me; for I expect him with the Brethren. As to Brother [t] *Apollos*, I have earnestly endeavoured to prevail with him to come to you with the Brethren [u]; but he has no mind to it at all at present: He will come however, when there shall be a fit Occasion.

10.

11.

12.

NOTES.

12 [t] There be few, perhaps, who need to be told it, yet it may be convenient here, once for all, to remark, that in the Apostle's Time *Brother* was the ordinary Compellation that Christians used to one another.

[u] The *Brethren* here mentioned, seem to be *Stephanas*, and those others, who with him came with a Message or Letter to St. *Paul* from the Church of *Corinth*, by whom he returned this Epistle in answer.

SECT. XIII.
CHAP. XVI. 13——24.

CONTENTS.

THE Conclusion, wherein St. *Paul*, according to his Custom, leaves some, which he thinks most necessary, Exhortations, and sends particular Greetings.

TEXT.

13 Watch ye, stand fast in the faith, quit you like men, be strong.
14 Let all your things be done with charity.

PARAPHRASE.

BE upon your Guard, stand firm in the Faith, behave yourselves like Men, with Courage and Resolution. And whatever is done amongst you, either in your publick Assem-

13.

14.

U

I CORINTHIANS.

PARAPHRASE.

Assemblies, or elsewhere, let it all be done with Affection and Good-will, one to another [w].
15. You know the House of *Stephanas*, that they were the first Converts of *Achaia*, and have all along made it their business to minister to the
16. Saints: To such I beseech you to submit yourselves; let such as with us labour to promote
17. the Gospel, be your Leaders. I am glad that *Stephanas*, *Fortunatus*, and *Achaicus*, came to me; because they have supplied what was defi-
18. cient on your Side. For, by the Account they have given me of you, they have quieted my Mind, and yours too [x]: Therefore have a Re-
19. gard to such Men as these. The Churches of *Asia* salute you; and so do *Aquila* and *Priscilla*, with much Christian Affection; with the
20. Church that is in their House. All the Brethren here salute you: Salute one another with
21. an holy Kiss. That which followeth, is the Salutation of me *Paul*, with my own Hand.
22. If any one be an Enemy to the Lord Jesus Christ, and his Gospel, let him be accursed, or devoted to Destruction: The Lord cometh
23. to execute Vengeance on him [y]. The Favour
24. of the Lord Jesus Christ be with you. My Love be with you all, for Christ Jesus sake. *Amen*.

TEXT.

15. I beseech you, brethren, (ye know the house of Stephanas, that it is the first-fruits of Achaia, and that they have addicted themselves to the ministry of the saints.)
16. That ye submit yourselves unto such, and to every one that helpeth with us and laboureth.
17. I am glad of the coming of Stephanas, and Fortunatus, and Achaicus: for that which was lacking on your part they have supplied.
18. For they have refreshed my spirit and yours: therefore acknowledge ye them that are such.
19. The churches of Asia salute you. Aquila and Priscilla salute you much in the Lord, with the church that is in their house.
20. All the brethren greet you. Greet you one another with an holy kiss.
21. The salutation of me Paul with mine own hand.
22. If any man love not the Lord Jesus Christ, let him be Anathema, Maranatha.
23. The grace of our Lord Jesus Christ be with you.
24. My love be with you all in Christ Jesus. Amen.

NOTES.

14 [w] His main Design being to put an end to the Faction and Division which the false Apostle had made amongst them, 'tis no wonder that we find Unity and Charity so much, and so often pressed, in this and the second Epistle.

18 [x] *Viz.* By removing those Suspicions and Fears that were on both Sides.

22 [y] This being so different a Sentence from any of those writ with St. *Paul*'s own Hands, in any of his other Epistles, may it not with Probability be understood to mean the false Apostle, to whom St. *Paul* imputes all the Disorders in this Church, and of whom he speaks not much less severely, 2 *Cor.* XI. 13 ———— 15 ?

A

A

PARAPHRASE *and* NOTES

ON THE

Second EPISTLE of St. *PAUL*

TO THE

CORINTHIANS.

An. Chrif.
57. Nero-
nis 3.

SYNOPSIS.

Aint *Paul* having writ his first Epistle to the *Corinthians*, to try, as he says himself, *Chap*. II. 9. what Power he had still with that Church, wherein there was a great Faction against him, which he was attempting to break, was in pain till he found what Success it had, *Chap*. II. 12, 13. and VII. 5. But when he had by *Titus* received an Account of their Repentance, upon his former Letter; of their Submission to his Orders, and of their good Disposition of Mind towards him; he takes Courage, speaks of himself more freely, and justifies himself more boldly, as may be seen, *Chap*. I. 12. & II. 14. & VI. 10. & X. 1. & XIII. 10. And as to his Opposers, he deals more roundly and sharply with them, than he had done in his former Epistle, as appears from *Chap*. II. 17. & IV. 2—5. & V. 12. & VI. 11—16. & XI. 11. & XII. 15.

The Observation of these Particulars may possibly be of use to give us some light, for the better understanding of this second Epistle; especially if we add, that the main Business of this, as of his former Epistle, is to take off the People from the new Leader they had got, who was St. *Paul*'s Opposer; and wholly to put an end to the Faction and Disorder which that false Apostle had caused in the Church of *Corinth*. He also, in this Epistle, stirs them

U 2

up

Chap. I. up again to a liberal Contribution to the poor Saints at *Jerusalem*.

This Epistle was writ in the same Year, not long after the former.

SECTION I.

CHAP. I. 1, 2.

INTRODUCTION.

1. PAUL an Apostle of Jesus Christ, by the Will of God, and *Timothy* our Brother [a], to the Church of God which is in *Corinth*, with
2. all the Christians that are in all *Achaia* [b]; Favour and Peace be to you from God our Father, and from the Lord Jesus Christ.

TEXT.

1 PAUL an apostle of Jesus Christ by the will of God, and Timothy our brother, unto the church of God which is at Corinth, with all the saints which are in all Achaia:

2 Grace be to you, and peace from God our Father, and from the Lord Jesus Christ.

NOTES.

1 [a] *Brother*, i. e. either in the common Faith; and so as we have already remarked, he frequently calls all the Converted, as *Rom.* I. 13. and in other Places; or *Brother* in the Work of the Ministry, *vid.* Rom. XVI. 21. 1 Cor. XVI. 10. To which we may add, that St. *Paul* may be supposed to have given *Timothy* the Title of *Brother* here for Dignity's sake, to give him a Reputation above his Age amongst the *Corinthians*, to whom he had before sent him, with some kind of Authority to rectify their Disorders. *Timothy* was but a young Man, when St. *Paul* writ his first Epistle to him, as appears, 1 *Tim.* IV. 12. Which Epistle, by the Consent of all, was writ to *Timothy* after he had been at *Corinth*; and in the Opinion of some very learned Men, not less that Eight Years after: And therefore his calling him Brother here, and joining him with himself in writing this Epistle, may be to let the *Corinthians* see, that though he were so young, who had been sent to them, yet it was one whom St. *Paul* thought fit to treat very much as an Equal.

[b] *Achaia*, the Country wherein *Corinth* stood.

II CORINTHIANS

SECT. II.
CHAP. I. 3——VII. 16.

CONTENTS.

THIS first Part of this Second Epistle of St. *Paul* to the *Corinthians*, is spent in justifying himself against several Imputations from the opposite Faction, and setting himself right in the Opinion of the *Corinthians*: The Particulars whereof we shall take notice of in the following Numbers.

SECT. II. N. I.
CHAP. I. 3——14.

CONTENTS.

HE begins with justifying his former Letter to them, which had afflicted them, *vid. Chap.* VII. 7, 8. by telling them, that he thanks God for his Deliverance out of his Afflictions, because it enables him to comfort them, by the Example both of his Affliction and Deliverance; acknowledging the Obligation he had to them and others, for their Prayers and Thanks for his Deliverance, which he presumes they could not but put up for him, since his Conscience bears him witness (which was his Comfort) that in his Carriage to all Men, and to them more especially, he had been direct and sincere, without any self or carnal Interest, and that what he writ to them had no other Design but what lay open, and they read in his Words; and did also acknowledge, and he doubted not but they should always acknowledge, part of them acknowledging already, that he was the Man they gloried in, as they shall be his Glory in the Day of the Lord. From what St. *Paul* says in this Section, (which, if read with Attention, will appear to be writ with a Turn of great Infinuation) it may be gathered, that the opposite Faction endeavoured to evade the Force of the former Epistle, by suggesting, that

Chap. I. that whatever he might pretend, St. *Paul* was a cunning, artificial, self-interested Man, and had some hidden Design in it; which Accusation appears in other Parts also of this Epistle, as *Chap*. IV. 2, 5.

PARAPHRASE.

3. Blessed be the God ᶜ and Father of our
4. Lord Jesus Christ, the Father of Mercies, and God of all Consolation, who comforteth me in all my Tribulations, that I may be able to comfort them ᵈ, who are in any Trouble, by the Comfort which I receive from
5. him: Because, as I have suffered abundantly for Christ, so through Christ I have been abundantly comforted; and both these for your
6. Advantage. For my Affliction is for your Consolation and Relief ᵉ; which is effected by a patient enduring those Sufferings, whereof you see an Example in me: And again, when I am comforted, it is for your Consolation and Relief, who may expect the like from the same
7. compassionate God and Father. Upon which Ground I have firm Hopes, as concerning you; being assured, that as you have had your Share of Sufferings, so ye shall likewise have of
8. Consolation. For I would not have you ignorant, Brethren, of the Load of the Afflictions in *Asia*, that were beyond Measure heavy upon me, and beyond my Strength; so that I could see no Way of escaping with Life,

TEXT.

3 Blessed be God, even the Father of our Lord Jesus Christ, the Father of mercies, and the God of all comfort;

4 Who comforteth us in all our tribulation, that we may be able to comfort them which are in any trouble, by the comfort wherewith we ourselves are comforted of God.

5 For as the sufferings of Christ abound in us, so our consolation also abounderh by Christ.

6 And whether we be afflicted, it is for your consolation and salvation, which is effectual in the enduring of the same sufferings which we also suffer: or whether we be comforted, it is for your consolation and salvation.

7 And our hope of you is stedfast, knowing that as you are partakers of the sufferings, so shall ye be also of the consolation.

8 For we would not, brethren, have you ignorant of our trouble which came to us in Asia, that we were pressed out of mea-

NOTES.

3 ᶜ That this is the right Translation of the *Greek* here, see *Eph*. I. 3. and 1 *Pet*. I. 3. where the same Words are so translated; and that it agrees with St. *Paul's* Sense, see *Eph*. I. 17.

4 ᵈ He means here the *Corinthians*, who were troubled for their Miscarriage towards him; vid. *Chap*. VII. 7.

6 ᵉ Σωτηρία, *Relief*, rather than *Salvation*; which is understood of Deliverance from Death and Hell, but here it signifies only Deliverance from their present Sorrow.

But

II CORINTHIANS.

Chap. I.

TEXT.

sure, above strength, insomuch that we despaired even of life:

9 But we had the sentence of death in ourselves, that we should not trust in ourselves, but in God which raiseth the dead.

10 Who delivered us from so great a death, and doth deliver: in whom we trust that he will yet deliver us:

11 You also helping together by prayer for us, that for the gift bestowed upon us by the means of many persons, thanks may be given by many on our behalf.

12 For our rejoicing is this, the testimony of our conscience, that in simplicity and godly sincerity, not with fleshly wisdom, but by the grace of God, we have had our conversation in the world, and more abundantly to you-wards.

13 For we write none other things unto you, than what you read or acknowledge, and I trust you shall acknowledge even to the end.

14 As also you have acknowledged us in part, that we are your rejoicing, even as ye also are ours in the day of the Lord Jesus.

PARAPHRASE.

But I have the Sentence of Death in myself, that I might not trust in myself, but in God, who can restore to Life even those who are actually dead; who delivered me from so imminent a Danger of Death, who doth deliver, and in whom I trust he will yet deliver me: You also joining the Assistance of your Prayers for me; so that Thanks may be returned by many, for the Deliverance procured me by the Prayers of many Persons. For I cannot doubt of the Prayers and Concern of you, and many others for me, since my Glorying is this, *viz.* the Testimony of my own Conscience, that in Plainness of Heart, and Sincerity before God, not in fleshly Wisdom [f], but by the Favour of God directing me [g], I have behaved myself towards all Men, but more particularly towards you. For I have no Design, no Meaning in what I write to you, but what lies open, and is legible in what you read: And you yourselves cannot but acknowledge it to be so; and I hope you shall always acknowledge it to the End; as Part of you have already acknowledged that I am your Glory [h], as you will be mine at the Day of Judgment, when being my Scholars and Converts, ye shall be saved.

9.

10.

11.

12.

13.

14.

NOTES.

12 [f] What *Fleshly Wisdom* is, may be seen *Chap.* IV. 2, 5.

[g] This ἀλλ᾽ ἐν χάριτι Θεοῦ, *But in the Favour of God*, is the same with ἀλλὰ χάρις Θεοῦ, ἡ σὺν ἐμοί, *The Favour of God that is with me,* i. e. by God's favourable Assistance.

14 [h] *That I am your Glory;* whereby he signifies that Part of them which stuck to him, owned him as their Teacher: In which Sense *Glorying* is much used, in these Epistles to the *Corinthians,* upon the Occasion of the several Partisans boasting, some that they were of *Paul*, and others of *Apollos*.

SECT.

II CORINTHIANS.

SECT. II. N. 2.

CHAP. I. 15——II. 17.

CONTENTS.

THE next Thing St. *Paul* justifies, is his not coming to them. St. *Paul* had promised to call on the *Corinthians* in his way to *Macedonia*, but failed. This his Opposers would have to be from Levity in him, or a Mind that regulated itself wholly by carnal Interest, *vid. ver.* 17. To which he answers, that God himself having confirmed him amongst them, by the Unction and Earnest of his Spirit, in the Ministry of the Gospel of his Son, whom St. *Paul* had preached to them steadily the same, without any the least Variation, or unsaying any thing he had at any Time delivered, they could have no ground to suspect him to be an unstable uncertain Man, that would play fast and loose with them, and could not be depended on in what he said to them. This is what he says, *Chap.* I. 15——22.

In the next Place he, with a very solemn Asseveration, professes that it was to spare them, that he came not to them. This he explains, *Chap.* I. 23. and II. 2, 3.

He gives another Reason, *Chap.* II. 12, 13. why he went on to *Macedonia*, without coming to *Corinth*, as he had purposed; and that was the Uncertainty he was in, by the not coming of *Titus*, what Temper they were in at *Corinth*. Having mentioned his Journey to *Macedonia*, he takes notice of the Success which God gave to him there and every where, declaring of what Consequence his Preaching was both to the Salvation and Condemnation of those who received or rejected it; professing again his Sincerity and Disinterestedness, not without a severe Reflection on their false Apostle. All which we find in the following Verses, *viz. Chap.* II. 14—17. and is all very suitable, and pursuant to his Design in this Epistle, which was to establish his Authority and Credit amongst the *Corinthians*.

Having

II CORINTHIANS.

Chap. I.

TEXT.

15 AND in this confidence I was minded to come unto you before, that you might have a second benefit:
16 And to pass by you into Macedonia, and to come again out of Macedonia unto you, and of you to be brought on my way toward Judea.
17 When I therefore was thus minded, did I use lightness? or the things that I purpose, do I purpose according to the flesh, that with me there should be yea, yea, and nay, nay?
18 But as God is true, our word toward you was not yea, and nay.
19 For the Son of God, Jesus Christ, who was preached among you by us, even by me, and Silvanus, and Timotheus, was not yea and nay, but in him was yea.
20 For all the promises of God in him are yea, and in him amen, unto the glory of God by us.
21 Now he which stablisheth us with you in Christ, and hath anointed us, is God:
22 Who hath also sealed us

PARAPHRASE.

HAVING this Persuasion *(viz.)* of your Love and Esteem of me, I purposed to come unto you ere this, that you might have a second Gratification ¹; and to take you in my Way to *Macedonia*, and from thence return to you again, and by you be brought on in my Way to *Judea*. If this fell not out so as I purposed, am I therefore to be condemned of Fickleness? or am I to be thought an uncertain Man, that talks forwards and backwards; one that has no regard to his Word, any farther than may suit his carnal Interest? But God is my Witness, that what you have heard from me has not been uncertain, deceitful, or variable. For Jesus Christ, the Son of God, who was preached among you by me, and *Silvanus*, and *Timotheus*, was not, sometimes one thing, and sometimes another; but has been shewn to be uniformly one and the same, in the Counsel or Revelation of God, (for all the Promises of God do all consent and stand firm in him) to the Glory of God by my Preaching. Now it is God who establishes me with you, for the preaching of the Gospel, who has anointed ᵏ, and also sealed ˡ me, and given me the Ear-

15.
16.
17.
18.
19.
20.
21.
22.

NOTES.

15 ¹ By the Word χάριν, which our Bibles translate *Benefit* or *Grace*, 'tis plain the Apostle means his being present among them a second Time, without giving them any Grief or Displeasure. He had been with them before, almost two Years together, with Satisfaction and Kindness: He intended them another Visit; but it was, he says, that they might have the like Gratification, *i. e.* the like Satisfaction in his Company a second Time; which is the same he says, 2 *Cor.* II. 1.

21 ᵏ *Anointed*, i. e. set apart to be an Apostle by an extraordinary Call. Priests and Prophets were set apart by Anointing, as well as Kings.

22 ˡ *Sealed*, i. e. by the miraculous Gifts of the Holy Ghost; which are an Evidence of the Truths he brings from God, as a Seal is of a Letter.

X   nest

PARAPHRASE.

23. rest ᵐ of his Spirit in my Heart. Moreover, I call God to witness, and may I die if it is not so, that it was to spare you, that I came not
24. yet to *Corinth*: Not that I pretend to such a Dominion over your Faith, as to require you to believe what I have taught you without coming to you, when I am expected there to maintain and make it good, for 'tis by that Faith you stand; but I forbore to come, as one concerned to preserve and help forwards your Joy, which I am tender of, and therefore declined coming to you, whilst I thought you in an Estate that would require Severity from me, that would trouble you ⁿ.
1. I purposed in myself, 'tis true, to come to you again; but I resolved too, it should be

TEXT.

and given the earnest of the Spirit in our hearts.

23 Moreover, I call God for a record upon my soul, that to spare you I came not as yet unto Corinth.

24 Not for that we have dominion over your faith, but are helpers of your joy: for by faith ye stand.

1 But I determined this with myself, that I would

NOTES.

ᵐ *Earnest* of Eternal Life; for of that the Spirit is mentioned as a Pledge, in more Places than one, *vid.* 2 Cor. V. 5. Eph. I. 13, 14. All these are Arguments to satisfy the *Corinthians* that St. *Paul* was not, nor could be, a shuffling Man, that minded not what he said, but as it served his Turn.

The Reasoning of St. *Paul,* ver. 18 ——— 22. whereby he would convince the *Corinthians* that he is not a fickle, unsteady Man, that says and unsays, as may suit his Humour or Interest, being a little obscure, by reason of the Shortness of his Style here, which has left many Things to be supplied by the Reader, to connect the Parts of the Argumentation, and make the Deduction clear; I hope I shall be pardoned, if I endeavour to set it in its clear Light, for the sake of ordinary Readers.

God hath set me apart to the Ministry of the Gospel by an extraordinary Call, has attested my Mission by the miraculous Gifts of the Holy Ghost, and given me the Earnest of eternal Life in my Heart by his Spirit, and hath confirmed me amongst you in preaching the Gospel, which is all uniform, and of a piece, as I have preached it to you, without tripping in the least; and there, to the Glory of God, have shewn that all the Promises concur, and are unalterably certain in Christ: I therefore having never faultered in any thing I have said to you, and having all these Attestations of being under the special Direction and Guidance of God himself, who is unalterably true, cannot be suspected of dealing doubly with you in any thing relating to my Ministry.

24 ⁿ It is plain St. *Paul*'s Doctrine had been opposed by some of them at *Corinth,* vid. 1 Cor. XV. 12. his Apostleship questioned, 1 Cor. IX. 1, 2. 2 Cor. XIII. 3. he himself triumphed over, as if he durst not come, 1 Cor. IV. 18. they saying, his Letters were weighty and powerful, but his bodily Presence weak, and his Speech contemptible, 2 Cor. X. 10. This being the State his Reputation was then in at *Corinth,* and he having promised to come to them, 1 Cor. XVI. 5. he could not but think it necessary to excuse his failing them, by Reasons that should be both convincing and kind; such as are contained in this Verse, in the Sense given of it.

without

II *CORINTHIANS.*   Chap. II.

TEXT.	PARAPHRASE.	
not come again to you in heaviness.	without bringing Sorrow with me °: For if I grieve you, who is there, when I am with you, to comfort me, but those very Persons whom I have discomposed with Grief? And this very Thing P, which made me sad, I writ to you, not coming myself, on purpose, that when I came, I might not have Sorrow from those from whom I ought to receive Comfort; having this Belief and Confidence in you all, that you, all of you, make my Joy and Satisfaction so much your own, that you would remove all Cause of Disturbance before I came. For I writ unto you with great Sadness of Heart, and many Tears; not with intention to grieve you, but that you might know the Overflow of Tenderness and Affection which I have for you. But if the Fornicator has been the Cause of Grief, I do not say he has been so to me, but in some degree to you all, that I may not lay load on him q;	2.
2. For if I make you sorry, who is he then that maketh me glad, but the same which is made sorry by me?		3.
3 And I wrote this same unto you, lest when I came, I should have sorrow from them of whom I ought to rejoice, having confidence in you all, that my joy is the joy of you all.		
4 For out of much affliction and anguish of heart, I wrote unto you with many tears; not that you should be grieved, but that ye might know the love which I have more abundantly unto you.		4.
5 But if any have caused grief, he hath not grieved me, but in part: that I may not overcharge you all.		5.

NOTES.

1 ° That this is the Meaning of this Verse, and not that he would not come to them in Sorrow a second Time, is past doubt, since he had never been with them in Sorrow a first Time; *vid.* 2 *Cor.* I. 15.

3 P Καὶ ἔγραψα ὑμῖν τοῦτο αὐτὸ. *And I writ to you this very Thing.* That ἔγραψα, *I writ,* relates here to the first Epistle to the *Corinthians,* is evident, because it is so used in the very next Verse; and again, a little lower, *ver.* 9. What, therefore, is it, in his first Epistle, which he here calls τοῦτο αὐτὸ, *this very Thing,* which he had writ to them? I answer, the Punishment of the Fornicator. This is plain by what follows here, to *ver.* 11. especially if it be compared with 1 *Cor.* IV. 21. and V. 8. For there he writes to them to punish that Person; whom if he, St. *Paul,* had come himself before it was done, he must have come, as he calls it, with a Rod, and have himself chastised: But now that he knows that the *Corinthians* had punished him in compliance to his Letter, and he had this Trial of their Obedience, he is so far from continuing the Severity, that he writes to them to forgive him, and take him again into their Affection.

5 q St. *Paul* being satisfied with the *Corinthians* for their ready Compliance with his Orders, in his former Letter, to punish the Fornicator, intercedes to have him restored; and to that end lessens his Fault, and declares, however he might have caused Grief to the *Corinthians,* yet he had caused none to him.

X 2   the

II. CORINTHIANS.

PARAPHRASE.

6. the Correction he hath received from the Majority of you, is sufficient in the Case: So that,
7. on the contrary ʳ, it is fit rather that you forgive and comfort him, lest he ˢ should be swal-
8. lowed up by an Excess of Sorrow. Wherefore, I beseech you, to confirm your Love to
9. him; which I doubt not of. For this also was one End of my writing to you, *viz.* to have a Trial of you, and to know whether you are
10. ready to obey me in all Things. To whom you forgive any thing, I also forgive. For if I have forgiven any thing, I have forgiven it to him for your sakes, by the Authority and in the
11. Name of Christ; that we may not be overreached by Satan, for we are not ignorant of
12. his Wiles. Furthermore, being arrived at *Troas*, because *Titus*, whom I expected from *Corinth* with News of you, was not come, I was very uneasy ᵗ there; in so much that I made not use of the Opportunity which was put into my Hands, by the Lord, of preaching the Gospel of Christ, for which I came thither.
13. I hastily left those of *Troas*, and departed thence
14. to *Macedonia*. But thanks be to God, in that he

TEXT.

6. Sufficient to such a man is this punishment which was inflicted of many.
7. So that contrariwise ye ought rather to forgive him, and comfort him, lest perhaps such a one should be swallowed up with overmuch sorrow.
8. Wherefore, I beseech you, that ye would confirm your love towards him.
9. For to this end also did I write, that I might know the proof of you, whether ye be obedient in all things.
10. To whom ye forgive any thing, I forgive also: for if I forgave any thing, to whom I forgave it, for your sakes forgave I it, in the person of Christ:
11. Lest Satan should get an advantage of us: for we are not ignorant of his devices.
12. Furthermore, when I came to Troas to preach Christ's gospel, and a door was opened unto me of the Lord,
13. I had no rest in my spirit, because I found not Titus my brother: but taking my leave of them, I went from thence into Macedonia.
14. Now thanks be unto

NOTES.

7 ʳ Τὐναντίον, *On the contrary*, here, has nothing to refer to but ἐπιτιμία, *Over-charge*, in the 5th Verse; which makes that to belong to the Fornicator, as I have explained it.

ˢ Ὁ τοιοῦτος, *such an one*, meaning the Fornicator. It is observable how tenderly St. *Paul* deals with the *Corinthians* in this Epistle; for though he treats of the Fornicator from the 5th to the 10th Verse inclusively, yet he never mentions him under that or any other disobliging Title, but in the soft and inoffensive Terms of *any one*, or *such an one*. And that possibly may be the Reason why he says μὴ ἐπιτιμία, indefinitely, without naming the Person it relates to.

12 ᵗ How uneasy he was, and upon what account, see *Chap.* VII. ⸔——16. It was not barely for *Titus*'s Absence, but for want of the News he brought with him, *Chap.* VII. 7.

always

II CORINTHIANS

Chap. II.

TEXT.

God, which always cauſeth us to triumph in Chriſt, and maketh manifeſt the favour of his knowledge by us in every place.
15 For we are unto God a ſweet favour of Chriſt, in them that are ſaved, and in them that periſh.
16 To the one we are the favour of death unto death; and to the other the favour of life unto life: and who is ſufficient for theſe things?

17 For we are not as many, which corrupt the word of God: but as of ſincerity, but as of God, in the ſight of God ſpeak we in Chriſt.

PARAPHRASE.

always makes me triumph every where ᵘ, thro' Chriſt, who gives me Succeſs in preaching the Goſpel, and ſpreads the Knowledge of Chriſt by me. For my Miniſtry and Labour in the Goſpel, is a Service or ſweet-ſmelling Sacrifice to God, through Chriſt, both in regard of thoſe that are ſaved, and thoſe that periſh: To the one my Preaching is of ill Savour, unacceptable and offenſive, by their rejecting whereof they draw Death on themſelves; and to the other, being as a ſweet Savour, acceptable, they thereby receive eternal Life: And who is ſufficient for theſe Things ʷ? And yet, as I ſaid, my Service in the Goſpel is well-pleaſing to God. For I am not as ſeveral ˣ are, who are Huckſters of the Word of God, preaching it for Gain; but I preach the Goſpel of Jeſus Chriſt in Sincerity: I ſpeak as from God himſelf, and I deliver it as in the Preſence of God.

15.

16.

17.

NOTES.

14 ᵘ *Who makes me triumph every where*, i. e. in the Succeſs of my Preaching in my Journey to *Macedonia*; and alſo in my Victory, at the ſame Time, at *Corinth*, over the falſe Apoſtles, my Oppoſers, that had raiſed a Faction againſt me amongſt you. This, I think, is St. *Paul*'s Meaning, and the Reaſon of his uſing the Word *Triumph*, which implies Conteſt and Victory, though he places that Word ſo, as modeſtly to cover it.
16 ʷ *Vid. Chap.* III. 5, 6.
17 ˣ This, I think, may be underſtood of the falſe Apoſtle.

II CORINTHIANS.

SECT. II. N. 3.
CHAP. III. 1——VII. 16.

CONTENTS.

HIS speaking well of himself, (as he did sometimes in his first Epistle, and with much more Freedom in this, which, as it seems, had been objected to him amongst the *Corinthians*) his Plainness of Speech, and his Sincerity in preaching the Gospel, are the Things which he chiefly justifies in this Section many ways. We shall observe his Arguments, as they come in the Order of St. *Paul*'s Discourse; in which are mingled, with great Insinuation, many Expressions of an overflowing Kindness to the *Corinthians*, not without some Exhortations to them.

PARAPHRASE.

1. DO I begin again to commend myself[y]; or need I, as some [z], commendatory Letters to, or from you? You are my commendatory Epistle, written in my Heart, known
2. and read by all Men. I need no other commendatory Letter, but you, being manifested
3. to be the commendatory Epistle of Christ, written on my behalf; not with Ink, but with the Spirit of the living God; not on Tables of Stone [a], but of the Heart, whereof I was the Ama-

TEXT.

1 DO we begin again to commend ourselves; or need we, as some others, epistles of commendation to you, or letters of commendation from you?

2 Ye are our epistle written in our hearts, known and read of all men:

3 Forasmuch as ye are manifestly declared to be the epistle of Christ, ministered by us, written not with ink, but with the

NOTES.

1 [y] This is a plain Indication that he had been blamed amongst them for commending himself.

[z] Seems to intimate, that their false Apostle had got himself recommended to them by Letters, and so had introduced himself into that Church.

3 [a] The Sense of St. *Paul* in this 3d Verse, is plainly this, That he needed no Letters of Commendation to them, but that by their Conversion, and the Gospel written not with Ink, but with the Spirit of God, in the Tables of their Hearts, and not in Tables of Stone, by his Ministry, was as clear an Evidence and Testimony to them of his Mission from Christ, as the Law writ in Tables of Stone was an Evidence of *Moses*'s Mission; so that he, St. *Paul*, needed no other Recommendation: This is what is to be understood by this Verse, unless we will make *the Tables*

II CORINTHIANS.

Chap. III.

TEXT.

Spirit of the living God; not in tables of stone, but in fleshly tables of the heart.

4 And such trust have we through Christ to Godward.

5 Not that we are sufficient of ourselves to think any thing as of ourselves: but our sufficiency is of God.

6 Who also hath made us able ministers of the new testament, not of the letter, but of the Spirit: for

PARAPHRASE.

Amanuensis, *i. e.* your Conversion was the Effect of my Ministry. ᵇ And this so great Confidence have I, thro' Christ, in God. Not as if I were sufficient of myself to reckon ᶜ upon any thing, as of myself; but my Sufficiency, my Ability to perform any thing, is wholly from God: Who has fitted and enabled me to be a Minister of the New Testament; not of the Letter ᵈ, but of the Spirit; for the Letter kills ᵉ, but the

4.
5.
6.

NOTES.

of *Stone* to have no Signification here. But, to say as he does, that the *Corinthians*, being writ upon, in their Hearts, not with Ink, but with the Spirit of God, by the Hand of St. *Paul*, was Christ's commendatory Letter of him, being a pretty bold Expression, liable to the Exception of the captious Part of the *Corinthians*; he, to obviate all Imputation of Vanity or Vainglory herein, immediately subjoins what follows in the next Verse.

4 ᵇ As if he had said, But mistake me not, as if I boasted of myself; this so great Boasting that I use, is only my Confidence in God, through Christ: For it was God that made me a Minister of the Gospel, that bestowed on me the Ability for it; and whatever I perform in it, is wholly from him.

5 ᶜ Πεποίθησις, *Trust*, a milder Term for *Boasting*; for so St. *Paul* uses it, Chap. X. 7. compared with *ver.* 8. where also λογίζεσθαι, *ver.* 7. is used, as here, for counting upon one's self. St. *Paul* also used πέποιθα, for *thou boastest*, Rom. II. 19. which will appear, if compared with *ver.* 17. Or if λογίζεσθαι shall rather be thought to signify here, to discover by Reasoning, then the Apostle's Sense will run thus: "Not as if I were sufficient of myself, by the Strength of " my own natural Parts, to attain the Knowledge of the Gospel Truths that I preach; but " my Ability herein is all from God." But in whatever Sense λογίζεσθαι is here taken, 'tis certain τι, which is translated *any thing*, must be limited to the Subject in hand, *viz.* the Gospel that he preached to them.

6 ᵈ Ου γράμματος, αλλα πνεύματος, *Not of the Letter, but of the Spirit*. By expressing himself, as he does here, St. *Paul* may be understood to intimate that *the New Testament*, or *Covenant*, was also, tho' obscurely, held forth in the Law: For he says he was constituted a Minister, πνεύματος, *of the Spirit*, or spiritual Meaning of the Law, which was Christ, (as he tells us himself, *ver.* 17.) and giveth Life, whilst the *Letter* killeth. But both *Letter* and *Spirit* must be understood of the same Thing, *viz. The Letter* of the Law, and *the Spirit* of the Law. And, in fact, we find St. *Paul* truly a Minister of the Spirit of the Law; especially in his Epistle to the *Hebrews*, where he shews what a spiritual Sense ran through the Mosaical Institution and Writings.

ᵉ *The Letter kills*, i. e. pronouncing Death, without any Way of Remission, on all Transgressors, leaves them under an irrevocable Sentence of Death; but the Spirit, *i. e.* Christ, *ver.* 17. who is a quickening Spirit, 1 *Cor.* XV. 45. giveth Life.

Spirit

II CORINTHIANS.

PARAPHRASE.

7. Spirit gives Life. But if the Ministry of the Law written in Stone, which condemns to Death, were so glorious to *Moses*, that his Face shone so that the Children of *Israel* could not steadily behold the Brightness of it, which was but temporary, and was quickly to vanish ᶠ;
8. how can it be otherwise, but that the Ministry of the Spirit, which giveth Life, should confer more Glory and Lustre on the Ministers
9. of the Gospel? For if the Ministration of Condemnation were Glory, the Ministry of Justification ᵍ in the Gospel doth certainly
10. much more exceed in Glory: Though even the Glory that *Moses*'s Mnistration had, was no Glory, in comparison of the far more excelling Glory of the Gospel-Ministry ʰ. Far-
11. ther, if that which is temporary, and to be done away, were delivered with Glory, how

TEXT.

the letter killeth, but the Spirit giveth life.

7 But if the ministration of death written and engraven in stones, was glorious, so that the children of Israel could not stedfastly behold the face of Moses, for the glory of his countenance; which glory was to be done away;

8 How shall not the ministration of the Spirit be rather glorious?

9 For if the ministration of condemnation be glory, much more doth the ministration of righteousness exceed in glory.

10 For even that which was made glorious, had no glory in this respect, by reason of the glory that excelleth.

11 For if that which is done away was glorious,

NOTES.

7 ᶠ Καταργουμένην, *done away*, is applied here to the Shining of *Moses*'s Face, and to the Law, ver. 11. and 13. In all which Places it is used in the Present Tense, and has the Signification of an Adjective, standing for temporary, or of a Duration, whose End was determined, and is opposed to τῷ μένοντι, *that which remaineth*, i. e. that which is lasting, and hath no predetermined End set to it, as ver. 11. where the Gospel Dispensation is called τὸ μένον, *that which remaineth*. This may help us to understand ἀπὸ δόξης εἰς δόξαν, ver. 18. *from Glory to Glory*, which is manifestly opposed to δόξῃ καταργουμένῃ, the *Glory done away*, of this Verse, and so plainly signifies a continued, lasting Glory of the Ministers of the Gospel; which, as he tells us there, consisted in their being changed into the Image and clear Representation of the Lord himself, as the Glory of *Moses* consisted in the transitory Brightness of his Face, which was a faint Reflection of the Glory of God appearing to him in the Mount.

9 ᵍ Διακονία τῆς δικαιοσύνης, *the Ministration of Righteousness*; so the Ministry of the Gospel is called, because, by the Gospel, a Way is provided for the Justification of those who have transgressed: But the Law has nothing but rigid Condemnation for all Transgressors, and therefore is called here *the Ministration of Condemnation*.

10 ʰ Though the shewing that the Ministry of the Gospel is more glorious than that of the Law, be what St. *Paul* is upon here, thereby to justify himself, if he has assumed some Authority and Commendation to himself, in his Ministry and Apostleship; yet, in his thus industriously placing the Ministry of the Gospel in Honour above that of *Moses*, may he not possibly have an Eye to the Judaizing, false Apostle of the *Corinthians*, to let them see what little Regard was to be had to that Ministration, in comparison of the Ministry of the Gospel?

much

II CORINTHIANS.

TEXT.

much more that which remaineth is glorious.
12 Seeing then that we have such hope, we use great plainness of speech.
13 And not as Moses, which put a vail over his face, that the children of Israel could not stedfastly

PARAPHRASE.

much rather is that which remains, without being done away, to appear in Glory ^{l}? Wherefore having such Hope ^{k}, we use great Freedom and Plainness of Speech. And not as *Moses*, who put a Vail over his Face, do we vail the Light, so that the Obscurity of what we deliver, should hinder ^{l} the Children of *Israel* from

12.
13.

NOTES.

11 ^{i} Here St. *Paul* mentions another Pre-eminency and Superiority of Glory in the Gospel over the Law, *viz.* That the Law was to cease and to be abolished, but the Gospel to remain and never to be abolished.

12 ^{k} *Such Hope:* That St. *Paul*, by these Words, means the so honourable Employment of an Apostle and Minister of the Gospel, or the Glory belonging to his Ministry in the Gospel, is evident by the whole foregoing Comparison which he has made, which is all along between διακονία, *the Ministry* of the Law and of the Gospel, and not between the Law and the Gospel themselves. The calling of it *Hope*, instead of Glory here, where he speaks of his having of it, is the Language of Modesty, which more particularly suited his present Purpose: For the Conclusion, which in this Verse he draws from what went before, plainly shews the Apostle's Design, in this Discourse, to be the justifying his speaking freely of himself and others, his Argument amounting to thus much:

Having therefore so honourable an Employment, as is the Ministry of the Gospel, which far exceeds the Ministry of the Law in Glory, tho' even that gave so great a Lustre to *Moses*'s Face, that the Children of *Israel* could not with fixed Eyes look upon him; I, as becomes one of such Hopes, in such a Post as sets me above all mean Considerations and Compliances, use great Freedom and Plainness of Speech in all Things that concern my Ministry.

13 ^{l} Πρὸς τὸ μὴ ἀτενίσαι, &c. *That the Children of* Israel *could not stedfastly look*, &c. St. *Paul* is here justifying in himself, and other Ministers of the Gospel, the Plainness and Openness of their Preaching, which he had asserted in the immediately preceding Verse. These Words therefore here, must, of necessity, be understood not of *Moses*, but of the Ministers of the Gospel, *viz.* That it was not the Obscurity of their Preaching, not any thing vailed, in their Way of proposing the Gospel, which was the Cause why the Children of *Israel* did not understand the Law to the Bottom, and see Christ, the End of it, in the Writings of *Moses*. What St. *Paul* says in the next Verse, *But their Minds were blinded, for until this Day remaineth the same Vail untaken away*, plainly determines the Words we are upon, to the Sense I have taken them in: For what Sense is this? *Moses put a Vail over his Face, so that the Children of* Israel *could not see the End of the Law; but their Minds were blinded, for the Vail remains upon them until this Day.* But this is very good Sense, and to St. *Paul*'s Purpose, *viz.* " We, the " Ministers of the Gospel, speak plainly and openly, and put no Vail upon ourselves, as " *Moses* did, whereby to hinder the *Jews* from seeing Christ in the Law; but that which hin- " ders them, is a Blindness on their Minds, which has been always on them, and remains to " this Day." This seems to be an obviating an Objection which some among the *Corinthians* might make to his boasting of so much Plainness and Clearness in his Preaching, *viz.* If you preach the Gospel, and Christ contained in the Law, with such a shining Clearness and Evidence, how comes it that the *Jews* are not converted to it? His Reply is, " Their Unbelief " comes not from any Obscurity in our Preaching, but from a Blindness which rests upon " their Minds to this Day; which shall be taken away, when they turn to the Lord.

II CORINTHIANS.

PARAPHRASE.

seeing in the Law, which was to be done a-
way, Christ, who was the End ᵐ of the Law:
14. But their not seeing it, is from the Blindness of
their own Minds; for unto this Day the same
Vail remains upon their Understandings, in
reading of the Old Testament, which Vail is
done away in Christ, *i. e.* Christ, now he is
come, so exactly answers all the Types, Prefi-
gurations, and Predictions of him in the Old
Testament, that presently, upon turning our
Eyes upon him, he visibly appears to be the
Person designed; and the Obscurity of those
Passages concerning him, which before were
not understood, is taken away and ceases.
15. Nevertheless, even until now, when the Writings of *Moses* are read, the Vail ⁿ remains upon
their Hearts; they see not the spiritual and
16. evangelical Truths contained in them. But
when their Heart shall turn to the Lord, and
laying by Prejudice and Aversion, shall be willing to receive the Truth, the Vail shall be
taken away, and they shall plainly see him
to be the Person spoken of and intended ᵒ.
17. But the Lord is the Spirit ᵖ whereof we are
Ministers; and they who have this Spirit,
have Liberty ᑫ, so that they speak openly and
18. freely: But we, all the faithful Ministers of

TEXT.

look to the end of that which is abolished.

14 But their minds were blinded: for until this day remaineth the same vail untaken away, in the read-ing of the Old Testament; which vail is done away in Christ.

15 But even unto this day, when Moses is read, the vail is upon their heart.

16 Nevertheless, when it shall turn to the Lord, the vail shall be taken away.

17 Now the Lord is that Spirit: and where the Spi-rit of the Lord is, there is liberty.

18 But we all with open face, beholding as in a

NOTES.

ᵐ *Vid.* Rom. X. 2-4.
15 ⁿ St. *Paul* possibly alludes here to the Custom of the *Jews*, which continues still in the Sy-nagogue, that when the Law is read, they put a Vail over their Faces.
16 ᵒ When this shall be, see *Rom.* XI. 25, 27.
17 ᵖ Ὁ δὲ κύριος τὸ πνεῦμά ἐστι, *but the Lord is that Spirit:* These Words relate to *ver.* 6. where he says, that he is a Minister, not of the Letter of the Law, nor of the outside and literal Sense, but of the mystical and spiritual Meaning of it; which here he tells us is Christ.
ᑫ *There is Liberty;* because the Spirit is given only to Sons, or those that are free. See *Rom.* VIII. 15. *Gal.* IV. 6, 7.

the

TEXT.

glass the glory of the Lord, are changed into the same image, from glory to glory, even as by the Spirit of the Lord.

PARAPHRASE.

the New Testament, not vailed ʳ, but with open Countenances, as Mirrors reflecting the Glory of the Lord, are changed into his very Image by a continued Succession of Glory, as it were streaming upon us from the Lord, who is the Spirit who gives us this Clearness and Freedom.

NOTES.

18 ˢ St. *Paul* justifies his Freedom and Plainness of Speech, by his being made by God himself a Minister of the Gospel, which is a more glorious Ministry than that of *Moses*, in promulgating the Law. This he does, from *ver.* 6. to *ver.* 12. inclusively. From thence, to the End of the Chapter, he justifies his Liberty of speaking; in that he, as a Minister of the Gospel, being illuminated with greater and brighter Rays of Light than *Moses*, was to speak (as he did) with more Freedom and Clearness than *Moses* had done. This being the Scope of St. *Paul* in this Place, 'tis visible, all from these Words, *Who put a Vail upon his Face,* ver. 13. to the Beginning of *ver.* 18. is a Parenthesis; which being laid aside, the Comparison between the Ministers of the Gospel and *Moses*, stands clear: "*Moses* with a Vail covered the Brightness and Glory "of God, which shone in his Countenance; but we, the Ministers of the Gospel, with open "Countenance, κατοπτριζομενοι, reflecting as Mirrors the Glory of the Lord." So the Word κατοπτριζομενοι must signify here, and not *beholding as in a Mirror*; because the Comparison is between the Ministers of the Gospel and *Moses*, and not between the Ministers of the Gospel and the Children of *Israel*: Now the Action of *beholding*, was the Action of the Children of *Israel*, but of *shining* or *reflecting the Glory received in the Mount*, was the Action of *Moses*; and therefore it must be something answering that in the Ministers of the Gospel wherein the Comparison is made, as is farther manifest in another express Part of the Comparison between the vailed Face of *Moses*, ver. 13. and the open Face of the Ministers of the Gospel in this Verse. The Face of *Moses* was vailed, that the bright Shining, or Glory of God, remaining on it, or reflected from it, might not be seen, and the Faces of the Ministers of the Gospel are open, that the bright Shining of the Gospel, or the Glory of Christ, may be seen. Thus the Justness of the Comparison stands fair, and has an easy Sense; which is hard to be made out, if κατοπτριζομενοι be translated *beholding as in a Glass*.

Την αυτην εικονα μεταμορφουμεθα, *We are changed into that very Image,* i. e. the Reflection of the Glory of Christ from us is so very bright and clear, that we are changed into his very Image; whereas the Light that shone in *Moses*'s Countenance, was but a faint Reflection of the Glory which he saw when God shewed him his Back-Parts, *Exod.* XXXIII. 23.

Απο δοξης εις δοξαν, *from Glory to Glory,* i. e. with a continued Influx and renewing of Glory; in opposition to the shining of *Moses*'s Face, which decayed and disappeared in a little while, *ver.* 7.

Καθαπερ απο κυριου πνευματος, *as from the Lord the Spirit,* i. e. as if this Irradiation of Light and Glory came immediately from the Source of it, the Lord himself, who is that Spirit whereof we are the Ministers, *ver.* 6. which giveth Life and Liberty, *ver.* 17.

This Liberty he here speaks of, *ver.* 17 is παρρησια, *Liberty of Speech,* mentioned *ver.* 12. the Subject of St. *Paul*'s Discourse here; as is farther manifest from what immediately follows in the six first Verses of the next Chapter, wherein an attentive Reader may find a very clear Comment on this 18th Verse we are upon, which is there explained in the Sense we have given of it.

Y 2

Seeing

PARAPHRASE.

1. Seeing therefore I am intrusted with such a Ministry as this, according as I have received great Mercy, being extraordinarily and miraculously called when I was a Prosecutor, I do not fail ᵗ nor flag; I do not behave myself unworthily in it, nor misbecoming the Honour and Dignity of such an Employment:

2. But, having renounced all unworthy and indirect Designs, which will not bear the Light, free from Craft, and from playing any deceitful Tricks in my preaching the Word of God, I recommend myself to every one's Conscience, only by making plain ᵘ the Truth which I deliver, as in the Presence of God.

3. But if the Gospel which I preach, be obscure and hidden, it is so only to those who are lost:

4. In whom being Unbelievers, the God of this World ᵛ has blinded their Minds ʷ, so that the glorious ˣ Brightness of the Light of the Gospel of Christ, who is the Image of

TEXT.

1. Therefore seeing we have this ministry, as we have received mercy, we faint not:

2. But have renounced the hidden things of dishonesty, not walking in craftiness, nor handling the word of God deceitfully, but by manifestation of the truth, commending ourselves to every man's conscience in the sight of God.

3. But if our gospel be hid, it is hid to them that are lost:

4. In whom the god of this world hath blinded the minds of them which believe not, lest the light of the glorious gospel of Christ, who is the image of God, should shine unto them.

NOTES.

1 ᵗ Ουκ ἐκκακοῦμεν, *we faint not*, is the same with πολλῇ παρρησίᾳ χρώμεθα, *we use great Plainness of Speech*, ver. 12. of the foregoing Chapter, and signifies, in both Places, the clear, plain, direct, disinterested Preaching of the Gospel; which is what he means in that figurative Way of Speaking in the former Chapter, especially the last Verse of it, and which he more plainly expresses in the five or six first Verses of this: The whole Business of the first Part of this Epistle being, as we have already observed, to justify to the *Corinthians* his Behaviour in his Ministry, and to convince them, that in his preaching the Gospel he hath been plain, clear, open and candid, without any hidden Design, or the least Mixture of any concealed, secular Interest.

2 ᵘ Απειπάμεθα τὰ κρυπτὰ τῆς αἰσχύνης, *have renounced the hidden Things of Dishonesty*, and τῇ φανερώσει τῆς ἀληθείας, *by Manifestation of the Truth*: These Expressions explain ἀνακεκαλυμμένῳ προσώπῳ, *with open Face*, Chap. iii. 18.

4 ᵛ *The God of this World*, i. e. the Devil: so called, because the Men of the World worshipped and obeyed him as their God.

ʷ Ἐτύφλωσε τὰ νοήματα, *blinded their Minds*, answers ἐπωρώθη τὰ νοήματα, *their Minds were blinded*, Chap. III. 14. And the second and third Verse of this, explains the 13th and 14th Verses of the preceding Chapter.

ˣ Δόξα, *Glory*, here, as in the former Chapter, is put for Shining and Brightness; so that ἐπαυγάσαι τῆς δόξης τοῦ Χριστοῦ, is the Brightness or Clearness of the Doctrine wherein Christ is manifested in the Gospel.

God,

II CORINTHIANS.

Chap. IV.

TEXT.

5 For we preach not ourselves, but Christ Jesus the Lord; and ourselves your servants for Jesus sake.
6 For God who commanded the light to shine out of darkness, hath shined in our hearts, to give the light of the knowledge of the glory of God, in the face of Jesus Christ.
7 But we have this treasure in earthen vessels, that the excellency of the power may be of God, and not of us.
8 We are troubled on every side, yet not distressed; we are perplexed, but not in despair:
9 Persecuted, but not forsaken; cast down, but not destroyed.
10 Always bearing about in the body, the dying of the Lord Jesus, that the life also of Jesus might be made manifest in our body.

PARAPHRASE.

God, cannot enlighten them. For I seek not my own Glory or secular Advantage in preaching, but only the propagating of the Gospel of the Lord Jesus Christ; professing myself your Servant for Jesus sake. For God, who made Light to shine out of Darkness, hath enlightened also my dark Heart, who before saw not the End of the Law; that I might communicate the Knowledge and Light of the Glory of God, which shines in the Face ʸ of Jesus Christ. But yet we, to whom this Treasure of Knowledge, the Gospel of Jesus Christ, is committed to be propagated in the World, are but frail Men; that so the exceeding great Power that accompanies it, may appear to be from God, and not from us. I am pressed on every side, but do not shrink; I am perplexed, but yet not so as to despond; persecuted, but yet not left to sink under it; thrown down, but not slain: Carrying about every where in my Body the Mortification, *i. e.* a Representation of the Sufferings of the Lord Jesus; that also the Life of Jesus, risen from the Dead, may be made manifest by the Energy that accompanies my preach-

5.
6.
7.
8.
9.
10.

NOTES.

6 ʸ This is a Continuation still of the Allegory of *Moses*, and the Shining of his Face, &c. so much insisted on in the foregoing Chapter.

For the Explication whereof, give me leave to add here one Word more to what I have said upon it already. *Moses*, by approaching to God in the Mount, had a Communication of *Glory* or *Light* from him, which irradiated from his Face when he descended from the Mount: *Moses* put a Vail over his Face, to hide this *Light* or *Glory*; for both these Names St. *Paul* uses in this, and the foregoing Chapter, for the same Thing. But the *Glory* or *Light* of the Knowledge of God, more fully and clearly communicated by Jesus Christ, is said here to *shine in his Face*: And in that Respect it is that Christ, in the foregoing Verse, is called by St. *Paul*, *the Image of God*; and the Apostles are said, in the last Verse of the precedent Chapter, to be *transformed into the same Image from Glory to Glory*, *i. e.* by their large and clear Communications of the Knowledge of God in the Gospel, they are said to be transformed into the same Image, and to represent, as Mirrors, the Glory of the Lord; and to be, as it were, the Images of Christ, as Christ is (as we are told here, ver. 4.) the Image of God.

ing

PARAPHRASE.

11. ing in this frail Body. For as long as I live, I shall be exposed to the Danger of Death for the sake of Jesus, that the Life of Jesus risen from the Dead, may be made manifest by my Preaching and Sufferings in this mortal Flesh
12. of mine. So that the Preaching of the Gospel procures Sufferings and Danger of Death to me, but to you it procures Life, *i. e.* the Energy of the Spirit of Christ, whereby he lives in, and
13. gives Life to those who believe in him. Nevertheless, though Suffering and Death accompany the preaching the Gospel, yet having the same Spirit of Faith that *David* had, when he said, I believe, therefore have I spoken; I also
14. believing, therefore speak: Knowing that he who raised up the Lord Jesus, shall raise me up also by Jesus, and present me with you to God.
15. For I do and suffer all Things for your sakes, that the exuberant Favour of God may abound, by the Thanksgiving of a greater Number, to the Glory of God; *i. e.* I endeavour by my Sufferings and Preaching to make as many Converts as I can; that so the more partaking of the Mercy and Favour of God, of which there is a plentiful and inexhaustible Store, the more may give Thanks unto him; it being more for the Glory of God, that a greater Num-
16. ber should give Thanks, and pray to him. For which Reason I faint not ⁿ, I flag not; but tho' my bodily Strength decay, yet the Vigour of my

TEXT.

11. For we which live, are alway delivered unto death for Jesus sake, that the life also of Jesus might be made manifest in our mortal flesh.
12. So then death worketh in us, but life in you.
13. We having the same spirit of faith, according as it is written, I believed, and therefore have I spoken: we also believe, and therefore speak;
14. Knowing that he which raised up the Lord Jesus, shall raise up us also by Jesus, and shall present us with you.
15. For all things are for your sakes, that the abundant grace might, through the thanksgiving of many, redound to the glory of God.
16. For which cause we faint not; but tho' our outward man perish, yet the inward man is renewed day by day:

NOTES.

16 ⁿ *I faint not.* What this signifies, we have seen, *ver.* 1. Here St. *Paul* gives another Proof of his Sincerity in his Ministry, and that is the Sufferings and Danger of Death, which he daily incurs by his preaching the Gospel: And the Reason why those Sufferings and Dangers deter him not, nor make him at all flag, he tells them, is the Assurance he has that God, through Christ, will raise him again, and reward him with Immortality in Glory. This Argument he pursues, *Chap.* IV. 17. & V. 9.

Mind

II CORINTHIANS.

Chap. IV.

TEXT.

17 For our light affliction, which is but for a moment, worketh for us a far more exceeding and eternal weight of glory;
18 While we look not at the things which are seen, but at the things which are not seen: for the things which are seen, are temporal; but the things which are not seen, are eternal.

1 For we know, that if our earthly house of this tabernacle were dissolved, we have a building of God, an house not made with hands, eternal in the heavens.
2 For in this we groan earnestly, desiring to be cloathed upon with our house which is from heaven.
3 If so be, that being cloathed, we shall not be found naked.
4 For we that are in this tabernacle do groan, being burdened: not for that we would be uncloathed, but cloathed upon, that mortality might be swallowed up of life.

PARAPHRASE.

17. Mind is daily renewed: For the more my Sufferings are here in propagating the Gospel, which at worst are but transient and light, the more will they procure me an exceedingly far greater Addition of that Glory [a] in Heaven, which is solid and eternal;
18. I having no regard to the visible Things of this World, but to the invisible Things of the other; for the Things that are seen, are temporal, but those that are not seen, are eternal.

Chap. V.

1. For I know, that if this my Body, which is but as a Tent for my sojourning here upon Earth for a short Time, were dissolved, I shall have another of a divine Original; which shall not, like Buildings made with Mens Hands, be subject to decay, but shall be eternal in the Heavens.
2. For in this Tabernacle [b] I groan earnestly, desiring, without putting off this mortal, earthly Body, by Death to have that celestial Body superinduced;
3. if so be, the coming [c] of Christ shall overtake me in this Life, before I put off this Body.
4. For we that are in the Body, groan under the Pressures and Inconveniencies that attend us in it; which yet we are not therefore willing to put off, but had rather, without dying, have it changed [d] into a celestial, immortal Body; that so this mortal State may be put an End to, by an immediate

NOTES.

17 [a] *Weight of Glory.* What an Influence St. *Paul's Hebrew* had among his *Greek*, is every where visible: כבד in *Hebrew* signifies *to be heavy*, and *to be glorious*; St. *Paul* in the *Greek* joins them, and says, *Weight of Glory.*

2 [b] Vid. Ver. 4.

3 [c] That the Apostle looked on the Coming of Christ as not far off, appears by what he says, 1 *Thess.* IV. 15. & V. 6. which Epistle was written some Years before this. See also to the same Purpose, 1 *Cor.* I. 7. & VII. 29, 31. & X. 11. *Rom.* XIII. 11, 12. *Heb.* X. 37.

4 [d] The same that he had told them in the first Epistle, *Cap.* XV. 51. should happen to those who should be alive at Christ's coming. This, I must own, is no very easy Passage: Whether we understand by γυμνοὶ, *naked*, as I do here, the State of the Dead, uncloathed

II CORINTHIANS.

PARAPHRASE.

5. mediate Entrance into an immortal Life. Now it is God who prepares and fits us for this immortal State; who also gives us the Spirit, as
6. a Pledge ᵉ of it. Wherefore, being always undaunted ᶠ, and knowing that whilst I dwell or sojourn in this Body, I am absent from my
7. proper Home, which is with the Lord (for I regulate my Conduct, not by the Enjoyment of the visible Things of this World, but by my Hope and Expectation of the invisible Things
8. of the World to come) I, with Boldness ᶠ, preach the Gospel; preferring in my Choice the quitting this Habitation, to get home to
9. the Lord. Wherefore, I make this my only Aim, whether staying ᵍ here in this Body, or departing ᵍ out of it, so to acquit myself, as

TEXT.

5. Now he that hath wrought us for the self-same thing, is God, who also hath given unto us the earnest of the Spirit.
6. Therefore we are always confident, knowing that whilst we are at home in the body, we are absent from the Lord:
7. (For we walk by faith, not by sight)
8. We are confident, I say, and willing rather to be absent from the body, and to be present with the Lord.
9. Wherefore we labour, that whether present or absent, we may be accepted of him.

NOTES.

with immortal Bodies, till the Resurrection; which Sense is favoured by the same Word, 1 *Cor.* XV. 37. or whether we understand the *Cloathing upon*, which the Apostle desires, to be those immortal Bodies which Souls shall be cloathed with at the Resurrection; which Sense of *cloathing upon*, seems to be favoured by 1 *Cor.* XV. 53, 54. and is that which one should be inclined to, were it not accompanied with this Difficulty, *viz.* that then it would follow that the Wicked should not have immortal Bodies at the Resurrection: For whatever it be, that St. *Paul* here means by being *cloathed upon*, it is something that is peculiar to the Saints, who have the Spirit of God, and shall be with the Lord, in contra-distinction to others, as appears from the following Verses, and the whole Tenor of this Place.

5 ᵉ The Spirit is mentioned, in more Places than one, as the Pledge and Earnest of Immortality; more particularly *Eph.* I. 13, 14. which, compared with *Rom.* VIII. 23. shews that the Inheritance, whereof the Spirit is the Earnest, is the same which the Apostle speaks of here, *viz.* the Possession of immortal Bodies.

6, 8 ᶠ Θαρρῶυτες and Θαρροῦμεν, *we are confident*, signifies, in these Verses, the same that ἐμ ἐκκακοῦμεν, *we faint not*, does, *Chap.* IV. 1, & 16. *i. e.* I go on undauntedly, without flagging, preaching the Gospel with Sincerity, and direct Plainness of Speech. This Conclusion, which he draws here from the Consideration of the Resurrection and Immortality, is the same that he makes upon the same Ground, *Chap.* IV. 14, 16.

9 ᵍ Εἴτε ἐνδημοῦντες, Ἐίτε ἐκδημοῦντες, *whether staying in the Body, or going out of it,* i. e. whether I am to stay longer here, or suddenly to depart. This Sense the foregoing Verse leads us to: And what he says in this Verse, that he endeavours (whether ἐνδημῶν, or ἐκδημῶν) *to be well-pleasing to the Lord,* i. e. do what is well-pleasing to him, shews, that neither of these Words can signify here his being with Christ in Heaven: For when he is there, the Time of endeavouring to approve himself is over.

II CORINTHIANS.

Chap. V.

TEXT.

10 For we must all appear before the judgment-seat of Christ, that every one may receive the things done in his body, according to that he hath done, whether it be good or bad.

11 Knowing therefore the terror of the Lord, we persuade men; but we are made manifest unto God, and I trust also are made manifest in your consciences.

12 For we commend not ourselves again unto you, but give you occasion to glory on our behalf, that you may have somewhat to answer them

PARAPHRASE.

to be acceptable to him [h]. For we must all 10. appear before the Judgment-Seat of Christ, that every one may receive according to what he has done in the Body, whether it be good or bad. Knowing therefore this terrible Judg- 11. ment of the Lord, I preach the Gospel, persuading Men to be Christians: And with what Integrity I discharge that Duty, is manifest to God; and I trust you also are convinced of it in your Consciences. And this I say, not 12. that I commend [i] myself again, but that I may give you an occasion not to be ashamed of me, but to glory on my behalf; having wherewithal to reply to those who make a shew of glorying in outward Appearance,

NOTES.

[h] St. *Paul*, from *Chap.* IV. 12. to this Place, has, to convince them of his Uprightness in his Ministry, been shewing that the Hopes and sure Expectation he had of eternal Life, kept him steady and resolute, in an open, sincere Preaching of the Gospel, without any Tricks, or deceitful Artifice. In which his Argument stands thus: "Knowing that God, who raised up Christ, will raise me up again, I, without any Fear or Consideration of what it may draw upon me, preach the Gospel faithfully, making this Account, that the momentaneous Afflictions which for it I may suffer here, which are but slight in comparison of the eternal Things of another Life, will exceedingly increase my Happiness in the other World, where I long to be; and therefore Death, which brings me home to Christ, is no Terror to me; all my Care is, that whether I am to stay longer in this Body, or quickly to leave it, living or dying, I may approve myself to Christ in my Ministry." In the next two Verses he has another Argument, to fix in the *Corinthians* the same Thoughts of him; and that is the Punishment he shall receive at the Day of Judgment, if he should neglect to preach the Gospel faithfully, and not endeavour sincerely and earnestly to make Converts to Christ.

12 [i] From this Place, and several others in this Epistle, it cannot be doubted but that his speaking well of himself had been objected to him, as a Fault. And in this lay his great Difficulty, how to deal with this People: If he answered nothing to what was talked of him, his Silence might be interpreted Guilt and Confusion; if he defended himself, he was accused of Vanity, Self-commendation, and Folly. Hence it is that he uses so many Reasons to shew, that his whole Carriage was upon Principles far above all worldly Considerations; and tells them here, once for all, that the Account he gives of himself is only to furnish them who are his Friends, and stuck to him, with Matter to justify themselves in their Esteem of him, and to reply to the contrary Faction.

Z

without

II CORINTHIANS.

PARAPHRASE.

13. without doing so inwardly in their Hearts [k]. For if [l] I am besides myself [m], in speaking as I do of myself, it is between God and me, he must judge, Men are not concerned in it, nor hurt by it; or if I do it soberly, and upon good ground; if what I profess of myself be in reality true, it is for your Sake and Ad-
14. vantage. For 'tis the Love of Christ constraineth me; judging, as I do, that if Christ
15. died for all, then all were dead; and that if he died for all, his Intention was, that they, who by him have attained to a State of Life, should not any longer live to themselves alone, seeking only their own private Advantage, but should employ their Lives in promoting the Gospel and Kingdom of Christ, who for them
16. died, and rose again. So that from henceforth I have no regard to any one, according to the Flesh [n], *i. e.* for being circumcised, or a *Jew*

TEXT.

13. which glory in appearance, and not in heart.
For whether we be besides ourselves, it is to God: or whether we be sober, it is for your cause.
14. For the love of Christ constraineth us, because we thus judge, that if one died for all, then were all dead:
15. And that he died for all, that they which live, should not henceforth live unto themselves, but unto him which died for them, and rose again.
16. Wherefore henceforth know we no man after the flesh: yea, though we have known Christ after the flesh, yet now henceforth

NOTES.

[k] This may be understood of the Leaders of the opposite Faction, who, as 'tis manifest from *Chap.* X. 7, 15. and XI. 12, 22, 23. pretended to something that they gloried in, though St. *Paul* assures us, they were satisfied in Conscience that they had no solid ground of glorying.

13 [l] St. *Paul*, from the 13th Verse of this Chapter, to *Chap.* VI. 12. gives another Reason for his disinterested Carriage in Preaching the Gospel; and that is his Love to Christ, who, by his Death, having given him Life, who was dead, he concludes, that in Gratitude he ought not to live to himself any more. He therefore being as in a new Creation, had now no longer any Regard to the Things or Persons of this World; but being made by God a Minister of the Gospel, he minded only the faithful Discharge of his Duty in that Ambassy, and pursuant thereunto, took care that his Behaviour should be such as he describes, *Chap.* VI. 3 —— 10.

[m] *Besides myself*, i. e. in speaking well of myself in my own Justification. He that observes what St. *Paul* says, *Chap.* XI. 1. & 16 —— 21. *Chap.* XII. 6. & 11. will scarce doubt but that the speaking of himself, as he did, was by his Enemies called Glorying, and imputed to him as Folly and Madness.

16 [n] This may be supposed to be said with Reflection on their *Jewish* false Apostle, who gloried in his Circumcision, and, perhaps, that he had seen Christ in the Flesh, or was some way related to him.

For

II CORINTHIANS.

Chap. V.

TEXT.

know we him no more.

17 Therefore if any man be in Christ, he is a new creature: old things are past away, behold, all things are become new.

18 And all things are of God, who hath reconciled us to himself by Jesus Christ, and hath given to us the ministry of reconciliation;

19 To wit, that God was in Christ, reconciling the world unto himself, not imputing their trespasses upon them; and hath committed unto us the word of reconciliation.

20 Now then we are ambassadors for Christ, as though God did beseech you by us: we pray you in Christ's stead, be ye reconciled to God.

21 For he hath made him to be sin for us, who knew no sin; that we might be made the righteousness of God in him.

PARAPHRASE.

For if I myself have gloried in this, that Christ himself was circumcised, as I am, and was of my Blood and Nation, I do so now no more any longer. So that if any one be in Christ, it is as if he were in a new Creation°, wherein all former mundane Relations, Considerations and Interests ᵖ are ceased, and at an end; all Things in that State are new to him, and he owes his very Being in it, and the Advantages he therein enjoys, not in the least measure to his Birth, Extraction, or any legal Observances or Privileges, but wholly and solely to God alone; reconciling the World to himself by Jesus Christ, and not imputing their Trespasses to them. And therefore I, whom God hath reconciled to himself, and to whom he hath given the Ministry, and committed the Word of this Reconciliation, as an Ambassador for Christ, as tho' God did by me beseech you, I pray you, in Christ's stead, be ye reconciled to God. For God hath made him subject to Sufferings and Death, the Punishment and

17.

18.

19.

20.

21.

NOTES.

17 ° Gal. VI. 14. may give some light to this Place. To make the 16th and 17th Verses coherent to the rest of St. Paul's Discourse here, they must be understood in reference to the false Apostle, against whom St. Paul is here justifying himself; and makes it his main Business in this, as well as his former Epistle, to shew what that false Apostle gloried in was no just Cause of boasting. Pursuant to this Design of sinking the Authority and Credit of that false Apostle, St. Paul, in these and the following Verses, dexterously insinuates these two Things: 1ˢᵗ, That the Ministry of Reconciliation being committed to him, they should not forsake him, to hearken to, and follow that Pretender. 2dly, That they being in Christ, and the new Creation, should, as he does, not know any Man in the Flesh; not esteem or glory in that false Apostle, because he might, perhaps, pretend to have seen our Saviour in the Flesh, or have heard him, or the like. Κτίσις signifies *Creation*; and is so translated, Rom. VIII. 22.

ᵖ Τὰ ἀρχαῖα *old Things*, perhaps, may here mean the *Jewish* Oeconomy; for the false Apostle was a *Jew*, and, as such, assumed to himself some Authority, probably by Right of Blood and Privilege of his Nation, vid. 2 Cor. XI. 21, 22. But that St. *Paul* here tells them, now under the Gospel, is all antiquated, and quite out of doors.

Z 2

Conse-

II CORINTHIANS.

PARAPHRASE.

Consequence of Sin, as if he had been a Sinner, though he were guilty of no Sin; that we, in and by him, might be made righteous by a Righteousness imputed to us by God.

1. I therefore working together with him, beseech you also, that you receive not the Favour of God, in the Gospel preached to you,
2. in vain ^a. (For he saith, I have heard thee in a Time accepted, and in the Day of Salvation have I succoured thee: Behold, now is the accepted Time; behold, now is the Day of Sal-
3. vation) Giving no Offence to any one in any
4. thing, that the Ministry be not blamed: But in every thing approving myself as becomes the Minister of God, by much Patience in Afflic-
5. tions, in Necessities, in Streights, in Stripes, in Imprisonments, in being tossed up and down, in
6. Labours, in Watchings, in Fastings; by a Life undefiled, by Knowledge, by Long-Sufferings, by the Gifts of the Holy Ghost, by Love un-
7. feigned; by preaching the Gospel of Truth sincerely, by the Power of God assisting my Ministry, by Uprightness of Mind, wherewith I am armed at all Points, both to do and to suffer;
8. by Honour and Disgrace, by good and bad Re-
9. port; as a Deceiver ^r, and yet faithful; as an obscure, unknown Man, but yet known and owned; as one often in danger of Death, and yet, behold, I live; as chastened, but yet not
10. killed; as sorrowful, but yet always rejoicing;

TEXT.

1 We then as workers together with him, beseech you also, that ye receive not the grace of God in vain.

2 (For he saith, I have heard thee in a time accepted, and in the day of salvation have I succoured thee: behold, now is the accepted time: behold, now is the day of salvation.)

3 Giving no offence in any thing, that the ministry be not blamed:

4 But in all things approving ourselves as the ministers of God, in much patience, in afflictions, in necessities, in distresses,

5 In stripes, in imprisonments, in tumults, in labours, in watchings, in fastings,

6 By pureness, by knowledge, by long-suffering, by kindness, by the Holy Ghost, by love unfeigned,

7 By the word of truth, by the power of God, by the armour of righteousness, on the right hand and on the left;

8 By honour and dishonour, by evil report and good report; as deceivers, and yet true;

9 As unknown, and yet well known; as dying, and behold, we live; as chastened, and not killed;

10 As sorrowful, yet al-

NOTES.

1 ^a *Receive the Grace of God in vain*, is the same with *believing in vain*, 1 Cor. XV. 2. *i. e.* receiving the Doctrine of the Gospel for true, and professing Christianity, without persisting in it, or performing what the Gospel requires.

8 *Deceiver*; a Title, 'tis like, he had received from some of the opposite Faction at *Corinth*, vid. Chap. XII. 16.

II CORINTHIANS.

Chap. VI.

TEXT.

way rejoicing; as poor, yet making many rich; as having nothing, and yet possessing all things.

11 O ye Corinthians, our mouth is open unto you, our heart is enlarged.

12 Ye are not straitened in us, but ye are straitened in your own bowels.

13 Now for a recompense in the same, (I speak as unto my children) be ye also enlarged.

14 Be ye not unequally yoked together with unbelievers: for what fellowship hath righteousness with unrighteousness? and what communion hath light with darkness?

15 And what concord hath Christ with Belial? or what part hath he that believeth with an infidel?

16 And what agreement hath the temple of God with idols? for ye are the temple of the living God; as God hath said, I will dwell in them, and walk in them; and I will be their God, and they shall be my people.

17 Wherefore come out from among them, and be ye separate, saith the Lord, and touch not the unclean thing; and I will receive you,

18 And will be a father unto you, and ye shall be my sons and daughters, saith the Lord almighty.

PARAPHRASE.

as poor, yet making many rich; as having nothing, and yet possessing all things.

O ye *Corinthians*, my Mouth is opened to you, my Heart is enlarged ᵃ to you, my Affection, my Tenderness, my Compliance for you, is not streight or narrow. 'Tis your own Narrowness makes you uneasy. Let me speak to you as a Father to his Children; in return do you likewise enlarge your Affections and Deference to me. Be ye not associated with Unbelievers, have nothing to do with them in their Vices or Worship ᵗ; for what Fellowship hath Righteousness with Unrighteousness? What Communion hath Light with Darkness? What Concord hath Christ with Belial ᵘ? Or what Part hath a Believer with an Unbeliever? What Agreement hath the Temple of God with Idols? For ye are the Temple of the living God, as God hath said, I will dwell in them, among them will I walk, and I will be their God, and they shall be my People. Wherefore come out from among them, and be separate, saith the Lord, and touch not the unclean Thing; and I will receive you to me. And I will be a Father to you, and ye shall be my Sons and Daughters, saith the Lord Almighty.

11.
12.
13.
14.
15.
16.
17.
18.

NOTES.

11 ᵗ Another Argument St. *Paul* makes use of to justify and excuse his Plainness of Speech to the *Corinthians*, is, the great Affection he has for them, which he here breaks out into an Expression of, in a very pathetical Manner. This, with an Exhortation to separate from Idolaters and Unbelievers, is what he insists on, from this Place to *Ch.* VII. 16.

14 ᵗ *Vid.* Ch. VII. 1.

15 ᵘ *Belial* is a general Name for all the false Gods worshipped by the idolatrous *Gentiles*.

Having

PARAPHRASE.

1. Having therefore these Promises, (dearly Beloved) let us cleanse ourselves from the Defilement of all Sorts of Sins, whether of Body or Mind, endeavouring after perfect Holiness in the Fear of God.
2. Receive me, as one to be hearkened to, as one to be followed, as one that hath done nothing to forfeit your Esteem. I have wronged no Man: I have corrupted no Man: I have defrauded no Man ʷ: I say not this to reflect on your Carriage towards me: ˣ For I have already assured you, that I have so great an Affection for you, that I could live
4. and die with you. But in the Transport of my Joy, I use great Liberty of Speech towards you. But let it not be thought to be of ill Will, for I boast much of you; I am filled with Comfort, and my Joy abounds exceedingly in all my Afflictions.
5. For when I came to *Macedonia*, I had no Respite from continual Trouble that befet me on every Side. From without I met with Strife and Opposition in Preaching the Gospel: And within I was filled with Fear upon your Account, lest the false Apostle continuing his Credit and Faction amongst you, should pervert you from the Simplicity of the
6. Gospel ʸ. But God, who comforteth those who are cast down, comforted me by the coming of *Titus*, not barely by his Presence, but by the Comfort I received from you by him, when he acquainted me with your great Desire of conforming yourselves to my Orders; your Trouble for any Neglects you have been guilty

TEXT.

1. Having therefore these promises (dearly beloved) let us cleanse ourselves from all filthiness of the flesh and spirit, perfecting holiness in the fear of God.
2. Receive us: we have wronged no man, we have corrupted no man, we have defrauded no man.
3. I speak not this to condemn you: for I have said before, that you are in our hearts to die and live with you.
4. Great is my boldness of speech toward you, great is my glorying of you. I am filled with comfort, I am exceeding joyful in all our tribulation.
5. For when we were come into Macedonia, our flesh had no rest, but we were troubled on every side; without were fightings, within were fears.

6. Nevertheless, God that comforteth those that are cast down, comforted us by the coming of Titus:
7. And not by his coming only, but by the consolation wherewith he was comforted in you, when he told us your earnest desire, your mourning, your fervent mind toward me;

NOTES.

2 ʷ This infinuates the contrary Behaviour of their false Apostle.
3 ˣ *Vid.* 1 Cor. IV. 3. 2. Cor. X. 2. & XI. 20, 21. & XIII. 3.
5 ʸ *Vid.* Chap. XI. 3.

II CORINTHIANS.

Ch. VII.

TEXT.

so that I rejoiced the more.

8 For though I made you sorry with a letter, I do not repent, though I did repent: for I perceive that the same epistle made you sorry, though it were but for a season.

9 Now I rejoice, not that ye were made sorry, but that ye sorrowed to repentance: for ye were made sorry after a godly manner, that ye might receive damage by us in nothing.

10 For godly sorrow worketh repentance to salvation not to be repented of: but the sorrow of the world worketh death.

11 For behold, this self same thing that ye sorrowed after a godly sort, what carefulness it wrought in you, yea, what clearing of yourselves, yea, what indignation, yea, what fear, yea, what vehement desire, yea, what zeal, yea, what revenge: in all things ye have approved yourselves to be clear in this matter.

PARAPHRASE.

of towards me; the great Warmth of your Affection and Concern for me; so that I rejoiced the more for my past Fears, having writ to you a Letter, which I repented of, but now do not repent of, perceiving that though that Letter grieved you, it made you sad but for a short Time: But now I rejoice not that you were made sorry, but that you were made sorry to Repentance. For this proved a beneficial Sorrow, acceptable to God, that in nothing you might have cause to complain that you were damaged by me. For godly Sorrow worketh Repentance to Salvation not to be repented of: But Sorrow rising from worldly Interest, worketh Death. In the present Case mark it, ᶻ that godly Sorrow which you had, what Carefulness it wrought in you, to conform yourselves to my Orders, *ver.* 15. yea, what clearing yourselves from your former Miscarriages; yea, what Indignation against those who led you into them; yea, what Fear to offend meᵃ; yea, what vehement Desire of satisfying me; yea, what Zeal for me; yea, what Revenge against yourselves for having been so misled. You have shewn yourselves to be set right *, and be as you should be in every

8.

9.

10.

11.

NOTES.

11 ᶻ St. *Paul* writing to those who knew the Temper they were in, and what were the Objects of the several Passions which were raised in them, doth both here, and in the 7*th* Verse, forbear to mention by, and to what they were moved, out of Modesty and Respect to them. This is necessary for the Information of ordinary Readers, to be supplied as can be best collected from the main Design of the Apostle in these two Epistles, and from several Passages giving us light in it.

* *Vid.* Ver. 15. * *Clear.* This Word answers very well ἁγνὸς in the *Greek*; but then to be clear in *English*, is generally understood to signify not to have been guilty; which could not be the Sense of the Apostle, he having charged the *Corinthians* so warmly in his first Epistle. His Meaning must therefore be, that they had now resolved on a contrary Course, and were so far clear, *i. e.* were set right, and in good Disposition again, as he describes it in the former

II CORINTHIANS.

PARAPHRASE.

12. every thing by this Carriage of yours †. If therefore I wrote unto you concerning the Fornicator, it was not for his Sake that had done, nor his that had suffered the Wrong, but principally that my Care and Concern for you might be made known to you, as in the Presence of
13. God; therefore I was comforted in your Comfort: But much more exceedingly rejoiced I in the Joy of *Titus*, because his Mind was set at ease by the good Disposition he found you all
14. in towards me ᵇ. So that I am not ashamed of having boasted of you to him. For as all that I have said to you is Truth, so what I said to *Titus* in your Commendation he has found to be
15. true, whereby his Affection to you is abundantly increased, he carrying in his Mind the universal Obedience of you all unanimously to me, and the Manner of your receiving him

TEXT.

12 Wherefore though I wrote unto you, I did it not for his cause that had done the wrong, nor for his cause that suffered wrong, but that our care for you in the sight of God might appear unto you.

13 Therefore we were comforted in your comfort: yea, and exceedingly the more joyed we for the joy of Titus, because his spirit was refreshed by you all.

14 For if I have boasted any thing to him of you, I am not ashamed; but as we speak all things to you in truth, even so our boasting which I made before Titus is found a truth.

15 And his inward affection is more abundant toward you, whilst he remembereth the obedience of you all, how with fear and trembling you received him.

NOTES.

former Part of this Verse. † And therefore I think ἐν τῷ πράγματι may best be rendered *in fact*, i. e. by your Sorrow, your Fear, your Indignation, your Zeal, &c. I think it cannot well be translated *in this Matter*, understanding thereby the Punishment of the Fornicator. For that was not the Matter St. *Paul* had been speaking of; but the *Corinthians* siding with the false Apostle against him, was the Subject of the preceding Part of this, and of the three or four foregoing Chapters, wherein he justifies himself against their Slanders, and invalidates the Pretences of the adverse Party. This is that which lay chiefly upon his Heart, and which he labours might and main both in this and the former Epistle to rectify, as the Foundation of all the Disorders amongst them; and consequently is the Matter wherein he rejoices to find them all set right. Indeed, in the immediately following Verse, he mentions his having writ to them concerning the Fornicator, but it is only as an Argument of Kindness and Concern for them: But that what was the great Cause of his Rejoicing, what it was that gave him the great Satisfaction, was the breaking the Faction, and the re-uniting them *all* to himself, which he expresses in the Word *all*, emphatically used, ver. 13, 15. and from thence he concludes thus, ver. 16. *I rejoice therefore that I have Confidence in you in all Things.* His Mind was now at rest; the Partizans of his Opposer, the false Apostle, having forsaken that Leader whom they had so much gloried in, and being all now come over to St. *Paul*, he doubted not but all would go well, and so leaves off the Subject he had been upon in the seven foregoing Chapters, viz. the Justification of himself, with here and there Reflections on that false Apostle.

13 ᵇ *Vid.* ver. 15.

with

II CORINTHIANS.

Ch. VIII.

TEXT.	PARAPHRASE.
16 I rejoice therefore, that I have confidence in you in all things.	with Fear and Trembling. I rejoice therefore, that I have Confidence in you in all Things. 16.

SECT. III.
CHAP. VIII. 1.——IX. 15.

CONTENTS.

THE Apostle having employed the seven foregoing Chapters in his own Justification, in the Close whereof he expresses the great Satisfaction he had in their being united again in their Affection and Obedience to him; he, in the two next Chapters, exhorts them, especially by the Example of the Churches of *Macedonia*, to a liberal Contribution to the poor Christians in *Judea*.

TEXT.	PARAPHRASE.	
1 Moreover, brethren, we do you to wit of the grace of God bestowed on the churches of Macedonia:	Moreover, Brethren, I make known to you the Gift ^{c}, which, by the Grace of God, is given in the Churches of *Macedonia*,	1.
2 How that in a great trial of affliction, the abundance of their joy, and their deep poverty, abounded unto the riches of their liberality.	*viz.* that amidst the Afflictions ^{d} they have been much tried with, they have, with exceeding Chearfulness and Joy, made their very low Estate of Poverty yield a rich Contribution of Liberality; being forward of themselves (as I	2.
3 For to their power (I bear record) yea, and be-	must bear them witness) to the utmost of their	3.

NOTES.

1 ^{c} Χάρις, which is translated *Grace*, is here used by St. *Paul* for *Gift* or *Liberality*; and is so used, *ver.* 4, 6, 7, 9, 19. & 1 *Cor.* XVI. 3. It is also χάρις Θεοῦ, *the Gift of God*; because God is the Author and Procurer of it, moving their Hearts to it. Besides, διδομένη cannot signify *bestowed on*, but *given in* or *by*.

2 ^{d} How ill disposed and rough to the Christians the *Macedonians* were, may be seen, *Acts* XVI. & XVII.

A a

Power;

PARAPHRASE.

4. Power; nay, and beyond their Power, earnestly intreating me to receive their Contribution, and be a Partner with others in the Charge of conveying and distributing it to the Saints.
5. And in this they out-did my Expectation, who could not hope for so large a Collection from them. But they gave themselves first to the Lord; and to me, to dispose of what they had, according as the good Pleasure of God should direct.
6. Insomuch, that I was moved to persuade *Titus*, that as he had begun, so he would also see this charitable Contribution carried on among you till it was perfected;
7. that as you excel in every thing, abounding in Faith, in Well-speaking, in Knowledge, in every good Quality, and in your Affection to me, ye might abound in this Act of charitable Liberality also.
8. This I say to you, not as a Command from God, but on occasion of the great Liberality of the Churches of *Macedonia*, and to shew the World a Proof of the genuine, noble Temper of your Love ᵉ. For ye know the

TEXT.

yond their power, they were willing of themselves.
4 Praying us with much intreaty, that we would receive the gift, and take upon us the fellowship of the ministring to the saints.
5 And this they did, not as we hoped, but first gave their own selves to the Lord, and unto us by the will of God.
6 Insomuch that we desired Titus, that as he had begun, so he would also finish in you the same grace also.
7 Therefore, as ye abound in every thing, in faith, in utterance, and knowledge, and in all diligence, and in your love to us; see that ye abound in this grace also.
8 I speak not by commandment, but by occasion of the forwardness of others, and to prove the sincerity of your love.

NOTES.

8 ᵉ Τὸ γνήσιον ὑμετέρας ἀγάπης γνήσιον δοκιμάζων, *shewing the World a Proof of the genuine Temper of their Love*: Thus, I think, it should be rendered. St. *Paul*, who is so careful all along in this Epistle, to shew his Esteem and good Opinion of the *Corinthians*, taking all Occasions to speak and presume well of them, whereof we have an eminent Example in these Words, *ye abound in your Love to us*, in the immediately preceding Verse; he could not, in this Place, so far forget his Design of treating them very tenderly, now they were newly returned to him, as to tell them, that he sent *Titus* for the promoting their Contribution, to make a Trial of the *Sincerity of their Love*. This had been but an ill Expression of that *Confidence*, which, *Chap.* VII. 16. he tells them, he has *in them in all Things*. Taking therefore, as without Violence to the Words one may, δοκιμάζων for drawing out a Proof, and γνήσιον for *genuine*, the Words very well express St. *Paul*'s obliging Way of stirring up the *Corinthians* to a liberal Contribution, as I have understood them: For St. *Paul*'s Discourse to them briefly stands thus: " The great Liberality of the poor *Macedonians*, made me send *Titus* to you, to carry on the Collection of your Charity, which he " had begun, that you who excel in all other Virtues, might be eminent also in this. But " this I urge, not as a Command from God, but upon Occasion of others Liberality, lay before " you an Opportunity of giving the World a Proof of the genuine Temper of your Charity; " which, like that of your other Virtues, loves not to come behind that of others."

II CORINTHIANS. Ch. VIII.

TEXT.

9 For ye know the grace of our Lord Jesus Christ, that though he was rich, yet for our sakes he became poor, that ye through his poverty might be rich.
10 And herein I give my advice: for this is expedient for you who have begun before, not only to do, but also to be forward a year ago.
11 Now therefore perform the doing of it; that as there was a readiness to will, so there may be a performance also out of that which you have.
12 For if there be first a willing mind, it is accepted according to that a man hath, and not according to that he hath not.
13 For I mean not that other men may be eased, and you burdened:
14 But by an equality, that now at this time your abundance may be a supply for their want, that their abundance also may be a supply for your want, that there may be equality:
15 As it is written, He that had gathered much, had nothing over; and he that had gathered little, had no lack.
16 But thanks be to God, which put the same earnest care into the heart of Titus for you.
17 For indeed he accepted the exhortation, but being

PARAPHRASE.

Munificence [f] of our Lord Jesus Christ, who being rich, made himself poor for your sakes, that you by his Poverty might become rich. I give you my Opinion in the Case, because it becomes you so to do; as having begun not only to do something in it, but to shew a Willingness to it above a Year ago. Now therefore apply yourselves to the doing of it in earnest; so that as you undertook it readily, so you would as readily perform it, out of what you have: For every Man's Charity is accepted by God according to the Largeness and Willingness of his Heart in giving, and not according to the Narrowness of his Fortune. For my Meaning is, not that you should be burdened to ease others, but that at this Time your Abundance should make up what they through Want come short in, that in another Occasion their Abundance may supply your Deficiency, that there may be an Equality: As it is written, He that had much, had nothing over; and he that had little, had no lack. But Thanks be to God, who put into the Heart of *Titus* the same Concern for you; who not only yielded to my Exhortation [g], but being more than ordinary concerned for you, of his own Accord went un-

9.
10.
11.
12.
13.
14.
15.
16.
17.

NOTES.

9 [f] Τὴν χάριν, the *Grace*, rather the *Munificence*; the Signification wherein St. Paul uses χάρις, over and over again in this Chapter, and is translated *Gift*, ver. 4.
17 [g] *Vid.* Ver. 6.

II CORINTHIANS.

Ch. VIII.

PARAPHRASE.

18. to you; with whom I have sent the Brother [h], who has Praise through all the Churches for
19. his Labour in the Gospel, (and not that only, but who was also chosen of the Churches to accompany me in the carrying this Collection, which Service I undertook for the Glory of our Lord, and for your Encouragement to a liberal
20. Contribution) to prevent any Aspersion might be cast on me by any one, on occasion of my meddling with the Management of so great a
21. Sum; and to take care, by having such Men joined with me in the same Trust, that my Integrity and Credit should be preserved, not only in the Sight of the Lord, but also in the
22. Sight of Men. With them I have sent our Brother, of whom I have had frequent Experience in sundry Affairs, to be a forward, active Man; but now much more earnestly intent, by reason of the strong Persuasion he has of your contri-
23. buting liberally. Now whether I speak of *Titus*, he is my Partner, and one who with me promotes your Interest; or the two other Brethren sent with him, they are the Messengers of the Churches of *Macedonia*, by whom their Collection is sent, and are Promoters of the Glory
24. of Christ. Give therefore to them, and by them to those Churches, a Demonstration of your Love, and a Justification of my boasting of you.
1. For as touching the Relief of the poor Christians in *Jerusalem*, it is needless for me
2. to write to you. For I know the Forwardness of your Minds, which I boasted of on

TEXT.

more forward, of his own accord he went unto you.

18 And we have sent with him the brother, whose praise is in the gospel, throughout all the churches:

19 (And not that only, but who was also chosen of the churches to travel with us with this grace, which is administered by us to the glory of the same Lord, and declaration of your ready mind)

20 Avoiding this, that no man should blame us in this abundance, which is administered by us:

21 Providing for honest things, not only in the sight of the Lord, but also in the sight of men.

22 And we have sent with them our brother, whom we have oftentimes proved diligent in many things, but now much more diligent, upon the great confidence which I have in you.

23 Whether any do enquire of Titus, he is my partner, and fellow helper concerning you: or our brethren be enquired of, they are the messengers of the churches, and the glory of Christ.

24 Wherefore shew ye to them, and before the churches, the proof of your love, and of our boasting on your behalf.

1 For as touching the ministering to the saints, it is superfluous for me to write to you.

2 For I know the for-

NOTES.

18 [h] This Brother most take to be St. *Luke*, who now was, and had been a long while St. *Paul's* Companion in his Travels.

your

TEXT.

wardness of your mind, for which I boast of you to them of Macedonia, that Achaia was ready a year ago; and your zeal hath provoked very many.

3 Yet have I sent the brethren, lest our boasting of you should be in vain in this behalf; that, as I said, ye may be ready:

4 Lest haply if they of Macedonia come with me, and find you unprepared, we (that we say not, you) should be ashamed in this same confident boasting.

5 Therefore I thought it necessary to exhort the brethren, that they would go before unto you, and make up beforehand your bounty, whereof ye had notice before, that the same might be ready as a matter of bounty, and not as of covetousness.

6 But this I say, He which soweth sparingly, shall reap also sparingly; and he which soweth bountifully, shall reap also bountifully.

7 Every man according as he purposeth in his heart, so let him give; not grudgingly, or of necessity: for God loveth a chearful giver.

8 And God is able to make all grace abound towards you; that ye always having all sufficiency in all things, may abound to every good work:

PARAPHRASE.

your behalf to the *Macedonians*, that [i] *Achaia* was ready a Year ago, and your Zeal in this Matter hath been a Spur to many others. Yet I have sent these Brethren, that my boasting of you may not appear to be vain and groundless in this part: But that you may, as I said, have your Collection ready, lest if perchance the *Macedonians* should come with me, and find it not ready, I (not to say you) should be ashamed in this Matter whereof I have boasted. I thought it therefore necessary to put the Brethren upon going before unto you, to prepare things by a timely Notice before-hand, that your Contribution may be ready, as a free Benevolence of yours, and not as a niggardly Gift extorted from you. This I say, He who soweth sparingly, shall reap also sparingly; and he who soweth plentifully, shall also reap plentifully. So give as you find yourselves disposed every one in his own Heart, not grudgingly, as if it were wrung from you; for God loves a chearful Giver. For God is able to make every charitable Gift [k] of yours redound to your Advantage, that you having in every thing always a Fulness of Plenty, ye may abound in every good Work (as it is written,

3.

4.

5.

6.

7.

8.

NOTES.

2 [i] *Achaia*, i. e. the Church of *Corinth*, which was made up of the Inhabitants of that Town, and of the circumjacent Parts of *Achaia*. Vid. Ch. I. 1.

8 [k] Χάρις, *Grace*, rather *Charitable Gift* or *Liberality*, as it signifies in the former Chapter, and as the Context determines the Sense here.

II CORINTHIANS.

Chap. IX.

| PARAPHRASE. | TEXT. |

9. He hath scattered, he hath given to the Poor;
10. and his Liberality¹ remaineth for ever. Now he that supplies Seed to the Sower, and Bread for Food; supply and multiply your Stock of Seed ᵐ, and increase the Fruit of your Libe-
11. rality) enriched in every thing to all Benefi- cence, which by me, as instrumental in it, pro-
12. cureth Thanksgiving to God. For the Perfor- mance of this Service doth not only bring Sup- ply to the Wants of the Saints, but reacheth farther, even to God himself, by many Thanks-
13. givings (whilst they having such a Proof of you in this your Supply, glorify God for your professed Subjection to the Gospel of Christ, and for your Liberality in communicating to
14. them, and to all Men) and to the procuring their Prayers for you, they having a great In- clination towards you, because of that gracious Gift of God bestowed on them by your Libe-
15. rality. Thanks be to God for this his un- speakable Gift.

(As it is written, He 9 hath dispersed abroad; he hath given to the poor: his righteousness remain- eth for ever.

Now he that ministereth 10 seed to the sower, both minister bread for your food, and multiply your seed sown, and increase the fruits of your righte- ousness)

Being enriched in every 11 thing to all bountifulness, which causeth through us thanksgiving to God.

For the administration 12 of this service, not only supplieth the want of the saints, but is abundant al- so by many Thanksgivings unto God;

(Whiles by the experi- 13 ment of this ministration, they glorify God for your professed subjection unto the gospel of Christ, and for your liberal distribu- tion unto them, and unto all men)

And by their prayer for 14 you, which long after you, for the exceeding grace of God in you.

Thanks be unto God 15 for his unspeakable gift.

NOTES.

9, 10 ¹ Δικαιοσύνη, *Righteousness*, rather *Liberality*; for so δικαιοσύνην in Scripture Language often signifies. And so *Matt.* VI. 1. for ἐλεημοσύνην, *Alms*, some Copies have δικαιοσύνην, *Libe- rality*. And so *Joseph*, Mat. I. 19. is called δίκαιος, *just, benign*.

10 ᵐ Σπόρον, *Seed sown*, rather your *Seed and Seed-plot*, i. e. Increase your Plenty to be laid out in charitable Uses.

II CORINTHIANS.

SECT. IV.
CHAP. X. 1.——XIII. 10.

CONTENTS.

ST. *Paul* having finished his Exhortation to Liberality in their Collection for the Christians at *Jerusalem*, he here reassumes his former Argument, and prosecutes the main Purpose of this Epistle, which was totally to reduce and put a final End to the adverse Faction, (which seems not yet to be entirely extinct) by bringing the *Corinthians* wholly off from the false Apostle they had adhered to; and to re-establish himself, and his Authority, in the Minds of all the Members of that Church. And this he does by the Steps contained in the following Numbers.

SECT. IV. N. 1.
CHAP. X. 1——6.

CONTENTS.

HE declares the extraordinary Power he hath in Preaching the Gospel, and to punish his Opposers amongst them.

TEXT.   *PARAPHRASE.*

1. NOW I Paul myself beseech you, by the meekness and gentleness of Christ, who in presence am base among

1. NOW I the same *Paul*, who am (as 'tis said amongst ⁿ you) base and mean when present with you, but bold towards you when absent, beseech you by the Meekness and Gen-

NOTES.

1 ⁿ Vid. *ver.* 10.

tleness,

II CORINTHIANS.

PARAPHRASE.

2. tleness ᵉ of Christ; I beseech you, I say, that I may not, when present among you, be bold after that manner. I have resolved to be bold towards some, who account that in my Conduct and Ministry I regulate myself wholly by car-
3. nal Considerations. For though I live in the Flesh, yet I do not carry on the Work of the Gospel (which is a Warfare) according to the
4. Flesh. (For the Weapons of my Warfare are not fleshly ᶠ, but such as God hath made mighty to the pulling down of strong Holds, *i. e.* whatever is made use of in Opposition)
5. Beating down human Reasonings, and all the towering and most elevate Superstructures raised thereon by the Wit of Men against the Knowledge of God, as held forth in the Gospel, captivating all their Notions, and bringing
6. them into Subjection to Christ; and having by me in a Readiness, Power wherewithal to punish and chastise all Disobedience; when you, who have been misled by your false Apostle, withdrawing yourselves from him, shall return to a perfect Obedience ᵍ.

TEXT.

you, but being absent am bold toward you.
2 But I beseech you, that I may not be bold when I am present, with that confidence wherewith I think to be bold against some which think of us, as if we walked according to the flesh.
3 For though we walk in the flesh, we do not war after the flesh:
4 (For the weapons of our warfare are not carnal, but mighty through God, to the pulling down of strong holds,)
5 Casting down imaginations, and every high thing that exalteth itself against the knowledge of God, and bringing into captivity every thought to the obedience of Christ:
6 And having in a readiness to revenge all disobedience, when your obedience is fulfilled.

SECT.

NOTES.

ᵉ St. *Paul* thinking it fit to forbear all Severity till he had, by fair Means, reduced as many of the contrary Party as he could, to a full Submission to his Authority, (*vid.* Ver. 6) begins here his Discourse, by conjuring them by the Meekness and Gentleness of Christ, as an Example that might excuse his Delay of exemplary Punishment on the Ringleaders and chief Offenders, without giving them reason to think it was for want of Power.

ᶠ What the ὅπλα ϲαρκικὰ, the *carnal Weapons*, and those other opposed to them, which he calls δυνατὰ τῷ Θεῷ, *mighty through God*, are, may be seen, if we read and compare 1 *Cor.* I. 23, 24. & II. 1, 2, 4, 5, 12, 13. 2 *Cor.* IV. 2, 6.

ᵍ Those whom he speaks to here, are the *Corinthian* Converts, to whom this Epistle is written. Some of these had been drawn into a Faction against St. *Paul*; these he had been, and was endeavouring to bring back to that Obedience and Submission which the rest had continued in to him as an Apostle of Jesus Christ. The *Corinthians* of these two Sorts are those he means, when he says to them, *Ch.* II. 3. & *Ch.* VII. 13, 15. *You all*, *i. e.* all the Christians of *Corinth* and *Achaia*. For he that had raised the Faction amongst them, and given so much Trouble to St. *Paul*, was a Stranger and a *Jew*, Vid. *Ch.* XI. 22.

crept

II CORINTHIANS.

SECT. IV. N. 2.

CHAP. X. 7—18.

CONTENTS.

ST. *Paul* examines the false Apostle's Pretensions, and compares his own with his Performances.

TEXT.

7 Do ye look on things after the outward appearance? if any man trust to himself, that he is Christ's, let him of himself think this again, that as he is Christ's, even so are we Christ's.
8 For though I should boast somewhat more of our authority, (which the Lord hath given us for edification, and not for your destruction) I should not be ashamed:
9 That I may not seem as if I would terrify you by letters.
10 For his letters (say they) are weighty and powerful, but his bodily presence is weak, and his speech contemptible.

PARAPHRASE.

7. Do ye judge of Men by the outward Appearance of Things? Is it by such Measures you take an Estimate of me and my Adversaries? If he has Confidence in himself that he is Christ's, *i. e.* assumes to himself the Authority of one employed and commissioned by Christ ᶠ; let him, on the other side, count thus with himself, that as he is Christ's, so I also am Christ's.
8. Nay, if I should boastingly say something more ᵍ of the Authority and Power, which the Lord has given me for your Edification, and not for your Destruction *, I should not be put to shame ʰ.
9. But that I may not seem to terrify you by Letters, as is objected to me by some, who say, that my Letters are weighty and powerful, but my bodily Presence weak, and my Discourse contemptible;

NOTES.

crept in amongst them, after St. *Paul* had gathered and established that Church, 1 *Cor.* III. 6, 10. 2 *Cor.* X. 15, 16. Of whom St. *Paul* seems to have no Hopes, *Chap.* XI. 13—15. and therefore he every where threatens, 1 *Cor.* IV. 19. and here particularly, *ver.* 6, & 11. to make an Example of him and his Adherents, (if any were so obstinate to stick to him) when he had brought back again all the *Corinthians* that he could hope to prevail on.

7 ᶠ Vid. *Chap.* XI. 33.
8 ᵍ *More*, vid. *Chap.* XI. 23. * Another Reason insinuated by the Apostle for his forbearing Severity to them.
ʰ *I should not be put to shame*, i. e. the Truth would justify me in it.

B b

let

II CORINTHIANS.

PARAPHRASE.

11. let him that says so, reckon upon this, that such as I am in Word by Letters when I am absent, such shall I be also in Deed when present.
12. For I dare not be so bold, as to rank or compare myself with some who vaunt themselves: But they measuring themselves within themselves ᵘ, and comparing themselves with themselves, do not understand ʷ.
13. But I, for my Part, will not boast of myself in what has not been measured out, or allotted to me ˣ, *i. e.* I will not go out of my own Province to seek Matter of Commendation, but proceeding orderly in the Province which God hath measured out and allotted to me, I have reached even unto you. *i. e.* I preached the Gospel in every Country as I went, till I came as far as to you.
14. For I do not extend myself farther than I should, as if I had skipped over other Countries in my way, without proceeding gradually to you; no, for I have reached even unto you in Preaching of the Gospel in all Countries as I passed along ʸ;

TEXT.

11. Let such an one think this, that such as we are in word by letters, when we are absent, such will we be also in deed when we are present.
12. For we dare not make ourselves of the number, or compare ourselves with some that commend themselves; but they measuring themselves by themselves, and comparing themselves amongst themselves, are not wise.
13. But we will not boast of things without our measure, but according to the measure of the rule which God hath distributed to us, a measure to reach even unto you.
14. For we stretch not ourselves beyond our measure, as though we reached not unto you; for we are come as far as to you also, in preaching the gospel of Christ:

NOTES.

12 ᵘ This is spoken ironically; ἐν ἑαυτοῖς, *amongst themselves*, rather *within themselves*: For in all likelihood, the Faction and Opposition against St. Paul was made by one Person, as we before observed. For though he speaks here in the Plural Number, which is the softer and decenter way in such Cases, yet we see, in the foregoing Verse, he speaks directly and expresly as of one Person; and therefore ἐν ἑαυτοῖς may, most consonantly to the Apostle's Meaning here, be understood to signify *within themselves*, i. e. with what they find in themselves: The whole Place shewing, that this Person made an Estimate of himself only by what he found in himself; and thereupon preferred himself to St. Paul, without considering what St. Paul was, or had done.

ʷ *Do not understand;* that they ought not to intrude themselves into a Church planted by another Man, and there vaunt themselves, and set themselves above him that planted it; which is the Meaning of the four next Verses.

13 ˣ Ἄμετρα, here, and in ver. 15. doth not signify immense, or immoderate, but something that hath not been measured out and allotted to him; something that is not committed to him, nor within his Province.

14 ʸ This seems to charge the false, pretended Apostle, who had caused all this Disturbance in the Church of *Corinth*, that, without being appointed to it, without preaching the Gospel in his way thither, as became an Apostle, he had crept into the Church of *Corinth*.

Not

II CORINTHIANS.

TEXT.

15 Not boasting of things without our measure, that is, of other mens labour; but having hope when your faith is increased, that we shall be enlarged by you, according to our rule abundantly;

16 To preach the gospel in the regions beyond you, and not to boast in another man's line, of things made ready to our hand.

17 But he that glorieth, let him glory in the Lord.

18 For not he that commendeth himself is approved, but whom the Lord commendeth.

PARAPHRASE.

15. Not extending my Boasting [z] beyond my own Bounds, into Provinces not allotted to me, nor vaunting myself of any thing I have done in another's Labour [a], *i. e.* in a Church planted by another Man's Pains; but having hope that your Faith increasing, my Province will be enlarged by you yet farther: So that I may

16. preach the Gospel to the yet unconverted Countries beyond you, and not take Glory to myself from another Man's Province, where all Things are made ready to my Hand [a]. But he

17. that will glory, let him glory or seek Praise from that which is committed to him by the Lord, or in that which is acceptable to the Lord. For not he who commends himself,

18. does thereby give a Proof of his Authority or Mission; but he whom the Lord commends, by the Gifts of the Holy Ghost [b].

NOTES.

15 [z] *Boasting*, i. e. intermeddling, or assuming to myself Authority to meddle, or Honour for meddling.

15, 16 [a] Here St. *Paul* visibly taxes the false Apostle for coming into a Church, converted and gathered by another, and there pretending to be some-body, and to rule all. This is another Thing that makes it probable, that the Opposition made to St. *Paul*, was but by one Man, that had made himself the Head of an opposite Faction: For it is plain it was a Stranger, who came thither after St. *Paul* had planted this Church; who pretending to be more an Apostle than St. *Paul*, with greater Illumination, and more Power, set up against him to govern that Church, and withdraw the *Corinthians* from following St. *Paul*, his Rules and Doctrine. Now this can never be supposed to be a Combination of Men, who came to *Corinth* with that Design; nor that they were different Men that came thither separately, each setting up for himself, for then they would have fallen out one with another, as well as with St. *Paul*: And, in both Cases, St. *Paul* must have spoken of them in a different Way from what he does now. The same Character and Carriage is given to them all, throughout both these Epistles; and 1 *Cor.* III. 10. he plainly speaks of one Man. That setting up thus to be a Preacher of the Gospel amongst those that were already Christians, was looked upon by St. *Paul* to be a Fault, we may see, *Rom.* XV. 20.

18 [b] 'Tis of these Weapons of his Warfare that St. *Paul* speaks in this Chapter; and 'tis by them that he intends to try which is the true Apostle, when he comes to them.

II CORINTHIANS.

SECT. IV. N. 3.
CHAP. XI. 1——6.

CONTENTS.

HE shews, that their pretended Apostle bringing to them no other Saviour, or Gospel; nor conferring greater Power of Miracles than he [St. *Paul*] had done, was not to be preferred before him.

PARAPHRASE.

1. Would you could bear with me a little in my Folly^c; and indeed do bear with me.
2. For I am jealous over you, with a Jealousy that is for God: For I have fitted and prepared you for one alone to be your Husband, *viz.* that I might deliver you up a pure Virgin to Christ.
3. But I fear lest some way or other, as the Serpent beguiled *Eve* by his Cunning, so your Minds should be debauched from that Singleness which is due to Christ^d. For if

TEXT.

1. Would to God ye could bear with me a little in my folly: and indeed bear with me.
2. For I am jealous over you with godly jealousy: for I have espoused you to one husband, that I may present you as a chaste virgin to Christ.
3. But I fear, lest by any means, as the serpent beguiled Eve through his subtilty, so your minds should be corrupted from the simplicity that is in Christ.

NOTES.

1 ^{c} *Folly*, so he modestly calls his speaking in his own Defence.

3 ^{d} Ἁπλότης τῆς εἰς τὸν Χριςὸν, *The Simplicity that is in*, rather, *towards Christ*, answers to ἑνὶ ἀνδρὶ Χριςῷ, *to one Husband Christ*, in the immediately foregoing Verse: For ἑνὶ, *one*, is not put there for nothing, but makes the Meaning plainly this; "I have formed and fitted you "for one Person alone, one Husband, who is Christ: I am concerned, and in care, that you "may not be drawn aside from that Submission, that Obedience, that Temper of Mind that is "due singly to him; for I hope to put you into his Hands possessed with pure Virgin Thoughts, "wholly fixed on him, not divided, nor roving after any other, that he may take you to Wife, "and marry you to himself for ever." 'Tis plain that Perverter, who opposed St. *Paul*, was a *Jew*, as we have seen. 'Twas from the *Jews*, from whom, of all professing Christianity, St. *Paul* had most Trouble and Opposition; for they having their Hearts set upon their old Religion, endeavoured to mix Judaism and Christianity together. We may suppose the Case here to be much the same with that which he more fully expresses in the Epistle to the *Galatians*; particularly *Gal.* I. 6——12. & *Chap.* IV. 9——11. & 16——21. & *Chap.* V. 1——13. The Meaning of this Place here seems to be this: "I have taught you the Gospel alone, in "its pure and unmixed Simplicity, by which only you can be united to Christ; but I fear, "lest this your new Apostle should draw you from it, and that your Minds should not stick to "that singly, but should be corrupted by a Mixture of *Judaism*." After the like manner St. *Paul* expresses Christians being delivered from the Law, and their Freedom from the ritual Observances of the *Jews*, by being married to Christ, *Rom.* VII. 4 which Place may give some light to this.

TEXT.

4 For if he that cometh, preacheth another Jesus whom we have not preached, or if ye receive another spirit, which ye have not received, or another gospel, which ye have not accepted, ye might well bear with him.
5 For I suppose I was not a whit behind the very chiefest apostles.
6 But though I be rude in speech, yet not in knowledge; but we have been thoroughly made manifest among you in all things.

PARAPHRASE.

4. this Intruder who has been a Leader amongst you, can preach to you another Saviour, whom I have not preached; or if you receive from him other or greater Gifts of the Spirit, than those you received from me; or another Gospel than what you accepted from me, you might well bear with him, and allow his Pretensions of being a new and greater Apostle. 5. For as to the Apostles of Christ, I suppose I am not a whit behind the chiefest of them. 6. For though I am but a mean Speaker, yet I am not without Knowledge, but in every thing have been made manifest unto you, *i. e.* to be an Apostle.

SECT. IV. N. 1.
CHAP. XI. 7——15.

CONTENTS.

HE justifies himself to them, in his having taken nothing of them. There had been great Talk about this, and Objections raised against St. *Paul* thereupon; *Vid.* 1 Cor. IX. 1——3. As if by this he had discovered himself not to be an Apostle: To which he there answers, and here touches it again, and answers another Objection, which it seems was made, *viz.* that he refused to receive Maintenance from them out of Unkindness to them.

II CORINTHIANS.

PARAPHRASE.

7. HAVE I committed an Offence *ᵉ* in abasing myself to work with my Hands, neglecting my Right of Maintenance due to me as an Apostle, that you might be exalted in Christianity, because I preached the Gospel of
8. God to you *gratis*? I robbed other Churches,
9. taking Wages of them to do you Service: And being with you, and in want, I was chargeable to not a Man of you. For the Brethren who came from *Macedonia*, supplied me with what I needed: And in all things I have kept myself from being burdensome to you, and so will
10. I continue to do. The Truth and Sincerity I owe to Christ, is in what I say to you, *viz.* This Boasting of mine shall not in the Regions
11. of *Achaia* be stopped in me. Why so? Is it because I love you not? For that God can be my
12. Witness, he knoweth. But what I do and shall do *ᶠ* is, that I may cut off all Occasion from those who, if I took any thing of you, would be glad of that Occasion to boast, that in it they had me for a Pattern, and did nothing
13. but what even I myself had done. For these are false *ᵍ* Apostles, deceitful Labourers in the Gospel, having put on the counterfeit Shape

TEXT.

7. HAVE I committed an offence in abasing myself, that you might be exalted, because I have preached to you the gospel of God freely?
8. I robbed other churches, taking wages of them to do you service.
9. And when I was present with you and wanted, I was chargeable to no man: for that which was lacking to me, the brethren which came from Macedonia supplied: and in all things I have kept myself from being burdensome unto you, and so will I keep myself.
10. As the truth of Christ is in me, no man shall stop me of this boasting in the regions of Achaia.
11. Wherefore? because I love you not? God knoweth.
12. But what I do, that I will do, that I may cut off occasion from them which desire occasion, that wherein they glory, they may be found even as we.
13. For such are false apostles, deceitful work-

NOTES.

7 *ᵉ* The adverse Party made it an Argument against St. *Paul*, as an Evidence that he was no Apostle, since he took not from the *Corinthians* Maintenace, 1 *Cor.* IX. 1 —— 3. Another Objection raised against him from hence, was, That he would receive nothing from them, because he loved them not, 2 *Cor.* XI. 11. This he answers here, by giving another Reason for his so doing. A third Allegation was, that it was only a crafty Trick in him to catch them, 2 *Cor.* XII. 16. which he answers there.

12 *ᶠ* Καὶ ποιήσω, *that I will do*, rather *and will do*; so the Words stand in the *Greek*, and do not refer to *ver.* 10. as a Profession of his Resolution to take nothing of them; but to *ver.* 11. to which it is joined; shewing that his refusing any Reward from them, was not out of Unkindness, but for another Reason.

13 *ᵍ* They had questioned St. *Paul*'s Apostleship, 1 *Cor.* IX. because of his not taking Maintenance of the *Corinthians*. He here directly declares them to be no true Apostles.

and

II CORINTHIANS

TEXT.	PARAPHRASE.	
ers, transforming themselves into the Apostles of Christ.	and Outside of Apostles of Christ: And no marvel; for Satan himself is sometimes transformed into an Angel of Light. Therefore it is not strange, if so be his Ministers are disguised so as to appear Ministers of the Gospel; whose End shall be according to their Works.	14.
14 And no marvel; for Satan himself is transformed into an angel of light.		15.
15 Therefore it is no great thing if his ministers also be transformed as the ministers of righteousness; whose end shall be according to their works.		

SECT. IV. N. 5.

CHAP. XI. 16——33.

CONTENTS.

HE goes on in his Justification, reflecting upon the Carriage of the false Apostle towards the *Corinthians*, v. 16——21. He compares himself with the false Apostle in what he boasts of, as being in *Hebrew*, v. 21, 22. or Minister of Christ, v. 23, and here St. *Paul* enlarges upon his Labours and Sufferings.

TEXT.	PARAPHRASE.	
16 I Say again, Let no man think me a fool: if otherwise, yet as a fool receive me, that I may boast myself a little.	I Say again, Let no Man think me a Fool, that I speak so much of myself: Or at least, if it be a Folly in me, bear with me as a Fool, that I too, as well as others [h], may boast myself a little. That which I say on this Occasion is not by Command from Christ, but, as it were, foolishly in this Matter of Boasting.	16.
17 That which I speak, I speak it not after the Lord, but as it were foolishly in this confidence of boasting.		17.

NOTES.

16 [h] Vid. *ver.* 18.

Since

II CORINTHIANS.

PARAPHRASE.

18, 19. Since many glory in their Circumcision or Extraction [i], I will glory also. For ye bear with Fools [k] easily, being yourselves wise.
20. [l] For you bear with it if a Man bring you into Bondage [m], *i. e.* domineer over you, and use you like his Bondmen; If he make a Prey of you; If he take or extort Presents or a Salary from you; If he be elevated and high amongst you; If he smite you on the Face,
21. *i. e.* treat you contumeliously. I speak according to the Reproach that has been cast upon me, as if I were weak, *i. e.* destitute of what might support me in Dignity and Authority equal to this false Apostle, as if I had not as fair Pretences to Power and Profit amongst you as he.
22. Is he an *Hebrew* [n], *i. e.* by Language an *Hebrew*? so am I: Is he an *Israelite*, truly of the *Jewish* Nation, and bred up in that Religion? so am I: Is he of the Seed of *Abraham*, really descended from him? and not a Proselyte of a foreign Extraction?
23. so am I: Is he a

TEXT.

Seeing that many glory 18 after the flesh, I will glory also.

For ye suffer fools glad-19 ly, seeing ye yourselves are wise.

For ye suffer if a man 20 bring you into bondage, if a man devour you, if a man take of you, if a man exalt himself, if a man smite you on the face.

I speak as concerning 21 reproach, as though we had been weak: howbeit, wherein soever any is bold (I speak foolishly) I am bold also.

Are they Hebrews? so 22 am I: are they Israelites? so am I: are they the seed of Abraham? so am I:

Are they ministers of 23 Christ? (I speak as a fool) I am more: in labours

NOTES.

18 [i] *Vid.* Ch. XII. 11.

19 [k] *After the Flesh.* What this Glorying *after the Flesh* was in particular here, *vid.* ver. 22. *viz.* being a *Jew* by descent.

20 [l] Spoken ironically for their bearing with the Insolence and Covetousness of their false Apostle.

[m] The *Bondage* here meant, was Subjection to the Will of their false Apostle, as appears by the following Particulars of this Verse; and not Subjection to the *Jewish* Rites. For if that had been, St. *Paul* was so zealous against it, that he would have spoke more plainly and warmly, as we see in his Epistle to the *Galatians*, and not have touched it thus, only by the bye, slightly, in a doubtful Expression. Besides, it is plain no such thing was yet attempted openly, only St. *Paul* was afraid of it; *Vid.* ver. 3.

22 [n] *Is he an Hebrew?* Having in the foregoing Verse spoke in the Singular Number, I have been fain to continue on the same Number here, though different from that in the Text, to avoid an Inconsistency in the Paraphrase, which could not but shock the Reader. But this I would be understood to do, without imposing my Opinion on any body, or pretending to change the Text: But as an Expositor, to tell my Reader that I think, that though St. *Paul* says *they*, he means but one; as often, when he says *we*, he means only himself, the Reason whereof I have given elsewhere.

Mini-

II CORINTHIANS.

TEXT.

more abundant, in stripes above measure, in prisons more frequent, in deaths oft.

24 Of the Jews five times received I forty stripes, save one.

25 Thrice was I beaten with rods, once was I stoned, thrice I suffered shipwrack; a night and a day I have been in the deep:

26 In journeying often, in perils of waters, in perils of robbers, in perils by mine own countrymen, in perils by the heathen, in perils in the city, in perils in the wilderness, in perils in the sea, in perils among false brethren;

27 In weariness and painfulness, in watchings often, in hunger and thirst, in fastings often, in cold and nakedness.

28 Besides those things that are without, that which cometh upon me daily, the care of all the churches.

29 Who is weak, and I am not weak? who is offended, and I burn not?

30 If I must needs glory, I will glory of the things

PARAPHRASE.

Minister of Jesus Christ? (I speak in my foolish way of boasting). I am more so: In toilsome Labours I surpass him; in Stripes I am exceedingly beyond him°; in Prisons I have been oftner; and in the very Jaws of Death more than once. Of the *Jews* I have five Times received forty Stripes, save one: Thrice was I whipped with Rods; once was I stoned; thrice shipwracked: I have passed a Night and a Day in the Sea: In Journeyings often; in Perils by Water, in Perils by Robbers, in Perils by my own Countrymen, in Perils from the Heathen, in Perils in the City, in Perils in the Country, in Perils at Sea, in Perils amongst false Brethren: In Toil and Trouble, and sleepless Nights often, in Hunger and Thirst; in Fastings often; in Cold and Nakedness. Besides these Troubles from without, the Disturbance that comes daily upon me from my Concern for all the Churches. Who is a weak Christian, in danger through Frailty or Ignorance to be misled, whose Weakness I do not feel and suffer in, as if it were my own? Who is actually misled, for whom my Zeal and Concern does not make me uneasy, as if I had a Fire in me? If I must be compelled ᵖ to glory ᑫ, I will

24.
25.
26.
27.
28.
29.
30.

NOTES.

23 ° Ἐν πληγαῖς ὑπερβαλλόντως, *in Stripes above Measure*, rather *in Stripes exceeding.* For these Words, as the other Particulars of this Verse, ought to be taken comparatively with reference to the false Apostle, with whom St. *Paul* is comparing himself in the Ministry of the Gospel: Unless this be understood so, there will seem to be a disagreeable Tautology in the following Verses; which, taking these Words in a comparative Sense, are Proofs of his saying, *In Stripes I am exceedingly beyond him, for of the Jews five Times*, &c.

30 ᵖ *Compelled,* vid. *Chap.* XII. 11.

ᑫ By Καυχᾶσθαι, which is translated sometimes to *glory,* and sometimes to *boast,* the Apostle all along, where he applies it to himself, means nothing but the mentioning some commendable Action of his without Vanity or Ostentation, but barely upon Necessity on the present Occasion.

II CORINTHIANS.

PARAPHRASE.

glory of those Thhings which are of my weak and suffering side. The God and Father of our Lord Jesus Christ, who is blessed for ever, knoweth that I lie not. In *Damascus*, the Governour under *Aretas* the King, who kept the Town with a Garrison, being desirous to apprehend me, I was through a Window let down in a Basket, and escaped his Hands.

31.
32.
33.

TEXT.

which concern mine infirmities.

The God and Father of 31 our Lord Jesus Christ, which is blessed for evermore, knoweth that I lie not.

In Damascus, the gover- 32 nour under Aretas the king, kept the city of the Damascenes with a garrison, desirous to apprehend me:

And through a window 33 in a basket was I let down by the wall, and escaped his hands.

SECT. IV. N. 6.

CHAP. XII. 1——11.

CONTENTS.

HE makes good his Apostleship by the extraordinary Visions and Revelations which he had received.

PARAPHRASE.

1. IF I must be forced to glory ' for your sakes, for me it is not expedient, I will come to Visions and Revelations of the Lord.
2. I knew a Man, by ' the Power of Christ, above fourteen Years ago, caught up into the third Heaven; whether the intire Man, Body and all, or out of the Body in an Extasy, I know not, God knows. And I know such an one',
3.

TEXT.

IT is not expedient for 1 me doubtless to glory: I will come to visions and revelations of the Lord.

I knew a man in Christ, 2 above fourteen years ago, (whether in the body, I cannot tell; or whether out of the body, I cannot tell: God knoweth) such an one caught up to the third heaven.

And I knew such a man 3

NOTES.

1. ' Ει καυχᾶσθαι δεῖ, *If I must glory*, is the Reading of some Copies, and is justified by ver. 30. of the foregoing Chapter, by the vulgar Translation, and by the *Syriac*, much to the same Purpose, and suiting better with the Context, renders the Sense clearer.

2 & 3 Modestly speaking of himself in a third Person.

whether

II CORINTHIANS.

Ch. XII.

TEXT.

(whether in the body, or out of the body, I cannot tell: God knoweth.).

4 How that he was caught up into paradife, and heard unspeakable words, which it is not lawful for a man to utter.

5 Of such an one will I glory: yet of myself I will not glory, but in mine infirmities.

6 For though I would defire to glory, I shall not be a fool; for I will say the truth: but now I forbear, left any man should think of me above that which he seeth me to be, or that he heareth of me.

7 And left I should be exalted above measure thro' the abundance of the revelations, there was given to me a thorn in the flesh, the messenger of Satan to buffet me, left I should be exalted above measure.

8 For this thing I besought the Lord thrice, that it might depart from me.

9 And he said unto me, My grace is sufficient for thee: for my strength is made perfect in weakness. Most gladly therefore will I rather glory in my infirmities, that the power of Christ may rest upon me.

10 Therefore I take pleasure in infirmities, in re-

PARAPHRASE.

whether in the Body, or out of the Body, I know not, God knows; that he was caught up into Paradife, and there heard what is not in the Power of Man to utter: Of such an one I will glory; but myself I will not mention with any boafting, unless in Things that carry the Marks of Weakness, and shew my Sufferings. But if I should have a mind to glory in other Things, I might do it without being a Fool; for I would speak nothing but what is true, having Matter in abundance: ᵗ But I forbear, left any one should think of me beyond what he sees me, or hears commonly reported of me. And that I might not be exalted above measure, by reason of the abundance of Revelations that I had, there was given me a Thorn in the Flesh ᵘ, the Messenger of Satan to buffet me, that I might not be over-much elevated. Concerning this Thing I besought the Lord thrice, that it might depart from me: And he said, My Favour is sufficient for thee; for my Power exerts itself, and its Sufficiency is seen the more perfectly, the weaker thou thyself art. I therefore most willingly choose to glory, rather in Things that shew my Weakness, than in my Abundance of glorious Revelations, that the Power of Christ may the more visibly be seen to dwell in me: Wherefore I have Satisfaction in Weaknesses, in Reproaches, in Necessities, in Persecutions, in Distresses for Christ's sake. For when I, looked upon in my outward State,

4.
5.
6.
7.
8.
9.
10.

NOTES.

6 ᵗ Vid. ver. 7.

7 ᵘ *Thorn in the Flesh:* What this was in particular, St. *Paul* having thought fit to conceal it, is not easy for those who come after to discover, nor is it much material.

appear

II CORINTHIANS.

PARAPHRASE.

appear weak; then by the Power of Christ which dwelleth in me, I am found to be strong.
11. I am become foolish in glorying thus; but it is you who have forced me to it. For I ought to have been commended by you, since in nothing came I behind the chiefest of the Apostles, though in myself I am nothing.

TEXT.

proaches, in necessities, in persecutions, in distresses for Christ's sake: for when I am weak, then am I strong.

11 I am become a fool in glorying, ye have compelled me: for I ought to have been commended of you: for in nothing am I behind the very chiefest apostles, though I be nothing.

SECT. IV. N. 7.

CHAP. XII. 12, 13.

CONTENTS.

HE continues to justify himself to be an Apostle, by the Miracles he did, and the supernatural Gifts he bestowed amongst the *Corinthians*.

PARAPHRASE.

12. Truly the Signs whereby an Apostle might be known, were wrought amongst you by me in all Patience ʷ and Submission under the Difficulties I there met with, in miraculous, wonderful and mighty Works, performed by me.
13. For what is there which you were any way shortened in, and had not equally with other Churches ˣ, except it be that I myself was not burdensome to you? Forgive me this Injury.

TEXT.

12 Truly the signs of an apostle were wrought among you in all patience, in signs, and wonders, and mighty deeds.
13 For what is it wherein ye were inferior to other churches, except it be that I myself was not burdensome to you? Forgive me this wrong.

NOTES.

12 ʷ This may well be understood to reflect on the Haughtiness and Plenty wherein the false Apostle lived amongst them.
13 ˣ Vid. 1 *Cor.* I. 4 ———— 7.

SECT.

II CORINTHIANS.
SECT. IV. N. 8.
CHAP. XII. 14——21.

CONTENTS.

HE farther justifies himself to the *Corinthians*, by his passed Disinterestedness, and his continued kind Intentions to them.

TEXT.

14 Behold, the third time I am ready to come to you; and I will not be burdensome to you: for I seek not yours, but you: for the children ought not to lay up for the parents, but the parents for the children.
15 And I will very gladly spend and be spent for you, though the more abundantly I love you, the less I be loved.
16 But be it so, I did not burden you: nevertheless being crafty, I caught you with guile.
17 Did I make a gain of you by any of them whom I sent unto you?
18 I desired Titus, and with him I sent a brother: did Titus make a gain of you? walked we not in the same spirit? walked we not in the same steps?

PARAPHRASE.

14. Behold, this is the third time I am ready to come unto you, but I will not be burdensome to you; for I seek not what is yours, but you: for 'tis not expected, nor usual, that Children should lay up for their Parents, but Parents[a] for their Children.
15. I will gladly lay out whatever is in my Possession or Power; nay, even wear out and hazard myself for your Souls[b], though it should so fall out, that the more I love you, the less I should be beloved by you[c].
16. Be it so, as some suggest, that I was not burdensome to you; but it was in Truth out of Cunning, with a Design to catch you with that Trick, drawing from you by others what I refused in Person.
17. In answer to which I ask, Did I by any of those I sent unto you make a Gain of you?
18. I desired *Titus* to go to you, and with him I sent a Brother: Did *Titus* make a Gain of you? Did not they behave themselves with the same Temper that I did amongst you? Did we not walk in the same Steps, *i. e.* neither they nor I received any thing from you.

NOTES.

14 [a] Vid. 1 *Cor.* iv. 14, 15.
5 [b] Vid. 2 *Tim.* ii. 10.
  [c] Vid. *Chap.* vi. 12, 13.

Again,

II CORINTHIANS.

Ch. XII.

PARAPHRASE.

19. Again, ᵈ Do not, upon my mentioning my sending of *Titus* to you, think that I apologize for my not coming myself: I speak as in the Presence of God, and as a Christian, there is no such thing. In all my whole Carriage towards you, Beloved, all that has been done has been done only for your Edification. No, there is no need of an Apology for my not coming to you
20. sooner: For I fear when I do come I shall not find you such as I would, and that you will find me such as you would not. I am afraid, that among you there are Disputes, Envyings, Animosities, Strifes, Backbitings, Whisperings,
21. Swellings of Mind, Disturbances; and that my God, when I come to you again, will hum-

TEXT.

19 Again, think you that we excuse ourselves unto you? we speak before God in Christ: but we do all things, dearly beloved, for your edifying.

20 For I fear, lest when I come I shall not find you such as I would, and that I shall be found unto you such as ye would not: lest there be debates, envyings, wraths, strifes, backbitings, whisperings, swellings, tumults:

21 And lest when I come again, my God will humble me among you, and that I shall bewail many which have sinned alrea-

NOTES.

19 ¹ He had before given the Reason, *Chap.* I. 23. of his not coming to them, with the like Asseveration that he uses here. If we trace the Thread of St. *Paul*'s Discourse here, we may observe, that having concluded the Justification of himself and his Apostleship by his past Actions, *ver.* 13. he had it in his Thoughts to tell them how he would deal with the false Apostle and his Adherents when he came, as he was ready now to do; and therefore solemnly begins, *ver.* 14. with *behold*, and tells them now *the third time* he was ready to come to them, to which joining (what was much upon his Mind) that he would not be burdensome to them when he came, this suggested to his Thoughts an Objection, (*viz.*) that this personal Shyness in him was but Cunning, for that he designed to draw Gain from them by other Hands. From which he clears himself by the Instance of *Titus* and the Brother whom he had sent together to them, who were as far from receiving any thing from them as he himself. *Titus* and his other Messenger being thus mentioned, he thought it necessary to obviate another Suspicion that might be raised in the Minds of some of them, as if he mentioned the sending of those two, as an Apology for his not coming himself: This he disclaims utterly; and to prevent any Thoughts of that kind, solemnly protests to them, that in all his Carriage to them, he had done nothing but for their Edification, nor had any other Aim in any of his Actions but purely that; and that he forbore coming merely out of Respect and Good-Will to them. So that all from *Beheld this third time I am ready to come to you*, ver. 14. to this *Third time I am coming to you*, ch. xiii. 1. must be looked on as an incident Discourse that fell in occasionally, though tending to the same Purpose with the rest: A Way of writing very usual with our Apostle, and with other Writers who abound in Quickness and Variety of Thoughts as he did. Such Men are often, by new Matter rising in their way, put by from what they were going and had begun to say; which therefore they are fain to take up again, and continue at a distance; which St. *Paul* does here after the Interposition of eight Verses. Other Instances of the like kind may be found in other Places of St. *Paul*'s Writings.

ble

II CORINTHIANS.

TEXT.

dy, and have not repented of the uncleanness, and fornication, and lasciviousness which they have committed.

PARAPHRASE.

ble me amongst you, and I shall bewail many who have formerly sinned, and have not yet repented of the Uncleanness, Fornication, and Lasciviousness, whereof they are guilty.

SECT. IV. N. 9.
CHAP. XIII. 1——10.

CONTENTS.

HE re-assumes what he was going to say, *Chap.* xii. 14. and tells them how he intends to deal with them when he comes to them, and assures them, that however they question it, he shall be able, by Miracles, to give proof of his Authority and Commission from Christ.

TEXT.

1 THIS is the third time I am coming to you: in the mouth of two or three witnesses shall every word be established.
2 I told you before, and foretel you as if I were present the second time; and being absent, now I write to them which heretofore have sinned, and to all other, that if I come again, I will not spare:
3 Since ye seek a proof of Christ speaking in me,

PARAPHRASE.

1. THIS is now the third time I am coming to you; and when I come I shall not spare you, having proceeded according to our Saviour's Rule, and endeavoured by fair means first to reclaim you, before I come to the last Extremity.
2. And of this my former Epistle, wherein I applied myself to you, and this wherein I now, as if I were present with you, foretel those who have formerly sinned, and all the rest, to whom, being now absent, I write, that when I come I will not spare you; I say, these two Letters are my Witnesses according to our Saviour's Rule, which says, In the Mouth of two or three Witnesses every Word shall be established [e]. Since you demand a Proof of
3. my

NOTES.

2 [e] *In the Mouth of two or three Witnesses shall every Word be established.* These Words seem to be quoted from the Law of our Saviour, *Matth.* xviii. 16. and not from the Law of
Moses

II CORINTHIANS.

PARAPHRASE.

4. my Mission, and of what I deliver, that it is dictated by Christ speaking in me, who must be acknowledged not to be weak to you-ward, but has given sufficient Marks of his Power amongst you. For though his Crucifixion and Death were with Appearance ᶠ of Weakness, yet he liveth with the Manifestation ᶠ of the Power of God appearing in my punishing you.

TEXT.

which to you-ward is not weak, but is mighty in you.
4 For though he was crucified through weakness, yet he liveth by the power of God: for we also are weak in him, but we shall live with him by the power of God toward you.

NOTES.

Moses in *Deuteronomy*, not only because the Words are the same with those in St. *Matthew*, but from the Likeness of the Case. In *Deuteronomy* the Rule given concerns only judicial Trials: In St. *Matthew* it is a Rule given for the Management of Persuasion used for the reclaiming an Offender, by fair Means, before coming to the utmost Extremity, which is the Case of St. *Paul* here. In *Deuteronomy* the Judge was to hear the Witnesses, *Deut*. xvii. 6. and xix. 15. In St. *Matthew* the Party was to hear the Witnesses, *Matth*. xviii. 17. which was also the Case of St. *Paul* here; the Witnesses which he means that he made use of to persuade them being his two Epistles. That by Witnesses he means his two Epistles, is plain from his Way of expressing himself here, where he carefully sets down his telling them twice, *(viz.)* before in his former Epistle, *Chap*. iv. 19. and now a *second time* in his second Epistle; and also by these words, ὡς παρὼν τὸ δεύτερον, *As if I were present* with you *a second time*. By our Saviour's Rule the offended Person was to go twice to the Offender; and therefore St. *Paul* says, *As if I were with you a second time*, counting his Letters as two personal Applications to them, as our Saviour directed should be done before coming to rougher Means. Some take the Witnesses to be the three Messengers by whom his first Epistle is supposed to be sent. But this would not be according to the Method prescribed by our Saviour in the Place from which St. *Paul* takes the Words he uses; for there were no Witnesses to be made use of in the first Application; neither, if those had been the Witnesses meant, would there have been any need for St. *Paul* so carefully and expresly to have set down ὡς παρὼν τὸ δεύτερον, *as if present a second time*, Words which in that case would be superfluous. Besides, those three Men are no where mentioned to have been sent by him to persuade them, nor the *Corinthians* required to hear them, or reproved for not having done it: And lastly, they could not be better Witnesses of St. *Paul*'s Endeavours twice to gain the *Corinthians* by fair Means, before he proceeded to Severity, than the Epistles themselves.

4 ᶠ Εἰ ἀσθενείας, *through Weakness*; ἐκ δυνάμεως Θεοῦ, *by the Power of God*, I have rendered *with Appearance of Weakness*, and *with the Manifestation of the Power of God*; which I think the Sense of the Place, and the Style of the Apostle, will justify. St. *Paul* sometimes uses the *Greek* Prepositions in a larger Sense than that Tongue ordinarily allows. Farther it is evident, that ἐκ joined to ἰσχυρίζω has not a casual Signification; and therefore in the Antithesis ἐκ δυνάμεως Θεοῦ, it cannot be taken casually. And it is usual for St. *Paul* in such Cases to continue the same Word, though it happens sometimes seemingly to carry the Sense another way. In short, the Meaning of the Place is this: " Though Christ in his Crucifixion appeared weak " and despicable, yet he now lives to shew the Power of God in the Miracles and mighty " Works which he does: So I, though I by my Sufferings and Infirmities appear weak and " contemptible, yet shall I live to shew the Power of God in punishing you miraculously."

You

II CORINTHIANS.   Ch. XIII.

TEXT.

5 Examine yourselves, whether ye be in the faith, prove your own selves: know ye not your own selves, how that Jesus Christ is in you, except ye be reprobates?

6 But I trust that ye shall know that we are not reprobates.

7 Now I pray to God that ye do no evil; not that we should appear approved, but that ye should do that which is honest, though we be as reprobates.

8 For we can do nothing against the truth, but for the truth.

9 For we are glad when we are weak, and ye are strong: and this also we wish, even your perfection.

10 Therefore I write these things being absent, lest being present I should use sharpness, according to

PARAPHRASE.

5. You examine me whether I can by any miraculous Operation give a Proof that Christ is in me. Pray examine yourselves whether you be in the Faith; make a Trial upon yourselves, whether you yourselves are not somewhat destitute of Proofs ʰ; or are you so little acquainted with yourselves, as not to know whether Christ be in

6. you? But if you do not know yourselves whether you can give Proofs or no, yet I hope you shall know that I am not unable to give

7. Proofs ʰ of Christ in me. But I pray to God that you may do no Evil, wishing not for an Opportunity to shew my Proofs ʰ; but that you doing what is right, I may be as if I had no Proofs ʰ, no supernatural Power: For

8. though I have the Power of punishing supernaturally, I cannot shew this Power upon any of you, unless it be that you are Offenders, and your Punishment be for the Advantage of the Gospel. I am therefore glad when I am weak,

9. and can inflict no Punishment upon you, and you are so strong, *i. e.* clear of Faults, that ye cannot be touched. For all the Power I have is only for promoting the Truth of the Gospel; whoever are faithful and obedient to that, I can do nothing to, I cannot make Examples of them, by all the extraordinary Power I have, if I would. Nay, this also I wish, even your Perfection. These things therefore I write to 10.

NOTES.

5, 6, 7. ʰ Ἀδόκιμοι, translated here *Reprobates*, 'tis plain, in these three Verses, has no such Signification, Reprobation being very remote from the Argument the Apostle is here upon: But the Word ἀδόκιμος is here used for one that cannot give proof of Christ being in him; one that is destitute of a supernatural Power: For thus stands St. *Paul's* Discourse, ver. 3. ἐπεὶ δοκιμὴν ζητεῖτε, ver. 6. γνώσεσθε ὅτι οὐκ ἀδόκιμοί ἐσμὲν, *Since you seek a Proof, you shall know that I am not destitute of a Proof.*

D d   you,

II CORINTHIANS.

PARAPHRASE.

you, being absent, that when I come I may not use Severity, according to the Power which the Lord hath given me for Edification, not for Destruction.

TEXT.

the power which the Lord hath given me to edification, and not to destruction.

SECT. V.

CHAP. XIII. 11—14.

CONCLUSION.

11. FINALLY, Brethren, farewel. Bring yourselves into one well united, firm, unjarring Society[i]. Be of good Comfort; be of one Mind; live in Peace, and the God of Love and
12. Peace shall be with you: Salute one another
13. with a holy Kiss: All the Saints salute you. The
14. Grace of our Lord Jesus Christ, and the Love of God, and the Communion of the Holy Ghost be with you all. *Amen.*

Finally, Brethren, farewell: be perfect, be of good comfort, be of one mind, live in peace; and the God of love and peace shall be with you. 11

Greet one another with an holy kiss. 12

All the saints salute you. 13

The grace of our Lord Jesus Christ, and the love of God, and the communion of the Holy Ghost, be with you all. *Amen.* 14

NOTES.

11 [i] The same that he exhorts them to in the Beginning of the first Epistle, *ch.* i. *ver.* 10.

A PARA-

A

PARAPHRASE *and* NOTES

ON THE

EPISTLE of St. *PAUL*

TO THE

ROMANS.

From Corinth, Anno Æræ Vulg. 57. *Neronis* 3.

SYNOPSIS.

BEFORE we take into Confideration the Epiftle to the *Romans* in particular, it may not be amifs to premife, That the miraculous Birth, Life, Death, Refurrection and Afcenfion of our Lord Jefus Chrift, were all Events that came to pafs within the Confines of *Judea*; and that the ancient Writings of the Jewifh Nation, allowed by the Chriftians to be of Divine Original, were appealed-to as witneffing the Truth of his Miffion and Doctrine, whereby it was manifeft that the Jews were the Depofitaries of the Proofs of the Chriftian Religion. This could not chufe but give the Jews, who were owned to be the People of God, even in the Days of our Saviour, a great Authority among the Convert Gentiles, who knew nothing of the Meffias they were to believe in, but what they derived from that Nation, out of which he and his Doctrine fprung. Nor did the Jews fail to make ufe of this Advantage feveral ways, to the Difturbance of the Gentiles that embraced Chriftianity. The Jews, even thofe of them that received the Gofpel, were, for the moft part, fo devoted to the Law of *Mofes* and their ancient Rites, that they could by no means bring them-

Synopsis. themselves to think that they were to be laid aside. They were every where stiff and zealous for them, and contended that they were necessary to be observed even by Christians, by all that pretended to be the People of God, and hoped to be accepted by him. This gave no small Trouble to the newly converted Gentiles, and was a great Prejudice to the Gospel, and therefore we find it complained of in more Places than one: *Vid. Acts* xv. 1. 2 *Cor*. xi. 3. *Gal.* ii. 4. and v. 1, 10, 12. *Phil.* iii. 2. *Col.* ii. 4, 8, 16. *Tit.* i. 10, 11, 14, *&c.* This Remark may serve to give Light, not only to this Epistle to the *Romans*, but to several other of St. *Paul*'s Epistles written to the Churches of converted Gentiles.

As to this Epistle to the *Romans*, the Apostle's principal Aim in it seems to be to persuade them to a steady Perseverance in the Profession of Christianity, by convincing them that God is the God of the Gentiles, as well as the Jews; and that now under the Gospel there is no Difference between Jew and Gentile. This he does several ways.

1. By shewing that though the Gentiles were very sinful, yet the Jews, who had the Law, kept it not, and so could not, upon account of their having the Law (which being broken, aggravated their Faults, and made them as far from righteous as the Gentiles themselves) have a Title to exclude the Gentiles from being the People of God under the Gospel.

2. That *Abraham* was the Father of all that believe, as well Uncircumcised as Circumcised; so that those that walk in the Steps of the Faith of *Abraham*, though uncircumcised, are the Seed to which the Promise is made, and shall receive the Blessing.

3. That it was the Purpose of God from the Beginning, to take the Gentiles to be his People under the Messias, in the Place of the Jews, who had been so till that Time, but were then nationally rejected, because they nationally rejected the Messias, whom he sent to them to be their King and Deliverer; but was received by but a very small Number of them; which Remnant was received into the Kingdom of Christ, and so continued to be his People with the converted Gentiles, who all together made now the Church and People of God.

4. That the Jewish Nation had no Reason to complain of any Unrighteousness in God, or Hardship from him in their being cast off for their Unbelief, since they had been warned of it, and they might find it threatened in their ancient Prophets. Besides, the raising

sing or depressing of any Nation is the Prerogative of God's Sovereignty; Preservation in the Land that God has given them being not the Right of any one Race of Men above another. And God might, when he thought fit, reject the Nation of the Jews by the same Sovereignty whereby he at first chose the Posterity of *Jacob* to be his People, passing by other Nations, even such as descended from *Abraham* and *Isaac*: But yet he tells them, that at last they shall be restored again.

Besides the Assurance he labours to give the *Romans*, that they are by Faith in Jesus Christ the People of God, without Circumcision or other Observances of the Jews, whatever they may say, which is the main Drift of this Epistle, it is farther remarkable, that this Epistle being writ to a Church of Gentiles in the Metropolis of the Roman Empire, but not planted by St. *Paul* himself, he as Apostle of the Gentiles, out of care that they should rightly understand the Gospel, has woven into his Discourse the chief Doctrines of it, and given them a comprehensive View of God's dealing with Mankind, from first to last, in reference to eternal Life. The principal Heads whereof are these.

That by *Adam*'s Transgression Sin entered into the World, and Death by Sin, and so Death reigned over all Men from *Adam* to *Moses*.

That by *Moses* God gave the Children of *Israel* (who were his People, *i. e.* owned him for their God, and kept themselves free from the Idolatry and Revolt of the Heathen World) a Law, which if they obeyed, they should have Life thereby, *i. e.* attain to Immortal Life, which had been lost by *Adam*'s Transgression.

That though this Law, which was righteous, just and good, were ordained to Life, yet not being able to give Strength to perform what it could not but require, it failed by reason of the Weakness of human Nature to help Men to Life. So that though the Israelites had Statutes, which if a Man did he should live in them; yet they all transgressed, and attained not to Righteousness and Life by the Deeds of the Law.

That therefore there was no way to Life left to those under the Law, but by the Righteousness of Faith in Jesus Christ, by which Faith alone they were that Seed of *Abraham*, to whom the Blessing was promised.

This was the State of the *Israelites*.
As to the *Gentile* World, he tells them,
I. That

Synopsis. That though God made himself known to them by legible Characters of his Being and Power visible in the Works of the Creation, yet they glorified him not, nor were thankful to him: They did not own nor worship the one only true invisible God, the Creator of all things, but revolted from him, to Gods set up by themselves in their own vain Imaginations, and worshipped Stocks and Stones, the corruptible Images of corruptible Things.

That they having thus cast off their Allegiance to him their proper Lord, and revolted to other Gods, God therefore cast them off, and gave them up to vile Affections, and to the Conduct of their own darkened Hearts, which led them unto all Sorts of Vices.

That both Jews and Gentiles being thus all under Sin, and coming short of the Glory of God; God, by sending his Son Jesus Christ, shews himself to be the God both of Jews and Gentiles, since he justifieth the Circumcision by Faith, and the Uncircumcision through Faith, so that all that believe are freely justified by his Grace.

That though Justification unto Eternal Life be only by Grace, through Faith in Jesus Christ, yet we are to the utmost of our Power sincerely to endeavour after Righteousness, and from our Hearts obey the Precepts of the Gospel, whereby we become the Servants of God; for his Servants we are whom we obey, whether of Sin unto Death, or of Obedience unto Righteousness.

These are but some of the more general and comprehensive Heads of the Christian Doctrine, to be found in this Epistle. The Design of a Synopsis will not permit me to descend more minutely to Particulars. But this let me say, that he that would have an enlarged View of true Christianity, will do well to study this Epistle.

Several Exhortations suited to the State that the Christians of *Rome* were then in, make up the latter Part of the Epistle.

This Epistle was writ from *Corinth* the Year of our Lord, according to the common Account, 57, the third Year of *Nero*, a little after the second Epistle to the *Corinthians*.

SECT.

ROMANS.

SECT. I.

CHAP. I. 1——15.

CONTENTS.

INTRODUCTION, with his Profession of a Desire to see them.

TEXT.

1 PAUL a servant of Jesus Christ, called to be an apostle, separated unto the gospel of God,
2 (Which he had promised afore by his prophets in the holy scriptures,)
3 Concerning his Son Jesus Christ our Lord, which was made of the seed of David according to the flesh,
4 And declared to be the Son of God with power, according to the spirit of holiness, by the resurrection from the dead:

PARAPHRASE.

1. *PAUL* a Servant of Jesus Christ, called ᵏ to
2. be an Apostle, separated ˡ to the preaching of the Gospel of God (which he had heretofore promised by his Prophets in the Holy
3. Scriptures) concerning his Son Jesus Christ our Lord, who according to the Flesh, *i. e.* as to the Body which he took in the Womb of the blessed Virgin his Mother, was of the Posterity and Lineage of *David* ᵐ according to the Spirit
4. of Holiness ⁿ, *i. e.* as to that more pure and spiritual Part, which in him over-ruled all, and kept even his frail Flesh holy and spotless from the least Taint of Sin °, and was of another Extraction, with most mighty Power ᵖ decla-

NOTES.

1 ᵏ *Called.* The Manner of his being called, see *Acts* ix. 1 – 22.
ˡ *Separated,* vid. *Acts* xiii. 2.
3 ᵐ *Of David,* and so would have been registered of the House and Lineage of *David*, as both his Mother and reputed Father were, if there had been another Tax in his Days. Vid. *Luke* ii. 4. *Matth.* xiii. 55.
4 ⁿ *According to the Spirit of Holiness,* is here manifestly opposed to, *according to the Flesh,* in the foregoing Verse; and so must mean that more pure and spiritual Part in him, which by divine Extraction he had immediately from God; unless this be so understood, the Antithesis is lost.
° See Paraphrase, *Chap.* viii. 3.
ᵖ Ἐν δυνάμει, *with Power:* He that will read in the Original what St. *Paul* says, *Eph.* i. 19, 20. of the Power which God exerted in raising Christ from the Dead, will hardly avoid thinking that he there sees St. *Paul* labouring for Words to express the Greatness of it.

red,

PARAPHRASE.

5. red ᵠ to be the Son of God by his Resurrection from the Dead, by whom I have received Favour, and the Office of an Apostle, for the bringing of the Gentiles every where to the Obedience
6. of Faith, which I preach in his Name; of which Number, *i. e.* Gentiles that I am sent to
7. preach to, are ye who are already called, ʳ and become Christians: To all the beloved of God ˢ, and called to be Saints, who are in *Rome*, Favour and Peace be to you from God our Father, and the Lord Jesus Christ.
8. In the first Place I thank my God through Jesus Christ for you all, that your Faith is spoken
9. of throughout the whole World. For God is my Witness, whom I serve with the whole Bent of my Mind in preaching the Gospel of his Son, that without ceasing I constantly make
10. mention of you in my Prayers, requesting (if it be God's Will, that I may now at length, if possible, have a good Opportunity) to come
11. unto you. For I long to see you, that I may communicate to you some spiritual Gift ᵗ for your Establishment ᵘ in the Faith; that is,

TEXT.

5. By whom we have received grace and apostleship, for obedience to the faith among all nations for his name:
6. Among whom are ye also the called of Jesus Christ.
7. To all that be in Rome, beloved of God, called to be saints: Grace to you, and peace from God our Father, and the Lord Jesus Christ.
8. First, I thank my God through Jesus Christ for you all, that your faith is spoken of throughout the whole world.
9. For God is my witness, whom I serve with my spirit in the Gospel of his Son, that without ceasing I make mention of you always in my prayers.
10. Making request (if by any means now at length I might have a prosperous journey by the will of God) to come unto you.
11. For I long to see you, that I may impart unto you some spiritual gift,

NOTES.

4 ᵠ *Declared* does not exactly answer the Word in the Original, nor is it perhaps easy to find a Word in *English* that perfectly answers ὁρισθέντος, in the Sense the Apostle uses it here; ὁρίζειν signifies properly to bound, terminate, or circumscribe; by which Termination the Figure of Things sensible is made, and they are known to be of this or that Race, and are distinguished from others. Thus St. *Paul* takes Christ's Resurrection from the Dead, and his entering into Immortality, to be the most eminent and characteristical Mark, whereby Christ is certainly known, and, as it were, determined to be the Son of God.

7 ʳ To take the Thread of St. *Paul's* Words here right, all from the Word *Lord* in the Middle of *ver.* 3. to the Beginning of this 7th, must be read as a Parenthesis.

6 & 7 ˢ *Called of Jesus Christ; called to be Saints; beloved of God;* are but different Expressions for Professors of Christianity.

11 ᵗ *Spiritual Gift.* If any one desire to know more particularly the spiritual Gifts, he may read 1 *Cor.* xii.

ᵘ *Establishment.* The *Jews* were the Worshippers of the true God, and had been for many Ages his People: This could not be denied by the Christians. Whereupon they were very apt to persuade

ROMANS.   Chap. I.

TEXT.

to the end you may be established;
12 That is, that I may be comforted together with you, by the mutual faith both of you and me.
13 Now I would not have you ignorant, brethren, that oftentimes I purposed to come unto you (but was let hitherto) that I might have some fruit among you also, even as among other Gentiles.
14 I am debtor both to the Greeks, and to the Barbarians; both to the wise, and to the unwise.
15 So, as much as in me is, I am ready to preach the gospel to you that are at Rome also.

PARAPHRASE.

is [x], that when I am among you, I may be comforted together with you, both with your Faith and my own. This I think fit you should know, Brethren, that I often purposed to come unto you, that I may have some Fruit of my Ministry among you also, even as among other Gentiles. I owe what Service I can do to the Gentiles of all kinds, whether Greeks or Barbarians, to both the more knowing and civilized, and the uncultivated and ignorant; so that as much as in me lies, I am ready to preach the Gospel to you also who are at *Rome*.

12.

13.

14.

15.

NOTES.

persuade the convert Gentiles, that the Messias was promised, and sent to the Jewish Nation alone, and that the Gentiles could claim, or have no Benefit by him; or if they were to receive any Benefit by the Messias, they were yet bound to observe the Law of *Moses*, which was the Way of Worship which God had prescribed to his People. This in several Places very much shook the Gentile Converts. St. *Paul* makes it (as we have already observed) his Business in this Epistle, to prove that the Messias was intended for the Gentiles as much as for the Jews; and that to make any one Partaker of the Benefits and Privileges of the Gospel, there was nothing more required but to believe and obey it: And accordingly here in the Entrance of the Epistle, he wishes to come to *Rome*, that by imparting some miraculous Gifts of the Holy Ghost to them, they might be established in the true Notion of Christianity against all Attempts of the Jews, who would either exclude them from the Privileges of it, or bring them under the Law of *Moses*. So where St. *Paul* expresses his Care that the *Colossians* should be *established in the Faith*, Col. ii. 7. it is visible by the Context, that what he opposed was Judaism.

12 [x] *That is.* St. *Paul* in the former Verse had said, that he desired to come amongst them to establish them; in these Words, *that is*, he explains, or, as it were, recals what he had said, that he might not seem to think them not sufficiently instructed or established in the Faith; and therefore turns the End of his coming to them, to their mutual Rejoicing in one another's Faith, when he and they came to see and know one another.

E e   SECT.

ROMANS.

SECT. II.

CHAP. I. 16——II. 29.

CONTENTS.

ST. *Paul* in this Section shews, that the Jews exclude themselves from being the People of God under the Gospel, by the same Reason that they would have the Gentiles excluded.

It cannot be sufficiently admired how skilfully, to avoid offending those of his own Nation, St. *Paul* here enters into an Argument so unpleasing to the Jews, as this of persuading them, that the Gentiles had as good a Title to be taken in to be the People of God under the Messias, as they themselves; which is the main Design of this Epistle.

In this latter Part of the first Chapter, he gives a Description of the Gentile World in very black Colours, but very adroitly interweaves such an Apology for them, in respect of the Jews, as was sufficient to beat that assuming Nation out of all their Pretences to a Right to continue to be alone the People of God, with an Exclusion of the Gentiles. This may be seen if one carefully attends to the Particulars that he mentions relating to the Jews and Gentiles, and observes how what he says of the Jews in the second Chapter, answers to what he had charged on the Gentiles in the first. For there is a secret Comparison of them one with another runs through these two Chapters, which as soon as it comes to be minded, gives such a Light and Lustre to St. *Paul*'s Discourse, that one cannot but admire the skilful Turn of it; and look on it as the most soft, the most beautiful, and most pressing Argumentation that one shall any where meet with, all together; since it leaves the Jews nothing to say for themselves, why they should have the Privilege continued to them under the Gospel, of being alone the People of God; all the Things they stood upon, and boasted in, giving them no Preference in this Respect to the Gentiles; nor any Ground to judge them to be uncapable or unworthy to be their Fellow-Subjects in the Kingdom of the Messias. This is what he says, speaking of them nationally. But as to every one's personal Concerns in a future State, he assures them, both Jews and Gentiles, that the Unrighteous of both Nations, whether admitted or not into the visible Communion of the People of God, are liable to Condemnation. Those who have sinned without Law, shall perish without Law; and those who have sinned in the Law, shall be judged, *i. e.* condemned by the Law.

Perhaps some Readers will not think it superfluous, if I give a short Draught of St. *Paul*'s Management of himself here, for allaying the Sourness of the Jews against the Gentiles, and their Offence at the Gospel for allowing any of them place among the People of God under the Messias.

After he had declared that the Gospel is the Power of God unto Salvation to those who believe, to the Jew first, and also to the Gentile, and that the Way of this Salvation is revealed to be by the Righteousness of God, which is by Faith; he tells them, that the Wrath of God is also now revealed against all Atheism, Polytheism, Idolatry, and Vice whatsoever of Men, holding the Truth in Unrighteousness; because they might come to the Knowledge of the true God, by the visible Works of the Creation, so that the Gentiles were without Excuse for turning from the true God to Idolatry, and the Worship of false Gods; whereby their Hearts were darkened, so that they were without God in the World. Wherefore God gave them up to vile Affections, and all Manner of Vices; in which State, though by the Light of Nature they knew what was right, yet understanding not that such Things were worthy of Death, they not only do them themselves, but abstaining from Censure, live fairly, and in Fellowship with those that do them. Whereupon he tells the Jews, that they are more inexcusable than the Heathen, in that they judge, abhor, and have in Aversion the Gentiles for what they themselves do with greater Provocation. Their Censure and Judgment in the Case is unjust and wrong: But the Judgment of God is always right and just, which will certainly overtake those who judge others for the same Things they do themselves; and do not consider that God's Forbearance to them ought to bring them to Repentance. For God will render to every one according to his Deeds; to those that in Meekness and Patience continue in well-doing, everlasting Life; but to those who are censorious, proud and contentious, and will not obey the Gospel, Condemnation and Wrath at the Day of Judgment, whether they be Jews or Gentiles: For God puts no Difference between them. Thou that art a Jew boastest that God

Chap. I. is thy God; that he has enlightened thee by the Law that he himself gave thee from Heaven, and hath by that immediate Revelation taught thee what Things are excellent and tend to Life, and what are evil and have Death annexed to them. If therefore thou transgressest, dost not thou more dishonour God and provoke him, than a poor Heathen that knows not God, nor that the Things he doth deserve Death, which is their Reward? Shall not he, if by the Light of Nature he do what is conformable to the revealed Law of God, judge thee who hast received that Law from God by Revelation, and breakest it? Shall not this rather than Circumcision make him an Israelite? For he is not a Jew, *i. e.* one of God's People, who is one outwardly by Circumcision of the Flesh, but he that is one inwardly by the Circumcision of the Heart.

PARAPHRASE.   TEXT.

16. FOR I am not ashamed to preach the Gospel of Christ, even at *Rome* itself, that Mistress of the World: For whatever it may be thought of there [y] by that vain and haughty People, it is that wherein God exerts himself, and shews his Power [z] for the Salvation of those who believe, of the Jews in the first [a]
17. place, and also of the Gentiles. For therein is the Righteousness [b] which is the Free Grace of God through Jesus Christ revealed to be wholly by Faith [c], as it is written, *The Just*

FOR I am not ashamed of the gospel of Christ; for it is the power of God unto salvation, to every one that believeth, to the Jew first, and also to the Greek. 16

For therein is the righteousness of God revealed from faith to faith: as it is written, The just shall live by faith. 17

NOTES.

16 [y] Vid. *ver.* 22. & 1 *Cor.* i. 21.
   [z] Vid. *Eph.* i. 19.
   [a] *First.* The Jews had the first Offers of the Gospel, and were always considered as those who were first regarded in it. Vid. *Luke* xxiv. 47. *Matth.* x. 6. & xv. 24. *Acts* xii. 46. & xvii. 2.
17 [b] Διχαιοσύνη Θεȣ, *The Righteousness of God;* called so, because it is a Righteousness of his Contrivance, and his bestowing. *It is God that justifieth,* Chap. iii. 21—24, 26, 30. & viii. 33. Of which St. *Paul* speaks thus, Phil. iii. 9. *Not having mine own Righteousness which is of the Law, but that which is through the Faith of Christ, the Righteousness which is of God by Faith.*
   [c] *From Faith to Faith.* The Design of St. *Paul* here being to shew, that neither Jews nor Gentiles could by Works attain to Righteousness, *i. e.* such a perfect and complete Obedience whereby they could be justified, which he calls their own Righteousness, Chap. x. 3.

ROMANS. Chap. I.

TEXT.

18 For the wrath of God is revealed from heaven against all ungodliness, and unrighteousness of men, who hold the truth in unrighteousness.

19 Because that which may be known of God, is manifest in them; for God hath shewed it unto them.

PARAPHRASE.

Just shall live by Faith. And 'tis no more than need, that the Gospel, wherein the Righteousness of God by Faith in Jesus Christ is revealed, should be preached to you Gentiles, since the Wrath of God is now revealed ᵈ from Heaven by Jesus Christ, against all Ungodliness ᵉ and Unrighteousness of Men ᶠ, who live not up to the Light that God has given them ᵍ. Because God, in a clear Manifestation of himself amongst them, has laid before them, ever since the Creation of the World, his Divine Nature

18.

19.

NOTES.

he here tells them, that in the Gospel *the Righteousness of God,* i. e. the Righteousness of which he is the Author, and which he accepts in the Way of his own Appointment, *is revealed from Faith to Faith,* i. e. to be all through, from one End to the other, founded in Faith. If this be not the Sense of this Phrase here, it will be hard to make the following Words, *as it is written, The Just shall live by Faith,* cohere: But thus they have an easy and natural Connexion, *(viz.)* whoever are justified either before, without, or under the Law of *Moses,* or under the Gospel, are justified, not by Works, but by Faith alone. Vid. *Gal.* iii. 11. which clears this Interpretation. The same Figure of speaking St. *Paul* uses in other Places to the same Purpose; Chap. vi. 19. *Servants to Iniquity unto Iniquity,* i. e. wholly to Iniquity. 2 Cor. iii. 18. *From Glory to Glory,* i. e. wholly glorious.

18 ᵈ *Now revealed.* Vid. *Acts* xvii. 30, 31. *God now commandeth all Men every where to repent, because he hath appointed a Day, in the which he will judge the World in Righteousness, by the Man whom he hath ordained.* These Words of St. *Paul* to the *Athenians* give light to these here to the *Romans.* A Life again after Death, and a Day of Judgment, wherein Men should be all brought to receive Sentence according to what they had done, and be punished for their Misdeeds, was what was before unknown, and was brought to light by the Revelation of the Gospel from Heaven, 2 *Tim.* i. 10. *Matth.* xiii. 40. *Luke* xiii. 27. & *Rom.* ii. 5. he calls the Day of Judgment *the Day of Wrath,* consonant to his saying here, *the Wrath of God is revealed.*

ᵉ Ἀσέβειαν, *Ungodliness,* seems to comprehend the Atheism, Polytheism, and Idolatry of the Heathen World; as ἀδικίαν, *Unrighteousness,* their other Miscarriages and vicious Lives, according to which they are distinctly threatened by St. *Paul* in the following Verses. The same Appropriation of these Words, I think, may be observed in other Parts of this Epistle.

ᶠ *Of Men,* i. e. Of all Men, or as in that xviith of *Acts* before cited, all Men every where, i. e. all Men of all Nations: Before it was only to the Children of *Israel,* that Obedience and Transgression were declared and proposed as Terms of Life and Death.

ᵍ *Who hold the Truth in Unrighteousness,* i. e. Who are not wholly without the Truth, but yet do not follow what they have of it, but live contrary to that Truth they do know, or neglect to know what they might. This is evident from the next Words, and from the same Reason of God's Wrath given, Chap. ii. 8. in these Words, *Who do not obey the Truth, but obey Unrighteousness.*

and

PARAPHRASE.

20. and eternal Power; so that what is to be known of his invisible Being, might be clearly discovered and understood from the visible Beauty, Order, and Operations observable in the Constitution and Parts of the Universe, by all those that would cast their Regards, and apply their Minds ʰ that Way: Insomuch that
21. they are utterly without Excuse: For that when the Deity was so plainly discovered to them, yet they glorified him not as was suitable to the Excellency of his Divine Nature; nor did they with due Thankfulness acknowledge him as the Author of their Being, and the Giver of all the Good they enjoyed: But following the vain Fancies of their own vain ⁱ Minds, set up to themselves fictitious no Gods, and their foolish Understandings were
22. darkened: Assuming to themselves the Opinion and Name ᵏ of being wise, they became
23. Fools; and putting the incomprehensible Majesty and Glory of the eternal incorruptible Deity, set up to themselves the Images of corruptible Men, Birds, Beasts, and Insects, as fit Objects of their Adoration and Worship.

TEXT.

For the invisible things 20 of him from the creation of the world are clearly seen, being understood by the things that are made, even his eternal power and Godhead; so that they are without excuse:

Because that when they 21 knew God, they glorified him not as God, neither were thankful, but became vain in their imaginations, and their foolish heart was darkened.

Professing themselves to 22 be wise, they became fools:

And changed the glory 23 of the uncorruptible God, into an image made like to corruptible man, and to birds and four footed beasts, and creeping things.

NOTES.

20 ʰ St. *Paul* says, νοούμενα καθοράται, *If they are minded they are seen*: The invisible Things of God lie within the Reach and Discovery of Mens Reason and Understandings, but yet they must exercise their Faculties, and employ their Minds about them.

21 ⁱ Ἐματαιώθησαν ἐν τοῖς; διαλογισμοῖς αὐτῶν, *became vain in their Imaginations* or *Reasonings*. What it is to become vain in the Scripture Language, one may see in these Words, *And they followed Vanity, and became vain, and went after the Heathen, and made to themselves molten Images, and worshipped all the Host of Heaven, and served* Baal, 2 *Kings* xvii. 15, 16. And accordingly the forsaking of Idolatry, and the Worship of false Gods, is called by St. *Paul, turning from Vanity to the living God*, Acts xiv. 15.

22 ᵏ Φάσκοντες εἶναι σοφοί, *Professing themselves to be wise:* Though the Nations of the Heathens generally thought themselves wise in the Religions they embraced, yet the Apostle here having all along in this and the following Chapter used Greeks for Gentiles, he may be thought to have an Eye to the Greeks, among whom the Men of Study and Enquiry had assumed to themselves the Name of σοφοί, *wise*.

Where-

ROMANS.

Chap. I.

TEXT.

24 Wherefore God also gave them up to uncleanness, through the lusts of their own hearts, to dishonour their own bodies between themselves:
25 Who changed the truth of God into a lie, and worshipped and served the creature more than the Creator, who is blessed for ever, Amen.
26 For this cause God gave them up unto vile affections: For even their women did change the natural use into that which is against nature:
27 And likewise also the men, leaving the natural use of the woman, burned in their lust one toward another, men with men, working that which is unseemly, and receiving in themselves that recompence of their error which was meet.
28 And even as they did not like to retain God in their knowledge, God

PARAPHRASE.

Wherefore they having forsaken God, he also left them to the Lusts of their own Hearts, and that Uncleanness their darkened Hearts led them into, to dishonour their Bodies among themselves: Who so much debased themselves, as to change the true God who made them for a Lie ¹ of their own making, worshiping and serving the Creature, and Things even of a lower Rank than themselves, more than the Creator, who is God over all, blessed for evermore, Amen. For this Cause God gave them up to shameful and infamous Lusts and Passions: For even their Women did change their natural Use into that which is against Nature: And likewise their Men leaving also the natural Use of the Women, burned in their Lusts one towards another, Men with Men practising that which is shameful, and receiving in themselves a fit Reward of their Error, *i. e.* Idolatry ᵐ. And ⁿ as they did not search out ᵒ God whom they had in the World, so as to have him with a due Acknow-

24.

25.

26.

27.

28.

NOTES.

25 ¹ The false and fictitious Gods of the Heathen are very fitly called in the Scripture *Lies*, *Amos* ii. 4. *Jer.* xvi. 19, 20.

27 ᵐ *Error*; so Idolatry is called, 2 *Pet.* ii. 18. As they against the Light of Nature debased and dishonoured God by their Idolatry, 'twas a just and fit Recompence they received, in being left to debase and dishonour themselves by unnatural Lusts.

28 ⁿ *And.* This Copulative joins this Verse to the 25th, so that the Apostle will be better understood, if all between be looked on as a Parenthesis; this being a Continuation of what he was there saying, or rather a Repetition of it in short, which led him into the Thread of his Discourse.

ᵒ Οὐκ ἐδοκίμασαν, *did not like*, rather *did not try* or *search*, for the Greek Word signifies to search and find out by searching: So St. *Paul* often uses it, *Chap.* ii. 18. & xii. 2. compared, & xiv. 22. *Eph.* v. 10.

ledgment

ROMANS.

Chap. I.

PARAPHRASE.

ledgment ᵖ of him, God gave them up to an unsearching and unjudicious ᵠ Mind, to do Things incongruous, and not meet ʳ to be
29. done: Being filled with all Manner of Iniquity, Fornication, Wickedness, Covetousness, Malice, full of Envy, Contention, Deceit, Malig-
30. nity even to Murder, Backbiters, Haters of God, Insulters of Men, Proud, Boasters, Inventers of new Arts of Debauchery, disobedient
31. to Parents, without Understanding, Covenant-breakers, without natural Affection, implaca-
32. ble, unmerciful: Who though they acknowledge the Rule of Right ˢ prescribed them by God, and discovered by the Light of Nature, did not yet understand ᵗ that those who did

TEXT.

gave them over to a reprobate mind, to do those things which are not convenient:

29 Being filled with all unrighteousness, fornication, wickedness, covetousness, maliciousness, full of envy, murder, debate, deceit, malignity; whisperers,

30 Backbiters, haters of God, despiteful, proud, boasters, inventers of evil things, disobedient to parents,

31 Without understanding, covenant-breakers, without natural affection, implacable, unmerciful.

32 Who knowing the judgment of God (that they which commit such

NOTES.

ᵖ Ἐν ἐπιγνώσει, *with Acknowledgment.* That the Gentiles were not wholly without the Knowledge of God in the World, St. *Paul* tells us in this very Chapter; but they did not acknowledge him as they ought, ver. 21. They had God εἶχον Θεὸν, but οὐκ ἐδοκίμασαν ἔχειν αὐτὸν ἐν ἐπιγνώσει, but did not so improve that Knowledge, as to acknowledge or honour him as they ought. This Verse seems in other Words to express the same that is said, ver. 21.

ᵠ Εἰς ἀδόκιμον νοῦν, *to a reprobate Mind,* rather to an *unsearching Mind,* in the Sense of St. *Paul,* who often uses Compounds and Derivatives in the Sense wherein a little before he used the Primitive Words, though a little varying from the precise Greek Idiom; an Example whereof we have in this very Word ἀδόκιμος, 2 *Cor.* xiii. where having, ver. 3. used δοκιμὴ for a Proof of his Mission by supernatural Gifts, he uses ἀδόκιμος for one that was destitute of such Proofs. So here he tells the *Romans,* that the Gentiles not exercising their Minds to search out the Truth, and form their Judgments right, God left them to an unsearching unjudicious Mind.

Non explorantibus permisit mentem non exploratricem.

ʳ A Discourse like this of St. *Paul* here, wherein Idolatry is made the Cause of the enormous Crimes and profligate Lives Men run into, may be read, *Wisdom* xiv. 11, &c.

32 ˢ Τὸ δικαίωμα τοῦ Θεοῦ, *the Judgment of God,* might it not be translated, *the Rectitude of God?* i. e. That Rule of Rectitude which God had given to Mankind in giving them Reason: As that Righteousness which God requires for Salvation, in the Gospel is called *the Righteousness of God,* ver. 17. *Rectitude* in the Translation being used in this appropriated Sense, as δικαίωμα is in the Original. *Vid.* Note, Chap. ii. 26.

ᵗ Οὐκ ἐνόησαν ὅτι, *Did not understand that they who commit,* &c. This Reading is justified by the *Clermont,* and another ancient Manuscript, as well as by that which the old *Latin* Version followed, as well as *Clement, Isidore,* and *Oecumenius,* and will probably be thought the

TEXT.	PARAPHRASE.
things are worthy of death) not only do the same, but have pleasure in them that do them. 1 Therefore thou art inexcusable, O man, who-	did such things were worthy of Death, do ⁿ not only do them themselves, but live well together, without any Mark of Dis-esteem or Censure, with them that do them. ˣ Therefore thou art unexcusable, O Man, whosoever thou art

1.

NOTES.

the more genuine by those who can hardly suppose that St. *Paul* should affirm, that the Gentile World did know, that he who offended against any of the Directions of this natural Rule of Rectitude, taught, or discoverable by the Light of Reason, was worthy of Death; especially if we remember what he says, *chap.* v. 13. *That Sin is not imputed, when there is no positive Law*; and *chap.* vii. 9. *I was alive without the Law once*: Both which Places signifying that Men did not know Death to be the Wages of Sin in general, but by the Declaration of a positive law.

ⁿ Συνευδοκȣσι τοις πρασσȣσι, *have pleasure in these that do them.* He that considers that the Design of the Apostle here, manifest in the immediately following Words, is to combat the Animosity of the Jews against the Gentiles; and that there could not be a more effectual way to shame them into a more modest and mild Temper, than by shewing them that the Gentiles, in all the Darkness that blinded them, and the Extravagancies they run into, were never guilty of such an Absurdity as this, to censure and separate from others, and shew an implacable Aversion to them, for what they themselves were equally guilty of: He, I say, that considers this, will be easily persuaded to understand συνευδοκȣσι here, as I do, for a Complacency that avoided censuring or breaking with them who were in the same State and Course of Life with themselves, that did nothing amiss but what they themselves were equally guilty of. There can be nothing clearer than that συνευδοκȣσι, *have pleasure*, in this Verse, is opposed to κρινεις, *judgest*, in the next Verse; without which I do not see how it is possible to make out the Inference which the Apostle draws here.

1 ˣ *Therefore:* This is a Term of Illation, and shews the Consequence here drawn from the foregoing Words. *Therefore* the Jew is inexcusable in judging, because the Gentiles, with all the Darkness that was on their Minds, were never guilty of such a Folly, as to judge those who were no more faulty than themselves. For the better understanding of this Place, it may not perhaps be amiss to set the whole Argumentation of the Apostle here in its due Light. It stands thus: "The Gentiles acknowledged the Rectitude of the Law of Nature, but knew not
"that those who break any of its Rules, incurred Death by their Transgression: But as much
"in the dark as they were, they are not guilty of such Absurdity as to condemn others,
"or refuse Communication with them as unworthy of their Society, who are no worse than
"themselves, nor do any thing but what they themselves do equally with them; but live in
"Complacency on fair Terms with them, without Censure or Separation, thinking as well of
"their Condition as of their own: *Therefore* if the blinded Heathen do so, thou, O Jew, art
"inexcusable, who having the Light of the revealed Law of God, and knowing by it that
"the Breaches of the Law merit Death, dost judge others to Perdition, and shut them out
"from Salvation, for that which thou thyself art equally guilty of, *viz.* Disobedience to the
"Law. Thou, a poor, ignorant, conceited, fallible Man, sittest in Judgment upon others, and com-
"mittest the same things thou condemnest them for:' But this thou mayest be sure, that the Judg-
"ment and Condemnation of God is right and firm, and will certainly be executed upon those
"who do such things. For thou who adjudgest the Heathen to Condemnation for the same things
"which thou dost thyself, canst thou imagine that thou thyself shalt escape the same Judgment

ROMANS.

PARAPHRASE.

art ʸ that judgeſt ᶻ or cenſureſt another; for wherein thou judgeſt another, thou condemneſt thyſelf: For thou that judgeſt art alike guilty in doing the ſame things. But this we are ſure of, that the Judgment that God paſſes upon any Offenders, is according to Truth, right and juſt. Canſt thou who doſt thoſe things, which thou condemneſt in another, think that thou ſhalt eſcape the condemn-

2.

3.

TEXT.

ſoever thou art that judgeſt: for wherein thou judgeſt another, thou condemneſt thyſelf, for thou that judgeſt doſt the ſame things.

But we are ſure that the judgment of God is according to truth, againſt them which commit ſuch things.

And thinkeſt thou this, O man, that judgeſt them which do ſuch things, and

2

3

NOTES.

" of God? God, whatever thou mayeſt think, is no Reſpecter of Perſons: Both Jews as well
" as Gentiles, that are perverſly contentious againſt others, and do not themſelves obey the
" Goſpel, ſhall meet with Wrath and Indignation from God: And Gentiles as well as Jews,
" whom the Goodneſs and Forbearance of God bringeth to Repentance, and an humble ſub-
" miſſive Acceptance of the Goſpel, ſhall find Acceptance with God, and eternal Life in the
" Kingdom of the Meſſias; for which if thou are contentious to ſhut out the Gentiles, thou
" manifeſtly ſhutteſt out thyſelf."

ʸ *O Man, whoſoever thou art.* It is plain from *ver.* 17 & 27. and the whole Tenor of this Chapter, that St. *Paul* by theſe Words means the Jews; but there are two viſible Reaſons why he ſpeaks in theſe Terms: 1ſt, He makes his Concluſion general, as having the more Force, but leſs Offence, than if he had bluntly named the Jews, whom he is very careful in all this Epiſtle to treat in the ſofteſt manner imaginable. 2dly, He uſes the Term *Man* emphatically, in Oppoſition to *God* in the next Verſe.

ᶻ *Judgeſt.* There will need nothing to be ſaid to thoſe who read this Epiſtle with the leaſt Attention, to prove that the *judging*, which St. *Paul* here ſpeaks of, was that Averſion which the Jews generally had to the Gentiles; ſo that the unconverted Jews could not bear with the Thoughts of a Meſſias, that admitted the Heathen equally with them into his Kingdom; nor could the converted Jews be brought to admit them into their Communion, as the People of God now equally with themſelves; ſo that they generally, both one and t'other, judged them unworthy the Favour of God, and out of Capacity to become his People any other way, but by Circumciſion, and an Obſervance of the ritual Parts of the Law; the Inexcuſableneſs and Abſurdity whereof St. *Paul* ſhews in this Chapter.

2 ᵃ *According to Truth*, doth, I ſuppoſe, ſignify not barely a true Judgment, which will ſtand in Oppoſition to erroneous, and that will not take effect, but ſomething more, *i. e.* according to the Truth of his Predictions and Threats. As if he had ſaid, " But if God in Judg-
" ment caſt off the Jews from being any longer his People, we know this to be according to
" his Truth, who hath forewarned them of it. Ye Jews judge the Gentiles not to be received
" into the People of God, and refuſe them Admittance into the Kingdom of the Meſſias,
" though you break the Law as well as they; you judge as prejudiced paſſionate Men. But
" the Judgment of God againſt you will ſtand firm." The Reaſon why he does it ſo covertly, may be that which I have before mentioned, his great Care not to ſhock the Jews, eſpecially here in the beginning, till he had got faſt hold upon them. And hence poſſibly it is that he calls obeying the Goſpel, *obeying the Truth*, ver. 8. and uſes other the like ſoft Expreſſions in this Chapter.

ing

ROMANS.

TEXT.

doſt the ſame, that thou ſhalt eſcape the judgment of God?

4 Or deſpiſeſt thou the riches of his goodneſs, and forbearance, and long-ſuffering, not knowing that the goodneſs of God leadeth thee to repentance?

5 But after thy hardneſs and impenitent heart, treaſureſt up unto thyſelf wrath againſt the day of wrath, and revelation of the righteous judgment of God;

6 Who will render to every man according to his deeds:

7 To them who by patient continuance in well-doing, ſeek for glory, and honour, and immortality, eternal life:

8 But unto them that are contentious, and do not obey the truth, but obey unrighteouſneſs, indignation, and wrath;

9 Tribulation and anguiſh upon every ſoul of man that doth evil, of the Jew firſt, and alſo of the Gentile.

PARAPHRASE.

ing Sentence of God? or ſlighteſt thou the Riches of his Goodneſs, Forbearance and Long-Suffering, not knowing nor conſidering that the Goodneſs of God ought to lead thee to Repentance? But layeſt up to thyſelf Wrath and Puniſhment, which thou wilt meet with at the Day of Judgment, and that juſt Retribution which ſhall be awarded thee by God in Proportion to thy Impenitency, and the Hardneſs of thy Heart; who will retribute to every one according to his Works, *viz.* Eternal Life to all thoſe who by Patience [b] and Gentleneſs in Well-doing ſeek Glory and Honour, and a State of Immortality: But to them who are contentious [*] and froward, and will not obey the Truth [c], but ſubject themſelves to Unrighteouſneſs, Indignation and Wrath; Tribulation and Anguiſh, ſhall be poured out upon every Soul of Man that worketh Evil, on the Jew firſt, and alſo on the Gentile. But Glory, Honour, and Peace, ſhall be beſtowed on every Man that worketh Good, on the Jew

4.

5.

6.
7.

8.

9.

10.

NOTES.

7 [b] *Patience* in this Verſe is oppoſed to *Contentious* [*] in the next, and ſeems principally to regard the Jews, who had no Patience for any Conſideration of the Gentiles, but with a ſtrange Peeviſhneſs and Contention, oppoſed the Freedom of the Goſpel in admitting the believing Gentiles to the Franchiſes of the Kingdom of the Meſſias, upon equal Terms with themſelves.

8 [c] Though by *Truth* the Goſpel be here meant, yet I doubt not but St. *Paul* uſed the Term Truth with an Eye to the Jews, who though ſome few of them received the Goſpel, yet even a great Part of thoſe few joined with the reſt of their Nation in oppoſing this great Truth of the Goſpel, That under the Meſſias the Gentiles who believed were the People of God, as well as the Jews, and as ſuch were to be received by them.

ROMANS. Chap. II.

PARAPHRASE.

11. first ᵈ, and also on the Gentile. For with
12. God there is no Respect of Persons. For all that have sinned without having the positive Law of God, which was given the Israelites, shall perish ᵉ without the Law; and all who have sinned being under the Law, shall be
13. judged by the Law. (For the bare Hearers of the Law are not thereby just or righteous in the Sight of God; but the Doers of the Law, they who exactly perform all that is commanded in it, shall be justified. For when the Gentiles,
14. who have no positive Law given them by God ᶠ, do by the Direction of the Light of

TEXT.

10 But glory, honour, and peace to every man that worketh good, to the Jew first, and also to the Gentile.
11 For there is no respect of persons with God.
12 For as many as have sinned without law, shall also perish without law: and as many as have sinned in the law, shall be judged by the law.
13 (For not the hearers of the law are just before God, but the doers of the law shall be justified.
14 For when the Gentiles which have not the law,

NOTES.

9 & 10 ᵈ *The Jew first, and also the Gentile.* We see by these two Verses, and *chap.* i. 16. that St. *Paul* carefully lays down, that there was now under the Gospel no other National Distinction between the Jews and the Gentiles, but only a Priority in the Offer of the Gospel, and in the Design of Rewards and Punishments, according as the Jews obeyed, or not. Which may farther satisfy us, that the Distinction which St. *Paul* insists on so much here, and all through the first Part of this Epistle, is national; the Comparison being between the Jews as nationally the People of God; and the Gentiles, as not the People of God before the Messias; and that under the Messias, the Professors of Christianity, consisting most of converted Gentiles, were the People of God, owned and acknowledged as such by him, the unbelieving Jews being rejected, and the unbelieving Gentiles never received; but that yet personally both Jews and Gentiles, every single Person, shall be punished for his own particular Sin, as appears by the two next Verses.

12 ᵉ Ἀπολοῦνται, *shall perish*; κριθήσονται, *shall be judged*. Those under the Law, St. *Paul* says, shall be *judged* by the Law; and this is easy to conceive, because they were under a positive Law, wherein Life and Death were annexed, as the Reward and Punishment of Obedience and Disobedience; but of the Gentiles, who were not under that positive Law, he says barely that they shall *perish*. St. *Paul* does not use these so eminently differing Expressions for nothing; they will, I think, give some light to *chap.* v. 13. and my Interpretation of it, if they lead us no farther.

14 ᶠ Μὴ νόμον ἔχοντες, *having not the Law,* or *not having a Law.* The Apostle by the Word *Law* generally in this Epistle signifying a positive Law given by God, and promulgated by a Revelation from Heaven, with the Sanction of declared Rewards and Punishments annexed to it, it is not improbable that in this Verse (where by the Greek Particle he so plainly points out the Law of *Moses*) by ὁ νόμος, without the Article, may intend Law in general, in his Sense of a Law; and so this Verse may be translated thus; *For when the Gentiles, who have not a Law, do by Nature the things contained in the Law; these not having a Law, are a Law to themselves.* And to ver. 12. *As many as have sinned, being under a Law, shall be judged by a Law.* For though from *Adam* to Christ there was no revealed positive Law, but that given to the *Israelites*; yet it is certain, that by Jesus Christ a positive Law from Heaven is given to all Mankind, and that those to whom this has been promulgated by the Preaching of the Gospel, are all under it, and shall be judged by it.

Nature

ROMANS.

TEXT.

do by nature the things contained in the law, these having not the law, are a law unto themselves:

15 Which shew the work of the law written in their hearts, their conscience also bearing witness, and their thoughts the mean while accusing, or else excusing one another.)

16 In the day when God shall judge the secrets of men by Jesus Christ, according to my gospel.

17 Behold, thou art called a Jew, and restest in the law, and makest thy boast of God;

18 And knowest his will, and approvest the things that are more excellent,

PARAPHRASE.

Nature observe or keep to the moral Rectitude contained in the positive Law given by God to the Israelites, they being without any positive Law given them, have nevertheless a Law within themselves; and shew the Rule of 15. the Law written in their Hearts, their Consciences also bearing witness to that Law, they amongst themselves, in the reasoning of their own Minds, accusing or excusing one another.) At 16. the Day of Judgment, when as I make known in my preaching the Gospel ^{g}, God shall judge all the Actions of Men by Jesus Christ. Behold thou art named ^{h} a Jew; and thou 17. with Satisfaction restest in the Privilege of having the Law, as a Mark of God's peculiar Favour ^{i}, whom thou gloriest in, as being thy God, and thou one of his People; a People who alone know and worship the true God: And thou knowest his Will, and hast the 18. Touchstone of things excellent ^{k}, having

NOTES.

16 ^{g} *According to my Gospel*, i. e. as I make known in my preaching the Gospel. That this is the Meaning of this Phrase, may be seen 2 *Tim.* ii. 8. And of St. *Paul*'s declaring of it in his Preaching, we have an Instance left upon Record, *Acts* xvii. 31.

17 ^{h} ἐπονομάζη, *thou art named*, emphatically said by St. *Paul*; for he that was such a Jew as he describes in the following Verses, he insists on it, was a Jew only in Name, not in Reality; for so he concludes, *ver.* 28 & 29. he is not in the Esteem of God a Jew, who is so outwardly only.

17——20 ^{i} In those four Verses St. *Paul* makes use of the Titles the Jews assumed to themselves, from the Advantages they had of Light and Knowledge above the Gentiles, to shew them how inexcusable they were in judging the Gentiles, who were even in their own Account so much beneath them in Knowledge, for doing those Things which they themselves were also guilty of.

17 Vid. *Mic.* iii. 11.

18 ^{k} Τὰ διαφέροντα signifies *things excellent, convenient, controverted,* or *differing.* In either of these Senses it may be understood here, though the last, *viz.* their Difference in respect of lawful and unlawful, I think may be pitched on, as most suited to the Apostle's Design here, and that which the Jews much stood upon, as giving them one great Pre-eminence above the defiled Gentiles.

been

PARAPHRASE.

19. been educated in the Law; and takest upon thee as one who art a Guide to the Blind¹, a Light to the ignorant Gentiles who are in
20. darkness¹, an Instructor of the Foolish¹, a Teacher of Babes, having an exact Draught, and a compleat System ᵐ of Knowledge and
21. Truth in the Law. Thou therefore who art a Master in this Knowledge, and teachest others, teachest thou not thyself? Thou that preachest that a Man should not steal, dost thou steal?
22. Thou that declarest Adultery to be unlawful, dost thou commit it? Thou that abhorrest I-
23. dols, dost thou commit Sacrilege? Thou who gloriest in the Law, dost thou by breaking of
24. the Law dishonour God? For the Name of God is blasphemed amongst the Gentiles, by reason of your Miscarriages, as it is written ⁿ.
25. Circumcision ᵒ indeed, and thy being a Jew, profiteth ᵖ, if thou keep the Law: But if thou be a Transgressor of the Law, thy Circumcision is made Uncircumcision; thou art no way

TEXT.

being instructed out of the law,

19 And art confident that thou thyself art a guide of the blind, a light of them which are in darkness,

20 An instructor of the foolish, a teacher of babes, which hast the form of knowledge and of the truth in the law.

21 Thou therefore which teachest another, teachest thou not thyself? Thou that preachest a man should not steal, dost thou steal?

22 Thou that sayest a man should not commit adultery, dost thou commit adultery? Thou that abhorrest idols, dost thou commit sacrilege?

23 Thou that makest thy boast of the law, through breaking the law dishonourest thou God?

24 For the name of God is blasphemed among the Gentiles through you, as it is written.

25 For circumcision verily profiteth, if thou keep the law: but if thou be a

NOTES.

19, 20 ¹ *Blind*, in *Darkness*, *Foolish*, *Babes*, were Appellations which the Jews gave to the Gentiles, signifying how much inferior to themselves they thought them in Knowledge.

20 ᵐ Μόρφωσις, *Form*, seems here to be the same with τύπΘ-, *Form*, ch. vi. 17. *i. e.* such a Draught as contained and represented the Parts and Lineaments of the whole. For it is to be remembered, that the Apostle uses these Expressions and Terms here in the same Sense the Jews spoke of themselves vaunting it over the Gentiles, he thereby aggravating their Fault in judging the Gentiles as they did.

24 ⁿ See 2 *Sam.* xii. 14. *Ezek.* xxxvi. 23.

25 ᵒ *Circumcision* is here put for being a Jew, as being one of the chief and most discriminating Rites of that People.

ᵖ *Profiteth if thou keep the Law*; because a Jew that kept the Law was to have Life therein, *Lev.* xviii. 5.

better

ROMANS.

Chap. II.

TEXT.

breaker of the law, thy circumcision is made uncircumcision.

26 Therefore, if the uncircumcision keep the righteousness of the law, shall not his uncircumci-

PARAPHRASE.

better than an Heathen. If therefore an uncircumcised Gentile keep the moral Rectitudes ^q of the Law, shall he not be reckoned and accounted of, as if he were circumcised and

26.

NOTES.

26 ^q Τὰ δικαιώματα τοῦ νόμου, *The Righteousness of the Law.* I have taken the Liberty to render it, *The Rectitudes of the Law,* in an appropriated Sense of the word *Rectitude,* in Imitation of St. *Paul,* who uses δικαίωμα here for all those Precepts of the Law which contain in them any Part of the natural and eternal Rule of *Rectitude,* which is made known to Men by the Light of Reason. This Rule of their Actions all Mankind, uncircumcised as well as circumcised, had, and is that which St. *Paul* calls δικαίωμα τοῦ Θεοῦ, *ch.* i. 32. Because it came from God, and was made by him the moral Rule to all Mankind, being laid within the Discovery of their Reason, which if they kept to, it was δικαίωμα, Righteousness to them, or they were justified. And this Rule of Morality St. *Paul* says the Gentile World did acknowledge. So that δικαίωμα τοῦ Θεοῦ, *ch.* i. 32. signifies that Rule of Right taken in general, and δικαιώματα τοῦ νόμου here signifies the particular Branches of it contained in the Law of *Moses*. For no other Part of the Law of *Moses* could an Heathen be supposed to observe or be concerned in: And therefore those only can be the δικαιώματα τοῦ νόμου here meant. If we consider the various Senses that Translators and Expositors have given to this Term δικαίωμα, in the several Places of St. *Paul*'s Epistles, where it occurs, we shall have occasion to think, that the Apostle used this Word with great Latitude and Variety of Significations; whereas I imagine, that if we carefully read those Passages, we shall find that he used it every where in the same Sense, *i. e.* for that Rule which, if complied with, justified, or rendered perfect, the Person or Thing it referred to. For Example,

Rom. i. 32. Δικαίωμα Θεοῦ, translated *The Judgment of God,* is that Rule of Right which if the Heathen World had kept and perfectly obeyed, they had been righteous before God.

Rom. ii. 26. Δικαιώματα τοῦ νόμου, *The Righteousness of the Law,* are those Precepts of the Law of *Moses,* which if the Uncircumcised whom he there speaks of had kept, they had been righteous before God.

Rom. v. 16. Εἰς δικαίωμα, *to Justification,* is to the obtaining of Righteousness.

Rom. v. 18. Δι' ἑνὸς δικαιώματος, *By one Righteousness,* is by one Act whereby he was justified or compleatly perfected to be what he had undertaken to be, *viz.* the Redeemer and Saviour of the World. For it was διὰ παθημάτων, or as some Copies read it, διὰ παθήματος, by his Suffering, *viz.* Death on the Cross, that he was perfected, *Heb.* ii. 9, 10. & xiv. 15. & v. 7 —— 9. *Rom.* v. 10. *Phil.* ii. 8. *Col.* i. 21, 21. *Rom.* viii. 4. τὸ δικαίωμα τοῦ νόμου, *The Righteousness of the Law.* Here, as *Rom.* ii. 26. it is that Rule of Right contained in the Law, which if a Man exactly performed, he was righteous and perfect before God.

Heb. ix. 1. Δικαιώματα λατρείας, *Ordinances of Divine Service,* are those Rules or Precepts concerning the outward Worship of God, which when conformed to render it perfect, and such as was right and unblameable before God.

Heb. ix. 10. Δικαιώματα σαρκὸς, *Carnal Ordinances,* are such Rules concerning ritual Performances, as, when observed, justified the Flesh. By these Observances, according as they were prescribed, the Flesh or natural outward Man, obtained a legal outward Holiness or Righteousness, there was no Exception against him, but he was freely admitted into the Congregation, and into the Sanctuary.

L l

PARAPHRASE.

27. and every way a Jew? And shall not a Gentile, who in his natural State of Uncircumcision fulfils the Law, condemn ʳ thee, who notwithstanding the Advantage of having the Law and Circumcision, ˢ art a Transgressor

TEXT.

sion be counted for circumcision?
And shall not uncircumcision which is by nature, if it fulfil the law, judge thee, who by the letter and circumcision dost transgress the law? — 27

NOTES.

In the same Sense δικαίωμα is also used in the Apocalypse.

Rev. xv. 4. Τὰ δικαιώματά σου ἐφανερώθησαν, *Thy Judgments are made manifest,* i. e. those Terms whereupon Men are to be justified before God, were clearly and fully made known under the Gospel. Here, as *Rom.* i. they are called δικαιώματα Θεοῦ, the Terms which God had prescribed to Men for their Justification. And,

Rev. xix. 8. Τὰ δικαιώματα τῶν ἁγίων, *The Righteousness of the Saints,* i. e. The Performances whereby the Saints stand justified before God.

So that if we well observe it, δικαίωμα is the Rule of Right; As having God for its Author, it is δικαίωμα Θεοῦ; As contained in the Precepts of the Law, 'tis δικαιώματα τοῦ νόμου; As it concerns the external instituted Rites of the Levitical Worship of God, it is δικαιώματα λατρείας; As it concerns the outward Legal or Ritual Holiness of the Jews, it is δικαιώματα σαρκὸς; As it is in holy Men made perfect, it is δικαιώματα ἁγίων.

It may not be amiss to take a little Notice also of St. *Paul's* Use of the other Term here, νόμος, Law, which he commonly puts for a positive Rule given to Men, with the Sanction of a Penalty annexed; and in particular frequently (sometimes with, sometimes without the Particle) for the Law of *Moses*, without naming what Law he means, as if there had been no other Law in the World, as indeed there was not any other in St. *Paul's* Notion of a Law, from the Fall to our Saviour's Time, but only the Law given by God to the Israelites by the Hand of *Moses*. Under the Gospel the Law of *Moses* was abrogated: But yet the δικαιώματα τοῦ νόμου were not abrogated. The δικαίωμα τοῦ Θεοῦ not only stood firm, but was by the Divine Authority promulgated anew by Jesus Christ, the King and Saviour of the World. For 'tis of this that he says, that he *is not come to destroy the Law, but to fulfil it,* i. e. to give it positively and plainly its full Latitude and Extent, and set these δικαιώματα τοῦ νόμου in their due Light and full Force; and accordingly we see all the Branches of it more expressly commanded, and with Penalties more vigorously enforced on all his Subjects by our Saviour and his Apostles, than they were in the Law of *Moses*.

Thus we see by the Doctrine of St. *Paul* and the New Testament, there is one and the same Rule of Rectitude set to the Actions of all Mankind, Jews, Gentiles, and Christians; and that failing of a complete Obedience to it in every Tittle, makes a Man unrighteous, the Consequence whereof is Death. For the Gentiles that have sinned without a Law, shall perish without a Law; the Jews that have sinned having a Law, shall be judged by that Law; but that both Jews and Gentiles shall be saved from Death, if they believe in Jesus Christ, and sincerely endeavour after Righteousness, though they do not attain unto it, their Faith being accounted to them for Righteousness, *Rom.* iii. 19 —— 24.

27 ʳ *Judge thee.* This he saith prosecuting the Design he began with, *ver.* 1. of shewing the Folly and Unreasonableness of the Jews in judging the Gentiles, and denying them Admittance and Fellowship with themselves in the Kingdom of the Messias.

ˢ It is plain that *by Nature,* and *by the Letter and Circumcision,* are there opposed to one another, and mean the one a Man in his natural State, wholly a Stranger to the Law of God revealed by *Moses*, and the other a Jew observing the external Rites contained in the Letter of that Law.

of

TEXT.

28 For he is not a Jew, which is one outwardly; neither is that circumcision, which is outward in the flesh:

29 But he is a Jew, which is one inwardly, and circumcision is that of the heart, in the spirit, and not in the letter, whose praise is not of men, but of God.

PARAPHRASE.

of the Law? For he is not a Jew who is one in outward Appearance and Conformity ᵗ; nor is that the Circumcision which renders a Man acceptable to God, which is outwardly in the Flesh. But he is a Jew, and one of the People of God, who is one in an inward Conformity to the Law; and that is the Circumcision which avails a Man, which is of the Heart ᵘ, according to the spiritual Sense of the Law, which is the purging our Hearts from Iniquity by Faith in Jesus Christ, and not in an external Observance of the Letter ˣ, by which a Man cannot attain Life; such true Israelites as these, though they are judged, condemned, and rejected by Men of the Jewish Nation, are nevertheless honoured and accepted by God.

28.

29.

NOTES.

28 ᵗ Vid. *ch.* ix. 6, 7. *Gal.* vi. 15, 16.
29 ᵘ St. *Paul's* Exposition of this, See *Phil.* iii. 3. *Col.* ii. 11.
ˣ *Letter,* vid. *ch.* vii. 6. 2 *Cor.* iii. 6, 7. compared with xvii.

SECT. III.

CHAP. III. 1———13.

CONTENTS.

IN this third Chapter St. *Paul* goes on to shew that the national Privileges the *Jews* had over the *Gentiles,* in being the People of God, gave them no particular Right, or better Title to the Kingdom of the Messias, than what the *Gentiles* had. Because they as well as the *Gentiles* all sinned, and not being able to attain Righteousness by the Deeds of the Law more than the *Gentiles,* Justification was to be had only by the Free Grace of God through

Chap. III. Faith in Jesus Christ; so that upon their believing, God, who is the God not of the Jews alone, but also of the Gentiles, accepted the Gentiles as well as the Jews; and now admits all who profess Faith in Jesus Christ, to be equally his People.

To clear his Way to this, he begins with removing an Objection of the Jews, ready to say; If it be so as you have told us in the foregoing Section, that it is the Circumcision of the Heart alone that availeth, what Advantage have the Jews, who keep to the Circumcision of the Flesh, and the other Observances of the Law, by being the People of God? To which he answers, that the Jews had many Advantages above the Gentiles; but yet that in respect of their Acceptance with God under the Gospel, they had none at all. He declares that both Jews and Gentiles are Sinners, both equally uncapable of being justified by their own Performances: That God was equally the God both of Jews and Gentiles, and out of his Free Grace justified those, and only those who believed, whether Jews or Gentiles.

PARAPHRASE.

1. *IF it be thus, that Circumcision by a Failure of Obedience to the Law becomes Uncircumcision; and that the Gentiles, who keep the Righteousness or moral Part of the Law, shall judge the Jews that transgress the Law, what Advantage have the Jews? or what Profit is there of Circumcision?*

2. I answer, Much every Way ʸ; chiefly that God particularly present amongst them revealed his Mind and Will, and engaged himself in Promises to them, by *Moses*, and other his Prophets, which Oracles they had, and kept amongst them, whilst the rest of Mankind had no such Communication with the Deity, had no Revelation of his Purposes of Mercy to Mankind, but were, as it were, without God

TEXT.

1. What advantage then hath the Jew? or what profit is there of circumcision?

2. Much every way: chiefly, because that unto them were committed the oracles of God.

NOTES.

2 ʸ A List of the Advantages the Jews had over the Gentiles he gives, ch. ix. 4, 5. but here mentions only one of them that was most proper to his present Purpose.

ROMANS.

Chap. III.

TEXT.

3 For what if some did not believe: shall their unbelief make the Faith of God without effect?

4 God forbid: yea let God be true, but every man a liar; as it is written, That thou mightest be justified in thy Sayings, and mightest overcome when thou art judged.

5 But if our unrighteousness commend the righteousness of God, what shall we say? Is God unrighteous who taketh vengeance? (I speak as a man)

6 God forbid: for then how shall God judge the world?

PARAPHRASE.

in the World. For though some of the Jews, who had the Promise of the Messias, did not believe in him when he came, and so did not receive the Righteousness which is by Faith in Jesus Christ; yet their Unbelief cannot render the Faithfulness and Truth of God of no Effect, who had promised to be a God to *Abraham* and his Seed after him, and bless them to all Generations [z]. No, by no means. God forbid that any one should entertain such a Thought: Yea, let God be acknowledged to be true, and every Man a Liar, as it is written, *That thou mightest be justified in thy Sayings, and mightest overcome when thou art judged.*

But you will say farther, *If it be so that our Sinfulness commendeth* [a] *the Righteousness of God shewn in keeping his Word* [b] *given to our Forefathers, what shall I say, Is it not Injustice in God to punish us for it, and cast us off? (I must be understood to say this in the Person of a carnal Man pleading for himself)* God forbid: For if God be unrighteous, how shall he judge the World [b]?

3.

4.

5.

6.

NOTES.

3 [z] How this was made good, St. *Paul* explains more at large in the following Chapter, and ch. ix. 6 ——— 13.

5 [a] That by *the Righteousness of God*, St. *Paul* here intends God's Faithfulness in keeping his Promise of saving Believers, Gentiles as well as Jews, by Righteousness through Faith in Jesus Christ, is plain, *ver.* 4, 7, 26. St. *Paul*'s great Design here, and all through the eleven first Chapters of this Epistle, being to convince the *Romans*, that God purposed, and in the Old Testament declared, that he would receive and save the Gentiles by Faith in the Messias, which was the only Way whereby Jews or Gentiles (they being all Sinners, and equally destitute of Righteousness by Works) were to be saved. This was a Doctrine which the Jews could not bear, and therefore the Apostle here in the Person of a Jew urges, and in his own Person answers their Objections against it, confirming to the *Romans* the Veracity and Faithfulness of God, on whom they might with all Assurance depend for the Performance of whatever he said.

-6 [b] This which is an Argument in the Mouth of *Abraham*, Gen. xviii. 25. St. *Paul* very appositely makes use of to stop the Mouths of the blasphemous Jews.

PARAPHRASE.

7. ‘ *For if the Truth and Veracity of God hath the more appeared to his Glory, by reason of my Lie* ᵈ, *i. e. my Sin, why yet am I condemned for a Sin-*
8. *ner, and punished for it? Why rather should not this be thought a right Consequence, and a just Excuse? Let us do Evil, that Good may come of it, that Glory may come to God by it.* Thus ᵉ some maliciously and slanderously report us Christians to say, for which they deserve and will from God receive Punishment as they deserve.
9. *Are we Jews then in any whit a better Condition than the Gentiles* ᶠ *?* Not at all. For I have already ᵍ brought a Charge of Guilt and Sin

TEXT.

For if the truth of 7 God hath more abounded through my lie unto his glory; why yet am I also judged as a sinner?

And not rather, as we 8 be slanderously reported, and as some affirm that we say, Let us do evil, that good may come? whose damnation is just.

What then? are we 9 better than they? No in no wise: for we have before proved both Jews and Gentiles, that they are all under sin;

NOTES.

7 ᶜ *For.* This Particle plainly joins what follows in this and the next Verse to *Vengeance* in the 5th Verse, and shews it to be, as it is, a Continuation of the Objection begun in that Verse; why St. *Paul* broke it into Pieces by intruding the 6th Verse in the Middle of it, there is a very plain Reason. In the Objection there were two Things to be corrected; 1st, The charging God with Unrighteousness, which as soon as mentioned, it was a becoming Interruption in St. *Paul* to quash immediately, and to stop the Jews Mouth with the Words of *Abraham.* 2dly, The other Thing in the Objection was a false Calumny upon the Christians, as if they preaching Justification by Free Grace, said, *Let us do Evil, that Good may come of it.* To which the Apostle's Answer was the more distinct, being subjoined to that Branch separated from the other.

ᵈ *Lie.* The Sense of the Place makes it plain, that St. *Paul* by Lie here means Sin in general, but seems to have used the Word *Lie*, as having a more forcible and graceful Antithesis to the *Truth of God*, which the Objection pretends to be thereby illustrated.

8 ᵉ *Some.* 'Tis past doubt that these were the Jews. But St. *Paul*, always tender towards his own Nation, forbears to name them, when he pronounces this Sentence, that their casting off and Destruction now at hand, for this Scandal and other Opposition to the Christian Religion, was just.

9 ᶠ Having in the six foregoing Verses justified the Truth of God, notwithstanding his casting off the Jews, and vindicated the Doctrine of Grace against the Cavils of the Jews, which two Objections of theirs came naturally in his way, the Apostle takes up here again the Jews Question proposed *ver.* 1. and urges it home to the Case in hand. Τί οὖν προεχόμεθα, being but the same with Τί οὖν τὸ περισσὸν τοῦ Ἰουδαίου, ver. 1. *Have Jews then any Preference in the Kingdom of the Messias?* To which he answers, No, not at all. That this is the Meaning, is visible from the whole Chapter, where he lays both Jews and Gentiles in an equal State in reference to Justification.

ᵍ *Already,* viz. *ch.* ii. 3. where St. *Paul*, under the gentler Compellation of O Man, charges the Jews to be Sinners as well as the Gentiles, and *ver.* 17 — 24. shews, that by having the Law they were no more kept from being Sinners than the Gentiles were without the Law. And this Charge against them, that they were Sinners, he here proves against them from the Testimony of their own Sacred Books contained in the Old Testament.

both

ROMANS

Chap. III.

TEXT.

10. As it is written, There is none righteous, no not one:
11. There is none that understandeth, there is none that seeketh after God.
12. They are all gone out of the way, they are together become unprofitable, there is none that doth good, no not one.
13. Their throat is an open sepulchre; with their tongues they have used deceit; the poison of asps is under their lips;
14. Whose mouth is full of cursing and bitterness.
15. Their feet are swift to shed blood.
16. Destruction and misery are in their ways:
17. And the way of peace have they not known.
18. There is no fear of God before their eyes.
19. Now we know that what things soever the law saith, it saith to them who are under the law; that every mouth may be stopped, and all the world

PARAPHRASE.

both against Jews and Gentiles, and urged that there is not one of them clear, which I shall prove now against you Jews; For it is written, *There is none righteous, no not one: There is none that understandeth, there is none that seeketh after God. They are all gone out of the way, they are together become unprofitable, there is none that doth good, no not one. Their Throat is an open Sepulchre; with their Tongues they have used Deceit; the Poison of Asps is under their Lips; whose Mouth is full of Cursing and Bitterness. Their Feet are swift to shed Blood: Destruction and Misery are in their Ways, and the Way of Peace have they not known. There is no Fear of God before their Eyes.* This is all said in the Sacred Book of our Law ʰ: And what is said there, we know is said to the Jews, who are under the Law, that the Mouth of every Jew that would justify himself might be stopped, and all the World, Jews as well as Gentiles, may be forced to acknowledge themselves guilty before God. From whence it is evident, that by his own Performances, in Obedience to a Law ⁱ

10.
11.
12.
13.
14.
15.
16.
17.
18.
19.

20.

NOTES.

19 ʰ *The Law* here signifies the whole Old Testament, which containing Revelations from God in the Time of the Law, and being to those under the Law of Divine Authority, and a Rule as well as the Law itself, it is sometimes in the New Testament called *the Law*, and so our Saviour himself uses the Term *Law*, John x. 34. The Meaning of St. *Paul* here is, That the Declarations of God, which he had cited out of the Old Testament, were spoken of the Jews, who were under the Dispensation of the Old Testament, and were, by the Word of God to them, all of them pronounced Sinners.

20 ⁱ Ἐξ ἔργων νόμου, I should render, *by Deeds of Law*, i. e. by Actions of Conformity to a Law requiring the Performance of the δικαίωμα Θεοῦ, *the right Rule of God* (mentioned chap. i. 32.) with a Penalty annexed, no Flesh can be justified: But every one failing of an exact Conformity of his Actions to the immutable Rectitude of that eternal Rule of Right, will be found unrighteous, and so incur the Penalty of the Law. That this is the Meaning of ἔργα νόμου, is evident, because the Apostle's Declaration here is concerning all Men, πᾶσα σάρξ. But we say, ἐξ ἔργων τοῦ νόμου, *by the Deeds of the Law*, but ἐξ ἔργων νόμου, *by Deeds of Law*. Though in the foregoing and following Verse, where he would specify the Law of *Moses*, he uses the Article with νόμου three times.

ROMANS.

PARAPHRASE.

no ᵏ Man can attain to an exact Conformity to the Rule of Right, so as to be righteous in the Sight of God. For by Law, which is the publishing the Rule with a Penalty, we are not delivered from the Power of Sin, nor can it help Men to Righteousness ˡ; but by Law we come experimentally to know Sin in the Force and Power of it, since we find it prevail upon us notwithstanding the Punishment

21. of Death is by the Law annexed to it ᵐ. But the Righteousness of God, that Righteousness which he intended, and will accept, and is a Righteousness not within the Rule and Rigour of Law, is now made manifest and confirmed by the Testimony of the Law and the Prophets, which bear witness to this Truth, that Jesus is the Messias, and that it is accord-

22. ing to his Purpose and Promise, That the Righteousness of God by Faith in Jesus the Messias, is extended to and bestowed on all who believe in him ⁿ (for there is no Diffe-

23. rence between them. They have all, both Jews and Gentiles, sinned, and fail of attaining that Glory ᵒ which God hath appointed

24. for the Righteous) being made righteous *gratis* by the Favour of God through the Re-

TEXT.

may become guilty before God.

Therefore by the deeds 20 of the Law there shall no flesh be justified in his sight: for by the Law is the knowledge of sin.

But now the righteous- 21 ness of God without the law is manifested, being witnessed by the law and the prophets;

Even the righteousness 22 of God, which is by faith of Jesus Christ unto all, and upon all them that believe; for there is no difference:

For all have sinned, and 23 come short of the glory of God;

Being justified freely by 24 his grace, through the redemption that is in Jesus Christ;

NOTES.

ᵏ *No Man.* St. *Paul* uses here the Word *Flesh* for Man emphatically, as that wherein the Force of Sin is seated. Vid *chap.* vii. 14, 18. & viii. 14.

ˡ *The Law cannot help Men to Righteousness.* This, which is but implied here, is large and express in *chap.* vii. and is said expressly, *chap.* viii 3. *Gal.* iii. 21.

ᵐ *Chap.* vii. 13.

22 ⁿ Vid. *chap.* x. 12. *Gal.* iii. 22——28.

23 ᵒ Here the Glory that comes from God, or by his Appointment, is called the *Glory of God*, as the Righteousness which comes from him, or by his Appointment, is called *the Righteousness of God*, chap. i. 17. and the Rule of moral Rectitude, which has God for its Author, or is appointed by him, is called δικαίωμα Θεȣ, *chap.* i. 32. That this is the Glory here meant, vid. chap. ii. 7, 10. In the same Sense the *Glory of God* is used, chap. v. 2.

demption

ROMANS.

TEXT.

25 Whom God hath set forth to be a propitiation, through faith in his blood, to declare his righteousness for the remissi-

PARAPHRASE.

demption ᵖ which is by Jesus Christ; whom God hath set forth to be the Propitiatory or Mercy-seat ᵍ in his own Blood ʳ, for the Manifestation of his [God's] Righteousness ˢ, 25.

NOTES.

24 ᵖ *Redemption* signifies Deliverance, but not Deliverance from every thing, but Deliverance from that, to which a Man is in Subjection or Bondage. Nor does Redemption by Jesus Christ import there was any Compensation made to God by paying what was of equal Value, in consideration whereof they were delivered; for that is inconsistent with what St. *Paul* expresly says here, *viz.* that Sinners are justified by God *gratis*, and of his free Bounty. What this *Redemption* is, St. *Paul* tells us, *Eph.* i. 7. *Col.* i. 14. even the Forgiveness of Sins. But if St. *Paul* had not been so express in defining what he means by *Redemption*, they yet would be thought to lay too much Stress upon the Criticism of a Word in the Translation, who would thereby force from the Word in the Original a necessary Sense, which it is plain it hath not. That Redeeming in the sacred Scripture Language signifies not precisely paying an Equivalent, is so clear, that nothing can be more. I shall refer my Reader to three or four Places amongst a great Number; *Exod.* vi. 6. *Deut.* vii. 8. & xv. 15. & xxiv. 18. But if any one will, from the literal Signification of the Word in *English*, persist in it against St. *Paul*'s Declarations, that it necessarily implies an equivalent Price paid, I desire him to consider to whom: And that if we will strictly adhere to the Metaphor, it must be to those whom the Redeemed are in Bondage to, and from whom we are redeemed, *viz.* Sin and Satan. If he will not believe his own System for this, let him believe St. *Paul*'s Words, *Tit.* ii. 14. *Who gave himself for us, that he might redeem us from all Iniquity*. Nor could the Price be paid to God in Strictness of Justice, (for that is made the Argument here) unless the same Person ought, by that strict Justice, to have both the Thing redeemed, and the Price paid for its Redemption. For 'tis to God we are redeemed by the Death of Christ, *Rev.* v. 9. *Thou wast slain, and hast redeemed us to God by thy Blood*.

25 ᵍ Ἱλαστήριον signifies *Propitiatory*, or *Mercy Seat*, and not *Propitiation*, as Mr. *Mede* has rightly observed upon this Place in his Discourse of God's House, §. 1.

ʳ The *Alexandrine* Copy omits the Words διὰ πίστεως, by Faith; which seems conformable to the Sense of the Apostle here: He says, that *God hath set forth Christ to be the Propitiatory in his Blood*. The Atonement under the Law was made by Blood sprinkled on the Propitiatory or Mercy-Seat, *Lev.* xvi. 14. Christ, says St. *Paul* here, is now set out and shewn by God to be the real Propitiatory or Mercy-Seat in his own Blood; see *Heb.* ix. 25, 26. where the Sacrifice of himself is opposed to the Blood of others. God has set him out to be so, to declare his Righteousness; the Mercy-Seat being the Place wherein God spake and declared his Pleasure, *Exod.* xxv. 22. *Numb.* xvii. 8, 9. And it was there where God always appeared, *Lev.* xvi. 2. It was the Place of his Presence, and therefore he is said to dwell between the Cherubims, *Psal.* lxxx. 1. 2 *Kings* xix. 15. For between the Cherubim was the Mercy-Seat. In all which Respects, our Saviour, who was the Antitype, is properly called the *Propitiatory*.

ˢ Δικαιοσύνη, *Righteousness*, seems to be used here in the same Sense it is *ver.* 5. for the Righteousness of God, in keeping his Word with the Nation of the *Jews*, notwithstanding their Provocations: And indeed, with the following Words of this Verse, contains in it a farther Answer to the Jews Insinuation of God's being hard to their Nation, by shewing that God had been very favourable to them, in not casting them off as they had deserved, till, according to his Promise, he had sent them the Messias, and they had rejected him.

by

PARAPHRASE.

by passing over ᵗ their Transgressions formerly committed, which he hath borne with hitherto, so as to with-hold his Hand from casting off the Nation of the Jews as their past 26. Sins deserved, for the manifesting of his Righteousness ᵘ at this time ˣ, that he might be just in keeping his Promise, and be the Justifier of every one, not who is of the Jewish Nation or Extraction, but of the Faith ʸ in Jesus Christ.

TEXT.

on of sins that are past, through the forbearance of God;

To declare, I say, at 26 this time his righteousness: that he might be just, and the justifier of him which believeth in Jesus.

NOTES.

ᵗ Διὰ τὴν πάρεσιν, *by passing over*. I do not remember any Place where πάρεσις signifies Remission or Forgiveness, but passing by, or *passing over*, as our Translation has it in the Margin, *i. e.* over-looking, or as it were, not minding; in which Sense it cannot be applied to the past Sins of private Persons, for God neither remits nor passes them by so as not to take notice of them. But this πάρεσις τῶν προγεγονότων ἁμαρτημάτων, *passing over past Sins*, is spoken nationally, in respect of the People of the Jews; who though they were a very sinful Nation, as appears by the Places here brought against them by St. *Paul*, yet God passed by all that, and would not be hindered by their past Sinfulness, from being just in keeping his Promise, in exhibiting to them Christ the Propitiatory. But though he would not be provoked by their past Sins, so as to cast them off from being his People before he had sent them the promised Messias to be their Saviour; yet after that, when at the due time he had manifested his Righteousness to them, that he might be just, and the Justifier of those who believe in Jesus, he no longer bore with their sinful Obstinacy; but when they rejected the Saviour (whom he had sent according to his Promise) from being their King, God rejected them from being his People, and took the Gentiles into his Church, and made them his People jointly and equally with the few believing Jews. This is plainly the Sense of the Apostle here, where he is discoursing of the Nation of the Jews, and their State in comparison with the Gentiles; not of the State of private Persons. Let any one without Prepossession attentively read the Context, and he will find it to be so.

26 ᵘ Δικαιοσύνης αὐτῶ, *his Righteousness*, is here to be understood in both Senses in which St. *Paul* had used it before in this Chapter, *viz. ver.* 5. & 22. as it is manifest by St. *Paul's* explaining of it himself in these Words immediately following: That he might be just, and the Justifier of him who believeth in Jesus, which are the two Senses wherein *the Righteousness of God* is used.

ˣ *At this time, viz.* The Fulness of Time, according to his Promise.

ʸ Τὸν ἐκ πίστεως Ἰησοῦ: If this Phrase had been translated, *him that is of the Faith of Jesus*, as it is, *chap.* iv. 6. & Gal. iii. 7. rather than *him which believeth in Jesus*, it would better have expressed the Apostle's Meaning here, which was to distinguish οἱ ἐκ πίστεως, *those who are of Faith*, from οἱ ἐκ περιτομῆς, or οἱ ἐκ νόμου, *those who are of the Circumcision*, or *those who are of the Law*, speaking of them as of two Sorts or Races of Men, of two different Extractions. To understand this Place fully, let any one read *chap.* iv. 12——16. Gal. iii. 7——10. where he will find the Apostle's Sense more at large.

What

TEXT.

27 Where is boasting then? It is excluded. By what law? Of works? Nay: but by the law of faith.
28 Therefore we conclude, that a man is justified by faith without the deeds of the law.
29 Is he the God of the Jews only? Is he not also of the Gentiles? Yes, of the Gentiles also:
30 Seeing it is one God which shall justify the circumcision by faith, and uncircumcision through faith.

PARAPHRASE.

27. What Reason then have you Jews to glory ª and set yourselves so much above the Gentiles in judging them as you do? None at all: Boasting is totally excluded. By what Law? By the Law of Works? No, but by the Law of Faith. I conclude therefore ᵇ, that a 28. Man is justified by Faith, and not by the Works of the Law ᶜ. Is God the God of the 29. Jews only, and not of the Gentiles also? Yea 30. certainly of the Gentiles also. Since the Time is come that God is no longer one to the Jews, and another to the Gentiles, but he is now become one and the same ᵈ God to them all, and will justify the Jews by Faith, and the Gentiles also through Faith, who by the Law of *Moses* were heretofore shut out ᵉ from be-

NOTES.

27 ª The *Glorying* here spoken of, is that of the Jews, *i. e.* their judging of the Gentiles, and their Contempt of them, which St. *Paul* had before in several Places taken notice of. And here, to take down their Pride and Vanity, he tells them, it is wholly excluded by the Gospel, wherein God, who is the God of the Gentiles as well as of the Jews, justifieth by Faith alone the Jews as well as the Gentiles, since no Man could be justified by the Deeds of the Law. This seems to be said to the converted Jews, to stop their thinking that they had any Advantage over the Gentiles under the Gospel. No, says he, the Gospel, which is the Law of Faith, lays you equal with the Gentiles; and you have no Ground to assume any thing to yourselves, or set yourselves above them now under the Messias. This, and all the rest to this purpose in this Epistle, is said to establish the converted *Romans* in their Title to the Favour of God, equally with the Jews in the Gospel, and fortifying them against any Disturbance that might be given them by the pretending Jews; which is the principal Design of this Epistle, as we have already observed.

28 ᵇ *Therefore*, this Inference is drawn from what he had taught, *ver.* 23.

ᶜ Vid *Acts* xiii. 29. *chap.* viii. 3. *Gal.* ii. 16.

30 ᵈ Ἐπείπερ εἷς ὁ Θεὸς, *since God is one.* He that will see the Force of St. *Paul*'s Reasoning here, must look to *Zachary* xiv. 9. from whence these Words are taken; where the Prophet speaking of the Time when *the Lord shall be King over all the Earth*, and not barely over the little People shut up in the Land of *Canaan*, he says, In that Day there shall be one Lord, i. e. God shall not be as he is now, the God of the Jews alone, whom only he hath known of all the People of the Earth; but he shall be the God of the Gentiles also, the same merciful, reconciled God to the People of all Nations. This Prophecy the Jews understood of the Times of the Messias, and St. *Paul* here presses them with it.

ᵉ It was impossible for remote Nations to keep the Law of *Moses*, a great Part of the Worship required by it being local, and confined to the Temple at *Jerusalem*.

ROMANS.

PARAPHRASE.

31. ing the People of God. Do we then make the Law ᶠ infignificant or ufelefs by our Doctrine of Faith? By no means: But on the contrary we eftablifh ᵍ and confirm the Law.

TEXT.

Do we then make void 31 the Law through Faith? God forbid: yea we eftablifh the Law.

NOTES.

31 ᶠ Νόμον, *Law*, is here repeated twice without the Article, and it is plain that by it St. *Paul* does not mean precifely the Mofaical Law, but fo much of it as is contained in the natural and eternal Rule of Right mentioned, *ch.* i. 32. and xi. 26. and is again by a pofitive Command re-enacted and continued as a Law under the Meffias. *Vid.* Matt. xxviii. 20.

ᵍ *Eftablifh*. The Doctrine of Juftification by Faith neceffarily fuppofeth a Rule of Righteoufnefs, which thofe who are juftified by Faith come fhort of; and alfo a Punifhment incurred, from which they are fet free by being juftified, and fo this Doctrine eftablifhes a Law, and accordingly the moral Part of the Law of *Mofes*, that δικαίωμα τῦ Θεῦ, as the Apoftle calls it in the Place above quoted, *ch.* i. 32. is enforced again by our Saviour and the Apoftles in the Gofpel, with Penalties annexed to the Breach of it.

SECT. IV.

CHAP. IV. 1——25.

CONTENTS.

ST. *Paul* having in the foregoing Section cut off all glorying from the Jews upon the account of their having the Law, and fhewn that that gave them no manner of Title or Pretence to be the People of God, more than the Gentiles, under the Meffias; and fo they had no Reafon to *judge* or exclude the Gentiles as they did; he comes here to prove that their lineal Extraction from their Father *Abraham*, gave them no better a Pretence of glorying, or of fetting themfelves upon that account above the Gentiles now in the time of the Gofpel.

1. Becaufe *Abraham* himfelf was juftified by Faith, and fo had not whereof to glory, for as much as he that receiveth Righteoufnefs as a Boon, has no Reafon to glory: But he that attains it by Works.

2. Becaufe

2. Because neither they who had Circumcision derived down to them, as the Posterity of *Abraham*, nor they who had the Law; but they only who had Faith were the Seed of *Abraham*, to whom the Promise was made. And therefore the Blessing of Justification was intended for the Gentiles, and bestowed on them as well as on the Jews, and upon the same Ground.

TEXT.

1. WHAT shall we say then, that Abraham our Father, as pertaining to the Flesh, hath found?
2. For if Abraham were justified by works, he hath whereof to glory, but not before God.
3. For what saith the scripture? Abraham believed God, and it was counted unto him for righteousness.

PARAPHRASE.

1. WHAT then shall we say of *Abraham* our Father according to the Flesh ^{h}, what has he obtained? Has not he found matter of glorying?
2. Yes, if he were justified by Works, he had matter of glorying ^{i}, he might then have gloried over the rest of the Gentile World in having God for his God, and he and his Family being God's People; but he had no Subject of glorying before God, as it is evident
3. from Sacred Scripture, which telleth us that *Abraham* believed God, and it was counted to him for Righteousness. Now there had been no need of any such Counting, any such Allowance, if he had attained Righteousness by

NOTES.

1 ^{h} *Our Father according to the Flesh*. St. *Paul* speaks here as lineally descended from *Abraham*, and joins himself herein with the rest of his Nation, of whom he calls *Abraham* the Father *according to the Flesh*, to distinguish the Jews by Birth, from those who were *Abraham*'s Seed according to the Promise, *viz.* those who were of the Faith of *Abraham*, whether Jews or Gentiles, a Distinction which he insists on all through this Chapter.

2 ^{i} Καύχημα, translated here *glorying*, I take to signify the same with καυχᾶσαι, translated *boasting*, chap. ii. 17, 23. in which Places it is used to signify the Jews valuing themselves upon some national Privileges above the rest of the World, as if they had thereby some peculiar Right to the Favour of God above other Men. This Jewish Nation thinking themselves alone to have a Title to be the People of God, expressed in their judging the Gentiles whom they despised, and looked on as unworthy and uncapable to be received into the Kingdom of the Messias, and admitted into Fellowship with their Nation under the Gospel. This Conceit of theirs St. *Paul* opposes here, and makes it his Business to shew the Falshood and Groundlesness of it all through the eleven first Chapters of this Epistle. I ask, whether it would not help the English Reader the better to find and pursue the Sense of St. *Paul*, if the Greek Term were every where rendered by the same English Word? Whether *boasting* or *glorying*, I think of no great Consequence, so one of them be kept to.

PARAPHRASE.	TEXT.

Works of Obedience exactly conformable and coming up to the Rule of Righteousness.
4. For what Reward a Man has made himself a Title to by his Performances, that he receives as a Debt that is due, and not as a Gift of Favour.
5. But to him that by his Works attains not Righteousness, but only believeth on God who justifieth him, being ungodly [k], to him Justification is a Favour of Grace: Because his Believing is accounted to him for Righteousness, or perfect Obedience.
6. Even as *David* speaks of the Blessedness of the Man to whom God
7. reckoneth Righteousness without Works, saying, Blessed are they whose Iniquities are
8. forgiven, and whose Sins are covered. Blessed is the Man to whom the Lord will not
9. reckon [l] Sin. Is this Blessedness then upon the Circumcised only, or upon the Uncircumcised also? For we say that Faith was
10. reckoned to *Abraham* for Righteousness. When therefore was it reckoned to him? When he was in Circumcision or in Uncircumcision? Not in Circumcision, but in Uncircumcision.
11. For he received the Sign of Circumcision, a Seal of the Righteousness of the Faith, which he had being yet uncircumcised [m], that he might

4. Now to him that worketh, is the reward not reckoned of grace, but of debt.
5. But to him that worketh not, but believeth on him that justifieth the ungodly, his Faith is counted for righteousness.
6. Even as David also describeth the blessedness of the man unto whom God imputeth righteousness without works,
7. Saying, Blessed are they whose iniquities are forgiven, and whose sins are covered.
8. Blessed is the man to whom the Lord will not impute sin.
9. Cometh this blessedness then upon the circumcision only, or upon the uncircumcision also? For we say that faith was reckoned to Abraham for righteousness.
10. How was it then reckoned? when he was in circumcision, or in uncircumcision? not in circumcision, but in uncircumcision.
11. And he received the sign of circumcision, a

NOTES.

5 [k] Τὸν ἀσεβῆ, *him being ungodly*. By these Words St. *Paul* plainly points out *Abraham*, who was ἀσεβής, *ungodly*, *i. e.* a Gentile, not a Worshipper of the true God when God called him. *Vid.* Note, chap. i. 18.

8 [l] Λογίσηται, *reckoneth*. What this imputing or *reckoning* of Righteousness is, may be seen in *ver.* 8. *viz.* the not reckoning of Sin to any one, the not putting Sin to his Account: The Apostle in these two Verses using these two Expressions as equivalent. From hence the Expression of blotting out of Iniquity, so frequently used in Sacred Scripture, may be understood, *i. e.* the striking it out of the Account. Λογίζεσθαι signifies to reckon or account, and with a Dative Case, to put to any one's Account; and accordingly, *ver.* 3, 4, 5. it is translated *counted* or *reckoned*; which Word for the sake of English Readers I have kept to in this, and *ver.* 9, 10, & 11.

11 [m] See *Gen.* xvii. 11.

ROMANS.

Chap. IV.

TEXT.

seal of the Righteousness of the Faith, which he had yet being uncircumcised: that he might be the Father of all them that believe, though they be not circumcised; that righteousness might be imputed unto them also:

12 And the Father of circumcision to them who are not of the circumcision only, but also walk in

PARAPHRASE.

be the Father of all those who believe, being uncircumcised, that Righteousness might be reckoned to them also; and the Father of the 12. Circumcised, that Righteousness might be reckoned not to those who were barely of the Circumcision, but to such of the Circumcision as did also walk in the Steps of the Faith of our Father *Abraham*, which he had being uncircumcised ⁿ. For the Promise ᵒ that he 13.

NOTES.

11 & 12 ⁿ What Righteousness reckoned to any one, or as it is usually called imputed Righteousness, is, St. *Paul* explains, *ver.* 6 — 8. Whom this Blessing belongs to, he enquires, *ver.* 9. and here, *ver.* 11, and 12. he declares who are the Children of *Abraham*, that from him inherit this Blessing, *ver.* 11. he speaks of the Gentiles, and there shews that *Abraham*, who was justified by Faith before he was circumcised, (the Want whereof the Jews looked on as a distinguishing Mark of a Gentile) was the Father of all those among the Gentiles, who should believe without being circumcised. And here, *ver.* 12. he speaks of the Jews, and says, that *Abraham* was their Father: But not that all should be justified who were only circumcised; but those who to their Circumcision added the Faith of *Abraham*, which he had before he was circumcised. That which misled those who mistook the Sense of St. *Paul* here, seems to be their not observing, that τοῖς ἐκ περιτομῆς, is referred to, and governed by εἰς τὸ λογισθῆναι, which must be supposed repeated here after πατέρα περιτομῆς. Or else the Apostle's Sense and Argument will not stand in its full Force, but the Antithesis will be lost; by preserving of which the Sense runs thus; *And the Father of the Circumcised, that Righteousness might be imputed to those who*, &c. Another Thing very apt to mislead them, was the joining of μόνον *only*, to ἐκ *not*, as if it were οἱ μόνον τότε, *not only those who are of the Circumcision*; whereas it should be understood as it stands joined to περιτομῆς, and so περιτομῆς μόνον are best translated *barely Circumcision*, and the Apostle's Sense runs thus; *That he might be the Father of the Gentiles that believe, though they be not circumcised, that Righteousness might be imputed to them also*; *And the Father of the Jews, that Righteousness might be imputed not to them who have Circumcision only, but to them who also walk in the Steps of the Faith of our Father* Abraham, *which he had being uncircumcised*. In which Way of Understanding this Passage, not only the Apostle's Meaning is very plain, easy and coherent, but the Construction of the Greek exactly corresponds to that of *ver.* 11. and is genuine, easy, and natural, which any other Way will be very perplexed.

13 ᵒ *The Promise* here meant is that which he speaks of, *ver.* 11. whereby *Abraham* was made the Father of all that should believe all the World over, and for that Reason he is called κληρονόμος κόσμου, *Heir or Lord of the World*. For the Believers of all Nations of the World being given to him for a Posterity, he becomes thereby Lord and Possessor (for so *Heir* amongst the Hebrews signified) of the World. For 'tis plain the Apostle in this Verse pursues the Argument he was upon in the two former. And 'tis also plain that St. *Paul* makes Circumcision to be the Seal of the Promise made to *Abraham*, *Gen.* xii. as well as of that made to him, *Gen.* xvii. and so both these to be but one Covenant, and that of *ch.* xvii. to be but a Repetition and farther Explication of the former, as is evident from this Chapter, compared with *Gal.* iii. In both which the Apostle argues, that the Gentiles were intended to be justified as well as the Jews, and that both Jews and Gentiles, who are justified, are justified by Faith, and not by the Works of the Law.

should

PARAPHRASE.

should be Possessor of the World, was not that *Abraham*, and those of his Seed, who were under the Law, should by virtue of their having and owning the Law, be possessed of it; but by the Righteousness of Faith, whereby those who were without the Law, scattered all over the World, beyond the Borders of *Canaan*, became his Posterity, and had him for their Father ᵖ, and inherited the Blessing of
14. Justification by Faith. For if they only who had the Law of *Moses* given them, were Heirs of *Abraham*, Faith is made void and useless ᑫ, it receiving no Benefit of the Promise which was made to the Heirs of *Abraham's* Faith, and
15. so the Promise becomes of no effect. Because the Law procures them not Justification ʳ, but renders them liable to the Wrath and Punishment of God ˢ, who by the Law has made known to them what is Sin, and what Punishment he has annexed to it. For there is no incurring Wrath or Punishment where there is no Law that says any thing of it ᵗ.

TEXT.

the steps of that Faith of our Father Abraham, which he had being yet uncircumcised.

13 For the promise that he should be the heir of the world, was not to Abraham, or to his seed through the law, but through the Righteousness of Faith.

14 For if they which are of the law be heirs, faith is made void, and the promise made of none effect.

15 Because the law worketh wrath: for where no law is, there is no transgression.

NOTES.

ᵖ *Gal.* iii. 7.
14 ᑫ See *Gal.* iii. 18.
15 ʳ *Ch.* viii. 3. *Gal.* iii. 21.
ˢ See *ch.* iii. 19, 20. & v. 10, 13, 20. & vii. 7, 8, 10. 1 *Cor.* xv. 56. *Gal.* iii. 19. *John* ix. 41. & xv. 22.
ᵗ Οὐκ ἔστιν νόμος, οὐδὲ παράβασις, *of that, concerning which there is no Law with the Sanction of a Punishment annexed, there can be no Transgression incurring Wrath or Punishment.* Thus it may be rendered if we read οὗ with an Aspiration, as some do. But whether it be taken to signify *where* or *whereof*, the Sense will be the same. For παράβασις here, to make St. *Paul's* Argument of Force, must signify such a *Transgression* as draws on the Transgressor Wrath and Punishment by the Force and Sanction of a Law. And so the Apostle's Proposition is made good, that 'tis the Law alone that exposes us to Wrath, and that is all that the Law can do, for it gives us no Power to perform.

Therefore

ROMANS. Chap. IV

TEXT.

16 Therefore it is of Faith, that it might be by grace, to the end the promise might be sure to all the seed, not to that only which is of the law, but to that also which is of the faith of Abraham, who is the Father of us all,

17 (As it is written, I have made thee a father of many nations) before him whom he believed, even God who quickeneth the dead, and calleth those things which be not, as though they were:

18 Who against hope believed in hope, that he might become the father of many nations, according to that which was spoken, So shall thy seed be.

19 And being not weak in faith, he considered not his own body now dead, when he was about an hundred years old, neither yet the deadness of Sarah's womb.

20 He staggered not at the promise of God through unbelief; but was strong in faith, giving glory to God:

21 And being fully persuaded, that what he had

PARAPHRASE.

16. Therefore the Inheritance ᵘ is of Faith, that it might be merely of Favour, to the end that the Promise might be sure to all the Seed of *Abraham*; not to that Part of it only which has Faith, being under the Law; but to that Part also who without the Law inherit the Faith of *Abraham*, who is the Father of us all who believe, whether Jews or Gentiles, (as it is

17. written ˣ, I have made thee a Father of many Nations) I say the Father of us all (in the Account of God, whom he believed, and who accordingly quickened the Dead, *i. e. Abraham* and *Sarah*, whose Bodies were dead; and calleth Things that are not as if they were ʸ:)

18. Who without any Hope, which the natural Course of Things could afford, did in hope believe, that he should become the Father of many Nations, according to what God had spoken, by God's shewing him the Stars of Heaven, saying, *So shall thy Seed be*. And being

19. firm and unshaken in his Faith, he regarded not his own Body now dead, he being about an hundred Years old; nor the Deadness of *Sarah*'s Womb; he staggered not at the Pro-

20. mise of God through Unbelief, but was strong in Faith, thereby giving Glory to God;

21. by the full Persuasion he had that God was able to perform what he had promised:

NOTES.

16 ᵘ The Grammatical Construction does not seem much to favour *Inheritance*, as the Word to be supplied here, because it does not occur in the preceding Verses. But he that observes St. *Paul*'s Way of Writing, who more regards Things than Forms of Speaking, will be satisfied, that it is enough that he mentioned Heirs, *ver.* 13, & 14. and that he does mean *Inheritance* here, *Gal.* iii. 18. puts it past doubt.

17 ˣ See *Gen.* xvii. 16.
ʸ *Gen.* xvii. 5, 6.

PARAPHRASE.

22, 23, 24. And therefore it was accounted to him for Righteousness. Now this of its being reckoned to him, was not written for his sake alone, but for ours also, to whom Faith also shall be reckoned for Righteousness, *viz.* to as many as believe in him who raised Jesus our Lord from the
25. dead ʳ, who was delivered to Death for our Offences ᵃ, and was raised again for our ᵇ Justification.

TEXT.

promised, he was able also to perform.

22 And therefore it was imputed to him for righteousness.

23 Now it was not written for his sake alone, that it was imputed to him;

24 But for us also, to whom it shall be imputed, if we believe on him that raised up Jesus our Lord from the dead,

25 Who was delivered for our offences, and was raised again for our Justification.

NOTES.

24 ᶻ St. *Paul* seems to mention this here in particular, to shew the Analogy between *Abraham*'s Faith, and that of Believers under the Gospel; see ver. 17.

25 ᵃ See *Rom.* iii. 25. & v. 6, 10. *Eph.* i. 7, 11, 14. & v. 2. *Col.* i. 14, 20—— 22. 1 *Tim.* ii. 6. *Tit.* ii. 14.

ᵇ 1 *Cor.* xv. 17. I have set down all these Texts out of St. *Paul*, that in them might be seen his own Explication of what he says here, *viz.* That our Saviour by his Death atoned for our Sins, and so we were innocent, and thereby freed from the Punishment due to Sin. But he rose again to ascertain to us eternal Life, the Consequence of Justification: For the Reward of Righteousness is eternal Life, which Inheritance we have a Title to by Adoption in Jesus Christ. But if he himself had not that Inheritance, if he had not rose into the Possession of eternal Life, we who hold by and under him, could not have risen from the dead, and so could never have come to be pronounced righteous, and to have received the Reward of it, everlasting Life. Hence St. *Paul* tells us, 1 *Cor.* xv. 17. that *if Christ be not raised, our Faith is vain, we are yet in our Sins*, *i. e.* as to the Attainment of eternal Life 'tis all one as if our Sins were not forgiven. And thus he rose for our Justification, *i. e.* to assure to us eternal Life, the Consequence of Justification. And this I think is confirmed by our Saviour in these Words, *Because I live ye shall live also*, John xiv. 19.

SECT.

ROMANS.

SECT. V.

CHAP. V. 1——11.

CONTENTS.

ST. *Paul* in the foregoing Chapters has examined the glorying of the Jews, and their valuing themselves so highly above the Gentiles, and shewn the Vanity of their boasting in Circumcision and the Law, since neither they nor their Father *Abraham* were justified, or found Acceptance with God by Circumcision, or the Deeds of the Law: And therefore they had no Reason so, as they did, to press Circumcision and the Law on the Gentiles, or exclude those who had them not, from being the People of God, and unfit for their Communion in and under the Gospel. In this Section he comes to shew what the Convert Gentiles, by Faith without Circumcision or the Law, had to glory in, *viz.* The Hope of Glory, *ver.* 2. Their Sufferings for the Gospel, *ver.* 3. And God as their God, *ver.* 11. In these three it is easy to observe the Thread and Coherence of St. *Paul*'s Discourse here, the intermediate Verses (according to that abounding with Matter, and overflowing of Thought he was filled with) being taken up with an incidental Train of Considerations, to shew the Reason they had to glory in Tribulations.

TEXT.

1 Therefore being justified by Faith, we have peace with God, through our Lord Jesus Christ.
2 By whom also we have access by faith into this

PARAPHRASE.

1. THerefore being justified by Faith, we ᶜ have Peace with God through our Lord Jesus Christ, by whom we have had admit-
2. tance through Faith into the Favour in which

NOTES.

ᶜ *We, i. e.* we Gentiles that are not under the Law. 'Tis in their Names that St. *Paul* speaks in the three last Verses of the foregoing Chapter, and all through this Section, as is evident from the Illation here, *Therefore being justified by Faith, we.* It being an Inference drawn from his having proved in the former Chapter, that the Promise was not to the Jews alone, but to the Gentiles also: And that Justification was not by the Law, but by Faith, and consequently designed for the Gentiles as well as the Jews.

ROMANS.

PARAPHRASE.

3. we have stood, and glory ᵈ in the Hope of the Glory which God has in store for us. And not only so, but we glory in Tribulation also, knowing that Tribulation worketh Patience;
4. And Patience giveth us a Proof of ourselves,
5. which furnishes us with Hope; And our Hope maketh not ashamed, will not deceive us, because ᵉ the Sense of the Love of God is poured out into our Hearts by the Holy Ghost,
6. which is given unto us *. For when we Gentiles were yet without Strength †, void of all Help or Ability to deliver ourselves, Christ in the Time that God had appointed and foretold, died for us, who lived without the Acknowledgment and Worship of the true God †.
7. Scarce is it to be found, that any one will die for a just Man, if peradventure one should
8. dare to die for a good Man; but God recommends, and herein shews the Greatness of his Love ᶠ towards us, in that whilst we Gentiles were a Mass of profligate Sinners ᵍ, Christ died

TEXT.

grace wherein we stand, and rejoice in hope of the glory of God.

5 And not only so, but we glory in tribulations also, knowing that tribulation worketh patience;

4 And patience, experience; and experience, hope;

5 And hope maketh not ashamed, because the love of God is shed abroad in our hearts, by the holy Ghost which is given unto us.

6 For when we were yet without strength, in due time, Christ died for the ungodly.

7 For scarcely for a righteous man will one die: yet peradventure for a good man some would even dare to die.

8 But God commendeth his love towards us, in that while we were yet sinners, Christ died for us.

NOTES.

2 ᵈ Καυχώμεθα, *we glory*. The same Word here for the Convert Gentiles that he had used before for the Boasting of the Jews, and the same Word he used where he examined what *Abraham* had found. The taking notice whereof, as we have already observed, may help to lead us into the Apostle's Sense: And plainly shews us here, that St. *Paul* in this Section opposes the Advantages the Gentile Converts to Christianity have by Faith, to those the Jews gloried in with so much Haughtiness and Contempt of the Gentiles.

5 ᵉ *Because*. * The Force of his Inference seems to stand thus. The Hope of eternal Happiness, which we glory in, cannot deceive us, because the Gifts of the Holy Ghost bestowed upon us, assure us of the Love of God towards us, the Jews themselves acknowledging that the Holy Ghost is given to none but those who are God's own People.

8 ᶠ Another Evidence St. *Paul* gives them here of the Love of God towards them, and the Ground they had to glory in the Hopes of eternal Salvation, is the Death of Christ for them, whilst they were yet in their Gentile Estate, which he describes by calling them,

6, 8 ᵍ † Ἀσθενεῖς, *without Strength*; Ἀσεβεῖς, *ungodly*; Ἁμαρτωλοί, *Sinners*; Ἐχθροί, *Enemies*: These four Epithets are given to them as Gentiles, they being used by St. *Paul*, as the proper Attributes of the Heathen World, as considered in Contradistinction to the Jewish Nation. What St. *Paul* says of the Gentiles in other Places will clear this. The helpless Condition of the Gentile World in the State of Gentilism, signified here by Ἀσθενεῖς, *without Strength*, he terms,

Col.

ROMANS.

NOTES.

Col. ii. 13. *dead in Sin*, a State, if any, of Weakness. And hence he says to the Romans converted to Jesus Christ; *Yield yourselves unto God, as those that are alive from the Dead, and yourselves as Instruments of Righteousness unto God*, *ch.* vi. 13. How he describes ἀσεβεῖς, *Ungodliness*, mentioned *ch.* i. 18. as the proper State of the Gentiles, we may see *ver.* 21, 23. That he thought the Title ἁμαρτωλοί, *Sinners*, belonged peculiarly to the Gentiles, in Contradistinction to the Jews, he puts it past doubt in these Words, *We who are Jews by Nature, and not Sinners of the Gentiles*, Gal. ii. 15. See also ch. vi. 17 — 22. And as for ἐχθροί, *Enemies*, you have the Gentiles before their Conversion to Christianity so called, *Col.* i. 21. St. *Paul*, Eph. ii. 1 — 13. describes the Heathens a little more at large; but yet the Parts of the Character he there gives them, we may find comprised in these four Epithets; the ἀσθενεῖς, *weak*, ver. 1, 5. the ἀσεβεῖς, *ungodly*, and ἁμαρτωλοί, *Sinners*, ver. 2, 3. and the ἐχθροί, *Enemies*, ver. 11, 12.

If it were remembered that St. *Paul* all along, through the eleven first Chapters of this Epistle, speaks nationally of the Jews and Gentiles, as 'tis visible he does, and personally of single Men, there would be less Difficulty and fewer Mistakes in understanding this Epistle. This one Place we are upon is a sufficient Instance of it. For if by these Terms here, we shall understand him to denote all Men personally, Jews as well as Gentiles, before they are savingly ingrafted into Jesus Christ, we shall make his Discourse here disjointed, and his Sense mightily perplexed, if at all consistent.

That there were some among the Heathen as innocent in their Lives, and as far from Enmity to God, as some among the Jews, cannot be questioned. Nay, that many of them were not ἀσεβεῖς, but σεβόμενοι, Worshippers of the true God, if we could doubt of it, is manifest out of the *Acts of the Apostles*; but yet St. *Paul*, in the Places above quoted, pronounces them all together, ἀσεβεῖς, and ἐθνοί, (for that by these two Terms applied to the same Persons, he means the same, *i. e.* such as did not acknowledge and worship the true God, seems plain) *ungodly*, and *Sinners of the Gentiles*, as nationally belonging to them, in Contradistinction to the People of the Jews, who were the People of God, whilst the other were the Provinces of the Kingdom of Satan: Not but that there were Sinners, hainous Sinners, among the Jews; but the Nation, considered as one Body and Society of Men, disowned and declared against, and opposed itself to those Crimes and Impurities which are mentioned by St. *Paul*, chap. i. 24, &c. as woven into the religious and politick Constitutions of the Gentiles. There they had their full Scope and Swing, had Allowance, Countenance and Protection. The idolatrous Nations had, by their Religions, Laws and Forms of Government, made themselves the open Votaries, and were the professed Subjects of Devils. So St. *Paul*, 1 Cor. x. 20, 21. truly calls the Gods they worshipped and paid their Homage to. And suitably hereunto, their religious Observances, 'tis well known, were not without great Impurities, which were of right charged upon them, when they had a Place in their sacred Offices, and had the Recommendation of Religion to give them Credit. The rest of the Vices in St. *Paul*'s black List, which were not warmed at their Altars, and fostered in their Temples, were yet by the Connivance of the Law cherished in their private Houses, and made a Part of the uncondemned Actions of common Life, and had the Countenance of Custom to authorize them, even in the best regulated and most civilized Governments of the Heathen. On the contrary, the Frame of the Jewish Commonwealth was founded on the Acknowledgment and Worship of the one only true and invisible God, and their Laws required an extraordinary Purity of Life, and Strictness of Manners.

That the Gentiles were stiled ἐχθροί, *Enemies*, in a political or national Sense, is plain from *Eph.* ii. where they are called, *Aliens from the Commonwealth of Israel, and Strangers from the Covenant*. *Abraham*, on the other side, was called *the Friend of God, i. e.* one in Covenant with him, and his professed Subject, that owned God to the World: And so were his Posterity the People of the Jews, whilst the rest of the World were under Revolt, and lived in open Rebellion against him, *vid.* Isa. xli. 8. And here in this Epistle St. *Paul* expresly teaches, that when the Nation of the Jews, by rejecting of the Messias, put themselves out of the Kingdom of God, and were cast off from being any longer the People of God, they became *Enemies*, and the Gentile World were reconciled. See *Chap.* xi. 15, 28. Hence St. *Paul*, who was the Apostle of the Gentiles, calls his performing that Office, *the Ministry of Reconciliation*, 2 Cor. v. 18.

I i 2   And

ROMANS.

NOTES.

And here in this Chapter, ver. 1. the Privilege which they receive by the accepting of the Covenant of Grace in Jesus Christ, he tells them is this, that *they have Peace with God*, i. e. are no longer incorporated with his Enemies, and of the Party of the open Rebels against him in the Kingdom of Satan, being returned to their natural Allegiance in their owning the one true supreme God, in submitting to the Kingdom he had set up in his Son, and being received by him as his Subjects. Suitably hereunto St. *James*, speaking of the Conversion of the Gentiles to the Profession of the Gospel, says of it, that *God did visit the Gentiles, to take out of them a People for his Name*, Acts xv. 14. & ver. 19. he calls the Converts, *those who from among the Gentiles are turned to God.*

Besides what is to be found in other Parts of St. *Paul*'s Epistles to justify the taking of these Words here, as applied nationally to the Gentiles, in Contradistinction to the Children of *Israel*, that which St. *Paul* says, ver. 10, 11. makes it necessary to understand them so. *We*, says he, *when we were Enemies were reconciled to God*, and so *we now glory in him*, as our God. *We* here must unavoidably be spoken in the Name of the Gentiles, as is plain not only by the whole Tenor of this Section, but from this Passage of *glorying in God*, which he mentions as a Privilege now of the believing Gentiles, surpassing that of the Jews, whom he had taken notice of before, *chap.* ii. 17. as being forward to glory in God as their peculiar Right, though with no great Advantage to themselves. But the Gentiles who were reconciled now to God by Christ's Death, and taken into Covenant with God, as many as received the Gospel, had a new and better Title to this Glorying than the Jews. Those that now are reconciled, and glory in God as their God, he says, were Enemies. The Jews who had the same corrupt Nature common to them with the rest of Mankind, are no where that I know called ἐχθροί, *Enemies*, or ἀσεβεῖς, *ungodly*, whilst they publickly owned him for their God, and professed to be his People. But the Heathen were deemed Enemies, for being Aliens to the Commonwealth of *Israel*, and Strangers from the Covenants of Promise. There were never but two Kingdoms in the World, that of God, and that of the Devil: These were opposite, and therefore the Subjects of the latter could not but be in the State of *Enemies*, and fall under that Denomination. The Revolt from God was universal, and the Nations of the Earth had given themselves up to Idolatry, when God called *Abraham*, and took him into Covenant with himself, as he did afterwards the whole Nation of the Israelites, whereby they were re-admitted into his Kingdom, came under his Protection, and were his People and Subjects, and no longer Enemies, whilst all the rest of the Nations remained in the State of Rebellion, the professed Subjects of other Gods, who were Usurpers upon God's Right, and Enemies of this Kingdom. And indeed if the four Epithets be not taken to be spoken here of the Gentile World in this political and truly evangelical Sense, but in the ordinary systematical Notion applied to all Mankind, as belonging universally to every Man personally, whether by Profession Gentile, Jew or Christian, before he be actually regenerated by a saving Faith, and an effectual thorough Conversion, the illative Particle *Wherefore*, in the Beginning of *ver.* 12. will hardly connect it and what follows to the foregoing Part of this Chapter. But the eleven first Verses must be taken for a Parenthesis, and then the *Therefore* in the Beginning of this fifth Chapter, which joins it to the fourth with a very clear Connexion, will be wholly insignificant; and after all, the Sense of the 12th Verse will but ill sodder with the End of the fourth Chapter, notwithstanding the *Wherefore* which is taken to bring them in as an Inference. Whereas these eleven first Verses being supposed to be spoken of the Gentiles, makes them not only of a Piece with St. *Paul*'s Design in the foregoing and following Chapters, but the Thread of the whole Discourse goes very smooth, and the Inferences (ushered in with *Therefore* in the 1st Verse, and with *Wherefore* in the 12th Verse) are very easy, clear and natural from the immediately preceding Verses. That of the 1st Verse may be seen in what we have already said, and that of the 12th Verse in short stands thus: *We Gentiles have by Christ received the Reconciliation, which we cannot doubt to be intended for us as well as for the Jews, since Sin and Death entered into the World by Adam, the common Father of us all. And as by the Disobedience of that one, Condemnation of Death came on all; so by the Obedience of one, Justification to Life came upon all.*

died

ROMANS.

TEXT.

9. Much more then, being now justified by his blood, we shall be saved from wrath through him.
10. For if, when we were enemies, we were reconciled to God, by the death of his Son: much more, being reconciled, we shall be saved by his life.
11. And not only so, but we also joy in God, through our Lord Jesus Christ, by whom we have now received the atonement.

PARAPHRASE.

died for us. Much more therefore, now being justified by his Death, shall we through him be delivered from Condemnation ʰ at the Day of Judgment. For if, when we were Enemies †, we were reconciled to God, by the Death of his Son, much more being reconciled, shall we be saved by his Life. And not only ⁱ do we glory in Tribulation, but also in God, through our Lord Jesus Christ, by whom now ᵏ we have received Reconciliation.

9.
10.
11.

NOTES.

9 ʰ What St. *Paul* here calls *Wrath*, he calls the *Wrath to come*, 1 Thess. i. 10. and generally in the New Testament *Wrath* is put for the Punishment of the Wicked at the last Day.

11 ⁱ Οὐ μόνον δὲ, *And not only so*; I think no body can with the least Attention read this Section, without perceiving that these Words join this Verse to the 3d. The Apostle in the 2d Verse says, *We the Gentiles who believe, glory in the Hopes of an eternal splendid State of Bliss*. In the 3d Verse he adds ἢ μόνον δὲ, *And not only so*, but our Afflictions are to us matter of glorying; which he proves in the seven following Verses; and then ver. 11. adds οὐ μόνον δὲ, *And not only so*; but we glory in God also as our God, being reconciled to him in Jesus Christ. And thus he shews that the Convert Gentiles had whereof to glory, as well as the Jews; and were not inferior to them, though they had not Circumcision and the Law, wherein Jews gloried so much, but with no Ground in comparison of what the Gentiles had to glory in, by Faith in Jesus Christ, now under the Gospel.

ᵏ It is true, the Gentiles could not formerly glory in God as our God; that was the Privilege of the Jews, who alone of all the Nations owned him for their King and God, and were his People, in Covenant with him. All the rest of the Kingdoms of the Earth had taken other Lords, and given themselves up to false Gods, to serve and worship them; and so were in a State of War with the true God, the God of *Israel*. But now we, being reconciled by Jesus Christ, whom we have received, and own for our Lord, and thereby being returned into his Kingdom, and to our ancient Allegiance, we can truly glory in God as our God, which the Jews cannot do, who have refused to receive Jesus for their Lord, whom God hath appointed Lord over all things.

SECT.

ROMANS.

SECT. VI.

CHAP. V. 12——VII. 25.

CONTENTS.

THE Apostle here goes on with his Design of shewing that the Gentiles under the Gospel have as good a Title to the Favour of God as the Jews, there being no other way for either Jew or Gentile to find Acceptance with God [but] by Faith in Jesus Christ. In the foregoing Section he reckoned up several Subjects of glorying, which the Convert Gentiles had, without the Law, and concludes them with this chief and principal Matter of glorying, even God himself, whom, now that they were by Jesus Christ their Lord reconciled to him, they could glory in as their God.

To give them a more full and satisfactory Comprehension of this, he leads them back to the Times before the giving of the Law, and the very Being of the Jewish Nation; and lays before them in short the whole Scene of God's Oeconomy, and his Dealing with Mankind from the Beginning, in reference to Life and Death.

1. He teaches them, that by *Adam's* Lapse all Men were brought into a State of Death, and by Christ's Death all are restored to Life.

2. That the Law, when it came, laid the *Israelites* faster under Death, by enlarging the Offence which had Death annexed to it. For by the Law every Transgression, that any one under the Law committed, had Death for its Punishment, notwithstanding which, by Christ, those under the Law, who believe, receive Life.

3. That though the Gentiles who believe come not under the Rigour of the Law, yet the Covenant of Grace, which they are under, requires that they should not be Servants and Vassals to Sin, to obey it in the Lusts of it, but sincerely endeavour after Righteousness, the End whereof would be everlasting Life.

4. That the Jews also who receive the Gospel, are delivered from the Law; not that the Law is Sin; but because, though the Law forbid the obeying of Sin, as well as the Gospel; yet not ena-

bling

bling them to refift their finful Lufts, but making each Compliance with any finful Luft deadly, it fettles upon them the Dominion of Sin by Death, from which they are delivered by the Grace of God alone, which frees them from the Condemnation of the Law for every actual Tranfgreffion, and requires no more, but that they fhould, with the whole Bent of their Mind, ferve the Law of God, and not their carnal Lufts. In all which Cafes the Salvation of the Gentiles is wholly by Grace, without their being at all under the Law. And the Salvation of the Jews is wholly by Grace alfo, without any Aid or Help from the Law: From which alfo by Chrift they are delivered.

Thus lies the Thread of St. *Paul*'s Argument; wherein we may fee how he purfues his Defign of fatisfying the Gentile Converts at *Rome*, that they were not required to fubmit to the Law of *Mofes*; and of fortifying them againft the Jews, who troubled them about it.

For the more diftinct and eafy Apprehenfion of St. *Paul*'s difcourfing on thefe four Heads, I fhall divide this Section into the four following Numbers, taking them up as they lie in the Order of the Text.

SECT. VI. N. I.

CHAP. V. 12——19.

CONTENTS.

HERE he inftructs them in the State of Mankind in general before the Law, and before the Separation that was made thereby of the *Ifraelites* from all the other Nations of the Earth. And here he fhews, that *Adam*, tranfgreffing the Law, which forbad him the eating of the Tree of Knowledge upon pain of Death, forfeited Immortality, and becoming thereby mortal, all his Pofterity defcending from the Loins of a mortal Man, were mortal too, and all died, though none of them broke that Law but *Adam* himfelf: But by Chrift they are all reftored to Life again. And God juftifying thofe who believe in Chrift, they are reftored to their Primitive State of Righteoufnefs and Immortality; fo that the
Gentiles,

Chap. V. Gentiles, being the Descendants of *Adam*, as well as the Jews, stand as fair for all the Advantages that accrue to the Posterity of *Adam* by Christ as the Jews themselves, it being all wholly and solely from Grace.

PARAPHRASE.

12. WHEREFORE, to give you a State of the whole Matter, from the Beginning, you must know, that as by the Act of one Man, *Adam*, the Father of us all, Sin entered into the World, and Death, which was the Punishment annexed to the Offence of eating the forbidden Fruit, entered by that Sin, for that all *Adam*'s Posterity thereby became mortal¹. It is

13. true indeed, Sin was universally committed in the World by all Men, all the Time before the positive Law of God delivered by *Moses*: But

TEXT.

12 Wherefore, as by one man sin entered into the world, and death by sin; and so death passed upon all men, for that all have sinned.

13 For until the law sin was in the world, but sin

NOTES.

12 ¹ *Have sinned*, I have rendered *became mortal*, following the Rule I think very necessary for the understanding St. *Paul*'s Epistles (*viz.*) the making him, as much as is possible, his own Interpreter, 1 *Cor.* xv. 22. cannot be denied to be parallel to this Place. This and the following Verses here being, as one may say, a Comment on that Verse in the *Corinthians*, St. *Paul* treating here of the same matter, but more at large. There he says, *As in Adam all die*; which Words cannot be taken literally, but thus, That in *Adam* all became mortal. The same he says here, but in other Words, putting, by a no very unusual Metonymy, the Cause for the Effect, (*viz.*) the Sin of eating the forbidden Fruit, for the Effect of it on *Adam*, *viz.* Mortality, and in him on all his Posterity: A mortal Father infected now with Death, being able to produce no better than a mortal Race. Why St. *Paul* differs in his Phrase here from that which we find he used to the *Corinthians*, and prefers here that which is harder and more figurative, may perhaps be easily accounted for, if we consider his Stile and usual Way of Writing, wherein is shewn a great Liking of the Beauty and Force of Antithesis, as serving much to Illustration and Impression. In the xvth Chapter of *Corinthians*, he is speaking of Life restored by Jesus Christ, and to illustrate and fix that in their Minds, the *Death* of Mankind best served: Here to the *Romans* he is discoursing of *Righteousness* restored to Men by Christ, and therefore here the Term Sin is the most natural and properest to set that off. But that neither actual or imputed Sin is meant here, *ver.* 19. where the same Way of Expression is used, he that has need of it may see proved in Dr. *Whitby* upon the Place. If there can be any need of any other Proof, when it is evidently contrary to St. *Paul*'s Desire here, which is to shew, that all Men, from *Adam* to *Moses*, died solely in consequence of *Adam*'s Transgression, see *ver.* 17.

ROMANS.

TEXT.

is not imputed when there is no law.
14 Nevertheless, death reign-

PARAPHRASE.

it is as true ᵐ that there is no certain determined Punishment affixed to Sin, without a positive ⁿ Law declaring it. Nevertheless we 14.

NOTES.

13 ᵐ Οὐκ ἐλλογεῖται, *is not imputed*; so our Translation, but possibly not exactly to the Sense of the Apostle: Ἐλλογεῖν signifies to *reckon*, but cannot be interpreted *reckon to*, which is the Meaning of *impute*, without a Person assigned to whom it is imputed. And so we see when the Word is used in that Sense, the Dative Case of the Person is subjoined. And therefore it is well translated, *Philem*. 18. if he owes thee any thing, ἐμοὶ ἐλλόγει, *put it to my Account*, reckon or impute it to me. Besides, St. *Paul* here tells us, the Sin here spoken of, as not reckoned, was in the World, and had actual Existence during the Time between *Adam* and *Moses*; but the Sin, which is supposed to be imputed, is *Adam*'s Sin which he committed in Paradise, and was not in the World during the Time from *Adam* till *Moses*, and therefore ἐλλογεῖται cannot here signify *imputed*. Sins in sacred Scripture are called Debts; but nothing can be brought to account, as a Debt, till a Value be set upon it. Now Sins can no way be taxed, or a Rate set upon them, but by the positive Declaration and Sanction of the Lawmaker. Mankind, without the positive Law of God, knew, by the Light of Nature, that they transgressed the Rule of their Nature, Reason, which dictated to them what they ought to do. But without a positive Declaration of God their Sovereign, they could not tell at what Rate God taxed their Trespasses against this Rule; till he pronounced that Life should be the Price of Sin, that could not be ascertained, and consequently Sin could not be brought to account: And therefore we see that where there was no positive Law affixing Death to Sin, Men did not look on Death as the Wages or Retribution for their Sin; they did not account that they paid their Lives as a Debt and Forfeit for their Transgression. This is the more to be considered, because St. *Paul* in this Epistle treats of Sin, Punishment and Forgiveness, by way of an Account, as it were of Debtor and Creditor.
He will be farther confirmed in this Sense of these Words, who will be at the Pains to compare *chap*. iv. 15. & v. 13, 20. & vii. 8, 9. together. St. *Paul*, *chap*. iv. 15. says, *The Law worketh Wrath*, i. e. carrieth Punishment with it. *For where there is no Law, there is no Transgression*. Whereby no Sin where meant, that there is no Sin where there is no positive Law, (the contrary whereof he says in this Verse, *viz. that Sin was in the World* all the Time before *the Law*) but that there is no Transgression with a Penalty annexed to it without a positive Law. And hence he tells the *Romans*, *chap*. i. 32. that they knew not that those Things deserved Death, [*vid*. Note, *chap*. i. 32.] but it was by the positive Law of God only, that Men knew that Death was certainly annexed to Sin, as its certain and unavoidable Punishment; and so St. *Paul* argues, *chap*. vii. 8, 9.
ⁿ Νόμος, *Law*. Whether St. *Paul* by νόμος here means *Law* in general, as for the most part he does where he omits the Article; or whether he means *the Law of Moses* in particular, in which Sense he commonly joins the Article to νόμος; this is plain, that St. *Paul*'s Notion of a Law was conformable to that given by *Moses*; and so he uses the Word νόμος, in English, *Law*, for the positive Command of God, with a Sanction of a Penalty annexed to it; of which kind there never having been any one given to any People, but that by *Moses* to the Children of *Israel*, till the Revelation of the Will of God by *Jesus Christ* to all Mankind; which for several Reasons is always called the Gospel, in Contradistinction to the Law of *Moses*; when St. *Paul* speaks of Law in general, it reduces itself in Matter of Fact to the Law of *Moses*.

K k   see

ROMANS.

PARAPHRASE.

see that in all that Space of Time, which was before the positive Law of God by *Moses*, Men from the Beginning of the World died, all as well as their Father *Adam*, though none of them but he alone had eaten of the forbidden Fruit°, and thereby, as he had committed that Sin, to which Sin alone the Punishment of Death was annexed by the positive Sanction of God denounced to *Adam*, he was the Figure and Type of Christ who was to come. But

15. yet though he were the Type of Christ, yet the Gift or Benefit received by Christ, is not exactly conformed and confined to the Dimensions of the Damage received by *Adam*'s Fall. For if by the Lapse of one Man the Multitude ᵖ, *i. e.* all Men died ᵠ, much more did the Favour of God, and the Free Gift by the Bounty or Good-will which is in Jesus Christ, exceed to the Multitude ᵖ, *i. e.* to all Men.

TEXT.

ed from *Adam* to *Moses*, even over them that had not sinned, after the similitude of *Adam*'s transgression, who is the figure of him that was to come:

But not as the offence, 15 so also is the free gift. For if through the offence of one many be dead, much more the grace of God, and the gift by grace, which is by one man, Jesus Christ, hath abounded unto many.

NOTES.

14 ° In this Verse St. *Paul* proves, that all Men became mortal by *Adam*'s eating the forbidden Fruit, and by that alone, because no Man can incur a Penalty without the Sanction of a positive Law declaring and establishing that Penalty; but Death was annexed by no positive Law to any Sin, but the eating the forbidden Fruit: And therefore Mens dying before the Law of *Moses*, was purely in consequence of *Adam*'s Sin, in eating the forbidden Fruit; and the positive Sanction of Death annexed to it, an evident Proof of Man's Mortality coming from thence.

15 ᵖ Οἱ πολλοὶ and τοῖς πολλοῖς, I suppose may be understood to stand here for the *Multitude* or collective Body of Mankind. For the Apostle in express Words assures us, 1 *Cor.* xv. 22. *That in Adam all died*, and *in Christ all are made alive:* And so here, *ver.* 18. *All Men* fell under the Condemnation of Death, and *all Men* were restored unto Justification of Life; which *all Men*, in the very next Words, *ver.* 19. are called οἱ πολλοὶ, *the many*. So that *the many* in the former Part of this Verse, and *the many* at the End of it, comprehending all Mankind, must be equal. The Comparison therefore, and the Inequality of the things compared, lies not here between the Numbers of those that died, and the Numbers of those that shall be restored to Life: But the Comparison lies between the Persons by whom this general Death, and this general Restoration to Life came, *Adam* the Type, and Jesus Christ the Antitype; and it seems to lie in this, that *Adam*'s Lapse came barely for the Satisfaction of his own Appetite and Desire of Good to himself, but the Restoration was from the exuberant Bounty and Good-will of Christ towards Men, who at the Cost of his own painful Death purchased Life for them. The

want

ROMANS.

Chap. V.

TEXT.

16 And not as it was by one that sinned, so is the gift: for the judgment was by one to condemnation; but the free gift is of many offences unto Justification.

17 For if by one man's offence, death reigned by one; much more they which receive abundance of grace, and of the gift of righteousness, shall

PARAPHRASE.

Men. Furthermore, neither is the Gift as was the Lapse, by one Sin ᑫ. For the Judgment or Sentence was for one ᑫ Offence to Condemnation: But the Gift of Favour reaches, notwithstanding many ᑫ Sins, to Justification of Life ʳ. For if by one Lapse Death reigned by reason of one Offence, much more shall they who receive the ˢ Surplusage of Favour, and of the Gift of Righteousness, reign

16.

17.

NOTES.

want of taking the Comparison here right, and the placing it amiss, in a greater Number restored to Life by Jesus Christ, than those brought into Death by *Adam*'s Sin, hath led some Men so far out of the way, as to alledge, that Men in the Deluge died for their own Sins. It is true they did so, and so did the Men of *Sodom* and *Gomorrah*, and the Philistines cut off by the Israelites, and Multitudes of others: But it is as true, that by their own Sins they were not made mortal: They were so before by their Father *Adam*'s eating the forbidden Fruit; so that what they paid for their own Sins was not Immortality, which they had not, but a few Years of their own finite Lives; which having been let alone, would every one of them, in a short Time, have come to an End. It cannot be denied therefore, but that it is as true of these, as any of the rest of Mankind before *Moses*, that they died solely in *Adam*, as St. *Paul* has proved in the three preceding Verses. And it is as true of them, as of any of the rest of Mankind in general, that they died in *Adam*. For this St. *Paul* expresly asserts of *all*, that in *Adam* all died, 1 *Cor.* xv. 22. and in this very Chapter, *ver.* 18. in other Words. It is then a flat Contradiction to St. *Paul* to say, that those whom the Flood swept away did not die in *Adam*.

16 ᑫ Δι' ἑνὸς ἁμαρτήματος, by *one* Sin; so the *Alexandrine* Copy reads it, more conformable to the Apostle's Sense. For if ἑνὸς *one*, in this Verse, be to be taken for the Person of *Adam*, and not for his *one* Sin of eating the forbidden Fruit, there will be nothing to answer πολλῶν παραπτωμάτων, many *Offences* here, and so the Comparison St. *Paul* is upon will be lost; whereas it is plain that in this Verse he shews another Disproportion in the Case, wherein *Adam* the Type comes short of Christ the Antitype; and that is, that 'twas but for one only Transgression that Death came upon all Men: But Christ restores Life unto all, notwithstanding multitudes of Sins. These two Excesses, both of the Good-will of the Donor, and of the Greatness of the Gift, are both reckoned up together in the following Verse, and are there plainly expressed in περισσείαν τῆς χάριτος ϰ τῆς δωρεᾶς, the Excess of the Favour in the greater Good-will and Cost of the Donor: And the Inequality of the Gift itself, which exceeds, as *many* exceeds *one*; or the Deliverance from the Guilt of *many* Sins, does the Deliverance from the Guilt of *one*.

ʳ Ζωῆς, *Of Life*, is found in the *Alexandrine* Copy. And he that will read *ver.* 18. will scarce incline to the leaving of it out here.

17 ˢ *Surplusage*, so περισσεία signifies. The Surplusage of χάριτος, *Favour*, was the painful Death of Christ, whereas the Fall cost *Adam* no more Pains but eating the Fruit. The Surplusage of δωρεᾶς, the Gift or Benefit received, was Justification to Life from a multitude of Sins, whereas the Loss of Life came upon all Men only for one Sin; but all Men, how guilty soever of many Sins, are restored to Life.

PARAPHRASE.

18. in Life by one, even Jesus Christ. Therefore ᵗ as by one ᵘ Offence *(viz.)* *Adam*'s eating the forbidden Fruit, all Men fell under the Condemnation of Death, so by one Act of Righteousness, *viz.* Christ's Obedience to Death upon the Cross ˣ, all Men are restored

TEXT.

reign in life by one, Jesus Christ.

18. Therefore as by the offence of one, judgment came upon all men to condemnation: even so by the righteousness of one, the free gift came upon all men unto justification of life.

NOTES.

18 ᵗ *Therefore* here is not used as an Illative, introducing an Inference from the immediately preceding Verses; but is the same *therefore* which began *ver.* 12. repeated here again with Part of the Inference that was there begun and left incomplete, the Continuation of it being interrupted by the Intervention of the Proofs of the first Part of it. The Particle *As* immediately following *therefore*, ver. 12. is a convincing Proof of this, having there or in the following Verses nothing to answer it; and so leaves the Sense imperfect and suspended, till you come to this Verse, where the same Reasoning is taken up again, and the same *Protasis* or first Part of Comparison repeated: And then the *Apodosis* or latter Part is added to it, and the whole Sentence made complete; which, to take right, one must read thus, *ver.* 12. *Therefore as by one Man Sin entered into the World, and Death by Sin, and so Death passed upon all Men,* &c.—— *ver.* 18. *I say therefore, as by the Offence of one, Judgment came upon all Men to Condemnation; even so by the Righteousness of one, the free Gift came upon all Men to Justification of Life.* A like Interruption of what he began to say, may be seen 2 Cor. xii. 14. and the same Discourse, after the Interposition of eight Verses, began again, *chap.* xiii. 1. not to mention others that I think may be found in St. *Paul*'s Epistles.

ᵘ That ἑνὸς παραπτώματος ought to be rendered *one Offence*, and not *the Offence of one Man*; and so ἑνὸς δικαιώματος, *one Act of Righteousness*, and not *the Righteousness of one*, is reasonable to think: Because in the next Verse St. *Paul* compares one Man to one Man, and therefore it is fit to understand him here (the Construction also favouring it) of one Fact compared with one Fact, unless we will make him here (where he seems to study Conciseness) guilty of a Tautology. But, taken as I think they should be understood, one may see a Harmony, Beauty, and Fulness in this Discourse, which at first Sight seems somewhat obscure and perplexed. For thus in these two Verses, 18, 19. he shews the Correspondence of *Adam* the Type with Christ the Antitype, as we may see, *ver.* 14. he designed; as he had shewn the Disparity between them, *ver.* 15, 16, 17.

ˣ That this is the Meaning of δι ἑνὸς δικαιώματος, is plain by the following Verse. St. *Paul* every one may observe to be a Lover of Antithesis. In this Verse it is ἑνὸς παραπτώματος, *one perverse Act of Transgression*; and ἑνὸς δικαιώματος, *one right Act of Submission*: In the next Verse it is παρακοὴ, *Disobedience*, and ὑπακοὴ, *Obedience*, the same Thing being meant in both Verses. And that this δικαίωμα, this Act of Obedience, whereby he procured Life to all Mankind, was his Death upon the Cross, I think no body questions, see *ver.* 7—9. *Heb.* ii. 10, 14. *Phil.* ii. 8. And that δικαίωμα, when applied to Men, signifies Actions conformable to the Will of God, see *Rev.* xix. 8.

ROMANS.

TEXT.	PARAPHRASE.	
19 For as by one man's disobedience many were made sinners: so by the obedience of one, shall many be made righteous.	to Life ʸ. For as by one Man's Disobedience many were brought into a State of Mortality, which is the State of Sinners ᶻ; so by the Obedience of one, shall many be made righteous, *i. e.* be restored to Life again as if they were not Sinners.	19.

NOTES.

ʸ By δικαιωσις ζωης, *Justification of Life*, which are the Words of the Text, is not meant that Righteousness by Faith which is to eternal Life. For eternal Life is no where in Sacred Scripture mentioned, as the Portion of all Men, but only of the Saints. But the *Justification of Life*, here spoken of, is what all Men partake in by the Benefit of Christ's Death, by which they are justified from all that was brought upon them by *Adam's* Sin, *i. e.* they are discharged from Death, the Consequence of *Adam's* Transgression; and restored to Life, to stand or fall by that Plea of Righteousness, which they can make, either of their own by Works, or of the Righteousness of God by Faith.

19 ᶻ *Sinners.* Here St. *Paul* uses the same Metonymy as above, *ver.* 12. putting *Sinners* for *Mortal*, whereby the Antithesis to Righteous is the more lively.

SECT. VI. N. 2.

CHAP. V. 20, 21.

CONTENTS.

ST. *Paul* pursuing his Design in this Epistle, of satisfying the Gentiles, that there was no need of their submitting to the Law, in order to their partaking of the Benefits of the Gospel, having in the foregoing eight Verses taught them, that *Adam's* one Sin had brought Death upon them all, from which they were all restored by Christ's Death, with Addition of eternal Bliss and Glory to all those who believe in him; all which being the Effect of God's Free Grace and Favour to those who were never under the Law, excludes the Law from having any Part in it, and so fully makes out the Title of the Gentiles to God's Favour, through Jesus Christ, under the Gospel, without the Intervention of the Law. Here, for

Chap. V. for the farther Satisfaction of the Gentile Converts, he shews them, in these two Verses, That the Nation of the Hebrews, who had the Law, were not delivered from the State of Death by it, but rather plunged deeper under it by the Law, and so stood more in need of Favour, and indeed had a greater Abundance of Grace afforded them for their Recovery to Life by Jesus Christ, than the Gentiles themselves. Thus the Jews themselves, not being saved by the Law, but by an Excess of Grace, this is a farther Proof of the Point St. *Paul* was upon, *(viz.)* that the Gentiles had no need of the Law for the obtaining of Life under the Gospel.

PARAPHRASE.

20. THIS was the State of all [a] Mankind before the Law, they all died for the one παράπτωμα, *Lapse* or *Offence* of one Man, which was the only Irregularity that had Death annexed to it: But the Law entered, and took Place over a small Part of Mankind [b], that this παράπτωμα, *Lapse* or *Offence*, to which

TEXT.

20. Moreover, the law entered, that the offence might abound: but where sin abounded,

NOTES.

20 [a] There can be nothing plainer, than that St. *Paul* here, in these two Verses, makes a Comparison between the State of the Jews, and the State of the Gentiles, as it stands described in the eight preceding Verses, to shew wherein they differed or agreed, so far as was necessary to his present Purpose of satisfying the Convert Romans, that in reference to their Interest in the Gospel, the Jews had no Advantage over them by the Law. With what reference to those eight Verses St. *Paul* writ these two, appears by the very Choice of his Words. He tells them, ver. 12. that Death by Sin, εἰσῆλθε, *entered* into the World; and here he tells them, that the Law (for Sin and Death were entered already) παρεισῆλθεν, *entered a little*; a Word that, set in opposition to εἰσῆλθε, gives a distinguishing Idea of the Extent of the Law, such as really it was, little and narrow, as was the People of *Israel* (whom alone it reached) in respect of all the other Nations of the Earth, with whom it had nothing to do. For the Law of *Moses* was given to *Israel* alone, and not to all Mankind. The *Vulgate* therefore translates this Word right, *subintravit*, it *entered*, *but not far*; i. e. the Death which followed, upon the account of the Mosaical Law, reigned over but a small Part of Mankind, *viz.* the Children of *Israel*, who alone were under that Law; whereas by *Adam's* Transgression of the positive Law given him in Paradise, Death passed upon all Men.

[b] *Ἵνα, that.* Some would have this signify barely the Event, and not the Intention of the Lawgiver, and so understand by these Words, *that the Offence might abound*, the Increase of Sin, or the Aggravations of it, as a Consequence of the Law. But it is to be remembered, that St. *Paul* here sets forth the Difference which God intended to put by the Law which he gave them, between the Children of *Israel* and the Gentile World, in respect of Life and Death, Life and Death being the Subject St. *Paul* was upon. And therefore to mention

ROMANS.

Chap. V.

TEXT.	PARAPHRASE.
grace did much more a-bound:	which Death was annexed, might abound, *i. e.* the multiplied Transgressions of many Men, *viz.* all that were under the Law of *Moses*, might have Death annexed to them by the positive Sanction of that Law, whereby the Offence^c, to which Death was annexed, did abound, *i. e.* Sins that had Death for their Punishment were increased. But by the Good-

NOTES.

mention barely accidental Consequences of the Law that made the Difference, had come short of St. *Paul's* Purpose.

All Mankind was in an irrecoverable State of Death by *Adam*'s Lapse. It was plainly the Intention of God to remove the *Israelites* out of this State by the Law: And so he says himself, that he *gave them Statutes and Judgments, which if a Man do, he shall live in them,* Lev. xviii. 5. And so St. *Paul* tells us here, *chap.* vii. 10. that *the Law was ordained for Life.* Whence it necessarily follows, that if Life were intended them for their Obedience, Death was intended them for their Disobedience: And accordingly *Moses* tells them, *Deut.* xxx. 19. that *he had set before them Life and Death.* Thus by the Law the Children of *Israel* were put into a new State: And by the Covenant God made with them, their remaining under Death, or their Recovery of Life, was to be the Consequence, not of what another had done, but of what they themselves did. They were thenceforth put to stand or fall by their own Actions, and the Death they suffered was for their Transgressions. Every Offence they committed against the Law, did, by this Covenant, bind Death upon them. It is not easy to conceive that God should give them a Law, to the end Sin and Guilt should abound amongst them; but yet he might and did give them a Law, that the Offence which had Death annexed should abound, *i. e.* that Death, which before was the declared Penalty of but one Offence, should to the Jews be made the Penalty of every Breach by the Sanction of this new Law; which was not a Hardship, but a Privilege to them. For in their former State, common to them with the rest of Mankind, Death was unavoidable to them. But by the Law they had a Trial for Life: Accordingly our Saviour to the young Man, who asked what he should do to obtain eternal Life, answers, *Keep the Commandments.* The Law, increasing *the Offence* in this Sense, had also another Benefit, *viz.* That the Jews perceiving they incurred Death by the Law, which was ordained for Life, might thereby, as by a School-master, be led to Christ to seek Life by him. This St. *Paul* takes notice of, *Gal.* iii. 24.

^c Παράπτωμα is another Word, shewing St. *Paul's* having an Eye, in what he says here, to what he said in the foregoing Verses. Our Bibles translate it *Offence*; it properly signifies *Fall*, and is used in the foregoing Verses, for that Transgression which, by the positive Law of God, had Death annexed to it, and in that Sense the Apostle continues to use it here also. There was but one such Sin before the Law given by *Moses*, viz. *Adam*'s eating the forbidden Fruit. But the positive Law of God, given to the *Israelites*, made all their Sins such, by annexing the Penalty of Death to each Transgression; and thus *the Offence abounded*, or was increased by the Law.

Chap. V.

PARAPHRASE.

ness of God where Sin ᵈ, with Death annexed to it, did abound, Grace did much more a-
21. bound ᵉ. That as Sin had reigned or shewed its Mastery in the Death of the *Israelites*, who were under the Law, so Grace in its Turn might reign, or shew its Mastery, by justifying them from all those many Sins which they had committed, each whereof by the Law brought Death with it, and so bestowing on them the Righteousness of Faith, instate them in eternal Life through Jesus Christ our Lord.

TEXT.

21. That as sin has reigned unto death, even so might grace reign through righteousness unto eternal life, by Jesus Christ our Lord.

NOTES.

ᵈ *Sin.* That by *Sin* St. *Paul* means here such Failure, as by the Sanction of a positive Law had Death annexed to it, the Beginning of the next Verse shews, where it is declared to be such Sin as *reigned* in or *by Death*; which all Sin doth not, all Sin is not taxed at that Rate, as appears by *ver.* 13. see the Note. The Article joined here both to παράπτωμα and ἁμαρτία, for it is τὸ παράπτωμα, and ἡ ἁμαρτία, *the Offence* and *the Sin*, limiting the general Signification of those Words to some particular Sort, seems to point out this Sense. And that this is not a mere groundless Criticism, may appear from *ver.* 12, & 13. where St. *Paul* uses ἁμαρτία in these two different Senses, with the Distinction of the Article and no Article.

ᵉ *Grace might much more abound.* The rest of Mankind were in a State of Death only for one Sin of one Man. This the Apostle is express in, not only in the foregoing Verses, but elsewhere. But those who were under the Law (which made each Transgression they were guilty of mortal) were under the Condemnation of Death, not only for that one Sin of another, but also for every one of their own Sins. Now to make any one Righteous to Life from many, and those his own Sins, besides that one, that lay on him before, is greater Grace, than to bestow on him Justification to Life only from one Sin, and that of another Man. To forgive the Penalty of many Sins, is a greater Grace than to remit the Penalty of one.

SECT.

ROMANS.

SECT. VI. N. 3.

CHAP. VI. 1——23.

CONTENTS.

ST. *Paul* having, in the foregoing Chapter, very much magnified Free Grace, by shewing that all Men, having lost their Lives by *Adam*'s Sin, were by Grace, through Christ, restored to Life again; and also as many of them as believed in Christ, were re-establishd in Immortality by Grace; and that even the Jews, who by their own Trespasses against the Law had forfeited their Lives over and over again, were also by Grace restored to Life, Grace superabounding where Sin abounded, he here obviates a wrong Inference, which might be apt to mislead the Convert Gentiles, *(viz.) Therefore let us continue in Sin, that Grace may abound.* The contrary whereof he shews, their very taking upon them the Profession of Christianity, required of them by the very initiating Ceremony of Baptism, wherein they were typically buried with Christ, to teach them that they, as he did, ought to die to Sin; and as he rose to live to God, they should rise to a new Life of Obedience to God, and be no more Slaves to Sin, in an Obedience and Resignation of themselves to its Commands. For if their Obedience were to Sin, they were Vassals of Sin, and would certainly receive the Wages of that Master, which was nothing but Death: But if they obeyed Righteousness, *i. e.* sincerely endeavoured after Righteousness, though they did not attain it, Sin should not have Dominion over them, by Death, *i. e.* should not bring Death upon them. Because they were not under the Law, which condemned them to Death for every Transgression; but under Grace, which by Faith in Jesus Christ justified them to eternal Life from their many Transgressions. And thus he shews the Gentiles not only the no Necessity, but the Advantage of their not being under the Law.

ROMANS.

PARAPHRASE.

1. WHAT shall we say then? Shall we continue in Sin, that Grace may abound?
2. God forbid: How can it be that we ᶠ, who, by our embracing Christianity, have renounced our former sinful Courses, and have professed a Death to Sin, should live any longer in it?
3. For this I hope you are not ignorant of, that we Christians, who by Baptism were admitted into the Kingdom and Church of Christ, were baptized into a Similitude of his Death; we did own some Kind of Death by
4. being buried under Water; which being buried with him, *i. e.* in Conformity to his Burial, as a Confession of our being dead, was to signify, that as Christ was raised up from the Dead ᵍ into a glorious Life with his Father, even so we, being raised from our typical Death and

TEXT.

1. WHAT shall we say then? shall we continue in sin, that grace may abound?
2. God forbid: how shall we that are dead to sin, live any longer therein?
3. Know ye not, that so many of us as were baptized into Jesus Christ, were baptized into his death?
4. Therefore we are buried with him by baptism into death: that like as Christ was raised up from the dead by the glory of the Father, even so we

NOTES.

2 ᶠ *We, i. e.* I and all Converts to Christianity. St. *Paul* in this Chapter shews it to be the Profession and Obligation of all Christians, even by their Baptism, and the typical Signification of it, to be dead to Sin, and alive to God, *i. e.* as he explains it, not to be any longer Vassals to Sin in obeying our Lusts, but to be Servants to God in a sincere Purpose and Endeavour of obeying him. For whether under the Law, or under Grace, whoever is a Vassal to Sin, *i. e.* indulges himself in a compliance with his sinful Lusts, will receive the Wages which Sin pays, *i. e.* Death. This he strongly represents here to the Gentile Converts of *Rome*, (for it is to them he speaks in this Chapter) that they might not mistake the State they were in, by being not under the Law, but under Grace; of which, and the Freedom and Largeness of it, he had spoken so much, and so highly in the foregoing Chapter, to let them see, that to be under Grace was not a State of Licence, but of exact Obedience, in the Intention and Endeavour of every one under Grace, though in the Performance they came short of it. This strict Obedience to the utmost Reach of every one's Aim and Endeavours, he urges as necessary, because Obedience to Sin unavoidably produces Death; and he urges as reasonable for this very Reason, that they were not under the Law, but under Grace. For as much as all the Endeavours after Righteousness, of those who were under the Law were lost Labour, since any one Slip forfeited Life: But the sincere Endeavours after Righteousness of those, who were under Grace, were sure to succeed, to the attaining the Gift of eternal Life.

4 ᵍ Διὰ, in the Hellenistick Greek, sometimes signifies *into*, and so our Translation renders it, 2 *Pet.* i. 3. And if it be not so taken here, the Force of St. *Paul's* Argument is lost, which is to shew *into* what State of Life we ought to be raised out of Baptism, in a Similitude and Conformity to that State of Life Christ was raised into from the Grave.

Burial

ROMANS.

Chap. VI.

TEXT.

also should walk in newness of Life.
5 For if we have been planted together in the likeness of his Death: we shall be also in the likeness of his resurrection:
6 Knowing this, that our old man is crucified with him, that the body of sin might be destroyed, that henceforth we should not serve sin.
7 For he that is dead, is freed from sin.

PARAPHRASE.

Burial in Baptism, should lead a new sort of Life, wholly different from our former, in some Approaches towards that heavenly Life that Christ is risen to. For if we had been ingrafted into him in the Similitude of his Death, we shall be also in a Conformity to the Life, which he is entered into by his Resurrection. Knowing this, that we are to live so, as if our Old Man, our wicked and corrupt fleshly self *h* which we were before, were crucified with him, that the Prevalency of our carnal sinful Propensities, which are from our Bodies, might be destroyed, that henceforth we should not serve Sin *i*, as Vassals to it. For he that is dead is set free from the Vassalage *k* of Sin, as a Slave is from the Vassalage of his Master.

5.

6.

7.

NOTES.

6 *h* See *Gal.* v. 24. *Eph.* iv. 22. *Col.* ii. 11. 1 *Pet.* iv. 1.
i It will conduce much to the understanding of St. *Paul*, in this and the two following Chapters, if it be minded that these Phrases, to *serve Sin*, to *be Servants of Sin*, *Sin reign in our mortal Bodies*, to *obey Sin in the Lusts of our Bodies*, to *yield our Members Instruments of Unrighteousness unto Sin*, or *Servants of Uncleanness*, and to *Iniquity unto Iniquity*, to *be free from Righteousness*, to *walk, live, or to be after the Flesh*, to be *carnally minded*, all signify one and the same Thing, *viz.* the giving ourselves up to the Conduct of our sinful, carnal Appetites, to allow any of them the Command over us, and the Conduct and Prevalency in determining us. On the contrary, that *walking after the Spirit*, or in *Newness of Life*, the *Crucifixion of the Old Man*, the *Destruction of the Body of Sin*, the *Deliverance from the Body of Death*, to *be freed from Sin*, to *be dead to Sin*, *alive unto God*, to *yield yourselves unto God*, *as those who are alive from the Dead*, *yield your Members Servants of Righteousness unto Holiness*, or *Instruments of Righteousness unto God*, to be *Servants of Obedience unto Righteousness*, *made free from Sin*, *Servants of Righteousness*, to be *after the Spirit*, to be *spiritually minded*, to *mortify the Deeds of the Body*, do all signify a constant and steady Purpose, and sincere Endeavour to obey the Law and Will of God in every thing: These several Expressions being used in several Places, as best serves the Occasion, and illustrates the Sense.
7 *k* The Tenor of St. *Paul's* Discourse here shews this to be the Sense of this Verse; and to be assured that it is so, we need go no farther than *ver.* 11, 12, 13. He makes it his Business in this Chapter, not to tell them what they certainly and unchangeably are, but to exhort them to be what they ought and are engaged to be, by becoming Christians, *viz.* that they ought to emancipate themselves from the Vassalage of Sin; not that they were so emancipated without any Danger of Return, for then he could not have said what he does, *ver.* 11, 12, 13. which supposes it in their Power to continue in their Obedience to Sin, or return to that Vassalage if they would.

PARAPHRASE.

8. Now if we understand by our being buried in Baptism, that we died with Christ, we cannot but think and believe, that we should live a
9. Life conformable to his; knowing that Christ being raised from the dead, returns no more to a mortal Life, Death hath no more Dominion over him, he is no more subject to Death.
10. For in that he died, he died unto Sin; *i. e.* upon the Account of Sin, once ¹ for all: But his Life, now after his Resurrection, is a Life wholly appropriated to God, with which Sin or Death shall never have any more to do, or
11. come in reach of. In like manner do you also make your Reckoning, account yourselves dead to Sin ᵐ, freed from that Master; so as not to suffer yourselves any more to be commanded or employed by it, as if it were still your Master; but alive to God, *i. e.* that it is your Business now to live wholly for his Service, and to his Glory ⁿ, through Jesus
12. Christ our Lord. Permit not, therefore, Sin to reign over you, by ᵒ your mortal Bodies, which you will do if you obey your carnal

TEXT.

Now if we be dead 8 with Christ, we believe that we shall also live with him:

Knowing that Christ 9 being raised from the dead, dieth no more; death hath no more dominion over him.

For in that he died, he 10 died unto sin once: but in that he liveth, he liveth unto God.

Likewise reckon ye also 11 yourselves to be dead indeed unto sin; but alive unto God, through Jesus Christ our Lord.

Let not sin therefore 12 reign in your mortal body, that ye should obey it in the lusts thereof.

NOTES.

10 ¹ See *Heb.* ix 26—28. 1 *Pet.* iv. 1, 2.

11 ᵐ *Sin* is here spoken of as a Person, a Prosopopœia made use of, all through this and the following Chapter, which must be minded if we will understand them right. The like Exhortation upon the same Ground, see 1 *Pet.* iv. 1—3.

ⁿ See *Gal.* ii. 19. 2 *Cor.* v. 15. *Rom.* vii. 4. The Force of St. *Paul's* Argument here seems to be this; in your Baptism you are engaged into a Likeness of Christ's Death and Resurrection. He once died to Sin, so do you count yourselves dead to Sin. He rose to Life, wherein he lives wholly to God, so must your new Life, after your Resurrection from your typical Burial in the Water, be under the Vassalage of Sin no more, but you must live entirely to the Service of God, to whom you are devoted, in Obedience to his Will in all things.

12 ᵒ *In your mortal Bodies*, is in the Apostle's Writings often signifies *by*. And he here, as also in the following Chapter, *ver.* 18, & 24. and elsewhere, placing the Root of Sin in the Body, his Sense seems to be, *Let not Sin reign over you by the Lusts of your mortal Bodies.*

Lusts:

ROMANS.
Chap. VI.

TEXT.

13 Neither yield ye your members as inſtruments of unrighteouſneſs unto ſin: but yield yourſelves unto God, as thoſe that are alive from the dead; and your members as inſtruments of righteouſneſs unto God.

14 For ſin ſhall not have dominion over you: for ye are not under the law, but under grace.

15 What then? ſhall we ſin, becauſe we are not

PARAPHRASE.

Luſts: Neither deliver up your Members to Sin, to be employed by Sin, as Inſtruments of Iniquity, but deliver up yourſelves unto God, as thoſe who have got to a new Life from among the Dead q, and chuſing him for your Lord and Maſter, yield your Members to him, as Inſtruments of Righteouſneſs. For if you do ſo, Sin ſhall not have Dominion over you r, you ſhall not be as its Slaves, in its Power, to be by it delivered over to Death. s For you are not under the Law in the legal State, but you are under Grace, in the Goſpel State of the Covenant of Grace. What then, ſhall we ſin becauſe we are not under the

p 13.

14.

15.

NOTES.

13 p Sinful Luſts, at leaſt thoſe to which the Gentiles were moſt eminently enſlaved, ſeem ſo much placed in the Body and the Members, that they are called the Members, Col. iii. 5.

q Ἐκ νεκρῶν, From among the Dead. The Gentile World were dead in Sins, Eph. ii. 1, 5. Col. ii. 13. thoſe who were converted to the Goſpel were raiſed to Life from among thoſe dead.

14 r Sin ſhall not have Dominion over you, i. e. Sin ſhall not be your abſolute Maſter to diſpoſe of your Members and Faculties in its Drudgery and Service as it pleaſes; you ſhall not be under its Controul in abſolute Subjection to it, but your own Men that are alive, and at your own Diſpoſal, unleſs by your own free Choice you enthral yourſelves to it, and by a voluntary Obedience give it the Command over you, and are willing to have it your Maſter. It muſt be remembered, that St. Paul here, and in the following Chapter, perſonates Sin as ſtriving with Men for Maſtery to deſtroy them.

s For. The Force of St. Paul's Reaſoning here ſtands thus: You are obliged by your taking on you the Profeſſion of the Goſpel, not to be any longer Slaves and Vaſſals to Sin, nor to be under the Sway of your carnal Luſts, but to yield yourſelves up to God to be his Servants in a conſtant and ſincere Purpoſe and Endeavour of obeying him in all things; this if you do, Sin ſhall not be able to procure your Death; for you Gentiles are not under the Law which condemns to Death for every the leaſt Tranſgreſſion, though it be but a Slip of Infirmity; but by your Baptiſm are entered into the Covenant of Grace, and being under Grace, God will accept of your ſincere Endeavours, in the Place of exact Obedience, and give you eternal Life through Jeſus Chriſt; but if you by a willing Obedience to your Luſts make yourſelves Vaſſals to Sin, Sin, as the Lord Maſter to whom you belong, will pay you with Death, the only Wages that Sin pays.

Law,

PARAPHRASE.

Law, but under the Covenant of Grace ᵗ? God forbid! Know ye not that to whom you subject yourselves ᵘ as Vassals, to be at his beck, his Vassals you are whom you thus obey, whether it be of Sin, which Vassalage ends in Death; or of Christ in obeying the Gospel, to the obtaining of Righteousness and Life. But God be thanked, that you who were the Vas-

TEXT.

under the law, but under Grace? God forbid.

Know ye not, that to whom you yield yourselves servants to obey, his servants ye are to whom ye obey, whether of sin unto death, or of obedience unto righteousness?

But God be thanked, that ye were the servants

NOTES.

15 ᵗ What is meant by being *under Grace*, is understood by the undoubted and obvious Meaning of the Phrase *under the Law*. They, it is unquestioned, were *under the Law*, who having by Circumcision, the Ceremony of Admittance, been received into the Commonwealth of the Jews, owned the God of the Jews for their God and King, professing Subjection to the Law he gave by *Moses*. And so, in like manner, he is *under Grace*, who having by Baptism, the Ceremony of Admittance, been received into the Kingdom of Christ, or the Society of Christians, called by a peculiar Name the Christian Church, owns Jesus of *Nazareth* to be the Messias his King, professing Subjection to his Law delivered in the Gospel. By which it is plain, that being under Grace is spoken here, as being under the Law is, in a political and national Sense. For whoever was circumcised, and owned God for his King, and the Authority of his Law, ceased not to be a Jew or Member of that Society by every or any Transgression of the Precepts of that Law, so long as he owned God for his Lord, and his Subjection to that Law; so likewise he who by Baptism is incorporated into the Kingdom of Christ, and owns him for his Sovereign, and himself under the Law and Rule of the Gospel, ceases not to be a Christian, though he offend against the Precepts of the Gospel, till he denies Christ to be his King and Lord, and renounces his Subjection to his Law in the Gospel. But God, in taking a People to himself to be his, not doing it barely as a temporal Prince, or Head of a politick Society in this World, but in order to his having as many as in obeying him perform the Conditions necessary, his Subjects for ever in the State of Immortality restored to them in another World, has, since the Fall, erected two Kingdoms in this World, the one of the Jews immediately under himself, another of Christians under his Son Jesus Christ, for that farther and more glorious End of attaining eternal Life; which Prerogative and Privilege of eternal Life does not belong to the Society in general, nor is the Benefit granted nationally to the whole Body of the People of either of these Kingdoms of God, but personally to such of them who perform the Conditions required in the Terms of each Covenant. To those who are Jews, or under the Law, the Terms are perfect and complete Obedience to every Tittle of the Law, *Do this and live*. To those who are Christians, or under Grace, the Terms are sincere Endeavours after perfect Obedience, though not attaining it, as is manifest in the remaining Part of this Chapter, where St. *Paul* acquaints those who ask whether *they shall sin, because they are not under the Law, but under Grace*; that though they are *under Grace*, yet they who obey Sin, are the Vassals of Sin; and those who are the Vassals of Sin shall receive Death, the Wages of Sin.

16 ᵘ Ὑπακοὴν, *Obedience*. That which he calls here simply ὑπακοὴ, *Obedience*, he in other Places call ὑπακοὴ πίστεως, *Obedience of Faith*, and ὑπακοὴ τῶ Χριςῶ, *Obedience of Christ*, meaning a Reception of the Gospel of Christ.

ROMANS. Chap. VI.

TEXT.

of sin; but ye have obeyed from the heart that form of Doctrine which was delivered you.

18 Being then made free from sin, ye became the servants of righteousness.

19 I speak after the manner of men, because of the infirmity of your flesh; for as ye have yielded your members servants to uncleanness, and to iniquity, unto iniquity; even so now yield your members servants to righteousness, unto holiness.

20 For when ye were the servants of sin, ye were free from righteousness.

PARAPHRASE.

sals of Sin, have sincerely, and from your Heart, obeyed so as to receive the Form, or be cast into the Mould of that Doctrine under whose Direction or Regulation ˣ you were put, that you might conform yourselves to it. Being therefore set free from the Vassalage of 18. Sin, you became the Servants or Vassals of Righteousness ʸ. (I make use of this Meta- 19. phor of the passing of Slaves from one Master to another ᶻ, well known to you *Romans*, the better to let in my Meaning into your Understandings that are yet weak in these Matters, being more accustomed to fleshly than spiritual Things.) For as you yielded your natural ᵃ Faculties obedient slavish Instruments to Uncleanness, to be wholly employed in all manner of Iniquity ᵇ, so now ye ought to yield up your natural Faculties to a perfect and ready Obedience to Righteousness. For when you 20. were the Vassals of Sin, you were not at all subject to, nor paid any Obedience to Righteousness: Therefore by a Parity of Reason, now Righteousness is your Master, you ought to

NOTES.

17 ˣ Εἰς ὃν παρεδόθητε, *unto which you were delivered*; no harsh, but an elegant Expression, if we observe that St. *Paul* here speaks of Sin and the Gospel, as of two Masters, and that those to were taken out of the Hands of the one, and delivered over to the other, which they having from their Hearts obeyed, were no longer the Slaves of Sin, he whom they obeyed being by the Rule of the foregoing Verse, truly their Master.

18 ʸ Ἐδουλώθητε τῇ δικαιοσύνῃ, *Ye became the Slaves of Unrighteousness*. This will seem an harsh Expression, unless we remember that St. *Paul* going on still with the Metaphor of Master and Servant, makes *Sin* and *Righteousness* here two Persons, two distinct Masters, and Men passing from the Dominion of the one into the Dominion of the other.

19 ᶻ Ἀνθρώπινον λέγω, *I speak after the manner of Men*. He had some reason to make some little kind of Apology, for a Figure of Speech which he dwells upon quite down to the End of this Chapter.

ᵃ *Members*, see *ch*. vii. 5. Note.

ᵇ *To Iniquity unto Iniquity*, see Note, *ch*. i. 17.

pay

PARAPHRASE.

21. pay no Obedience to Sin. What Fruit or Benefit had you then in thoſe Things, in that Courſe of Things, whereof you are now aſhamed?
22. For the End of theſe Things, which are done in Obedience to Sin, is Death. But now being ſet free from Sin, being no longer Vaſſals to that Maſter, but having God now for your Lord and Maſter, to whom you are become Subjects or Vaſſals, your Courſe of Life tends to Holineſs, and will end in everlaſting Life.
23. For the Wages ^c that Sin pays is Death: But that which God's Servants receive from his Bounty, is the Gift ^d of eternal Life through Jeſus Chriſt our Lord.

TEXT.

21. What fruit had ye then in thoſe things whereof ye are now aſhamed? for the end of thoſe things is death.
22. But now being made free from Sin, and become ſervants to God, ye have your fruit unto holineſs, and the end everlaſting life.
23. For the wages of ſin is death: but the gift of God is eternal life, through Jeſus Chriſt our Lord.

NOTES.

23 ^c *The Wages of Sin*, does not ſignify here the Wages that are paid for ſinning, but the Wages that Sin pays. This is evident not only by the Oppoſition that is put here in this Verſe between *the Wages of Sin* and *the Gift of God*, *viz.* That Sin rewards Men with Death for their Obedience; but that which God gives to thoſe, who believing in Jeſus Chriſt, labour ſincerely after Righteouſneſs, is Life eternal. But it farther appears by the whole Tenor of St. Paul's Diſcourſe, wherein he ſpeaks of Sin as a Perſon and a Maſter, who hath Servants, and is ſerved and obeyed; and ſo the Wages of Sin being the Wages of a Perſon here, muſt be what it pays.

^d *The Gift of God.* Sin pays Death to thoſe who are its obedient Vaſſals: But God rewards the Obedience of thoſe, to whom he is Lord and Maſter, by the Gift of eternal Life. Their utmoſt Endeavours and higheſt Performances can never entitle them to it of Right; and ſo it to them not Wages, but a free Gift. See *chap.* iv. 4.

ROMANS.

SECT. VI. N. IV.

CHAP. VII. 1——25.

CONTENTS.

ST. *Paul* in the foregoing Chapter addressing himself to the Convert Gentiles, shews them, that not being under the Law, they were obliged only to keep themselves free from a Vassalage of Sin, by a sincere Endeavour after Righteousness, forasmuch as God gave eternal Life to all those who being under Grace, *i. e.* being converted to Christianity, did so.

In this Chapter addressing himself to those of his own Nation in the Roman Church, he tells them, that the Death of Christ having put an end to the Obligation of the Law, they were at their Liberty to quit the Observances of the Law, and were guilty of no Disloyalty in putting themselves under the Gospel. And here St. *Paul* shews the Deficiency of the Law, which rendered it necessary to be laid aside by the Coming and Reception of the Gospel. Not that it allowed any Sin, but on the contrary forbad even Concupiscence, which was not known to be Sin without the Law. Nor was it the Law that brought Death upon those who were under it, but Sin, that herein it might shew the extreme malignant Influence it had upon our weak fleshly Natures, in that it could prevail on us to transgress the Law (which we could not but acknowledge to be holy, just and good) though Death was the declared Penalty of every Transgression: But herein lay the Deficiency of the Law as spiritual, and opposite to Sin as it was, that it could not master and root it out, but Sin remained and dwelt in Men as before, and by the Strength of their carnal Appetites, which were not subdued by the Law, carried them to Transgressions that they approved not. Nor did it avail them to disapprove or struggle, since though the Bent of their Minds were the other Way, yet their Endeavours after Obedience delivered them not from that Death which their Bodies or carnal Appetites, running them into Transgressions, brought upon them. That Deliverance was to be had from Grace, by which those who putting themselves from under the Law into the Gospel-State, were accepted, if with the Bent of their Minds they

Ch. VII. they sincerely endeavoured to serve and obey the Law of God, though sometimes through the Frailty of their Flesh they fell into Sin.

This is a farther Demonstration to the converted Gentiles of *Rome*, that they are under no Obligation of submitting themselves to the Law, in order to be the People of God, or partake of the Advantages of the Gospel, since it was necessary even to the Jews themselves to quit the Terms of the Law, that they might be delivered from Death by the Gospel. And thus we see how steadily and skilfully he pursues his Design, and with what Evidence and Strength he fortifies the Gentile Converts against all Attempts of the Jews, who went about to bring them under the Observances of the Law of *Moses*.

PARAPHRASE.

1. I HAVE let those of you who were formerly Gentiles, see that they are not under the Law, but under Grace ᵉ: I now apply myself to you, my Brethren of my own Nation ᶠ, who know the Law. You cannot be ignorant that the Authority of the Law reaches or concerns a Man ᵍ so long as he liveth, and no
2. longer. For ʰ a Woman who hath a Hus-

TEXT.

1 KNOW ye not, brethren, (for I speak to them that know the law) how that the law hath dominion over a man as long as he liveth?

2 For the woman which hath an husband, is bound

NOTES.

1 ᵉ See *chap.* vi. 14.

ᶠ That his Discourse here is addressed to those Converts of this Church, who were of the Jewish Nation, is so evident from the whole Tenor of this Chapter, that there needs no more but to read it with a little Attention to be convinced of it, especially *ver.* 1, 4, 6.

ᵍ Κυριεύει τȣ̃ ἀνθρώπȣ, *Hath Dominion over a Man*. So we render it rightly: But I imagine we understand it in too narrow a Sense, taking it to mean only that Dominion or Force which the Law has to compel or restrain us in Things which we have otherwise no mind to; whereas it seems to me to be used in the Conjugation *Hiphil*, and to comprehend here that Right and Privilege also of doing or enjoying, which a Man has by Virtue and Authority of the Law, which all ceases as soon as he is dead. To this large Sense of these Words, St. *Paul*'s Expressions in the two next Verses seem suited; and so understood, have a clear and easy Meaning, as may be seen in the Paraphrase.

2 ʰ *For*. That which follows in the 2d Verse, is no Proof of what is said in the 1st Verse, either as a Reason or an Instance of it, unless κρατεῖται be taken in the Sense I propose, and then the whole Discourse is easy and uniform.

band,

ROMANS.

Ch. VII.

TEXT.

by the law to her husband, so long as he liveth: but if the husband be dead, she is loosed from the law of her husband.

3 So then if while her husband liveth, she be married to another man, she shall be called an adulteress: but if her husband be dead, she is free from that law; so that she is no adulteress, tho' she be married to another man.

4 Wherefore, my brethren, ye also are become dead to the law by the

PARAPHRASE.

band, is bound by the Law ⁱ to her living Husband; but if her Husband dieth, she is loosed from the Law which made her her Husband's, because the Authority of the Law whereby he had a Right to her, ceased in respect of him as soon as he died. Wherefore she shall be called an Adulteress, if while her Husband liveth she become another Man's. But if her Husband dies, the Right he had to her by the Law ceasing, she is freed from the Law, so that she is not an Adulteress, though she become another Man's. So that even ye, my Brethren ᵏ, by the Body of Christ ˡ, are become dead ᵐ to the Law, whereby the Dominion

3.

4.

NOTES.

ⁱ Ἀπὸ τοῦ νόμου τοῦ ἀνδρὸς, *From the Law of her Husband.* This Expression confirms the Sense above-mentioned. For it can in no Sense be termed *the Law of her Husband,* but as it is the Law whereby he has the Right to his Wife. But this Law, as far as it is her Husband's Law, as far as he has any Concern in it, or Privilege by it, dies with him, and so she is loosed from it.

4 ᵏ Καὶ ὑμεῖς, *Ye also,* is not added here by Chance, and without any Meaning, but shews plainly that the Apostle had in his Mind some Person or Persons beforementioned, who were free from the Law; and that must be either the Woman mentioned in the two foregoing Verses, as free from the Law of her Husband, because he was dead; or else the Gentile Converts, mentioned *chap.* vi. 14. as free from the Law, because they were never under it. If we think καὶ refers to the Woman, then St. Paul's Sense is this; *Ye also are free from the Law, as well as such a Woman, and may without any Imputation subject yourselves to the Gospel.* If we take καὶ to refer to the Gentile Converts, then his Sense is this; *Even ye also, my Brethren, are free from the Law as well as the Gentile Converts, and as much at liberty to subject yourselves to the Gospel as they.* I confess myself most inclined to this latter, both because St. *Paul's* main Drift is to shew, that both Jews and Gentiles are wholly free from the Law; and because ἐθανατώθητε τῷ νόμῳ, *Ye have been made dead to the Law,* the Phrase here used to express that Freedom, seems to refer rather to the 1st Verse, where he says, *The Law hath Dominion over a Man as long as he liveth,* implying *and no longer,* rather than to the two intervening Verses, where he says, not the Death of the Woman, but the Death of the Husband sets the Woman free; of which more by and by.

ˡ *By the Body of Christ,* in which you as his Members died with him; see *Col.* ii. 20. and so by a like Figure Believers are said to be circumcised with him, *Col.* ii. 11.

ᵐ *Are become dead to the Law.* There is a great deal of needless Pains taken by some to reconcile this Saying of St. *Paul* to the two immediately preceding Verses, which they suppose do require he should have said here what he does *ver.* 6. that *the Law was dead,* that so the Persons here spoken of might rightly answer to the Wife, who there represents them.

M m 2

ROMANS.

PARAPHRASE.

minion of the Law over you has ceased, that you should subject yourselves to the Dominion of Christ in the Gospel, which you may do with as much Freedom from Blame, or the Imputation of Disloyalty ⁿ, as a Woman whose Husband is dead, may without the Imputation of Adultery marry another Man. And this making yourselves another's, even Christ's, who is risen from the Dead, is that we º should bring forth Fruit unto God ᵖ. For

TEXT.

body of Christ; that ye should be married to another, even to him who is raised from the dead, that we should bring forth fruit unto God.

NOTES.

them. But he that will take this Passage together, will find that the first Part of this 4th Verse refers to *ver.* 1. and the latter Part of it to *ver.* 2, and 3. and consequently that St. *Paul* had spoken improperly, if he had said what they would make him say here. To clear this, let us look into St. *Paul*'s Reasoning, which plainly stands thus; *The Dominion of the Law over a Man ceases when he is dead,* ver. 1. *You are become dead to the Law by the Body of Christ,* ver. 4. *And so the Dominion of the Law over you is ceased; then you are free to put yourselves under the Dominion of another, which can bring on you no Charge of Disloyalty to him who had before the Dominion over you, any more than a Woman can be charged with Adultery, when the Dominion of her former Husband being ceased by his Death, she marrieth herself to another Man.* For the Use of what he says, *ver.* 2, and 3, is to satisfy the Jews, that the Dominion of the Law over them being ceased by their Death to the Law in Christ, they were no more guilty of Disloyalty by putting themselves wholly under the Law of Christ in the Gospel, than a Woman was guilty of Adultery, when the Dominion of her Husband ceasing, she gave herself up wholly to another Man in Marriage.

ⁿ *Disloyalty.* One Thing that made the Jews so tenacious of the Law was, that they looked upon it as a Revolt from God, and a Disloyalty to him their King, if they retained not the Law that he had given them. So that even those of them who embraced the Gospel, thought it necessary to observe those Parts of the Law which were not continued, and as it were re-enacted by Christ in the Gospel. Their Mistake herein is what St. *Paul* by the Instance of a Woman marrying a second Husband, the former being dead, endeavours to convince them of.

º *We.* It may be worth our taking notice of, that St. *Paul* having all along from the Beginning of the Chapter, and even in this very Sentence, said *Ye*, here with neglect of Grammar on a sudden changes it into *We*, and says, *that we should,* &c. I suppose to press the Argument the stronger, by shewing himself to be in the same Circumstances and Concern with them, he being a Jew as well as those he spoke to.

ᵖ *Fruit unto God.* In these Words St. *Paul* visibly refers to *chap.* vi. 10. where he saith, that *Christ in that he liveth, he liveth unto God*; and therefore he mentions here his *being raised from the Dead,* as a Reason for their *bringing forth Fruit unto God,* i. e. living to the Service of God, obeying his Will to the utmost of their Power, which is the same that he says, *chap.* viii. 11.

when

ROMANS.   Ch. VII.

TEXT.

5 For when we were in the flesh, the motions of sins which were by the law, did work in our members to bring forth fruit unto death.

PARAPHRASE.

5. when we were after so fleshly ⁹ a Manner under the Law, as not to comprehend the spiritual Meaning of it, that directed us to Christ the spiritual End of the Law, our sinful Lust ʳ that remained in us under the Law ˢ, or in the State under the Law, wrought in our Members, *i. e.* set our Members and Faculties ᵗ on Work in doing that whose End was

NOTES.

5 ⁹ *When we were in the Flesh.* The Understanding and Observance of the Law in a bare literal Sense, without looking any farther for a more spiritual Intention in it, St. *Paul* calls *being in the Flesh*. That the Law had besides a literal and carnal Sense, a spiritual and evangelical Meaning, see 2 *Cor.* iii. 6, and 17. compared. Read also *ver.* 14, 15, 16 where the Jews in the Flesh are described; and what he says of the ritual Part of the Law, see *Heb.* ix. 9, 10. which whilst they lived in the Observance of, they were in the Flesh. That Part of the Mosaical Law was wholly about fleshly Things, *Col.* ii. 14—23. was sealed in the Flesh, and proposed no other but temporal fleshly Rewards.

ʳ Παθήματα τῶν ἁμαρτιῶν, literally *Passions of Sin*, in the Scripture Greek (wherein the Genitive Case of the Substantive is often put for the Adjective) *sinful Passions* or *Lusts*.

ˢ Τὰ διὰ τοῦ νόμου, *which were by the Law*, is a very true literal Translation of the Words, but leads the Reader quite away from the Apostle's Sense, and is fain to be supported (by Interpreters that so understand it) by saying that the Law excited Men to sin by forbidding it. A strange Imputation on the Law of God; such as, if it be true, must make the Jews more defiled with the Pollutions set down in St. *Paul*'s black List, *chap.* i. than the Heathens themselves. But herein they will not find St. *Paul* of their Mind, who besides the visible Distinction wherewith he speaks of the Gentiles all through his Epistles, in this respect doth here, *ver.* 7. declare quite the contrary; see also 1 *Pet.* iv. 3, 4. If St. *Paul*'s Use of the Preposition διὰ a little backwards in this very Epistle were remembered, this and a like Passage or two more in this Chapter would not have so harsh and hard a Sense put on them as they have. Τῶν πιστευόντων δι᾽ ἀκροβυστίας our Translation renders *chap.* iv. 11. *that believe though they be not circumcised*; where they make δι᾽ ἀκροβυστίας, to signify during the State, or during their being under Uncircumcision. If they had given the same Sense to διὰ νόμου here, which plainly signifies their being in the contrary State, *i. e.* under the Law, and rendered it, *sinful Affections which they had, though they were under the Law*, the Apostle's Sense here would have been easy, clear and conformable to the Design he was upon. This Use of the Word διὰ I think we may find in other Epistles of St. *Paul*, τὰ διὰ τοῦ σώματος, 2 *Cor.* v. 10. may possibly with better Sense be understood of Things done *during the Body*, or *during the bodily State*, than *by the Body*; and so 1 *Tim.* ii. 15. διὰ τεκνογονίας; *during the State of Child bearing*. Nor is this barely an Hellenistical Use of διὰ; for the Greeks themselves say δι᾽ ἡμέρας; *during the Day*; and διὰ νυκτὸς, *during the Night*. And so I think διὰ τῆς εὐαγγελίας, *Eph.* iii. 6. should be understood to signify in the Time of the Gospel, or under the Gospel Dispensation.

ᵗ *Members* here doth not signify barely the fleshly Parts of the Body in a restrained Sense, but the animal Faculties and Powers, all in us that is employed as an Instrument in the Works of the Flesh, which are reckoned up. *Gal.* v. 19—21. some of which do not require the *Members* of our Body, taken in a strict Sense for the outward gross Parts, but only the Faculties of our Minds for their Performance.

Death.

ROMANS.

PARAPHRASE.

6. Death ᵘ. But now the Law under which we were heretofore held in Subjection being dead, we are set free from the Dominion of the Law, that we should perform our Obedience as under the new ʷ and spiritual Covenant of the Gospel, wherein there is Remission of Frailties, and not as still under the old Rigor of the Letter of the Law, which condemns every one who does not perform exact Obedience to every Tittle ˣ.
7. What shall we then think, that the Law, because it is set aside, was unrighteous, or gave any Allowance, or contributed any thing to Sin ʸ? By no means: For the Law on the contrary tied Men stricter up from

TEXT.

6 But now we are delivered from the law, that being dead wherein we were held; that we should serve in newness of spirit, and not in the oldness of the letter.

7 What shall we say then; is the law sin? God forbid. Nay, I had not known sin, but by the law: for I had not known

NOTES.

ᵘ Καρποφορησαι τῷ θανατῳ, *Bringing forth Fruit unto Death*, here is opposed to *bringing forth Fruit unto God*, in the End of the foregoing Verse. Death here being considered as a Master whom Men serve by Sin, as God in the other Place is considered as a Master, who gives Life to them who serve him in performing Obedience to his Law.

6 ʷ *In Newness of Spirit, i. e.* Spirit of the Law, as appears by the Antithesis, *Oldness of the Letter, i. e.* Letter of the Law. He speaks in the former Part of the Verse of the Law as being dead, here he speaks of its being revived again with a new Spirit. Christ by his Death abolished the Mosaical Law, but revived as much of it again, as was serviceable to the Use of his spiritual Kingdom under the Gospel, but left all the Ceremonial and purely Typical Part dead, *Col.* ii. 14——18. The Jews were held before Christ in an Obedience to the whole Letter of the Law, without minding the spiritual Meaning which pointed at Christ. This the Apostle calls here *serving in the Oldness of the Letter*, and this he tells them they should now leave, as being freed from it by the Death of Christ, who was the End of the Law for the attaining of Righteousness, *ch.* x. 4. *i. e.* in the spiritual Sense of it, which 2 *Cor.* iii. 6. he calls Spirit, which Spirit, *ver.* 17. he explains to be Christ. That Chapter and this Verse here give light to one another. *Serving in the Spirit* then is obeying the Law, as far as it is revived, and as it is explained by our Saviour in the Gospel, for the attaining of Evangelical Righteousness.

ˣ That this Sense also is comprehended in *not serving in the Oldness of the Letter*, is plain from what St. *Paul* says, 2 *Cor.* iii. 6. *The Letter killeth, but the Spirit giveth Life.* From this killing Letter of the Law, whereby it pronounced Death for every the least Transgression, they were also delivered, and therefore St. *Paul* tells them here, *ch.* viii. 15. that they *have not received the Spirit of Bondage again to fear, i. e.* to live in perpetual Bondage and Dread under the inflexible Rigor of the Law, under which it was impossible for them to expect aught but Death.

7 ʸ *Sin.* That *Sin* here comprehends both these Meanings expressed in the Paraphrase, appears from this Verse, where the Strictness of the Law against Sin is asserted in its prohibiting of Desires, and from *ver.* 12. where its Rectitude is asserted.

Sin,

ROMANS.

TEXT.

luſt, except the law had ſaid, Thou ſhalt not covet.

8 But ſin taking occaſion by the commandment, wrought in me all manner of concupiſcence. For without the law ſin was dead.

PARAPHRASE.

Sin, forbidding Concupiſcence, which they did not know to be Sin but by the Law. For I ᶻ had not known Concupiſcence to be Sin, unleſs the Law had ſaid, *Thou ſhalt not covet.* Nevertheleſs Sin taking Opportunity ᵃ during the Law ᵇ, or whilſt I was under the Commandment, wrought in me all manner of Concupiſcence: For without the Law Sin is dead, ᶜ not able to hurt me; and there was a Time

8.

NOTES.

ᶻ *I.* The Skill St. *Paul* uſes in dexterouſly avoiding as much as poſſible the giving Offence to the Jews, is very viſible in the Word *I* in this Place. In the Beginning of this Chapter, where he mentions their Knowledge in the Law, he ſays *Ye*. In the 4th Verſe he joins himſelf with them, and ſays *We*. But here, and ſo to the End of this Chapter, where he repreſents the Power of Sin, and the Inability of the Law to ſubdue it wholly, he leaves them out, and ſpeaks altogether in the firſt Perſon, though it be plain he means all thoſe who were under the Law.

8 ᵃ St. *Paul* here, and all along this Chapter, ſpeaks of Sin as a Perſon endeavouring to compaſs his Death; and the Senſe of this Verſe amounts to no more but this, that in matter of Fact that Concupiſcence which the Law declared to be Sin, remained and exerted itſelf in him, notwithſtanding the Law. For if Sin, from St. *Paul's* Proſopopeia, or making it a Perſon, ſhall be taken to be a real Agent, the carrying this Figure too far will give a very odd Senſe to St. *Paul's* Words, and, contrary to his Meaning, make Sin to be the Cauſe of itſelf, and of Concupiſcence, from which it has its Riſe.

ᵇ See Note, *ver.* 5.

ᶜ *Dead.* It is to be remembered, not only that St. *Paul* all along this Chapter makes Sin a Perſon, but ſpeaks of that Perſon and himſelf as two incompatible Enemies, the Being and Safety of the one conſiſting in the Death or Inability of the other to hurt. Without carrying this in mind, it will be very hard to underſtand this Chapter. For Inſtance; in this Place St. *Paul* has declared, *ver.* 7. that the Law was not aboliſhed, becauſe it at all favoured or promoted Sin; for it lays Reſtraints upon our very Deſires, which Men without the Law did not take notice to be ſinful: Nevertheleſs Sin perſiſting in its Deſign to deſtroy me, took the Opportunity of my being under the Law, to ſtir up Concupiſcence in me; for without the Law, which annexes Death to Tranſgreſſion, Sin is as good as dead, is not able to have its Will on me, and bring Death upon me. Conformable hereunto St. *Paul* ſays, 1 *Cor.* xv. 56. *The Strength of Sin is the Law*, i. e. it is the Law that gives Sin the Strength and Power to kill Men. Laying aſide the Figure which gives a lively Repreſentation of the State of a well-minded Jew under the Law, the plain Meaning of St. *Paul* here is this: "Though the Law " lays a ſtricter Reſtraint upon Sin than Men have without it, yet it betters not my Condition " thereby, becauſe it enables me not wholly to extirpate Sin, and ſubdue Concupiſcence, " though it hath made every Tranſgreſſion a mortal Crime. So that being no more totally ſe-" cured from offending under the Law than I was before, I am under the Law expoſed to " certain Death." This deplorable Eſtate could not be more feelingly expreſſed than it is here, by making Sin (which ſtill remained in Man under the Law) a Perſon who implacably aiming at his Ruin, cunningly took the Opportunity of exciting Concupiſcence in thoſe to whom the Law had made it mortal.

once

PARAPHRASE.

9. once ᵈ when I being without the Law, was in a State of Life; but the Commandment com-
10. ing, Sin got Life and Strength again, and I found myself a dead Man; and that very Law which was given me for the attaining of Life ᵉ, was found to produce Death ᶠ to
11. me. For my mortal Enemy Sin taking the Opportunity of my being under ᵍ the Law, slew me by the Law, which it inveigled ʰ me to disobey, *i. e.* The Frailty and vicious Inclinations of Nature remaining in me under the Law, as they were before, able still to bring

TEXT.

9 For I was alive without the law once: but when the commandment came, sin revived, and I died.
10 And the commandment which was ordained to life, I found to be unto death.
11 For sin taking occasion by the commandment, de-

NOTES.

9 ᵈ Ποτὲ, *once*. St. *Paul* declares there was a Time *once* when he was in a State of Life. When this was, he himself tells us, *viz.* when he was without the Law, which could only be before the Law was given. For he speaks here in the Person of one of the Children of *Israel*, who never ceased to be under the Law since it was given. This ποτὲ therefore must design the Time between the Covenant made with *Abraham* and the Law. By that Covenant *Abraham* was made *Blessed*, i. e. delivered from Death. That this is so, *vid. Gal.* iii. 9, &c. And under him the *Israelites* claimed the Blessing, as his Posterity, comprehended in that Covenant, and as many of them as were of the Faith of their Father, faithful *Abraham*, were blessed with him. But when the Law came, and they put themselves wholly into the Covenant of Works, wherein each Transgression of the Law became mortal, then Sin recovered Life again, and a Power to kill; and an *Israelite* now under the Law, found himself in a State of Death, a dead Man. Thus we see it corresponds with the Design of the Apostle's Discourse here. In the six first Verses of this Chapter he shews the *Jews* that they were at Liberty from the Law, and might put themselves solely under the Terms of the Gospel. In the following Part of this Chapter he shews them, that it is necessary for them so to do; since the Law was not able to deliver them from the Power Sin had to destroy them, but subjected them to it: This Part of the Chapter shewing at large what he says, *chap.* viii. 3. and so may be looked on as an Explication and Proof of it.

10 ᵉ That the Commandments of the Law were given to the *Israelites*, that they might have Life by them; see *Lev.* xviii. 5. *Matth.* xix. 17.

ᶠ The Law which was just, and such as it ought to be, in having the Penalty of Death annexed to every Transgression of it, *Gal.* iii. 10. came to produce Death, by not being able so to remove the Frailty of human Nature, and subdue carnal Appetites, as to keep Men entirely free from all Trespasses against it, the least whereof by the Law brought Death. See *chap.* viii. 3. *Gal.* iii. 21.

11 ᵍ The Sense wherein I understand διὰ τοῦ νόμου, *by the Law*, *ver.* 5. is very much confirmed by διὰ τῆς ἐντολῆς, in this and *ver.* 8. by which Interpretation the whole Discourse is made plain, easy, and consonant to the Apostle's Purpose.

ʰ *Inveigled.* St. *Paul* seems here to allude to what *Eve* said in a like Case, *Gen.* iii. 13. and uses the Word *deceived* in the same Sense she did, *i. e.* drew me in.

me

ROMANS. Ch. VII.

TEXT.	PARAPHRASE.

ceived me, and by it slew me.

12. Wherefore the law is holy; and the commandment holy, and just, and good.

13. Was then that which is good, made death unto me? God forbid. But sin that it might appear sin, working death in me by that which is good; that sin by the commandment might become exceeding sinful.

me into Transgressions, each whereof was mortal Sin, had by my being under the Law, a sure Opportunity of bringing Death upon me. So that ⁱ the Law is holy, just and good, such as the eternal, immutable Rule of Right and Good required it to be. Was then the Law, that in itself was good, made Death to me? No ᵏ, by no means: But it was Sin that by the Law was made Death unto me, to the end that the Power ˡ of Sin might appear, by its being able to bring Death upon me, by that very Law that was intended for my Good, that so by the Commandment the Power ᵐ of

12.

13.

NOTES.

12 ⁱ *Ὅτι, so that,* ver. 7. he laid down this Position, that *the Law was not Sin,* ver. 8, 9, 10, 11. he proves it by shewing, that the Law was very strict in forbidding of Sin, so far as to reach the very Mind and the internal Acts of Concupiscence, and that it was Sin, that remaining under the Law (which annexed Death to every Transgression) brought Death on the *Israelites,* he here infers, that the Law was not sinful, but *righteous, just, and good,* just such as by the eternal Rule of Right it ought to be.

13 ᵏ *No.* In the five foregoing Verses the Apostle had proved, that the Law was not Sin. In this and the ten following Verses he proves the Law not to be made Death; but that it was given to shew the Power of Sin which remained in those under the Law, so strong, notwithstanding the Law, that it could prevail on them to transgress the Law, notwithstanding all its Prohibition, with the Penalty of Death annexed to every Transgression. Of what Use this shewing the Power of Sin by the Law was, we may see, *Gal.* iii. 24.

ˡ That ἁμαρτία καθ' ὑπερβολὴν ἁμαρτωλὸς, *Sin exceeding sinful,* is put here to signify the great Power of Sin or Lust, is evident from the following Discourse, which wholly tends to shew that let a Man under the Law be right in his Mind and Purpose, yet the Law in his Members, *i. e.* his carnal Appetites, would carry him to the committing of Sin, though his Judgment and Endeavours were averse to it. He that remembers that Sin in this Chapter is all along represented as a Person whose very Nature it was to seek and endeavour his Ruin, will not find it hard to understand, that the Apostle here by *Sin exceedingly sinful,* means Sin strenuously exerting its sinful, *i. e.* destructive Nature with mighty Force.

ᵐ *Ἵνα γένηται, that Sin might become,* i. e. *might appear to be.* It is of Appearance he speaks in the former Part of this Verse, and so it must be understood here, to conform to the Sense of the Words, not only to what immediately precedes in this Verse, but to the Apostle's Design in this Chapter, where he takes pains to prove that the Law was not intended any way to promote Sin; and to understand by these Words that it was, is an Interpretation that neither Holy Scripture nor good Sense will allow. Though the sacred Scripture should not, as it does, give many Instances of putting *being* for *appearing.* Vid. *chap.* iii. 19.

Ch. VII.

PARAPHRASE.

14. Sin and Corruption in me might be shewn to be exceeding great; for we know that the Law is spiritual, requiring Actions quite opposite ⁿ to our carnal Affections. But I am so carnal as to be enslaved to them, and forced against my Will to do the Drudgery of Sin, as if I were a Slave that had been sold into the
15. Hands of that my domineering Enemy. For what I do is not of my own Contrivance °. For that which I have a Mind to, I do not; and what I have an Aversion to, that I
16. do. If then my transgressing the Law be what I in my Mind am against, it is plain the Consent of my Mind goes with the Law, that it is
17. good. If so, then it is not I a willing Agent of my own free Purpose that do what is contrary to the Law, but as a poor Slave in Captivity, not able to follow my own Understanding and Choice, forced by the Prevalency of my own sinful Affections, and Sin that remains still in
18. me, notwithstanding the Law. For I know by woful Experience, that in me *(viz.)* in my Flesh ᵖ, that part which is the Seat of car-

TEXT.

For we know that the law is spiritual: but I am carnal, sold under sin. 14

For that which I do, I allow not: for what I would, that do I not; but what I hate, that do I. 15

If then I do that which I would not, I consent unto the law, that it is good. 16

Now then, it is no more I that do it, but sin that dwelleth in me. 17

For I know that in me (that is, in my flesh) dwelleth no good thing: for 18

NOTES.

14 ⁿ Πνευματικὸς, *spiritual*, is used here to signify the Opposition of the Law to our carnal Appetites. The Antithesis in the following Words makes it clear.

15 ° Οὐ γινώσκω, *I do not know*, i. e. it is not from my own Understanding or Forecast of Mind. The following Words, which are a Reason brought to prove this Saying, give it this Sense. But if οὐ γινώσκω be interpreted, *I do not approve*, what in the next Words is brought for a Reason will be but a Tautology.

18 ᵖ St. *Paul* considers himself, and in himself other Men, as consisting of two Parts which he calls *Flesh* and *Mind*, see ver. 25. meaning by the one the Judgment and Purpose of his Mind, guided by the Law or right Reason; by the other his natural Inclination pushing him to the Satisfaction of his irregular sinful Desires. These he also calls, the one *the Law of his Members*, and the other *the Law of his Mind*, ver. 23. and *Gal*. v. 16, 17. a Place parallel to the ten last Verses of this Chapter, he calls the one *Flesh*, and the other *Spirit*. These two are the Subject of his Discourse in all this Part of the Chapter, explaining particularly how by the Power and Prevalency of the fleshly Inclinations, not abated by the Law, it come to pass, which he says, *ch*. viii. 2, 3. that *the Law being weak by reason of the Flesh could not set a Man free from the Power and Dominion of Sin and Death*.

nal

ROMANS.

TEXT.

to will is present with me, but how to perform that which is good, I find not.
19 For the good that I would, I do not: but the evil which I would not, that I do.
20 Now if I do that I would not, it is no more I that do it, but sin that dwelleth in me.
21 I find then a law, that when I would do good, evil is present with me.
22 For I delight in the law of God, after the inward man.
23 But I see another law in my members, warring against the law of my mind, and bringing me

PARAPHRASE.

nal Appetites, there inhabits no good. For in the Judgment and Purpose of my Mind, I am readily carried into a Conformity and Obedience to the Law: But the Strength of my carnal Affections not being abated by the Law, I am not able to execute what I judge to be right, and intend to perform. For the Good that is 19. my Purpose and Aim, that I do not: But the Evil that is contrary to my Intention, that in my Practice takes place, *i. e.* I purpose and aim at universal Obedience, but cannot in fact attain it. Now if I do that which is against the 20. full Bent and Intention of me ᵠ myself, it is as I said before, not I my true self who do it, but the true Author of it is my old Enemy Sin, which still remains and dwells in me, and I would fain get rid of. I find it therefore as by 21. a Law settled in me, that when my Intentions aim at Good, Evil is ready at hand, to make my Actions wrong and faulty. For that which 22. my inward Man is delighted with, that which with Satisfaction my Mind would make its Rule, is the Law of God. But I see in my 23. Members ʳ another Principle of Action equivalent to a Law ˢ directly waging War against

NOTES.

20 ᵠ Οὐ θέλω ἐγὼ, *I would not.* I in the Greek is very emphatical, as is obvious, and denotes the Man in that Part which is chiefly to be counted himself, and therefore with the like Emphasis, *ver.* 25. is called αὐτὸς ἐγὼ, *I my own self.*

23 ʳ St. *Paul* here, and in the former Chapter, uses the Word *Members* for the lower Faculties and Affections of the animal Man, which are as it were the Instruments of Actions.

ˢ He having in the foregoing Verse spoken of the Law of God as a Principal of Action, but yet such as had not a Power to rule and influence the whole Man so as to keep him quite clear from Sin, he here speaks of *natural Inclinations* as of a Law, also a *Law in the Members*, and a *Law of Sin in the Members*, to shew that it is a Principle of Operation in Men even under the Law, as steady and constant in its Direction and Impulse to Sin, as the Law is to Obedience, and failed not, through the Frailty of the Flesh, often to prevail.

PARAPHRASE.

24. that Law which my Mind would follow, leading me captive into an unwilling Subjection to the constant Inclination and Impulse of my carnal Appetite, which as steadily as if it were a Law, carries me to Sin. O miserable
25. Man that I am, who shall deliver me ' from this Body of Death? The Grace of God "

TEXT.

into captivity to the law of sin, which is in my members.

24 O wretched man that I am, who shall deliver me from the body of this death!

25 I thank God, through

NOTES.

24 ' What is it that St. *Paul* so pathetically desires to be delivered from? The State he had been describing was that of human Weakness, wherein notwithstanding the Law, even those who were under it, and sincerely endeavouring to obey it, were frequently carried by their carnal Appetites into the Breach of it. This State of Frailty he knew Men in this World could not be delivered from. And therefore, if we mind him, it is not that, but the Consequence of it, Death, or so much of it as brings Death, that he enquires after a Deliverer from. *Who shall deliver me*, says he, *from this Body?* He does not say of Frailty, but *of Death? What shall hinder that my carnal Appetites, that so often make me fall into Sin, shall not bring Death upon me, which is awarded me by the Law?* And to this he answers, *The Grace of God through our Lord Jesus Christ*. It is the Favour of God alone through Jesus Christ that delivers frail Man from Death. Those under Grace obtain Life upon sincere Intentions and Endeavours after Obedience, and those Endeavours a Man may attain to in this State of Frailty. But good Intention and sincere Endeavours are of no behoof against Death to those under the Law, which requires complete and punctual Obedience, but gives no Ability to attain it. And so it is Grace alone through Jesus Christ, that accepting of what a frail Man can do, delivers from the Body of Death. And thereupon he concludes with Joy, *So then I being now a Christian, not any longer under the Law, but under Grace, this is the State I am in, whereby I shall be delivered from Death, I with my whole Bent and Intention devote myself to the Law of God in sincere Endeavours after Obedience, though my carnal Appetites are enslaved to, and have their natural Propensity towards Sin.*

25 " Our Translators read εὐχαριςῶ τῷ Θεῷ, *I thank God:* The Author of the Vulgate, χάρις τῷ Θ.ᾶ, *The Grace* or *Favour of God*, which is the reading of the *Clermont* and other Greek Manuscripts. Nor can it be doubted which of these two Readings should be followed by one who considers, not only that the Apostle makes it his Business to shew that the Jews stood in need of Grace for Salvation, as much as the Gentiles: But also that *the Grace of God* is a direct and apposite Answer to *who shall deliver me?* which if we read it, *I thank God*, has no Answer at all; an Omission the like whereof I do not remember any where in St. *Paul*'s Way of Writing. This I am sure, it renders the Passage obscure and imperfect in itself; but much more disturbs the Sense, if we observe the Illative *therefore*, which begins the next Verse, and introduces a Conclusion easy and natural, if the Question, *who shall deliver me?* has for Answer, *The Grace of God*. Otherwise it will be hard to find Premises from whence it can be drawn. For thus stands the Argument plain and easy. The Law cannot deliver from the Body of Death, *i. e.* from those carnal Appetites which produce Sin, and so bring Death. But the Grace of God through Jesus Christ, which pardons Lapses, where there is sincere Endeavour after Righteousness, delivers us from this Body that it doth not destroy us. From whence naturally results this Conclusion, *There is therefore now no Condemnation*, &c. But what it is grounded on in the other Reading, I confess I do not see.

through

ROMANS.

Ch. VII.

TEXT.

Jesus Christ our Lord. So then with the mind I myself serve the law of God; but with the flesh the law of sin.

PARAPHRASE.

through Jesus Christ our Lord. To comfort myself therefore as that State requires for my Deliverance from Death, I myself [x] with full Purpose and sincere Endeavours of Mind, give up myself to obey the Law of God, though my carnal Inclinations are enslaved, and have a constant Tendency to Sin. This is all I [y] can do, and this is all, I being under Grace, that is required of me, and through Christ will be accepted.

NOTES.

[x] Αὐτὸς ἐγώ, *I myself*, i. e. I the Man, with all my full Resolution of Mind. Αὐτὸς and ἐγώ might have both of them been spared, if nothing more had been meant here than the Nominative Case to δυλεύω; see Note, ver. 20.

[y] Δηλεύω, *I serve*, or *I make myself a Vassal*, i. e. I intend and devote my whole Obedience. The Terms of Life to those under Grace St. *Paul* tells us at large, *chap.* vi. are δυλωθῆναι τῇ δικαιοσύνῃ, and τῷ Θεῷ, to become Vassals to Righteousness and to God; consonantly he says here, αὐτὸς ἐγώ, *I myself*, *I the Man*, being now a Christian, and so no longer under the Law, but under Grace, do what is required of me in that State; δυλεύω, I become a Vassal to the Law of God, *i. e.* dedicate myself to the Service of it, in sincere Endeavours of Obedience; and so αὐτὸς ἐγώ, *I the Man*, shall be delivered from Death: For he that, being under Grace, makes himself a Vassal to God in a steady Purpose of sincere Obedience, shall from him receive the Gift of eternal Life, though his carnal Appetite, which he cannot get rid of, having its Bent towards Sin, makes him sometimes transgress; which would be certain Death to him, if he were still under the Law. See *chap.* vi. 18, and 22.

And thus St. *Paul* having shewn here in this Chapter, that the being under Grace alone, without being under the Law, is necessary even to the *Jews*, as in the foregoing Chapter he had shewn it to be to the *Gentiles*, he hereby demonstratively confirms the *Gentile* Converts in their Freedom from the Law, which is the Scope of this Epistle thus far.

SECT. VII.

CHAP. VIII. 1———39.

CONTENTS.

ST. *Paul* having, *ch.* vi. shewn that the Gentiles who were not under the Law, were saved only by Grace, which required that they should not indulge themselves in Sin, but steadily and sincerely endeavour after perfect Obedience: Having also, *ch.* vii. shewn that the Jews, who were under the Law, were also saved by Grace only, because the Law could not enable them wholly to avoid Sin, which by the Law was in every the least Slip made Death; he in this Chapter shews, that both Jews and Gentiles who are under Grace, *i. e.* Converts to Christianity, are free from Condemnation, if they perform what is required of them; and thereupon he sets forth the Terms of the Covenant of Grace, and presses their Observance, *viz.* not to live after the Flesh, but after the Spirit mortifying the Deeds of the Body; forasmuch as those that do so are the Sons of God. This being laid down, he makes use of it to arm them with Patience against Afflictions, assuring them, that whilst they remain in this State nothing can separate them from the Love of God, nor shut them out from the Inheritance of eternal Life with Christ in Glory, to which all the Sufferings of this Life bear not any the least Proportion.

PARAPHRASE.	TEXT.
1. THERE is therefore ^z now ^a no Condemnation ^b to, *i. e.* no Sentence of Death	1 THERE is therefore now no condemna-

NOTES.

1 ^z *Therefore.* This is an Inference drawn from the last Verse of the foregoing Chapter, where he saith, that it is Grace that delivers from Death, as we have already observed.

^a *Now.* Now that under the Gospel the Law is abolished to those who entertain the Gospel.

^b The Condemnation here spoken of, refers to the Penalty of Death annexed to every Transgression by the Law, whereof he had discoursed in the foregoing Chapter.

[shall]

ROMANS.
Ch. VIII.

TEXT.	PARAPHRASE.

tion to them which are in Christ Jesus, who walk not after the flesh, but after the spirit.

2 For the law of the spirit of life in Christ Jesus, hath made me free from the law of sin and death.

3 For what the law could

shall pass upon those who are Christians [c], if so be they obey [d] not the sinful Lusts of the Flesh, but follow with Sincerity of Heart the Dictates of the [e] Spirit [f] in the Gospel. For the [g] Grace of God, which is effectual to 2. Life, has set me free from that Law in my Members which cannot now produce Sin in me unto Death [h]. For this *(viz.* the delivering 3. us from Sin) being beyond the Power of the

NOTES.

[c] *In Christ Jesus* expressed *chap.* vi. 14. by *under Grace*, and *Gal.* iii. 27. by *having put on Christ*, all which Expressions plainly signify, to any one that reads and considers the Places, the professing the Religion, and owning a Subjection to the Law of Christ contained in the Gospel; which is, in short, the Profession of Christianity.

[d] Περιπατᾶσι, *Walking*, or *who walk*, does not mean that all who are in Christ Jesus do walk not after the Flesh, but after the Spirit; but all who being in Christ Jesus, omit not to walk so. This, if the Tenor of St. *Paul*'s Discourse here can suffer any one to doubt of, he may be satisfied, is so from *ver.* 13. *If ye live after the Flesh.* The *ye* he there speaks to, are no less than those that, *chap.* i. 6, 7. he calls *the Called of Jesus Christ*, and *the Beloved of God*, Terms equivalent to *being in Jesus Christ*, see *chap.* vi. 12—14. *Gal.* v. 16—18. which Places compared together, shew that by Christ we are delivered from the Dominion of Sin and Lust; so that it shall not reign over us unto Death, if we will set ourselves against it, and sincerely endeavour to be free: A voluntary Slave who enthrals himself by a willing Obedience, who can set free?

[e] *Flesh* and *Spirit* seem here plainly to refer to *Flesh*, wherewith, he says, he serves Sin, and *Mind*, wherewith he serves the Law of God, in the immediately preceding Words.

[f] *Walking after the Spirit*, is, *ver.* 13. explained by *mortifying the Deeds of the Body through the Spirit*.

[g] That it is *Grace* that delivers from the Law in the Members, which is the Law of Death, is evident from *chap.* vii. 23—25. why it is called *a Law*, may be found in the Antithesis to *the Law of Sin and Death*, Grace being as certain a Law to give Life to *Christians* that live not after the Flesh, as the Influence of sinful Appetites is to bring Death on those who are not under Grace. In the next Place, why it is called the *Law of the Spirit of Life*, has a Reason, in that the Gospel which contains this Doctrine of Grace, is dictated by the same Spirit that raised Christ from the dead, and that quickens us to Newness of Life, and has for its End the conferring of eternal Life.

[h] *The Law of Sin and Death.* Hereby is meant that which he calls the Law in his Members, *chap.* vii. 23. where it is called the Law of Sin; and *ver.* 24. it is called the Body of Death, from which Grace delivers. This is certain, that no body who considers what St. *Paul* has said, *ver.* 7, & 13. of the foregoing Chapter, can think that he can call the Law of *Moses*, *the Law of Sin*, or *the Law of Death*. And that the Law of *Moses* is not meant, is plain from his Reasoning in the very next Words. For the Law of *Moses* could not be complained of as being weak, for not delivering those under it from its self; yet its Weakness might, and is all along, *chap.* vii. as well as *ver.* 3. complained of, as not being able to deliver those under it from their carnal sinful Appetites and the Prevalence of them.

Law,

ROMANS.
Ch. VIII.

PARAPHRASE.

Law, which was too weak ¹ to master the Propensities of the Flesh, God sending his Son in Flesh, that in all Things except Sin, was like unto our frail sinful Flesh ᵏ, and sending ˡ him also to be an Offering ᵐ for Sin, he put to Death, or extinguished or suppressed Sin ⁿ

TEXT.

not do, in that it was weak through the flesh, God sending his own Son in the likeness of sinful

NOTES.

³ ¹ *Weak*; *the Weakness*, and as he there also calls it, *the Unprofitableness* of the Law, is again taken notice of by the Apostle, *Heb.* vii. 18, 19. There were two Defects in the Law whereby it became unprofitable, as the Author to the *Hebrews* says, so as to *make nothing perfect*. The one was its inflexible Rigour, against which it provided no Allay or Mitigation; it left no place for Atonement; the least Slip was mortal; Death was the inevitable Punishment of Transgression by the Sentence of the Law, which had no Temperament: Death the Offender must suffer, there was no Remedy. This St. *Paul*'s Epistles are full of; and how we are delivered from it by the Body of Christ, he shews, *Heb.* x. 5–10. The other Weakness or Defect of the Law was, that it could not enable those who were under it, to get a Mastery over their Flesh, or fleshly Propensities, so as to perform the Obedience required. The Law exacted complete Obedience, but afforded Men no Help against their Frailty or vicious Inclinations. And this reigning of Sin in their mortal Bodies, St. *Paul* shews here how they are delivered from, by the Spirit of Christ enabling them, upon their sincere Endeavours after Righteousness, to keep Sin under in their mortal Bodies in Conformity to Christ in whose Flesh it was condemned, executed, and perfectly extinct, having never had there any Life or Being, as we shall see in the following Note. The Provision that is made in the New Covenant against both these Defects of the Law, is in the Epistle to the *Hebrews* expressed thus: God will make a new Covenant with the House of *Israel*, wherein he will do these two Things; *He will write his Law in their Hearts, and he will be merciful to their Iniquities*. See *Heb.* viii. 7–12.

ᵏ See *Heb.* iv. 15.

ˡ Καὶ, *and*, joins here *in the Likeness*, &c. with *to be an Offering*; whereas if *and* be made to copulate *sending* and *condemned*, neither Grammar nor Sense would permit it: Nor can it be imagined the Apostle should speak thus: *God sending his Son, and condemned Sin*: But *God sending his own Son in the Likeness of sinful Flesh*, and sending him *to be an Offering for Sin* with very good Sense joins the Manner and End of his sending.

ᵐ Περὶ ἁμαρτίας, which in the Text is translated *for Sin*, signifies *an Offering for Sin*, as the Margin of our Bibles takes notice: See 2 *Cor.* v. 21. *Heb.* x. 5–10. So that the plain Sense is, *God sent his Son in the Likeness of sinful Flesh, and sent him an Offering for Sin*.

ⁿ Κατέκρινε, *condemned*. The *Prosopopœia* whereby Sin was considered as a Person all the foregoing Chapter, being continued here, *the condemning of Sin* here cannot mean, as some would have it, that Christ was condemned for Sin, or in the Place of Sin; for that would be to save Sin, and leave that Person alive which Christ came to destroy. But the plain Meaning is, that Sin itself was condemned or put to death in his Flesh, *i. e.* was suffered to have no Life nor Being in the Flesh of our Saviour: He was in all Points tempted as we are, yet without Sin, *Heb.* iv. 15. By the Spirit of God the Motions of the Flesh were suppressed in him, Sin was crushed in the Egg, and could never fasten in the least upon him. This farther appears to be the Sense by the following Words. The *Antithesis* between κατάκριμα, ver. 1. und κατέκρινε here, will also shew why that Word is used here to express the Death or No being of Sin in our Saviour, 2 *Cor.* v. 2. 1 *Pet.* ii. 22. That St. *Paul* sometimes uses *Condemnation* for putting to death. See *chap.* v. 16, & 18.

ROMANS.

Ch. VIII.

TEXT.

flesh, and for sin condemned sin in the flesh:

4 That the righteousness of the law might be fulfilled in us, who walk not after the flesh, but after the spirit.

5 For they that are after the flesh, do mind the things of the flesh: but they that are after the spirit, the things of the spirit.

6 For to be carnally minded, is death; but to be

PARAPHRASE.

in the Flesh, *i. e.* sending his Son into the World with the Body wherein the Flesh could never prevail to the producing of any one Sin, to the end, That under this Example of Flesh wherein Sin was perfectly mastered and excluded from any Life, the moral Rectitude of the Law ° might be conformed to ᵖ by us, who abandoning the Lusts of the Flesh, follow the Guidance of the Spirit in the Law of our Minds, and make it our Business to live not after the Flesh, but after the Spirit. For as for those who ᵠ are still under the Direction of the Flesh and its sinful Appetites, who are under Obedience to the Law in their Members, they have the Thoughts and Bent of their Minds set upon the Things of the Flesh, to obey it in the Lusts of it: But they who are under the spiritual Law of their Minds, the Thoughts and Bent of their Hearts is to follow the Dictates of the Spirit in that Law. For ʳ to have our Minds set upon the Satisfaction of the Lusts of the Flesh, in a slavish Obedience to them, does certainly produce and

4.

5.

6.

NOTES.

4 ° Τὸ δικαίωμα τȣ νόμȣ, *The Righteousness of the Law*. See Note, *chap.* ii. 26.

ᵖ *Fulfilled* does not here signify a complete exact Obedience, but such an unblameable Life, by sincere Endeavours after Righteousness, as shews us to be the faithful Subjects of Christ, exempt from the Dominion of Sin, see *chap.* xiii. 8. *Gal.* vi. 2. A Description of such who thus fulfilled the Righteousness of the Law, we have *Luke* i. 6. As Christ in the Flesh was wholly exempt from all Taint of Sin, so we by that Spirit which was in him shall be exempt from the Dominion of our carnal Lusts, if we make it our Choice and Endeavour to live after the Spirit, *ver.* 9, 10, 11. For that which we are to perform by that Spirit, is the Mortification of the Deeds of the Body, *ver.* 13.

5 ᵠ Οἱ κατὰ σάρκα ὄντες, *Those that are after the Flesh*, and *those that are after the Spirit*, are the same with *those that walk after the Flesh*, and *after the Spirit*. A Description of these two different Sorts of Christians, see *Gal.* v. 16—26.

6 ʳ *For* joins what follows here to *ver.* 1. as the Reason of what is here laid down, (*viz.*) Deliverance from Condemnation is to such Christian Converts only, who walk not after the Flesh, but after the Spirit. For, *&c.*

O o

bring

PARAPHRASE.

bring Death upon us; but our setting ourselves seriously and sincerely to obey the Dictates and Direction of the Spirit, produces Life ˢ and Peace, which are not to be had in the
7. contrary carnal State, because to be carnally minded ᵗ is direct Enmity and Opposition against God; for such a Temper of Mind, given up to the Lusts of the Flesh, is in no Subjection to the Law of God, nor indeed can be ᵘ, it
8. having a quite contrary Tendency. So then ˣ they that are in the Flesh, *i. e* under the fleshly Dispensation of the Law ʸ; without regarding Christ the Spirit of it, in it cannot please

TEXT.

spiritually minded, is life and peace;

7 Because the carnal mind is enmity against God; for it is not subject to the law of God, neither indeed can be.

8 So then they that are in the flesh, cannot please God.

NOTES.

ˢ See *Gal.* vi. 8.

7 ᵗ Φρόνημα τῆς σαρκὸς, should have been translated here *to be carnally minded*, as it is in the foregoing Verse which is justified by Φρονοῦσι τὰ τῆς σαρκὸς, *do mind the Things of the Flesh*, ver. 5. which signifies the employing the Bent of their Minds, or subjecting the Mind entirely to the fulfilling the Lusts of the Flesh.

ᵘ Here the Apostle gives the Reason why even those that are in Christ Jesus, have received the Gospel, and are Christians (for to such he is here speaking) are not saved, unless they cease to walk after the Flesh, because that runs directly counter to the Law of God, and can never be brought into Conformity and Subjection to his Commands. Such a settled Contravention to his Precepts cannot be suffered by the supreme Lord and Governor of the World in any of his Creatures, without foregoing his Sovereignty, and giving up the eternal immutable Rule of Right, to the overturning the very Foundations of all Order and moral Rectitude in the intellectual World. This even in the Judgment of Men themselves will be always thought a necessary Piece of Justice for the keeping out of Anarchy, Disorder and Confusion, that those refractory Subjects who set up their own Inclinations for their Rule against the Law, which was made to restrain those very Inclinations, should feel the Severity of the Law, without which the Authority of the Law, and Law-maker, cannot be preserved.

8 ˣ This is a Conclusion drawn from what went before. The whole Argumentation stands thus: They that are under the Dominion of their carnal Lusts cannot please God; therefore they who are under the carnal or literal Dispensation of the Law, cannot please God, because they have not the Spirit of God: Now it is the Spirit of God alone that enlivens Men so as to enable them to cast off the Dominion of their Lusts. See *Gal.* iv. 3——6.

ʸ Οἱ ἐν σαρκὶ ὄντες, *They that are in the Flesh.* He that shall consider that this Phrase is applied, *ib.* vii. 5. to the Jews, as resting in the bare literal or carnal Sense and Observance of the Law, will not be averse to the understanding the same Phrase in the same Sense here, which I think is the only Place besides in the New Testament, where ἐν σαρκὶ εἶναι is used in a moral Sense. This I dare say, it is hard to produce any one Text wherein εἶναι ἐν σαρκὶ is used to signify a Man's being under the Power of his Lusts, which is the Sense wherein

ROMANS. Ch. VIII.

TEXT.

9 But ye are not in the flesh, but in the spirit, if so be that the spirit of God dwell in you. Now if any man have not the spirit of Christ, he is none of his.
10 And if Christ be in you, the body is dead, because of sin; but the spirit is life, because of righteousness.
11 But if the spirit of him that raised up Jesus from the dead dwell in you; he that raised up Christ from the dead, shall also quicken your mortal bo-

PARAPHRASE.

please God. But ye are not in that State of 9. having all your Expectation from the Law, and the Benefits that are to be obtained barely by that, but are in the spiritual State of the Law, *i. e.* the ª Gospel, which is the End of the Law, and to which the Law leads you. And so having received the Gospel, you have therewith received the Spirit of God: For as many as receive Christ, he gives Power to become the ª Sons of God: And to those that are his Sons God gives his Spirit ᵇ. And if Christ 10. be in you by his Spirit, the Body is dead as to all Activity to Sin ᶜ, Sin no longer reigns in you, but your sinful carnal Lusts are mortified. But the Spirit ᵈ of your Mind liveth, *i. e.* is enlivened in order to Righteousness, or living righteously. But if the Spirit of God, who 11. had Power able to raise Jesus Christ from the dead, dwell in you, as certainly it does, he that raised Christ from the Dead, is certainly able, and will, by his Spirit, that dwells in you, enliven even ᵉ your mortal Bodies,

NOTES.

wherein it is and must be taken here, if what I propose be rejected. Let it be also remembered, that St. *Paul* makes it the chief Business of this Epistle (and he seldom forgets the Design he is upon) to persuade both Jew and Gentile from a Subjection to the Law, and that the Argument he is upon here, is the Weakness and Insufficiency of the Law to deliver Men from the Power of Sin; and then perhaps it will not be judged that the Interpretation I have given of these Words is altogether remote from the Apostle's Sense.

9 ˠ See 2 *Cor.* iii. 6 —— 18. particularly *ver.* 6, 13, 16.
ª See *John* i. 12.
ᵇ See *Gal.* iv. 6.
10 ᶜ See *chap.* vi. 1 —— 14. which explains this Place, particularly *ver.* 2, 6, 11, 12. *Gal.* ii. 20. *Eph.* iv. 22, 23. *Col.* ii. 11. and iii. 8 —— 10.
ᵈ See *Eph.* iv. 23.
11 ᵉ To lead us into the true Sense of this Verse, we need only observe, that St. *Paul* having in the four first Chapters of this Epistle shewn, that neither Jew nor Gentile could be justified by the Law; and in the fifth Chapter, how Sin entered into the World by *Adam*, and reigned by Death, from which it was Grace, and not the Law, that delivered Men: In the

sixth

NOTES.

sixth Chapter he sheweth the Convert Gentiles, that though they were not under the Law, but under Grace, yet they could not be saved, unless they cast off the Dominion of Sin, and became the devoted Servants of Righteousness, which was what their very Baptism taught and required of them: And in *chap.* vii. he declares to the Jews the Weakness of the Law, which they so much stood upon; and shews that the Law could not deliver them from the Dominion of Sin; that Deliverance was only by the Grace of God, through Jesus Christ: From whence he draws the Consequence which begins this eighth Chapter, and so goes on with it here in two Branches, relating to his Discourse in the foregoing Chapter, that complete it in this. The one is to shew, that the Law of the Spirit of Life, *i. e.* the new Covenant in the Gospel, required that those that are in Christ Jesus should not live after the Flesh, but after the Spirit. The other is to shew how, and by whom, since the Law was weak, and could not enable those under the Law to do it, they are enabled to keep Sin from reigning in their mortal Bodies, which is the Sanctification required. And here he shews, that Christians are delivered from the Dominion of their carnal sinful Lusts, by the Spirit of God, that is given to them and dwells in them, as a new quickening Principle and Power, by which they are put into the State of a spiritual Life, wherein their Members are made capable of being made the Instruments of Righteousness, if they please, as living Men alive now to Righteousness, so to employ them. If this be not the Sense of this Chapter to *ver.* 14. I desire to know how ἄρα οὖν in the first Verse comes in, and what Coherence there is in what is here said. Besides the Connexion of this to the former Chapter contained in the illative *Therefore*, the very Antithesis of the Expressions in one and the other, shews that St. Paul, in writing this very Verse, had an Eye to the foregoing Chapter. There it was *Sin that dwelleth in me*, that was the active and over-ruling Principle: Here it is, *the Spirit of God that dwelleth in you*, that is the Principle of your spiritual Life. There it was, *who shall deliver me from this Body of Death?* Here it is, *God by his Spirit shall quicken your mortal Bodies, i. e.* Bodies, which as the Seat and Harbour of sinful Lusts that possess it, are indisposed and dead to the Actions of a spiritual Life, and have a natural Tendency to Death. In the same Sense, and upon the same Account, he calls the Bodies of the Gentiles their *mortal Bodies*, chap. vi. 12. where his Subject is as here, Freedom from the Reign of Sin, upon which account they are there stiled, *ver.* 13. *Alive from the Dead.* To make it yet clearer, that it is Deliverance from the Reign of Sin in our Bodies that St. Paul speaks of here, I desire any one to read what he says, *chap.* vi. 1 —— 14. to the Gentiles on the same Subject, and compare it with the thirteen first Verses of this Chapter; and then tell me whether they have not a mutual Correspondence, and do not give a great Light to one another? If this be too much Pains, let him at least read the two next Verses, and see how they could possibly be, as they are, an Inference from this 11th Verse, if the *quickening of your mortal Bodies* in it mean any thing but a quickening to Newness of Life, or to a spiritual Life of Righteousness. This being so, I cannot but wonder to see a late learned Commentator and Paraphrast positive, that ζωοποιήσει τὰ θνητὰ σώματα ὑμῶν, *shall quicken your mortal Bodies*, does here signify, *shall raise your dead Bodies out of the Grave*, as he contends in his Preface to his Paraphrase on the Epistles to the *Corinthians*; ζωοποιεῖν, *quicken*, he says, imports the same with ἐγείρειν, *raise*. His Way of proving it is very remarkable; his Words are, ζωοποιεῖν and ἐγείρειν, are, *as to this Matter* [*viz.* the Resurrection] *Words of the same Import, i. e.* where in discoursing of the Resurrection, ζωοποιεῖν, *quicken*, is used, it is of the same Import with ἐγείρειν, *raise*. But what if St. *Paul*, which is the Question, be not here speaking of the Resurrection? why then, according to our Author's own Confession, ζωοποιεῖν, *quicken*, does not necessarily import the same with ἐγείρειν, *raise*. So that this Argument to prove that St. *Paul* here, by the Words in question, means the raising of their dead Bodies out of the Grave, is but a fair begging of the Question: which is enough, I think, for a Commentator that hunts out of his Way for Controversy. He might therefore have spared the ζωοποιεῖν, *quicken*, which he produces out of St. *John* v. 21. as of no Force to his Purpose, till he had proved that St. *Paul* here in *Romans* viii. 11. was speaking of the Resurrection of Men's Bodies out of the Grave, which he will never do till

he

ROMANS.

Ch. VIII.

TEXT.
dies, by his Spirit that dwelleth in you.

PARAPHRASE.
dies ᶠ, (that Sin shall not have the sole Power and Rule there) but your Members may be made

NOTES.

he can prove that θνητα, *mortal*, here signifies the same with νεκρα, *dead*. And I demand of him to shew θνητον, *mortal*, any where in the New Testament attributed to any thing void of Life. Ουκ εν, *mortal*, always signifies the Thing it is joined to, to be living; so that ζωοποιησει κ. τα θνητα σωματα ὑμων, *shall quicken even your mortal Bodies*, in that learned Author's Interpretation of these Words of St. *Paul*, here signify, *God shall raise to Life your living dead Bodies*; which no one can think, in the softest Terms can be given to it, a very proper Way of Speaking; though it be very good Sense and very emphatical to say, *God shall by his Spirit put into even your mortal Bodies a Principle of Immortality*, or *spiritual Life*, which is the Sense of the Apostle here; see *Gal.* vi. 8. And so he may find ζωοποιησαι used, *Gal.* iii. 21. to the same Purpose it is here. I next desire to know of this learned Writer, how he will bring in the Resurrection of the Dead into this Place, and to shew what Coherence it has with St. *Paul*'s Discourse here, and how he can join this Verse with the immediately preceding and following, when the Words under Consideration are rendered, *Shall raise your dead Bodies out of their Graves at the last Day?* It seems as if he himself found this would make but an awkward Sense standing in this Place with the rest of St. *Paul*'s Words here, and so never attempted it by any sort of Paraphrase, but has barely given us the English Translation to help us, as it can, to so uncouth a Meaning as he would put upon this Passage; which must make St. *Paul*, in the midst of a very serious, strong and coherent Discourse, concerning walking not after the Flesh, but after the Spirit, skip on a sudden into the Mention of the Resurrection of the Dead; and having just mentioned it, skip back again into his former Argument. But I take the Liberty to assure him, that St. *Paul* has no such Starts from the Matter he has in Hand, to what gives no Light or Strength to his present Argument. I think there is not any where to be found a more pertinent close Arguer, who has his Eye always on the Mark he drives at. This Men would find, if they would study him as they ought, with more Regard to Divine Authority than to Hypotheses of their own, or to Opinions of the Season. I do not say that he is every way clear in his Expressions to us now: But I do say he is every way a coherent, pertinent Writer: and wherever in his Commentators and Interpreters any Sense is given to his Words, that disjoints his Discourse, or deviates from his Argument, and looks like a wandering Thought, it is easy to know whose it is, and whose the Impertinence, his, or theirs that father it on him. One Thing more the Text suggests concerning this Matter, and that is, If by *quickening your mortal Bodies*, &c. be meant here the raising them into Life after Death, how can this be mentioned as a peculiar Favour to those who have the Spirit of God? For God shall also raise the Bodies of the Wicked, and as certainly as those of Believers. But that which is promised here, is promised to those only who have the Spirit of God: And therefore it must be something peculiar to them, (*viz.*) that God shall so enliven their mortal Bodies by his Spirit, which is the Principal and Pledge of immortal Life, that they may be able to yield up themselves to God, as those that are alive from the Dead, and their Members Servants to Righteousness unto Holiness, as he expresses himself, *chap.* vi. 13, and 19. If any one can yet doubt whether this be the Meaning of St. *Paul* here, I refer him for farther Satisfaction to St. *Paul* himself in *Eph.* iv. 4—6. where he will find the same Notion of St. *Paul* expressed in the same Terms, but so, that it is impossible to understand by ζωοποιειν or εγειρειν (which are both used there as well as here) the Resurrection of the Dead out of their Graves. The full Explication of this Verse may be seen, *Eph.* i. 19. and ii. 10. See also *Col.* ii. 12, 13. to the same Purpose; and *Rom.* vii 4.

ᶠ ζωοποιησει κ. *shall quicken even your mortal Bodies*, seems more agreable to the Original, than *shall also quicken your mortal Bodies*; for the κ. doth not copulate ζωοποιησει with ὁ εγειρας ;

PARAPHRASE.

made living Instruments of Righteousness.
12. Therefore Brethren, we are not under any Obligation to the Flesh to obey the Lusts of it.
13. For if ye live after the Flesh, that mortal Part shall lead you to Death irrecoverable; but if by the Spirit, whereby Christ totally suppressed and hindered Sin from having any Life in his Flesh, you mortify the Deeds of the Body g,
14. ye shall have Eternal Life. For as many as are led by the Spirit of God, they are the Sons of God, of an immortal Race, and consequently like their Father immortal h.
15. For ye have not received the Spirit of Bondage i again, k to fear; but ye have received the l Spirit of God (which is given to those who having received Adoption are Sons) whereby we are
16. all enabled to call God our Father m. The Spirit of God himself beareth witness n with our Spirits, that we are the Children of God.
17. And if Children, then Heirs of God, Joint-Heirs with Christ, if so be we suffer o with him, that we may also be glorified with him.

TEXT.

12 Therefore brethren, we are debtors not to the flesh to live after the flesh.
13 For if ye live after the flesh, ye shall die: but if ye through the spirit do mortify the deeds of the body, ye shall live.
14 For as many as are led by the spirit of God, they are the sons of God.
15 For ye have not received the spirit of bondage again to fear; but ye have received the spirit of adoption, whereby we cry, Abba, Father.
16 The spirit itself beareth witness with our spirit, that we are the children of God.
17 And if children, then heirs; heirs of God, and joint-heirs with Christ: if so be that we suffer with him, that we may be also glorified together.

NOTES.

i ἴνα: for then it must have been ἐὰν ζωοποιήσει; for the Place of the Copulative is between the two Words that it joins, and so must necessarily go before the latter of them.

13 g *Deeds of the Body:* what they are may be seen, *Gal.* v. 19, &c. as we have already remarked.

14 h In that lies the Force of his Proof, that they shall live. The Sons of mortal Men are mortal; the Sons of God are like their Father, Partakers of the Divine Nature, and are immortal. See 2 *Pet.* i. 4. *Heb.* ii. 13—15.

15 i *What the Spirit of Bondage is,* the Apostle hath plainly declared, *Heb.* ii. 15. See Note, ver. 21.

k *Again,* i. e. Now again under Christ, as the Jews did from *Moses* under the Law.

l See *Gal.* iv. 5, 6.

m *Abba, Father.* The Apostle here expresses this filial Assurance in the same Words that our Saviour applies himself to God, *Mark* xiv. 36.

16 n See the same Thing taught, 2 *Cor.* i. 21, 22. and v. 5. *Eph.* i. 11——14. and *Gal.* iv. 6.

17 o The full Sense of this you may take in St. *Paul's* own Words, 2 *Tim.* ii. 11, 12.

For

TEXT.	PARAPHRASE.	
18 For I reckon, that the sufferings of this present time, are not worthy to be compared with the glory which shall be revealed in us.	For I count that the Sufferings of this transitory Life, bear no Proportion to that glorious State that shall be hereafter ᵖ revealed and set before the Eyes of the whole World at our Admittance into it. For the whole Race of ᵠ Mankind, in an earnest Expectation of this unconceivable glorious ʳ Immortality that shall be bestowed on the ˢ Sons of God, (For Mankind created in a better State, was made subject to the ᵗ Vanity of this calamitous fleeting Life, not of its own Choice, but by the Guile of the Devil ᵘ, who brought Mankind into this mortal State) Waiteth in Hope ˣ, that even they also shall be delivered from	18.
19 For the earnest expectation of the creation waiteth for the manifestation of the sons of God.		19.
20 For the creature was made subject to vanity, not willingly, but by reason of him who hath subjected the same in hope:		20.
21 Because the creature itself also shall be delivered from the bondage of cor-		21.

NOTES.

18 ᵖ *Revealed.* St. *Paul* speaks of this Glory here, as what needs to be revealed to give us a right Conception of it. It is impossible to have a clear and full Comprehension of it till we taste it. See how he labours for Words to express it, 2 *Cor.* iv. 17. &c. a Place to the same Purpose with this here.

19 ᵠ Κτίσις, *Creature,* in the Language of St. *Paul,* and of the New Testament, signifies Mankind; especially the Gentile World, as the far greater Part of the Creation. See *Col.* i. 23. *Mark* xvi. 15. compared with *Matth.* xxviii. 19.

ʳ *Immortality.* That the Thing here expected was immortal Life, is plain from the Context, and from that parallel Place, 2 *Cor.* iv. 17. and v. 5. the Glory whereof was so great, that it could not be comprehended, till it was by an actual exhibiting of it revealed. When this Revelation is to be, St. *Peter* tells us, 1 *Pet.* i. 4—7.

ˢ Ἀποκάλυψιν τῶν υἱῶν, *Revelation of the Sons,* i. e. *Revelation to the Sons.* The Genitive Case often in the New Testament denotes the Object. So *Rom.* i. 5. ὑπακοὴν πίστεως signifies Obedience to Faith: *Chap.* iii. 22. δικαιοσύνη Θεοῦ διὰ πίστεως Χριστοῦ, *The Righteousness that God accepts by Faith in Christ:* *Chap.* iv. 11. δικαιοσύνη πίστεως, *Righteousness by Faith.* If ἀποκάλυψις here be rendered *Revelation,* as ἀποκαλύπτεται in the foregoing Verse is rendered *revealed,* (and it will be hard to find a Reason why it should not) the Sense in the Paraphrase will be very natural and easy. For the Revelation in the foregoing Verse is not *of,* but *to* the Sons of God. The Words are ἀποκαλυφθῆναι εἰς ἡμᾶς.

20 ᵗ The State of Man in this frail short Life, subject to Inconveniencies, Sufferings, and Death, may very well be called *Vanity,* compared to the impassible Estate of eternal Life, the Inheritance of the Sons of God.

ᵘ *Devil.* That by *he that subjected it,* is meant the Devil, is probable from the History, *Gen.* iii. and from *Heb.* ii. 14, 15. *Col.* ii. 15.

21 ˣ Ἀπεκδέχεται ἐπ' ἐλπίδι ὅτι, *Waiteth in hope;* that the not joining *in hope* to *waiteth,* by placing it in the Beginning of the 21st Verse, as it stands in the Greek, but joining it to *subjected the same,* by placing it at the End of the 20th Verse, has mightily obscured the Meaning of this Passage; which taking all the Words between *of God* and *in Hope* for a Parenthesis, is as easy and clear as any thing can be, and then the next Word ὅτι, will have its proper Signification *that,* and not *because.*

this

Ch. VIII.

PARAPHRASE.

this Subjection to Corruption ʸ, and shall be brought into that glorious Freedom from Death, which is the proper Inheritance of the Children of God. For we know that Mankind, all ᶻ of them, groan together, and unto this Day are in pain, as a Woman in Labour, to be delivered out of the Uneasiness of this mortal State. And not only they, but even those who have the first Fruits of the Spirit, and therein the Earnest ᵃ of eternal Life, we ourselves groan ᵇ within ourselves, waiting for the Fruit of our Adoption, which is, that as we are by Adoption made Sons, and Co-heirs with Jesus Christ, so we may have Bodies like unto his most glorious Body, spiritual and immortal. But we must wait with Patience, for we have hitherto been saved but in Hope and Expectation: But Hope is of Things not in present Possession or Enjoyment. For what a Man hath, and seeth in his own Hands, he no longer hopes for. But if we hope for what is out of sight, and yet to come, then do we with Patience wait for it ᶜ. Such therefore are our Groans, which the Spirit in aid to our

TEXT.

ruption, into the glorious liberty of the children of God.

For we know that the 22 whole creation groaneth and travaileth in pain together until now:

And not only they, but 23 ourselves also, which have the first fruits of the spirit, even we ourselves groan within ourselves, waiting for the adoption, to wit, the redemption of our body.

For we are saved by 24 hope: but hope that is seen, is not hope: for what a man seeth, why doth he yet hope for?

But if we hope for that 25 we see not, then do we with patience wait for it.

Likewise the spirit al- 26 so helpeth our infirmities: for we know not what

NOTES.

ʸ Δουλεία τῆς Φθορᾶς, *Bondage of Corruption*, i. e. the Fear of Death; see *ver.* 15. and *Heb.* ii. 15. *Corruption* signifies Death or Destruction, in opposition to Life everlasting. See *Gal.* vi. 8.

22 ᶻ How *David* groaned under the Vanity and Shortness of this Life, may be seen, *Psa.* lxxxix. 47, 48. which Complaint may be met with in every Man's Mouth; so that even those who have not the first Fruits of the Spirit, whereby they are assured of a future happy Life in Glory, do also desire to be freed from a Subjection to Corruption, and have uneasy Longings after Immortality.

23 ᵃ See 2 *Cor.* v. 2, 5. *Eph.* i. 13, 14.

ᵇ Read the parallel Place, 2 *Cor.* iv. 17. and v. 5.

25 ᶜ What he says here of Hope, is to shew them, that the Groaning in the Children of God before spoken of, was not the Groaning of Impatience, but such wherewith the Spirit of God makes Intercession for us, better than if we expressed ourselves in Words, *ver.* 19—23.

Infirmity

ROMANS   293
Ch. VIII.

TEXT.   PARAPHRASE.

we should pray for as we ought: but the spirit itself maketh intercession for us with groanings which cannot be uttered.

27 And he that searcheth the hearts, knoweth what is the mind of the spirit, because he maketh intercession for the saints, according to the will of God.

28 And we know that all things work together for good to them that love God, to them who are the called according to his purpose.

29 For whom he did foreknow, he also did predestinate to be conformed to the image of his Son, that he might be the first-born among many brethren.

30 Moreover, whom he did predestinate, them he also called: and whom he called, them he also justified; and whom he justified, them he also glorified.

Infirmity makes use of. For we know not what Prayers to make as we ought, but the Spirit itself layeth for us our Requests before God in Groans that cannot be expressed in Words. And God the Searcher of Hearts, 27. who understandeth this Language of the Spirit, knoweth what the Spirit would have, because the Spirit is wont to make Intercession for the Saints ᵈ acceptably to God. Bear 28. therefore your Sufferings with Patience and Constancy, for we certainly know, that all Things work together for Good to those that love God, who are the Called according to his Purpose of calling the Gentiles ᵉ. In which 29. Purpose the Gentiles, whom he fore-knew as he did the Jews ᶠ, with an Intention of Kindness, and of making them his People, he pre-ordained to be conformable to the Image of his Son, that he might be the First-born, the Chief amongst many Brethren ᵍ. Moreover, 30. whom he did thus pre-ordain to be his People, them he also called, by sending Preachers of the Gospel to them: And whom he called, if they obeyed the Truth ʰ, those he also justified, by counting their Faith for Righteous-

NOTES.

27 ᵈ The Spirit promised in the Time of the Gospel, is called the Spirit of Supplications, *Zach.* xii. 10.

28 ᵉ Which Purpose was declared to *Abraham*, *Gen.* xviii. 18. and is largely insisted on by St. *Paul*, *Eph.* iii. 1——11. This, and the Remainder of this Chapter, seems said to confirm the Gentile Converts in the Assurance of the Favour and Love of God to them through Christ, though they were not under the Law.

29 ᶠ See *chap.* xi. 2. *Amos* iii. 2.

ᵍ See *Eph.* i. 3——7.

30 ʰ *Many are called, and few are chosen*, says our Saviour, *Matth.* xx. 16. Many, both Jews and Gentiles, were called, that did not obey the Call. And therefore, *ver.* 32. it is those who are chosen, who he saith are justified, *i. e.* such as were called, and obeyed, and consequently were chosen.

P p   ness:

PARAPHRASE.

ness: And whom he justified, them he also
31. glorified, *viz.* in his Purpose. What shall we
say then to these Things? If God be for us, as
by what he has already done for us it appears
32. he is, who can be against us? He that spared
not his own Son, but delivered him up to
Death for us all, Gentiles as well as Jews, how
shall he not with him also give us all Things?
33. Who shall be the Prosecutor of those whom
God hath chosen? Shall God who justifieth
34. them¹? Who as Judge shall condemn them?
Christ that died for us, yea rather that is risen
again for our Justification, and is at the Right
Hand of God, making Intercession for us?
35. Who shall separate us from the Love of Christ?
Shall Tribulation, or Distress, or Persecution,
or Famine, or Nakedness, or Peril, or Sword?
36. For this is our Lot, as it is written, *For thy sake
we are killed all the Day long, we are accounted as
37. Sheep for the Slaughter.* Nay in all these Things
we are already more than Conquerors by the
Grace and Assistance of him that loved us.
38. For I am steadfastly persuaded, that neither
the Terrors of Death, nor the Allurements of
Life, nor Angels, nor the Princes and Powers
of this World; nor Things present; nor any

TEXT.

What shall we then say 31
to these things? If God
be for us, who can be a-
gainst us?
He that spared not his 32
own Son, but delivered
him up for us all, how
shall he not with him also
freely give us all things?
Who shall lay any thing 33
to the charge of God's
elect? It is God that justifieth:
Who is he that con- 34
demneth? It is Christ that
died, yea rather that is risen again, who is even at
the right hand of God,
who also maketh interces-
sion for us.
Who shall separate us 35
from the love of Christ?
Shall tribulation, or distress, or persecution, or
famine, or nakedness, or
peril, or sword?
(As it is written, For 36
thy sake we are killed all
the day long; we are ac-
counted as sheep for the
slaughter)
Nay, in all these things 37
we are more than conque-
rors, through him that
loved us.
For I am persuaded, 38
that neither death, nor life,
nor angels, nor principa-
lities, nor powers, nor
things present, nor things
to come,

NOTES.

33 Reading this with an Interrogation, makes it needless to add any Words to the Text to make out the Sense, and is more conformable to the Scheme of his Argumentation here, as appears by *ver.* 35. where the Interrogation cannot be avoided; and is as it were an Appeal to them themselves to be Judges, whether any of those Things he mentions to them (reckoning up those which had most Power to hurt them) could give them just Cause of Apprehension, *Who shall accuse you? Shall God who justifies you? Who shall condemn you? Christ that died for you?* What can be more absurd than such an Imagination?

thing

TEXT.

39 Nor height, nor depth, nor any other creature, shall be able to separate us from the love of God which is in Christ Jesus our Lord.

PARAPHRASE.

thing future; Nor the Height of Prosperity; nor the Depth of Misery; nor any thing else whatsoever shall be able to separate us from the Love of God which is in Christ Jesus our Lord.

39.

SECT. VIII.

CHAP. IX. 1.——X. 21.

CONTENTS.

THERE was nothing more grating and offensive to the Jews, than the Thoughts of having the Gentiles joined with them, and partake equally in the Privileges and Advantages of the Kingdom of the Messiah: And which was yet worse, to be told that those Aliens should be admitted, and they who presumed themselves Children of that Kingdom to be shut out. St. *Paul* who had insisted much on this Doctrine, in all the foregoing Chapters of this Epistle, to shew that he had not done it out of any Aversion or Unkindness to his Nation and Brethren the Jews, does here express his great Affection to them, and declares an extreme Concern for their Salvation. But withal he shews, that whatever Privileges they had received from God above other Nations, whatever Expectation the Promises made to their Forefathers might raise in them, they had yet no just Reason of complaining of God's dealing with them now under the Gospel, since it was according to his Promise to *Abraham*, and his frequent Declarations in Sacred Scripture. Nor was it any Injustice to the Jewish Nation, if God now acted by the same Sovereign Power wherewith he preferred *Jacob* (the younger Brother, without any Merit of his) and his Posterity to be his People, before *Esau* and his Posterity, whom he rejected. The Earth is all his; nor have the Nations that possess it any Title of their own, but what he gives them, to the Countries they inhabit, nor to the good Things they enjoy, and he may dispossess or exter-

Chap. IX. exterminate them when he pleaseth. And as he destroyed the Ægyptians for the Glory of his Name, in the Deliverance of the Israelites, so he may according to his good Pleasure raise or depress, take into Favour or reject the several Nations of this World. And particularly as to the Nation of the Jews, all but a small Remnant were rejected, and the Gentiles taken in, in their room, to be the People and Church of God, because they were a gainsaying and disobedient People, that would not receive the Messiah, whom he had promised, and in the appointed Time sent to them. He that will with moderate Attention and Indifferency of Mind read this Ninth Chapter, will see that what is said of God's exercising of an absolute Power, according to the good Pleasure of his Will, relates only to Nations or Bodies Politick of Men incorporated in civil Societies, which feel the Effects of it only in the Prosperity or Calamity they meet with in this World, but extends not to their eternal State in another World, considered as particular Persons, wherein they stand each Man by himself upon his own Bottom, and shall so answer separately at the Day of Judgment. They may be punished here with their Fellow-Citizens, as Part of a sinful Nation, and that be but temporal Chastisement for their Good, and yet be advanced to eternal Life and Bliss in the World to come.

PARAPHRASE.

TEXT.

1. AS a Christian speak Truth, and my Conscience, guided and enlightened by the Holy Ghost, bears me witness, That I lie not in
2. my Profession of great Heaviness and continual Sorrow of Heart. I could even wish that ᵏ the
3. Destruction and Extermination to which my Brethren the Jews are devoted by Christ might, if it could save them from Ruin, be executed on me in the stead of those my Kins-

1. I Say the truth in Christ, I lie not, my conscience also bearing me witness in the Holy Ghost,
2. That I have great heaviness and continual sorrow in my heart.
3. For I could wish that myself were accursed from Christ for my brethren, my kinsmen, according to the flesh:

NOTES.

3 ᵏ 'Ανάθεμα, *accursed*, חרם, which the Septuagint render *Anathema*, signifies Persons or Things devoted to Destruction and Extermination. The Jewish Nation were now an *Anathema*, destined to Destruction. St. *Paul* to express his Affection to them, says, he could wish to save them from it, to become an *Anathema*, and be destroyed himself.

men

ROMANS.

Chap IX.

TEXT.

4 Who are Israelites; to whom pertaineth the adoption, and the glory, and the covenants, and the giving of the law, and the service of God, and the promises;

5 Whose are the fathers, and of whom as concerning the flesh, Christ came, who is over all, God blessed for ever. Amen.

6 Not as though the word of God had taken none effect. For they are not all Israel, which are of Israel:

PARAPHRASE.

men after the Flesh; who are *Israelites*, a Nation dignified with these Privileges, which were peculiar to them. Adoption, whereby they were in a particular Manner the Sons of God¹; the Glory ᵐ of the Divine Presence amongst them. Covenants ⁿ made between them and the great God of Heaven and Earth. The moral Law °, a Constitution of Civil Government, and a Form of Divine Worship prescribed by God himself, and all the Promises of the Old Testament, had the Patriarchs, to whom the Promises were made, for their Fore-fathers ᵖ; and of them as to his fleshly Extraction Christ is come, he who is over all, God be blessed for ever, Amen. I commiserate my Nation for not receiving the promised Messiah now he is come, and I speak of the great Prerogatives they had from God above other Nations; but I say not this as if it were possible that the Promise of God should fail of Performance, and not have its Effect ᑫ. But it is to be observed for a right understanding of the Promise, that the sole Descendants of *Jacob* or *Israel* do not make up the whole

4.

5.

6.

NOTES.

4 ˡ *Adoption*, Exod. iv. 22. Jer. xxxi. 9.

ᵐ *Glory*, which was present with the Israelites, and appeared to them in a great shining Brightness out of a Cloud. Some of the Places which mention it are these following, Exod. xiii. 21. Lev. ix. 6. and xxiii. 24. Numb. xvi. 42. 2 Chron. vii. 1—3. Ezek. x. 4. and xliii. 2, 3. compared with *chap.* i. 4, 28.

ⁿ Covenants. See *Gen.* xvii. 4. Exod. xxxiv. 27.

° Νομοθεσία, *The giving of the Law*, whether it signifies the extraordinary giving of the Law by God himself, or the exact Constitution of their Government in the moral and judicial Part of it (for the next Word, λατρεία, *Service of God*, seems to comprehend the religious Worship) this is certain, that in either of these Senses it was the peculiar Privilege of the Jews, and what no other Nation could pretend to.

5 ᵖ *Fathers*; who they were, see *Exod.* iii. 6, 16. *Acts* vii. 32.

6 ᑫ See *chap.* iii. 3. *Word of God*, i. e. Promise, see ver. 9.

Nation

PARAPHRASE.

7. Nation of *Ifrael*ʳ, or the People of God comprehended in the Promife; nor are they who are the Race of *Abraham* all Children, but only his Pofterity by *Ifaac*, as it is faid, In
8. *Ifaac* fhall thy Seed be called: That is, the Children of the Flefh defcended out of *Abraham*'s Loins, are not thereby the Children of God ˢ, and to be efteemed his People; but the Children of the Promife, as *Ifaac* was, are
9. alone to be accounted his Seed. For thus runs the Word of Promife, *At this Time I will come,*
10. *and* Sarah *fhall have a Son.* Nor was this the only Limitation of the Seed of *Abraham*, to whom the Promife belonged, but alfo when *Rebecca* had conceived by that one of *Abraham*'s Iffue to whom the Promife was made, *viz.* our Father *Ifaac*, and there were Twins in her Womb,
11. of that one Father, before the Children were born, or had done any Good or Evilᵗ, to

TEXT.

7 Neither becaufe they are the feed of Abraham, are they all children: but in Ifaac fhall thy feed be called.

8 That is, They which are the children of the flefh, thefe are not the children of God: but the children of the promife are counted for the feed.

9 For this is the word of promife, At this time will I come, and Sarah fhall have a fon.

10 And not only this, but when Rebecca alfo had conceived by one, even by our father Ifaac,

11 (For the children being not yet born, neither ha-

NOTES.

ʳ See *chap.* iv. 16. St. *Paul* ufes this as a Reafon to prove that the Promife of God failed not to have its Effect, though the Body of the Jewifh Nation rejected Jefus Chrift, and were therefore nationally rejected by God from being any longer his People. The Reafon he gives for it is this, That the Pofterity of *Jacob* or *Ifrael* were not thofe alone who were to make that *Ifrael*, or that chofen People of God, which were intended in the Promife made to *Abraham*; others befides the Defcendants of *Jacob* were to be taken into this *Ifrael*, to conftitute the People of God under the Gofpel: And therefore the calling and coming in of the Gentiles was a fulfilling of that Promife. And then he adds in the next Verfe, that neither were all the Pofterity of *Abraham* comprehended in that Promife; fo that thofe who were taken in, in the Time of the Meffiah, to make the *Ifrael* of God, were not taken in, becaufe they were the natural Defcendants from *Abraham*, nor did the Jews claim it for all his Race. And this he proves by the Limitation of the Promife to *Abraham*'s Seed by *Ifaac* only. All this he does to fhew the Right of the Gentiles to that Promife, if they believed: Since that Promife concerned not only the natural Defcendants either of *Abraham* or *Jacob*, but alfo thofe who were of the Faith of their Father *Abraham*, of whomfoever defcended; fee *chap.* iv. 11—17.

ˢ *Children of God*, i. e. People of God, fee *ver.* 26.

ᵗ *Neither having done good nor evil.* Thefe Words may poffibly have been added by St. *Paul* to the foregoing (which may perhaps feem full enough of themfelves) the more exprefsly to obviate an Objection of the Jews, who might be ready to fay, that *Efau* was rejected becaufe he was wicked; as they did of *Ifhmael*, that he was rejected becaufe he was the Son of a Bond-woman.

I fhew

ROMANS. Chap. IX.

TEXT.

ving done any good or e-
vil, that the purpose of
God according to election
might stand, not of works,
but of him that calleth)

12 It was said unto her,
The elder shall serve the
younger.

13 As it is written, Jacob
have I loved, but Esau
have I hated.

14 What shall we say then?
Is there unrighteousness
with God? God forbid.

15 For he saith to Moses,
I will have mercy on
whom I will have mer-
cy, and I will have com-

PARAPHRASE.

shew that his making any Stock or Race of
Men his peculiar People, depended solely on
his own Purpose and good Pleasure in chusing
and calling them, and not on any Works or
Deserts of theirs; he acting here in the Case of
Jacob and *Esau*, according to the Predetermina-
tion of his own Choice, it was declared unto 12.
her, that there were two Nations ᵘ in her
Womb, and that the Descendants of the elder
Brother should serve those of the younger, as 13.
it is written, Jacob *have I loved*ˣ, so as to
make his Posterity my chosen People; and *Esau*
I put so much behind himʸ, as to lay his
Mountains and his Heritage wasteᶻ. What 14.
shall we say then, is there any Injustice with
God in chusing one People to himself before
another according to his good Pleasure? By
no Means. My Brethren, the Jews themselves 15.
cannot charge any such Thing on what I say,
since they have it from *Moses* himselfᵃ, that

NOTES.

12 ᵘ See *Gen.* xxv. 23. And it was only in a national Sense that it is there said, *The Elder shall serve the Younger*, and not personally, for in that Sense it is not true; which makes it plain, that these Words, of *ver.*

13 ˣ *Jacob have I loved, and Esau have I hated*, are to be taken in a national Sense, for the Preference God gave to the Posterity of one of them to be his People, and possess the promised Land before the other. What this Love of God was, see *Deut.* vii. 6—8.

ʸ *Hated.* When it is used in sacred Scripture, as it is often comparatively, it signifies only to postpone in our Esteem or Kindness; for this I need only give that one Example, *Luke* xiv. 26. see *Mal.* i. 2, 3.

ᶻ From the 7th to this 13th Verse proves to the Jews, that though the Promise was made to *Abraham* and his Seed, yet it was not to all *Abraham*'s Posterity, but God first chose *Isaac* and his Issue: And then again of *Isaac*, (who was but one of the Sons of *Abraham*) when *Rebecca* had conceived Twins by him, God of his sole good Pleasure chose *Jacob* the younger, and his Posterity, to be his peculiar People, and to enjoy the Land of Promise.

15 ᵃ See *Exod.* xxxiii. 19. It is observable that the Apostle, arguing here with the Jews, to vindicate the Justice of God in casting them off from being his People, uses three Sorts of Ar-
guments; the first is the Testimony of *Moses* of God's asserting this to himself by the Right of his Sovereignty; and this was enough to stop the Mouths of the Jews. The second from Reason, *ver.* 19—24. and the third from his Predictions of it to the Jews, and the Warning he gave them of it before-hand, *ver.* 25—29. which we shall consider in their Places.

God

PARAPHRASE.

God declared to him that he would be gracious to whom he would be gracious; and shew Mercy on whom he would shew Mercy.

16. So then neither the Purpose of *Isaac* who designed it for *Esau*, and willed ᵇ him to prepare himself for it; nor the Endeavours of *Esau*, who ran a hunting for Venison to come and receive it, could place on him the Blessing; but the Favour of being made in his Posterity a great and prosperous Nation, the peculiar People of God, preferred to that which should descend from his Brother, was bestowed on *Jacob* by the mere Bounty and good

17. Pleasure of God himself. The like hath *Moses* left us upon Record of God's Dealing with *Pharaoh* and his Subjects the People of *Egypt*, to whom God saith ᶜ, *Even for this same Purpose have I raised thee up, that I might shew my Power in thee, and that my Name might be*

18. *renowned through all the Earth.* ᵈ Therefore that his Name and Power may be made known and taken notice of in the World, he is kind and bountiful ᵉ to one Nation, and lets another go on obstinately in their Opposition to him, that his taking them off by some signal Calamity and Ruin brought on them by

TEXT.

passion on whom I will have compassion.

16. So then it is not of him that willeth, nor of him that runneth, but of God that sheweth mercy.

17. For the scripture saith unto Pharaoh, Even for this same purpose have I raised thee up, that I might shew my power in thee, and that my name might be declared throughout all the earth.

18. Therefore hath he mercy on whom he will have

NOTES.

16 ᵇ *Willeth* and *runneth*, considered with the Context, plainly direct us to the Story, *Gen.* xxvii. where, *ver.* 3—5. we read *Isaac*'s Purpose, and *Esau*'s going a hunting: And *ver.* 28, 29. we find what the Blessing was.

17 ᶜ *Exod.* ix. 16.

18 ᵈ *Therefore.* That his Name and Power may be made known, and taken notice of in all the Earth, he is kind and bountiful to one Nation, and lets another go on in their Opposition and Obstinacy against him, till their taking off, by some signal Calamity and Ruin brought on them, may be seen and acknowledged to be the Effect of their standing out against God, as in the Case of *Pharaoh*.

ᵉ *Ἐλεεῖ, Hath Mercy.* That by this Word is meant being bountiful in his outward Dispensations of Power, Greatness, and Protection to one People above another, is plain from the three preceding Verses.

the

ROMANS.

Chap. IX.

TEXT.

mercy, and whom he will, he hardeneth.
19 Thou wilt say then unto me, Why doth he yet find fault? For who hath resisted his will?
20 Nay, but O man, who art thou that repliest against God? Shall the thing formed say to him that formed it, Why hast thou made me thus?

PARAPHRASE.

the visible Hand of his Providence, may be seen and acknowledged to be an Effect of their standing out against him, as in the Case of *Pharaoh*: For this End he is bountiful to whom he will be bountiful, and whom he will he permits to make such an Use of his Forbearance towards them, as to persist obdurate in their Provocation of him, and draw on themselves exemplary Destruction ᶠ. To this some may be ready to say, Why then does he find fault? For who at any Time hath been able to resist his Will? Say you so indeed? But who art thou, O Man, that repliest thus to God? Shall the Nations ᵍ that are made great or

19.

20.

NOTES.

ᶠ *Hardens.* That God's *hardening* spoke of here is what we have explained it in the Paraphrase, is plain in the Instance of *Pharaoh*, given *ver.* 17. as may be seen in that Story, *Exod.* vii.——xiv. which is worth the Reading for the understanding of this Place: See also *ver.* 22.

20 ᵍ Here St. *Paul* shews that the Nations of the World, who are by a better Right in the Hands and Disposal of God, than the Clay in the Power of the Potter, may, without any Question of his Justice, be made great and glorious, or pulled down, and brought into Contempt as he pleases. That he here speaks of Men nationally, and not personally, in reference to their eternal State, is evident not only from the Beginning of this Chapter, where he shews his Concern for the Nation of the Jews being cast off from being God's People, and the Instances he brings of *Isaac,* of *Jacob* and *Esau*, and of *Pharaoh* ; but it appears also very clearly in the Verses immediately following, where by *the Vessels of Wrath fitted for Destruction,* he manifestly means the Nation of the Jews, who were now grown ripe, and fit for the Destruction he was bringing upon them. And by *Vessels of Mercy* the Christian Church, gathered out of a small Collection of Convert Jews, and the rest made up of the Gentiles, who together were from thence-forwards to be the People of God in the room of the Jewish Nation, now cast off, as appears by *ver.* 24. The Sense of which Verses is this: "How darest thou, O Man, to "call God to account, and question his Justice in casting off his ancient People the Jews? "what if God willing to punish that sinful People, and to do it so as to have his Power known, "and taken notice of in the doing of it: (For why might he not raise them to that Purpose "as well as he did *Pharaoh* and his *Egyptians?*) what, I say, if God bore with them a long "Time, even after they had deserved his Wrath, as he did with *Pharaoh*, that his Hand might "be the more eminently visible in their Destruction? And that also at the same Time he might "with the more Glory make known his Goodness and Mercy to the Gentiles, whom, according "to his Purpose, he was in a Readiness to receive into the glorious State of being his "People under the Gospel."

Q q

little,

ROMANS.

PARAPHRASE.

little, shall Kingdoms that are raised or depressed, say to him in whose Hands they are, to dispose of them as he pleases, Why hast thou
21. made us thus? Hath not the Potter Power over the Clay of the same Lump, to make this a Vessel of Honour, and that of Dishonour ʰ?
22. But what hast thou to say, O Man of *Judea*, if God willing to shew his Wrath, and have his Power taken notice of in his Execution of it, did with much Long-suffering ⁱ bear with the

TEXT.

21. Hath not the potter power over the clay, of the same lump to make one vessel unto honour, and another unto dishonour?

22. What if God willing to shew his wrath, and to make his power known, endured with much long-suffering the vessels of wrath fitted to destruction:

NOTES.

21 ʰ *Vessel unto Honour*, and *Vessel unto Dishonour*, signifies a Thing designed by the Maker to an honourable or dishonourable Use: Now why it may not design Nations as well as Persons, and Honour and Prosperity in this World, as well as eternal Happiness and Glory or Misery and Punishment in the World to come, I do not see. In common Reason this figurative Expression ought to follow the Sense of the Context: And I see no peculiar Privilege it hath to wrest and turn the visible Meaning of the Place to something remote from the Subject in hand. I am sure no such Authority it has from such an appropriated Sense settled in sacred Scripture. This were enough to clear the Apostle's Sense in these Words, were there nothing else; but *Jer.* xviii. 6, 7. from whence this Instance of a Potter is taken, shews them to have a temporal Sense, and to relate to the Nation of the Jews.

22 ⁱ *Endured with much Long-suffering.* Immediately after the Instance of *Pharaoh*, whom God said he raised up to shew his Power in him, *ver.* 17. it is subjoined, *ver.* 18. *and whom he will he hardeneth*, plainly with reference to the Story of *Pharaoh*, who is said to harden himself, and whom God is said to harden, as may be seen, *Exod.* vii. 3, 22, 23. and viii. 15, 32. and ix. 7, 12, 34. and x. 1, 20, 27. and xi. 9, 10. and xiv. 5. What God's Part in hardening is, is contained in these Words, *endured with much Long-suffering.* God sends *Moses* to *Pharaoh* with Signs; *Pharaoh*'s Magicians do the like, and so he is not prevailed with. God sends Plagues; whilst the Plague is upon him, he is mollified, and promises to let the People go: But as soon as God takes off the Plague, he returns to his Obstinacy, and refuses, and thus over and over again; God's being intreated by him to withdraw the Severity of his Hand, his gracious Compliance with *Pharaoh*'s Desire to have the Punishment removed, was what God did in the Case, and this was all Goodness and Bounty: But *Pharaoh* and his People made that ill Use of his Forbearance and Long-suffering, as still to harden themselves the more for God's Mercy and Gentleness to them, till they bring on themselves exemplary Destruction from the visible Power and Hand of God employed in it. This Carriage of theirs God foresaw, and so made use of their obstinate perverse Temper for his own Glory, as he himself declares, *Exod.* vii. 3——5. and viii. 18. and ix. 14, 16. The Apostle, by the Instance of a Potter's Power over his Clay, having demonstrated, that God by his Dominion and Sovereignty, had a Right to set up or pull down what Nation he pleased; and might, without any Injustice, take one Race into his particular Favour to be his peculiar People, or reject them, as he thought fit, does in this Verse apply it to the Subject in hand, (*viz.*) the casting off the Jewish Nation, whereof he speaks here in Terms that plainly make

ROMANS.

TEXT.

23 And that he might make known the riches of his glory on the vessels of mercy, which he had afore prepared unto glory?

24 Even us whom he hath called, not of the Jews only, but also of the Gentiles.

PARAPHRASE.

the sinful Nation of the Jews, even when they were proper Objects of that Wrath, fit to have it poured out upon them in their Destruction; That [k] he might make known the Riches of his Glory [l] on those whom, being Objects of his Mercy, he had before prepared to Glory? Even us Christians, whom he had also called, not

23.

24.

NOTES.

make a Parallel between this and his dealing with the *Egyptians*, mentioned *ver.* 17. and therefore that Story will best explain this Verse, that thence will receive its full Light. For it seems a somewhat strange Sort of Reasoning, to say, God, to shew his Wrath, endured with much Long-suffering those who deserved his Wrath, and were fit for Destruction. But he that will read in *Exodus* God's Dealing with *Pharaoh* and the *Egyptians*, and how God passed over Provocation upon Provocation, and patiently endured those who by their first Refusal, nay, by their former Cruelty and Oppression of the *Israelites*, deserved his Wrath, and were fitted for Destruction, that in a more signal Vengeance on the *Egyptians*, and glorious Deliverance of the *Israelites*, he might shew his Power, and make himself be taken notice of, will easily see the strong and easy Sense of this and the following Verse.

23 [k] Καὶ ἵνα, *And that*: The Vulgate has not *And*, and there are Greek MSS. that justify that Omission, as well as the Sense of the Place, which is disturbed by the Conjunction *And*. For with that Reading it runs thus; *And God, that he might make known the Riches of his Glory, &c.* A learned Paraphrast, both against the Grammar and Sense of the Place, by his own Authority adds, *shewed Mercy*, where the sacred Scripture is silent, and says no such Thing; by which we may make it say any Thing. If a Verb were to be inserted here, it is evident it must some way or other answer to *endured* in the foregoing Verse; but such an one will not be easy to be found that will suit here. And indeed there is no need of it; for *and* being left out, the Sense, suitable to St. *Paul's* Argument, here runs plainly and smoothly thus; *What have you Jews to complain of, for God's rejecting you from being any longer his People, and giving you up to be over-run and subjected by the Gentiles, and his taking them in to be his People in your room?* He has as much Power over the Nations of the Earth, to make some of them mighty and flourishing, and others mean and weak, as a Potter has over his Clay, to make what Sort of Vessels he pleases of any Part of it. This you cannot deny. God might from the Beginning have made you a small, neglected People: But he did not; he made you the Posterity of Jacob, a greater and mightier People than the Posterity of his elder Brother Esau; and made you also his own People, plentifully provided for in the Land of Promise. Nay, when your frequent Revolts and repeated Provocations had made you fit for Destruction, he with Long-suffering forbore you, that now, under the Gospel, executing his Wrath on you, he might manifest his Glory on us whom he hath called to be his People, consisting of a small Remnant of Jews, and of Converts out of the Gentiles, whom he had prepared for this Glory, as he had foretold by the Prophets Hosea and Isaiah. This is plainly St. *Paul's* Meaning, That God dealt as is described, *ver.* 22. with the *Jews*, that he might manifest his Glory on the *Gentiles*; for so he declares over and over again, Chap. xi. *ver.* 11, 12, 15, 20, 28, 30.

[l] *Make known the Riches of his Glory on the Vessels of Mercy*. St. Paul, in a parallel Place, Col. i. has so fully explained these Words, that he that will read *ver.* 17. of that Chapter with the Context there, can be in no manner of doubt what St. *Paul* means here.

PARAPHRASE.

25. only of the Jews, but also of the Gentiles, as he hath declared in *Osee*: *I will call them my people, who were not my people, and her beloved,*
26. *who was not beloved. And it shall come to pass, that in the place where it was said unto them, Ye are not my people; there shall they be called, the Children*
27. *of the living God:* Isaiah crieth also concerning *Israel*: Though the number of the Children of Israel be as the sand of the Sea, yet it is but ᵐ a
28. remnant that shall be saved. For the Lord finishing and contracting the account in Righteousness, shall make a short or small remainder ⁿ in the earth.
29. And as Isaiah said before, Unless the Lord of Hosts had left us a seed °, we had been as Sodom, and been made like unto Gomorrah, we had utter-
30. ly been extirpated. What then remains to be said but this? That the Gentiles, who sought not after Righteousness, have obtained the Righteousness which is by Faith, and thereby
31. are become the People of God; but the Children of *Israel*, who followed the Law, which contained the Rule of Righteousness, have not attained to that Law whereby Righteousness is to be attained, *i. e.* have not received the Gospel ᵖ, and so are not the People of God.

TEXT.

25. As he saith also in O-see, I will call them my people, which were not my people; and her, beloved, which was not beloved.
26. And it shall come to pass, that in the place where it was said unto them, Ye are not my people; there shall they be called, the children of the living God.
27. Esaias also crieth concerning Israel, Though the number of the children of Israel be as the sand of the sea, a remnant shall be saved.
28. For he will finish the work, and cut it short in righteousness: because a short work will the Lord make upon the earth.
29. And as Esaias said before, Except the Lord of sabaoth had left us a seed, we had been as Sodoma, and been made like unto Gomorrah.
30. What shall we say then? That the Gentiles which followed not after righteousness, have attained to righteousness, even the righteousness which is of faith:

How

NOTES.

27 ᵐ *But a remnant.* There needs no more but to read the Text, to see this to be the Meaning.

28 ⁿ Λόγον συντετμημένον ποιήσει; Shall make a contracted or little Account, or Overplus; a Metaphor taken from an Account wherein the Matter is so ordered, that the Overplus or Remainder standing still upon the Account, is very little.

29 ° *A Seed,* Isaiah i. 9. The Words are, *a very small Remnant.*

31 ᵖ See *Chap.* x. 3. & xi. 6, 7. The Apostle's Design, in this and the following Chapter, is, to shew the Reason why the Jews were cast off from being the People of God, and the Gentiles admitted. From whence it follows, that by *attaining to Righteousness, and to the Law of Righteousness* here is meant not attaining to the Righteousness which puts particular Persons into the State of Justification and Salvation; but the Acceptance of that Law, the Profession of that Religion wherein that Righteousness is exhibited; which Profession of

that

ROMANS.

Chap. X.

TEXT.

31 But Israel, which followed after the law of righteousness, hath not attained to the law of righteousness.
32 Wherefore? Because they sought it, not by faith, but as it were by the works of the law: for they stumbled at that stumbling stone;
33 As it is written, Behold, I lay in Sion a stumbling-stone, and rock of offence: and whosoever believeth on him, shall not be ashamed.
1 Brethren, my heart's desire and prayer to God for Israel, is that they might be saved.
2 For I bear them record, that they have a zeal of God, but not according to knowledge.
3 For they being ignorant of God's righteousness, and going about to establish their own righteousness, have not submitted themselves unto the righteousness of God.
4 For Christ is the end of the law for righteousness to every one that believeth.

PARAPHRASE.

How came they to miss it? Because they 32. sought not to attain it by Faith; but as if it were to be obtained by the Works of the Law. A crucified Messiah was a Stumbling-block to them ^q; and at that they stumbled, as it is 33. written, *Behold I lay in Sion a stumbling-block, and a rock of offence, and whosoever believeth in him shall not be ashamed.* Brethren, my hearty 1. Desire and Prayer to God for *Israel* is, that they may be saved. For I bear them witness, that 2. they are zealous ^r, and as they think for God and his Law; but their Zeal is not guided by true Knowledge: For they being ignorant of 3. the Righteousness that is of God, *viz.* that Righteousness which he graciously bestows and accepts of; and going about to establish a Righteousness of their own, which they seek for in their own Performances, have not brought themselves to submit to the Law of the Gospel, wherein the Righteousness of God, *i. e.* Righteousness by Faith, is offered. For the End of 4. the Law ^s was to bring Men to Christ, that by believing in him every one that did so might be justified by Faith; For *Moses* describeth the 5.

NOTES.

that which is now the only true Religion, and owning ourselves under that Law which is now solely the Law of God, puts any collective Body of Men into the State of being the People of God. For every one of the Jews and Gentiles that *attained to the Law of Righteousness*, or to *Righteousness* in the Sense St. *Paul* speaks here, *i. e.* became a Professor of the Christian Religion, did not attain to eternal Salvation. In the same Sense must *Chap.* x. 3. and xi. 7, 8. be understood.

33 ^q See 1 *Cor.* i. 23.
2 ^r This their Zeal for God, see described, *Act.* xxi. 27——31. and xxii. 3.
4 ^s See *Gal.* iii. 24.

ROMANS

PARAPHRASE.

Righteousness that was to be had by the Law thus: *That the man which doth the things required in the law, shall have life thereby.* But the Righteousness which is of Faith speaketh after this manner: *Say not in thine heart, who shall ascend into Heaven,* that is, to bring down the Messiah from thence, whom we expect personally here on Earth to deliver us? *Or who shall descend into the deep,* i. e to bring up Christ again from the Dead to be our Saviour? You mistake the Deliverance you expect by the Messiah, there needs not the fetching him from the other World to be present with you: The Deliverance by him is a Deliverance from Sin, that you may be made righteous by Faith in him; and that speaks thus; *The word is nigh thee, even in thy mouth, and in thy heart;* that is, the Word of Faith, or the Doctrine of the Gospel which we preach ᵗ, viz. *If thou shalt confess with thy mouth* ᵘ, i. e. openly own Jesus the Lord,

6.
7.
8.
9.

TEXT.

For Moses describeth the righteousness which is of the law, That the Man which doth those things, shall live by them. 5

But the righteousness which is of faith, speaketh on this wise, Say not in thine heart, Who shall ascend into heaven? (that is, to bring Christ down from above.) 6

Or, who shall descend into the deep? (that is, to bring up Christ again from the dead) 7

But what saith it? The word is nigh thee, even in thy mouth, and in thy heart, that is the word of faith which we preach. 8

That if thou shalt confess with thy mouth the Lord Jesus, and shalt be- 9

i. e.

NOTES.

8 ᵗ St. *Paul* had told them *ver.* 4. That the End of the Law was to bring them to Life by Faith in Christ, that they might be justified, and so be saved. To convince them of this, he brings three Verses out of the Book of the Law itself, declaring that the Way to Life was by hearkening to that Word which was ready in their Mouth and in their Heart, and that therefore they had no Reason to reject Jesus the Christ, because he died and was now removed into Heaven, and was remote from them; their very Law proposed Life to them by something nigh them, that might lead them to their Deliverer: By Words and Doctrines that might be always at Hand, in their Mouths, and in their Hearts, and so lead them to Christ, *i. e.* to that Faith in him which the Apostle preached to them. I submit to the attentive Reader, whether this be not the Meaning of this Place.

9 ᵘ The Expectation of the Jews was, that the Messiah, who was promised them, was to be their Deliverer; and so far they were in the Right. But that which they expected to be delivered from, at his appearing, was the Power and Dominion of Strangers. When our Saviour came, their Reckoning was up; and the Miracles which Jesus did, concurred to persuade them that it was he: But his obscure Birth and mean Appearance suited not with that Power and Splendor, they had fancied to themselves he should come in. This, with his denouncing to them the Ruin of their Temple and State at hand, set the Rulers against him, and held the Body of the Jews in suspense till his Crucifixion; and that gave a full Turn of their Minds from him. They had figured him a mighty Prince, at the Head of their Nation, setting them free

from

ROMANS.

Chap. X.

TEXT.

lieve in thine heart, that God hath raised him from the dead, thou shalt be saved.
10 For with the heart man believeth unto righteousness, and with the mouth confession is made unto salvation.
11 For the scripture saith, Whosoever believeth on him, shall not be ashamed.
12 For there is no difference between the Jew and the Greek: for the same Lord over all, is rich unto all that call upon him.

PARAPHRASE.

i. e. Jesus to be the Messiah, thy Lord, and shalt believe in thy Heart, that God hath raised him from the Dead [x], otherwise he cannot be believed to be the Messiah, thou shalt be saved. 'Twas not for nothing that *Moses* in the Place above-cited mentioned both Heart and Mouth; there is Use of both in the Case. For with the Heart Man believeth unto Righteousness, and with the Mouth Confession [y] is made unto Salvation. For the Scripture saith, *whosoever believeth on him shall not be ashamed*, shall not repent his having believed, and owning it. The Scripture saith *whosoever*, for in this Case there is no Distinction of Jew and Gentile. For it is he the same who is Lord of them all, and is abundantly bountiful to all that call upon him.

10.

11.

12.

NOTES.

from all foreign Power, and themselves at ease, and happy under his glorious Reign. But when at the Passover the whole People were Witnesses of his Death, they gave up all Thought of Deliverance by him. He was gone, they saw him no more, and it was past doubt a dead Man could not be the Messiah or Deliverer, even of those who believed him. It is against these Prejudices that what St. *Paul* says in this and the three preceding Verses seems directed, wherein he teaches them, that there was no need to fetch the Messiah out of Heaven, or out of the Grave, and bring him personally among them. For the Deliverance he was to work for them, the Salvation by him was Salvation from Sin, and Condemnation for that; and that was to be had by barely believing and owning him to be the Messiah their King, and that he was raised from the Dead: by this they would be saved without his Personal Presence among them.

[x] *Raised him from the Dead.* The Doctrine of the Lord Jesus being raised from the Dead, is certainly one of the most fundamental Articles of the Christian Religion; but yet there seems another Reason why St. *Paul* here annexes Salvation to the Belief of it, which may be found, ver. 7. where he teaches, that it was not necessary for their Salvation, that they should have Christ out of his Grave personally present amongst them; and here he gives them the Reason, because if they did but own him for their Lord, and believe that he was raised, that sufficed, they should be saved.

10 [y] Believing and an open avowed Profession of the Gospel, are required by our Saviour, *Mark* xvi. 16.

For.

ROMANS.

PARAPHRASE.

13. For whosoever shall call ᵃ upon his Name shall be saved. But how shall they call upon him
14. on whom they have not believed? And how shall they believe on him of whom they have not heard? And how shall they hear without a
15. Preacher? And how shall they preach except they be sent ᵃ? As it is written, *How beautiful are the Feet of them that preach the Gospel of Peace, and bring glad Tidings of good Things?* But
16. though there be Messengers sent from God to preach the Gospel, yet it is not to be expected that all should receive and obey it ᵇ. For

TEXT.

For whosoever shall 13 call upon the name of the Lord, shall be saved.
How then shall they 14 call on him, in whom they have not believed? And how shall they believe in him of whom they have not heard? And how shall they hear without a preacher?
And how shall they 15 preach, except they be sent? As it is written, How beautiful are the feet of them that preach the gospel of peace, and

NOTES.

13 ᵃ Whoever hath with Care looked into St. *Paul*'s Writings, must own him to be a close Reasoner that argues to the Point; and therefore if in the three preceeding Verses he requires an open Profession of the Gospel, I cannot but think that *all that call upon him*, *ver.* 12. signifies all that are open professed Christians; and if this be the Meaning of calling upon him, *ver.* 12. it is plain it must be the Meaning *of calling upon his Name*, *ver.* 13. a Phrase not very remote from *naming his Name*, which is used by St. *Paul* for professing Christianity, 2 *Tim.* ii. 19. If the Meaning of the Prophet *Joel*, from whom these Words be taken, be urged, I shall only say, that it will be an ill Rule for interpreting St. *Paul*, to tie up his Use of any Text he brings out of the Old Testament, to that which is taken to be the Meaning of it there. We need go no farther for an Example than the 6, 7, 8, Verses of this Chapter, which I desire any one to read as they stand, *Deut.* xxx. 11 —— 14. and see whether St. *Paul* uses them here in the same Sense.

15 ᵃ St. *Paul* is careful every where to keep himself, as well as possibly he can, in the Minds and fair Esteem of his Brethren the *Jews*; may not therefore this, with the two foregoing Verses, be understood as an Apology to them for professing himself an Apostle of the Gentiles, as he does by the Tenor of this Epistle, and in the next Chapter in Words at length, *ver.* 13. In this Chapter *ver.* 12. he had shewed that both Jews and Greeks or Gentiles were to be saved only by receiving the Gospel of Christ. And if so, it was necessary that somebody should be sent to teach it them, and therefore the Jews had no Reason to be angry with any that was sent on that Employment.

16 ᵇ *But they have not all obeyed.* This seems an Objection of the Jews to what St. *Paul* had said, which he answers in this and the following Verse. The Objection and Answer seems to stand thus: You tell us that you are sent from God to preach the Gospel; if it be so, how comes it that all that have heard, have not received and obeyed; and since, according to what you would insinuate, the Messengers of good Tidings (which is the Import of *Evangil* in Greek, and *Gospel* in English) were so welcome to them? To this he answers out of *Isaiah*, that the Messengers sent from God were not believed by all. But from those Words of *Isaiah*, he draws an Inference to confirm the Argument he was upon, *viz.* that Salvation cometh by hearing and believing the *Word* of God. He had laid it down, *ver.* 8. that it was by their having ῥῆμα πίστεως, *the Word of Faith*, nigh them or present with them, and not by the bodily Presence of their Deliverer amongst them, that they were to be saved. This ῥῆμα, *Word*, he tells them, *ver.* 17. is by preaching brought to be actually present with them and the Gentiles; so that it was their own Fault if they believed it not to Salvation.

Isaiah

ROMANS.

Chap. XI.

TEXT.

bring glad tidings of good things?
16 But they have not all obeyed the gospel. For Esaias saith, Lord, who hath believed our report?
17 So then faith cometh by hearing, and hearing by the word of God.
18 But I say, Have they not heard? Yes verily, their sound went into all the earth, and their words unto the ends of the world.
19 But I say, Did not Israel know? First Moses saith, I will provoke you to jealousy by them that are no people, and by a foolish nation I will anger you.
20 But Esaias is very bold, and saith, I was found of them that sought me not; I was made manifest unto them that asked not after me.
21 But to Israel he saith, All day long I have stretched forth my hands unto a disobedient and gainsaying people.

PARAPHRASE.

Isaiah hath foretold that they should not, saying, *Lord, who hath believed our report?* That which we may learn from thence is, that Faith cometh by hearing, and hearing from the Word of God, *i. e.* the Revelation of the Gospel in the Writings of the sacred Scriptures, communicated by those whom God sends as Preachers thereof, to those who are ignorant of it; and there is no need that Christ should be brought down from Heaven, to be personally with you, to be your Saviour. It is enough that both Jews and Gentiles have heard of him by Messengers, whose Voice is gone out into the whole Earth, and his Words unto the Ends of the World, far beyond the Bounds of *Judea*.

But I ask, did not *Israel* know ᶜ this, that the Gentiles were to be taken in and made the People of God? First *Moses* tells it them from God, who says, *I will provoke you to Jealousy by them who are no People; and by a foolish Nation I will anger you.* But *Isaiah* declares it yet much plainer in these Words; *I was found of them that sought me not; I was made manifest to them that asked not after me.* And to *Israel*, to shew their Refusal, he saith; *All Day long have I stretched forth mine Hands unto a disobedient and gainsaying People.*

17.

18.

19.

20.

21.

NOTES.

19 ᶜ *Did not Israel know?* In this and the next Verses St. *Paul* seems to suppose a Reasoning of the Jews to this Purpose, *viz.* That they did not deserve to be cast off, because they did not know that the Gentiles were to be admitted, and so might be excused if they did not embrace a Religion wherein they were to mix with the Gentiles; and to this he answers in the following Verses.

R r

SECT.

ROMANS.

SECT. IX.

CHAP. XI. 1——36.

CONTENTS.

THE Apostle in this Chapter goes on to shew the future State of the Jews and Gentiles, in respect of Christianity, *viz.* That though the Nation of the Jews were for their Unbelief rejected, and the Gentiles taken in their room to be the People of God, yet there was a few of the Jews that believed in Christ, and so a small Remnant of them continued to be God's People, being incorporated with the converted Gentiles into the Christian Church. But they shall, the whole Nation of them, when the Fulness of the Gentiles is come in, be converted to the Gospel, and again be restored to be the People of God.

The Apostle takes occasion also from God's having rejected the Jews, to warn the Gentile Converts, that they take heed: Since if God cast off his ancient People the Jews for their Unbelief, the Gentiles could not expect to be preserved, if they apostatized from the Faith, and kept not firm in their Obedience to the Gospel.

PARAPHRASE.

1. I SAY then, Has ^d God wholly cast away his People the Jews from being his People? By no Means. For I myself am an Israelite, of the Seed of *Abraham*, of the Tribe of *Benja-*
2. *min.* God hath not utterly cast off his People whom he formerly owned ^e with so peculiar a Respect. Know ye not what the Scripture saith concerning *Elijah?* How he complained to

TEXT.

1 I SAY then, Hath God cast away his people? God forbid. For I also am an Israelite, of the seed of Abraham, of the tribe of Benjamin.

2 God hath not cast away his people which he foreknew. Wot ye not what the scripture saith of Elias? How he maketh in-

NOTES.

1 ^d This is a Question in the Person of a Jew, who made the Objections in the foregoing Chapter, and continues to object here.
2 ^e See *Chap.* viii. 29.

the

ROMANS.

Chap. XI.

TEXT.

tercession to God against Israel, saying,

3 Lord, they have killed thy prophets, and digged down thine altars; and I am left alone, and they seek my life.

4 But what saith the answer of God unto him? I have reserved to myself seven thousand men, who have not bowed the knee to the image of Baal.

5 Even so then at this present time also there is a remnant according to the election of grace.

6 And if by Grace, then is it no more of works: otherwise grace is no more grace. But if it be of works, then it is no more grace: otherwise work is no more work.

PARAPHRASE.

the God of *Israel* in these Words: *Lord, they have killed thy Prophets, and have digged down thine Altars, and of all that worshipped thee, I alone am left, and they seek my Life also.* But what saith the Answer of God to him? *I have reserved to myself seven thousand Men, who have not bowed the Knee to* Baal ᶠ, *i. e.* have not been guilty of Idolatry. Even so at this Time also there is a Remnant reserved and segregated by the Favour, and free Choice of God. Which Reservation of a Remnant, if it be by Grace and Favour, it is not of Works ᵍ, for then Grace would not be Grace. But if it were of Works, then it is not Grace: For then Work would not be Work, *i. e.* Work gives a Right, Grace bestows the Favour where there is no Right to it; so that what is conferred by

3.

4.

5.

6.

NOTES.

4 ᶠ *Baal* and *Baalim* was the Name whereby the false Gods and Idols which the Heathens worshipped were signified in Sacred Scripture; See *Judges* ii. 11——13. *Hos.* xi. 2.

6 ᵍ *It is not of works.* This Exclusion of Works seems to be mistaken by those who extend it to all manner of Difference in the Person chosen, from those that were rejected; for such a Choice as that excludes not Grace in the Chuser, but Merit in the Chosen. For it is plain that by *Works* here St. *Paul* means Merit, as is evident also from *chap.* iv. 2——4. The Law required complete perfect Obedience: He that performed that, had a Right to the Reward; but he that failed and came short of that, had by the Law no Right to any thing but Death. And so the Jews being all Sinners, God might without Injustice have cast them all off; none of them could plead a Right to his Favour. If therefore he chose out and reserved any, it was of mere Grace, though in his Choice he preferred those who were the best disposed and most inclined to his Service. A whole Province revolts from their Prince, and takes Arms against him: He resolves to pardon some of them. This is a Purpose of Grace. He reduces them under his Power, and then chuses out of them as Vessels of Mercy, those that he finds least infected with Malice, Obstinacy and Rebellion. This Choice neither voids nor abates his Purpose of Grace, that stands firm; but only executes it so as may best comport with his Wisdom and Goodness. And indeed without some Regard to a Difference in the Things taken from those that are left, I do not see how it can be called Choice. An Handful of Pebbles, for Example, may be taken out of a Heap; they are taken and separated indeed from the rest, but if it be without any Regard to any Difference in them from others rejected, I doubt whether any body can call them chosen.

PARAPHRASE.

7. the one, cannot be afcribed to the other. How is it then? Even thus; *Ifrael*, or the Nation of the Jews, obtained not what it feeks [h]; but the Election [i], or that Part which was to remain God's elect chofen People, obtained it,
8. but the reft of them were blinded [k]: According as it is written [l], *God hath given them the Spirit of Slumber; Eyes that they fhould not fee, and Ears that they fhould not hear, unto this*
9. *Day.* And *David* faith [m], *Let their Table be made a Snare and a Trap, and a Stumbling-block,*
10. *and a Recompence unto them: Let their Eyes be darkened, that they may not fee, and bow down their*
11. *Back alway.* What then, do I fay that they have fo ftumbled as to be fallen paft Recovery? By no Means: But this I fay, that by their Fall, by their Rejection for refufing [n] the Gofpel, the Privilege of becoming the People of God, by receiving the Doctrine of Salvation, is come to the Gentiles, to provoke the Jews to Jealoufy. Now if the Fall of the Jews
12. hath been to the enriching of the reft of the World, and their Damage an Advantage to

TEXT.

7 What then? Ifrael hath not obtained that which he feeketh for; but the election hath obtained it, and the reft were blinded:

8 According as it is written, God hath given them the fpirit of flumber, eyes that they fhould not fee, and ears that they fhould not hear, unto this day.

9 And David faith, Let their table be made a fnare, and a trap, and a ftumbling-block, and a recompence unto them.

10 Let their eyes be darkened, that they may not fee, and bow down their back alway.

11 I fay then, Have they ftumbled that they fhould fall? God forbid; but rather through their fall falvation is come unto the Gentiles, for to provoke them to jealoufy.

12 Now if the fall of them be the riches of the world, and the diminifh-

NOTES.

7 [h] *What it feeks*, i. e. That Righteoufnefs whereby it was to continue the People of God; fee *chap.* ix. 31. It may be obferved that St. *Paul's* Difcourfe being of the National Privilege of continuing the People of God, he fpeaks here, and all along of the Jews in the collective Term *Ifrael*. And fo likewife the *Remnant*, which were to remain his People, and incorporate with the Convert Gentiles, into one Body of Chriftians, owning the Dominion of the one true God, in the Kingdom he had fet up under his Son, and owned by God for his People, he calls the *Election*.

[i] *Election*, a collective Appellation of the Part elected, which in other Places he calls *Remnant*. This *Remnant* or *Election*, call it by which Name you pleafe, were thofe who fought Righteoufnefs by Faith in Chrift, and not by the Deeds of the Law, and fo became the People of God, that People which he had chofen to be his.

[k] *Blinded*, fee 2 *Cor.* iii. 13——16.

8 [l] *Written*, Ifa. xxix. 10. and vi. 9, 10.

9 [m] *Saith*, Pfal. lxix. 22, 23.

11 [n] That this is the Meaning of *Fall* here, fee *Acts* xiii. 46.

the

ROMANS.

Chap. XI.

TEXT.

ing of them the riches of the Gentiles: how much more their fulness?

13 For I speak to you Gentiles, in as much as I am the Apostle of the Gentiles, I magnify mine office:

14 If by any means I may provoke to emulation them which are my flesh, and might save some of them.

15 For if the casting away of them be the reconciling of the world; what shall the receiving of them be but life from the dead?

16 For if the first-fruit be holy, the lump is also holy: and if the root be holy, so are the branches.

17 And if some of the branches be broken off, and thou being a wild olive-tree, were graffed in amongst them, and with them partakest of the root and fatness of the olive-tree;

18 Boast not against the branches: but if thou

PARAPHRASE.

the Gentiles, by letting them into the Church, how much more shall their Completion be so, when their whole Nation shall be restored? This I say to you Gentiles, forasmuch as being Apostle of the Gentiles, I magnify ° mine Office: If by any Means I may provoke to Emulation the Jews, who are my own Flesh and Blood, and bring some of them into the Way of Salvation. For if the casting them off be a Means of reconciling the World, what shall their Restoration be, when they are taken again into Favour, but as it were Life from the Dead, which is to all Mankind of all Nations? For if the First-fruits ᵖ be holy ᑫ and accepted, the whole Product of the Year is holy, and will be accepted. And if *Abraham, Isaac* and *Jacob*, from whom the Jewish Nation had their Original, were holy, the Branches also that sprang from this Root are holy. If then some of the natural Branches were broken off: If some of the natural Jews, of the Stock of *Israel*, were broken off and rejected, and thou, a Heathen of the wild Gentile Race, were taken in, and ingrafted into the Church of God in their room; and there partakest of the Blessings promised to *Abraham* and his Seed, be not

13.

14.

15.

16.

17.

18.

NOTES.

13 ° St. *Paul* magnified his Office of Apostle of the Gentiles not only by preaching the Gospel to the Gentiles, but in assuring them farther, as he does, *ver.* 12. that when the Nation of the Jews shall be restored, the Fulness of the Gentiles shall also come in.

16 ᵖ These Allusions the Apostle makes use of here, to shew that the Patriarchs, the *Root* of the Jewish Nation, being accepted by God; and the few Jewish Converts, which at first entered into the Christian Church, being also accepted by God, are as it were *first Fruits* or Pledges, that God will in due Time admit the whole Nation of the Jews into his visible Church, to be his peculiar People again.

ᑫ *Holy:* By *Holy* is here meant that relative Holiness whereby any thing hath an Appropriation to God.

ROMANS.

PARAPHRASE.

so conceited of thyself, as to shew any Disrespect ᶠ to the Jews. If any such Vanity possesses thee, remember that the Privilege thou hast in being a Christian, is derived to thee from the Promise made to *Abraham* and his Seed; but nothing accrues to *Abraham* or his Race by any thing derived from thee. Thou wilt perhaps say, The Jews were rejected to make way for me. Well, let it be so: But remember that it was because of Unbelief that they were broken off, and that it is by Faith alone that thou hast obtained, and must keep thy present Station. This ought to be a Warning to thee, not to have any haughty Conceit of thyself, but with Modesty to fear. For if God spared not the Seed of *Abraham*, but cast off even the Children of *Israel*, for their Unbelief, he will certainly not spare thee, if thou art guilty of the like Miscarriage. Mind therefore the Benignity and Rigour of God; Rigour to them that stumbled at the Gospel and fell, but Benignity to thee, if thou continue within the Sphere of his Benignity, *i. e.* in the Faith by which thou partakest of the Privilege of being one of his People: Otherwise even thou also shalt be cut off. And the Jews, also, if they continue not in Unbelief, shall be again grafted into the Stock of *Abraham*, and be re-

TEXT.

boast, thou bearest not the root, but the root thee.

19 Thou wilt say then, The branches were broken off, that I might be grafted in.

20 Well; because of unbelief they were broken off, and thou standest by faith. Be not high minded, but fear.

21 For if God spared not the natural branches, take heed lest he also spare not thee.

22 Behold therefore the goodness and severity of God: on them which fell, severity; but towards thee, goodness, if thou continue in his goodness: otherwise, thou also shalt be cut off.

23 And they also, if they abide not still in unbelief,

NOTES.

18 ᶠ *Boast not against the Branches.* Though the great Fault that most disordered the Church, and principally exercised the Apostle's Care in this Epistle, was from the Jews pressing the Necessity of legal Observances, and not brooking that the Gentiles, though Converts to Christianity, should be admitted into their Communion, without being circumcised: Yet it is plain from this Verse, as also *ch.* xiv. 3, 10. that the Convert Gentiles were not wholly without Fault on their Side, in treating the Jews with Dis-esteem and Contempt. To this also, as it comes in his way, he applies his Remedies, particularly in this Chapter, and *ch.* xiv.

established

ROMANS.

Chap. XI.

TEXT.	PARAPHRASE.

shall be graffed in: for God is able to graff them in again.

24 For if thou wert cut out of the olive-tree which is wild by nature, and wert graffed contrary to nature into a good olive-tree; how much more shall these which be the natural branches, be graffed into their own olive-tree?

25 For I would not, brethren, that ye should be ignorant of this mystery (lest ye should be wise in your own conceits) that blindness in part is happened to Israel, until the fulness of the Gentiles be come in.

26 And so all Israel shall be saved: as it is written, There shall come out

established the People of God. For however they are now scattered, and under Subjection to Strangers, God is able to collect them again into one Body, make them his People, and set them in a flourishing Condition in their own Land ˢ. For if you who are Heathens by 24. Birth, and not of the promised Seed, were, when you had neither Claim nor Inclination to it, brought into the Church, and made the People of God; how much more shall those who are the Posterity and Descendants of him to whom the Promise was made, be restored to the State which the Promise vested in that Family? For to prevent your being conceited of 25. yourselves, my Brethren, let me make known to you, which has yet been undiscovered to the World, *(viz.)* that the Blindness which has fallen upon Part of *Israel*, shall remain upon them but till the Time be come wherein the whole ᵗ Gentile World shall enter into the Church, and make Profession of Christianity. And so all *Israel* shall be converted ᵘ to the 26.

NOTES.

23 ˢ This *grafting in again*, seems to import, that the Jews shall be a flourishing Nation again, professing Christianity in the Land of Promise, for that is to be re-instated again in the Promise made to *Abraham*, *Isaac* and *Jacob*. This St. *Paul* might, for good Reasons, be withheld from speaking out here: But in the Prophets there are very plain Intimations of it.

25 ᵗ Πλήρωμα, The *Fulness* of the Jews, *ver. 12.* is the whole Body of the Jewish Nation professing Christianity; and therefore here πλήρωμα τῶν ἐθνῶν, *The Fulness of the Gentiles*, must be the whole Body of the Gentiles professing Christianity. And this *ver 15.* seems to teach. For the Resurrection is of all.

26 ᵘ Σωθήσεται, *shall be saved*. It is plain that the Salvation that St. *Paul* in this Discourse concerning the Nation of the Jews, and the Gentile World in gross, speaks of, is not eternal Happiness in Heaven, but he means by it the Profession of the true Religion here on Earth. Whether it be that that is as far as Corporations or Bodies Politick can go, towards the Attainment of eternal Salvation, I will not enquire. But this is evident, that being saved, is used by the Apostle here in this Sense. That all the Jewish Nation may become the People of God again, by taking up the Christian Profession, may be easily conceived. But that every Person of such a Christian Nation, shall attain eternal Salvation in Heaven, I think no body can imagine to be here intended.

Christian

ROMANS.

PARAPHRASE.

Christian Faith, and the whole Nation become the People of God: As it is written, *There shall come out of* Sion *the Deliverer, and shall turn away Ungodliness from* Jacob. *For this is my Covenant to them, when I shall take away* ˣ *their*
27.
28. *Sins.* They are indeed at present Strangers to the Gospel, and so are in the State of Enemies ʸ, but this is for your sakes: Their Fall and Loss is your enriching, you having obtained Admittance through their being cast out: But yet they being within the Election that God made of *Abraham, Isaac* and *Jacob*, and their Posterity, to be his People, are still his beloved People, for *Abraham, Isaac* and *Jacob*'s
29. sake, from whom they are descended. For the Favours that God shewed those their Fathers, in calling them and their Posterity to be his People, he doth not repent of; but his Promise, that they shall be his People, shall stand
30. good ᶻ. For as you the Gentiles formerly stood out, and were not the People of God, but yet have now obtained Mercy so as to be taken in through the standing out of the Jews,

TEXT.

of Sion the deliverer, and shall turn away ungodliness from Jacob.

For this is my cove- 27 nant unto them, when I shall take away their sins.

As concerning the gos- 28 pel, they are enemies for your sake, but as touching the election, they are beloved for the fathers sakes.

For the gifts and call- 29 ing of God are without repentance.

For as ye in times past 30 have not believed God, yet have now obtained mercy through their unbelief:

NOTES.

27 ˣ *Take away*, i. e. Forgive *their Sins*, and take away the Punishment they lie under for them.

28 ʸ Ἐχθροὶ, *Enemies*, signifies Strangers or Aliens, *i. e.* such as are no longer the People of God. For they are called *Enemies* in Opposition to *Beloved*, in this very Verse. And the Reason given why they are *Enemies*, makes it plain, that this is the Sense, *(viz.) For the Gentiles sake*, i. e. They are rejected from being the People of God, that you Gentiles may be taken in to be the People of God in their room, *ver.* 30. The same Signification has ἐχθροὶ, *Enemies*, ch. v. 10. καὶ' εὐαγγέλιον ἐχθροὶ, *as concerning the Gospel-Enemies*, i. e. all those who not embracing the Gospel, not receiving Christ for their King and Lord, are Aliens from the Kingdom of God, and all such Aliens are called ἐχθροὶ, *Enemies*. And so indeed were the Jews now: But yet they were κατ' ἐκλογὴν ἀγαπητοὶ, *as touching the Election, beloved*, i. e. were not actually within the Kingdom of God his People, but were within the *Election*, which God had made of *Abraham, Isaac* and *Jacob*, and their Posterity to be his People, and so God had still Intentions of Kindness to them for their Fathers sake, to make them again his People.

29 ᶻ So God's not repenting is explained, *Numb.* xxiii. 19——24.

who

ROMANS.

Chap. XI.

TEXT.

1. Even so have these also so now not believed, that through your mercy they also may obtain mercy.
2. For God hath concluded them all in unbelief,

PARAPHRASE.

who submit not to the Gospel^a: Even so they now have stood out by reason of your being in Mercy admitted, that they also through the Mercy you have received, may again hereafter be admitted. For God hath put up together in a State of Revolt for their Allegiance^b 31.
32.

NOTES.

30 ^a See *Acts* xiii. 46.

32 ^b Εἰς ἀπείθειαν, *In Unbelief.* The *Unbelief* here charged nationally on Jews and Gentiles in their turns, in this and the two preceding Verses, whereby they ceased to be the People of God, was evidently the disowning of his Dominion, whereby they put themselves out of the Kingdom which he had and ought to have in the World, and so were no longer in the State of Subjects, but Aliens and Rebels. A general View of Mankind will lead us into an easier Conception of St. *Paul*'s Doctrine, who all through this Epistle considers the Gentiles, Jews, and Christians, as three distinct Bodies of Men.

God by Creation had no doubt an unquestionable Sovereignty over Mankind, and this was at first acknowledged in their Sacrifices and Worship of him. Afterwards they withdrew themselves for their Submission to him, and found out other Gods, whom they worshipped and served. This Revolt from God, and the Consequence of it, God's abandoning them, St. *Paul* describes, *chap.* i. 18 — 32.

In this State of Revolt from God were the Nations of the Earth in the Times of *Abraham*. And then *Abraham, Isaac* and *Jacob*, and their Posterity the Israelites, upon God's gracious Call, returned to their Allegiance to their ancient and rightful King and Sovereign, to own the one invisible God, Creator of Heaven and Earth, for their God, and so become his People again, to whom he, as to his peculiar People, gave a Law. And thus remained the Distinction between Jews and Gentiles, *i. e.* The Nations, as the Word signifies, till the Time of the Messiah, and then the Jews ceased to be the People of God, not by a direct renouncing the God of *Israel*, and taking to themselves other false Gods whom they worshipped; but by opposing and rejecting the Kingdom of God, which he purposed at that Time to set up with new Laws and Institutions, and to a more glorious and spiritual Purpose under his Son Jesus Christ: Him God sent to them, and him the Nation of the Jews refused to receive as their Lord and Ruler, though he was their promised King and Deliverer, answering all the Prophecies and Types of him, and evidencing his Mission by his Miracles. By this Rebellion against him, into whose Hand God had committed the Rule of his Kingdom, and appointed Lord over all Things, the Jews turned themselves out of the Kingdom of God, and ceased to be his People, who had now no other People but those who received and obeyed his Son as their Lord and Ruler. This was the ἀπείθεια, *Unbelief*, here spoken of. And I would be glad to know any other Sense of *Believing* or *Unbelief*, wherein it can be nationally attributed to a People (as visibly here it is) whereby they shall cease, or come to be the People of God, or visible Subjects of his Kingdom here on Earth. Indeed to enjoy Life and Estate in this, as well as other Kingdoms, not only the owning of the Prince, and the Authority of his Laws, but also Obedience to them is required. For a Jew might own the Authority of God, and his Law given by *Moses*, and so be a true Subject, and as much a Member of the Commonwealth of *Israel*, as any one in it, and yet forfeit his Life by Disobedience to the Law. And a Christian may own the Authority of Jesus Christ, and of the Gospel, and yet forfeit eternal Life by his Disobedience to the Precepts of it, as may be seen *chap.* vii. 8, 9.

S f   to

PARAPHRASE.

to him, as it were in one Fold, all Men, both Jews and Gentiles, that through his Mercy they might all, both Jews and Gentiles, come to be his People, *i. e.* he hath suffered both Jews and Gentiles in their turns not to be his People, that he might bring the whole Body, both of Jews and Gentiles, to be his People.

33. O the Depth of the Riches of the Wisdom and Knowledge of God^c! How unsearchable are his Judgments, and his Ways not to be traced!

34. For who hath known the Mind of the Lord? Or who hath sat in Counsel with him? Or

35. who hath been before-hand with him, in bestowing any thing upon him, that God may repay it to him again^d? The Thought of

36. any such Thing is absurd. For from him all Things have their Being and Original; by him they are all ordered and disposed of, and for him and his Glory they are all made and regulated, to whom be Glory for ever. Amen.

TEXT.

that he might have mercy upon all.

33 O the depth of the riches both of the wisdom and knowledge of God! how unsearchable are his judgments, and his ways past finding out!

34 For who hath known the mind of the Lord, or who hath been his counsellor?

35 Or who hath first given to him, and it shall be recompensed unto him again?

36 For of him, and through him, and to him, are all things, to whom be glory for ever. Amen.

NOTES.

33 ^c 'This emphatical Conclusion seems, in a special Manner, to regard the Jews, whom the Apostle would hereby teach Modesty and Submission to the over-ruling Hand of the all-wise God, whom they are very unfit to call to account for his dealing so favourably with the Gentiles. His Wisdom and Ways are infinitely above their Comprehension, and will they take upon them to advise him what to do? Or is God in their Debt? Let them say for what, and he shall repay it to them. This is a very strong Rebuke to the Jews, but delivered, as we see, in a Way very gentle and inoffensive. A Method which the Apostle endeavours every where to observe towards his Nation.

35 ^d This has a manifest Respect to the Jews, who claimed a Right to be the People of God so far, that St. *Paul*, ch. ix. 14. finds it necessary to vindicate the Justice of God in the Case, and does here in this Question expose and silence the Folly of any such Pretence.

SECT.

ROMANS.

SECT. X.

CHAP. XII. 1——21.

CONTENTS.

ST. *Paul* in the End of the foregoing Chapter, with a very solemn Epiphonema, closes that admirable Evangelical Discourse to the Church at *Rome*, which had taken up the eleven foregoing Chapters. It was addressed to the two Sorts of Converts, *viz.* Gentiles and Jews, into which, as into two distinct Bodies, he all along through this Epistle divides all Mankind, and considers them as so divided into two separate Corporations.

1. As to the Gentiles, he endeavours to satisfy them, that though they, for their Apostasy from God to Idolatry, and the Worship of False Gods, had been abandoned by God, had lived in Sin and Blindness, without God in the World, Strangers from the Knowledge and Acknowledgment of him, yet that the Mercy of God through Jesus Christ was extended to them, whereby there was a Way now opened to them to become the People of God, For since no Man could be saved by his own Righteousness, no not the Jews themselves, by the Deeds of the Law, the only Way to Salvation, both for Jews and Gentiles, was by Faith in Jesus Christ. Nor had the Jews any other Way now to continue themselves the People of God, than by receiving the Gospel, which Way was opened also to the Gentiles, and they as freely admitted into the Kingdom of God now erected under Jesus Christ, as the Jews, and upon the sole Terms of Believing. So that there was no need at all for the Gentiles to be circumcised to become Jews, that they might be Partakers of the Benefits of the Gospel.

2. As to the Jews, the Apostle's other great Aim in the foregoing Discourse, is to remove the Offence the Jews took at the Gospel, because the Gentiles were received into the Church as the People of God, and were allowed to be Subjects of the Kingdom of the Messiah. To bring them to a better Temper, he shews them from the Sacred Scripture, that they could not be saved by the Deeds of the Law, and therefore the Doctrine of Righteousness by Faith ought not to be so strange a Thing to them. And as to their being

Ch. XII. for their Unbelief rejected from being the People of God, and the Gentiles taken in in their room, he shews plainly, that this was foretold them in the Old Testament; and that herein God did them no Injustice. He was Sovereign over all Mankind, and might chuse whom he would to be his People, with the same Freedom that he chose the Posterity of *Abraham* among all the Nations of the Earth, and of that Race chose the Descendants of *Jacob* before those of his elder Brother *Esau*, and that before they had a Being, or were capable of doing Good or Evil. In all which Discourse of his it is plain the Elect spoken of, has for its Object only Nations or collective Bodies Politick in this World, and not particular Persons, in reference to their eternal State in the World to come.

Having thus finished the principal Design of his Writing, we here in this, as is usual with him in all his Epistles, conclude with practical and moral Exhortations, whereof there are several in this Chapter, which we shall take in their Order.

PARAPHRASE.

1. IT being so then that you are become the People of God in the room of the Jews, do not ye fail to offer him that Sacrifice that it is reasonable for you to do, I mean your Bodies ᵉ, not to be slain; but the Lusts thereof being mortified, and the Body cleansed from the Spots and Blemishes of Sin, will be an acceptable Offering to him, and such a Way of Worship as becomes a rational Creature, which therefore I beseech you by the Mercies of God to you, who has made you his People, to present to him. And be not conformed to the Fa-
2.

TEXT.

1 I Beseech you therefore, Brethren, by the mercies of God, that ye present your bodies a living sacrifice, holy, acceptable unto God, which is your reasonable service.

2 And be not conformed

NOTES.

1 ᵉ *Your Bodies.* There seem to be two Reasons why St. *Paul*'s first Exhortation to them is, to present their Bodies undefiled to God: (1.) Because he had before, especially *ch.* vii. so much insisted on this, that the Body was the great Source from whence Sin arose. (2.) Because the Heathen World, and particularly the *Romans*, were guilty of those vile Affections which he mentions, *ch.* i. 24 ——— 27.

shion

ROMANS.

Ch. XII.

TEXT.

to this world: but be ye transformed by the renewing of your mind, that ye may prove what is that good, and acceptable, and perfect will of God.

3 For I say, through the grace given unto me, to every man that is among you, not to think of himself more highly than he ought to think; but to think soberly, according as God hath dealt to every man the measure of faith.

4 For as we have many

PARAPHRASE.

shion of this World ᶠ: But be ye transformed in the renewing of your Minds ᵍ, that you may upon Examination find out, what is the good, the acceptable and perfect Will of God, which now under the Gospel has shewn itself to be in Purity and Holiness of Life: The ritual Observances which he once instituted not being that his good, acceptable and perfect Will which he always intended, they were made only the Types and preparatory Way to this more perfect State under the Gospel ʰ. For by virtue of that Commission, to be the Apostle of the Gentiles, which by the Favour of God is bestowed on me, I bid every one of you, not to think of himself more highly than he ought to think, but to have sober and modest Thoughts of himself, according to that Measure of spiritual Gifts ⁱ, which God has bestowed upon him. For as there are many

3.

4.

NOTES.

2 ᶠ *To the Fashion of this World*; or, as St. Peter expresses it, *not fashioning yourselves according to your former Lusts in the Time of Ignorance,* 1 Pet. i. 14.

ᵍ *Transformed in the renewing of your Minds.* The State of the Gentiles is thus described, Eph. iv. 17 – 19. *As walking in the Vanity of their Minds, having the Understanding darkened, being alienated from the Life of God through the Ignorance that is in them; because of the Blindness of their Hearts, who being past feeling have given themselves over unto Lasciviousness, to work all Uncleanness with Greediness, fulfilling the Lusts of the Flesh and of the Mind.* And Col. i. 21. *Alienated and Enemies in their Minds by wicked Works.* The *renewing* therefore *of their Minds,* or, as he speaks, *Eph.* iv. *in the Spirit of their Minds,* was the getting into an Estate contrary to what they were in before, (*viz.*) to take it in the Apostle's own Words; *That the Eyes of their Understandings might be enlightened;* and that they might *put on the new Man, that is renewed in Knowledge after the Image of him that created him;* that ye *walk as Children of the Light, proving what is acceptable to the Lord, having no Fellowship with the Works of Darkness:* That they *be not unwise, but understanding what is the Will of the Lord: For this is the Will of God, even your Sanctification.* That you should *abstain from Fornication.* That every one of you should *know how to possess his Vessel in Sanctification and Honour, not in the Lusts of Concupiscence, even as the Gentiles that know not God.*

ʰ In these two first Verses of this Chapter is shewn the Preference of the Gospel to the Gentile State and the Jewish Institution.

3 ⁱ Μέτρον πίστεως, *Measure of Faith;* some Copies read χάριτος, *of Favour;* either of them express the same thing, *i. e.* Gifts of the Spirit.

Members

ROMANS. Chap. X.

PARAPHRASE.

Members in one and the same Body, but all the Members are not appointed to the same Work:
5. So we who are many make all but one Body in Christ, and are all Fellow-Members one of
6. another [k]. But having according to the respective Favour that is bestowed upon us, every one of us different Gifts; whether it be Prophecy [l], let us prophesy, according to the Proportion of Faith [m], or Gift of Interpretation, which is given us, *i. e* as far forth as we are enabled by Revelation, and an extraordinary Illumination to understand and expound it, and

TEXT.

members in one body, and all members have not the same office:
5 So we being many are one body in Christ, and every one members one of another.
6 Having then gifts, differing according to the grace that is given to us, whether prophecy, let us prophesy according to the proportion of faith:

NOTES.

5 [k] The same Simile to the same Purpose, see 1 *Cor.* xii.

6 [l] *Prophecy* is enumerated in the New Testament among the Gifts of the Spirit, and means either the Interpretation of Sacred Scripture, and explaining of Prophecies already delivered, or foretelling Things to come.

[m] *According to the Proportion of Faith.* The Context in this and the three preceding Verses leads us, without any Difficulty, into the Meaning of the Apostle in this Expression. 1 *Cor.* xii. and xiv. shew us how apt the new Converts were to be puft up with the several Gifts that were bestowed on them; and every one, as in like Cases is usual, forward to magnify his own, and to carry it farther than in reality it extended. That it is St. *Paul's* Design here to prevent or regulate such Disorder, and to keep every one in the exercising of his particular Gift within its due Bounds, is evident, in that exhorting them, *ver.* 3. to a sober Use of their Gifts (for it is in reference to their spiritual Gifts he speaks in that Verse) he makes the Measure of that Sobriety to be that Measure of Faith or spiritual Gift which every one in particular enjoyed by the Favour of God, *i. e.* That no one should go beyond that which was given him, and he really had. But besides this, which is very obvious, there is another Passage in that Verse, which, rightly considered, strongly inclines this way. *I say through the Grace that is given unto me,* says St. *Paul.* He was going to restrain them in the Exercise of their distinct spiritual Gifts, and he could not introduce what he was going to say in the Case with a more persuasive Argument than his own Example: "I exhort (says he) that every one of you, in the Exercise and Use of his spiritual
"Gift, keep within the Bounds and Measure of that Gift which is given him. I myself, in
"giving you this Exhortation, do it *by the Grace given unto me*; I do it by the Commission
"and Power given me by God, and beyond that I do not go." In one that had before declared himself an Apostle, such an Expression, as this here (if there were not some particular Reason for it) might seem superfluous, and to some idle, but in this View it has a great Grace and Energy in it. There wants nothing but the Study of St. *Paul's* Writings to give us a just Admiration of his great Address, and the Skill wherewith all that he says is adapted to the Argument he has in Hand: "I (says he) according to the Grace given me, direct
"you every one in the Use of your Gifts, which according to the Grace given you are different, whether it be the Gift of Prophecy, to prophesy according to the Proportion or Measure of that Gift or Revelation that he hath. And let him not think that because some Things
"are,

ROMANS.

TEXT.

7 Or ministry, let us wait on our ministring; or he that teacheth, on teaching;
8 Or he that exhorteth, on exhortation: he that giveth, let him do it with simplicity; he that ruleth, with diligence; he that sheweth mercy, with chearfulness.
9 Let love be without dissimulation: Abhor that which is evil, cleave to that which is good.
10 Be kindly affectioned one to another; with brotherly love, in honour preferring one another.
11 Not slothful in business: fervent in spirit; serving the Lord:
12 Rejoicing in hope; patient in tribulation; continuing instant in prayer:
13 Distributing to the necessity of saints; given to hospitality.
14 Bless them which persecute you: bless, and curse not.
15 Rejoice with them that do rejoice, and weep with them that weep.
16 Be of the same mind one towards another. Mind not high things,

PARAPHRASE.

and no farther: Or if it be Ministry, let us wait on our Ministering: He that is a Teacher, let him take care to teach. He whose Gift is Exhortation, let him be diligent in exhorting: He that giveth, let him do it liberally, and without the Mixture of any Self-Interest: He that presideth ⁿ, let him do it with Diligence: He that sheweth Mercy, let him do it with Chearfulness. Let Love be without Dissimulation. Abhor that which is Evil, stick to that which is Good. Be kindly affectioned one towards another with brotherly Love; in Honour preferring one another. Not slothful in Business; but active and vigorous in Mind, directing all to the Service of Christ and the Gospel. Rejoicing in the Hope you have of Heaven and Happiness; patient in Tribulation; frequent and instant in Prayer: Forward to help Christians in Want according to their Necessities; given to Hospitality. Bless them who persecute you: Bless and curse not. Rejoice with them that rejoice, and weep with them that weep. Be of the same Mind one towards another. Do not mind only high Things; but suit yourselves to the mean Condition and

7.
8.
9.
10.
11.
12.
13.
14.
15.
16.

NOTES.

" are, therefore every thing is revealed to him." The same Rule concerning the same Matter St. *Paul* gives, *Eph.* iv. 16. that every Member should act according to the Measure of its own Strength, Power and Energy; 1 *Cor.* xiv. 29 —— 32. may also give light to this Place. This therefore is far from signifying that a Man in interpreting of Sacred Scripture should explain the Sense according to the System of his particular Sect, which each Party is pleased to call the *Analogy of Faith*. For this would be to make the Apostle to set that for a Rule of Interpretation, which had not its Being till long after, and is the Product of fallible Men.

The *Measure of Faith*, ver. 3. and *Proportion of Faith*, in this Verse, signifies the same Thing, viz. so much of that particular Gift which God was pleased to bestow on any one.

8 ⁿ Ὁ προϊστάμενος, *He that ruleth*, says our Translation; the Context inclines to the Sense I have taken it in: See *Vitringa de Synagog.* l. 2. c. 3.

low

PARAPHRASE.

low Concerns of Persons beneath you. Be not
17. wise in your own Conceits. Render to no
Man Evil for Evil: But take care that your
Carriage be such as may be approved by all
18. Men. If it be possible, as much as lieth in
you, live peaceably with all Men. Dear-
19. ly beloved, do not avenge yourselves, but
rather leave that to God. For it is written,
Vengeance is mine, and I will repay it, saith the
20. *Lord.* Therefore if thine Enemy hunger, feed
him; if he thirst, give him Drink; if this
prevail on him, thou subduest an Enemy, and
gainest a Friend; if he persists still in his Enmity, in so doing thou heapest Coals of Fire
on his Head, *i. e.* exposest him to the Wrath
21. of God, who will be thy Avenger. Be not
overcome and prevailed on, by the Evil thou
receivest, to retaliate; but endeavour to master
the Malice of an Enemy in injuring thee, by a
Return of Kindness and good Offices to him.

TEXT.

but condescend to men of low estate. Be not wise in your own conceits.

17 Recompense to no man evil for evil. Provide things honest in the sight of all men.

18 If it be possible, as much as lieth in you, live peaceably with all men.

19 Dearly beloved, avenge not yourselves, but rather give place unto wrath: for it is written, Vengeance is mine; I will repay, saith the Lord.

20 Therefore if thine enemy hunger, feed him; if he thirst, give him drink: for in so doing thou shalt heap coals of fire on his head.

21 Be not overcome of evil, but overcome evil with good.

ROMANS.

SECT. XI.

CHAP. XIII. 1——7.

CONTENTS.

THIS Section contains the Duty of Christians to the Civil Magistrate. For the understanding this right, we must consider these two Things.

1. That these Rules are given to Christians that were Members of a Heathen Commonwealth, to shew them that by being made Christians and Subjects of Christ's Kingdom, they were not by the Freedom of the Gospel exempt from any Ties of Duty or Subjection, which by the Laws of their Country they were in, and ought to observe, to the Government and Magistrates of it, though Heathens, any more than any of their Heathen Subjects. But on the other Side, these Rules did not tie them up any more than any of their Fellow-Citizens, who were not Christians, from any of those due Rights, which by the Law of Nature, or the Constitutions of their Country, belonged to them. Whatsoever any other of their Fellow-Subjects, being in a like Station with them, might do without sinning, that they were not abridged of, but might do still being Christians. The Rule being here the same with that given by St. *Paul,* 1 Cor. vii. 17. *As God has called every one, so let him walk.* The Rules of Civil Right and Wrong that he is to walk by, are to him the same they were before.

2. That St. *Paul* in this Direction to the *Romans,* does not so much describe the Magistrates that then were in *Rome,* as tells whence they, and all Magistrates every where, have their Authority; and for what End they have it, and should use it. And this he does as becomes his Prudence, to avoid bringing any Imputation on Christians from Heathen Magistrates, especially those insolent and vicious ones of *Rome,* who could not brook any thing to be told them as their Duty, and so might be apt to interpret such plain Truths laid down in a dogmatical Way, into Sauciness, Sedition, or Treason; a Scandal cautiously to be kept off from the Christian Doctrine. Nor does he, in what he says, in the least flatter the *Roman* Emperor, let it be either *Claudius,* as some think; or *Nero,*

Ch. XIII. as others, who then was in Possession of that Empire. For he speaks here of the *Higher Powers*, i. e. the Supreme Civil Power, which is in every Commonwealth derived from God, and is of the same Extent every where, *i. e.* is absolute and unlimited by any thing but the End for which God gave it, *viz.* the Good of the People sincerely pursued, according to the best of the Skill of those who share that Power, and so not to be resisted. But how Men come by a rightful Title to this Power, or who has that Title, he is wholly silent, and says nothing of it. To have meddled with that would have been to decide of Civil Rights, contrary to the Design and Business of the Gospel, and the Example of our Saviour, who refused meddling in such Cases with this decisive Question, *Who made me a Judge or Divider over you?* Luke xii. 14.

PARAPHRASE.

1. LET every one of you, none excepted °, be subject to the over-ruling Powers ᵖ of the Government he lives in. There is no Power but

TEXT.

1. LET every soul be subject unto the higher powers. For there is no

NOTES.

1. ° *Every one*, however endowed with miraculous Gifts of the Holy Ghost, or advanced to any Dignity in the Church of Christ. For that these Things were apt to make Men over-value themselves, is obvious from what St. *Paul* says to the *Corinthians*, 1 *Cor.* xii. and here to the *Romans*, chap. xii. 3——5. But above all others, the Jews were apt to have an inward Reluctancy and Indignation against the Power of any Heathen over them, taking it to be an unjust and tyrannical Usurpation upon them, who were the People of God, and their Betters. These the Apostle thought it necessary to restrain, and therefore says in the Language of the Jews, *Every Soul*, i. e. every Person among you, whether Jew or Gentile, must live in Subjection to the Civil Magistrate. We see by what St. *Peter* says on the like Occasion, that there was great need that Christians should have this Duty inculcated to them, lest any among them should use their Liberty for a Cloak of Maliciousness or Misbehaviour, 1 *Pet.* ii. 13 - 16. The Doctrine of Christianity was a Doctrine of Liberty. And St. *Paul* in this Epistle had taught them, that all Christians were free from the Mosaical Law. Hence corrupt and mistaking Men, especially Jewish Converts, impatient, as we have observed, of any Heathen Dominion, might be ready to infer that Christians were exempt from Subjection to the Laws of Heathen Governments. This he obviates by telling them, That all other Governments derived the Power they had from God, as well as that of the Jews, though they had not the whole Frame of their Government immediately from him as the Jews had.

ᵖ Whether we take *Powers* here in the Abstract for Political Authority, or in the Concrete for the Persons, *de facto* exercising Political Power and Jurisdiction, the Sense will be the same, *viz.* that Christians, by Virtue of being Christians, are not any way exempt from Obedience to the Civil Magistrates, nor ought by any Means to resist them, though by what is said, *ver.* 3. it

seems

ROMANS. Ch. XIII.

TEXT.

power but of God: the powers that be, are ordained of God.

2 Whosoever therefore resisteth the power, resisteth the ordinance of God: and they that resist, shall receive to themselves damnation.

3 For rulers are not a terror to good works, but to the evil. Wilt thou then not be afraid of the power? do that which is good, and thou shalt have praise of the same:

4 For he is the minister of God to thee for good. But if thou do that which is evil, be afraid; for he beareth not the sword in vain: for he is the minister of God, a revenger to execute wrath upon him that doth evil.

5 Wherefore ye must needs be subject, not only for wrath, but also for conscience sake.

6 For, for this cause pay you tribute also: for they are God's ministers, attending

PARAPHRASE.

but what is from God: The Powers that are in Being are ordained by God: So that he who resisteth the Power, resisteth the Ordinance of God; and they that resist will be punished by those Powers that they resist. What should you be afraid of? Rulers are no Terror to those that do well, but to those that do ill. Wilt thou then not live in dread of the Civil Power? Do that which is good and right, and then Praise only is thy Due from the Magistrate. For he is the Officer and Minister of God appointed only for thy Good. But if thou doest amiss, then thou hast reason to be afraid. For he bears not the Sword in vain. For he is the Minister of God, and Executioner of Wrath and Punishment upon him that doth ill. This being the End of Government, and the Business of the Magistrate, to cherish the good, and punish ill Men, it is necessary for you to submit to Government, not only in Apprehension of the Punishment which Disobedience will draw on you, but out of Conscience, as a Duty required of you by God. This is the Reason why also you pay Tribute, which is due to the Magistrates, because they employ their Care, Time and Pains for the publick Weal, in pu-

2.

3.

4.

5.

6.

NOTES.

seems that St. *Paul* meant here Magistrates, having and exercising a lawful Power. But whether the Magistrates in being were or were not such, and consequently were or were not to be obeyed, that Christianity gave them no peculiar Power to examine. They had the common Right of others their Fellow-Citizens, but had no distinct Privilege as Christians. And therefore we see, *ver.* 7. where he enjoins the paying of Tribute and Custom, *&c.* it is in these Words: *Render to all their Dues, Tribute to whom Tribute is due, Honour to whom Honour*, &c. But who it was to whom any of these, or any other Dues of Right belonged, he decides not; for that he leaves them to be determined by the Laws and Constitutions of their Country.

T t 2   nishing

ROMANS.

PARAPHRASE.

nishing and restraining the Wicked and Vicious, and in countenancing and supporting the Virtuous and Good. Render therefore to all their Dues: Tribute to whom Tribute is due, Custom to whom Custom, Fear to whom Fear, and Honour to whom Honour.

TEXT.

continually upon this very thing.

7. Render therefore to all their dues: tribute to whom tribute is due, custom to whom custom, fear to whom fear, honour to whom honour.

SECT. XII.
CHAP. XIII. 8——14.

CONTENTS.

HE exhorts them to Love, which is in effect the fulfilling of the whole Law.

PARAPHRASE.

8. OWE nothing to any body but Affection and Good-will mutually to one another: For he that loves others sincerely, as he does

9. himself, has fulfilled the Law. For this Precept, Thou shalt not commit Adultery, Thou shalt not kill, Thou shalt not steal, Thou shalt not bear false Witness, Thou shalt not covet, and whatever other Command there be concerning social Duties, it in short is comprehended in this, Thou shalt love thy Neighbour

10. as thyself. Love permits us to do no Harm to our Neighbour, and therefore is the fulfilling

11. of the whole Law of the second Table. And all this do, considering that it is now high Time that we rouse ourselves up, shake off Sleep, and betake ourselves with Vigilancy and Vigor to the Duties of a Christian Life. For the Time of your Removal out of this Place of Exercise and Probationership is nearer than

TEXT.

8. OWE no man any thing, but to love one another: for he that loveth another, hath fulfilled the law.

9. For this, Thou shalt not commit adultery, Thou shalt not kill, Thou shalt not steal, Thou shalt not bear false witness, Thou shalt not covet; and if there be any other commandment, it is briefly comprehended in this saying, namely, Thou shalt love thy neighbour as thy self.

10. Love worketh no ill to his neighbour: therefore love is the fulfilling of the law.

11. And that, knowing the time, that now it is high time to awake out of sleep: for now is our sal-

when

Ch. XIII.

TEXT.

vation nearer than when we believed.

12 The night is far spent, the day is at hand: let us therefore cast off the works of darkness, and let us put on the armour of light.

13 Let us walk honestly as in the day; not in rioting and drunkenness, not in chambering and wantonness, not in strife and envying.

14 But put ye on the Lord Jesus Christ, and make not provision for the flesh, to fulfil the lusts thereof.

PARAPHRASE.

when you first entered into the Profession of Christianity ⁿ. The Night, the dark State of this World, wherein the Good and the Bad can scarce be distinguished, is far spent. The Day that will shew every one in his own Dress and Colours is at hand. Let us therefore put away the Works that we should be ashamed of but in the Dark; and let us put on the Dress ʳ and Ornaments, that we should be willing to appear in the Light. Let our Behaviour be decent, and our Carriage such as fears not the Light, nor the Eyes of Men; not in disorderly Feastings and Drunkenness; not in Dalliance and Wantonness ˢ; nor in Strife and Envy ᵗ. But walk in Newness of Life, in Obedience to the Precepts of the Gospel, as becomes those who are baptized into the Faith of Christ; and let not the great Employment of your Thoughts and Cares be wholly in making Provision for the Body, that you may have wherewithal to satisfy your carnal Lusts.

12.

13.

14.

NOTES.

11, 12 ⁿ It seems by these two Verses, as if St. *Paul* looked upon Christ's coming as not far off, to which there are several other concurrent Passages in his Epistles: See 1 *Cor.* i. 7.

12 ʳ *Ὅπλα, Armour*. The Word in the Greek is often used for the Apparel, Clothing, and Accoutrements of the Body.

13 ˢ These he seems to name with reference to the Night which he had mentioned, these being the Disorders to which the Night is usually set apart.

ᵗ These probably were set down with regard to universal Love and Good-will, which he was principally here pressing them to.

SECT.

ROMANS.

SECT. XIII.

CHAP. XIV. 1.——XV. 13.

CONTENTS.

ST. *Paul* instructs both the Strong and the Weak in their mutual Duties one to another in respect of Things indifferent, teaching them that the Strong should not use their Liberty where it might offend a weak Brother; nor the Weak censure the Strong for using their Liberty.

PARAPHRASE.

1. HIM that is weak in the Faith, *i. e.* not fully persuaded of his Christian Liberty in the Use of some indifferent Thing, receive you into your Friendship and Conversation ᵘ, without any Coldness or Distinction; but do not engage him in Disputes and Controversies
2. about it. For such Variety is there in Mens Persuasions about their Christian Liberty, that one believeth that he may without Restraint eat all Things; another is so scrupulous that he
3. eateth nothing but Herbs. Let not him that is persuaded of his Liberty, and eateth, despise him that through Scruple eateth not: And let not him that is more doubtful and eateth not, judge or censure him that eateth, for God hath

TEXT.

1 HIM that is weak in the faith receive you, but not to doubtful disputations.

2 For one believeth that he may eat all things: another who is weak, eateth herbs.

3 Let not him that eateth despise him that eateth not; and let not him which eateth not, judge

NOTES.

1 ᵘ That the Reception here spoken of is the receiving into familiar and ordinary Conversation, is evident from *chap.* xv. 7. where he directing them to receive one another mutually, uses the same Word προσλαμβάνεσθε, *i. e.* live together in a free and friendly Manner, the Weak with the Strong, and the Strong with the Weak, without any Regard to the Differences among you about the Lawfulness of any indifferent Things. Let those that agree or differ concerning the Use of any indifferent Thing, live together all alike.

received

ROMANS.

Ch. XIV.

TEXT.

him that eateth: for God hath received him.

4 Who art thou that judgest another man's servant? To his own master he standeth or falleth: yea, he shall be holden up: for God is able to make him stand.

5 One man esteemeth one day above another: another esteemeth every day alike. Let every man be fully persuaded in his own mind.

6 He that regardeth the day, regardeth it unto the Lord; and he that re-

PARAPHRASE.

received ʷ him into his Church and Family: And who art thou that takest upon thee to judge the Domestick of another, whether he be of his Family or no? It is his own Master alone who is to judge whether he be or shall continue his Domestick or no: What hast thou to do to meddle in the Case? But trouble not thyself, he shall stand and stay in the Family. For God is able to conform and establish him there. One Man judgeth ˣ one Day to be set apart to God more than another, another Man judgeth every Day to be God's alike. Let every one take care to be satisfied in his own Mind touching the Matter. But let him not censure ʸ another in what he doth. He that observeth a Day, observeth it as the Lord's Servant, in Obedience to him: And he that

4.

5.

6.

NOTES.

4 ʷ *By him that eateth*, ver. 3. St. *Paul* seems to mean the Gentiles, who were less scrupulous in the Use of indifferent Things; and by *him that eateth not*, the Jews, who made a great Distinction of Meats and Drinks, and Days, and placed in them a great, and as they thought necessary Part of the Worship of the true God. To the Gentiles the Apostle gives this Caution, that they should not contemn the Jews, as weak narrow minded Men, that laid so much Stress on Matters of so small Moment, and thought Religion so much concerned in those indifferent Things. On the other Side, he exhorts the Jews not to judge that those who neglected the Jewish Observances of Meats and Days were still Heathens, or would soon apostatize to Heathenism again: No, says he; God has received them, and they are of his Family; and thou hast nothing to do to judge whether they are or will continue of his Family, or no; that belongs only to him, the Master of the Family, to judge, whether they shall stay or leave his Family, or no. But, notwithstanding thy Censure or hard Thoughts of them, they shall not fall off or apostatize; for God is able to continue them in his Family, in his Church, notwithstanding thou suspectest, from their free Use of Things indifferent, they incline too much, or approach too near to Gentilism.

5 ˣ The Apostle having in the foregoing Verse used κρίνειν ἀδελφὸν ἑαυτοῦ, for judging any one to be or not to be another Man's Servant or Domestick, he seems here to continue the Use of the Word κρίνειν in the same Signification, *i. e.* for judging a Day to be more peculiarly God's.

ʸ This may be concluded to be the Apostle's Sense, because the Thing he is upon here, is to keep them from censuring one another in the Use of Things indifferent; particularly the Jews from judging the Gentiles in their Neglect of the Observance of Days or Meats. This judging being what St. *Paul* principally endeavoured here to restrain, as being opposite to the Liberty of the Gospel, which favoured a Neglect of these Rituals of the Law which were now antiquated. See *Gal.* iv. 9 —— 11. and v. 1, 2.

observeth

PARAPHRASE.

observeth it not, passes by that Observance as the Lord's Servant in Obedience also to the Lord. He that eateth, what another out of Scruple forbears, eateth it as the Lord's Servant: For he giveth God Thanks. And he that out of Scruple forbeareth to eat, does it also as the Lord's Servant: For he giveth God Thanks even for that which he doeth, and thinks he may not eat. For no one of us Christians liveth, as if he were his own Man, perfectly at his own Disposal: And no one ᵃ of us dies so. For whether we live, our Life is appropriated to the Lord; or whether we die, to him we die as his Servants. For whether we live or die, we are his, in his Family, his Domesticks ᵃ, appropriated to him. For to this End Christ died, and rose, and lived again, that he might be Lord and Proprietor of us ᵇ both dead and living. What hast thou then to do to judge thy Brother, who is none of thy Servant, but thy Equal? Or how darest thou

7.

8.

9.

10.

TEXT.

gardeth not the day, to the Lord he doth not regard it. He that eateth, eateth to the Lord, for he giveth God thanks; and he that eateth not, to the Lord he eateth not, and giveth God thanks.

For none of us liveth to 7 himself, and no man dieth to himself.

For whether we live, 8 we live unto the Lord; and whether we die, we die unto the Lord: whether we live therefore, or die, we are the Lord's.

For to this end Christ 9 both died, and rose, and revived, that he might be Lord both of the dead and living.

But why dost thou 10 judge thy brother? Or

NOTES.

7 ᵃ Οὐδεὶς, should, I suppose, be taken here with the same Limitation it hath in the former Part of the Verse with the Pronoun ἡμῶν; and so should here, as there, be rendered in English, *no one of us*, and not, *no Man*. St. *Paul* speaking here only of Christians, this Sense of οὐδεὶς the next Verse seems to confirm.

8 ᵃ These Words, *we are the Lord's*, give an easy Interpretation to these Phrases of *eating and living*, &c. *to the Lord*: For they make them plainly refer to what he had said at the latter End of ver. 3. *For God hath received him*; signifying that God had received all those who profess the Gospel, and had given their Names up to Jesus Christ, into his Family, and had made them his Domesticks. And therefore we should not judge or censure one another, for that every Christian was the Lord's Domestick, appropriated to him as his menial Servant: And therefore all that he did in that State, was to be looked on as done to the Lord, and not to be accounted for to any body else.

9 ᵇ Κυριεύσῃ, *might be Lord*; must be taken so here as to make this agree with the foregoing Verse. There it was *we*, i. e. *we* Christians, whether we live or die, are the Lord's Property: For the Lord died and rose again, that we, whether living or dying, should be his.

to

ROMANS.

Ch. XIV

TEXT.

why doſt thou ſet at nought thy brother? For we ſhall all ſtand before the judgment-ſeat of Chriſt.

11 For it is written, As I live, ſaith the Lord, every knee ſhall bow to me, and every tongue ſhall confeſs to God.

12 So then every one of us ſhall give account of himſelf to God.

13 Let us not therefore judge one another any more: but judge this rather, that no man put a ſtumbling block, or an occaſion to fall in his brother's way.

14 I know, and am perſuaded by the Lord Jeſus, that there is nothing unclean of itſelf: but to him that eſteemeth any thing to be unclean, to him it is unclean.

15 But if thy brother be grieved with thy meat, now walkeſt thou not charitably. Deſtroy not him with thy meat, for whom Chriſt died.

16 Let not then your good be evil ſpoken of.

17 For the Kingdom of God is not meat and drink, but righteouſneſs, and peace, and joy in the Holy Ghoſt.

PARAPHRASE.

to think contemptibly of him. For we ſhall, thou, and he, and all of us, be brought before the Judgment-Seat of Chriſt, and there we ſhall anſwer every one for himſelf to our Lord and Maſter. For it is written, *As I live,* ſaith the Lord, *every Knee ſhall bow to me, and every Tongue ſhall confeſs to God.* So then every one of us ſhall give an Account of himſelf to God. Let us not therefore take upon us to judge one another; but rather come to this Judgment or Determination of Mind, that no Man put ᶜ a Stumbling-Block, or an Occaſion of falling in his Brother's Way. I know, and am fully aſſured by the Lord Jeſus, that there is nothing unclean or unlawful to be eaten of itſelf. But to him that accounts any thing to be unclean, to him it is unclean. But if thy Brother be grieved ᵈ with thy Meat, thy Carriage is uncharitable to him. Deſtroy not him with thy Meat, for whom Chriſt died. Let not then your Liberty, which is a Good ᵉ you enjoy under the Goſpel, be evil ſpoken of. For the Privileges and Advantages of the Kingdom of God do not conſiſt in the Enjoyment of greater Variety of Meats and Drinks, but in Uprightneſs of Life, Peace of all Kinds, and Joy in the Gifts and Benefits of the Holy Ghoſt

11.
12.
13.
14.
15.
16.
17.

NOTES.

13 ᶜ He had before reproved the Weak that cenſured the Strong in the Uſe of their Liberty. He comes now to reſtrain the Strong from offending their weak Brethren by a free Uſe of their Liberty, in not forbearing the Uſe of it where it might give Offence to the Weak.

15 ᵈ *Grieved* does not here ſignify ſimply, made ſorrowful for what thou doeſt; but brought into Trouble and Diſcompoſure, or receive an Hurt or Wound, as every one does, who by another's Example does what he ſuppoſes to be unlawful. This Senſe is confirmed in the Words, *Deſtroy not him with thy Meat*: And alſo by what he ſays, 1 *Cor.* viii. 9——13. in the like Caſe.

16 ᵉ See 1 *Cor.* x. 30.

U u   under

PARAPHRASE.

18. under the Gospel. For he that in these Things pays his Allegiance and Service to Jesus Christ, as a dutiful Subject of his Kingdom, is accep-
19. table to God, and approved of Men. The Things therefore that we set our Hearts upon to pursue and promote, let them be such as tend to Peace and Good-will, and the mutual
20. Edification of one another. Do not for a little Meat destroy a Man, that is the Work [f] of God, and no ordinary Piece of Workmanship. It is true, all Sort of wholesome Food is pure, and defileth not a Man's Conscience. But yet it is evil to him who eateth any Thing, so as to
21. offend his Brother. It is better to forbear Flesh, and Wine, and any Thing, rather than in the Use of thy Liberty, in any indifferent Things, to do that whereby thy Brother stumbleth, or is offended, or is made weak [g].
22. Thou art fully persuaded of the Lawfulness of eating the Meat which thou eatest: It is well. Happy is he that is not self-condemned in the Thing that he practises. But have a care to keep this Faith or Persuasion to thyself: Let it be between God and thy own Conscience: Raise no Dispute about it; neither make Ostentation of it [h] by thy Practice before others. But he
23. that is in doubt, and balanceth [i], is self-con-

TEXT.

For he that in these 18 things serveth Christ, is acceptable to God, and approved of men.

Let us therefore follow 19 after the things which make for peace, and things wherewith one may edify another.

For meat destroy not 20 the work of God. All things indeed are pure; but it is evil for that man who eateth with offence.

It is good neither to 21 eat flesh, nor to drink wine, nor any thing whereby thy brother stumbleth, or is offended, or is made weak.

Hast thou faith? have 22 it to thyself before God. Happy is he that condemneth not himself in that thing which he alloweth.

And he that doubteth is 23 damned if he eat, be-

NOTES.

20 [f] *The Force of this Argument, see* Matth. vi. 25. *The Life is more than Meat.*

21 [g] *Offended and made weak,* i. e. drawn to the doing of any thing, of whose Lawfulness not being fully persuaded, it becomes a Sin to him.

22 [h] *These two, viz.* not disputing about it, which he forbad, *v.* 1. and not using his Liberty before any one whom possibly it may offend, may be supposed to be contained in these Words, *Have it to thyself.*

23 [i] Διακρινόμενος, translated here *doubteth,* is, *Rom.* iv. 20. translated *staggered;* and is there opposed to ἐνεδυναμώθη τῇ πίστει, *strong in the Faith;* or to πληροφορηθεὶς, *fully persuaded,* as it follows in the next Verse.

demned,

ROMANS.

Ch. XV.

TEXT.

cause he eateth not of faith: for whatsoever is not of faith, is sin.

1 We then that are strong, ought to bear the infirmities of the weak, and not to please ourselves.

2 Let every one of us please his neighbour for his good to edification.

3 For even Christ pleased not himself; but as it is writen, The reproaches of them that reproached thee, fell on me.

4 For whatsoever things were written aforetime, were written for our learning; that we through patience and comfort of the scriptures might have hope.

5 Now the God of patience and consolation grant you to be like minded one towards another, according to Christ Jesus:

6 That ye may with one mind and one mouth glorify God; even the Father of our Lord Jesus Christ.

7 Wherefore receive ye one another, as Christ

PARAPHRASE.

demned, if he eat; because he doth it without a full Persuasion of the Lawfulness of it. For whatever a Man doth, which he is not fully persuaded in his own Mind to be lawful, is Sin. We then that are strong ought to bear the Infirmities of the Weak, and not to indulge our own Appetites or Inclinations, in such an Use of indifferent Things as may offend the Weak. But let every one of us please his Neighbour, comply with his Infirmities for his Good, and to Edification. For even Christ our Lord pleased not himself; but as it is written, *The Reproaches of them that reproached thee are fallen upon me.* For whatsoever was heretofore written, *i. e.* in the Old Testament, was written for our Learning, that we through Patience, and the Comfort which the Scriptures give us, might have Hope. Now God, who is the Giver of Patience and Consolation, make you to be at Unity one with another, according to the Will of Christ Jesus; That you may with one Mind and one Mouth glorify the God and Father of our Lord Jesus Christ. Wherefore admit and receive one another ^k into Fellowship

1.

2.

3.

4.

5.

6.

7.

NOTES.

7 ^k Προσλαμβάνεσθε, *receive one another*, cannot mean receive one another into Church-Communion: For there is no Appearance, that the convert Jews and Gentiles separated Communion in *Rome* upon account of Differences about Meats and Drinks, and Days. We should have heard more of it from St. *Paul*, if there had been two separate Congregations, *i. e.* two Churches of Christians in *Rome* divided about these indifferent Things. Besides, Directions cannot be given to private Christians to *receive* one another in that Sense. The *receiving* therefore here, must be understood of *receiving* as a Man doth another into his Company, Converse and Familiarity, *i. e.* He would have them, Jews and Gentiles, lay by all Distinction, Coldness, and Reservedness in their Conversation one with another; and as Domesticks of the same Family, live friendly and familiar, notwithstanding their different Judgments about those ritual Observances. Hence, *ver.* 5. he exhorts them to be united in Friendship one to another, that with one Heart and one Voice they might conjointly glorify God, and receive one another with the same Good-will that Christ has received us the Jews, εἰς δόξαν τῦ Θεῦ, to the glorifying of God for

U u 2

his

ROMANS. Ch. XV.

PARAPHRASE.

ship and Familiarity, without Shiness or Distance, upon occasion of Differences about Things indifferent, even as Christ received us Jews to
8. glorify ¹ God. (For ᵐ I must tell you, ye converted *Romans*, that Christ was sent to the Jews, and employed all his Ministry ⁿ on those of the Circumcision) for his Truth in making good his Promise made to the Fathers, *i. e.*
9. *Abraham*, *Isaac*, and *Jacob*; and received you the Gentiles to glorify God for his Mercy to you, as it is written; *For this Cause I will confess to thee among the Gentiles, and sing unto thy*
10. *Name.* And again he saith, *Rejoice, ye Gentiles,*
11. *with his People.* And again, *Praise the Lord, all ye Gentiles, and laud him, all ye Nations.* And
12. again *Isaiah* saith, *There shall be a Root of Jesse, and he that shall rise to reign over the Gentiles, in*

TEXT.

also received us, to the glory of God.

8 Now I say, that Jesus Christ was a minister of the circumcision for the truth of God, to confirm the promises made unto the fathers:

9 And that the Gentiles might glorify God for his mercy; as it is written, For this cause I will confess to thee among the Gentiles, and sing unto thy name.

10 And again he saith, Rejoice, ye Gentiles, with his people.

11 And again, Praise the Lord, all ye Gentiles, and laud him, all ye people.

12 There shall be a root of Jesse, and he that shall rise to reign over the

NOTES.

his Truth, in fulfilling the Promises he made to the Patriarchs, and received the Gentiles to glorify God for his Mercy to them. So that we have Reason, both Jews and Gentiles, laying aside these little Differences about Things indifferent, to join together heartily in glorifying God.

¹ Εἰς δόξαν τȣ̃ Θεȣ̃, *to the Glory of God*; i. e. to glorify God by the same Figure of Speech that he uses πίϛις Ἰησȣ̃, *the Faith of Jesus*, for believing in *Jesus*, *Rom.* iii. 22, and 26. The Thing that St. *Paul* is exhorting them to here, is to the glorifying of God with one accord; as is evident from the immediately preceding Words, *ver.* 6. and that which follows, *ver.* 9, 10, 11. is to the same purpose: So that there is no room to doubt that his Meaning in these Words is this, *(viz.)* Christ received or took us believing Jews to himself, that we might magnify the Truth of God; and took the Gentiles that believe to himself, that they might magnify God's Mercy. This stands easy in the Construction of his Words, and Sense of his Mind.

ᵐ *(Now I say, that Jesus Christ was a Minister of the Circumcision.)* These Words are plainly a Parenthesis, and spoken with some Emphasis, to restrain the Gentile Converts of *Rome*; who, as it is plain from *chap.* xiv. 3. were apt, ἐξȣθενεῖτε]αι, to set at nought and despise the converted Jews for sticking to their ritual Observances of Meats and Drinks, &c.

ⁿ Διακονον περιτομῆς; *a Minister of*, or *to the Circumcision*. What it was that Christ ministred to the Jews, we may see by the like Expression of St. *Paul*, applied to himself, *ver.* 16. where he calls himself *a Minister of Jesus Christ to the Gentiles, ministring the Gospel of God*.

him

ROMANS.

Ch. XV.

TEXT.

Gentiles; in him shall the Gentiles trust.
13 Now the God of hope fill you with all joy and peace in believing, that ye may abound in hope through the power of the Holy Ghost.

PARAPHRASE.

him shall the Gentiles trust °. Now the God of Hope fill you with all Joy and Peace in Believing, that ye may abound in Hope, through the Power of the Holy Ghost ᴾ.

13.

NOTES.

12 ° Επ' αυτῷ ἔθνη ἐλπιοῦσι, *in him shall the Gentiles trust*, rather *hope*; not that there is any material Difference in the Signification of *trust* and *hope*, but the better to express and answer St. *Paul's* Way of writing, with whom it is familiar, when he had been speaking of any Virtue or Grace whereof God is the Author, to call God thereupon the God of that Virtue or Favour. An eminent Example whereof we have a few Verses backwards, *ver.* 4. ἵνα διὰ τῆς ὑπομονῆς κỳ τῆς παρακλήσεως τῶν γραφῶν τὴν ἐλπίδα ἔχωμεν, *That we through Patience and Comfort*, rather *Consolation of the Scripture might have hope*; and then subjoins, ὁ δὲ Θεὸς τῆς ὑπομενῆς κỳ τῆς παρακλήσεως, *Now the God of Patience and Consolation*. And so here, ἔθνη ἐλπιοῦσι, ὁ δὲ Θεὸς ἐλπίδος, *The Gentiles shall hope*, *now the God of Hope*.

13 ᴾ The Gifts of the *Holy Ghost* bestowed upon the Gentiles, were a Foundation of Hope to them, that they were, by believing, the Children or People of God as well as the Jews.

SECT. XIV.

CHAP. XV. 14——33.

CONTENTS.

IN the remaining Part of this Chapter St. *Paul* makes a very kind and skilful Apology to them for this Epistle: Expresses an earnest Desire of coming to them: Touches upon the Reasons that hitherto had hindred him: Desires their Prayers for his Deliverance from the Jews in his Journey to *Jerusalem*, whither he was going; and promises that from thence he will make them a Visit in his way to *Spain*.

ROMANS.

PARAPHRASE.

14. As to my own Thoughts concerning you, my Brethren, I am persuaded that you also, as well as others, are full of Goodness, abounding in all Knowledge, and able to instruct
15. one another. Nevertheless, Brethren, I have written to you in some Things pretty freely, as your Remembrancer, which I have been imboldened to do, by the Commission which God has been graciously pleased to bestow on me,
16. whom he hath made to be the Minister of Jesus Christ to the Gentiles in the Gospel of God, in which holy Ministration I officiate, that the Gentiles may be made an acceptable Offering ^q to God, sanctified by the pouring out of the
17. Holy Ghost upon them. I have therefore Matter of glorying through Jesus Christ, as to
18. those Things that pertain ^r to God. For I shall not venture to trouble you with any concerning myself, but only what Christ hath wrought by me, for the bringing of the Gentiles to Christianity, both in Profession and
19. Practice, through mighty Signs and Wonders, by the Power of the Holy Ghost, so that from *Jerusalem* and the neighbouring Countries, all along quite to *Illyricum*, I have effectually preach-
20. ed the Gospel of Christ, but so as studiously to avoid the carrying of it to those Places where it was already planted, and where the People

TEXT.

And I myself also am 14 persuaded of you, my brethren, that ye also are full of goodness, filled with all knowledge, able also to admonish one another.

Nevertheless, brethren, 15 I have written the more boldly unto you, in some sort, as putting you in mind, because of the grace that is given to me of God.

That I should be the 16 minister of Jesus Christ to the Gentiles, ministring the Gospel of God, that the offering up of the Gentiles might be acceptable, being sanctified by the Holy Ghost.

I have therefore where- 17 of I may glory through Jesus Christ, in those things which pertain to God.

For I will not dare to 18 speak of any of those things which Christ hath not wrought by me, to make the Gentiles obedient, by word and deed,

Through mighty signs 19 and wonders, by the power of the Spirit of God; so that from Jerusalem and round about unto Illyricum I have fully preached the Gospel of Christ.

Yea, so have I strived 20

NOTES.

16 ^q *Offering.* See *Isa.* lxvi. 20.

17 ^r Τὰ πρὸς Θεὸν, *Things that pertain to God.* The same Phrase we have *Heb.* v. 1. where it signifies the Things that were offered to God in the Temple-ministration. St. *Paul*, by way of Allusion, speaks of the Gentiles in the following Verse, as an Offering to be made to God; and of himself, as the Priest by whom the Sacrifice or Offering was to be prepared and offered; and then he here tells them, that he had Matter of glorying in this Offering, *i. e.* that he had had Success in converting the Gentiles, and bringing them to be a living, holy, and acceptable Sacrifice to God; an Account whereof he gives them in the four following Verses.

were

ROMANS.

Ch. XV.

TEXT.

to preach the gospel, not where Christ was named, lest I should build upon another man's foundation:

21 But as it is written, To whom he was not spoken of, they shall see: and they that have not heard, shall understand.

22 For which cause also I have been much hindred from coming to you:

23 But now having no more place in these parts, and having a great desire these many years to come unto you;

24 Whensoever I take my journey into Spain, I will come to you; for I trust to see you in my journey, and to be brought on my way thitherward by you, if first I be somewhat filled with your company.

25 But now I go unto Jerusalem to minister unto the saints.

26 For it hath pleased them of Macedonia and Achaia, to make a certain contribution for the poor saints which are at Jerusalem.

27 It hath pleased them verily, and their debtors they are. For if the Gentiles have been made partakers of their spiritual things, their duty is also to minister unto them in carnal things.

28 When therefore I have performed this, and have sealed to them this fruit, I will come by you into Spain.

PARAPHRASE.

were already Christians, lest I should build upon another Man's Foundation ⁵. But as 21. it is written ᵗ, *To whom he was not spoken of they shall see: And they that have not heard shall understand.* This has often hindred me from 22. coming to you: But now having in these Parts 23. no Place, where Christ hath not been heard of, to preach the Gospel in; and having had for these many Years a Desire to come to you, I will, when I take my Journey to *Spain*, take 24. you in my Way: For I hope then to see you, and to be brought on my Way thitherward by you, when I have for some Time enjoyed your Company, and pretty well satisfied my Longing upon that Account. But at present I am setting 25. out for *Jerusalem*, going to minister to the Saints there. For it hath pleased those of *Ma-* 26. *cedonia* and *Achaia*, to make a Contribution for the Poor among the Saints at *Jerusalem*. It hath 27. pleased them to do so, and they are indeed their Debtors. For if the Gentiles have been made Partakers of their spiritual Things, they are bound on their Side to minister to them for the Support of this temporal Life. When therefore 28. I have dispatched this Business, and put this Fruit of my Labours into their Hands, I will come to you in my Way to *Spain*. And I know

NOTES.

20 ˢ See 1 *Cor.* iii. 10. 2 *Cor.* x. 16.
21 ᵗ *Isa.* lii. 15.

that

ROMANS.

PARAPHRASE.

29. that when I come unto you, I shall bring with me to you full Satisfaction concerning the Blessedness which you receive by the Gospel " of
30. Christ. Now I beseech you, Brethren, by our Lord Jesus Christ, and by the Love which comes from the Spirit of God, to join with me
31. in earnest Prayers to God for me, that I may be delivered from the Unbelievers in *Judea*; and that the Service I am doing the Saints there
32. may be acceptable to them. That if it be the Will of God, I may come to you with Joy, and
33. may be refreshed together with you. Now the God of Peace be with you all. Amen.

TEXT.

And I am sure that 29 when I come unto you, I shall come in the fulness of the blessing of the gospel of Christ.

Now I beseech you, 30 brethren, for the Lord Jesus Christ's sake, and for the love of the spirit, that ye strive together with me in your prayers to God for me:

That I may be deliver-31 ed from them that do not believe in Judea; and that my service which I have for Jerusalem may be accepted of the saints:

That I may come unto 32 you with joy by the will of God, and may with you be refreshed.

Now the God of peace 33 be with you all. Amen.

NOTES.

29 " He may be understood to mean here, that he should be able to satisfy them, that by the Gospel the Forgiveness of Sins was to be obtained. For that he shews, *chap.* iv. 6 — 9. And they had as much Title to it by the Gospel as the Jews themselves; which was the Thing he had been making out to them in this Epistle.

ROMANS.
SECT. XV.
CHAP. XVI. 1——27.
CONTENTS.

THE foregoing Epistle furnishes us with Reasons to conclude, that the Divisions and Offences that were in the Roman Church were between the Jewish and Gentile Converts; whilst the one over-zealous for the Rituals of the Law endeavoured to impose Circumcision and other Mosaical Rites, as necessary to be observed by all that professed Christianity: And the other, without due Regard to the Weakness of the Jews, shewed a too open Neglect of those their Observances, which were of so great Account with them. St. *Paul* was so sensible how much the Churches of Christ suffered on this Occasion, and so careful to prevent this, which was a Disturbance almost every where (as may be seen in the History of the *Acts*, and collected out of the Epistles) that after he had finished his Discourse to them, (which we may observe solemnly closed in the End of the foregoing Chapter) he here, in the middle of his Salutation, cannot forbear to caution them against the Authors and Fomenters of these Divisions, and that very pathetically, ver. 17——20. All the rest of this Chapter is spent almost wholly in Salutations. Only the four last Verses contain a Conclusion after St. *Paul*'s Manner.

PARAPHRASE.

1. I Commend to you *Phebe* our Sister, who is a Servant of the Church, which is at *Ken-*
2. *chrea* ˣ, that you receive her for Christ's Sake, as becomes Christians, and that you assist her in whatever Business she has need of you, for she has assisted ʸ many, and me in particular.
3. Salute *Priscilla* and *Aquila*, my Fellow-Labour-
4. ers in the Gospel (Who have for my Life exposed their own to Danger, unto whom not only I give Thanks, but also all the Churches
5. of the Gentiles.) Greet also the Church that is in their Houses. Salute my well-beloved *Epenetus*, who is the First-fruits of *Achaia* un-
6. to Christ. Greet *Mary*, who took a great deal of Pains for our Sakes. Salute *Andronicus* and
7. *Junia* my Kinsfolk and Fellow-Prisoners, who are of Note among the Apostles, who also were

TEXT.

1. I Commend unto you Phebe our sister, which is a servant of the Church, which is at Cenchrea.
2. That ye receive her in the Lord, as becometh saints, and that ye assist her in whatsoever business she hath need of you: for she hath been a succourer of many, and of myself also.
3. Greet Priscilla and Aquila my helpers in Christ Jesus:
4. (Who have for my life laid down their own necks, unto whom not only I give thanks, but also all the Churches of the Gentiles)
5. Likewise greet the church that is in their house. Salute my well beloved Epenetus, who is the first fruits of Achaia unto Christ.
6. Greet Mary, who bestowed much labour on us.
7. Salute Andronicus and Junia my kinsmen and my fellow-prisoners, who are of note among the apostles, who also were in Christ before me.

NOTES.

1 ˣ *Kenchrea* was the Port to *Corinth*.

2 ʸ Προςᾶτις, *Succour*, seems here to signify *Hostess*, not in a common Inn; for there was no such thing as our Inns in that Country; but one whose House was the Place of Lodging and Entertainment of those who were received by the Church as their Guests, and these she took care of. And to that προςᾶτις may be very well applied. But whether St. *Paul* was induced to make use of it here, as somewhat corresponding to παρακᾶτις, which he used in her Behalf just before in this Verse, I leave to those who nicely observe St. *Paul's* Stile.

Christians

ROMANS.
Ch. XVI.

TEXT.

8 Greet Amplias, my beloved in the Lord.
9 Salute Urban, our helper in Christ, and Stachys, my beloved.
10 Salute Apelles, approved in Christ. Salute them which are of Aristobulus houshold.
11 Salute Herodion, my kinsman. Greet them that be of the houshold of Narcissus, which are in the Lord.
12 Salute Tryphena and Tryphosa, who labour in the Lord. Salute the beloved Persis, which laboured much in the Lord.
13 Salute Rufus, chosen in the Lord, and his mother and mine.
14 Salute Asyncritus, Phlegon, Hermas, Patrobas, Hermes, and the brethren which are with them.
15 Salute Philologus and Julia, Nereus and his sister, and Olympas, and all the saints which are with them.
16 Salute one another with an holy kiss; the churches of Christ salute you.
17 Now I beseech you, brethren, mark them which cause divisions and offences, contrary to the doctrine which ye have learned; and avoid them.
18 For they that are such, serve not our Lord Jesus Christ, but their own belly; and by good words

PARAPHRASE.

Christians before me. Greet *Amplias*, my Beloved in the Lord. Salute *Urban* our Helper in Christ, and *Stachys* my Beloved. Salute *Apelles* approved in Christ. Salute those who are of the Houshold of *Aristobulus*. Salute *Herodion* my Kinsman. Salute all those of the Houshold of *Narcissus*, who have embraced the Gospel. Salute *Tryphena* and *Tryphosa*, who take pains in the Gospel. Salute the beloved *Persis*, who laboured much in the Lord. Salute *Rufus*, chosen or selected to be a Disciple of the Lord; and his Mother and mine. Salute *Asyncritus*, *Phlegon*, *Hermas*, *Patrobas*, *Hermes*, and the Brethren who are with them. Salute *Philologus*, and *Julius*, *Nereus* and his Sister, and all the Saints who are with them. Salute one another with an holy Kiss. The Churches of Christ salute you.

Now I beseech you, Brethren, mark those who cause Divisions and Offences contrary to the Doctrine which you have learned, and avoid them. For they serve ᶻ not our Lord Jesus Christ, but their own Bellies, and by good Words and fair Speeches, insinuating themselves, deceive well-meaning simple Men.

8.
9.
10.
11.
12.
13.
14.
15.
16.
17.
18.

NOTES.

18 ᶻ Such as these we have a Description of, *Tit.* i. 10, 11.

PARAPHRASE.

19. Your Conversion and ready Compliance with the Doctrine of the Gospel, when it was brought to you, is known in the World [a] and generally talked of: I am glad for your Sakes that you so forwardly obeyed the Gospel. But give me leave to advise you to be wise and cautious in preserving yourselves steady in what is wise and good [b]; but employ no Thought or Skill how to circumvent or injure another: Be in this regard very plain
20. and simple. For God who is the Giver and Lover of Peace, will soon rid you of these Ministers of Satan [c], the Disturbers of your Peace who make Divisions amongst you [d]. The Grace of our Lord Jesus Christ be with you. Amen.
21. *Timothy* my Work-fellow, and *Lucius*, and *Jason*, and *Sosipater* my Kinsmen salute you.
22. I *Tertius*, who wrote this Epistle, salute you in
23. the Lord. *Gaius* mine Host, and of the whole Church, saluteth you. *Erastus* the Chamberlain of the City saluteth you; and *Quartus* a
24. Brother. The Grace of our Lord Jesus Christ be with you all. Amen.

TEXT.

and fair speeches, deceive the hearts of the simple.

19 For your obedience is come abroad unto all men. I am glad therefore on your behalf: but yet I would have you wise unto that which is good; and simple concerning evil.

20 And the God of peace shall bruise Satan under your feet shortly. The Grace of our Lord Jesus Christ be with you. Amen.

21 Timotheus, my workfellow, and Lucius, and Jason, and Sosipater, my kinsmen salute you.

22 I Tertius, who wrote this epistle, salute you in the Lord.

23 Gaius, mine host, and of the whole church, saluteth you. Erastus, the chamberlain of the city, saluteth you, and Quartus a brother.

24 The grace of our Lord Jesus Christ be with you all. Amen.

NOTES.

19 [a] See *chap.* i. 8.
[b] A Direction much like this you have, 1 *Cor.* xiv. 20. and *Eph.* iv. 13——15.
20 [c] So those who made Divisions in the Church of *Corinth* are called, 2 *Cor.* xi. 14, 15.
[d] *Shall bruise Satan,* i. e. shall break the Force and Attempts of Satan upon your Peace by these his Instruments, who would engage you in Quarrels and Discords.

Now

ROMANS.

TEXT.

25 Now to him that is of power to ſtabliſh you according to my goſpel, and the preaching of Jeſus Chriſt, according to the revelation of the myſtery which was kept ſecret ſince the world began,
26 But now is made manifeſt, and by the ſcriptures of the prophets according to the commandment

PARAPHRASE.

Now to him that is able to ſettle and eſta- 25. bliſh you in an Adherence to my ᵉ Goſpel, and to that which I deliver concerning Jeſus Chriſt in my Preaching, conformable to the Revelation of the ᶠ Myſtery which lay unexplained in the ᵍ ſecular Times; but now is 26. laid open, and by the Writings of the Prophets made

NOTES.

25 ᵉ *My Goſpel.* St. *Paul* cannot be ſuppoſed to have uſed ſuch an Expreſſion as this, unleſs he knew that what he preached had ſomething in it that diſtinguiſhed it from what was preached by others; which was plainly the Myſtery, as he every where calls it, God's Purpoſe of taking in the Gentiles to be his People under the Meſſiah, and that without ſubjecting them to Circumciſion, or the Law of *Moſes.* This is that which he calls here τὸ κήρυγμα Ἰησοῦ Χριστοῦ, *the preaching of Jeſus Chriſt*; for without this, he did not think that Chriſt was preached to the Gentiles as he ought to be: And therefore in ſeveral places of his Epiſtle to the *Galatians,* he calls it, *the Truth,* and, *the Truth of the Goſpel*; and uſes the like Expreſſions to the *Epheſians* and *Coloſſians.* This is that Myſtery which he is ſo much concerned that the *Epheſians* ſhould underſtand and ſtick firm to, which was revealed to him according to that Goſpel, whereof he was made the Miniſter; as may be ſeen at large in that Epiſtle, particularly *chap.* iii. 6, 7. The ſame thing he declares to the *Coloſſians* in his Epiſtle to them, particularly *chap.* i. 27——29. and ii. 6——8. For that he in a peculiar manner preached this Doctrine, ſo as none of the other Apoſtles did, may be ſeen *Acts* xxi. 18——25. *Acts* xv. 6, 7. For though the other Apoſtles and Elders of the Church at *Jeruſalem* had determined, that the Gentiles ſhould only keep themſelves from Things offered to Idols, and from Blood, and from ſtrangled, and from Fornication; yet it is plain enough from what they ſay, *Acts* xxi. 20——24. that they taught not, nay, probably did not think what St. *Paul* openly declares to the *Epheſians,* that the Law of *Moſes* was aboliſhed by the Death of Chriſt, *Eph.* ii. 15. Which if St. *Peter* and St. *James* had been as clear in as was St. *Paul,* St. *Peter* would not have incurred his Reproof, as he did by his Carriage, mentioned *Gal.* ii. 12, &c. But in all this may be ſeen the Wiſdom and Goodneſs of God to both Jews and Gentiles. See Note, *Eph.* ii. 15.

ᶠ That the *Myſtery* he here ſpeaks of, is the calling of the Gentiles, may be ſeen in the following Words; which is that which in many of his Epiſtles he calls *Myſtery.* See *Eph.* i. 9. and iii. 3——9. *Col.* i. 25——27.

ᵍ Χρόνοις αἰωνίοις, *in the ſecular Times,* or in the Times under the Law. Why the Times under the Law were called χρόνοι αἰώνιοι, we may find a Reaſon in their Jubilees, which were αἰῶνες, *Sæcula,* or Ages, by which all the Time under the Law was meaſured: And ſo χρόνος αἰώνιος is uſed 2 *Tim.* i. 9. *Tit.* i. 2. And ſo αἰῶνες are put for the Times of the Law, or the Jubilees, *Luke* i. 70. *Acts* iii. 21. 1 *Cor.* ii. 7. and x. 11. *Eph.* iii. 9. *Col.* i. 26. *Heb.* ix. 26. And ſo God is called the Rock עולמי αἰώνων, of *Ages, Iſa.* xxvi. 4. in the ſame Senſe that he is called *the Rock of Iſrael, Iſa.* xxx. 29. *i. e.* the Strength and Support of the Jewiſh State: For it is of the Jews the Prophet here ſpeaks. So *Exod.* xxi. 6. לעולם עד τὸν αἰῶνα, ſignifies not as we tranſlate it *for ever,* but to the Jubilee; which will appear if we compare *Lev.* xxv. 39——41. and *Exod.* xxi. 2. See *Burthogg's Chriſtianity a Revealed Myſtery,* p. 17, 18. Now that the Times of the Law were the Times ſpoken of here by St. *Paul,* ſeems plain

from

ROMANS.

PARAPHRASE.

made known (according to the Commandment of the Everlasting God) to the Gentiles of all Nations, for the bringing them in to the Obedience of the Law of Faith. To the only wise God be Glory, through Jesus Christ for ever. Amen.

27.

TEXT.

of the everlasting God, made known to all nations for the obedience of faith.

27 To God only wise, be glory through Jesus Christ for ever. Amen.

NOTES.

from that which he declares to have continued a Mystery during all those Times; to wit, God's Purpose of taking in the Gentiles to be his People under the Messiah: For this could not be said to be a Mystery at any other time, but during the time that the Jews were the peculiar People of God, separated to him from among the Nations of the Earth. Before that time there was no such Name or Notion of Distinction as Gentiles. Before the Days of *Abraham*, *Isaac*, and *Jacob*, the calling of the Israelites to be God's peculiar People, was as much a Mystery, as the calling of others out of other Nations was a Mystery afterwards. All that St. *Paul* insists on here, and in all the Places where he mentions this Mystery, is to shew, that though God has declared this his Purpose to the Jews, by the Predictions of his Prophets amongst them; yet it lay concealed from their Knowledge, it was a Mystery to them, they understood no such thing; there was not any where the least Suspicion or Thought of it, till the Messiah being come, it was openly declared by St. *Paul* to the Jews and Gentiles, and made out by the Writings of the Prophets, which were now understood.

A PARA-

A PARAPHRASE and NOTES

ON THE

EPISTLE of St. *PAUL*

TO THE

EPHESIANS.

SYNOPSIS.

OUR Saviour had so openly and expressly declared to his Disciples the Destruction of the Temple, that they could by no Means doubt of it, nor of this Consequence of it, *viz.* that the ἔθη, Customs or Rites of the Mosaical Law, as they are called, *Acts* vi. 14. and xxi. 21. were to cease with it. And this St. *Stephen*, by what is laid to his Charge, *Acts* vi. 13, 14. seems to have taught. And upon this Ground it might very well be, that the Apostles and Church of *Jerusalem* required no more of the Convert Gentiles, than the Observance of such Things as were sufficient to satisfy the Jews that they were not still Heathens and Idolaters. But as for the rest of the Mosaical Rites, they required not the Convert Gentiles (to whom the Mosaical Law was not given) to observe them. This being a very natural and obvious Consequence, which they could not but see, that if by the Destruction of the Temple and Worship of the Jews, those Rites were speedily to be taken away, they were not Observances necessary to the People of God, and of perpetual Obligation. Thus far it is

4   plain

Synopsis. plain the other Apostles were instructed and satisfied of the Freedom of the Gentile Converts from complying with the Ritual Law. But whether it was revealed to them with the same Clearness as it was to St. *Paul*, that the Jews too, as well as the Gentiles, who were converted to the Christian Faith, were discharged from their former Obligation to the Ritual Law of *Moses*, and freed from those Observances, may be doubted: Because as we see they had not at all instructed their Converts of the Circumcision, of their being set at Liberty from that Yoke, which it is very likely they should not have forborn to have done, if they had been convinced of it themselves. For in all that Discourse concerning this Question, *Acts* xv. 1—21. there is not one Syllable said of the Jews being discharged, by Faith in the Messiah, from the Observance of any of the Mosaical Rites. Nor does it appear that the Apostles of the Circumcision ever taught their Disciples, or suggested to them any such thing; which one can scarce imagine they could have neglected, if it had been revealed to them, and so given them in charge. It is certain, their Converts had never been taught any such thing. For St. *James* himself acquaints us, *Acts* xxi. 20. that the *many thousands that believed were all zealous of the Law*. And what his own Opinion of those Rites was, may be seen *ver.* 24. where he calls keeping this Part of the Law, *walking orderly*: And he is concerned to have St. *Paul* thought a strict Observer thereof. All which could not have been, if it had been revealed to him as positively and expresly as it was to St. *Paul*, that all Believers in the Messiah, Jews as well as Gentiles, were absolved from the Law of *Moses*, and were under no Obligation to observe those Ceremonies any longer, they being now no longer necessary to the People of God in this his new Kingdom erected under the Messiah; nor indeed was it necessary that this particular Point should have been from the Beginning revealed to the other Apostles, who were sufficiently instructed for their Mission, and the Conversion of the Brethren the Jews by the Holy Ghost's bringing to their Minds (as was promised) all that our Saviour had said unto them in his Life-time here amongst them, in the true Sense of it. But the sending them to the Jews with this Message, that the Law was abolished, was to cross the very Design of sending them; it was to bespeak an Aversion to their Doctrine, and to stop the Ears of the Jews, and turn their Hearts from them. But St. *Paul* receiving his whole Knowledge of the Gospel immediately from Heaven by Revelation, seems to have this parti-

particular Instruction added, to fit him for the Mission he was chosen to, and make him an effectual Messenger of the Gospel, by furnishing him presently with this necessary Truth concerning the Cessation of the Law, the Knowledge whereof could not but come in time to the other Apostles, when it should be seasonable. Whether this be not so, I leave it to be considered.

 This at least is certain, that St. *Paul* alone, more than all the rest of the Apostles, was taken notice of to have preached that the coming of Christ put an end to the Law; and that in the Kingdom of God erected under the Messiah, the Observation of the Law was neither required, nor availed aught: Faith in Christ was the only Condition of Admittance both for Jew and Gentile, all who believed being now equally the People of God, whether circumcised or uncircumcised. This was that which the Jews, zealous of the Law, which they took to be the irrevocable, unalterable Charter of the People of God, and the standing Rule of his Kingdom, could by no means bear. And therefore provoked by this Report of St. *Paul,* the Jews, both Converts as well as others, looked upon him as a dangerous Innovator, and an Enemy to the true Religion, and as such seized on him in the Temple, *Acts* xxi. upon Occasion whereof it was that he was a Prisoner at *Rome* when he writ this Epistle, where he seems to be concerned, lest now he that was the Apostle of the Gentiles, from whom alone the Doctrine of their Exemption from the Law had its Rise and Support, was in Bonds upon that very Account, it might give an Opportunity to those judaizing Professors of Christianity, who contended that the Gentiles, unless they were circumcised after the Manner of *Moses,* could not be saved, to unsettle the Minds, and shake the Faith of those whom he had converted. This being the Controversy from whence rose the great Trouble and Danger that in the Time of our Apostle disturbed the Churches collected from among the Gentiles. That which chiefly disquieted the Minds, and shook the Faith of those who from Heathenism were converted to Christianity, was this Doctrine, that except the Converts from Paganism were circumcised, and thereby subjected themselves to the Law and the Jewish Rites, they could have no Benefit by the Gospel, as may be seen all through the *Acts,* and in almost all St. *Paul's* Epistles. Wherefore when he heard that the *Ephesians* stood firm in the Faith, whereby he means their Confidence of their Title to the Privileges and Benefits of the Gospel, without Submission to the Law, (for the introducing the legal Observances into the Kingdom of the Messiah, he declared to be a Subversion of the Gospel, and contrary to the great and glorious Design of that Kingdom) he thanks God for them; and setting forth the gracious and glorious Design of God towards them, prays that they may be enlightned, so as to be able to see the mighty Things done for them, and the immense Advantages they receive by it. In all which he displays the glorious State of that Kingdom, not in the ordinary way of Argumentation and formal Reasoning, which had no Place in an Epistle writ as this is, all as it were in a Rapture, and in a Stile far above the plain didactical Way; he pretends not to teach them any thing, but couches all that he would drop into their Minds, in Thanksgivings and Prayers; which affording a greater Liberty and Flight to his Thoughts, he gives Utterance to them in noble and sublime Expressions, suitable to the unsearchable Wisdom and Goodness of God, shewn to the World in the Work of Redemption. This, though perhaps at first Sight it may render his Meaning a little obscure, and his Expressions the harder to be understood; yet by the Assistance of the two following Epistles, which were both writ whilst he was in the same Circumstances, upon the same Occasion, and to the same Purpose, the Sense and Doctrine of the Apostle here may be so clearly seen, and so perfectly comprehended, that there can be hardly any doubt left about it, to any one who will examine them diligently, and carefully compare them together. The Epistle to the *Colossians* seems to be writ the very same Time, in the same Run and Warmth of Thoughts, so that the very same Expressions, yet fresh in his Mind, are repeated in many Places; the Form, Phrase, Matter, and all the Parts quite through of these two Epistles, do so perfectly correspond, that one cannot be mistaken in thinking one of them very fit to give Light to the other. And that to the *Philippians*, writ also by St. *Paul* during his Bonds at *Rome*, when attentively looked into, will be found to have the same Aim with the other two; so that in these three Epistles taken together, one may see the great Design of the Gospel laid down as far surpassing the Law, both in Glory, Greatness, Comprehension, Grace and Bounty; and therefore they were Opposers, not Promoters of the true Doctrine of the Gospel, and the Kingdom of God under the Messiah, who would confine it to the narrow and beggarly Elements of this World, as St. *Paul* calls the positive Ordinances of the Mosaical Institution. To confirm the Gentile Churches, whom he had converted, in this Faith which

EPHESIANS.

which he had inſtructed them in; and keep them from ſubmitting to the Moſaical Rites in the Kingdom of Chriſt, by giving them a nobler and more glorious View of the Goſpel, is the Deſign of this and the two following Epiſtles. For the better underſtanding theſe Epiſtles, it might be worth while to ſhew their Harmony all through; but this Synopſis is not a Place for it, the following Paraphraſe and Notes will give an Opportunity to point out ſeveral Paſſages wherein their Agreement will appear.

The latter End of this Epiſtle, according to St. *Paul*'s uſual Method, contains practical Directions and Exhortations.

He that deſires to inform himſelf in what is left upon Record in ſacred Scripture, concerning the Church of the *Epheſians*, which was the Metropolis of *Aſia*, ſtrictly ſo called, may read the xixth and xxth of the *Acts*.

SECT. I.

CHAP. I. 1, 2.

CONTENTS.

THESE two Verſes contain St. *Paul*'s Inſcription or Introduction of this Epiſtle; what there is in it remarkable for its Difference from what is to be found in his other Epiſtles, we ſhall take notice of in the Notes.

TEXT.	PARAPHRASE.	
PAUL, an apoſtle of Jeſus Chriſt, by the will of God, to the ſaints which are at Epheſus, and to the	PAUL, an Apoſtle of Jeſus Chriſt, by the declared Will and ſpecial Appointment of God to the Profeſſors of the Goſpel ⁱ, who	1.

NOTES.

1 ⁱ Τοῖς ἁγίοις, though rightly tranſlated Saints, yet it does not mean any other than a national Sanctification, ſuch as the Jews had by being ſeparated from the Gentiles, and appropriated to God as his peculiar People; not that every one that was of the holy Nation of the Jews heretofore, or of the holy Church of Chriſt under the Goſpel, were Saints in that Senſe that the Word is uſually taken now among Chriſtians, *viz.* ſuch Perſons as were every one of them actually in a State of Salvation.

PARAPHRASE.

2. are in *Ephesus*, Converts who stand firm in the Faith ᵇ of Christ Jesus: Favour and Peace be to you from God our Father, and the Lord Jesus Christ.

TEXT.

faithful in Christ Jesus: Grace be to you, and 2 peace from God our Father, and from the Lord Jesus Christ.

NOTES.

ᵇ Πιϛοῖς, *Faithful*. We have observed above, that this Epistle, and that of the *Colossians*, have all through a very great Resemblance; their Lineaments do so correspond, that I think they may be Twin-Epistles, conceived and brought forth together; so that the very Expressions of the one occurred fresh in St. *Paul*'s Memory, and were made use of in the other. Their being sent by the same Messenger *Tychicus*, is a farther Probability that they were writ at the same time. Πιϛοῖς therefore being found in the Introduction of both Epistles, and no one other of St. *Paul*'s, there is just Reason to think that it was a Term suited to the present Notion he had of those he was writing to, with reference to the Business he was writing about. I take it therefore, that by *faithful in Christ Jesus*, he means here such as stood firm to Jesus Christ; which he did not count them to do, who made Circumcision necessary to Salvation, and an Observance of Jewish Rites a requisite Part of the Christian Religion. This is plain from his express Words, Gal. v. 1, 2. *Stand fast therefore in the Liberty wherewith Christ hath made us free, and be not entangled again with the Yoke of Bondage. Behold I Paul say unto you, That if ye be circumcised, Christ shall profit you nothing*, &c. And those that contended for Submission to the Law, he calls *Perverters of the Gospel of Christ*, Gal. i. 7. And more to the same Purpose may be seen in that Epistle: We shall have an Occasion to confirm this Interpretation of the Word πιϛὸς, *faithful*, here, when we come to consider the Import of the Word πίϛις, *Faith*, ver. 15. They that would have ᾳ, *and*, not exegetical here, but used only to join under the Title of *faithful in Christ Jesus*, the Converts in *Asia*, I shall desire, besides *Col*. i. 2. to read also 1 *Cor*. i. 2. and thereby judge in what Sense they are to understand, *And to the faithful in Christ Jesus* here.

EPHESIANS.

SECT. II.

CHAP. I. 3——14.

CONTENTS.

IN this Section St. *Paul* thanks God for his Grace and Bounty to the Gentiles, wherein he so sets forth both God's gracious Purpose of bringing the Gentiles into his Kingdom under the Messiah, and his actual bestowing on them Blessings of all kinds in Jesus Christ, for a compleat re-instating them in that his heavenly Kingdom, that there could be nothing stronger suggested to make the *Ephesians*, and other Gentile Converts not to think any more of the Law, and that much inferior Kingdom of his, established upon the Mosaical Institution, and adapted to a little Canton of the Earth, and a small Tribe of Men, as now necessary to be retained under this more spiritual Institution, and celestial Kingdom erected under Jesus Christ, intended to comprehend Men of all Nations, and extend itself to the utmost Bounds of the Earth for the greater Honour of God, or as St. *Paul* speaks, to the Praise of the Glory of God.

TEXT.

3 Blessed be the God and Father of our Lord Jesus Christ, who hath blessed us with all spiritual blessings in heavenly places in Christ.

PARAPHRASE.

3. Blessed and magnified be the God and Father of our Lord Jesus Christ, who has in and by Jesus Christ [b], furnished us [c] Gentiles with all sorts of Blessings that may fit us to be Partakers of his heavenly Kingdom, without need of any Assistance from the Law, according

NOTES.

3 [b] Ἐν Χριϛῷ, *In Christ*, I take to be put here emphatically, and to signify the same with *filleth all in all*, v. 23. which is more fully explained, *Col.* iii. 11. *Where there is neither Greek nor Jew, Circumcision nor Uncircumcision, Barbarian, Scythian, Bond or Free, but Christ is all, and in all.*

[c] *Us*. The right understanding of this Section, and indeed of this whole Epistle, depends very much on understanding aright who are more especially comprehended under the Terms, *Us* and *We,*

EPHESIANS.

NOTES.

We, from *ver.* 3. to 12. For *Us* must signify either, 1. St. *Paul* himself personally; but that the visible Tenor of the Discourse at first sight plainly destroys: Besides it suits not St. *Paul*'s Modesty to attribute so much in particular to himself, as is spoken of *Us* and *We* in this Section; or if we could think he would give himself the Liberty, yet *ver.* 12. overturns it all; for ἡμᾶς τοὺς προηλπικότας, *We who first trusted in Christ*, can by no means be admitted to be spoken by St. *Paul* personally of himself. Add to this, that in this very Chapter, no farther off than *ver.* 15. St. *Paul* speaking of himself, says I, in the Singular Number; and so he does *Chap.* iii. *ver.* 7, 8. Or,

2. It must signify Believers in general; but that προηλπικότας joined to it will not admit, for ἡμᾶ, the first Believers, cannot signify we all that are Believers, but restrains the Persons to some sort of Men that then began to believe, *i. e.* the Gentiles: And then the next Words, *v.* 13. have an easy and natural Connexion; We other Gentiles who first believed in Christ, in whom also ye Gentiles, also of *Ephesus*, after ye heard, believed. Or,

3. It must signify the Convert Jews. But would it not be somewhat preposterous for St. *Paul* so much to magnify God's Goodness and Bounty to the Jews in particular, in an Epistle writ to a Church of converted Gentiles; wherein he addresses himself to the Gentiles, in Contradistinction to the Jews, and tells them they were to be made Co-partners with them in the Kingdom of the Messiah, which was opened to them by abolishing the Law of *Moses*, intimated plainly in this very Section, *ver.* 7——10. Wherein he magnifies the Riches of the Favour of God, to the Persons he is speaking of under the Denomination *Us*, in gathering again *all things*, i. e. Men of all sorts, under Christ the Head; which could not mean the Jews alone: But of this he speaks more openly afterwards. Farther, *We* here, and *We*, chap. ii. 3. must be the same, and denote the same Persons; but the *We*, chap. ii. 3. can neither be St. *Paul* alone, nor Believers in general, nor Jewish Converts in particular, as the obvious Sense of the Place demonstrates: For neither St. *Paul* can be called ἡμεῖς ἅπαντες, nor is it true that all the Convert Jews *had their Conversation among the Gentiles*, as our Bible renders the Greek; which if otherwise to be understood, is more directly against signifying the Jews. These therefore being excluded from being meant by *We* and *Us* here, who can remain to be signified thereby but the Convert Gentiles in general? That St. *Paul*, who was the Apostle of the Gentiles, did often in an obliging manner join himself with the Gentile Converts under the Terms Us and We, as if he had been one of them, there are so many Instances, that it cannot seem strange that he should do so in this Section, *Rom.* v. 1——11. where it is plain all along under the Term Us, he speaks of the Gentile Converts. And many other Passages might be brought out of this Epistle to evince it. *Chap.* i. 11. he saith, *We* have obtained an Inheritance. Those *We's*, it is plain, *chap.* iii. 6. were Gentiles. So *chap.* ii. 5. when *We*, i. e. Converts of the Gentiles, were dead in Sins: For I do not remember that the Jews are any where said by St. *Paul* to be dead in Sins; that is one of the distinguishing Characters of the Gentiles: And there we see in the same Verse *we* is changed into *ye*: And so *ver.* 6, and 7, having spoke of the Gentiles in the first Person *us*, in the Beginning of the next Verse it is changed into *ye*, i. e. ye Ephesians, a Part of those Gentiles. To this I shall add one Place more out of the parallel Epistle to the *Colossians*, chap. i. 12, 13. where he uses ἡμᾶ;, *us*, for the Convert Gentiles, changing the *ye* in the 10th Verse to *us* in the 12th; the Matter of giving Thanks being the same all along from *ver.* 3. where it begins, and is repeated here again, *ver.* 12. i. e. the removing of the Gentiles out of the Kingdom of the Devil and Darkness, into the Kingdom of his beloved Son: Or as he expresses it, *Eph.* i. 6. *Wherein he hath made us accepted in the Beloved*. And in the same Sense he uses ὑμᾶν, *us*, Col. ii. 14. For those that the Hand-writing of Ordinances was against and contrary to, were the Gentiles, as he declares, *Eph.* ii. 14, 15. who were kept off from coming to be the People of God by those Ordinances, which were that wherein the Enmity between the Jews and Gentiles consisted, and was kept up; which therefore Christ abolished, to make way for their Union into one Body under Christ their Head. Other Passages tending to the clearing of this, we shall have occasion to take notice of as they occur in the Sequel of this Epistle.

EPHESIANS.

Chap. I.

TEXT.

4 According as he hath chosen us in him before the foundation of the world, that we should be holy, and without blame before him in love:

5 Having predestinated us unto the adoption of

PARARAPHRASE.

cording as he chose us Gentiles upon Christ's Account alone [d], before the Law was, even before the Foundation of the World, to be his People [e] under Jesus the Messiah, and to live unblameable Lives [f] before him in all Love and Affection [g] to all the Saints or Believers, of what Nation soever; having predetermined to take us Gentiles by Jesus Christ [h], to be

4.

5.

NOTES.

4 [d] Ἐν αὐτῷ, *in him, i. e.* Christ: In the former Verse it is εὐλογήσας ἡμᾶς ἐν πάσῃ εὐλογίᾳ πνευματικῇ ἐν Χριστῷ. Καθὼς ἐξελέξατο ἡμᾶς ἐν αὐτῷ. All which together make up this Sense; "As it was in Consideration of Christ alone, that God heretofore, before the Foundation of "the World, designed us Gentiles to be his People; so now the Messiah is come, all the "Blessings and Benefits we are to receive in his heavenly Kingdom, are laid up in him, and "to be had only by our Faith and Dependance on him, without any Respect to the Law, or "any other Consideration."

[e] Ἅγιοι, *Saints,* in St. *Paul's* Epistle, is known to signify Christians, *i. e.* such as made Profession of the Gospel, for those were now the People of God.

[f] See in *Col.* i. 22. this Verse explained, where comparing it with the immediate preceding Words, *ver.* 21. one may find a farther Reason to take *us* here to signify the Gentile Converts, the same thing being applied there solely to the Gentile Converts of *Colosse.*

[g] *Affection to all the Saints.* That this is the Meaning may be seen *ver.* 15. where to their true Faith in Christ, which he was rejoiced with, he joined τὴν ἀγάπην εἰς πάντας τοὺς ἁγίους, *Love unto all the Saints.* The very same thing which he takes notice of in the *Colossians* in the very same Words, *Col.* i. 4. Why Love is so often mentioned in this Epistle, as *chap.* iii. 18. and iv. 2, 15, 16. and v. 2. and vi. 23. we may find a Reason, *chap.* ii. 11—22. wherein there is an Account given of the Enmity between the Jews and Gentiles, which Christ had taken away the Cause of; and therefore the ceasing of it was one great Mark of Men's being right in the Faith, and of their having true and worthy Notions of Christ, who had broke down the Wall of Partition, and opened the Kingdom of Heaven to all equally who believed in him without any the least Distinction of Nation, Blood, Profession or Religion that they were of before; all that being now done away, and superseded by the Prince of Peace, Jesus Christ the Righteous, to make way for a more enlarged and glorious Kingdom solely by Faith in him, which now made the only Distinction among Men; so that all who agreed in that were thereby brought to the same Level, to be all Brethren and Fellow-Members in Christ, and the People or Sons of God, as he says in the next Verse.

5 [h] It was not by the Observances of the Law, but by Faith alone in Jesus Christ, that God predetermined to take the Gentiles into the State of Sonship or Adoption. This was another particular for which St. *Paul* blesses God in the Name of the Gentiles; the Consideration whereof was fit to raise the *Ephesians* Thoughts above the Law, and keep them firm in Adherence to the Liberty of the Gospel.

his

EPHESIANS. Chap. I.

PARAPHRASE.

his Sons ^{i} and People according to the good
6. Pleasure of his Will ^{k}, to the End that the Gentiles too might praise him for his Grace and Mercy to them, and all Mankind magnify his Glory for his abundant Goodness to them, by receiving them freely into the Kingdom of the Messiah, to be his People again in a State of Peace with him ^{l}, barely for the sake of him
7. that is his Beloved ^{m}: In whom *we* ^{n} have Redemption by his Blood, *viz.* the Forgiveness of Transgressions, according to the Great-

TEXT.

children by Jesus Christ to himself, according to the good pleasure of his will.

6 To the praise of the glory of his grace, wherein he hath made us accepted in the beloved:

7 In whom we have redemption through his blood, the forgiveness of sins according to the riches of his grace;

NOTES.

^{i} Υἱοθεσία, Adoption or Sonship belonged only to the Jews before the coming of the Messiah, *Rom.* ix. 4. For after the Nations of the Earth had revolted from God their Lord and Maker, and became Servants and Worshippers of the Devil, God abandoned them to the Vassalage they had chosen, and owned none of them for his but the Israelites, whom he had adopted to be his Children and People. See *Exod.* iv. 22. *Jer.* xxxi. 9. *Luke* i. 54. Which Adoption is expressed to *Abraham* in these Words, *Gen.* xvii. 7. *I will be a God to thee, and to thy Seed after thee, and to the Israelites.* Exod. vi. 7. *I will take you to me for a People, and I will be your God*; and so *Lev.* xxvi. 12. *I will walk amongst you, and be your God, and ye shall be my People.* And so we see that those whom, *Exod.* iv. he calls his Sons, he calls in several other Places his People, as standing both when spoken nationally for one and the same Thing.

^{k} *According to the good Pleasure of his Will*; spoken here in the same Sense with what is said, *Rom.* ix. 18, 23, 24. God under the Law took the Nation of *Israel* to be his People, without any Merit in them; and so it is of his mere good Pleasure that he even then purposed to enlarge his Kingdom under the Gospel, by admitting all that of all the Nations whatsoever would come in and submit themselves, not to the Law of *Moses*, but to the Rule and Dominion of his Son Jesus Christ; and this, as he says in the next Words, for the Praise of the Glory of his Grace.

6 ^{l} See *chap.* ii. 12 —— 14. *Acts* xv. 14, &c.

^{m} I do not think that any thing of greater Force can be imagined to raise the Minds of the *Ephesians* above the Jewish Rituals, and keep them steady in the Freedom of the Gospel, than what St. *Paul* says here, *viz.* That God before the Foundation of the World freely determined within himself to admit the Gentiles into his Kingdom to be his People, for the Manifestation of his free Grace all the World over, that all Nations might glorify him; and this for the sake of his Son Jesus Christ, who was his Beloved, and so was chiefly regarded in all this; and therefore it was to mistake or pervert the End of the Gospel, and debase this glorious Dispensation, to make it subservient to the Jewish Ritual, or to suppose that the Law of *Moses* was to support, or to be supported by the Kingdom of the Messiah, which was to be of a larger Extent, and settled upon another Foundation; whereof the Mosaical Institution was but a narrow, faint and typical Representation.

7 ^{n} *We* does as plainly here stand for the Gentile Converts, as it is manifest it does in the parallel Place, *Col.* i. 13, 14.

ness

EPHESIANS.

TEXT.

8 Wherein he hath abounded toward us in all wisdom and prudence.
9 Having made known unto us the mystery of his will according to his good pleasure, which he hath purposed in himself:
10 That in the dispensation of the fulness of times he might gather together in one all things in Christ, both which are in heaven, and which are on earth, even in him:
11 In whom also we have

PARAPHRASE.

ness of his Grace and Favour, which he has overflowed in towards us, in bestowing on us so full a Knowledge and Comprehension of the Extent and Design of the Gospel °, and Prudence to comply with it, as becomes you ᵖ; in that he hath made known to you the good Pleasure of his Will and Purpose, which was a ᑫ Mystery that he had proposed in himself ʳ, until the Coming of the due Time of that Dispensation wherein he had predetermined to reduce all Things again both in Heaven and Earth, under one Head ˢ in Christ; in whom we became

8.

9.

10.

11.

NOTES.

8 ° That by πάση σοφία, St. *Paul* means a Comprehension of the revealed Will of God in the Gospel, more particularly the Mystery of God's Purpose of calling the Gentiles, and making out of them a People and Inheritance to himself in his Kingdom under the Messiah, may be perceived by reading and comparing, *chap.* i. 8. *Col.* i. 9, 10, 28. and ii. 2, 3. Which Verses read with Attention to the Context, plainly shew what St. *Paul* means here.

ᵖ That this is the Meaning of this Verse, I refer my Reader to *Col.* i. 9, 10.

9 ᑫ I cannot think that God's Purpose of calling the Gentiles, so often termed a Mystery, and so emphatically declared to be concealed from Ages, and particularly revealed to himself, and as we find in this Epistle, where it is so called by St. *Paul* five times, and four times in that to the *Colossians*, is by Chance, or without some particular Reason. The Question was, whether the converted Gentiles should hearken to the Jews, who would persuade them it was necessary for them to submit to Circumcision and the Law, or to St. *Paul*, who had taught them otherwise? Now there could be nothing of more Force to destroy the Authority of the Jews in the Case, than the shewing them that the Jews knew nothing of the Matter; that it was a perfect Mystery to them, concealed from their Knowledge, and made manifest in God's good Time, at the coming of the Messiah, and most particularly discovered to St. *Paul* by immediate Revelation, to be communicated by him to the Gentiles, who therefore had Reason to stick firm to this great Truth, and not to be led away from the Gospel which he had taught them.

ʳ See *chap.* iii. 9.

10 ˢ 'Ανακεφαλαιώσασθαι properly signifies to recapitulate or recollect, and put together the Heads of a Discourse. But since that cannot possibly be the Meaning of this Word here, we must search for the Meaning which St. *Paul* gives it here in the Doctrine of the Gospel, and not in the Propriety of the Greek.

1. It is plain in sacred Scripture, that Christ at first had the Rule and Supremacy over all, and was Head over all. See *Col.* i. 15——17. *Heb.* i. 8.

2. There are also manifest Indications in Scripture, that a principal Angel, with great Numbers of Angels his Followers joining with him, revolted from this Kingdom of God, and standing out in Rebellion, erected to themselves a Kingdom of their own, in Opposition to the Kingdom of God, *Luke* x. 17——20. and had all the heathen World Vassals and Subjects of that their Kingdom, *Luke* iv. 5——8. *Matth.* xii. 26——30. *John* xiii. 31. and xiv. 30. and xvi. 11. *Eph.* vi. 12. *Col.* i. 13. *Rom.* i. 18. *Acts* xxvi. 18, &c.

3. That

EPHESIANS.

NOTES.

3. That Christ recovered this Kingdom, and was re-instated in the Supremacy and Headship, in the Fulness of Time (when he came to destroy the Kingdom of Darkness, as St. *Paul* calls it here) at his Death and Resurrection. Hence, just before his Suffering, he says, *John* xii. 31. *Now is the Judgment of this World; now shall the Prince of this World be cast out.* From whence may be seen the Force of Christ's Argument, *Matt.* xii. 28. *If I cast out Devils by the Spirit of God, then the Kingdom of God is come upon you:* For the Jews acknowledged that the Spirit of God, which had been withdrawn from them, was not to be given out again till the coming of the Messiah, under whom the Kingdom of God was to be erected. See also *Luke* x. 18, 19.

4. What was the State of his Power and Dominion from the Defection of the Angels, and setting up the Kingdom of Darkness, till his being re-instated in the Fulness of Time, there is little revealed in sacred Scripture, as not so much pertaining to the Recovery of Men from their Apostasy, and re-instating them in the Kingdom of God. It is true, God gathered to himself a People, and set up a Kingdom here on Earth, which he maintained in the little Nation of the Jews till the setting up the Kingdom of his Son, *Acts* i. 3. and ii. 36. which was to take place as God's only Kingdom here on Earth for the future. At the Head of this, which is called the Church, he sets Jesus Christ his Son; but that is not all, for he having by his Death and Resurrection conquered Satan, *John* xii. 31. and xvi. 11. *Col.* ii. 15. *Heb.* ii. 14. *Ephes.* iv. 8. has all Power given him in Heaven and Earth, and is made the Head over all Things for the Church. [*Matth.* xxviii. 18. and xi. 27. *John* iii. 35. and xi. 3. *Ephes.* i. 20——22. *Heb.* i. 2——4. and ii. 9. 1 *Cor.* xv. 25, 27. *Phil.* ii. 8 - 11. *Col.* ii. 10. *Heb.* x. 12, 13. *Acts* ii. 33. and v. 31. In both which Places it should be translated, *to the Right Hand of God.*] Which re-instating him again in the supreme Power, and restoring him, after the Conquest of the Devil, to that compleat Headship which he had over all Things, being now revealed under the Gospel, as may be seen in the Texts here quoted, and in other Places; I leave to the Reader to judge, whether St. *Paul* might not probably have an Eye to that in this Verse, and in his Use of the word ἀνακεφαλαιώσασθαι. But to search thoroughly into this Matter (which I have not in my small Reading found any where sufficiently taken notice of) would require a Treatise.

It may suffice at present, to take notice that this Exaltation of his is expressed, *Phil.* ii. 9, 10. by all Things in Heaven and Earth bowing the Knee at his Name; which we may see farther explained, *Rev.* v. 13. Which Acknowledgment of his Honour and Power, was that perhaps which the proud Angel that fell refusing, thereupon rebelled.

If our Translators have rendered the Sense of ἀνακεφαλαιώσασθαι right, by *gather together into one,* it will give countenance to those who are inclined to understand by *things in Heaven,* and *things on Earth,* the Jewish and Gentile World: For of them St. *John* plainly says, *John* xi. 52. *That Jesus should die, not for the Nation of the Jews only, but that also* συναγάγῃ εἰς ἓν, *he should gather together in one the Children of God that were scattered abroad,* i. e. the Gentiles that were to believe, and were by Faith to become the Children of God; whereof Christ himself speaks thus, *John* x. 16. *Other Sheep I have which are not of this Fold, them also I must bring, and they shall hear my Voice, and there shall be one Fold, and one Shepherd.* This is the gathering together into one that our Saviour speaks of, and is that which very well suits with the Apostle's Design here, where he says in express Words, that Christ makes τὰ ἀμφότερα ἓν both Jews and Gentiles one, *Ephes.* ii. 14. Now that St. *Paul* should use Heaven and Earth for Jews and Gentiles, will not be thought so very strange, if we consider that *Daniel* himself expresses the Nation of the Jews by the Name of *Heaven, Dan.* viii. 10. Nor does he want an Example of it in our Saviour himself, who *Luke* xxi. 26. by *Powers of Heaven,* plainly signifies the great Men of the Jewish Nation: Nor is this the only Place in this Epistle of St. *Paul* to the *Ephesians,* which will bear this Interpretation of *Heaven* and *Earth;* he who shall read the fifteen first Verses of *chap.* iii. and carefully weigh the Expressions, and observe the Drift of the Apostle in them, will not find that he does manifest Violence to St. *Paul's* Sense, if he understands by *the Family in Heaven and Earth,* ver. 15. the united Body of Christians, made up of Jews and Gentiles, living still promiscuously among those two Sorts of People, who continued

in

EPHESIANS.

TEXT.

obtained an inheritance, being predestinated according to the purpose of him who worketh all things after the counsel of his own will:

12 That we should be to the praise of his glory, who first trusted in Christ,

PARAPHRASE.

became his Possession ^{t}, and the Lot of his Inheritance, being predetermined thereunto according to the Purpose of him who never fails to bring to pass what he hath purposed within himself ^{u}: That we of the Gentiles, who first 12. through Christ entertained Hope ^{w}, might

NOTES.

in their Unbelief. However, this Interpretation I am not positive in, but offer it as a Matter of Enquiry, to such who think an impartial Search into the true Meaning of the sacred Scripture the best Employment of all the Time they have.

11 ^{t} So the Greek Word ἐκληρώθημεν will signify, if taken, as I think it may, in the Passive Voice, *i. e.* we Gentiles who were formerly in the Possession of the Devil, are now by Christ brought into the Kingdom, Dominion and Possession of God again. This Sense seems very well to agree with the Design of the Place, *viz.* That the Gentile World had now in Christ a Way opened for their returning into the Possession of God under their proper Head Jesus Christ. To which suit the Words that follow, *that we who first amongst the Gentiles* entertained Terms of Reconciliation by Christ, *might be to the Praise of his Glory,* i. e. so that we of the Gentiles who first believed, did, as it were, open a new Scene of Praise and Glory to God, by being restored to be his People, and become again a Part of his Possession; a thing not before understood, nor looked for. See *Acts* xi. 18. and xv. 3, 14——19. the Apostle's Design here being to satisfy the *Ephesians*, that the Gentiles were by Faith in Christ restored to all the Privileges of the People of God, as far forth as the Jews themselves. See *chap.* ii. 11——22. particularly *ver.* 19. As to ἐκληρώθημεν, it may, I humbly conceive, do no Violence to the Place to suggest this Sense, *we became the Inheritance,* instead of *we have obtained an Inheritance*; that being the Way wherein God speaks of his People the *Israelites,* of whom he says, *Deut.* xxxii. 9. *The Lord's Portion is his People, Jacob is the Lot of his Inheritance.* See also *Deut.* iv. 20. 1 *Kings* viii. 51. and other Places. And the Inheritance which the Gentiles were to obtain, was to be obtained, we see, *Col.* i. 12, 13. by their being translated out of the Kingdom of Satan into the Kingdom of Christ: So that take it either Way, that *we have obtained an Inheritance,* or *we are become his People and Inheritance*; it in effect amounts to the same thing, and so I leave it to the Reader.

^{u} *i. e.* God had purposed, even before the taking the *Israelites* to be his People, to take in the Gentiles by Faith in Christ to be his People again; and what he purposes he will do without asking the Counsel or Consent of any one; and therefore you may be sure of this your Inheritance, whether the Jews consent to it or no.

12 ^{w} It was a Part of the Character of the Gentiles, to be *without Hope*; see *chap.* ii. 12. But when they received the Gospel of Jesus Christ, then they ceased to be Aliens from the Commonwealth of *Israel,* and became the People of God, and had Hope as well as the Jews, or, as St. *Paul* expresses it in the Name of the converted *Romans, Rom.* v. 2. *We rejoice in Hope of the Glory of God.* This is another Evidence that ἡμᾶς, *we,* here stands for the Gentile-Converts. That the Jews were not without Hope, or without God in the World, appears from that very Text, *Eph.* ii. 12. where the Gentiles are set apart under a discriminating Description properly belonging to them, the sacred Scripture no where speaks of the Hebrew Nation, that People of God, as without God, or without Hope, the contrary appears every where. See *Rom.* ii. 17. and xi. 1. *Acts* xxiv. 15. and xxvi. 6, 7. and xxviii. 20. And therefore the Apostle might well say, that those of the Gentiles who first entertained Hopes in Christ were *to the Praise of the Glory of God.* All Mankind having thereby now a new and greater Subject of praising and glorifying God for this great and unspeakable Grace and Goodness to them, of which before they had no Knowledge, no Thought, no Expectation.

EPHESIANS.

PARAPHRASE.

13. bring Praise and Glory to God. And ye *Ephesians* are also in Jesus Christ become God's People and Inheritance ˣ, having heard the Word of Truth, the good Tidings of your Salvation, and having believed in him, have been sealed by
14. the Holy Ghost; Which was promised, and is the Pledge and Evidence of being the People of God ʸ, his Inheritance given out ᶻ for the Redemption ᵃ of the purchased Possession,

TEXT.

In whom ye also trusted 13 after that ye heard the word of truth, the gospel of your salvation: in whom also after that ye believed, ye were sealed with that holy Spirit of promise,

Which is the earnest of 14 our inheritance, until the redemption of the purcha-

NOTES.

13 ˣ Ἐν ᾧ καὶ ὑμεῖς; seems in the Tenor and Scheme of the Words to refer to ἐν ᾧ ἐκληρώθημεν, ver. 11. St. *Paul* making a Parallel here between those of the *Gentiles* that first believed, and the *Ephesians*, tells them, that as those who heard and received the Gospel before them, became the People of God, &c. to the Praise and Glory of his Name, so they the *Ephesians*, by believing became the People of God, &c. to the Praise and Glory of his Name; only in this Verse there is an Ellypsis of ἐκληρώθητε.

14 ʸ The Holy Ghost was neither promised nor given to the Heathen, who were Apostates from God, and Enemies, but only to the People of God, and therefore the Convert *Ephesians* having received it, might be assured thereby that they were now the People of God, and rest satisfied in this Pledge of it.

ᶻ The giving out of the Holy Ghost, and the Gift of Miracles, was the great Means whereby the Gentiles were brought to receive the Gospel, and become the People of God.

ᵃ *Redemption* in Sacred Scripture signifies not always strictly paying a Ransom for a Slave delivered from Bondage, but Deliverance from a slavish Estate into Liberty: So God declares to the Children of *Israel* in *Egypt*, Exod. vi. 6. *I will redeem you with a stretched out Arm*. What is meant by it is clear from the former Part of the Verse, in these Words, *I will bring you out from under the Burden of the Egyptians, and I will rid you out of their Bondage*. And in the next Verse he adds, *And I will take you to me for my People, and I will be to you a God*: The very Case here. As God in the Place cited promised to deliver his People out of Bondage under the word *redeem*, so *Deut*. vii. 8. he telleth them, that he *had brought them out with a mighty Hand, and redeemed them out of the House of Bondage from the Hand of* Pharaoh *King of* Egypt: Which Redemption was performed by God, who is called the Lord of Hosts their Redeemer, without the Payment of any Ransom. But here there was περιποίησις, *a Purchase*; and what the Thing purchased was we may see, *Acts* xx. 28. *viz*. the *Church of God*, ἣν περιεποιήσατο, which he *purchased with his own Blood*, to be a People that should be the Lord's Portion, and the Lot of his Inheritance, as *Moses* speaks of the Children of *Israel*, Deut. xxxii. 9. And hence St. *Peter* calls the Christians, 1 *Pet*. xi. 9. λαὸς εἰς περιποίησιν, which in the Margin of our Bible is rightly translated *a purchased People*: But if any one takes ἐκληρώθημεν, ver. 11. to signify *we obtained an Inheritance*, then κληρονομία, in this Verse, will signify that Inheritance, εἰς ἀπολύτρωσιν τῆς περιποιήσεως, *until the Redemption of that purchased Inheritance*, i. e. until the Redemption of our Bodies, *viz*. Resurrection unto eternal Life. But besides that, this seems to have a more harsh and forced Sense, the other Interpretation is more consonant to the Stile and Current of the Sacred Scripture, and (which weighs more with me) answers St. *Paul's* Design here, which is to establish the *Ephesians* in a settled Persuasion, that they, and all the other Gentiles that believed in Christ, were as much the People of God, his Lot, and his Inheritance, as the

Jews

EPHESIANS.

TEXT.　　PARAPHRASE.

sed possession, unto the praise of his glory.　　on, that ye also might bring Praise and Glory to God ᵇ.

NOTES.

Jews themselves, and equally Partakers with them of all the Privileges and Advantages belonging thereunto, as is visible by the Tenor of the second Chapter. And this is the Use St. *Paul* mentions of God setting his Seal, 2 *Tim.* ii. 19. that it might mark who are his: And accordingly we find it applied, *Rev.* vii. 3. to the Foreheads of his Servants, that they might be known to be his, *chap.* iv. 1. For so did those who purchased Servants, as it were take Possession of them, by setting their Marks on their Foreheads.

14 ᵇ As he declared, *ver.* 6, and 12. that the other Gentiles, by believing and becoming the People of God, enhanced thereby the Praise and Glory of his Grace and Goodness; so here, *ver.* 14. he pronounces the same thing of the *Ephesians* in particular, to whom he is writing, to possess their Minds with the Sense of the happy Estate they were now in by being Christians; for which he thanks God, *ver.* 3. and here again in the next Words.

SECT. III.

CHAP. I. 15.——II. 10.

CONTENTS.

HAVING in the foregoing Section thanked God for the great Favours and Mercies which from the Beginning he had purposed for the Gentiles under the Messiah, in such a Description of that Design of the Almighty, as was fit to raise their Thoughts above the Law, and, as St. *Paul* calls them, beggarly Elements of the Jewish Constitution, which was nothing in Comparison of the great and glorious Design of the Gospel, taking notice of their standing firm in the Faith he had taught them, and thanking God for it, he here in this prays God that he would enlighten the Minds of the *Ephesian* Converts, to see fully the great Things that were actually done for them, and the glorious Estate they were in under the Gospel, of which in this Section he gives such a Draught, as in every Part of it shews, that in the Kingdom of Christ they are set far above the Mosaical Rites, and enjoy the spiritual and incomprehensible Benefits of it, not by the Tenure of a few outward Ceremonies,

Chap. I. remonies, but by their Faith alone in Jesus Christ, to whom they are united, and of whom they are Members, who is exalted to the top of all Dignity, Dominion and Power, and they with him their Head.

PARAPHRASE.   TEXT.

15. WHerefore I also in my Confinement, having heard ᶜ of the Continuance of your Faith in Christ Jesus, and your Love to

WHerefore I also, af- 15 ter I heard of your faith in the Lord Jesus, and

NOTES.

15 ᶜ Ἀκούσας τὴν καθ᾽ ὑμᾶς πίστιν ἐν τῷ κυρίῳ Ἰησοῦ, *Wherefore I also after I heard of your Faith in the Lord Jesus.* St. *Paul's* hearing of their Faith here mentioned, cannot signify his being informed that they had received the Gospel, and believed in Christ, this would have looked impertinent for him to have told them, since he himself had converted them, and had lived a long time amongst them, as has been already observed. We must therefore seek another Reason of his mentioning his hearing of their Faith, which must signify something else than his being barely acquainted that they were Christians, and this we may find in these Words *chap*. iii. 13. *Wherefore I desire that ye faint not at my Tribulations for you.* He, as Apostle of the Gentiles, had alone preached up Freedom from the Law, which the other Apostles who had not that Province (see *Gal.* ii. 9.) in their converting the Jews, seem to have said nothing of, as is plain from *Acts* xxi. 20, 21. It was upon account of his preaching that the Christian Converts were not under any Subjection to the Observances of the Law, and that the Law was abolished by the Death of Christ, that he was seized at *Jerusalem*, and sent as a Criminal to *Rome* to be tried for his Life, where he was now a Prisoner. He being therefore afraid that the *Ephesians* and other Convert Gentiles, seeing him thus under Persecution, in Hold, and in danger of Death, upon the Score of his being the Preacher and zealous Propagater and Minister of this great Article of the Christian Faith, which seemed to have had its Rise and Defence wholly from him, might give it up, and not stand firm in the Faith which he had taught them, was rejoiced when in his Confinement he heard that they persisted stedfast in that Faith, and in their Love to all the Saints, *i. e.* as well the Convert Gentiles that did not, as those Jews that did conform to the Jewish Rites. This I take to be the Meaning of his hearing of their Faith here mentioned; and conformably hereunto, *ch*. vi. 19, 20. he desires their Prayers, that he may with Boldness preach the Mystery of the Gospel of which he is the Ambassador in Bonds. This *Mystery of the Gospel*, it is plain from *ch*. i. 9, *&c*. and *ch* iii. 3 — 7. and other Places, was God's gracious Purpose of taking the Gentiles, as Gentiles, to be his People under the Gospel. St. *Paul*, whilst he was a Prisoner at *Rome*, writ to two other Churches, that at *Philippi* and that at *Colofs*: To the *Colossians*, *ch*. i. 4. he uses almost *verbatim* the same Expression that he does here, *having heard of your Faith in Christ Jesus, and of your Love which ye have to all the Saints*: He gives Thanks to God for their knowing and sticking to the Grace of God in Truth, which had been taught them by *Epaphras*, who had informed St. *Paul* of this, and their Affection to him; whereupon he expresses his great Concern that they should continue in that Faith, and not be drawn away to Judaizing, which may be seen from *ver*. 14. of this Chapter, to the End of the Second. So that the hearing of their Faith, which he says both to the *Ephesians* and *Colossians*, is not his being told that they were Christians, but their continuing in the Faith they were converted to and instructed in, *viz*. that they became the People of God, and were admitted into his Kingdom only by Faith in Christ, without submitting to the Mosaical Institution, and legal Observances, which was the Thing he was afraid they should be drawn to, either through any Despondency in themselves, or Importunity of others now that he was removed from them, and in Bonds, and thereby give up that Truth and Freedom of the Gospel which he had preached to them.

5   To

EPHESIANS.

TEXT.	PARAPHRASE.
love unto all the faints, 16 Ceafe not to give thanks for you, making mention of you in my prayers;	to all the Saints ᵈ, ceafe not to give Thanks for you, making mention of you in my Prayers 16.

NOTES.

To the fame Purpofe he writes to the *Philippians*, chap. i. 3 —— 5. telling them that he gave Thanks to God, ἐπὶ πάσῃ τῇ μνείᾳ αὐτῶν, upon every Mention was made of them, upon every Account he received of their continuing in the Fellowſhip and Profeſſion of the Goſpel, as it had been taught them by him, without changing or wavering at all, which is the ſame with *hearing of their Faith*, and that thereupon he prays amongſt other things, chiefly that they might be kept from Judaizing: As appears *ver.* 27, 28. where the Thing he defired to hear of them was, that *they ſtood firm in one Spirit, and one Mind, jointly contending for the Faith of the Goſpel, in nothing ſtartled by thoſe who are Oppoſers*; ſo the Words are, and not *their Adverſaries*. Now there was no Party at that time, who were in Oppofition to the Goſpel which St. *Paul* preached, and with whom the Convert Gentiles had any Difpute, but thoſe who were for keeping up Circumciſion, and the Jewiſh Rites under the Goſpel. Theſe were they whom St. *Paul* apprehended alone as likely to affright the Convert Gentiles, and make them ſtart out of the way from the Goſpel, which is the proper Import of πτυρόμενοι. Though this Paſſage clearly enough indicates what it was that he was and ſhould always be glad to hear of them, yet he more plainly ſhews his Aprehenſion of Danger to them, to be from the Contenders for Judaiſm, in the expreſs Warning he gives them againſt that Sort of Men. *ch.* iii. 2, 3. So that this *Hearing* which he mentions, is the Hearing of theſe three Churches perſiſting firmly in the Faith of the Goſpel which he had taught them, without being drawn at all towards Judaizing. It was that for which St. *Paul* gave Thanks; and it may reaſonably be preſumed that if he had writ to any other Churches of Converted Gentiles, whilſt he was a Priſoner at *Rome*, upon the like Carriage of theirs, ſomething of the ſame Kind would have been ſaid to them. So that the great Buſineſs of theſe three Epiſtles written during his being a Priſoner at *Rome*, was to explain the Nature of the Kingdom of God under the Meſſiah, from which the Gentiles were now no longer ſhut out by the Ordinances of the Law; and confirm the Churches in the Belief of it. St. *Paul* being choſen and ſent by God to preach the Goſpel to the Gentiles, had in all his preaching ſet forth the Largeneſs and Freedom of the Kingdom of God now laid open to the Gentiles, by taking away the Wall of Partition that kept them out. This made the Jews his Enemies, and upon this Account they had ſeized him, and he was now a Priſoner at *Rome*. Fearing that the Gentiles might be wrought upon to ſubmit to the Law, now that he was thus removed, or ſuffering for this Goſpel, he tells theſe three Churches, that he rejoices at their ſtanding firm in the Faith, and thereupon writes to them, to explain and confirm to them the Kingdom of God under the Meſſiah, into which now all Men had an Entrance by Faith in Chriſt, without any Regard to the Terms whereby the Jews were formerly admitted. The ſetting forth the Largeneſs and free Admittance into this Kingdom, which was ſo much for the Glory of God, and ſo much ſhewed his Mercy and Bounty to Mankind, that he makes it as it were a new Creation, is, I ſay, plainly the Buſineſs of theſe three Epiſtles, which tend all viſibly to the ſame Thing, that any one that reads them cannot miſtake the Apoſtle's Meaning, they giving ſuch a clear Light one to another.

15 ᵈ *All the Saints.* One finds in the very reading of theſe Words, that the word *All* is emphatical here, and put in for ſome particular Reaſon. I can, I confeſs, ſee no other but this, *viz.* That they were not by the Judaizers in the leaſt drawn away from their Eſteem and Love of thoſe who were not circumciſed, nor obſerved the Jewiſh Rites; which was a Proof to him, that they ſtood firm in the Faith and Freedom of the Goſpel, which he had inſtructed them in.

EPHESIANS.

PARAPHRASE.

17. ers; that the God of our Lord Jesus Christ, the Father of Glory, would endow your Spirits with Wisdom ^{f}, and Revelation ^{g},
18. whereby ye may know him; and enlighten the Eyes of your Understandings, that you may see what Hopes his calling you to be Christians carries with it, and what an abundant Glory it is to the Saints to become his People,
19. and the Lot of his Inheritance; and what an exceeding great Power he has employed upon us ^{h}: Who believe a Power corresponding to
20. that mighty Power which he exerted in the raising Christ from the dead, and in setting him next to himself over all Things relating to his heavenly Kingdom ^{i}, far above all Principality,

TEXT.

17 That the God of our Lord Jesus Christ, the father of glory, may give unto you the spirit of wisdom and revelation, in the knowledge of him:
18 The eyes of your understanding being enlightned; that you may know what is the hope of his calling, and what the riches of the glory of his inheritance in the saints;
19 And what is the exceeding greatness of his power to us-ward who believe, according to the working of his mighty power;
20 Which he wrought in Christ when he raised him from the dead, and set him at his own right hand, in the heavenly places,

NOTES.

17 ^{e} *Father of Glory*: An Hebrew Expression which cannot be well changed, since it signifies his being glorious himself, being the Fountain from whence all Glory is derived, and to whom all Glory is to be given. In all which Senses it may be taken here, where there is nothing that appropriates it in peculiar to any one of them.

^{f} *Wisdom* is visibly used here for a right Conception and Understanding of the Gospel. See Note, *ver.* 8.

^{g} *Revelation* is used by St. *Paul*, not only for immediate Inspiration, but as it is meant here, and in most other Places, for such Truths which could not have been found out by human Reason, but had their first Discovery from Revelation, though Men afterwards came to the Knowledge of those Truths by reading them in the Sacred Scripture, where they are set down for their Information.

19 ^{h} *Us* here, and *you*, ch. ii. 1. and *us*, ch. ii. 5. it is plain signify the same, who being dead, partook of the Energy of that great Power that raised Christ from the Dead, *i. e.* the Convert Gentiles; and all those glorious Things he in *v.* 18——23. intimates to them, by praying they may see them, he here in this 19th Verse tells us, are bestowed on them as Believers, and not as Observers of the Mosaical Rites.

20 ^{i} Ἐν τοῖς, ἐπουρανίοις, *in heavenly Places*, says our Translation, and so *v.* 3. but possibly the marginal Reading, *Things*, will be thought the better, if we compare, *v.* 22. *He set him at his right Hand*, i. e. transferred on him his Power; Ἐν ἐπουρανίοις, *i. e.* in his Heavenly Kingdom; that is to say, set him at the Head of his Heavenly Kingdom; see *v.* 22. This Kingdom in the Gospel is called indifferently βασιλεία Θεοῦ, *the Kingdom of God*; and βασιλεία τῶν οὐρανῶν, *the Kingdom of Heaven.* God had before a Kingdom and People in this World, *viz.* that Kingdom which he erected to himself of the Jews, selected and brought back to himself out of the apostatized Mass of revolted and rebellious Mankind: With this his People he dwelt, among them he had his Habitation, and ruled as their King in a peculiar Kingdom; and therefore we see that our Saviour calls the Jews, *Matt.* viii. 12. *The Children of the Kingdom.* But that Kingdom, though God's, was not

EPHESIANS.

TEXT.

21 Far above all principality, and power, and might, and dominion, and every name that is named, not only in this world, but also in that which is to come:

22 And hath put all things under his feet, and gave him to be the head over all things to the Church,

PARAPHRASE.

lity, and Power, and Might, and Dominion [k], 21. and any other, either Man or Angel, of greater Dignity and Excellency, that we may come to be acquainted with, or hear the Names of, either in this World, or the World to come.

And hath put all Things in Subjection to him; 22. and him, invested with a Power over all Things, he hath constituted Head of the Church, which

NOTES.

not yet βασιλεία τῶν οὐρανῶν, *the Kingdom of Heaven*; that came with Christ: See *Mat.* iii. 2. & x. 7. That was but ἐπίγειος, of the Earth, compared to this ἐπουράνιος, heavenly Kingdom, which was to be erected under Jesus Christ; and with that Sort of Distinction our Saviour seems to speak and use those Words, ἐπίγεια, *earthly*, and ἐπουράνια, *heavenly*, John iii. 12. ¶ In his Discourse there with *Nicodemus*, he tells him, unless a Man were born again he could not see the Kingdom of God. This being *born again* stuck with *Nicodemus*, which Christ reproaches him with, since being a Teacher in *Israel*, he understood not that which belonged to the Jewish Constitution, wherein to be baptized, for Admittance into that Kingdom, was called and counted to be born again; and therefore says, if having spoken to you ἐπίγεια, things relating to your own *earthly* Constitution, you comprehend me not, how shall you receive what I say, if I speak to you τὰ ἐπουράνια, *heavenly things*, i. e. of that Kingdom which is purely heavenly? And according to this St. *Paul's* Words here, *Eph.* i. 10. τά τε ἐν τοῖς οὐρανοῖς καὶ τὰ ἐπὶ τῆς γῆς, (which occur again, *ch.* iii. 15. *Col.* i. 16, 20.) may perhaps not unfitly be interpreted of the spiritual heavenly Kingdom of God, and that also of the more earthly one of the Jews, whose Rites and positive Institutions St. *Paul* calls *Elements of the World*, Gal. iv. 3. Col. ii. 8, 9. which were both at the coming of the *Messiah* consolidated into one, and together re-established under one Head, *Christ Jesus*. The whole Drift of this and the two following Chapters, being to declare the Union of Jews and Gentiles into one Body, under Christ the Head of the heavenly Kingdom. And he that sedately compares *Eph.* ii. 16. with *Col.* i. 20. in both which Places it is evident the Apostle speaks of the same Thing, *viz.* God's reconciling of both *Jews* and *Gentiles* by the Cross of Christ, will scarce be able to avoid thinking, that Things in Heaven, and Things on Earth, signify the People of the one and the other of these Kingdoms.

21 [k] These abstract Names are frequently used in the New Testament, according to the Stile of the Eastern Languages, for those vested with *Power* and *Dominion*, &c. and that not only here on Earth amongst Men, but in Heaven among superior Beings: And so often are taken to express Ranks and Degrees of Angels; and though they are generally agreed to do so here, yet there is no Reason to exclude earthly Potentates out of this Text, when πάσης necessarily includes them; for that Men in Power are one Sort of ἀρχαὶ and ἐξουσίαι, in a Scripture-Sense, our Saviour's own Words shew, *Luke* xii. 11. & xx. 2. Besides, the Apostle's chief Aim here being to satisfy the *Ephesians*, that they were not to be subjected to the Law of *Moses*, and the Government of those who ruled by it, but they were called to be of the Kingdom of the *Messiah*: It is not to be supposed, that here, where he speaks of Christ's Exaltation to a Power and Dominion paramount to all other, he should not have an Eye to that *little* and low Government of the Jews, which it was beneath the Subjects of so glorious a Kingdom as that of Jesus Christ to submit themselves to: And this the next Words do farther enforce.

A a a   is

EPHESIANS.

PARAPHRASE. | *TEXT.*

23. is his Body, which is compleated by him alone ¹, from whom comes all that gives any thing of Excellency and Perfection to any of the Members of the Church: Where to be a Jew or a Greek, circumcised, or uncircumcised, a Barbarian or a Scythian, a Slave, or a Freeman, matters not; but to be united to him, to partake of his Influence and Spirit, is all in all.

1. And ᵐ you also being dead in Trespasses and Sins, in which you Gentiles, before you were converted to the Gospel, walked according to the State and Constitution of this World,

23 Which is his body, the fulness of him that filleth all in all.

1 And you hath he quick'ned who were dead in trespasses and sins,

NOTES.

23 ¹ Πληρωμα, *Fulness*, here is taken in a passive Sense, for a Thing to be filled or compleated, as appears by the following Words, *of him that filleth all in all*, i. e. It is Christ the Head who perfecteth the Church, by supplying and furnishing all Things to all the Members, to make them what they are and ought to be in that Body. See *chap.* v. 18. *Col.* ii. 10. & iii. 10, 11.

1 ᵐ Και, *And*, gives us here the Thread of St. *Paul*'s Discourse, which is impossible to be understood without seeing the Train of it; without that View it would be like a Rope of Gold Dust, all the Parts would be excellent, and of Value, but would seem heaped together, without Order or Connexion. This *And* h're, it is true, ties the Parts together, and points out the Connexion and Coherence of St. *Paul*'s Discourse; but yet it stands so far from ἐκάθισεν, *set*, in *v.* 20. of the foregoing Chapter; and συνεζωοποίησε, *quickened*, *v.* 5. of this Chapter, which are the two Verbs it copulates together; that by one not acquainted with St. *Paul*'s Stile, it would scarce be observed or admitted; and therefore it may not be amiss to lay it in its due Light, so as to be visible to an ordinary Reader. St. *Paul*, v. 18 — 20. prays that the *Ephesians* may be so enlightened, as to see the great Advantages they received by the Gospel: Those that he specifies are these; 1. What great Hopes it gave them. 2. What an exceeding Glory accompanied the Inheritance of the Saints. 3. The mighty Power exerted by God on their Behalf, which bore some Proportion to that which he employed in the raising Christ from the Dead, and placing him at his Right Hand: Upon the Mention of which his Mind being filled with that glorious Image, he lets his Pen run into a Description of the Exaltation of Christ; which lasts to the End of that Chapter, and then re-assumes the Thread of his Discourse; which in short stands thus, "I pray God that the Eyes of your Understandings " may be enlightened, that you may see the exceeding great Power of God, which is em- " ployed upon us who believe: [κατα την] corresponding to that Energy wherewith he raised " Christ from the Dead, and seated him at his Right Hand; for so also has he raised you " who were dead in Trespasses and Sins: *Us*, I say, who were dead in Trespasses and Sins, " has he quickened and raised together with Christ, and seated together with him in his " heavenly Kingdom." This is in short the Train and Connexion of his Discourse from *ch.* i. 18. to ii. 5. though it be interrupted by many incident Thoughts; which, as his Manner is, he enlarges upon by the Way, and then returns to the Thread of his Discourse. For here again in this first Verse of the second Chapter, we must observe, that having mentioned their being

dead

EPHESIANS.

TEXT.

Wherein in time paſt ye walked according to the courſe of this world, ac-

PARAPHRASE.

World ⁿ, Conforming yourſelf to the Will and Pleaſure of the Prince of the Power of the Air,

2.

NOTES.

dead in Treſpaſſes and Sins, he enlarges upon that forlorn Eſtate of the Gentiles before their Converſion; and then comes to what he deſigned, that God out of his great Goodneſs quickened, raiſed, and placed them together with Chriſt in his heavenly Kingdom. In all which, it is plain, he had more Regard to the Things he declared to them, than to a nice grammatical Conſtruction of his Words: For it is manifeſt, ϗ, *and*, ver. 1. and ϗ, *and*, ver. 5. copulate συνεζωοποίησε, *quickened*, with ἐκάθισεν, *ſet*, ver. 20. of the foregoing Chapter, which the two following Words, *ver.* 6. ϗ, συνήγειρε ϗ, συνεκάθισεν ἐν ἐπουρανίοις, and hath *raiſed up together*, and *hath made ſit together in heavenly Places*. St. Paul, to diſplay the great Power and Energy of God ſhewed towards the Gentiles, in bringing them into his heavenly Kingdom, declares it to be κατὰ τὴν ἐνέργειαν, proportionable to that Power wherewith he raiſed Jeſus from the Dead, and ſeated him at his Right Hand: To expreſs the Parallel, he keeps to the parallel Terms concerning Chriſt; he ſays, *chap.* i. 20. ἐγείρας αὐτὸν ἐκ τῶν νεκρῶν ϗ, ἐκάθισεν ἐν δεξιᾷ αὐτοῦ ἐν τοῖς ἐπουρανίοις, *raiſing him from the dead, and ſet him at his own right hand in heavenly places*. Concerning the Gentile Converts his Words are, *chap.* ii. 5, 6. ϗ, ὄντας ἡμᾶς νεκρὸς τοῖς παραπτώμασι συνεζωοποίησε τῷ Χριστῷ ϗ, συνήγειρε ϗ, συνεκάθισεν ἐν ἐπουρανίοις· *And us being dead in treſpaſſes, he hath quickened together with Chriſt, and hath raiſed us up together, and made us ſit together in heavenly places*. It is alſo viſible, that ὑμᾶς *you*, ver. 1. and ἡμᾶς, *us*, ver. 5. are both governed by the Verb συνεζωοποίησε, *quickened together*, ver. 5. though the grammatical Conſtruction be ſomewhat broken, but is repaired in the Senſe, which lies thus, " God by his mighty Power raiſed Chriſt from the Dead;
" by the like mighty Power, you Gentiles of *Epheſus* being dead in Treſpaſſes and Sins; what
" do I ſay, you of *Epheſus*, nay, us all Converts of the Gentiles being dead in Treſpaſſes
" and Sins, has he quickened and raiſed from the Dead: You *Epheſians* were dead in Treſpaſſes
" and Sins; in which you walked according to the Courſe of this World, according to the Prince
" of the Power of the Air, the Spirit that yet worketh in the Children of Diſobedience; and ſo
" were we, all the reſt of us who are converted from Gentiliſm; we, all of us, of the ſame
" Stamp and Strain, involved in the ſame Converſation, living heretofore according to the Luſts
" of our Fleſh, to which we were perfectly obedient, doing what our carnal Wills and blinded
" Minds directed us, being then no leſs Children of Wrath, no leſs liable to Wrath and Puniſh-
" ment, than thoſe that remained ſtill Children of Diſobedience, *i. e.* unconverted; but God,
" rich in Mercy (for it is by Grace *ye* are ſaved) and raiſed us, &c." This is St. *Paul's* Senſe drawn out more at length, which in his compendious Way of Writing, wherein he crowds many Ideas together, as they abounded in his Mind, could not eaſily be ranged under Rules of Grammar. The promiſcuous Uſe St. *Paul* here makes of *we* and *you*, and his ſo eaſy changing one into the other, plainly ſhews, as we have already obſerved, that they both ſtand for the ſame Sort of Perſons, *i. e.* Chriſtians that were formerly Pagans, whoſe State and Life, whilſt they were ſuch, he here expreſly deſcribes.

2 ⁿ Αἰών may be obſerved in the New Teſtament to ſignify the laſting State and Conſtitution of Things, in the great Tribes or Collections of Men, conſidered in reference to the Kingdom of God; wherefore there were two moſt eminent and principally intended, if I miſtake not, by the Word αἰῶνες, when that is uſed alone, and that is ὁ νῦν αἰών, *this preſent World*, which is taken for that State of the World wherein the Children of *Iſrael* were his People, and made up his Kingdom upon Earth; the Gentiles, *i. e.* all the other Nations of the World, being in a

A a a 2

State

EPHESIANS.

PARAPHRASE.

3. Air º, the Spirit that now yet poſſeſſes and works ᵖ in the Children of Diſobedience ᵍ. Of which Number even we all having formerly been ʳ, lived in the Luſts of our Fleſh, fulfilling the Deſires thereof, and of our blinded perverted Minds ˢ. But ᵗ God who is

TEXT.

cording to the prince of the power of the air, the ſpirit that now worketh in the children of diſobedience.

3 Among whom alſo we all had our converſation in times paſt, in the luſts of our fleſh, fulfilling the

NOTES.

State of Apoſtaſy and Revolt from him, the profeſſed Vaſſals and Subjects of the Devil, to whom they paid Homage, Obedience and Worſhip: And αἰὼν μελλῶν, *the World to come*, i. e. the Time of the Goſpel, wherein God by Chriſt broke down the Partition Wall between Jew and Gentile, and opened a Way for reconciling the reſt of Mankind, and taking the Gentiles again into his Kingdom under Jeſus Chriſt, under whoſe Rule he had put it.

º In theſe Words St. *Paul* points out the Devil, the Prince of the revolted Part of the Creation, and Head of that Kingdom which ſtood in oppoſition to, and was at War with the Kingdom of Jeſus Chriſt.

ᵖ 'Ενεργῶν is the proper Term whereby in the *Greek* is ſignified the Poſſeſſion and Acting of any Perſon by an evil Spirit.

ᵍ *Children of Diſobedience* are thoſe of the Gentiles, who continued ſtill in their Apoſtaſy under the Dominion of Satan, who ruled and acted them, and returned not from their Revolt, deſcribed *Rom*. i. 18, &c. into the Kingdom of God, now that Jeſus Chriſt had opened an Entrance into it to all thoſe who diſobeyed not his Call; and thus they are called, *chap*. v. 6.

ʳ 'Εν οἷς cannot ſignify, *Amongſt whom we alſo all had our Converſation*: For if ἡμεῖς, *we*, ſtands for either the converted Jews or Converts in general, it is not true. If *we* ſtands (as is evident it doth) for the converted Gentiles, of what Force or Tendency is it for the Apoſtle to ſay, We the converted Gentiles heretofore lived among the unconverted Gentiles? But it is of great Force, and to his Purpoſe, in magnifying the Free Grace of God to them, to ſay, We of the Gentiles, who are now admitted to the Kingdom of God, were formerly of that very ſort of Men in whom the Prince of the Power of the Air ruled, leading Lives in the Luſts of our Fleſh, obeying the Will and Inclinations thereof, and ſo as much expoſed to the Wrath of God, as thoſe who ſtill remain in their Apoſtaſy under the Dominion of the Devil.

ˢ This was the State that the Gentile World were given up to. See *Rom*. i. 21, 24. Parallel to this third Verſe of the ſecond Chapter, we have a Paſſage in *chap*. iv. 17——20. of this ſame Epiſtle, where καθὼς ἢ τὰ λοιπὰ ἔθνη, *even as the other Gentiles*, plainly anſwers ὡς ἢ οἱ λοιποὶ, *even as the others* here; and ἐν ματαιότητι τοῦ νοὸς αὐτῶν ἐσκοτισμένοι τῇ διανοίᾳ, *in the Vanity of their Mind, having their Underſtandings darkned*, anſwers ἐν ταῖς ἐπιθυμίαις τῆς σαρκὸς ὑμῶν ποιοῦντες τὰ θελήματα τῆς σαρκὸς ἢ τῶν διανοιῶν, *in the Luſts of our Fleſh, fulfilling the Deſires of the Fleſh, and of the Minds*. He that compares theſe Places, and conſiders that what is ſaid in the fourth Chapter contains the Character of the Gentile World, of whom it is ſpoken, I ſay, he that reads and conſiders theſe two Places well together, and the Correſpondency between them, cannot doubt of the Senſe I underſtand this Verſe in; and that St. *Paul* here, under the Terms *we* and *our*, ſpeaks of the Gentile Converts.

ᵗ 'Ο δὲ, *but*, connects this Verſe admirably well with the immediately preceding, which makes the Parts of that incident Diſcourſe cohere, which ending in this Verſe, St. *Paul* in the Beginning of *ver*. 5. takes up the Thread of his Diſcourſe again, as if nothing had come between; though ὁ δὲ, *but*, in the Beginning of this 4th Verſe, rather breaks than continues the Senſe of the whole. See Note, *ver*. 1.

EPHESIANS.

Chap. II.

TEXT.

desires of the flesh, and of the mind; and were by nature the children of wrath, even as others.

4 But God, who is rich in mercy, for his great love wherewith he loved us,

5 Even when we were dead in sins, hath quickned us together with Christ (by grace ye are saved)

6 And hath raised us up together, and made us sit together in heavenly places in Christ Jesus.

7 That in the ages to come he might shew the

PARAPHRASE.

rich in Mercy ᵘ, through his great Love wherewith he loved us, Even us Gentiles who were dead ˣ in Trespasses, hath he quickened ʸ, together with Christ, (by Grace ye are saved) And hath raised ᶻ us up together with Christ, and made us Partakers in and with Jesus Christ, of the Glory and Power of his heavenly Kingdom, which God has put into his Hands, and put under his Rule: That in the Ages ᵃ to come he might shew the exceeding

NOTES.

ᵘ *Rich in Mercy.* The Design of the Apostle being in this Epistle to set forth the exceeding great Mercy and Bounty of God to the Gentiles under the Gospel, as is manifest at large, *ch.* iii. it is plain that ὑμᾶς, *us*, here in this Verse, must mean the Gentile Converts.

5 ˣ *Dead in Trespasses*, does not mean here, under the Condemnation of Death, or obnoxious to Death for our Transgressions, but so under the Power and Dominion of Sin, so helpless in that State, into which for our Apostasy we were delivered up by the just Judgment of God, that we had no more Thought, nor Hope, nor Ability to get out of it, than Men dead and buried have to get out of the Grave. This State of Death he declares to be the State of Gentilism *Col.* ii. 13. in these Words; *And you being dead in Trespasses, and the Uncircumcision of your Flesh, hath God* quickened together with him, *i. e.* Christ.

ʸ *Quickened*. This quickening was by the Spirit of God given to those who by Faith in Christ were united to him, became Members of Christ, and Sons of God, partaking of the Adoption, by which Spirit they were put into a State of Life; see *Rom.* viii. 9 —— 15. and made capable, if they would, to live to God, and not to obey Sin in the Lusts thereof, nor to yield their Members Instruments of Sin unto Iniquity; but to give up themselves to God, as Men alive from the Dead, and their Members to God, as Instruments of Righteousness; as our Apostle exhorts the converted *Romans* to do, *Rom.* vi. 11 —— 13.

6 ᶻ Wherein this *raising* consists, may be seen, *Rom.* vi. 1 —— 10.

7 ᵃ The great Favour and Goodness of God manifests itself in the Salvation of Sinners in all Ages: But that which most eminently sets forth the Glory of his Grace, was those who were first of all converted from Heathenism to Christianity, and brought out of the Kingdom of Darkness, in which they were as dead Men, without Life, Hope, or so much as a Thought of Salvation, or a better State, into the Kingdom of God. Hence it is that he says, *ch.* i. 12. *That we should be to the Praise of his Glory who first believed.* To which he seems to have an Eye in this Verse; the first Conversion of the Gentiles being a surprizing and wonderful Effect and Instance of God's exceeding Goodness to them, which, to the Glory of his Grace, should be admired and acknowledged by all future Ages; and so *Paul* and *Barnabas* speaks of it, *Acts* xiv. 27. *They rehearsed all that God had done with them, and how he had opened the Door of Faith to the Gentiles.* And so *James* and the Elders at *Jerusalem*, when they heard what Things God had wrought by St. *Paul's* Ministry amongst the Gentiles, *they glorified the Lord*, *Acts* xxi. 19, 20.

Riches

EPHESIANS

PARAPHRASE.

8. Riches of his Grace, in his Kindness towards us, through Christ Jesus. For by God's Free Grace it is that ye ᵇ are, through Faith in Christ, saved ᶜ and brought into the Kingdom of God, and made his People, not by any thing you did yourselves to deserve it, it is the Free Gift of God, who might, if he had so pleased, with Justice have left you in that for-
9. lorn Estate. That no Man might have any Pretence of boasting of himself, or his own Works

TEXT.

8 exceeding riches of his grace in his kindness towards us, through Christ Jesus.

For by grace are ye saved, through faith; and that not of yourselves: it is the gift of God:

9 Not of works, lest any man should boast:

NOTES.

8 ᵇ *Ye.* The Change of *we* in the foregoing Verse, to *ye* here, and the like Change observable *v.* 1. & 5. plainly shews, that the Persons spoken of under these two Denominations, are of the same Kind, *i. e.* Gentile Converts; only St. *Paul* every now and then, the more effectually to move those he is writing to, changes *we* into *ye*, and *vice versa*; and so makes, as it were, a little Sort of Distinction, that he may the more emphatically apply himself to them.

ᶜ *Saved.* He that reads St. *Paul* with Attention, cannot but observe, that speaking of the Gentiles, he calls their being brought back again from their Apostasy into the Kingdom of God, their being *saved.* Before they were thus brought to be the People of God again under the *Messiah,* they were, as they are here described, Aliens, Enemies, without Hope, without God, dead in Trespasses and Sins; and therefore when by Faith in Christ they came to be reconciled, and to be in Covenant again with God, and his Subjects and liege People, they were in the Way of Salvation, and if they persevered, could not miss attaining to it, though they were not yet in actual Possession. The Apostle, whose Aim it is in this Epistle to give them an high Sense of God's extraordinary Grace and Favour to them, and to raise their Thoughts above the mean Observances of the Law, shews them that there was nothing in them; no Deeds or Works of theirs, nothing that they could do to prepare or recommend themselves, contributed aught to the bringing them into the Kingdom of God under the Gospel; that it was all purely the Work of Grace, for they were all dead in Trespasses and Sins, and could do nothing, not make one Step or the least Motion towards it. Faith, which alone gained them Admittance, and alone opened the Kingdom of Heaven to Believers, was the sole Gift of God; Men, by their natural Faculties could not attain to it. It is Faith which is the Source and Beginning of this new Life; and the Gentile World who were without Sense, without Hope of any such thing, could no more help themselves, or do any thing to procure it themselves, than a dead Man can do any thing to procure himself Life. It is God here does all; by Revelation of what they could never discover by their own natural Faculties, he bestows on them the Knowledge of the *Messiah,* and the *Faith* of the Gospel; which as soon as they have received, they are in the Kingdom of God, in a new State of Life; and being thus quickened by the Spirit, may as Men alive work if they will. Hence St. *Paul* says, *Rom.* x. *Faith cometh by hearing, and hearing by the Word of God*; having in the foregoing Verses declared, there is no believing without hearing, and no hearing without a Preacher, and no Preacher unless he be sent, *i. e.* the good Tidings of Salvation by the Messiah, and the Doctrine of Faith was not, nor could be known to any, but to those to whom God communicated it, by the preaching of Prophets and Apostles, to whom he revealed it, and whom he sent on this Errand with this Discovery. And thus God now gave *Faith* to the *Ephesians,* and the other Gentiles, to whom he sent St. *Paul,* and others his Fellow-Labourers, to bestow on them the Knowledge of Salvation,

Recon-

EPHESIANS.

NOTES.

Reconciliation, and Restoration into his Kingdom of the Messiah. All which, though revealed by the Spirit of God in the Writings of the Old Testament, yet the Gentile World was kept wholly Strangers from the Knowledge of, by the Ceremonial Law of *Moses*, which was the Wall of Partition that kept the Gentiles at a Distance, Aliens and Enemies, which Wall God, according to his gracious Purpose before the erecting of it, having now broke down, communicated to them the Doctrine of Faith, and admitted them, upon their Acceptance of it, to all the Advantages and Privileges of his Kingdom; all which was done of his free Grace, without any Merit or Procurement of theirs; *he was found of them who sought him not, and was made manifest to them that asked not after him.* I desire him that would clearly understand this, *ch.* ii. of the *Ephesians*, to read carefully with it, *Rom.* x. & 1 *Cor.* ii. 9—16. where he will see, that *Faith* is wholly owing to the Revelation of the Spirit of God, and the Communication of that Revelation by Men sent by God, who attained this Knowledge, not by the Assistance of their own natural Parts, but from the Revelation of the Spirit of God. Thus *Faith* we see is the Gift of God, and with it, when Men by Baptism are admitted into the Kingdom of God, comes the Spirit of God, which brings Life with it: For the attaining this Gift of Faith, Men do or can do nothing; Grace hitherto does all, and Works are wholly excluded; God himself creates them to do good Works, but when by him they are made living Creatures in this new Creation, it is then expected, that being quickened, they should act; and from henceforwards Works are required, not as the meritorious Cause of Salvation, but as a necessary, indispensible Qualification of the Subjects of God's Kingdom under his Son Jesus Christ; it being impossible that any one should at the same Time be a Rebel and a Subject too: And though none can be Subjects of the Kingdom of God, but those who continuing in the Faith that has been once bestowed on them, sincerely endeavour to conform themselves to the Laws of their Lord and Master Jesus Christ; and God gives eternal Life to all those, and those only that do so; yet eternal Life is the Gift of God, the Gift of Free Grace, since their Works of sincere Obedience afford no manner of Title to it; their Righteousness is imperfect, *i. e.* they are all unrighteous, and so deserve Death; but God gives them Life upon the Account of his Righteousness. *vid. Rom.* i. 17. the Righteousness of Faith which is by Jesus Christ; and so they are still saved by Grace.

Now when God hath, by calling them into the Kingdom of his Son, thus quickened Men, and they are by his free Grace created in Christ Jesus unto good Works, that then Works are required of them, we see in this that they are called on, and pressed to *walk worthy of God, who hath called them to his Kingdom and Glory*, 1 Thess. ii. 12. And to the same Purpose here, *ch.* iv. 1. *Phil.* i. 27. *Col.* i. 10——12. So that of those who are in the Kingdom of God, who are actually under the Covenant of Grace, good Works are strictly required, under the Penalty of the Loss of Eternal Life; *If ye live after the Flesh ye shall die, but if through the Spirit ye mortify the Deeds of the Body, ye shall live*, Rom. viii. 13. And so *Rom.* vi. 11, 13. they are commanded to obey God as living Men. This is the Tenor of the whole New Testament: The Apostate Heathen World were dead, and were of themselves in that State not capable of doing any thing to procure their Translation into the Kingdom of God, that was purely the Work of Grace: But when they received the Gospel, they were then made alive by Faith, and by the Spirit of God; and then they were in a State of Life, and Working and Works were expected of them. Thus Grace and Works consist without any Difficulty; that which has caused the Perplexity and seeming Contradiction, has been Mens Mistake concerning the Kingdom of God: God in the Fulness of Time set up his Kingdom in this World under his Son; into which he admitted all those who believed on him, and received Jesus the Messiah for their Lord. Thus by Faith in Jesus Christ Men became the People of God, and Subjects of his Kingdom; and being by Baptism admitted into it, were from henceforth, during their continuing in the Faith, and Profession of the Gospel, accounted Saints, the Beloved of God, the Faithful in Christ Jesus, the People of God, saved, &c. for in these Terms, and the like, the Sacred Scripture speaks of them. And indeed those who were thus translated into the Kingdom of the Son of God, were no longer in the dead State of the Gentiles; but having passed from Death to Life, were in the State of the Living, in the Way to eternal Life; which they were sure to attain, if they persevered in that Life which the Gospel required, *viz.* Faith and sincere Obedience. But yet this was not an actual Possession of eternal

EPHESIANS.

PARAPHRASE.

10. *Works or Merit.* So that, in this new State in the Kingdom of God, we are, and ought to look upon ourselves, not as deriving any thing from ourselves, but as the mere Workmanship of God created ᵈ in Christ Jesus, to the end we should do good Works, for which he had prepared and fitted us to live in them ᵉ.

TEXT.

10 For we are his workmanship, created in Christ Jesus unto good works, which God hath before ordained that we should walk in them.

NOTES.

Life in the Kingdom of God in the World to come; for by Apostasy or Disobedience, this, though sometimes called Salvation, might be forfeited and lost; whereas he that is once possessed of the other, hath actually an eternal Inheritance in the Heavens, which fadeth not away. These two Considerations of the Kingdom of Heaven some Men have confounded and made one; so that a Man being brought into the first of these, wholly by Grace without Works, Faith being all that was required to instate a Man in it, they have concluded that for the attaining eternal Life, or the Kingdom of God in the World to come, Faith alone, and not good Works, are required, contrary to express Words of Scripture, and the whole Tenor of the Gospel: But yet not being admitted into that State of eternal Life for our good Works, it is by Grace here too that we are saved, our Righteousness after all being imperfect, and we by our Sins liable to Condemnation and Death: But it is by Grace we are made Partakers of both these Kingdoms; it is only into the Kingdom of God in this World we are admitted by Faith alone without Works; but for our Admittance into the other, both Faith and Obedience, in a sincere Endeavour to perform those Duties, all those good Works which are incumbent on us, and come in our Way to be performed by us, from the Time of our Believing till our Death.

10 ᵈ *Workmanship of God created.* It is not by Virtue of any Works of the Law, nor in Consideration of our submitting to the Mosaical Institution, or having any Alliance with the Jewish Nation, that we Gentiles are brought into the Kingdom of Christ; we are in this entirely the Workmanship of God, and are, as it were, created therein, framed and fitted by him, to the Performance of those good Works which we were from thence to live in; and so owe nothing of this our new Being, in this new State, to any Preparation or Fitting we received from the Jewish Church, or any Relation we stood in thereunto. That this is the Meaning of the new Creation under the Gospel, is evident from St. *Paul*'s own explaining of it himself, 2 *Cor.* v. 16——18. *viz.* That being in Christ was all one as if he were in a new Creation; and therefore from henceforth he knew no Body after the Flesh, *i. e.* he pretended to no Privilege for being of a Jewish Race, or an Observer of their Rites; all these old Things were done away; all Things under the Gospel are new, and of God alone.

ᵉ This is conformable to what he says, *v.* 5, 6. That God quickened and raised the Gentiles, that were dead in Trespasses and Sins, with Christ, being by Faith united to him, and partaking of the same Spirit of Life which raised him from the Dead; whereby, as Men brought to Life, they were enabled (if they would not resist nor quench that Spirit) to live unto God in Righteousness and Holiness, as before they were under the absolute Dominion of Satan and their own Lusts.

SECT.

EPHESIANS.
SECT. IV.
CHAP. II. 11——22.

CONTENTS.

FROM this Doctrine of his in the foregoing Section, that God of his Free Grace, according to his Purpose from the Beginning, had quickened and raised the Convert Gentiles, together with Christ, and seated them with Christ in his heavenly Kingdom, St. *Paul* here in this Section draws this Inference to keep them from Judaizing, that though they (as was the State of the Heathen World) were heretofore, by being uncircumcised, shut out from the Kingdom of God, Strangers to the Covenants of Promise, without Hope and without God in the World, yet they were by Christ, who had taken away the Ceremonial Law, that Wall of Partition, that kept them in that State of Distance and Opposition, now received, without any subjecting them to the Law of *Moses*, to be the People of God, and had the same Admittance into the Kingdom of God with the *Jews* themselves, with whom they were now created into one new Man or Body of Men; so that they were no longer to look on themselves any more as Aliens, or remoter from the Kingdom of God, than the *Jews* themselves.

TEXT.

11 Wherefore remember that ye being, in time past, Gentiles in the flesh, who are called uncircumcision, by that which is called the circumcision in the flesh, made by hands;

12 That at that time ye were without Christ, be-

PARAPHRASE.

11 Wherefore remember that ye who were heretofore Gentiles, distinguished and separated from the Jews, who are circumcised by a Circumcision made with Hands in their Flesh, by your not being circumcised in your Flesh [f], were at that time without all Knowledge of the Messiah, or any Expectation of

11.

12.

NOTES.

11 [f] This Separation was so great, that to a Jew the uncircumcised Gentiles were counted so polluted and unclean, that they were not shut out barely from their holy Places and Service, but from their Tables and ordinary Conversation.

EPHESIANS.

PARAPHRASE.

Deliverance or Salvation by him g, Aliens from the Commonwealth of *Israel* h, and Strangers to the Covenants of Promise i, not having any Hope of any such thing, and living in the World without having the true God for their God k, or they being his People. But now you that were formerly remote and at a Distance are by Jesus Christ brought near by his Death l. For it is he that reconcileth us m to the Jews, and hath brought us and them, who were before at an irreconcileable Distance, into Unity one with another, by removing the middle Wall of Partition n, that kept us at a Distance, having taken away the Cause of Enmity o, or Distance between us,

13.

14.

15.

TEXT.

ing aliens from the commonwealth of Israel, and strangers from the covenants of promise, having no hope, and without God in the world:

But now in Christ Jesus, ye who sometimes were far off, are made nigh by the blood of Christ.

For he is our peace, who hath made both one, and hath broken down the middle wall of partition between us;

Having abolished in his flesh the enmity, even the

13

14

15

NOTES.

12 g That this is the Meaning of being *without Christ* here, is evident from this, that what St. *Paul* says here, is to shew the different State of the Gentiles from that of the Jews, before the Coming of our Saviour.

h Who were alone then the People of God.

i *Covenants.* God more than once renewed his Promise to *Abraham, Isaac* and *Jacob*, and the Children of *Israel*, that upon the Conditions proposed he would be their God, and they should be his People.

k It is in this Sense that the Gentiles are called ἄθεοι; for there were few of them Atheists in our Sense of the Word, *i. e.* denying superior Powers; and many of them acknowledged one supreme Eternal God; but, as St. *Paul* says, Rom. i. 21. when they knew God, they glorified him not as God, they owned not him alone, but turned away from him the invisible God, to the Worship of Images, and the false Gods of their Countries.

13 l How this was done the following Words explain, and *Col.* ii. 14.

14 m Ἡμῶν, *Our*, in this Verse must signify Persons in the same Condition with those he speaks to under the Pronoun ὑμεῖς, *ye*, in the foregoing Verse, or else the Apostle's Argument here would be wide, and not conclusive; but *ye* in the foregoing Verse incontestibly signifies the Convert Gentiles, and so therefore must ἡμῶν in this Verse.

n See *Col.* i. 20.

15 o It was the Ritual Law of the Jews, that kept them and the Gentiles at an irreconcileable Distance; so that they could come to no Terms of a fair Correspondence; the Force whereof was so great, that even after Christ was come, and had put an End to the Obligation of that Law, yet it was almost impossible to bring them together; and this was that which in the Beginning most obstructed the Progress of the Gospel, and disturbed the Gentile Converts.

EPHESIANS.

Chap. II.

TEXT.	PARAPHRASE.
law of commandments contained in ordinances,	by abolishing ᵖ that Part of the Law which consisted in positive Commands and Ordinances,

NOTES.

ᵖ *By abolishing.* I do not remember that the Law of *Moses*, or any Part of it, is by an actual Repeal any where abrogated; and yet we are told here, and in other Places of the New Testament, that it is *abolished*. The Want of a right understanding of what this *abolishing* was, and how it was brought about, has, I suspect, given Occasion to the misunderstanding of several Texts of Sacred Scripture; I beg leave therefore to offer what the Sacred Scripture seems to me to suggest concerning this Matter, till a more thorough Enquiry by some abler Hand shall be made into it. After the general Revolt and Apostasy of Mankind, from the Acknowledgment and Worship of the one only true invisible God their Maker, the Children of *Israel*, by a voluntary Submission to him, and Acknowledgment of him to be their God and supreme Lord, came to be his People, and he, by a peculiar Covenant, to be their King; and thus erected to himself a Kingdom in this World out of that People, to whom he gave a Law by *Moses*, which was to be the Law of the *Israelites*, his People, with a Purpose at the same time, that he would in due Season transfer this his Kingdom in this World, into the Hands of the Messiah, whom he intended to send into the World, to be the Prince and Ruler of his People, as he had foretold and promised to the Jews. Into which Kingdom of his under his Son, he purposed also, and foretold that he would admit and incorporate the other Nations of the Earth, as well as those of the Posterity of *Abraham*, *Isaac*, and *Jacob*, who were to come into this his enlarged Kingdom upon new Terms that he should then propose; and that those, and those only, should from henceforth be his People. And thus it came to pass, that though the Law which was given by *Moses* to the *Israelites* was never repealed, and so ceased not to be the Law of that Nation; yet it ceased to be the Law of the People and Kingdom of God in this World, because the Jews not receiving him to be their King, whom God had sent to be the King and sole Ruler of his Kingdom for the future, ceased to be the People of God, and the Subjects of God's Kingdom. And thus Jesus Christ by his Death entering into his Kingdom, having then fulfilled all that was required of him for the obtaining of it, put an End to the Law of *Moses*, opening another Way to all People, both Jews and Gentiles, into the Kingdom of God, quite different from the Law of Ordinances given by *Moses*, viz. Faith in Jesus Christ, by which, and which alone, every one that would, had now Admittance into the Kingdom of God, by the one plain easy and simple Ceremony of Baptism. This was that which, though it was also foretold, the Jews understood not, having a very great Opinion of themselves, because they were the chosen People of God; and of their Law, because God was the Author of it; and so concluded that both they were to remain the People of God for ever, and also that they were to remain so under the same Law, which was never to be altered; and so never understood what was foretold them of the Kingdom of the Messiah, in Respect of the ceasing of their Law of Ordinances, and the Admittance of the Gentiles upon the same Terms with them into the Kingdom of the Messiah; which therefore St. *Paul* calls over and over again a Mystery, and a Mystery hidden from Ages.

Now he that will look a little farther into this Kingdom of God, under these two different Dispensations of the Law and the Gospel, will find that it was erected by God, and Men were recalled into it out of the general Apostasy from their Lord and Maker, for the unspeakable Good and Benefit of those who by entering into it, returned to their Allegiance, that thereby they might be brought into a Way and Capacity of being restored to that happy State of Eternal Life, which they had all lost in *Adam*, which it was impossible they could ever recover whilst they remained Worshippers and Vassals of the Devil, and so Outlaws and Enemies to God, in the Kingdom, and under the Dominion of Satan; since the most biassed and partial Inclination of an intelligent Being, could never expect that God should reward Rebellion and Apostasy with

B b b 2   eternal

eternal Happiness, and take Men that were actually Vassals and Adorers of his Arch-Enemy the Devil, and immediately give them eternal Bliss, with the Enjoyment of Pleasures in his Presence, and at his Right-Hand for evermore. The Kingdom of God therefore in this World, was, as it were, the Entrance to the Kingdom of God in the other World, and the Receptacle and Place of Preparation of those who aimed at a Share in that eternal Inheritance. And hence the People of the Jews were called holy, chosen, and Sons of God; as were afterward the Christians called Saints, Elect, Beloved, and Children of God, &c. But there is this remarkable Difference to be observed in what is said of the Subjects of this Kingdom, under the two different Dispensations of the Law and the Gospel, that the Converts to Christianity, and Professors of the Gospel, are often termed and spoke of as *saved*, which I do not remember that the Jews or Proselytes, Members of the Commonwealth, any where are: The Reason whereof is, that the Conditions of that Covenant whereby they were made the People of God, under that Constitution of God's Kingdom in this World, was, *Do this and live*; but he that continues not in all these Things to do them, shall die. But the Condition of the Covenant whereby they become the People of God, in the Constitution of his Kingdom under the Messiah, is, Believe and repent, and thou shalt be saved, *i. e.* Take Christ for thy Lord, and do sincerely but what thou canst to keep his Law, and thou shalt be saved. In the one of which, which is therefore called the Covenant of Works, those who were actually in that Kingdom could not attain the everlasting Inheritance: And in the other, called the Covenant of Grace, those, who if they would but continue as they began, *i. e.* in the State of Faith and Repentance, *i. e.* in a Submission to and owning of Christ, and a steady unrelenting Resolution of not offending against his Law, could not miss it, and so might truly be said to be saved, they being in an unerring Way to Salvation. And thus we see how the Law of *Moses* is by Christ abolished under the Gospel; not by any actual Repeal of it, but is set aside, by ceasing to be the Law of the Kingdom of God, translated into the Hands of the Messiah, and set up under him; which Kingdom so erected, contains all that God now does or will own to be his People in this World. This Way of *abolishing* of the Law, did not make those Observances unlawful to those who before their Conversion to the Gospel were circumcised, and under the Law; they were indifferent Things, which the converted Jews might or might not observe, as they found convenient: That which was unlawful and contrary to the Gospel, was the making those Ritual Observances necessary to be joined with Faith in Believers for Justification, as we see they did, who, *Acts* xv. taught the Brethren, that unless they were circumcised after the Manner of *Moses*, they could not be saved; so that the nailing it to Christ's Cross, *Col.* ii. xiv. was the taking away from thenceforth all Obligation for any one to be circumcised, and to put himself under the Observances of the Law, to become one of the People of God, but was no Prohibition to any one who was circumcised before Conversion to observe them. Accordingly we see, *Gal.* ii. 11. that what St. *Paul* blames in St. *Peter*, was compelling the Gentiles to live as the Jews do: Had not that been the Case, he would no more have blamed his Carriage at *Antioch*, than he did his observing the Law at *Jerusalem*.

The Apostle here tells us what Part of the Mosaical Law it was that Christ put an End to by his Death, *viz.* τὸν νόμον τῶν ἐντολῶν ἐν δόγμασι, *the Law of Commandments in Ordinances*; *i. e.* the positive Injunction of the Law of *Moses* concerning Things in their own Nature indifferent, which became obligatory merely by virtue of a direct positive Command; and are called by St. *Paul* in the parallel Place, *Col.* ii. 14. χειρόγραφον τοῖς δόγμασι, *the Hand-writing of Ordinances*. There were, besides these, contained in the Book of the Law of *Moses*, the Law of Nature, or as it is commonly called, the Moral Law, that unmoveable Rule of Right which is of perpetual Obligation: This Jesus Christ is so far from abrogating, that he has promulgated it anew under the Gospel, fuller and clearer than it was in the Mosaical Constitution, or any where else; and by adding to its Precepts the Sanction of his own Divine Authority, has made the Knowledge of that Law more easy and certain than it was before; so that the Subjects of his Kingdom whereof this is now the Law, can be at no Doubt or Loss about their Duty, if they will but read and consider the Rules of Morality, which our Saviour and his Apostles have delivered in very plain Words in the holy Scriptures of the New Testament.

that

EPHESIANS.

TEXT.

for to make in himself, of twain, one new man, so making peace;
16. And that he might reconcile both unto God in one body by the Cross, having slain the enmity thereby:
17. And came, and preached peace to you which were afar off, and to them that were nigh.
18. For through him we both have an access by

PARAPHRASE.

that so he might make ᵠ or frame the two, *viz.* Jews and Gentiles, into one new Society or Body of God's People, in a new Constitution under himself ʳ, so making Peace between them. And might reconcile them both to God, being thus united into one Body in him by the Cross, whereby he destroyed that Enmity or Incompatibility that was between them, by nailing to his Cross the Law of Ordinances that kept them at a Distance. And being come, preached the good Tidings of Peace to you Gentiles that were far off from the Kingdom of Heaven, and to the Jews that were near, and in the very Precincts of it. For it is by him

16.

17.

18.

NOTES.

15 ᵠ *Make*; the Greek Word is κτίση, which does not always signify Creation in a strict Sense.

ʳ This, as I take it, being the Meaning, it may not be amiss perhaps to look into the Reason why St. *Paul* expresses it in this more figurative Manner, *viz. to make in himself of twain one new Man*, which, I humbly conceive, was more suitable to the Ideas he had, and so were, in fewer Words, more lively and express to his Purpose: He always has Jesus Christ in his Mind, as the Head of the Church, which was his Body, from and by whom alone, by being united to him, the whole Body and every Member of it received Life, Vigour and Strength, and all the Benefits of that State; which admirably well shews, that whoever were united to this Head, must needs be united to one another, and also that all the Privileges and Advantages they enjoyed, were wholly owing to their Union with, and adhering to him their Head; which were the two Things that he was here inculcating to the Convert Gentiles of *Ephesus*, to shew them, that now under the Gospel Men became the People of God, merely by Faith in Jesus Christ, and having him for their Head, and not at all by keeping the Ritual Law of *Moses*, which Christ had abolished, and so had made way for the Jews and Gentiles to become one in Christ, since now Faith in him alone united them into one Body under that Head, with the Observance of the Law; which is the Meaning of *so making Peace*. I hope this single Note here may lead ordinary Readers into an Understanding of St. *Paul's* Stile, and by making them observe the Reason, give them an easier Entrance into the Meaning of St. *Paul's* figurative Expressions.

If the Nation of the Jews had owned and received Jesus the Messiah, they had continued as the People of God; but after that they had Nationally rejected him, and refused to have him rule over them, and put him to Death, and so had revolted from their Allegiance, and withdrawn themselves from the Kingdom of God, which he had now put into the Hands of his Son, they were no longer the People of God; and therefore all those of the Jewish Nation, who after that would return to their Allegiance, had need of Reconciliation to be re-admitted into the Kingdom of God, as part of his People, who were now received into Peace and Covenant with him upon other Terms, and under other Laws, than being the Posterity of *Jacob*, or Observers of the Law of *Moses*.

that

PARAPHRASE.

19. that we, both Jews and Gentiles, have access to the Father by one and the same Spirit. Therefore, ye *Ephesians*, though heretofore Gentiles, now Believers in Christ, you are no more Strangers and Foreigners, but without any more ado Fellow-Citizens of the Saints, and Domestics
20. of God's own Family; Built upon the Foundation laid by the Apostles and Prophets, where-
21. of Jesus Christ is the Corner-stone: In whom all the Building fitly framed together, groweth unto
22. an holy Temple in the Lord: In which even the Gentiles also are built up together with the believing Jews, for an Habitation of God, through the Spirit ⁵.

TEXT.

one Spirit unto the Father.

19. Now therefore ye are no more strangers and foreigners, but fellow-citizens with the saints, and of the houshold of God:
20. And are built upon the foundation of the Apostles and prophets, Jesus Christ himself being the chief corner-stone.
21. In whom all the building fitly framed together, groweth unto an holy temple in the Lord:
22. In whom you also are builded together for an habitation of God through the Spirit.

NOTES.

22 ⁵ The Sense of which Allegory I take to be this: It is plain from the Attestation of the Apostles and Prophets, that the Gentiles who believe in Christ are thereby made Members of his Kingdom, united together under him their Head into such a well-framed Body, wherein each Person has his proper Place, Rank and Function to which he is fitted, that God will accept and delight in them as his People, and live amongst them, as in a well-framed Building dedicated and set apart to him, whereof the Gentiles make a Part, and without any Difference put between you, are framed in Equality, and promiscuously with the believing Jews, by the Spirit of God, to be one People, amongst whom he will dwell, and be their God, and they shall be his People.

EPHESIANS.

SECT. V.

CHAP. III. 1——21.

CONTENTS.

THIS Section gives a great Light to those foregoing, and more clearly opens the Design of this Epistle: For here St. *Paul* in plain Words tells them, it is for preaching this Doctrine that was a Mystery till now, being hid from former Ages, (*viz.*) that the Gentiles should be Co-heirs with the believing Jews, and making one Body or People with them, should be equally Partakers of the Promises under the Messiah, of which Mystery he by particular Favour and Appointment was ordained the Preacher. Whereupon he exhorts them not to be dismayed, or flinch in the least from the Belief or Profession of this Truth, upon his being persecuted and in Bonds upon that Account. For his suffering for it, who was the Preacher and Propagator of it, was so far from being a just Discouragement to them, from standing firmly in the Belief of it, that it ought to be to them a Glory, and a Confirmation of this eminent Truth of the Gospel, which he peculiarly taught; and thereupon he tells them, he makes it his Prayer to God, that they may be strengthened herein, and be able to comprehend the Largeness of the Love of God in Christ, not confined to the Jewish Nation and Constitution, as the Jews conceited, but far surpassing the Thoughts of those who presuming themselves knowing, would confine it to such only who were Members of the Jewish Church, and Observers of their Ceremonies.

TEXT.   *PARAPHRASE.*

1 FOR this cause, I Paul, the prisoner of Jesus Christ for you Gentiles;

1. FOR my Preaching of this [1], I *Paul* am a Prisoner, upon Account of the Gospel of Jesus Christ, for the Sake and Service of you Gen-

NOTES.

1 [1] See *Col.* iv. 3. 2 *Tim.* ii. 9, 10.

EPHESIANS.

PARAPHRASE.

2. Gentiles ᵘ. Which you cannot doubt of, since ʷ ye have heard of the Dispensation of the Grace of God, which was given to me in
3. reference to you Gentiles: How that by especial Revelation he made known unto me in particular ˣ the Mystery ʸ, (as I hinted to you
4. above, viz. ch. i. 9. By the bare reading whereof ye may be assured of my Knowledge in this formerly concealed and unknown Part of the
5. Gospel of Christ ᶻ:) Which in former Ages was not made known to the Sons of Men, as it is now revealed to his holy Apostles and Pro-

TEXT.

If ye have heard of 2 the dispensation of the grace of God, which is given me to you-ward:

How that by revelati- 3 on he made known unto me the mystery, (as I wrote afore in few words,

Whereby when ye read 4 ye may understand my knowledge in the mystery of Christ)

Which in other ages 5 was not made known unto the sons of men, as it is now revealed unto his

NOTES.

ᵘ See *Phil.* i. 7. *Col.* i. 24.

2 ˣ Εἴγε, is sometimes an affirmative Particle, and signifies in Greek the same that *siquidem* does in Latin, and so the Sense requires it to be understood here: For it could not be supposed but the *Ephesians*, among whom St. *Paul* had lived so long, must have heard that he was by express Commission from God made Apostle of the Gentiles, and by immediate Revelation instructed in the Doctrine he was to teach them, whereof this of their Admittance into the Kingdom of God purely by Faith in Christ, without Circumcision or other legal Observances, was one great and necessary Point, whereof St. *Paul* was so little shy, that we see the World rung of it, *Acts* xxi. 28. And if his Preaching and Writing were of a-piece, as we need not doubt, this Mystery of God's Purpose to the Gentiles, which was communicated to him by Revelation, and we hear of so often in his Epistles, was not concealed from them he preached to.

3 ˣ Though St. *Peter* was by a Vision from God sent to *Cornelius* a Gentile, *Acts* x. yet we do not find that this Purpose of God's calling the Gentiles to be his People equally with the Jews, without any Regard to Circumcision, or the Mosaical Rites, was revealed to him, or to any other of the Apostles, as a Doctrine which they were to preach and publish to the World: Neither indeed was it needful that it should be any Part of their Commission, who were Apostles only of the Circumcision, to mix that in their Message to the Jews, which should make them stop their Ears, and refuse to hearken to the other Parts of the Gospel, which they were more concerned to know and be instructed in.

ʸ See *Col.* i. 26.

4 ᶻ One may be ready to ask, to what Purpose is this, which this Parenthesis contains here concerning himself? and indeed without having an Eye on the Design of this Epistle, it is pretty hard to give an Account of it; but that being carried in view, there is nothing plainer, nor more pertinent and persuasive than this here; for what can be of more Force to make them stand firm to the Doctrine which he had taught them, of their being exempt from Circumcision, and the Observances of the Law? If you have heard, and I assure you in my Epistle, that this Mystery of the Gospel was revealed in a particular Manner to me from Heaven; the very reading of this is enough to satisfy you, that I am well instructed in that Truth, and that you may safely depend upon what I have taught you concerning this Point, notwithstanding I am in Prison for it, which is a thing you ought to glory in, since I suffer for a Truth wherein you are so nearly concerned; see *chap.* vi. 19.

EPHESIANS

TEXT.

holy apostles and prophets by the Spirit;

6 That the Gentiles should be fellow-heirs, and of the same body, and partakers of his promise in Christ by the Gospel:

7 Whereof I was made a minister according to the gift of the grace of God

PARAPHRASE.

phets by the Spirit, *viz.* That the Gentiles should be Fellow-Heirs, be united into one Body, and partake of his Promise ᵃ in Christ jointly with the Jews ᵇ, in the time ᶜ of the Gospel; of which Doctrine I in particular was made the Minister ᵈ according to the free and gracious Gift of God, given unto me

NOTES.

6 ᵃ The Promise here intended, is the Promise of the Spirit: see *Gal.* iii. 14. which was not given to any but to the People and Children of God; and therefore the Gentiles received not the Spirit till they became the People of God, by Faith in Christ in the Times of the Gospel.

ᵇ Though the Jews are not expresly named here, yet it is plain from the foregoing Chapter, *v.* 11, &c. that it is of the Union of the Gentiles with the Jews, and making with them one Body of God's People equally sharing in all the Privileges and Benefits of the Gospel, that he is here speaking; the same which he teaches, *Gal.* iii. 26——29.

ᶜ Διὰ τοῦ εὐαγγελίου, signifies here, In the time of the Gospel, as δι ἀκροβυςίας signifies, In the time of Uncircumcision, *Rom.* iv. 11. see Note on *Rom.* vii. 5. The same thing being intended here, which, chap. i. 10. is thus expressed; *That in the Dispensation of the Fulness of Times*, i. e. in the Time of the Gospel, *all things might be gathered together*, or united, *in Christ*, or, by Christ.

7 ᵈ Though he does not in express Words deny others to be made Ministers of it, for it neither suited his Modesty, nor the Respect he had for the other Apostles, so to do, yet his Expression here will be found strongly to imply it, especially if we read and consider well the two following Verses; for this was a necessary Instruction to one who was sent to convert the Gentiles, though those who were sent to their Brethren the Jews were not appointed to promulgate it. This one Apostle of the Gentiles, by the Success of his preaching to the Gentiles the Attestation of Miracles, and the Gift of the Holy Ghost joined to what *Peter* had done by special Direction in the Case of *Cornelius*, would be enough in its due Season to convince the other Apostles of this Truth, as we may see it did, *Acts* xv. and *Gal.* ii. 6——9. And of what Consequence, and how much St. *Paul* thought the preaching of this Doctrine his peculiar Business, we may see by what he says, chap. vi. 19, 20. where any one may see by the different Treatment he received from the rest of the Apostles, being *in Bonds* upon that Account, that his Preaching herein differed from theirs, and he was thereupon, as he tells us himself, treated *as an evil Doer*, 1 Tim. ii. 9. The History whereof we have, *Acts* xxi. 17, &c. as we have elsewhere observed. And it is upon the Account of his preaching this Doctrine, and displaying to the World this concealed Truth, which he calls every where a hidden Mystery, that he gives to what he had preached the distinguishing Title of *my Gospel*, *Rom.* xvi. 25. which he is concerned that God should establish them in, that being the chief Design of his Epistle to the *Romans*, as here to the *Ephesians*. The insisting so much on this, that it was the special Favour and Commission of God to him in particular, to preach this Doctrine of God's Purpose of calling the Gentiles to the Word, was not out of Vanity or Boasting, but was here of great Use to his present Purpose, as carrying a strong Reason with it, why the *Ephesians* should rather believe him, to whom, as their Apostle, it was made manifest, and committed to be preached, than the Jews, from whom it had been concealed, and was kept as a Mystery, and was in itself ἀνεξιχνίαστον, inscrutable by Men, though of the best natural Parts and Endowments.

EPHESIANS.

PARAPHRASE.

by the effectual working of his Power, in his so wonderful converting the Gentiles by my Preaching ᵉ;
8. Unto me, I say, who am less than the least of all Saints, is this Favour given, that I should preach among the Gentiles the unsearchable Riches of Christ ᶠ;
9. And make all Men ᵍ perceive how this Mystery comes now to be communicated ʰ to the World, which has been concealed from all past Ages, lying hid in the secret Purpose of God, who frames and manages this whole new Creation by Jesus Christ ⁱ;
10. To the Intent that now under the Gospel

TEXT.

given unto me by the effectual working of his power.

8 Unto me, who am less than the least of all saints is this grace given, that I should preach among the Gentiles the unsearchable riches of Christ;

9 And to make all men see, what is the fellowship of the mystery which from the beginning of the world hath been hid in God, who created all things by Jesus Christ:

10 To the intent that now

NOTES.

ᵉ This seems to be the Energy of the Power of God which he here speaks of, as appears by what he says of St. *Peter*, and of himself, *Gal.* ii. 8. Ὁ ἐνηργήσας Πέτρῳ εἰς ἀποστολὴν τῆς περιτομῆς ἐνήργησε ᾐ ἐμοὶ εἰς τὰ ἔθνη, *He that* wrought effectually *in Peter to the Apostleship of the Circumcision, the same was mighty, or wrought effectually in me*, as ἐνέργεια is here translated, of which his very great Modesty could not hinder from speaking thus, 1 Cor. xv. 9, 10. *I am the least of the Apostles, that am not meet to be called an Apostle, because I persecuted the Church of God: But by the Grace of God I am what I am, and his Grace, which was bestowed upon me, was not in vain, but I laboured more abundantly than they all; yet not I, but the Grace of God that was with me:* A Passage very suitable to what he says in this and the next Verse.

ᶠ 8 *i. e.* That abundant Treasure of Mercy, Grace and Favour, laid up in Jesus Christ, not only to the Jews, but to the whole Heathen World, which was beyond the Reach of Human Sagacity to discover, and could be known only by Revelation.

ᵍ All Men, *i. e.* Men of all Sorts and Nations, Gentiles as well as Jews.

ʰ 9 Τί; ἡ κοινωνία, *What is the Communication*, i. e. that they may have Light from me, to see and look into the Reason and Ground of the Discovery or Communication of this Mystery to them now by Jesus Christ, who is now exhibited to the World, into whose Hands God has put the Management of this whole Dispensation.

ⁱ To open our Way to a right Sense of these Words, Τῷ τὰ πάντα κτίσαντι διὰ Ἰησοῦ, it will be necessary in the first Place to consider the Terms of it, and how they are used by St. *Paul*.

1. As to κτίσαντι, *created*, it is to be acknowledged, that it is the Word used in Sacred Scripture to express *Creation* in the Scriptural Sense of *Creation*, i. e. making out of nothing; yet that it is not always used in that Sense by St. *Paul*, is visible from the 15th Verse of the foregoing Chapter, where our Translators have rightly rendered κτίσῃ, *make*, and it would contain a manifest Absurdity to render it there *create*, in the Theological Sense of the Word *create*.

2. It is to be observed that St. *Paul* often chuses to speak of the Work of Redemption by Christ as a Creation. Whether it were because this was the chief End of the Creation, or whether it were because there was no less seen of the Wisdom, Power and Goodness of God,

in

EPHESIANS.

TEXT.

unto the principalities and powers in heavenly places, might be known by the Church the mani-

PARAPHRASE.

Gospel the manifold Wisdom of God, in the ordering and management of his heavenly Kingdom, might be made known to Principa-

NOTES.

in this, than in the first Creation, and the Change of lost and revolted Man from being dead in Sins, to Newness of Life, was as great, and by as great a Power, as at first making out of nothing; or whether it was because the ἀνακεφαλαίωσις, under Jesus Christ, the Head mentioned, *chap.* i. 10. was a Restitution of the Creation to its primitive State and Order, which, *Acts.* iii. 21. is called ἀποκατάστασις πάντων, *the Restitution of all things*, which was begun with the preaching of St. *John Baptist* (who was the *Elias* that restored all things, *Mat.* xvii. 11. *i. e.* opened the Kingdom of Heaven to Believers of all Nations, *Luke* xvi. 16.) and is compleated in Christ's coming with his Saints in the Glory of his Father at the last Day. But whether some or all of these Conjectures which I have mentioned be the Reason of it, this is certain, that St. *Paul* speaks of the Work of Redemption under the Name of Creation. So 2 *Cor.* v. 17. *If any one be in Christ,* καινὴ κτίσις, *he is a new Creature, or it is a new Creation.* And *Gal.* vi. 15. *In Christ Jesus neither Circumcision availeth any thing, nor Uncircumcision, but* καινὴ κτίσις, *the new Creation.*

It is then to be considered of which Creation τὰ πάντα κτίσαντι, *who created all things*, is here to be understood. The Business St. *Paul* is upon in this Place, is to shew that God's Purpose of taking in the Gentiles to be his People under the Gospel, was a Mystery unknown in former Ages, and now under the Kingdom of the Messiah committed to him to be preached to the World.

This is so manifestly the Design of St. *Paul* here, that no body can mistake it. Now if the Creation of the material World, of this visible Frame of Sun, Moon, and Stars, and heavenly Bodies, that are over us, and of the Earth we inhabit, hath no immediate Relation, as certainly it hath not to this Mystery, this Design of God's to call the Gentiles into the Kingdom of his Son, it is to make St. *Paul* a very loose Writer and weak Arguer, in the middle of a Discourse which he seems to lay much stress on, and to press earnestly on the *Ephesians* (for he urges it more than once) to bring in things not at all to his Purpose, and of no Use to the Business in Hand. We cannot therefore avoid taking the Creation, and things created, here to be those of the new Creation, (*viz.*) those of which the Kingdom of Christ, which was this new Creation, was to be made up; and in that Sense, τὰ πάντα κτίσαντι διὰ Ἰησοῦ Χριστοῦ, *who created all things by Jesus Christ*, is a Reason to shew why God kept his Purpose of making the Gentiles meet to be Partakers of the Inheritance of the Saints, or, as he expresseth it, *chap.* ii. 10. that they *should be his Workmanship created in Christ Jesus unto good Works*, concealed from former Ages, *viz.* because this new Creation was in Jesus Christ, and so proper to be preached and published when he was come; which is strongly confirmed by the Words of the following Verse, *viz.* that *NOW* in its due time, by this new Piece of Workmanship of his, *viz. the Church, might be made known the manifold Wisdom of God.* This taking in the Gentiles into the Kingdom of his Son, and after that the re-assuming again of the Jews, who had been rejected, St. *Paul* looks on as so great an Instance, and Display of the Wisdom of God, that it makes him cry out, *Rom.* xi. 33. *O the Depth of the Riches both of the Wisdom and Knowledge of God, how unsearchable are his Judgments, and his Ways past finding out!*

EPHESIANS.

PARAPHRASE.

lities and Powers by the Church [k], According to

TEXT.

fold wisdom of God,

NOTES.

[k] There be two things in this Verse that to me make it hard to determine the precise Sense of it; The first is, what is meant by ἀρχαῖς and ἐξουσίαις, Terms that sometimes in Sacred Scripture signify Temporal Magistrates, and so our Saviour uses them, *Luke* xii. 11. and St. *Paul*, *Tit*. iii. 1. Sometimes for those who are vested with any Power, whether Men or Angels, so 1 *Cor*. xv. 24. Sometimes for evil Angels, so they are understood, *eb*. vi. 12. Sometimes they are understood of good Angels, so *Col*. i. 16. Now to which of these to determine the Sense here, I confess myself not sufficiently enlightened. Indeed ἐν τοῖς ἐπουρανίοις, in the things of his heavenly Kingdom, would do something toward it, were it undoubtedly certain whether those Words were in construction to be joined to ἀρχαῖς and ἐξουσίαις, or to σοφία; *i. e.* whether we are to understand it of Principalities and Powers in the Kingdom of Heaven, or of the Wisdom of God in the ordering of that Kingdom: If the first of these, then it is evident they would signify the heavenly Host of good Angels employed in the Guard and Promotion of the Kingdom of Christ. But the Knowledge spoken of here, as communicated to these Principalities and Powers, being only in Consequence of St. *Paul*'s preaching, it is not easy to conceive, that the Revelation and Commission given to St. *Paul*, for the declaring the Mystery of God's Purpose, to take the Gentiles into the Church, was to the Intent they Angels, either good or bad, should be instructed in this great and important Truth, wherein the Wisdom of God so much shewed itself, and that they should have no Knowledge of it before nor otherwise. This is so great a Difficulty, that it seems strongly to persuade, that the Principalities and Powers here mentioned are of this World; but against this there lies this obvious Objection, that the Magistrates of the Heathen World did not much concern themselves in what St. *Paul* preached, nor upon his declaring that the Gentiles under the Messiah, were to be taken in to be the People of God, did in effect gather from the Church thus constituted, any Arguments of the Wisdom of God. If therefore I may venture my Conjecture, for I dare not be positive in a Place that I confess myself not fully to understand, I should take this to be the Meaning of it. The High-Priests, Scribes and Pharisees, who are the Rulers of the Jewish Nation, and alone pretend to any Authority in these Matters, deny the Converted Heathens to be the People of God, because they neglect the Law and Circumcision, and those other Rites, whereby God had appointed those who are his People to be separated from the rest of the World, and made holy to himself. And so far most of the converted Jews agree with them, that they will not allow the converted Gentiles to be Members and Subjects of the Kingdom of the Messiah without being circumcised, and submitting to the Laws and Ceremonies of the Jews, as the only Religion and Way of Worship wherein they can be allowed to be God's People, or be accepted by him. Now, says St. *Paul*, God of his special Grace has commissioned me to preach to the World this his hidden Purpose of taking the Gentiles into the Kingdom of his Son, that so by the Church, consisting of Members who are God's People, without being circumcised, or observing the other Mosaical Rites, might, which the Jews could by no means conceive, now be made known, and declared to the Leaders and chief of that Nation the manifold Wisdom of God, which is not, as the Jews imagine, tied up to their own Way, but can bring about his Purposes by sundry Manners, and in Ways that they thought not of. This seems suitable to the Apostle's Meaning here; for though the Jews were not hereby converted, yet when urged by the Converted Gentiles, it served to stop their Mouths, and thereby to confirm the Gentiles in the Liberty of the Gospel. And thus by the Church, to whom St. *Paul* says, *Col*. i. 24. and ii. 2. God would now have made it manifest by his Preaching, is this Mystery made known to Principalities and Powers, *i. e.* the Rulers and Teachers of the Jewish Nation, the Saints who were apprised of it by St. *Paul*'s preaching, urging and manifesting it to them. And to this Sense of this Passage these two Words, νῦν, *now*, and πολυποίκιλος, *manifold*, seem wholly accommodated, *i. e. now* that the uncircumcised Gentiles believe

EPHESIANS.

TEXT.

11 According to the eternal purpose which he purposed in Christ Jesus our Lord:
12 In whom we have boldness and access with confidence by the faith of him.
13 Wherefore I desire that ye faint not at my tribulations for you, which is your glory.
14 For this cause I bow my knees unto the Father of our Lord Jesus Christ,
15 Of whom the whole family in heaven and

PARAPHRASE.

to that Predisposition [1] of the Ages, or several Dispensations which he made in Christ Jesus our Lord; By whom *we* have Boldness and Access to God the Father, with Confidence by Faith [m] in him. Wherefore my Desire is, that ye be not dismayed by my present Affliction, which I suffer for your sake, and is in truth a Glory to you, that ought to raise your Hearts, and strengthen your Resolutions. Upon this Account I bend my Knees in Prayer to the Father of our Lord Jesus Christ [n]. From whom the whole Family or Lineage both in Heaven and Earth have their Domination, *(viz.)* Jesus Christ, that is already in Heaven,

11.
12.
13.
14.
15.

NOTES.

believe in Christ, and are by Baptism admitted into the Church, the Wisdom of God is made known to the Jews, not to be tied up to one invariable Way and Form, as they persuade themselves, but displays itself in sundry Manners, as he thinks fit.

11 [l] Whether by αἰῶνες, *Ages*, here, the several Dispensations Mankind was under from first to last, or whether the two great Dispensations of the Law and the Gospel (for that αἰῶνες are used in the Sacred Scripture to denote these, I think an attentive Reader cannot doubt) be here meant, this seems visibly the Sense of the Place, that all these Dispensations, in the several Ages of the Church, were all by the Preordination of God's Purpose regulated and constituted in Christ Jesus our Lord; that is, with regard to Christ, who was designed and appointed Lord and Head over all; which seems to me to answer τὰ πάντα κτίσαντι διὰ Ἰησοῦ Χριστοῦ, *Who created all things by Jesus Christ*, v. 9.

12 [m] πίστει αὐτοῦ, *Faith of him*, the Genitive Case of the Object, as well as of the Agent, is so frequent in Sacred Scripture, that there needs nothing to be said of it.

14 [n] *The Father of our Lord Jesus Christ*, set down as it is in the Beginning of this Verse, joined to the Design of the Apostle in this Place, makes me think that the Sense of it is so plainly that, which I have given of it, that I do not see any Difficulty can be made about it. In the foregoing Chapter, ver. 19. he tells the Convert Gentiles of *Ephesus*, that now they believe in Christ, they are no longer Strangers and Foreigners, but Fellow Citizens with the Saints, and of the Houshold of God; here he goes on, and tells them they are of the Family and Lineage of God, being jointly with Jesus Christ, who is already in Heaven, the Sons of God: What could be of greater Force to continue them stedfast in the Doctrine he had preached to them, and which he makes it his whole Business here to confirm them in, (*viz.*) That they need not be circumcised and submit to the Law of *Moses*, they being already by Faith in Christ the Sons of God, and of the same Lineage and Family with Christ himself, who was already by that Title possessed of his Inheritance in Glory.

and

EPHESIANS.

PARAPHRASE.

and Believers that are still on Earth, have all God for their Father, are all the Sons of God.

16. That he would grant you, according to the great Glory he designed to you Gentiles, who should receive the Gospel under the Messiah °, to be strengthened with Might by his Spirit in
17. the inward Man ᵖ; That Christ may dwell in your Hearts by Faith; that you being settled and established in the Sense of the Love of God
18. to you in Jesus Christ, May be able together with all Christians to comprehend the Length, and Breadth, and Height, and Depth of this Mystery of God's Purpose, of calling and taking in the Gentiles to be his People in the
19. Kingdom of his Son ᑫ: And to understand the exceeding ʳ Love of God, in bringing us to the Knowledge of Christ: That you may be filled with that Knowledge, and all other Gifts, with God's Plenty, or to that Degree of Fulness which is suitable to his Purpose of Muni-

TEXT.

earth is named.

That he would grant 16 you according to the riches of his glory, to be strengthened with might by his Spirit in the inner man:

That Christ may dwell 17 in your hearts by faith; that ye being rooted and grounded in love,

May be able to compre- 18 hend with all Saints, what is the breadth, and length, and depth, and height:

And to know the love 19 of Christ, which passeth knowledge, that ye might be filled with all the fulness of God.

NOTES.

16 ° See this Sense of this Passage as given, *Col.* i. 27. and not much different *chap.* i. 17, &c.

ᵖ What the *inward Man* signifies, see *Rom.* vii. 22. 2 *Cor.* iv. 16.

18 ᑫ This Mystery being the Subject St. *Paul* is here upon, and which he endeavours to magnify to them, and establish in their Minds, the Height and Breadth, &c. which he mentions in these Words, being not applied to any thing else, cannot, in good Sense, be understood of any thing else.

19 ʳ ὑπερβάλλουσα, *exceeding*, seems to be here a comparative Term, joined to the Love of God, in communicating the Knowledge of Christ, and declaring it superior to some other thing, if you desire to know what he himself tells you on the same Occasion, *Phil.* iii. 8. *viz.* To Circumcision, and the other Ritual Institutions of the Law, which the Jews looked on as the Marks of the highest Degree of God's Love to them, whereby they were sanctified and separated to him from the rest of the World, and secured of his Favour. To which, if any one will add what St. *Paul* says on the same Subject, *Col.* ii. 2, &c. For his Business is the very same in these three Epistles, he will not want Light to guide him in the Sense of this Place here.

ficence

EPHESIANS.

TEXT.

20 Now unto him that is able to do exceeding abundantly above all that we ask or think, according to the power that worketh in us,

21 Unto him be glory in the Church by Christ Jesus, throughout all ages, world without end. Amen.

PARAPHRASE.

ficence and Bounty towards you¹. Now to 20. him that worketh in us by a Power¹ whereby he is able to do exceedingly beyond all that we can ask or think; unto him be Glory in 21. the Church by Christ Jesus, throughout all Ages, World without end. Amen.

NOTES.

¹ Εἰς πᾶν τὸ πλήρωμα τοῦ Θεοῦ, *To the Fulness of God*; the *Fulness of God* is such Fulness as God is wont to bestow, *i. e.* wherein there is nothing wanting to any one, but every one is filled to the utmost of his Capacity. This I take to be the Meaning of εἰ; τὸ πλήρωμα Θεοῦ; and then πᾶν πλήρωμα may be understood, to shew that it is not a Fulness of one thing, and an Emptiness of another, but it is a Fulness of all those Gifts which any one shall need, and may be useful to him or the Church.

20 ¹ What Power that is, see *chap.* i. 19, 20.

SECT. VI.

CHAP. IV. 1——16.

CONTENTS.

ST. *Paul* having concluded the special Part of his Epistle with the foregoing Chapter, he comes in this, as his Manner is, to practical Exhortations. He begins with Unity, Love and Concord, which he presses upon them upon a Consideration that he makes use of in more of his Epistles than one, *i. e.* their being all Members of one and the same Body, whereof Christ is the Head.

I there-

EPHESIANS.

PARAPHRASE.

1. I Therefore who am in Bonds upon Account of the Gospel, beseech you to walk worthy of the Calling wherewith ye are called,
2. with Lowliness and Meekness, with Long-suffering, bearing with one another in Love;
3. taking care to preserve the Unity of the Spi-
4. rit in the Bond of Peace, considering yourselves as being one Body, enlivened and acted by one Spirit, as also was your Calling in one Hope:
5. There is one Lord, one Faith, one Baptism,
6. one God and Father of you all, who is above all, in the midst amongst you all, and in every
7. one of you. And to every one of us is made a free Donation, according to that Proportion of Gifts which Christ has allotted to every one.
8. Wherefore the Psalmist saith, *When he ascended up on high, he led Captivity captive, and*
9. *gave Gifts unto Men.* (Now that he ascended, what is it but that he descended first into the
10. lower Parts of the Earth? He that descended is the same also that ascended above all Heavens, that there receiving the Fulness of Power, he might be able to fill all his Members ʷ.)

TEXT.

1 I Therefore the prisoner of the Lord, beseech you that ye walk worthy of the vocation wherewith ye are called,
2 With all lowliness and meekness, with longsuffering, forbearing one another in love;
3 Endeavouring to keep the unity of the Spirit in the bond of peace.
4 There is one body, and one spirit, even as ye are called in one hope of your calling;
5 One Lord, one faith, one baptism,
6 One God and Father of all, who is above all, and through all, and in you all.
7 But unto every one of us is given grace according to the measure of the gift of Christ.
8 Wherefore he saith, when he ascended up on high, he led captivity captive, and gave gifts unto men.
9 (Now that he ascended, what is it but that he also descended first into the lower parts of the earth?
10 He that descended, is

NOTES.

8 ᵘ *Psal.* xlviii. 18.

9, 10. ʷ St. *Paul's* Argumentation in these two Verses is skilfully adapted to the main Design of his Epistle. The Convert Gentiles were attacked by the Unconverted Jews, who were declared Enemies to the Thoughts of a Messiah that died: St. *Paul* to enervate that Objection of theirs, proves by the Passage out of the Psalms, *v.* 8. that he must die and be buried. Besides the unbelieving Jews, several of them that were converted to the Gospel, or at least professed to be so, attacked the Gentile Converts on another Side, perswading them, that they could not be admitted to be the People of God in the Kingdom of the Messiah, nor receive any Advantage by him, unless they were circumcised, and put themselves wholly under the Jewish Constitution. He had said a great deal in the three first Chapters to free them from this Perplexity, but yet takes Occasion here to offer them a new Argument, by telling them, that Christ, the same Jesus that died, and was laid in his Grave, was exalted to the Right Hand of God above all the Heavens, in the highest State of Dignity and Power; that he himself being filled with the Fulness of God, Believers who were all his Members, might receive immediately from him their Head, a Fulness of Gifts and Graces, upon no other Terms, but barely as they were his Members.

and

EPHESIANS. Chap. IV.

TEXT.

the same also that ascended up far above all heavens, that he might fill all things)

11 And he gave some, apostles: and some, prophets: and some, evangelists: and some, pastors and teachers;

12 For the perfecting of the saints, for the work of the ministry, for the edifying of the body of Christ;

13 Till we all come in the unity of the faith, and of the knowledge of the Son of God, unto a perfect man, unto the measure of the stature of the fulness of Christ:

14 That we henceforth be no more children tossed to and fro, and carried about with every wind of doctrine, by the slight of men, and cunning craftiness, whereby they lie in wait to deceive;

15 But speaking the truth in love, may grow up into him in all things which is the head, even Christ:

16 From whom the whole body fitly joined together, and compacted by that which every joint supplieth, according to the effectual working in the measure of every part, maketh increase of the body, unto the edifying of itself in love.

PARAPHRASE.

And therefore he alone framing the Constitution of his new Government, by his own Power, and according to such a Model, and such Rules as he thought best, making some Apostles, others Prophets, others Evangelists, and others Pastors and Teachers, putting thus together in a fit Order and Frame, the several Members of his new collected People, that each in its proper Place and Function might contribute to the Whole, and help to build up the Body of Christ; till all cementing together in one Faith and Knowledge of the Son of God, to the full State of a grown Man, according to the Measure of that Stature which is to make up the Fulness of Christ: That we should be no longer Children tossed to and fro, and carried about with every Wind of Doctrine by Men, versed in the Slights of Cheating, and their cunning Artifices laid in train to deceive. But being steady in true and unfeigned Love, should grow up into a firm Union in all Things with Christ, who is the Head: From whom the whole Body fitly framed together, and compacted by that which every Joint supplies, according to the proper Force and Function of each particular Part, makes an Increase of the whole Body, building itself up in Love, or a mutual Concern of the Parts [x].

11.
12.
13.
14.
15.
16.

NOTES.

16 [x] The Sum of all that St. *Paul* says in this figurative Discourse, is, that Christians, all as Members of one Body whereof Christ is the Head, should each in his proper Place, according to the Gifts bestowed upon him, labour with Concern and Good-Will for the Good and Increase of the Whole, till it be grown up to that Fulness which is to compleat it in Christ Jesus. This is in short the Sense of the Exhortation contained in this Section, which carries a strong Insinuation with it, especially if we take in the rest of the Admonitions to the End of the Epistle, that the Mosaical Observances were no Part of the Business or Character of a Christian, but were wholly to be neglected and declined by the Subjects of Christ's Kingdom.

EPHESIANS.

SECT. VII.

CHAP. IV. 17——24.

CONTENTS.

IN this Section the Apostle exhorts them wholly to forsake their former Conversation, which they had passed their Lives in, whilst they were Gentiles, and to take up that which became them, and was proper to them, now they were Christians. Here we may see the Heathen and Christian State and Conversation described, and set in Opposition one to the other.

PARAPHRASE.

17. THIS I say therefore, and testify to you, from the Lord, that ye henceforth walk not as the unconverted Gentiles walk, in the Vanity of their Minds [y], having their Understandings darkened, being alienated from that Rule and Course of Life which they own and observe, who are the professed Subjects and Servants of the true God [z], through the Ignorance that is in them, because of the Blindness of their Hearts; who being past feeling, have given themselves over to Lasciviousness, to the committing of all Uncleanness even beyond the Bounds of natural Desires [a]. But you that have been instructed in the Religion of

TEXT.

17 THIS I say therefore, and testify in the Lord, that ye henceforth walk not as other Gentiles walk in the vanity of their mind,

18 Having the understanding darkened, being alienated from the love of God, through the ignorance that is in them, because of the blindness of their heart:

19 Who being past feeling, have given themselves over unto lasciviousness, to work all uncleanness with greediness.

20 But ye have not so

NOTES.

17 [y] This Vanity of Mind, if we look into *Rom.* i. 21, &c. we shall find to be the Apostatizing of the Gentiles from the true God to Idolatry, and in consequence of that, to all that profligate Way of Living which followed thereupon, and is there described by St. *Paul.*

18 [z] This Alienation was from owning Subjection to the true God, and the Observance of those Laws which he had given to those of Mankind that continued and professed to be his People; see *chap.* ii. 12.

19 [a] Πλεονεξία, *Covetousness,* in the common Acceptation of the Word, is the letting loose our Desires to that which by the Law of Justice we have no Right to. But St. *Paul* in some of his

EPHESIANS.

TEXT.

21 If so be that ye have heard him, and have been taught by him, as the truth is in Jesus;
22 That ye put off concerning the former conversation, the old man, which is corrupt according to the deceitful lusts:
23 And be renewed in the spirit of your mind;
24 And that ye put on the new man, which after God is created in righteousness and true holiness.

PARAPHRASE.

learned Christ; of Christ, have learned other Things; if you have been Scholars of his School, and have been taught the Truth, as it is in the Gospel of Jesus Christ: That you change your former Conversation, abandoning those deceitful Lusts wherewith you were entirely corrupted: And that being renewed in the Spirit of the Mind, you become new Men [b], framed and fashioned according to the Will of God, in Righteousness and true Holiness.

21.
22.
23.
24.

NOTES.

his Epistles uses it for intemperate and exorbitant Desires of carnal Pleasures, not confined within the Bounds of Nature. He that will compare with this Verse here, *ch.* v. 3. *Col.* iii. 5. 1 *Thess.* iv. 5. 1 *Cor.* v. 10, 11. and well consider the Context, will find Reason to take it here in the Sense I have given of it, or else it will be very hard to understand these Texts of Scripture. In the same Sense the learned Dr. *Hammond* understands πλεονεξία, *Rom.* i. 29. Which though perhaps the Greek Idiom will scarce justify, yet the Apostle's Stile will, who often uses Greek Terms in the full Latitude of the Hebrew Words which they are usually put for in translating, though in the Greek Use of them, they have nothing at all of that Signification, particularly the Hebrew Word בצע, which signifies Covetousness, the Septuagint translate μιασμὸς, *Ezek.* xxxiii. 31. In which Sense the Apostle uses πλεονεξία here. In these and the two preceding Verses, we have a Description of the State of the Gentiles without, and their wretched and sinful State whilst unconverted to the Christian Faith, and Strangers from the Kingdom of God, to which may be added what is said of these *Sinners of the Gentiles,* ch. ii. 11——13. Col. i. 21. 1 *Thess.* iv. 5. Col. iii. 5——7. Rom. i. 30, 31.

24 [b] What the παλαιὸς ἄνθρωπος, the *old* Man that is to be put off, is, and the καινὸς ἄνθρωπος, the *new Man* that is to be put on, is, may be seen in the opposite Characters of good and bad Men, in the following Part of this, and in several other of St. *Paul's* Epistles.

EPHESIANS.

SECT. VIII.

CHAP. IV. 25.——V. 2.

CONTENTS.

AFTER the general Exhortation in the Close of the foregoing Section to the *Ephesians*, to renounce the old Course of Life they led when they were Heathens, and to become perfectly new Men, conformed to the holy Rules of the Gospel, St. *Paul* descends to Particulars; and here in this Section presses several Particulars of those great social Virtues, Justice and Charity, &c.

PARAPHRASE.

25. Wherefore putting away Lying, let every Man speak Truth to his Neighbour;
26. for we are Members one of another. If you meet with Provocations that move you to Anger, take care that you indulge it not so far, as to make it sinful: Defer not its Cure till Sleep calm the Mind, but endeavour to recover yourself forthwith, and bring yourself into
27. Temper; Lest you give an Opportunity to the Devil to produce some Mischief by your Disor-
28. der. Let him that hath stole, steal no more, but rather let him labour in some honest Calling, that he may even have wherewithal to
29. relieve others that need it. Let not any filthy Language, or a misbecoming Word, come out of your Mouths, but let your Discourse be pertinent to the Occasion, and tending to Edification, and such as may have a becoming
30. Gracefulness in the Ears of the Hearers. And grieve not the Holy Spirit of God, whereby ye

TEXT.

25. Wherefore putting away lying, speak every man truth with his neighbour: for we are members one of another.
26. Be ye angry and sin not: let not the sun go down upon your wrath:
27. Neither give place to the devil.
28. Let him that stole, steal no more: but rather let him labour, working with his hands the thing which is good, that he may have to give him that needeth.
29. Let no corrupt communication proceed out of your mouth, but that which is good to the use of edifying, that it may minister grace unto the hearers.
30. And grieve not the holy Spirit of God, where-

EPHESIANS.

TEXT.

by ye are sealed unto the day of redemption.

31 Let all bitterness, and wrath, and anger, and clamour, and evil speaking be put away from you, with all malice.

32 And be ye kind one to another, tender-hearted, forgiving one another, even as God for Christ's sake hath forgiven you.

1 Be ye therefore followers of God, as dear children;

2 And walk in love, as Christ also hath loved us, and hath given himself for us, an offering and a sacrifice to God for a sweet smelling savour.

PARAPHRASE.

are sealed ᶜ to the Day of Redemption. Let all 31. Bitterness, and Wrath, and Anger, and Clamour, and Evil-speaking, be put away from you, with all Malice. And be ye kind one to another, 32. tender-hearted, forgiving one another, even as God for Christ's sake hath forgiven you. Therefore as becomes Children that are beloved and 1. cherished by God, propose him as an Example to yourselves, to be imitated; and let Love 2. conduct and influence your whole Conversation, as Christ also hath loved us, and hath given himself for us, an Offering and an acceptable Sacrifice ᵈ to God.

NOTES.

30 ᶜ *Sealed*; i. e. have God's Mark set upon you, that you are his Servants, a Security to you, that you shall be admitted into his Kingdom as such, at the Day of Redemption, *i. e.* at the Resurrection, when you shall be put in the actual Possession of a Place in his Kingdom, among those who are his, whereof the Spirit is now an Earnest; see *Note, ch.* i. 14.

2 ᵈ *Of a sweet smelling Savour*, was, in Scripture-Phrase, such a Sacrifice as God accepted, and was pleased with; see *Gen.* viii. 21.

EPHESIANS.

SECT. IX.

CHAP. V. 3——20.

CONTENTS.

THE next Sort of Sins, he dehorts them from, are those of Intemperance, especially those of Uncleanness, which were so familiar, and so unrestrained amongst the Heathens.

PARAPHRASE.	TEXT.
3. BUT Fornication, and all Uncleanness, or exorbitant Desires in venereal Matters ᵉ, let it not be once named amongst you, as becometh	3 BUT fornication, and all uncleanness, or covetousness, let it not be once named amongst you, as becometh saints:

NOTES.

3 ᵉ The Word in the Greek is πλεονεξία, which properly signifies Covetousness, or an intemperate ungoverned Love of Riches: But the chaste Stile of the Scripture makes use of it to express the letting loose of the Desires to irregular venereal Pleasures, beyond what was fit and right. This one can hardly avoid being convinced of, if one considers how it stands joined with these Sort of Sins, in those many Places which Dr. *Hammond* mentions in his Notes on *Rom.* i. 29. & *ch.* iv. *v.* 19. of this Epistle, & *v.* 5 of this *ch.* v. compared with this here, they are enough to satisfy one what πλεονεξία, Covetousness, means here; but if that should fail, these Words, *Let it not be once named amongst you, as becometh Saints*, which are subjoined to Covetousness, put it past doubt; for what Indecency or Misbecomingness is it amongst Christians to name Covetousness? πλεονεξία therefore must signify the Title of Sins that are not fit to be named amongst Christians, so that πᾶσα ἀκαθαρσία ἢ πλεονεξία, seem not here to be used definitively for several Sorts of Sins, but as two Names of the same thing explaining one another; and so this Verse will give us a true Notion of the Word πορνεία in the New Testament, the Want whereof, and taking it to mean *Fornication* in our *English* Acceptation of that Word, as standing for one distinct Species of Uncleanness, in the natural Mixture of an unmarried Couple, seems to me to have perplexed the Meaning of several Texts of Scripture; whereas taken in that large Sense which ἀκαθαρσία and πλεονεξία seem here to expound it, the Obscurity, which follows from the usual Notion of Fornication applied to it, will be removed. Some Men have been forward to conclude from the Apostle's Letter to the Convert Gentiles of *Antioch*, Acts xv. 28. wherein they find Fornication joined with two or three other Actions; that simple Fornication, as they call it, was not much distant, if at all, from an indifferent Action; whereby I think they very much confounded the Meaning of the Text. The Jews that were converted to the Gospel could by no means admit, that those of the Gentiles who retained any of their ancient Idolatry, though they professed Faith in Christ, could by any Means be received by them into the Communion of the Gospel, as the People of God under the Messiah; and so far they were in the right, to make sure of it, that they fully renounced Idolatry; the Generality insisted on it, that they should be circumcised, and so, by submitting to the Observances of the Law, gave the same Proof that Proselytes were wont to do, that they were perfectly clear from all Remains of Idolatry. This the Apostles thought more than was necessary; but the eating of things sacrificed to Idols, and Blood, whether let out of the Animal,

or

EPHESIANS.

Chap. V.

TEXT.

4 Neither filthiness, nor foolish talking, nor jesting, which are not convenient: but rather giving of thanks.

5 For this ye know, that no whoremonger, nor unclean person, nor covetous man who is an idolater, hath any inheritance in the Kingdom of Christ, and of God.

6 Let no man deceive you with vain words: for because of these

PARAPHRASE.

4. cometh Saints: Neither Filthiness, nor foolish Talking, nor Pleasantry of Discourse of this Kind, which are none of them convenient, but rather giving of Thanks. 5. For this you are thoroughly instructed in, and acquainted with, that no Fornicator, nor unclean Person, nor lewd, lascivious Libertine in such Matters, who is in truth an Idolater, shall have any Part in the Kingdom of Christ, and of God. 6. Let no Man deceive you with vain empty Talk ^{f}; these Things in themselves are highly offensive to

NOTES.

or contained in it, being strangled; and Fornication in the large Sense of the Word, as it is put for all Sorts of Uncleanness, being the presumed Marks of Idolatry to the Jews, they forbid the Convert Gentiles, thereby to avoid the Offence of the Jews, and prevent a Separation between the Professors of the Gospel upon this Account. This therefore was not given to the Convert Gentiles by the Apostles of the Circumcision, as a standing Rule of Morality required by the Gospel; if that had been the Design, it must have contained a great many other Particulars; what Laws of Morality they were under as Subjects of Jesus Christ, they doubted not but St. *Paul* their Apostle taught and inculcated to them: All that they instructed them in here, was necessary for them to do, so as to be admitted into one Fellowship and Communion with the Converts of the Jewish Nation, who would certainly avoid them, if they found that they made no Scruple of those things, but practised any of them. That Fornication, or all Sorts of Uncleanness, were the Consequence and Concomitants of Idolatry, we see, *Rom.* i. 29. and it is known were favoured by the Heathen Worship; and therefore the Practice of those Sins is every where set down, as the Characteristical Heathen Mark of the idolatrous Gentiles, from which Abominations the Jews, both by their Law, Profession, and general Practice, were Strangers; and this was one of those things wherein chiefly God severed his People from the idolatrous Nations, as may be seen, *Lev.* xviii. 20, &c. And hence I think that πλεονεξία, used for licentious Intemperance in unlawful and unnatural Lusts, is in the New Testament called Idolatry, and πλεονέκτης, an Idolater; see 1 *Cor.* v. 11. *Col.* iii. 5. *Eph.* v. 5. as being the sure and undoubted Mark of an Heathen Idolater.

6 ^{f} One would guess by this, that as there were Jews who would persuade them, that it was necessary for all Christians to be circumcised, and observe the Law of *Moses*; so there were others who retained so much of their ancient Heathenism, as to endeavour to make them believe, that those venereal Abominations and Uncleannesses, were no other than what the Gentiles esteemed them, barely indifferent Actions, not offensive to God, or inconsistent with his Worship, but only a Part of the peculiar and positive Ceremonial Law of the Jews, whereby they distinguished themselves from other People, and thought themselves holier than the rest of the World, as they did by their Distinctions of Food into clean and unclean, these Actions being in themselves as indifferent as those Meats, which the Apostle confutes in the following Words.

God,

EPHESIANS. Chap. V.

PARAPHRASE.

God, and are that which he will bring the Heathen World (who will not come in and submit to the Law of Christ) to Judgment
7. for ᵍ. Be ye not therefore Partakers with
8. them. For ye were heretofore in your Gentile-State, perfectly in the Dark ʰ, but now by believing in Christ, and receiving ⁱ the Gospel, Light and Knowledge is given to you, walk
9. as those who are in a State of Light (For the Fruit of the Spirit is in all Goodness, Righte-
10. ousness and Truth ᵏ) Practising that which upon Examination you find acceptable to the
11. Lord. And do not partake in the fruitless Works of Darkness ˡ; do not go on in the Practice of those shameful Actions, as if they were in-
12. different, but rather reprove them. For the Things that the Gentile Idolaters ᵐ do in secret, are so filthy and abominable, that it is a Shame so much as to name them. This you
13. now see, which is an Evidence of your being enlightened, for all Things that are discovered to be amiss are made manifest by the Light; for

TEXT.

things cometh the wrath of God upon the children of disobedience.

7 Be not ye therefore partakers with them.

8 For ye were sometimes darkness, but now are ye light in the Lord: walk as children of light.

9 (For the fruit of the Spirit is in all goodness, and righteousness, and truth)

10 Proving what is acceptable unto the Lord.

11 And have no fellowship with the unfruitful works of darkness, but rather reprove them.

12 For it is a shame even to speak of those things which are done of them in secret.

13 But all things that are reproved, are made manifest by the light: for

NOTES.

ᵍ *Children of Disobedience*, here, and *ch*. ii. 2. & *Col*. iii. 6. are plainly the Gentiles, who refused to come in and submit themselves to the Gospel, as will appear to any one who will read these Places and the Contexts with Attention.

8 ʰ St. *Paul* to express the great Darkness the Gentiles were in, calls them Darkness itself.

ⁱ Which is thus expressed, *Col*. i. 12, 13. *Giving Thanks to the Father, who hath made us meet to be Partakers of the Inheritance of his Saints in Light, who hath delivered us from the Power of Darkness, and translated us into the Kingdom of his dear Son*. The Kingdom of Satan over the Gentile World, was a Kingdom of Darkness; see *Eph*. vi. 12. And so we see Jesus is pronounced by *Simeon, a Light to lighten the Gentiles*, Luke ii. 32.

9 ᵏ This Parenthesis serves to give us the literal Sense of all that is here required by the Apostle in this allegorical Discourse of Light.

11 ˡ These Deeds of the unconverted Heathen who remained in the Kingdom of Darkness, are thus expressed by St. *Paul, Rom*. vi. 21. *What Fruit had you then in those Things whereof you are now ashamed, for the End of those Things is Death?*

12 ᵐ That by *them* here are meant the unconverted Gentiles, is so visible, that there needs nothing to be said to justify the Interpretation of the Word.

what-

EPHESIANS. Chap. V

TEXT.

whatsoever doth make manifest, is light.
14 Wherefore he saith, awake thou that sleepest, and arise from the dead, and Christ shall give thee light.
15 See then that ye walk circumspectly, not as fools, but as wise.
16 Redeeming the time, because the days are evil.
17 Wherefore be ye not unwise, but understanding what the will of the Lord is.
18 And be not drunk with wine, wherein is excess;

PARAPHRASE.

whatsoever shews them to be such is Light [n]. Wherefore he saith, awake thou that sleepest, 14. and arise from the dead, and Christ shall give thee Light. Since then you are in the Light, 15. make use of your Eyes to walk exactly in the right Way, not as Fools, rambling at Adventures, but as wise, in a steady right chosen 16. Course, securing yourselves [o] by your prudent Carriage, from the Inconveniences of those difficult Times, which threaten you with Danger. Wherefore be ye not unwise, 17. but understanding what the Will of the Lord is. And be not drunken with Wine, wherein 18. there is Excess [p]; seek not Diversion in the

NOTES.

13 [n] See *John* iii. 20. The Apostle's Argument here to keep the *Ephesian* Converts from being misled by those that would persuade them that the Gentile Impurities were indifferent Actions, was, to shew them that they were now better enlightened; to which Purpose, *v*. 5. he tells them, that they *know* that no such Person hath any Inheritance in the Kingdom of Christ or of God. This he tells them, *v*. 8, &c. was Light which they had received from the Gospel, which before their Conversion they knew nothing of, but were in perfect Darkness and Ignorance of it; but now they were better instructed, and saw the Difference, which was a Sign of Light, and therefore they should follow that Light which they had received from Christ, who had raised them from among the Gentiles, (who were so far dead, as to be wholly insensible of the evil Course and State they were in) and had given them Light, and a Prospect into a future State, and the Way to attain everlasting Happiness.

16 · St. *Paul* here intimates, *v*. 6. that the unconverted Heathens they lived among, would be forward to tempt them to their former lewd dissolute Lives; but to keep them from any Approaches that Way, that they have Light now by the Gospel, to know that such Actions are provoking to God, and will find the Effects of his Wrath in the Judgments of the World to come. All those Pollutions, so familiar among the Gentiles, he exhorts them carefully to avoid, but yet to take care, by their prudent Carriage to the Gentiles they lived amongst, to give them no Offence, that so they might escape the Danger and Trouble that otherwise might arise to them from the Intemperance and Violence of those Heathens Idolaters, whose shameful Lives the Christian Practice could not but reprove. This seems to be the Meaning of *redeeming the Time* here, which, Col. iv. 5. the other Place where it occurs, seems so manifestly to confirm and give Light to. If this be not the Sense of *redeeming the Time* here, I must own myself ignorant of the precise Meaning of the Phrase in this Place.

18 [ ] St. *Paul* dehorts them from Wine, in a too free Use of it, because therein is *Excess*; the Greek Word is ἀσωτία, which may signify *Luxury* or *Dissoluteness*; i. e. that Drinking is no Friend to Continency and Chastity, but gives up the Reins to Lust and Uncleanness, the Vice he had been warning them against: Or ἀσωτία may signify *Intemperance* and *Disorder*, opposite to that sober and prudent Demeanor advised in redeeming the Time.

E e e noisy

EPHESIANS.

PARAPHRASE.

noisy and intemperate Jollity of Drinking; but when you are disposed to a chearful Entertainment of one another, let it be with the Gifts of the holy Spirit that you are filled with,
19. singing Hymns and Psalms, and spiritual Songs among yourselves; this makes real and solid Mirth in the Heart, and is Melody well-pleasing
20. to God himself; giving Thanks always for all Things, in the Name of our Lord Jesus Christ, to God and the Father.

TEXT.

but be filled with the Spirit.
19 Speaking to yourselves in psalms and hymns, and spiritual songs, singing and making melody in your heart to the Lord.
20 Giving thanks always for all things unto God and the Father, in the name of our Lord Jesus Christ.

SECT. X.

CHAP. V. 21.——VI. 9.

CONTENTS.

IN this Section he gives Rules concerning the Duties arising from the several Relations Men stand in one to another in Society; those which he particularly insists on are these three, Husbands and Wives, Parents and Children, Masters and Servants.

PARAPHRASE.

21.
22. SUBMIT ⁹ yourselves one to another in the Fear of God. As for example, Wives, submit yourselves to your own Husbands, as being Members of the Church you submit

TEXT.

21 SUbmitting yourselves one to another in the fear of God.
22 Wives, submit yourselves unto your own

NOTES.

21 ⁹ This, though in Grammatical Construction it be joined to the foregoing Discourse, yet I think it ought to be looked on as introductory to what follows in this Section, and to be a general Rule given to the *Ephesians*, to submit to those Duties which the several Relations they stood in to one another required of them.

your

EPHESIANS. Chap. V.

TEXT.

husbands, as unto the Lord.
23 For the husband is the head of the wife, even as Christ is the head of the church: and he is the Saviour of the body.
24 Therefore as the church is subject unto Christ, so let the wives be to their own husbands in every thing.
25 Husbands, love your wives, even as Christ also loved the church, and gave himself for it:
26 That he might sanctify and cleanse it with the washing of water by the word,
27 That he might present it to himself a glorious church, not having spot or wrinkle, or any such thing; but that it should be holy, and without blemish.
28 So ought men to love their wives, as their own bodies: he that loveth his wife, loveth himself.
29 For no man ever yet

PARAPHRASE.

yourselves to the Lord. For the Husband is the Head of the Wife, as Christ himself is the Head of the Church, and it is he the Head that preserves that his Body [r]; so stands it between Man and Wife. Therefore as the Church is subject to Christ, so let Wives be to their Husbands in every thing. And you Husbands, do you on your Side, love your Wives, even as Christ also loved the Church, and gave himself to Death for it, that he might sanctify and fit it to himself, purifying it by the washing of Baptism, joined with the Preaching and Reception of the Gospel [s]; that so he himself [t] might present it to himself an honourable Spouse, without the least Spot of Uncleanness or misbecoming Feature, or any Thing amiss, but that it might be holy, and without all manner of Blemish. So ought Men to love their Wives, as their own Bodies; he that loveth his Wife, loveth himself. For no Man ever hated his own Flesh, but nourisheth and

23.

24.

25.

26.

27.

28.

29.

NOTES.

23 [r] It is from the Head that the Body receives its healthy and vigorous Constitution of Health and Life; this St. *Paul* pronounces here of Christ, as Head of the Church, that by that Parallel which he makes use of to represent the Relation between Husband and Wife, he may both shew the Wife the Reasonableness of her Subjection to her Husband, and the Duty incumbent on the Husband to cherish and preserve his Wife, as we see he pursues it in the following Verses.

26 [s] Ἐν ῥήματι, *by the Word.* The purifying of Men is ascribed so much throughout the whole New Testament to the *Word*, i. e. the preaching of the Gospel, and Baptism, that there needs little to be said to prove it; see *John* xv. 3. & xvii. 17. 1 *Pet.* i. 22. *Tit.* iii. 5. *Heb.* x. 22. *Col.* ii. 12, 13, and as it is at large explained in the former Part of the 6th Chapter to the *Romans.*

27 [t] *He himself*, so the Alexandrine Copy reads it αὐτὸς, and not αὐτὴν, more suitable to the Apostle's Meaning here, who, to recommend to Husbands Love and Tenderness to their Wives, in Imitation of Christ's Affection to the Church, shews, that whereas other Brides take care to spruce themselves, and set off their Persons with all manner of Neatness and Cleanness, to recommend themselves to their Bridegrooms, Christ himself, at the Expence of his own Pains and Blood, purified and prepared himself for his Spouse the Church, that he might present it to himself without Spot or Wrinkle.

E e e 2 che-

PARAPHRASE.

30. cherisheth it, even as the Lord Christ doth the Church: For we are Members of his Body, of
31. his Flesh, and of his Bones. For this Cause shall a Man leave his Father and Mother, and shall be joined unto his Wife, and they two
32. shall be one Flesh ᵘ. These Words contain a very mystical Sense in them ʷ, I mean in
33. reference to Christ and the Church. But laying that aside, their literal Sense lays hold on you; and therefore do you Husbands, every one of you in particular, so love his Wife, as his own self, and let the Wife reverence her
1. Husband. Children, obey your Parents, performing it as required thereunto by our Lord Jesus Christ; for this is right and conformable
2. to that Command, Honour thy Father and Mother, (which is the first Command with Pro-

TEXT.

hated his own flesh; but nourisheth and cherisheth it, even as the Lord the church:

30 For we are members of his body, of his flesh, and of his bones.

31 For this cause shall a man leave his father and mother, and shall be joined unto his wife, and they two shall be one flesh.

32 This is a great mystery: but I speak concerning Christ and the church.

33 Nevertheless, let every one of you in particular, so love his wife even as himself; and the wife see that she reverence her husband.

1 Children, obey your parents in the Lord: for this is right.

2 Honour thy father and

NOTES.

30 & 31 ᵘ These two Verses may seem to stand here disorderly, so as to disturb the Connexion, and make the Inferences disjointed and very loose, and inconsistent, to any one who more minds the Order and Grammatical Construction of St. *Paul's* Words written down, than the Thoughts that possessed his Mind when he was writing. It is plain the Apostle had here two things in View; the one was, to press Men to love their Wives, by the Example of Christ's Love to his Church; and the Force of that Argument lay in this, that a Man and his Wife were one Flesh, as Christ and his Church were one: But this latter being a Truth of the greater Consequence of the two, he was as intent on settling that upon their Minds, though it were but an Incident, as the other, which was the Argument he was upon; and therefore having said, *v.* 29. that every one nourisheth and cherisheth his own Flesh, *as Christ doth the Church,* it was natural to subjoin the Reason there, *viz.* because *we were Members of his Body, of his Flesh and of his Bones:* A Proposition he took as much Care to have believed, as that it was the Duty of Husbands to love their Wives; which Doctrine of Christ and the Church being one, when he had so strongly asserted, in the Words of *Adam* concerning *Eve,* Gen. ii. 23. which he, in his concise Way of expressing himself, understands both of the Wife and of the Church, he goes on with the Words in *Gen.* ii. 24. which makes their being one Flesh the Reason why a Man was more strictly to be united to his Wife, than to his Parents, or any other Relation.

32 It is plain by *v.* 30. here, and the Application therein of these Words, *Gen.* ii. 23. to Christ and the Church, that the Apostles understood several Passages in the Old Testament in reference to Christ and the Gospel, which evangelical or spiritual Sense was not understood, till by the Assistance of the Spirit of God the Apostles so explained and revealed it. This is that which St. *Paul,* as we see he does here, calls Mystery. He that has a Mind to have a true Notion of this Matter, let him carefully read 1 *Cor.* ii. where St. *Paul* very particularly explains this Matter.

EPHESIANS.

TEXT.

mother, (which is the first commandment with promise)

3 That it may be well with thee, and thou mayest live long on the earth.

4 And ye fathers, provoke not your children to wrath: but bring them up in the nurture and admonition of the Lord.

5 Servants, be obedient to them that are your masters according to the flesh, with fear and trembling, in singleness of your heart, as unto Christ;

6 Not with eye-service, as men-pleasers, but as the servants of Christ, doing the will of God from the heart;

7 With good-will doing service, as to the Lord, and not to men:

8 Knowing that whatsoever good thing any man doeth, the same shall he receive of the Lord, whether he be bond or free.

9 And ye masters, do the same things unto them, forbearing threatening: knowing that your master also is in heaven, neither is there respect of persons with him.

PARAPHRASE.

mise) That it may be well with thee, and thou mayest be long lived upon the Earth. And on the other Side, ye Fathers, do not, by the Austerity of your Carriage, despise and discontent your Children, but bring them up under such a Method of Discipline, and give them such Instruction as is suitable to the Gospel. Ye that are Bondmen, be obedient to those who are your Masters according to the Constitution of human Affairs with great Respect and Subjection, and with that Sincerity of Heart which should be used to Christ himself: Not with Service only in those outward Actions that come under their Observation, aiming at no more but the pleasing of Men, but as the Servants of Christ, doing what God requires of you from your very Hearts, in this with Good-Will paying your Duty to the Lord, and not unto Men, knowing that whatsoever good thing any one doth to another, he shall be considered and rewarded for it by God, whether he be Bond or Free. And ye Masters, have the like Regard and Readiness to do good to your Bond-slaves, forbearing the Roughness even of unnecessary Menaces, knowing that even you yourselves have a Master in Heaven above, who will call you, as well as them, to an impartial Account for your Carriage one to another, for he is no Respecter of Persons.

3.
4.

5.

6.

7.
8.

9.

EPHESIANS.

SECT. XI.

CHAP. VI. 10——20.

CONTENTS.

HE concludes this Epistle with a general Exhortation to them to stand firm against the Temptations of the Devil in the Exercise of Christian Virtues and Graces, which he proposes to them as so many Pieces of Christian Armour, fit to arm them *Cap-a-pee*, and preserve them in the Conflict.

PARAPHRASE.

10. FINALLY, my Brethren, go on resolutely in the Profession of the Gospel, in Reliance upon that Power, and in the Exercise of that Strength, which is ready for your Support in
11. Jesus Christ; putting on the whole Armour of God, that ye may be able to resist all the Attacks of the Devil. For our Conflict is not
12. barely with Men, but with Principalities, and with Powers[x], with the Rulers of the Darkness that is in Men in the present Constitution of the World, and the spiritual Managers of the
13. Opposition to the Kingdom of God. Wherefore take unto yourselves the whole Armour of God, that you may be able to make Resistance in the evil Day, when you shall be attacked, and having acquitted yourselves in every thing as you ought, to stand and keep
14. your Ground: Stand fast therefore, having your Loins girt with Truth, and having on the

TEXT.

Finally, my brethren, 10 be strong in the Lord, and in the power of his might.

Put on the whole ar- 11 mour of God, that ye may be able to stand against the wiles of the devil.

For we wrestle not a- 12 gainst flesh and blood, but against principalities, against powers, against the rulers of the darkness of this world, against spiritual wickedness in high places.

Wherefore take unto 13 you the whole armour of God, that ye may be able to withstand in the evil day, and having done all to stand.

Stand therefore, hav- 14 ing your loins girt about with truth, and having

NOTES.

12 [x] *Principalities* and *Powers*, are put here, it is visible, for those revolted Angels which stood in Opposition to the Kingdom of God.

Breast-

EPHESIANS.

Chap. VI.

TEXT.

on the breast-plate of righteousness;
15 And your feet shod with the preparation of the gospel of peace;
16 Above all, taking the shield of faith, wherewith ye shall be able to quench all the fiery darts of the wicked.
17 And take the helmet of salvation, and the sword of the spirit, which is the word of God:
18 Praying always with all prayer and supplication in the spirit, and watching thereunto with all perseverance, and supplication for all saints;
19 And for me, that utterance may be given unto me, that I may open my mouth boldly, to make known the mystery of the gospel:
20 For which I am an ambassador in bonds: that therein I may speak boldly, as I ought to speak.

PARAPHRASE.

Breast-Plate of Righteousness, and your Feet shod with a Readiness to walk in the Way of the Gospel of Peace, which you have well studied and considered. Above all taking the Shield of Faith, wherein you may receive, and so render ineffectual all the fiery Darts of the wicked one, *i. e.* the Devil——Take also the Hopes of Salvation for an Helmet: And the Sword of the Spirit, which is the Word of God ^y: Praying at all Seasons with all Prayer and Supplication in the Spirit, attending and watching hereunto with all Perseverance and Supplication for all the Saints; and for me in particular, that I may with Freedom and Plainness of Speech preach the Word, to the manifesting and laying open that Part of the Gospel that concerns the calling of the Gentiles, which has hitherto as a Mystery lain concealed, and not been at all understood: But I as an Ambassador am sent to make known to the World, and am now in Prison upon that very Account: But let your Prayers be, that in the Discharge of this my Commission, I may speak plainly and boldly, as an Ambassador from God ought to speak.

15.
16.
17.
18.
19.
20.

NOTES.

17 [y] In this foregoing Allegory St. *Paul* providing Armour for his Christian Soldier, to arm him at all Points, there is no need curiously to explain wherein the peculiar Correspondence between those Virtues and those Pieces of Armour consisted, it being plain enough what the Apostle means, and wherewith he would have Believers be armed for their Warfare.

SECT.

EPHESIANS.

SECT. XII.

CHAP. VI. 21——24.

EPILOGUS.

PARAPHRASE.	TEXT.
21. *TYCHICUS*, a beloved Brother, and faithful Minister of the Lord in the Work of the Gospel, shall acquaint you how Matters stand with me, and how I do, and give you a particular Account how all Things stand here. I 22. have sent him on purpose to you, that you might know the State of our Affairs, and that 23. he might comfort your Hearts. Peace be to the Brethren, and Love with Faith from God 24. the Father, and the Lord Jesus Christ. Grace be with all those that love our Lord Jesus Christ in Sincerity ᶻ.	21 BUT that ye also may know my affairs, and how I do, Tychicus, a beloved brother and faithful minister in the Lord, shall make known to you all things: 22 Whom I have sent unto you for the same purpose, that ye might know our affairs, and that he might comfort your hearts. 23 Peace be to the brethren, and love with faith from God the Father, and the Lord Jesus Christ. 24 Grace be with all them that love our Lord Jesus Christ in sincerity. Amen.

NOTES.

24 ᶻ Ἐν ἀφθαρσίᾳ, *in Sincerity*, so our Translation; the Greek Word signifies, *in Incorruption*. St. *Paul* closes all his Epistles with this Benediction, *Grace be with you*; but this here is so peculiar a Way of expressing himself, that it may give us some Reason to enquire what Thoughts suggested it. It has been remarked more than once, that the main Business of his Epistles, is that which fills his Mind, and guides his Pen in his whole Discourse. In this to the *Ephesians* he sets forth the Gospel, as a Dispensation so much in every thing superior to the Law, that it was to debase, corrupt and destroy the Gospel, to join Circumcision and the Observance of the Law as necessary to it. Having writ this Epistle to this End, he here in the Close, having the same Thought still upon his Mind, pronounces Favour on all those that love the Lord Jesus Christ *in Incorruption*, i. e. without the mixing or joining any thing with him in the Work of our Salvation, that may render the Gospel useless and ineffectual. For thus he says, *Gal.* v. 2. *If ye be circumcised, Christ shall profit you nothing.* This I submit to the Consideration of the judicious Reader.

www.ingramcontent.com/pod-product-compliance
Lightning Source LLC
Chambersburg PA
CBHW030543300426
44111CB00009B/843